SOCIOLOGY
and YOU

JON M. SHEPARD
Virginia Polytechnic Institute and State University

ROBERT W. GREENE
Greenfield High School
Greenfield, Wisconsin

Mc Graw Hill **Glencoe McGraw-Hill**

New York, New York   Columbus, Ohio   Chicago, Illinois   Peoria, Illinois   Woodland Hills, California

About the Authors

Jon M. Shepard

Jon M. Shepard earned a Ph.D. in sociology at Michigan State University before assuming a teaching position at the University of Kentucky. The eighth edition of his popular college sociology textbook has recently been published. He has also has written extensively for academic journals and professional sociology associations. Dr. Shepard has received teaching awards at both the University of Kentucky and Virginia Polytechnic Institute and State University where he currently teaches. His love of sociology and extensive experience with introductory sociology students have motivated and guided him in the creation of this unique text for high school students.

Robert W. Greene

Robert W. Greene has taught high school sociology for fifteen years. In that time, he has served as Secretary of the Wisconsin Sociological Association and is currently its President-elect. He has also served on the American Sociological Association's "Teaching Sociology in K-12 Committee," and chaired that committee in 1998. Mr. Greene was just recently nominated to the American Sociological Association's Task Force for the creation of an advanced placement sociology course and exam. Over the last four years, he has chaired the Sociology Special Interest Group of the National Council for the Social Studies. In addition to his high school teaching responsibilities, Mr. Greene teaches sociology part-time at Alverno College in Milwaukee and extension courses for Marian College of Wisconsin.

Glencoe/McGraw-Hill

A Division of The McGraw-Hill Companies

Send all inquiries to:
Glencoe/McGraw-Hill
8787 Orion Place
Columbus, OH 43240

ISBN 0-07-828576-3 (Student Edition)
Printed in the United States of America.

5 6 7 8 055/058 10 09 08 07 06 05 04 03

Reviewers/Contributors

Carolyn Andrews
Eisenhower High School
Houston, TX

Sandy Eichhorst
Centennial High School
Champaign, IL

Sally Raskoff
University of Southern California
Los Angeles, CA

Nancy Browning
Land O'Lakes High School
Land O'Lakes, FL

Dianne Brunt
Canyon Springs High School
Moreno Valley, CA

John D. Bush
Bedford No. Law High School
Bedford, IN

Candee Collins
Pine Tree High School
Longview, TX

Barb Damon
Merrimack High School
Merrimack, NH

Patricia Darnell
Killeen High School
Killeen, TX

Diane G. Dowler
Buena High School
Ventura, CA

Tom Dubay
Trinity High School
Louisville, KY

Frances D. Duncan
Hudson's Bay High School
Vancouver, WA

Richard B. DuRall
Evergreen High School
Seattle, WA

Beth Duron
Santa Clarita Christian School
Canyon Country, CA

Debbie Stuart Everett
Park Tudor High School
Indianapolis, IN

Matthew Ferren
Seminole High School
Sanford, FL

James E. Flora
New Holstein High School
New Holstein, WI

Glenn Gritzon
Preble High School
Green Bay, WI

Robin Heisig
South Grand Prairie High School
Grand Prairie, TX

Mark R. Henthorn
Shadyside High School
Shadyside, OH

Kim Ibach
Kelly Walsh High School
Casper, WY

Debra Ann Jones
Bloomington High School North
Bloomington, IN

Donna Juren
Denton High School
Denton, TX

B. Dale Kinney
Ralston High School
Omaha, NE

Kathleen M. Knoll
South Milwaukee High School
Milwaukee, WI

Jim Kraft
Wausau West High School
Wausau, WI

Kimberly Landers-George
McNeil High School
Austin, TX

Kathrine Leonard
Southern High School
Louisville, KY

Linda McDanal
Machebeaf High School
Denver, CO

Susan Mirra
West Genesee High School
Camillus, NY

Jeff Morgenstein
Land O'Lakes High School
Land O'Lakes, FL

Catherine Morris
Grapevine High School
Grapevine, TX

Ed Pottenger
Lakota West High School
West Chester, OH

Tom Ramos
Bay High School
Panama City, FL

Alison Record
A&M Consolidated High School
College Station, TX

Rebecca Reeves
Cullman High School
Cullman, AL

Tom Robertson
Carlsbad High School
Carlsbad, CA

Lianne K. Schneider
Msgr. Kelly Catholic High School
Beaumont, TX

Sandra Setter
Eagan High School
Eagan, MN

Dan Sheesley
North Platte High School
North Platte, NE

Toni C. Tropiak
Parkland High School
El Paso, TX

Bob Walls
Lakeview High School
Cortland, OH

Mary Beth Wilson
Gallatin County High School
Warsaw, KY

Table of Contents

Table of Contents

Features

Another Place Another Time

Focus on Research

Sociology Today

Tech Trends

Features

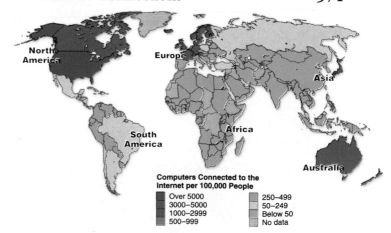

Computers Connected to the
Internet per 100,000 People

Over 5000
3000–5000
1000–2999
500–999

250–499
50–249
Below 50
No data

Focus on Theoretical Perspectives

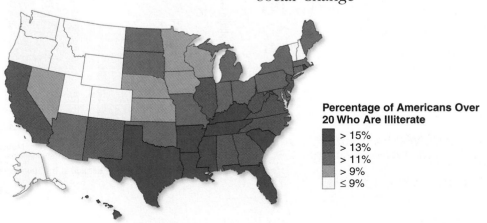

Percentage of Americans Over 20 Who Are Illiterate

- > 15%
- > 13%
- > 11%
- > 9%
- ≤ 9%

Charts & Graphs

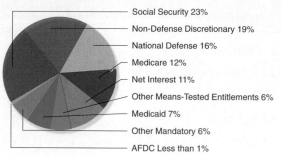

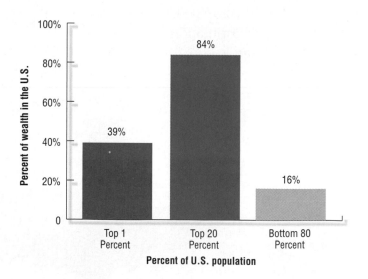

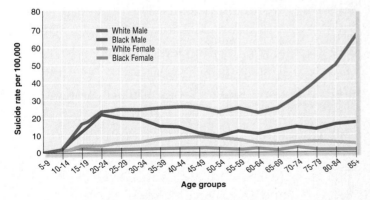

Charts & Graphs

Occupational Category
Farm   Blue collar   White collar

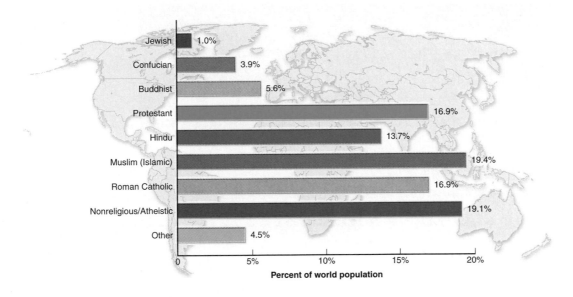

Percent of world population

Jewish	1.0%
Confucian	3.9%
Buddhist	5.6%
Protestant	16.9%
Hindu	13.7%
Muslim (Islamic)	19.4%
Roman Catholic	16.9%
Nonreligious/Atheistic	19.1%
Other	4.5%

ECONOMY	INSTITUTIONS	ARTS	LANGUAGE	ENVIRONMENT	RECREATION	BELIEFS
Trade						
Tools						
Technology						
Goods				Communities		
Services		Art		Geography		Values
Jobs		Literature		Geology	Games	Traditions
Business	Family	Dance	Words	Habitat	Toys	Ethnicity
Transportation	Government	Theater	Expressions	Wildlife	Arts	Customs
Communications	Education	Music	Pronunciations	Climates	Media	Religions
Food, Shelter,	Religion	Crafts	Alphabet	Resources	Holidays	Morals
Clothing	Economy	Folktales	Symbols		Festivals	

CULTURAL UNIVERSALS

Sociology Handbook

Contents

Thinking Like a Sociologist

Why Should You Study Sociology?

If someone in the United States is asked why he or she acted in a certain way, most of us would expect the person to provide an explanation that described the causes of the behavior in terms of his or her *individual* choices. Americans are generally taught to think that they totally determine their own thoughts, feelings, and actions. However, sociologists recognize that the groups, or social structures, that one belongs to have a profound influence over the way individuals think, feel, and act. Sociology provides tools to understand what these social structures are, how they affect our beliefs and behaviors, and how individuals relate to each other. Developing a sociological imagination—the mindset that enables individuals to see the relationship between events in their personal lives and events in their society—will help you to see how social forces affect your life in a way that a more individualistic perspective does not.

Sociologists recognize the influence that groups have on individuals.

What Should You Expect?

As you begin your study of sociology, you will probably find that it is very different from other classes you have taken. This is because sociology looks at groups rather than at individuals. It is this focus on groups, rather than on individuals, that distinguishes sociology from psychology, the study of individual behavior. Although sociology employs a distinct perspective, it does share some common features with other social sciences, including anthropology, psychology, economics, political science, and history. You will find elements of all of these disciplines in this sociology textbook. You will also find that you will begin to look at your life and your interactions with other people and with social institutions in a different way as you proceed through this course.

Sociologists as Scientists

In your study of sociology, you will learn to think like a social scientist. Scientists constantly question their own assumptions and look for alternative evidence and conclusions. All scientists—including sociologists—use the scientific method as a problem-solving tool. It teaches them to think critically by encouraging open-mindedness, intellectual curiosity, and evaluation of reasons. Using the scientific method will help you think critically and be objective when applying sociological principles to everyday events, issues, and problems.

Study and Writing Skills

Study Skills

To get the most out of any course you take, you must be active in learning the material. All fields of study have their own terminology, and sociology is no different in that respect. However, in sociology, understanding the central concepts is confounded by the fact that many of the terms used by sociologists are often also used in everyday language with different meanings. Because it is important for you to understand such definitional differences, sociological concepts are carefully defined throughout the textbook.

Learning the Skill

To understand the central concepts used in sociology:

◆ Identify the terms that sociologists use to represent specific scientific concepts. You must be careful at this point, because many of the words that sociologists use are also used in everyday language. You may mistakenly think that you already understand a word, when, in fact, its scientific meaning is different.

◆ Be sure that you understand the words that are used to define a sociological term.

◆ Try to put the definition in your own words. If you cannot do this at first, keep working at it until you can. But be careful not to lapse back into everyday usage of the term.

◆ Understand the context in which the term is used, not just its specific definition.

◆ Practice using sociological terms with their scientific meanings.

Practicing the Skill

Read the following paragraph and then answer the questions below.

Prejudice is a widely held preconception of a group and its individual members. These preconceptions are often based on strong emotions and unchallenged ideas. Consequently, they are difficult to change, even in the face of overwhelming evidence to the contrary. Prejudice involves an either/or type of logic: A group is either good or bad, and it is assumed that each of the members of that group possesses the characteristics attributed to the group. Prejudice, then, involves an overgeneralization based on biased or insufficient information. While prejudice refers to an attitude, discrimi-

Studying sociology can open doors for you.

nation describes unequal treatment of others. Prejudice does not always result in discrimination, but it often does.

1. Define *prejudice* in its sociological meaning. Do the same for *discrimination*.
2. Based on their sociological meanings, are prejudice and discrimination always negative?
3. Based on their sociological meanings, can discrimination occur without prejudice?

Applying the Skill

1. Look up the sociological definitions of culture and society. How are these meanings different from everyday usage?
2. How are these terms similar to each other?
3. How are they different?

The Writing Process

Researching and writing allow you to organize your ideas in a logical manner. Actually, writing a paper is only the final step in a process that involves using other skills you have already learned, such as identifying central issues, distinguishing fact from opinion, and making generalizations.

Learning the Skill

Use the following guidelines in the writing process:

◆ Select an interesting topic. As you identify possible topics, focus on resources that are available. Do preliminary research to determine whether your topic is too broad or too narrow.

◆ Write a thesis statement that defines what you want to prove, discover, or illustrate in your writing. This will be the focus of your entire paper.

◆ Research your topic. First, formulate a list of central questions. Prepare note cards on each question, listing the information sources.

◆ Organize your information by building an outline. Then follow your outline in writing a rough draft of your report.

The Internet has made certain kinds of research much quicker and easier. But, the researcher must still use critical thinking skills to evaluate the information obtained from the Internet.

◆ A report should have three main parts: the introduction, the body, and the conclusion. The introduction briefly presents the topic and gives your topic statement. In the body, follow your outline to develop the important ideas in your argument. The conclusion summarizes and restates your findings.

◆ Each paragraph should express one main idea in a topic sentence. Additional sentences support or explain the main idea by using details and facts.

◆ Revise the draft into a final report. Wait for a day, then reread and revise it.

Practicing the Skill

Suppose you are writing a report on the role family income plays in the children's educational attainment. Answer the following questions about the writing process.

1. How could you narrow the topic?
2. Write a thesis statement.
3. What are the main ideas?
4. What are three possible sources of information?

Applying the Skill

Use research resources in your library to find information on the role of the family in society. Narrow the topic and write a short report on it.

Critical Thinking Skills

Identifying Central Issues

Identifying central issues will help you organize information and assess the most important concepts to remember.

Good debaters must identify the central issues in a topic and in their opponents' arguments. Do you think political candidates do this well?

Learning the Skill

To identify a central issue, follow these steps:

1. Understand the context in which the reading was written.
2. Skim the material to identify its general subject. Look at headings and subheadings.
3. Read the information carefully to pinpoint the ideas that the details support.
4. Identify the central issue. Ask what part of the reading conveys the main idea.

Read the following excerpt from a paper entitled "The Crisis of the Young African American Male and the Criminal Justice System."

In recent years policy attention regarding the crisis of the African American male has focused on a variety of areas in which African American males have suffered disproportionately from social ills. These have included education, housing, employment, and health care, among others. Perhaps in no other area, though, have these problems been displayed as prominently as in the rate of crime and the criminal justice system. African Americans have been affected in this area in two significant regards. First, African Americans are more likely to be victimized by crime than are other groups.... Second, the dramatic rates at which African American males have come under some form of criminal justice supervision has created a complex set of consequences which affect not only individual victims and offenders, but families and communities as well (Mauer, 1999).

A first step in identifying the central issue is to find out who wrote the piece and understand the author's purposes in writing it. Marc Mauer is the Assistant Director of The Sentencing Project, a non-profit organization engaged in research on criminal justice issues. In this paper, Mr. Mauer wanted to explore the current status of African American males in America's criminal justice system and recommend policies that would help change the system's destructive impacts on public safety.

Practicing the Skill

Read another paragraph from Mr. Mauer's paper and answer the questions that follow.

In assessing the extent to which racial bias within the criminal justice system has contributed to these disparities, there is mixed research evidence. Imposition of the death penalty provides the most compelling evidence for ongoing racial disparity. A series of studies has demonstrated that . . . the race of both victim and offender has a significant impact on the determination of a sentence of death as opposed to life in prison. [M]urder defendants charged with killing whites faced a 4.3 times greater chance of receiving death than those charged with killing blacks (Mauer, 1999).

1. According to Mauer, is it clear that African Americans receive harsher treatment from the courts?
2. Summarize the central issue of this paragraph in one sentence.

Applying the Skill

1. Bring to class three editorials from your local newspaper, national newspaper, or a newsmagazine. Try to find examples written by the publications' readers ("Letters to the Editor" are a good source for these) and professional writers.
2. Identify the central issue in each editorial.
3. Discuss how clearly each writer made his or her main point(s).

Determining Cause and Effect

Understanding cause and effect involves determining *why* an event occurred. A *cause* is the action or situation that produces an event. What happens as a result of a cause is an *effect*. Despite the seeming simplicity of this relationship, determining the true cause of an event is often very difficult. This is the case because there is seldom a single cause of any effect. Like other scientists, sociologists realize that almost all events occur as a result of several factors operating in combination. This viewpoint is known as the principle of multiple causation.

Calvin has obviously discovered the difficulties of determining cause-and-effect relationships.

Learning the Skill

Just because two things happen at nearly the same time, or they seem to occur regularly together, does not mean that they have a causal relationship. To identify cause-and-effect relationships, follow these steps:

◆ Identify two or more events.

◆ Decide whether one event caused the other. Look for clue words such as *because, led to, brought about, produced, as a result of, so that, since,* and *therefore.*

◆ Look for logical relationships between events, such as "She overslept, and then she missed her bus."

◆ Identify the outcomes of events. Remember that some effects have more than one cause, and some causes lead to more than one effect. Also, an effect can become the cause of yet another effect.

Practicing the Skill

Sociologists have studied the relationship between violence on television and violent behavior for many years. For decades, no one was willing to conclude that there was a cause-and-effect relationship between the two, but in 1999 the Milton S. Eisenhower Foundation issued a report that established a causal link between viewing violence on television and increased levels of violent behavior among viewers.

1. Why do you think that earlier researchers were reluctant to say that watching violence on television caused violent behavior?
2. Why did the Milton S. Eisenhower Foundation conclude that a cause-and-effect relationship does exist (see page 126 of the text)?

Applying the Skill

1. Do some research on the causes of criminal behavior. Prepare a short report that summarizes your findings.
2. Discuss how the principle of multiple causation applies to criminal behavior.
3. What other questions does your research raise?

Separating Fact from Opinion

Separating fact from opinion can be very important to you in everyday life.

Being able to distinguish fact from opinion can help you make reasonable judgments about what others say and write. Unfortunately, fact and opinion are often confused with each other, and separating them can be difficult. Facts must be verified by evidence. Opinions are simply based on people's differing values and beliefs.

Learning the Skill

The following steps will help you distinguish facts from opinions:

◆ Read or listen to the information carefully. Identify the facts by asking: Can these statements be proved? Where would I find information to verify them?

◆ If a statement can be verified, it is factual. Check the sources for the facts. Often statistics sound impressive, but they may come from an unreliable source.

◆ Identify opinions by looking for statements of feelings or beliefs. If the statement refers to situations that are desirable or undesirable, important or unimportant, or likely or unlikely, then the statement is an opinion. Opinions may also contain words like *should, would, could, best, greatest, all, every,* or *always.*

Practicing the Skill

Read the following paragraph, then answer the questions below it.

According to data collected by the Census Bureau, African Americans who have received a high school diploma earned a median income in 1999 of $23,990, and their white counterparts earned $29,261, nearly 22 percent more. The gap between blacks and whites with bache-

lor's degrees is even greater—median earnings of $36,930 for African Americans and $45,737 for whites, or 24 percent more (U.S. Bureau of the Census, 2000). Does this discrepancy between blacks and whites extend to other areas of life as well? Almost seven out of ten whites say that blacks are treated the same as whites in their communities, but only 41 percent of African Americans agree with that statement. Less than half of African Americans believe they receive equal housing opportunities, while 83 percent of whites responded that their communities provide equal housing opportunities for everyone (Ludwig, 2001).

1. Which of the statements in the preceding paragraph are facts? How did you identify the facts?
2. Which of the statements in the preceding paragraph are opinions? How did you identify them?

Applying the Skill

1. Watch a television interview. List three facts and three opinions that were stated.
2. Can you verify the facts?
3. How did you identify the opinions?
4. What statements, if any, seemed to contain both fact and opinion?

Making Generalizations

Generalizations are statements assumed to represent the truth by those who make them. If you say, "People who work hard make more money," you are making a generalization. If you also say that every hardworking person you know makes more money, you are attempting to support your generalization. Keep in mind that making a generalization from a small number of observations does not provide strong evidence that your generalization is actually true.

Learning the Skill

To make a valid generalization, you must first collect factual information relevant to the topic. Follow these steps:
◆ Identify the subject matter.
◆ Gather related facts and examples.
◆ Identify similarities among these facts.
◆ Use these similarities to form some general conclusions about the subject.

Sociologists study processes of socialization and make generalizations about how these processes shape individuals' ways of thinking, feeling, and acting.

Practicing the Skill

Read this paragraph, and then answer the questions below:

Many people in America believe that people at the bottom of the economic scale belong there because they don't have the motivation to succeed in a competitive marketplace. In a series of surveys, Americans were asked to account for poverty in the U.S. The most popular reasons blamed the poverty on the poor themselves. However, in studies of the poor and those receiving welfare, researchers have consistently found that a majority want to work, to support themselves, and to get off the welfare rolls.

1. Based on the preceding paragraph, what generalizations are made about the poor?
2. Is the generalization about the poor based on facts?
3. Is the generalization accurate? If so, how does that influence our policies regarding the poor? If not, why does the generalization persist?

Applying the Skill

Read the editorials in your local or a national newspaper for one week. Then write a list of generalizations about the newspaper's position on issues such as political ideology, economic policy, or the environment.

Analyzing Graphics

Line and Bar Graphs

A graph, like a picture, may present information in a more concise way than words. Line graphs and bar graphs are drawings that compare numerical values. They often are used to compare changes over time or differences between places, groups of items, or other related events. Both types of graphs can be used to display the same information, and the choice between the two is often at the discretion of the author. In general, however, line graphs are used to show trends over time related to one type of data (e.g. percentage of the population that believes in God, average age at first marriage, or number of households headed by a single woman). Bar graphs may be used to show trends over time or to compare different types of information, such as median income for men and women or age groups of a population.

Learning the Skill

Follow these steps to learn how to understand and use line and bar graphs.

◆ Read the title of the graph. This should tell you what to expect or look for.

◆ Note the information on the left side of the graph—the vertical axis. The information being compared usually appears on this axis.

◆ Note the information along the bottom of the graph—the horizontal axis. Time often appears along this axis.

◆ Determine what the line(s) or bar(s) symbolizes.

◆ Select a point on the line or bar, then note the date below this point on the horizontal axis and the quantity measured on the vertical axis.

◆ Analyze the movement of the line (whether increasing or decreasing over time), or compare bars to determine the point being made.

Practicing the Skill

Review the graphs, then answer the questions. Note that both graphs present the same information.

1. About what percentage of families with children under 18 were headed by single parents in 1985? In 1996?
2. How would you describe the general trend shown by these graphs?
3. Based on the data for the last four years shown, can you state what the current trend is for families headed by single parents?
4. Which graph represents this data in a more meaningful way?

**Percent of Families with Children
Under 18 Headed by a Single
Parent, 1975-2000**

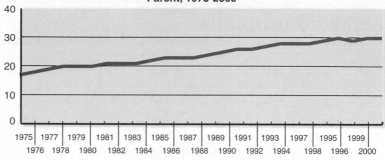

Source: *2001 Kids Count Data Sheet.* Baltimore, MD: The Annie E. Casey
Foundation, 2001.

**Percent of Families with Children Under 18
Headed by a Single Parent, 1975–2000**

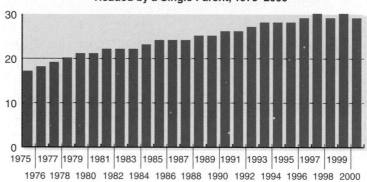

Source: *2001 Kids Count Data Sheet.* Baltimore, MD: The Annie E. Casey Foundation, 2001.

Applying the Skill

1. Create line and bar graphs that show the number and percent of children living in poverty in the United States from 1975 through 2000.
2. Pose two questions that the graphs you created raise in your mind.
3. Answer the questions you pose.
4. Which graph do you think is easier to understand and presents the information more meaningfully?

Circle Graphs and Tables

Circle graphs (also called pie charts) are often used to present information that shows the proportions of a whole. The particular data being presented can vary widely, but the common element in circle graphs is to show how

the entire population is divided into subgroups. The same information can be presented in tables, but in numerical, rather than graphic, form. Tables have the advantage of being able to present multiple categories of data in one location, whereas circle graphs are limited to one type of data.

Learning the Skill

Follow these steps to learn how to understand and use circle graphs and tables.

◆ Read the graph or table title to determine the content being presented.

◆ Read the labels (on circle graphs) or row headings (in tables). These will tell you what information is to be compared.

◆ For tables, examine the labels in the left-hand column. They describe ranges or subgroups and are often organized chronologically or alphabetically.

◆ Note the source of the data. It may tell you about the reliability of the data or where to go for further information.

◆ Compare the data presented to discover the relationships among categories.

Practicing the Skill

Study the table and circle graph, and then answer the following questions.

1. Which medium presents more information to the reader?
2. If you were concerned solely with the world's population, which graph/table would you prefer? Why?

Applying the Skill

1. Gather information on the demographics (for example, age, sex, parental income) of high school students in your state.
2. Present selected information in a table and in circle graphs.

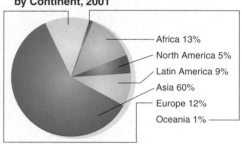

Percentage of World Population by Continent, 2001

Africa 13%
North America 5%
Latin America 9%
Asia 60%
Europe 12%
Oceania 1%

Source: *2001 World Population Data Sheet.* Washington, DC: Population Reference Bureau, 2001.

Demographic Data for Regions of the World

Location	Population 2001 (in millions)	Crude Birth Rate	Crude Death Rate	Life Expectancy
World	6,137	22	9	67
Africa	818	38	14	54
North America	316	14	9	77
Latin America	525	24	6	71
Oceania	31	18	7	74
Asia	3,720	22	8	67
Europe	727	10	11	74

Source: *2001 World Population Data Sheet.* Washington, D.C.: Population Reference Bureau, 2001.

Maps

Maps are visual tools that show the relative size and location of specific geographic areas. There are political maps, which show human-made

boundaries; physical maps, which show physical features of an area; and special purpose maps that can show historical change, cultural features, population, climate, land use, resources, or any other information of interest. Regardless of type, all maps use symbols to convey information.

Learning the Skill

Follow these steps to learn how to understand and use maps.

◆ Read the title to determine the map's content.

◆ Examine the map's scale, which indicates the ratio between the map's size and the actual area being represented. However, for many special purpose maps, this information will not be provided, and is not relevant to the information being presented.

◆ Read the legend, or key, to interpret any shapes, colors, boundary lines, or symbols. This step is, in many ways, the most important for maps of interest to sociologists.

◆ Interpret the information being presented. Determine patterns or other interesting points of interest. What questions does the map raise in your mind?

Practicing the Skill

Study the map and answer the questions that follow.

1. What information does this map present to the reader?
2. Do you see any patterns in the information?
3. What questions does the map raise for you?
4. Where could you find the answers to the questions you posed?

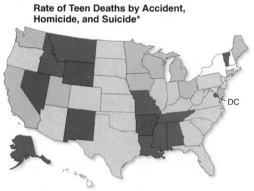

Rate of Teen Deaths by Accident, Homicide, and Suicide*

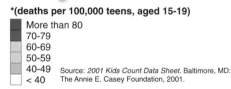

*(deaths per 100,000 teens, aged 15-19)

■ More than 80
■ 70-79
■ 60-69
■ 50-59
■ 40-49
□ < 40

Source: *2001 Kids Count Data Sheet.* Baltimore, MD: The Annie E. Casey Foundation, 2001.

Applying the Skill

1. Do research on participation of high school students in school-sponsored music programs, by state.
2. Summarize your findings by preparing a map of the United States that depicts the information you found.

Interpreting Data

Percentages

Sociologists use the concept of percentages quite often in their work on groups and social structures. Percent means "parts per hundred." So when a sociologist notes that, say, 18 percent of a group has a certain trait, she means that 18 out of 100 members of that group possess the trait in question. Changes in the size or number of a particular item (usually over time) can be expressed in percentages also. Stating the amount of change as a percentage allows you to analyze the relative size of the change. For example, if you knew that the populations of two states each increased by 250,000 people, you would have some information. But knowing that the percentage change in one state was 1 percent, while in the other state it was 15 percent, would provide you with substantially more information about the relative size of the increase, and would allow you to infer some of the possible consequences for the states.

Learning the Skill

Follow these steps to learn how to calculate and use percentages.

◆ Calculate the percent by dividing the number of the sub-group or change by the number of the original group population. Multiply your answer by 100 to express it as a percentage.

◆ Compare the percentage you calculated with other relevant measures.

◆ Remember that numbers or percentages by themselves tell you very little. This type of information is most useful when compared to other, similar types of information, so that you can put it into its proper context.

The individuals in this group can be categorized in many different ways. What percentage of the group is male? Female? African American? Redheaded?

Practicing the Skill

Complete the table on page HB-16 by calculating the missing percentages. Then answer the questions below the table.

1. Look at the percentages of students studying sociology at each school. Do you see a pattern? Does sociology seem to be more popular at some schools than others?
2. Now look at the differences between the percentages studying sociology in 1990 and 2000 at each school. Do you see a pattern of change during the ten-year period?
3. What might account for the changes you noticed?

School	1990			2000		
	# Student Body	# Studying Sociology	% Studying Sociology	# Student Body	# Studying Sociology	% Studying Sociology
Cave Spring	928	83	8.9%	1008	164	
Glenvar	316	40		421	44	10.5%
Northside	745	52		763	79	
Patrick Henry	866	54	6.2%	940	30	
William Byrd	643	37		715	55	
Wm. Fleming	872	91		948	116	

Applying the Skill

1. Survey 50 students at your high school to determine their favorite style of music. Based on the results of your survey, determine the percentages of your sample that listed each kind of music as their favorite.
2. Do the results of your survey surprise you? Why or why not?
3. How did you categorize students who named more than one style of music as their favorite?

Mean, Median, and Mode

Suppose a group of your friends wanted to compare scores on a college entrance exam. How would you calculate the group's mean score? Its median score? Its mode score? Which measure would be most meaningful?

The most commonly used summary statistic is the average. Generally speaking, an average is a measure of central tendency, indicating where the middle of a series of number lies. There are three ways to compute the average: the mean, median, and mode. The mean is the arithmetic average of a series of items. However, using the mean to represent the average can sometimes be misleading. This generally occurs when a few of the numbers in the series are much higher or lower than the others, resulting in a skewed or biased mean. When this happens, using the median or mode to represent the average may be more meaningful. The median is the midpoint in a series of numbers when they are arranged in order from low to high. The mode is the number that appears most frequently in the series.

Learning the Skill

Follow the steps below to learn how to determine and use measures of central tendency.

◆ To find the mean, add all of the numbers in the series. Then divide the sum by the number of observations in the series.

◆ Locate the median by arranging all of the numbers in the series from low to high. Then find the number that is the midpoint in the series. When an even number of figures is in the series, the median is the mean of the two middle numbers.

◆ The mode is the number in the series that appears most frequently. Simply look at the series and count which number appears the most.

◆ Compare the mean, median, and mode. Determine which one or combination is the most accurate in a particular case.

Practicing the Skill

Read the paragraph below and answer the questions.

An academic department at a major university conducts a survey each year of its recent graduates. One of the questions on the survey asks the respondents to report their annual income. Suppose this question drew the following responses from some graduates:

$23,500	$18,760	$43,000	$32,400
$26,750	$28,410	$1,466,980	$27,600
$26,750	$34,500	$24,580	

1. Determine the mean, median, and mode for these earnings figures.
2. Which measure of central tendency would you recommend using for this series? Why?

Applying the Skill

1. What are some of the data that you would want to know?
2. Which of the three measures of central tendency would you use for each type of data?
3. Explain your choices.

UNIT 1

SOCIOLOGICAL PERSPECTIVES

Chapter 1
An Invitation to Sociology

Chapter 2
Sociologists Doing Research

Enrichment Readings

Section 1

The Sociological Perspective

Key Terms

- perspective
- sociology
- sociological perspective
- social structure
- sociological imagination

Section Preview

Sociology studies human social behavior. It assumes a group, rather than an individual, perspective. Sociologists look for the patterns in social relationships. Individuals can benefit by using their sociological imaginations to look at events in their personal lives.

perspective
a particular point of view

sociology
the scientific study of social structure (human social behavior)

sociological perspective
a view that looks at behavior of groups, not individuals

The Nature of Sociology

A **perspective** is a particular point of view. Babies are usually brighter and better looking to their parents than they are to others. Newlyweds nearly always find their spouses much more attractive than do their friends. We all see what is happening around us through our own perspectives—our own points of view.

We normally do not realize how much of our attitudes and beliefs are determined by our perspectives. Sometimes, though, when our outlook is challenged, we may be jarred into realizing how much we take it for granted. As you will see, sociology has its own perspective. To understand it, you must have an idea of just what sociology is.

What is sociology?   As a newcomer to the field, you may at first view sociology as the study of human social behavior. As you go along, however, you will acquire a more precise understanding of **sociology** as the scientific study of *social structure*. (Social structure is discussed later in this section.)

What is unique about sociology?   Sociology, as stated earlier, has its own perspective. The **sociological perspective** never focuses on the individual. Psychologists may study the individual, but not sociologists. The view through the lens of sociology always remains at the social, or group, level.

These elephant tusks were burned to discourage trade in ivory. Whether you support this action depends upon your beliefs about conservation and national sovereignty.

The Social Sciences

Social science is a branch of learning that deals with human society. It includes a number of disciplines, which we generally refer to as the social sciences. These disciplines differ, but they share enough in common to overlap. Descriptions of the major social sciences are presented in this table.

Social Science	Description	Example
Sociology	Sociology investigates human social behavior from a group rather than an individual perspective. It concentrates on patterns of social relationships, primarily in modern societies.	Relationship between the employment of women and family size
Anthropology	Anthropology investigates culture, the customary beliefs and material traits of groups. It is the social science most closely related to sociology. Anthropologists, however, concentrate on the study of preliterate societies (societies that do not use writing). Sociologists focus on modern, industrial societies.	Nature of the family in preliterate societies
Psychology	Psychology investigates human mental and emotional processes. While sociologists concentrate on the group, psychologists also study the development and functioning of the individual.	Effects of birth order on emotional development
Economics	Economics is the study of the production, distribution, and consumption of goods and services.	Annual income levels of American families
Political science	Political science investigates the organization, administration, history, and theory of government. Political scientists are concerned, for example, with voting patterns and participation in political parties.	Relationship between a family's social class and voting behavior
History	History examines past events in human societies. Historians generally rely on newspapers, historical documents, and oral histories as sources of information.	Nature of family life in colonial society

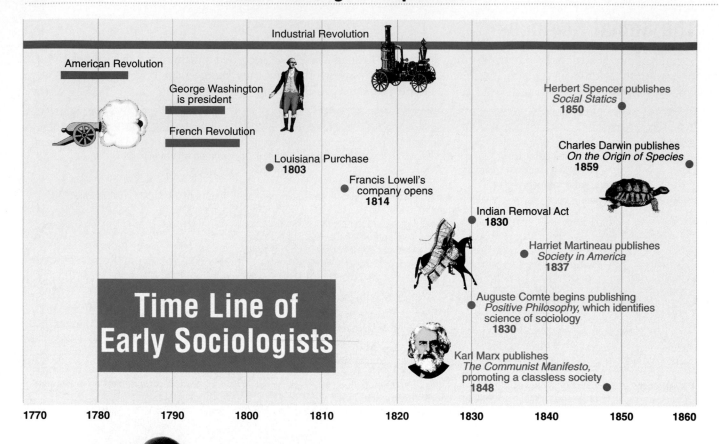

Industrial Revolution

American Revolution

George Washington
is president

French Revolution

Herbert Spencer publishes
Social Statics
1850

Charles Darwin publishes
On the Origin of Species
1859

Louisiana Purchase
● **1803**

Francis Lowell's
company opens
1814

Indian Removal Act
● **1830**

Harriet Martineau publishes
Society in America
1837

Time Line of Early Sociologists

Auguste Comte begins publishing
Positive Philosophy, which identifies
science of sociology
1830

Karl Marx publishes
The Communist Manifesto,
promoting a classless society
1848

| 1770 | 1780 | 1790 | 1800 | 1810 | 1820 | 1830 | 1840 | 1850 | 1860 |

Sociologists do not focus on the behavior of individuals but on the patterns of behavior shared by members of a group or society. The person on the street might explain human behavior in individualistic or personal terms—a young man joins a gang to prove his toughness; a woman divorces her husband to develop her potential; a teen commits suicide to escape depression.

Sociologists attempt to explain these same events *without* relying on personal factors. They look for social rather than personal explanations when they examine delinquency, divorce, or suicide. Sociologists might explain the events in the following ways:

❖ Young men join gangs because they have been taught by their society to be "masculine."

❖ More women divorce because of the social trend toward sexual equality.

❖ Teens commit suicide because of peer group expectations of performance, material possessions, and physical appearance.

Sociologists do not speak of *a* young man, *a* married woman, or *a* teenager. They concentrate on *categories* of people—young men, married women, and teenagers.

Joining a gang provides some young men—and women— with a sense of security and belonging they haven't found elsewhere.

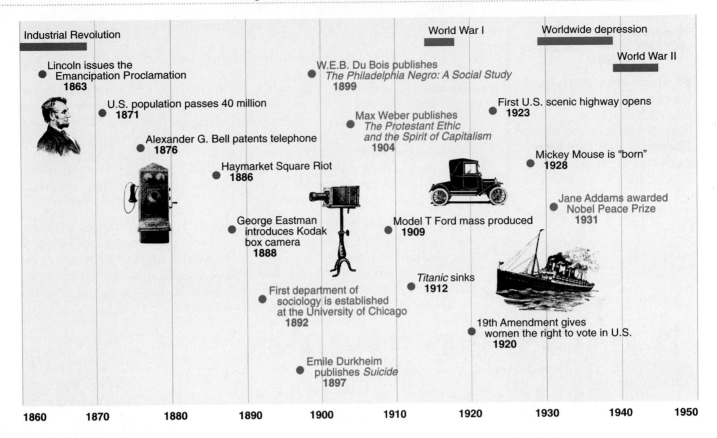

Industrial Revolution

World War I

Worldwide depression

World War II

Lincoln issues the
Emancipation Proclamation
1863

W.E.B. Du Bois publishes
The Philadelphia Negro: A Social Study
1899

U.S. population passes 40 million
1871

First U.S. scenic highway opens
1923

Max Weber publishes
*The Protestant Ethic
and the Spirit of Capitalism*
1904

Alexander G. Bell patents telephone
1876

Mickey Mouse is "born"
1928

Haymarket Square Riot
1886

Jane Addams awarded
Nobel Peace Prize
1931

George Eastman
introduces Kodak
box camera
1888

Model T Ford mass produced
1909

Titanic sinks
1912

First department of
sociology is established
at the University of Chicago
1892

19th Amendment gives
women the right to vote in U.S.
1920

Emile Durkheim
publishes *Suicide*
1897

1860   **1870**   **1880**   **1890**   **1900**   **1910**   **1920**   **1930**   **1940**   **1950**

The Importance of Patterns

As you well know, high school students in a classroom behave in different ways. Some students listen to everything their teacher says. Some tune in and out, and others spend much of the time daydreaming. Yet, if you visit almost any high school, you will find *patterned* relationships. Teachers walk around the room, work with students, lecture, and give tests. Students follow the teacher's lesson plan, make notes, and take tests. Although the personal characteristics of students and teachers may vary from school to school, students and teachers relate in similar patterned ways. It is the patterned interaction of people in social relationships—what sociologists call **social structure**—that captures the attention of sociologists.

How do group behavior and individual behavior differ?   Sociologists assume that social relationships are not determined by the particular characteristics of the individuals involved. Emile Durkheim, a pioneering nineteenth-century sociologist, helped develop the sociological perspective. He argued, for example, that we do not attempt to explain bronze in terms of its separate parts (lead, copper, and tin). Instead, we consider bronze a totally new metal created by the combination of several other metals. We cannot even predict the characteristics of bronze from the traits of its parts. For example, bronze is hard, while lead, copper, and tin are soft and pliable. The mixing of the individual parts creates a new whole with new characteristics. Durkheim reasoned that a similar process happens with groups of people.

Indeed, people's behavior within a group setting cannot be predicted from their personal characteristics. Something new is created when individuals

This time line shows when important developments in sociology occurred in relation to well-known events in American history. Entries marked with a blue dot indicate important sociology landmarks (The sociologists on this time line are discussed in the next sections of this chapter.) How might the development of the box camera in 1888 have influenced the growth of sociology as a field of study?

social structure
the patterned interaction of people in social relationships

Student Web Activity
Visit the *Sociology and You* Web site at soc.glencoe.com and click on **Chapter 1—Student Web Activities** for an activity on social patterns.

come together. For example, in 1999 the Denver Broncos won the Super Bowl championship. Following the game, a few otherwise law-abiding Bronco fans, as a group, disrupted the peace and challenged the police in ways they would not have done as individuals.

Tragedy, as well as joy, can change group behavior. The intense rivalry between the Texas A&M Aggies and the University of Texas Longhorns was banished the year twelve Aggie students died while preparing for the traditional football pregame bonfire. During the halftime, the Longhorn band played the song "Amazing Grace" and taps, and saluted the victims and their families by removing their hats. At a joint Aggie-Longhorn candlelight vigil two nights before the football game, the A&M student body president said that the communal sharing of the grief changed the relationship between the two schools forever.

Why do people conform?   Groups range in size from a family to an entire society. Regardless of size, all groups encourage conformity. We will study conformity in more detail later. For now, you need to know only that members of a group think, feel, and behave in similar ways. For example, Americans, Russians, and Nigerians have eating habits, dress, religious beliefs, and attitudes toward family life that reflect their group.

Another Time

A Native American's Speech

Virginia colonists had offered to "properly educate" some young Indian boys at the College of William and Mary in Williamsburg. To the surprise of the colonists, the benefits of a white gentleman's education were not highly valued by the tribal elders. Below is a Native American's reply to the white men's offer.

We know that you highly esteem the kind of learning taught in . . . [your] colleges. . . . But you, who are wise, must know that different nations have different conceptions of things; and you will not therefore take it amiss, if our ideas of this kind of education happen not to be the same with yours. We have had some experience of it; several of our young people were formerly brought up at the colleges of the northern provinces; they were instructed in all your sciences; but, when they came back to us, they were bad runners, ignorant of every means of living in the woods, unable to bear either cold or hunger, knew neither how to build a cabin, take a deer, nor kill an enemy, spoke our language imperfectly, were therefore neither fit for hunters, warriors, nor councellors; they were totally good for nothing.

We are however not the less obligated by your kind offer, though we decline accepting it; and, to show our grateful sense of it, if the gentlemen of Virginia will send us a dozen of their sons, we will take care of their education, instruct them in all we know, and make men of them.

Thinking It Over

1. Describe your reaction to this passage. What does it tell you about the importance of perspective in interpreting the social world?

2. Describe a social encounter where you personally experienced a "clash of perspectives" with someone from another culture.

3. Do you think your education is preparing you to succeed in the world outside school?

Conformity within a group occurs, in part, because members have been taught to value the group's ways. Members generally tend to conform even when their personal preferences are not the same as the group's. Some teens, for example, start smoking only to gain group acceptance.

Behavior within a group cannot be predicted simply from knowledge about its individual members. This could be because members truly value their group's ways or because they give in to social pressures. Like bronze, the group is more than the sum of its parts.

Acquiring the Sociological Imagination

The sociological perspective enables us to develop a sociological imagination. That is, knowing how social forces affect our lives can prevent us from being prisoners of those forces. C. Wright Mills (1959), an American sociologist, called this personal use of sociology the **sociological imagination**—the ability of individuals to see the relationship between events in their personal lives and events in their society.

To the outsider, these teenagers seem to be dressed alike. How does this photo show that a group is more than the sum of its parts?

sociological imagination
the ability to see the link between society and self

What is gained by using our sociological imagination? People do not make decisions, big or small, in isolation. Historically, for example, American society has shown a strong bias against childless and one-child marriages. Couples without children have been considered selfish, and an only child has often been labeled "spoiled" (Benokraitis, 1999). These values date back to a time when large families were needed for survival. Most people lived on family farms, where children were needed to help with the work. Furthermore, many children died at birth or in infancy. People responded to society's needs by having large families. Now, as the need for large families is disappearing, we are beginning to read about benefits of one-child families—to the child, to the family, and to society. This change in attitude is reflected in the decrease in family size.

The sociological imagination helps us understand the effects of events, such as the social pressures just discussed, on our daily lives. With this understanding, we are in a better position to make our own decisions rather than merely conform (Erikson, 1997; Game and Metcalfe, 1996).

This social awareness permits us to read the newspaper with a fuller understanding of the events. Instead of interpreting a letter opposing welfare as an expression of someone with no compassion, we might instead see the writer as a person who places great importance on independence and self-help. The sociological imagination questions common interpretations of human social behavior. It challenges *conventional social wisdom*—ideas people assume are true.

Sociology Today

Job Opportunities in Sociology

In general, all employers are interested in four types of skills regardless of what specific career path you choose. These skills are:

- ❖ the ability to work with others
- ❖ the ability to write and speak well
- ❖ the ability to solve problems
- ❖ the ability to analyze information

Because computers have revolutionized the office, for example, information analysis skills are becoming much more important to managers in all types of organizations. The increasing complexity of work demands greater critical thinking and problem-solving skills. Knowledge is of limited use if you can't convey what you know to others.

The study of sociology helps students to develop these general skills, so it is a solid base for many career paths. For sociology majors, the following list of possibilities is only the beginning—many other paths are open to you.

- ❖ **Social services**—in rehabilitation, case management, group work with youth or the elderly, recreation, or administration
- ❖ **Community work**—in fund-raising for social service organizations, nonprofits, child-care or community development agencies, or environmental groups
- ❖ **Corrections**—in probation, parole, or other criminal justice work
- ❖ **Business**—in advertising, marketing and consumer research, insurance, real estate, personnel work, training, or sales
- ❖ **College settings**—in admissions, alumni relations, or placement offices
- ❖ **Health services**—in family planning, substance abuse, rehabilitation counseling, health planning, hospital admissions, and insurance companies
- ❖ **Publishing, journalism, and public relations**—in writing, research, and editing
- ❖ **Government services**—in federal, state, and local government jobs in such areas as transportation, housing, agriculture, and labor
- ❖ **Teaching**—in elementary and secondary schools, in conjunction with appropriate teacher certification; also in universities, with research opportunities.

Doing Sociology

1. Which of the above career paths is most interesting to you? What is it about this area that you find interesting?
2. Evaluate your current strengths and weaknesses in the four primary skill areas.
3. Look at the employment opportunities in the Sunday edition of your local paper. Clip out ads for jobs that you might qualify for with a sociology degree.

Adapted from *Careers in Sociology,* 4th ed., American Sociological Association, 1995.

Snapshot of America

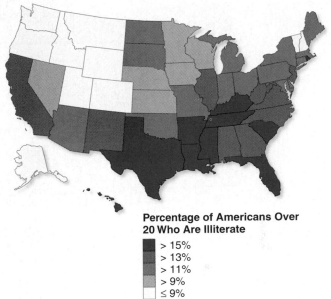

Illiteracy Rates

One of the assumptions of conventional wisdom is that nearly all American adults know how to read and write. Research has shown, however, that a large percentage of adults are illiterate. Literacy is defined as the ability to read at a fourth-grade level. This map shows, by state, the percentage of Americans over twenty years old who are illiterate.

Percentage of Americans Over 20 Who Are Illiterate

- > 15%
- > 13%
- > 11%
- > 9%
- ≤ 9%

Interpreting the Map

1. List the states with highest and lowest literacy rates.
2. How does your state rate on literacy?
3. What might be some reasons for adult illiteracy?

Adapted from Doug Henwood. *The State of the U.S.A. Atlas.*

Section 1 Assessment

1. Define sociology.
2. Explain the significance of patterns for sociologists.
3. Give an example from your life that illustrates conformity within a group.
4. How does the sociological imagination help people to understand the effects of society on their personal lives?

Critical Thinking

5. **Making Comparisons** Examine the idea of perspectives by identifying an issue that you look at in one way and your parent(s) or other adults look at in a different way. Write about the issue from both perspectives.

It is doubtless impossible to approach any human problem with a mind free of bias.

Simone de Beauvoir
feminist author

Section 2
The Origins of Sociology

Key Terms

- positivism
- social statics
- social dynamics
- bourgeoisie
- capitalist
- proletariat

- class conflict
- mechanical solidarity
- organic solidarity
- verstehen
- rationalization

Section Preview

Sociology is a young science. It started with the writings of European scholars like Auguste Comte, Harriet Martineau, Herbert Spencer, Karl Marx, Emile Durkheim, and Max Weber. Jane Addams and W.E.B. DuBois helped to focus America's attention on social issues. After World War II, America took the lead in developing the field of sociology.

positivism
the belief that knowledge should be derived from scientific observation

social statics
the study of social stability and order

social dynamics
the study of social change

European Origins

Sociology is a relatively new science. It began in late nineteenth-century Europe during a time of great social upheaval. The social and economic effects of the Industrial Revolution and the French Revolution were touching all aspects of life. People were moving from farms to factory life, losing a sense of community.

Some intellectuals were fascinated and troubled by the sudden changes. Auguste Comte, Harriet Martineau, and others began to grapple with ideas for bringing back a sense of community and for restoring order. These ideas led to the rise of the science of sociology. Examining the central ideas of the major pioneers of sociology will help you better understand what sociology is today.

What were Auguste Comte's major ideas?

Auguste Comte (1798–1857), a Frenchman, is recognized as the father of sociology. As a child he was often ill, but he proved early to be an excellent student. He had difficulty balancing his genuine interest in school and his rebellious and stubborn nature. In fact, he was expelled for protesting against the examination procedures at the elite *Ecole Polytechnique.*

As an adult, Comte's main concern was the improvement of society. If societies were to advance, Comte believed, social behavior had to be studied scientifically. Because no science of society existed, Comte attempted to create one himself. He coined the term *sociology* to describe this science.

Auguste Comte is considered to be the founder of sociology. He was the first to advocate the scientific study of society.

Comte wanted to use scientific observation in the study of social behavior. He called this **positivism.** He meant that sociology should be a science based on knowledge of which we can be "positive," or sure. Comte also distinguished between **social statics,** the study of social stability and order, and **social dynamics,** the study of social change. This distinction between social stability and social change remains at the center of modern sociology.

Comte published his theories in a book titled *Positive Philosophy,* but he died before people generally came to appreciate his work. His belief that sociology could use scientific procedures and promote social progress, however, was widely adopted by other European scholars.

What were Harriet Martineau's contributions?

Harriet Martineau (1802–1876), an Englishwoman, is another important figure in the founding of sociology. She was born into a solidly middle-class home. Never in good health, Martineau had lost her sense of taste, smell, and hearing before reaching adulthood. Her writing career, which included fiction as well as sociological work, began in 1825 after the Martineau's family textile mill was lost to a business depression. Without the family income, and following a broken engagement, Martineau was forced to seek a dependable source of income to support herself. She became a popular writer of celebrity status, whose work initially outsold Charles Dickens's.

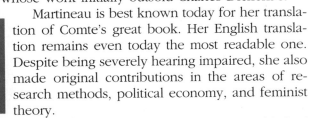

Harriet Martineau emphasized sociology as a science and introduced feminism. Her profound deafness prevented her earning a living as a teacher so she became an author.

Martineau is best known today for her translation of Comte's great book. Her English translation remains even today the most readable one. Despite being severely hearing impaired, she also made original contributions in the areas of research methods, political economy, and feminist theory.

In *Society in America,* Martineau established herself as a pioneering feminist theorist. Because she saw a link between slavery and the oppression of women, she was a strong and outspoken supporter of the emancipation of both women and slaves. Martineau believed women's lack of economic power helped keep them dependent. By writing about the inferior position of women in society, she helped inspire future feminist theorists.

An unexamined idea, to paraphrase Socrates, is not worth having.

Mark Van Doren
American poet

Why did Herbert Spencer oppose social reform?

Herbert Spencer (1820–1903), the sole survivor of nine children, was born to an English schoolteacher. Spencer was taught exclusively by his father and uncle, mostly in mathematics and the natural sciences. He did not enjoy scholarly work or the study of Latin, Greek, English, or history, and therefore he decided not to apply to Cambridge University, his uncle's alma mater. As a result, his higher education was largely the result of his own reading. Spencer's career became a mixture of engineering, drafting, inventing, journalism, and writing.

To explain social stability, Herbert Spencer compared society to the human body. He explained that, like a body, a society is composed of parts working together to promote its well-being and survival. People have brains, stomachs, nervous systems, limbs. Societies have economies, religions, governments, families. Just as the eyes and the heart make essential contributions to the functioning of the human body, religious and educational institutions are crucial for a society's functioning.

Herbert Spencer was an early proponent of Social Darwinism and evolutionary social change.

Spencer also introduced a theory of social change called *Social Darwinism,* based on Charles Darwin's theory of evolution. Spencer thought that evolutionary social change led to progress—provided people did not interfere. If left alone, natural social selection would ensure the survival of the fittest society. On these grounds, Spencer opposed social reform because it interfered with the selection process. The poor, he wrote, deserve to be poor and the rich to be rich. Society profits from allowing individuals to find their own social-class level without outside help or hindrance. To interfere with the existence of poverty—or the result of any other natural process—is harmful to society.

When Spencer visited America in 1882, he was warmly greeted, particularly by corporate leaders. After all, his ideas provided moral justification for their competitive actions. Later, public support for government intervention increased, and Spencer's ideas began to slip out of fashion. He reportedly died with a sense of having failed. His contribution in sociology was a discussion of how societies should be structured.

Who was Karl Marx? Karl Marx (1818–1883), a German scholar, did not consider himself a sociologist, but his ideas have had a major effect on the field. Marx felt great concern for the poverty and inequality suffered by the working class of his day. His life was guided by the principle that social scientists should try to change the world rather than merely study it. Marx's friend and coauthor Friedrich Engels helped put his ideas into writing.

Karl Marx was the social scientist who underscored the importance of conflict in social change. Parts of his writings were later used as a basis for communism.

Marx identified several social classes in nineteenth-century industrial society. Among them were farmers, servants, factory workers, craftspeople, owners of small businesses, and moneyed capitalists. He predicted that at some point all industrial societies would contain only two social classes: the *bourgeoisie* and the *proletariat.* The **bourgeoisie** (burzh-wa-zee) are those who own the means for producing wealth in industrial society (for example, factories and equipment). The means for producing wealth are called *capital.* Thus, those who own them are also called **capitalists.** The **proletariat** work for the bourgeoisie and are paid just enough to stay alive.

For Marx, the key to the unfolding of history was **class conflict**—a clash between the bourgeoisie, who controlled the means for producing wealth, and the proletariat, who labored for them. Just as slaves overthrew slave owners, wage workers would overtake capitalists. Out of this conflict would come a classless *(communistic)* society—one in which there would be no powerless proletariat.

Planned revolution, Marx was convinced, could speed up the change from capitalism to communism. His political objective was to explain the workings of capitalism in order to hasten its fall through revolution. He believed, though, that capitalism would eventually self-destruct anyway.

What were Emile Durkheim's greatest contributions? Emile Durkheim (1858–1917) was the son of a French rabbi. Durkheim was a brilliant student even during his early school years. In college, he was so intensely studious that his schoolmates nicknamed him "the metaphysician."

bourgeoisie
class owning the means for producing wealth

capitalist
person who owns or controls the means for producing wealth

proletariat
working class; those who labor for the bourgeoisie

class conflict
the ongoing struggle between the bourgeoisie (owners) and the proletariat (working) classes

According to Durkheim, society exists because of broad *consensus,* or agreement, among members of a society. In preindustrial times, societies were based on what sociologists call **mechanical solidarity.** With these societies, there was widespread consensus of values and beliefs, strong social pressures for conformity, and dependence on tradition and family. In contrast, industrial societies are based on **organic solidarity**—social interdependency based on a web of highly specialized roles. These specialized roles make members of a society dependent on one another for goods and services. For example, instead of being self-sufficient, people need bankers and bankers need customers.

Although early sociologists emphasized the need to make sociology scientific, they did not have the research tools that are available today. Later sociologists developed the methods to replace speculation with observation, to collect and classify data, and to use data for testing social theories.

Durkheim was the most prominent of these later sociologists. He first introduced the use of statistical techniques in his groundbreaking research on suicide, which we will discuss in Chapter 2. In that study, Durkheim demonstrated that suicide involves more than individuals acting alone and that suicide rates vary according to group characteristics. Durkheim showed that human social behavior must be explained by social factors rather than psychological ones.

Emile Durkheim was the first sociologist to use statistical methods in the study of human groups. He was also the first to teach a university sociology course.

Who was Max Weber?

Max Weber (1864–1920) was the eldest son of a father who was a well-to-do German lawyer and politician. His mother, in stark contrast, was a strongly devout Calvinist who rejected the worldly lifestyle of her husband. Weber was affected psychologically by the conflicting values of his parents. Weber eventually suffered a complete mental breakdown from which he recovered to do some of his best work. As a university professor trained in law and economics, Weber wrote on a wide variety of topics, including the nature of power, the religions of the world, the nature of social classes, and the development and nature of bureaucracy. His most famous book is *The Protestant Ethic and the Spirit of Capitalism,* published in 1906.

Through the quality of his work and the diversity of his interests, Weber has had the single most important influence on the development of sociological theory. Human beings act on the basis of their own understanding of a situation, Weber said. Thus, sociologists must discover the personal meanings, values, beliefs, and attitudes underlying human social behavior. Weber believed that an understanding of the personal intentions of people in groups can be best accomplished through the method of **verstehen**—understanding the social behavior of others by putting yourself mentally in their places. Putting yourself in someone else's "shoes" allows you to temporarily shed your values and see things from a different point of view.

Weber also identified *rationalization* as a key influence in the change from a preindustrial to an industrial society. **Rationalization** is the mind-set

Max Weber's model of a bureaucracy reflected greatly increased efficiency in business and government. Today, however, bureaucratic is often used as a synonym for unimaginative, plodding, or despotic.

mechanical solidarity
social dependency based on a widespread consensus of values and beliefs, enforced conformity, and dependence on tradition and family

organic solidarity
social interdependency based on a high degree of specialization in roles

verstehen
understanding social behavior by putting yourself in the place of others

rationalization
the mind-set emphasizing knowledge, reason, and planning

that emphasizes the use of knowledge, reason, and planning. It marked a change from the tradition, emotion, and superstition of preindustrial society. For example, agriculture became grounded in science rather than belief in luck, fate, or magic. In stressing rationality and objectivity, Weber pioneered research techniques that helped prevent personal biases from unduly affecting the results of sociological investigations.

Sociology in America

Although the early development of sociology occurred in Europe, the greatest development of sociology has taken place in the United States. Because sociology has become a science largely through the efforts of American sociologists, it is not surprising that the majority of all sociologists are from the United States. Sociological writings in English are used by sociologists throughout the world, reflecting the global influence of American sociologists.

In 1892, the first department of sociology was established at the University of Chicago. From its founding up to World War II, the sociology department at the University of Chicago stood at the forefront of American sociology. After World War II, sociology departments at eastern universities such as Harvard and Columbia, midwestern universities such as Wisconsin and Michigan, and western universities such as Stanford and the University of California at Berkeley emerged as leaders.

In later chapters we will be studying the works of major American sociologists. Two early contributors, however, who are often left out of the history of American sociology are Jane Addams and W.E.B. DuBois. Although

What is not good for the hive is not good for the bee.

**Marcus Aurelius
Roman emperor**

"Hmmm...what shall I wear today...?"

Everyone manages his or her behavior to create a desired impression. What face have you put on today?

Jane Addams was a social reformer who spent her life working on the social problems created by the imbalance of power among social classes.

neither of these remarkable people were researchers or scientists, both were greatly concerned with social problems in America.

Why should we remember Jane Addams? The best known of the early women social reformers in the United States was Jane Addams (1860–1935). Although her mother died when she was two years old, Addams's wealthy father provided a loving and comfortable home for her and her eight brothers and sisters. Addams was an excellent student. Her early education emphasized practical knowledge and the improvement of "the organizations of human society." She attended the Women's Medical College of Philadelphia but was compelled to drop out of the school because of illness.

When she was a child, Addams saw many examples of government corruption and business practices that harmed workers. She never forgot their suffering. While on one of her European trips, she saw the work being done to help the poor in London. With this example of social action, Addams began her life's work seeking social justice. She co-founded Hull House in Chicago's slums. Here, people who needed refuge—immigrants, the sick, the poor, the aged—could find help.

Addams focused on the problems caused by the imbalance of power among the social classes. She invited sociologists from the University of Chicago to Hull House to witness firsthand the effects of industrialism on the lower class. In addition to her work with the underclass, Addams was active in the woman suffrage and peace movements. As a result of her tireless work for social reform, Addams was awarded the Nobel Peace Prize in 1931—the only sociologist to receive this honor. The irony is that Addams herself suffered a sort of class discrimination. She was not considered a sociologist during her lifetime because she did not teach at a university. She was considered a social worker (then considered a less prestigious career) because she was a woman and because she worked directly with the poor.

Focus on Research

Secondary Analysis: The McDonaldization of Higher Education

Research is to sociology what lab experiments are to chemists. Through the research process sociologists gather information, or data, to help them understand how people behave in social settings. (In the next chapter, you will learn more about how sociologists do research.) The research project described below will give you some idea of how sociologists use already-collected data to study human social behavior.

In this study, George Ritzer investigated how Max Weber's process of *rationalization* (see pages 17–18) is being used by a popular fast-food company. Like Weber, Ritzer was interested in the movement of organizations toward ever-increasing efficiency, predictability, calculability, and control. After explaining each of these characteristics, Ritzer applies rationalization to the field of education in what he calls the "McDonaldization" of higher education.

According to George Ritzer, universities share some of the organizational characteristics of popular fast-food restaurants.

Efficiency refers to the relationship between effort and result. An organization is most efficient when the maximum results are achieved with minimum effort. For example, fast-food restaurants are efficient in part because they transfer work usually done by employees to customers. For example, self-service drink centers allow customers to get refills on drinks while disguising the fact they are waiting on themselves. *Calculability* involves estimation based on probabilities. High calculability exists when the output, cost, and effort associated with products can be predicted. A McDonald's manager trains employees to make *each* Big Mac within a rigid time limit. *Predictabilty* pertains to consistency of results. Predictability exists when products turn out as planned. Big Macs are the same everywhere. *Control* is increased by replacing human activity with technology. McDonald's drink machines stop after a cup has been filled to its prescribed limit.

Because Ritzer believes that McDonald's restaurants reflect the rationalization process, he refers to the "McDonaldization" of society (1998). His sources of information include newspapers, books, magazines, and industry publications. Since many of you are now thinking about attending college, Ritzer's findings on the "McUniversity" should be of interest.

Increasingly, students and parents view a college degree as a necessity to compete successfully in the job market. "Shopping" for the right college requires many of the consumer skills used in making any major purchase. This consumer orientation, Ritzer asserts, can be seen on most college campuses in the United States. For example, students want education to be conveniently located and they want it open as long as possible each day. They seek inexpensive parking, efficient service, and short waiting lines. Students want high-quality service at the lowest cost. A "best buy" label in national academic rankings catches the attention of parents and students.

Public colleges and universities, Ritzer contends, are responding to this consumer orientation. They are doing so in part because government funding for higher education is becoming more scarce. To meet reduced funding, colleges and universities are cutting costs and paying more attention to "customers." For example, Ritzer points to student unions. Many of them are being transformed into mini-malls with fast-food restaurants, video games, and ATMs.

Ritzer predicts that a far-reaching, customer-oriented tactic will be to "McDonaldize" through new technology. The "McUniversity" will still have a central campus, but it will also have convenient satellite locations in community colleges, high schools, businesses, and malls. "Students will 'drop by' for a course or two. Parking lots will be adjacent to McUniversity's satellites (as they are to fast-food restaurants) to make access easy" (Ritzer, 1998: 156).

McDonaldization, Ritzer contends, will dehumanize the process of education. Most instructors at satellites will be part-timers hired to teach one or more courses. They will come and go quickly, so students will not have the opportunity to form relationships as with more permanent faculty members. In order to make the courses alike from satellite to satellite, course content, requirements, and materials will be highly standardized, losing the flavor individual professors bring to their classes. Students will not be able to choose a particular instructor for a course because there will be only one per satellite. Often, there may be no teacher physically present at all. More courses will be delivered by professors televised from distant places.

In spite of these predictions, colleges and universities will not be a chain of fast-food restaurants or a shopping mall, Ritzer concludes. Institutions of higher education will retain many traditional aspects, but there will undoubtedly be a significant degree of McDonaldization.

Working with the Research

1. Do you think the benefits of the "McUniversity" outweigh the disadvantages? Why or why not?

2. What other industries or professions are being affected by McDonaldization? Give examples.

DuBois used science and sociology to disprove racist assumptions about African Americans.

W.E.B. DuBois focused on the question of race inside and outside the United States.

What were the contributions of W.E.B. DuBois?   W.E.B. DuBois (1868–1963), an African American educator and social activist, also influenced the early development of sociology in the United States. DuBois attended an integrated high school in Great Barrington, Massachusetts, and was the first black to receive a diploma there. He earned a doctorate degree from Harvard University in 1895 and taught at a number of predominantly black universities during his career.

DuBois learned firsthand about racial discrimination and segregation when he attended Fisk University in Nashville, Tennessee, as an undergraduate student. Partly from this experience, and from teaching in rural, all-black schools around Nashville, DuBois decided to attack the "Negro problem." This racist policy was based on the assumption that blacks were an inferior race. DuBois analyzed the sophisticated social structure of black communities, first in Philadelphia and later in many other places.

DuBois's concern for his race did not stop at the borders of the United States—he was also active in the *Pan African* movement, which was concerned with the rights of all African descendants, no matter where they lived. While documenting the experience and contributions of African people throughout the world, DuBois died in the African country of Ghana, at the age of ninety-five.

Section 2 Assessment

1. Define the term *positivism*.
2. Name and explain the theory of social change proposed by Herbert Spencer.
3. Give an example to illustrate Emile Durkheim's idea of organic solidarity.

Critical Thinking

4. **Evaluating Information** Max Weber introduced the concept of *verstehen*. How would you use this approach to social research if you wanted to investigate the importance of money to your peers? Explain.

Section 3

Theoretical Perspectives

Key Terms

- theoretical perspective
- functionalism
- manifest functions
- latent functions
- dysfunction
- conflict perspective
- power
- symbol
- symbolic interactionism
- dramaturgy

The Role of Theoretical Perspectives

Perception is the way the brain interprets an image or event. Similarly, perspective is the way you interpret the *meaning* of an image or event. Your perspective is influenced by beliefs or values you hold. It draws your attention to some things and blinds you to others. This is demonstrated in two drawings psychologists often use to illustrate the concept of perception. (See Figure 1.1.) If you stare at the old woman long enough, she becomes a beautiful young woman with a feather boa around her neck. If you stare at Figure 1.1b, it alternates between two facing profiles and a vase. You cannot, however, see the old woman and the young woman or the faces and the vase at the same time.

Which image is real depends on your focus—your perspective influences what you see. One perspective emphasizes certain aspects of an event, while another perspective accents different aspects of the same event. When a perspective highlights certain parts of something, it must place other parts in the background.

What is a theoretical perspective? A **theoretical perspective** is a set of assumptions about an area of study—in this case, about the workings

Section Preview

Sociology includes three major theoretical perspectives. Functionalism views society as an integrated whole. Conflict theory looks at class, race, and gender struggles. Symbolic interactionism examines how group members use shared symbols as they interact.

theoretical perspective
a set of assumptions accepted as true

a.

b.

Fig. 1.1 These two famous images are used by psychologists to illustrate perception and perspective. What did you see first in Figure 1.1a—an old woman or a beautiful young lady? What did you see first in Figure 1.1b—a vase or two human faces?

World View

A World Turned Upside Down

Without turning this book upside down, try to locate the United States. If you find this view of the world disorienting because you are used to conventional maps, you may reject this new worldview. So it is with any perspective. In this book you will be asked to abandon the conventional or psychological perspective in favor of the sociological perspective.

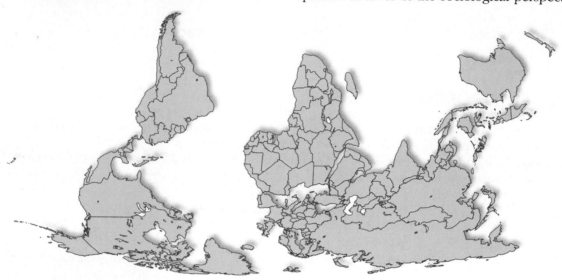

Interpreting the Map

1. What does your reaction to this map tell you about the power of the perspective you bring to a situation?

2. Look at world maps in your various social studies classes as you progress through the day. Where are North America and Europe located on these maps? What does that tell you about the perspective of these map publishers and their customers?

of society. A theoretical perspective is viewed as true by its supporters and it helps them organize their research.

Competing, even conflicting, theories in science usually exist at the same time. Perhaps not enough evidence exists to determine which theory is accurate, or different theories may explain different aspects of the problem. This is even true in the so-called "hard" sciences like modern physics. Einstein's theory of general relativity, for example, contradicts the widely accepted Big Bang theory of the origin of the physical universe. Einstein himself never accepted the quantum theory. Nonetheless, this theory has become the foundation of modern developments in such fields as chemistry and molecular biology (Hawking, 1998). Today theories are being put forth that hold promise for combining relativity and quantum theory. If theories still compete in physics, it should not be surprising that several major theoretical perspectives exist in sociology.

Sociology has three overarching theoretical perspectives: *functionalism, conflict theory,* and *symbolic interactionism.* Each of these perspectives provides a different slant on human social behavior. The exclusive use of any one of them prevents our seeing other aspects of social behavior, just as one cannot see the old woman and the young woman at the same time. All three perspectives together, however, allow us to see most of the important dimensions of human social behavior.

Functionalism

Functionalism emphasizes the contributions (functions) of each part of a society. For example, family, economy, and religion are "parts" of a society. The family contributes to society by providing for the reproduction and care of its new members. The economy contributes by dealing with production, distribution, and consumption of goods and services. Religion contributes by emphasizing beliefs and practices related to sacred things.

functionalism
approach that emphasizes the contributions made by each part of society

How does functionalism explain social change? Functionalists see the parts of a society as an integrated whole. A change in one part of a society leads to changes in other parts. A major change in the economy, for example, may change the family—which is precisely what happened as a result of the Industrial Revolution. Before the Industrial Revolution, when most people made their living by farming, a large farm labor force was needed. Families fulfilled this need by having many children. The need disappeared as industrialization proceeded, and smaller families became the norm.

Functionalism assumes that societies tend to return to a state of stability after some upheaval has occurred. A society may change over time, but functionalists believe that it will return to a stable state. It will do this by changing in such a way that society will be similar to what it was before. Student unrest and other protests during the late 1960s illustrate this. The activities of protesters helped bring about some changes:

❖ Many Americans became suspicious of the federal government's foreign policy.

❖ Schools and universities became more responsive to students' needs and goals.

❖ Environmental protection became an important political issue to many Americans.

These changes, however, have not revolutionized American society. They have been absorbed into it. As a result, our society is only somewhat different from the way it was before the student unrest. In fact, most of the student radicals are now part of the middle-class society they once rejected.

Because of social and economic changes, norms that dictate women's roles have changed greatly over the years. Functionalists study how a change in one part of a society affects other parts.

Do all functions have a positive effect?   Most aspects of a society exist to promote a society's survival and welfare. It is for this reason that all complex societies have economies, families, governments, and religions. If these elements did not contribute to a society's well-being and survival, they would disappear.

Recall that a function is a contribution made by some part of a society. According to Robert Merton (1996), there are two kinds of functions. **Manifest functions** are intended and recognized. **Latent functions** are unintended and unrecognized. One of the manifest functions of school, for example, is to teach math skills. A latent (and positive) function of schools is the development of close friendships.

Not all elements of a society make a positive contribution. Elements that have negative consequences result in **dysfunction.** Dysfunctions of bureaucracies, for example, include rigidity, inefficiency, and impersonality. When you go to the division of motor vehicles to register your car or get your driver's license, the clerk may treat you like a "number" rather than as an individual. You don't like his bureaucratic inflexibility and impersonality.

How does functionalism view values?   Finally, according to functionalism, there is a consensus on values. Most Americans, for example, agree on the desirability of democracy, success, and equal opportunity. This consensus of values, say the functionalists, accounts for the high degree of cooperation found in any society.

manifest functions
intended and recognized consequences of an aspect of society

latent functions
unintended and unrecognized consequences of an aspect of society

dysfunction
negative consequence of an aspect of society

How does this photo emphasize the approach to studying society that is taken by the conflict perspective?

Figure 1.2 Focus on Theoretical Perspectives

Assumptions of the Major Theoretical Perspectives. This table compares the most important assumptions of the functionalist, conflict, and symbolic interactionist perspectives. Do you believe, as the functionalists do, that society is relatively well integrated? Or do you support the conflict theorists' assumption that society experiences conflict on all levels?

Functionalism	Conflict Perspective	Symbolic Interactionism
1. A society is a relatively integrated whole. 2. A society tends to seek relative stability. 3. Most aspects of a society contribute to the society's well-being and survival. 4. A society rests on the consensus of its members.	1. A society experiences inconsistency and conflict everywhere. 2. A society is continually subjected to change. 3. A society involves the constraint and coercion of some members by others.	1. People's interpretations of symbols are based on the meanings they learn from others. 2. People base their interaction on their interpretations of symbols. 3. Symbols permit people to have internal conversations. Thus, they can gear their interaction to the behavior that they think others expect of them and the behavior they expect of others.

Conflict Perspective

The **conflict perspective** emphasizes conflict, competition, change, and constraint within a society (Giddens, 1987, 1997). Understanding the conflict perspective is easier when you understand functionalism, because the assumptions behind these two perspectives are the reverse of each other. This is shown in Figure 1.2 above.

What is the role of conflict and constraint?   Functionalists see a basic agreement on values within a society. This leads them to emphasize the ways people cooperate to reach common goals. The conflict perspective, in contrast, focuses on the disagreements among various groups in a society or between societies. Groups and societies compete as they attempt to preserve and promote their own special values and interests.

Supporters of the conflict perspective, then, see social living as a contest. Their central question is "Who gets what?" It is those with the most **power**— the ability to control the behavior of others—who get the largest share of

conflict perspective
approach emphasizing the role of conflict, competition, and constraint within a society

power
the ability to control the behavior of others

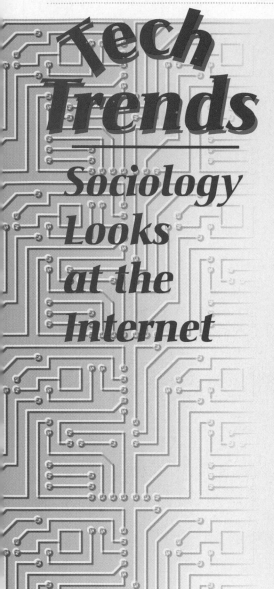

Tech Trends

Sociology Looks at the Internet

The number of Americans paying for an on-line Internet service is skyrocketing. The Internet began as a way for military and scientific users to share information after a nuclear war. ARPAnet (the Internet's forerunner) was formed in 1969 with only four connected computers. By 2000, an estimated 55 percent of Americans had access to the Internet. According to some estimates, there will be more than 500 million users worldwide by the year 2003.

Because of its rapid spread through American society, cyberspace technology is a timely example for showcasing the usefulness of the three theoretical perspectives. The viewpoints of functionalism, conflict theory, and symbolic interactionism contribute to an understanding of the social implications of this new technology in very different ways.

Functionalism.   Functionalists see cyberspace technology as having both positive and negative consequences. On the one hand, computer links bring advantages. Parents can work at home and spend more time with their children. Individuals with disabilities can do jobs at home that would be denied them otherwise, thus becoming more fully integrated into society. On the other hand, there are dysfunctions. Young people may have easy access to pornographic material, which can distort their view of the opposite sex. Hate groups can be formed by strangers who live hundreds or thousands of miles apart. Their anonymity may encourage them to engage in antisocial or violent behavior that they would otherwise avoid.

Conflict Theory.   The Internet is clearly changing American society. The Internet, conflict theorists point out, is contributing to the increasing speed of technological change. An advocate of conflict theory might investigate the social instability created by this rapid change. Workers may be let go by corporations in increasing numbers as more tasks are performed by computers.

Conflict theory could guide an investigation comparing the numbers of computers used in school districts of varying socioeconomic levels. Computer literacy is becoming an essential skill for obtaining a well-paying job. Thus, students who attend wealthy schools with

whatever is considered valuable in a society. Those with the most power have the most wealth, prestige, and privileges. Because some groups have more power than others, they are able to constrain, or limit, the less powerful.

How does the conflict perspective explain social change?   Many conflicting groups exist in a society. As the balance of power among these groups shifts, change occurs. For example, the women's movement is attempting to change the balance of power between men and women. As this movement progresses, we see larger numbers of women in occupations once limited to men. More women are either making or influencing decisions in business, politics, medicine, and law. Gender relations are changing in other ways as well. More women are choosing to remain single, to marry later in life, to have fewer children, and to divide household tasks with their husbands. According to the conflict perspective, these changes are the result of increasing power among women.

access to computers have an advantage over students in poorer schools.

Symbolic Interactionism. Symbolic interactionists are interested in how the Internet can affect a child's social development. The popularity of cartoon characters on television is reinforced by web pages that allow children to join fan clubs, interact with other fans, and view video clips of their favorite cartoon characters whenever they want. The popular cartoons *The Simpsons* and *South Park* feature children behaving in ways unacceptable in nearly all American homes. Television provides limited exposure to these characters, but the Internet allows them to become an important part of a child's daily life. What children come to accept as desirable behavior is being based increasingly on their interpretations of the symbols and behaviors represented by these characters. Symbolic interactionists might conclude that to the extent this occurs, the Internet lessens adult influence on children.

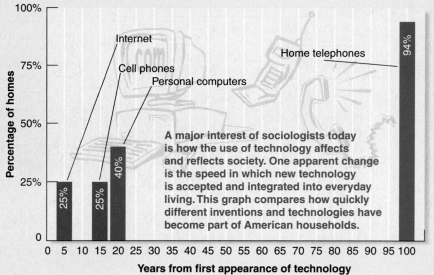

A major interest of sociologists today is how the use of technology affects and reflects society. One apparent change is the speed in which new technology is accepted and integrated into everyday living. This graph compares how quickly different inventions and technologies have become part of American households.

Analyzing the Trends

1. Which perspective would you choose to conduct an in-depth study of the Internet's effect on society? Explain why you chose this perspective.
2. Do you think that the Internet has some dysfunctions that Americans should consider? Consider the advantages and disadvantages of the Internet on society.

Which perspective is better? There is no "better" theoretical perspective. Each perspective highlights certain areas of social life. The advantages of one perspective are the disadvantages of the other. Functionalism explains much of the consensus, stability, and cooperation within a society. The conflict perspective explains much of the constraint, conflict, and change. Each chapter, throughout the text, will illustrate both perspectives, as well as the perspective discussed next—*symbolic interactionism.*

Symbolic Interactionism

Both functionalism and conflict theory deal with large social units, such as the economy, and broad social processes, such as conflict among social classes. At the close of the nineteenth century, some sociologists began to

According to conflict theory, the interests of groups will clash at times. If questioned, the men around the water cooler may offer a functionalist interpretation of their pastime—talking sports brings them together. Women who are not "sports savvy" may see their exclusion from such office talk more from a conflict perspective.

change their approach to the study of society. Instead of concentrating on large social structures, they began to recognize the importance of the ways people interact. Two sociologists, Charles Horton Cooley and George Herbert Mead, developed the insight that groups exist only because their members influence each other's behavior. These early American sociologists, in short, created symbolic interactionism, a perspective that focuses on the actual *interaction* among people.

What is the significance of symbols in symbolic interactionism?   To understand social interactionism, we need to talk first about symbols. A **symbol** is something chosen to represent something else. It may be an object, a word, a gesture, a facial expression, a sound. A symbol is something observable that often represents something not observable, something that is abstract. For example, your school's team mascot is often used as a symbol of school loyalty. The American flag is used as a symbol of the United States.

The meaning of a symbol is not determined by its own physical characteristics. Those who create and use the symbols assign the meanings to them. If people in a group do not share the same meanings for a given symbol, confusion results. For example, if some people interpreted the red light of a traffic signal to mean go, while others interpreted it to mean stop, chaos would result.

The importance of shared symbols is reflected in the formal definition of **symbolic interactionism.** It is the theoretical perspective that focuses on interaction among people—interaction based on mutually understood symbols.

What are the basic assumptions of symbolic interactionism? Herbert Blumer (1969a, 1969b), who coined the term *symbolic interactionism,* outlined three assumptions central to this perspective. (Refer to Figure 1.2 on page 27.)

First, according to symbolic interactionism, we learn the meaning of a symbol from the way we see others reacting to it. For example, American musicians in Latin America soon learn that when audience members whistle at the end of a performance, they are expressing disapproval. In other words, their whistling is a symbol of disapproval, as booing is in the United States.

symbol
anything that stands for something else and has an agreed-upon meaning attached to it

symbolic interactionism
approach that focuses on the interactions among people based on mutually understood symbols

Second, once we learn the meanings of symbols, we base our behavior (interaction) on them. Now that the musicians have learned that whistling symbolizes a negative response, they will definitely avoid an encore if the crowd begins whistling. (They would likely have the opposite response in the United States, where the symbol of whistling has a very different meaning.)

Finally, we use the meanings of symbols to imagine how others will respond to our behavior. Through this capability, we can have "internal conversations" with ourselves. These conversations enable us to visualize how others will respond to us *before* we act. This is crucial because we guide our interactions with people according to the behavior we think others expect of us and we expect of others. Meanwhile, these others are also having internal conversations. The interaction (acting on each other) that follows is therefore *symbolic* interaction.

In an attempt to better understand human interaction, Erving Goffman introduced **dramaturgy,** which depicts human interaction as theatrical performance (Goffman, 1961a, 1963, 1974, 1979, 1983; Lemert and Branaman, 1997). Like actors on a stage, people present themselves through dress, gestures, tone of voice. Teenagers sometimes act in a particular way in order to attract the attention of someone they want to like them. Goffman calls this *presentation of self* or *impression management.*

dramaturgy
approach that depicts human interaction as theatrical performances

According to symbolic interactionism, social life can be likened to a theatrical performance. Don't we convey as much about ourselves in the way we dress as do the actors above?

Section 3 Assessment

1. What is a theoretical perspective?
2. Indicate whether the following statements represent functionalism (F), the conflict perspective (C), or symbolic interactionism (S).
    a. Societies are in relative balance.
    b. Power is one of the most important elements in social life.
    c. Religion helps hold a society together morally.
    d. Symbols are crucial to social life.
    e. Many elements of a society exist to benefit the powerful.
    f. Different segments of a society compete to achieve their own self-interest rather than cooperate to benefit others.
    g. Social life should be understood from the viewpoint of the individuals involved.
    h. Social change is constantly occurring.
    i. Conflict is harmful and disruptive to society.
3. Does dramaturgy explain human interaction in a way that is meaningful to you? Why or why not?

Critical Thinking

4. **Analyzing Information** Think of an aspect of human social behavior (for example, dating or team sports) that you would like to know more about. Which of the three theoretical perspectives would you use to help you understand this aspect of behavior? Explain your choice.

A person gets from a symbol the meaning he puts into it, and what is one man's comfort and inspiration is another's jest and scorn.

William Shakespeare
English playwright

Summary

Section 1: The Sociological Perspective

Main Idea: Sociology studies human social behavior. It assumes a group, rather than an individual perspective. Sociologists look for the patterns in social relationships. Individuals can benefit by using their sociological imaginations to look at events in their personal lives.

Section 2: The Origins of Sociology

Main Idea: Sociology is a young science. It started with the writings of European scholars like Auguste Comte, Harriet Martineau, Herbert Spencer, Karl Marx, Emile Durkheim, and Max Weber. Jane Addams and W.E.B. DuBois helped to focus America's attention on social issues. After World War II, America took the lead in developing the field of sociology.

Section 3: Theoretical Perspectives

Main Idea: Sociology includes three major theoretical perspectives. Functionalism views society as an integrated whole. Conflict theory looks at class, race, and gender struggles. Symbolic interactionism examines how group members use shared symbols as they interact.

SOCIOLOGY Online

Self-Check Quiz
Visit the *Sociology and You* Web site at soc.glencoe.com and click on **Chapter 1—Self-Check Quizzes** to prepare for the chapter test.

Reviewing Vocabulary

Complete each sentence using each term once.

a. mechanical solidarity
b. positivism
c. social structure
d. bourgeoisie
e. sociology

f. symbol
g. latent function
h. conflict perspective
i. presentation of self
j. theoretical perspective

1. _____ is a set of assumptions accepted as true by supporters.
2. The perspective that emphasizes conflict is called _____.
3. _____ is an unintended and unrecognized consequence of some element of a society.
4. _____ is the way that people attempt to make a favorable impression of themselves in the minds of others.
5. The patterned interaction of people in social relationships is called _____.
6. _____ is the study of social structure from a scientific perspective.
7. The use of observation, experimentation and other methods to study social life is known as _____.
8. A _____ is something that stands for or represents something else.
9. _____ is social unity based on a consensus of values and norms, strong social pressure to conform and a dependence on family and tradition.
10. The _____ are members of an industrial society who own the means for producing wealth.

Reviewing the Facts

1. According to C. Wright Mills, what is the sociological imagination?
2. Explain "sociology" as defined in this chapter.

3. What did Herbert Spencer believe about the relationship between people, progress and social change?

4. List and explain the three sociological perspectives.

5. What are manifest functions and latent functions? Provide an example of each.

6. Using the chart below, give a major idea expressed by each of the sociologists listed. Briefly explain each idea. The first one has been completed. Use this as your model and complete the chart.

Sociologist	Major Idea	Brief Explanation
Karl Marx	class conflict	Struggle between bourgeoisie class (owners) and the proletariat class (workers)
Max Weber		
Auguste Comte		
Emile Durkheim		

Thinking Critically

1. **Applying Concepts** Give three examples of how the sociological perspective can be applied to your life.

2. **Analyzing Information** Using your own words, define the term sociology imagination. What is the relationship to the sociological perspective?

3. **Making Inferences** Select two early sociologists discussed in your text and construct a dialogue between them about the current social issue of homelessness.

4. **Summarizing Information** You have been selected to be on a panel to discuss illiteracy in your community. The panel also includes an economist, a psychologist, and an anthropologist. As a sociologist, what areas of this topic would be of most interest to you? Consider what aspects would be of interest to each of the other panel members. Complete the chart to summarize the aspects of interest to you and the other panel members.

Panel Member	Aspects of Interest
Sociologist (you)	
Economist	
Psychologist	
Anthropologist	

5. **Making Comparisons** Both a sociologist and a psychologist would be interested in the ACT (achievement) and SAT (assessment) test scores of high school students. Consider how the scientific interest of the sociologist would differ from that of the psychologist. Compare the similarities and contrast the differences.

6. **Categorizing Information** Merton's theory of manifest and latent functions (see page 26) could be easily applied to high schools. Using your particular school as a model, identify three manifest functions of high schools and three latent functions of high schools.

7. **Evaluating Information** You must select one of the job opportunities in sociology listed on page 12 for your career. Which one would you choose? Suggest ways in which the job fits your personality, abilities, interests, and ambitions.

8. **Analyzing Information** Spitting in public is not an appropriate behavior, but people "spit" all the time. When we drink soda, we usually leave a little spit in the can. When we kiss someone, we are transmitting spit. We don't think of it in these terms, because in some cases we call spit by a more scientific term—saliva. How would the sociologist perspective help to understand and explain why we flip back and forth between the two terms?

Sociology Projects

1. **Theoretical Perspectives** Based on what you read about the Internet from the functionalist, conflict, and symbolic interactionist perspectives, how is each perspective useful in understanding the popularity of the Internet? Write a brief statement describing how each perspective would approach this issue. You might see

positive or negative effects, depending upon your interpretation. (For instance, the conflict perspective may focus on the fact that the underprivileged classes would not have full access because of the cost of the hardware and therefore decreased power.)

2. **Developing a Commercial** Develop a commercial for sociology using a video camera. Think of the field of sociology as a product to sell. Market it as "a way to improve your understanding of the world around you."

3. **Observations** Go to a public place (such as a mass, school cafeteria, or restaurant) and discreetly observe people there for 15 minutes. It is important that you do not appear to be spying on individuals, both because it may be interpreted as being rude and also because it would probably affect their normal behaviors. Write down your observations, noting such details as the type of dress, general interactions, and level of activity. Do not assume any value judgments about your subjects; just make factual observations.

When you return home, rewrite your observations applying the sociological concepts in this chapter. Consider and list the ways your second analysis is different from the first. Compare and contrast them. How does sociology help to describe what you observed? What might you want to study from your observation?

4. **Sociology and Careers** Research one of the career options for sociology majors that interest you. Look for such important information as the education requirements, income expectations, and management opportunities. Write a short report on the advantages and disadvantages of that particular career in sociology.

Technology Activities

1. In this chapter, you learned about several of the founders of sociology and their contributions to the field. To learn more about these sociologists and others, go to the Dead Sociologists web page at http://raven.jmu.edu/~ridenelr/DSS. Select three sociologists named on the web site who were not included in the textbook and create a database including their year of birth, place of birth, and primary contributions they made to sociology.

2. Use the Internet to do further research on the pioneers of sociology. Design a poster representing the pioneers in sociology. Describe each one's basic ideas, including their theories and information attained through research. You may want to start your research at the Dead Sociologists web page listed above.

3. Write or use the Internet to contact the American Sociological Association and request the booklet "Majoring in Sociology." Using standard grammar, spelling, sentence structure, and punctuation, prepare a report for your class from the information. (The address is American Sociological Association, 1722 N. Street NW, Washington, DC 20036. For Internet access, the URL is www.asanet.org.)

Chapter 1
Enrichment Reading
Invitation to Sociology by *Peter L. Berger*

The sociologist . . . is a person intensively, endlessly, shamelessly interested in the doings of men. His natural habitat is all the human gathering places of the world, wherever men come together. The sociologist may be interested in many other things. But his consuming interest remains in the world of men, their institutions, their history, their passions. And since he is interested in men, nothing that men do can be altogether tedious for him. He will naturally be interested in the events that engage men's ultimate beliefs, their moments of tragedy and grandeur and ecstasy. But he will also be fascinated by the commonplace, the everyday. He will know reverence, but this reverence will not prevent him from wanting to see and to understand. He may sometimes feel revulsion or contempt. But this also will not deter him from wanting to have his questions answered. The sociologist, in his quest for understanding, moves through the world of men without respect for the usual lines of **demarcation.** Nobility and **degradation,** power and obscurity, intelligence and folly—these are equally interesting to him, however unequal they may be in his personal values or tastes. Thus his questions may lead him to all possible levels of society, the best and the least known places, the most respected and the most despised. And, if he is a good sociologist, he will find himself in all these places because his own questions have so taken possession of him that he has little choice but to seek for answers. . . .

The sociologist moves in the common world of men, close to what most of them would call real. As a result, there is a deceptive simplicity and obviousness about some sociological investigations. One reads them, nods at the familiar scene, remarks that one has heard all this before and concludes that people have better things to do than to waste their time on truisms—until one is suddenly brought up against an insight that radically questions everything one had previously assumed about this familiar scene. This is the point at which one begins to sense the excitement of sociology.

It can be said that the first wisdom of sociology is this—things are not what they seem. This . . . is a deceptively simple statement. It ceases to be simple after a while. Social reality turns out to have many layers of meaning. The discovery of each new layer changes the perception of the whole.

People who feel no temptation before closed doors, who have no curiosity about human beings, who are content to admire scenery without wondering about the people who live in those houses on the other side of that river, should probably . . . stay away from sociology. And people whose interest is mainly in their own **conceptual constructions** will do just as well to turn to the study of little white mice. Sociology will be satisfying, in the long run, only to those who can think of nothing more entrancing than to watch men and to understand things human.

Source: Excerpted from *Invitation to Sociology.* New York: Doubleday & Company, Inc., 1963.

What Does It Mean?

conceptual construction
personal idea of reality

degradation
low esteem, corruption

demarcation
setting apart, separation

Read and React

How is this excerpt different in style from most articles by scientists? Why do you think the author chose this style to describe his field of study?

CHAPTER 2
Sociologists Doing Research

Your Sociological Imagination

Two headlines appear on the front page of two different papers in the newsstand. The first reads "Cure for Alzheimer's disease just around the corner." The second, while more accurate, is less exciting. It reads "Scientists cautiously declare that a promising—but as yet unduplicated—test result may lead to some small progress in the long-term effort to prevent Alzheimer's disease."

Which paper do you think would sell more copies? Like savvy news editors, you probably know that both fear and hope are emotions that sell papers. For this reason, research results, especially on social and health studies, are often exaggerated by the media.

We routinely read that tomato sauce can prevent prostate cancer, that tea prevents heart disease, and that eating blueberries can reduce the effects of aging and improve short-term memory. On the other hand, milk, eggs, anger, too-strict parenting, too-lax parenting, and marrying before age thirty have all been blamed for various deadly diseases and social disorders. To further complicate matters, stories often contradict each other from week to week. Caffeine, fish, milk, and butter are only some of the products that can heal or harm, depending on the date.

People who know what questions to ask about research reports can better protect themselves from acting on inaccurate information. Chapter 2 will look at some of the basic research methods used by sociologists and explore the area of ethics in social research.

Sections

1. **Research Methods**
2. **Causation in Science**
3. **Procedures and Ethics in Research**

Learning Objectives

After reading this chapter, you will be able to

❖ describe the basic quantitative and qualitative research methods used by sociologists.

❖ discuss basic research concepts, including variables and correlations.

❖ list the standards for proving cause-and-effect relationships.

❖ explain the steps sociologists use to guide their research.

❖ discuss ethics in sociological research.

SOCIOLOGY Online

Chapter Overview
Visit the *Sociology and You* Web site at soc.glencoe.com and click on **Chapter 2— Chapter Overviews** to preview chapter information.

Section 1

Research Methods

Key Terms

- survey
- population
- sample
- representative sample
- questionnaire
- interview

- closed-ended questions
- open-ended questions
- secondary analysis
- field research
- case study
- participant observation

Section Preview

When sociologists do quantitative research, they generally use either surveys or precollected data. Each has its own advantages and disadvantages. Qualitative research uses descriptive rather than numerical data. Field studies are best used when interaction needs to be observed in a natural setting, and when in-depth analysis is needed. The case study is the most popular approach to field research.

survey
research method in which people respond to questions

Doing Research in the Social Sciences

Like all scientists, sociologists gain their knowledge by doing research. The goal of sociological research is to test common sense assumptions and replace false ideas with facts and evidence. Part of the sociological perspective is to ask "why" and "how" questions and then to form hypotheses to arrive at accurate understandings.

Social scientists differ from other scientists, however, in how they conduct much of their research. Unlike chemists, biologists, or physicists, sociologists (and often psychologists) are very limited in their ability to set up laboratory experiments to replicate real-life conditions. Even if they reproduce conditions as they are in the outside world, the ethical issues involved in manipulating people and controlling events would prevent most sociologists from pursuing this kind of research. For sociologists, the world is their laboratory.

How then do sociologists do research? The methods that sociologists rely on are described below. These methods are classified as either *quantitative* or *qualitative*. Quantitative research uses numerical data, while qualitative research rests on narrative and descriptive data. Quantitative research tools include *surveys* and *precollected data*. About 90 percent of the research published in major sociological journals is based on surveys, so this approach is discussed first.

Survey Research

The **survey,** in which people are asked to answer a series of questions, is the most widely used research method among sociologists. It is ideal for studying large numbers of people.

The survey is the most widely used research method for collecting data in sociology.

Survey researchers must guard against affecting a respondent's answer.

How are effective surveys conducted? In survey research, care must be taken that surveys are sent to the right number and type of people (Black, 1998). Researchers describe the people surveyed in terms of *populations* and *samples*.

A **population** is all those people with the characteristics a researcher wants to study. A population could be all high school seniors in the United States, all retired postal workers living in Connecticut, or the number of freshmen who buy school yearbooks.

Sociologists would like to collect information on all members of a population, but most populations are too large. Surveys including the entire population would cost too much and take too long for most research projects. Instead, a sample is drawn. A **sample** is a limited number of cases drawn from the larger population. A sample must be selected carefully if it is to have the same basic characteristics as the general population—that is, if it is to be a **representative sample.** If a sample is not representative of the population from which it is drawn, the survey findings cannot be used to make generalizations about the entire population. For example, if you were to conduct a survey using ten students from an advanced biology class, this sample would not be representative of your school. On the other hand, if you randomly selected ten students who walked into the school cafeteria for your survey, these students would probably be more representative of the student body. The sample would probably be too small, however, to give accurate results. The United States Census Bureau regularly uses sample surveys in its highly accurate work. The Gallup Poll and Harris Poll are recognized all over the country as reliable indicators of national trends and public opinion because they use representative samples in their surveys.

How are representative samples selected? The standard way of getting a representative sample is by random, or chance, selection. A random sample can be selected by assigning each member of the population a number and then drawing numbers from a container after they have been thoroughly scrambled. An easier and more practical method uses a table of random numbers. After each member of the population has been assigned a number, the researcher begins with any number in the table and goes down the list until enough subjects have been selected.

population
a group of people with certain specified characteristics

sample
a group of people that represents a larger population

representative sample
a sample that accurately reflects the characteristics of the population as a whole

Student Web Activity
Visit the *Sociology and You* Web site at soc.glencoe.com and click on **Chapter 2—Student Web Activities** for an activity on survey research.

Section 1

The Basis Of Culture

Key Terms

- culture
- society
- instincts

- reflexes
- drives
- sociobiology

Section Preview

Culture defines how people in a society behave in relation to others and to physical objects. Although most behavior among animals is instinctual, human behavior is learned. Even reflexes and drives do not completely determine how humans will behave, because people are heavily influenced by culture.

culture
knowledge, values, customs, and physical objects that are shared by members of a society

Culture and Society

Culture consists of the knowledge, language, values, customs, and physical objects that are passed from generation to generation among members of a group. On the *material* side, the culture of the United States includes such physical objects as skyscrapers, fast-food restaurants, cell phones, and cars. On the *nonmaterial* side, American culture includes beliefs, rules, customs, family systems, and a capitalist economy.

Culture helps to explain human social behavior. What people do and don't do, what they like and dislike, what they believe and don't believe, and what they value and discount are all based on culture. Culture provides the blueprint that people in a society use to guide their relationships with others. It is because of culture that teenage girls are encouraged to compete for a position on the women's basketball team. It is from culture that teenage boys come to believe that "pumping iron" is a gateway to masculinity.

Coming from a different culture than that of the other sunbathers doesn't prevent this Amish family from enjoying a day at the beach.

Culture and society are tightly interwoven. One cannot exist without the other, but they are not identical. A **society** is a group of people who live in a defined territory and participate in a common culture. Culture is that society's total way of life.

Human behavior, then, is based on culture. Since people are not born knowing their culture, human cultural behavior must be learned. In this section we will examine the relative importance of biology in influencing behavior.

society
a specific territory inhabited by people who share a common culture

Culture and Heredity

Instincts are genetically inherited patterns of behavior. Nonhuman animals, especially insects, are highly dependent on instincts for survival. Human infants, in contrast, cannot go very far on instincts alone. Instincts are not enough to solve the problems that humans face.

instincts
innate (unlearned) patterns of behavior

Why is culture more important than instinct in determining human behavior? If humans were controlled by instincts alone, they would all behave in the same way with respect to those instincts. If, for example, women had an instinct for mothering, then *all* women would want children, and all women would love and protect their children. In fact, some women do not want to have children, and some women who give birth abuse or abandon their children.

Without instincts to dictate the type of shelter to build, the kind of food to eat, the time of year to have children, or when to mate, humans are forced to create and learn their own ways of thinking, feeling, and behaving. Even for meeting basic needs such as those involving reproduction, food, and survival, humans rely on the culture they have created.

How does heredity affect behavior? Of course, culture is not the only influence on human behavior. Genetic inheritance plays a role. For example, you may have heard people argue about how much of personality is a result of heredity and how much is the product of the environment. (This is sometimes called the "nature versus nurture" argument.) Using studies of identical twins, researchers have determined that about half of your personality traits are determined by your genetic makeup and about half by environmental factors (Tellegen et al., 1993).

Studies of identical twins show that about half of your personality traits are inherited.

In addition, humans have **reflexes**—simple, biologically inherited, automatic reactions to physical stimuli. A human baby, for example, cries when pinched; the pupils of the eyes contract in bright light. We also have biologically inherited **drives,** or impulses, to reduce discomfort. We want to eat, drink, sleep, and associate with others.

You should realize, however, that genetically inherited personality traits, reflexes, and drives do not control human social behavior. Culture *channels* the expression of these biological characteristics. Boys in some Native American cultures, for example, are taught not to cry in response to pain. This is very different from boys in Jewish and Italian cultures, who are taught to pay more attention to physical discomfort and express it more openly (Zborowski, 1952, 1969).

reflex
automatic reaction to physical stimulus

drive
impulse to reduce discomfort

Sociobiology

sociobiology
the study of the biological basis of human behavior

Sociobiology is the study of the biological basis of human behavior. It combines Darwin's theory of natural selection with modern genetics.

How do sociobiologists view human behavior? According to Darwin's theory of evolution, organisms evolve through natural selection. The plants and animals best suited to an environment survive and reproduce, while the rest perish. Sociobiologists assume that the behaviors that best help people are biologically based and transmitted in the genetic code (Degler, 1991; Wright, 1996). Behaviors that would contribute to the survival of the human species include parental affection and care, friendship, sexual reproduction, and the education of children.

Sociobiologists do not draw a sharp line between human and nonhuman animals. They claim that nonhuman animals also act on knowledge—as when baboons use long sticks to pull ants from an anthill for a meal. Many nonhuman animals, claim sociobiologists, show intelligence of a kind formerly thought to be unique to humans, such as the ability to use language (Begley, 1993; Linden, 1993a).

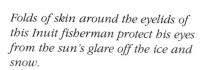

Folds of skin around the eyelids of this Inuit fisherman protect his eyes from the sun's glare off the ice and snow.

What are some criticisms of sociobiology? The major criticism of sociobiology is that the importance placed on genetics could be used as a justification to label specific races as superior or inferior. Critics of sociobiology also point out that there is too much variation in societies around the world for human behavior to be explained on strictly biological grounds. They believe that the capacity for using language is uniquely human and that humans have created a social life that goes far beyond what heredity alone could accomplish.

Is there a middle ground? Some common ground has emerged in this debate. A growing body of sociologists believe that genes work with culture in a complex way to shape and limit human nature and social life. They would like this relationship to be further examined (Lopreato, 1990; Weingart, 1997; Konner, 1999).

A 1998 study found that women look for one set of characteristics in men they marry while men value different characteristics in women (Buss,

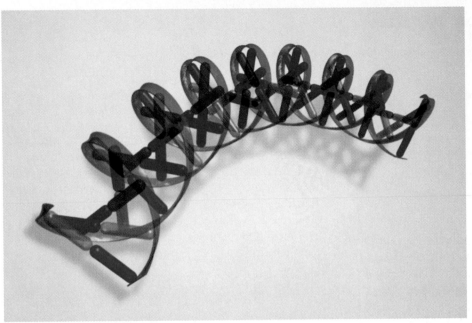

DNA, the genetic material in all cells, is the molecular basis of heredity. Sociobiology focuses on the relationship between heredity and human behavior.

Malamuth, and Windstad, 1998). The researchers believe this behavior is programmed into the genetic code. Studies have also determined that stepfathers are more likely than biological fathers to abuse their children (Daly and Wilson, 1997). Is this because men are more protective of their own biological offspring? Because of the speed of discoveries in the field of biology, the relationships between heredity, culture, and behavior are of growing interest to sociobiologists.

Men's natures are alike; it is their habits that carry them apart.

Confucius
Chinese philosopher

Section 1 Assessment

1. How is society different from culture?
2. About what percentage of personality is determined by genetics?
3. What are two arguments against the theory of sociobiology?
4. Predict which of the following are drives (D), which are reflexes (R), which are instincts (I), and which are creations of culture (C).
   a. eye blinking in dust storm   **d.** socialism
   b. need for sleep   **e.** reproduction
   c. reaction to a loud noise   **f.** racial inequality

Critical Thinking

5. **Synthesizing Information** Name three nonmaterial and three material elements that represent American culture to you.
6. **Making Generalizations** Do you think human behavior is more a result of culture or of heredity? Give reasons to support your answer.

Another Time

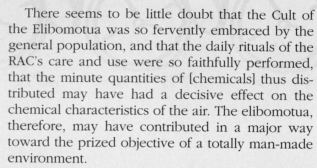

The Mysterious Fall of Nacirema

The following reading is excerpted from a review on a little-known North American culture.

Although the Nacirema left a large number of documents, our linguists have been unable to decipher any more than a few scattered fragments of the Nacirema language. Eventually, with the complete translation of these documents, we will undoubtedly learn a great deal about the reasons for the sudden disappearance of what . . . must have been an explosive and expansive culture . . . .

When we examine the area occupied by these people . . . it is immediately apparent that the Nacirema considered it of primary importance to completely remake the environment. . . . Trees . . . were removed. . . . Most of the land . . . was sowed each year with a limited variety of plants . . . .

For a period of about 300 solar cycles . . . the Nacirema devoted a major part of their effort to the special environmental problem of changing the appearance of air and water. Until the last fifty solar cycles of the culture's existence, they seemed

to have had only indifferent success. But during the short period before the fall of the culture, they mastered their art magnificently. They changed the color of the waters from the cool end of the spectrum (blues and greens) toward the warm ends (reds and browns). . . .

Early research has disclosed the importance of . . . the presence of the . . . Elibomotua [RAC] Cult, which sought to create an intense sense of individual involvement in the community effort to completely control the environment . . . .

There seems to be little doubt that the Cult of the Elibomotua was so fervently embraced by the general population, and that the daily rituals of the RAC's care and use were so faithfully performed, that the minute quantities of [chemicals] thus distributed may have had a decisive effect on the chemical characteristics of the air. The elibomotua, therefore, may have contributed in a major way toward the prized objective of a totally man-made environment.

In summary, our evaluation of . . . the Nacirema's man-made environmental alterations . . . lead us to advance the hypothesis that they may have been responsible for their own extinction. The Nacirema culture may have been so successful in achieving its objectives that . . . its people were unable to cope with its manufactured environment.

If the Nacirema seem vaguely familiar, it's because *Nacirema* is *American* spelled backward. Neil Thompson's description strikes us as strange. This is because Americans are not used to looking at their culture as others from the outside might see it. Like fish in water, Americans are so close to their own customs and rituals that they are in a sense unaware of them. Looking at culture from the sociological perspective will heighten your awareness of your own culture as well as the cultures of others.

Source: Neil B. Thompson, "The Mysterious Fall of Nacirema." *Natural History* (December, 1972). Copyright the American Museum of Natural History (1972). Reprinted with permission.

Thinking It Over

1. Describe how your feeling toward the Nacirema changed when you knew their true identity.

2. What other items in today's American culture might be misinterpreted by future anthropologists?

Section 2

Language and Culture

Key Terms

- symbols
- hypothesis of linguistic relativity

Symbols, Language, and Culture

If culture is to be transmitted, it must be learned anew by each generation. Both the creation and the transmission of culture depend heavily on the use of symbols. The most powerful symbols are those that make up language.

What are symbols? In Lewis Carroll's *Through the Looking Glass*, Humpty Dumpty says to Alice, "When I use a word, it means just what I choose it to mean—neither more nor less." So it is with **symbols**—things that stand for or represent something else.

Symbols range from physical objects to sounds, smells, and tastes. As you read in Chapter 1, the meaning of a symbol is not based on physical characteristics. For example, there is nothing naturally pleasing about the sound created by hands loudly clapping together. Applause warms the heart of an entertainer, a politician, or a high school athlete in the United States, but in Latin America the same sound means disapproval. The ball Mark McGwire hit for his 70th home run in 1998 is a symbol. The Confederate flag that represents oppression for many African Americans and a proud cultural heritage for many white Southerners is a symbol with different meanings attached.

How are language and culture related? Language frees humans from the limits of time and place. It allows us to create culture. The Wright brothers' successful flight did not come just from their own personal efforts. They built their airplane according to principles of flight already existing in American culture. Through language they could read, discuss, and recombine existing ideas and technology.

Equipped with language, humans can pass their experiences, ideas, and knowledge to others. Although it may take time and repetition, children can be taught the dangers of fire and heights without being burned or toppling down stairs. This process of social learning, of course, applies to other cultural patterns as well, such as eating, showing patriotism, or staying awake in class.

Section Preview

Humans can create and transmit culture. The symbols of language play a role in determining people's views of reality.

symbol
a thing that stands for or represents something else

Some symbols are recognized and understood by people all over the world.

How to Speak with Your Hands

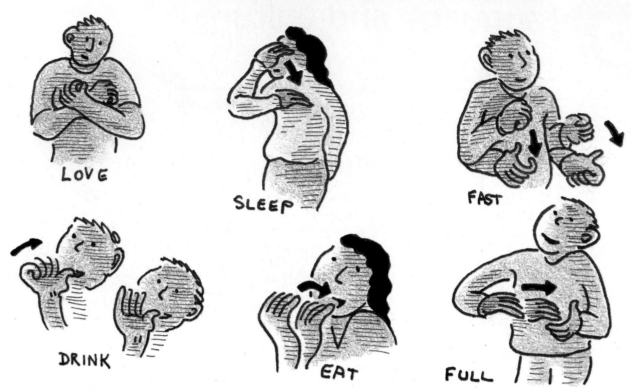

Figure 3.1 Sign Language. *Hand movements in sign language are symbols.*

The Sapir-Whorf Hypothesis

hypothesis of linguistic relativity
theory stating that our idea of reality depends largely upon language

> England and America are two countries separated by the same language.
>
> G. B. Shaw
> British playwright

According to Edward Sapir (1929) and Benjamin Whorf (1956), language is our guide to reality. How we think about a thing relates to the number and complexity of words available to describe that thing. In effect, our perceptions of the world depend in part on the particular language we have learned. Since languages differ, perceptions differ as well. This theory is known as the Sapir-Whorf Hypothesis, or the **hypothesis of linguistic relativity.**

What can vocabulary tell you about a culture?   When something is important to a society, its language will have many words to describe it. The importance of time in American culture is reflected in the many words that describe time intervals—*nanosecond, millisecond, moment, minute, hour, era, interim, recurrent, century, light-year, afternoon, eternal, annual, meanwhile,* and *regularly,* just to name a few. When something is unimportant to people, they may not have even one word for it. When Christian missionaries first went to Asia, they were dismayed because the Chinese language contained no word for sin. Other missionaries were no less distressed to learn that Africans and Polynesians had no word to express the idea of a single, all-powerful God. While English has only a few words that describe snow, the Inuit (Eskimo) language has over twenty.

Does the hypothesis of linguistic relativity mean we are prisoners of our language?
Even if our view of the world is shaped largely by language, we are not forever trapped by our own language. Exposure to another language or to new words can alter a person's perception of the world. (This is one reason why it is important to avoid using racist slurs and stereotypical labels.) People can begin to view the world differently as they learn a new language or vocabulary. However, most people do confine themselves to the language and vocabulary they learned from birth. They tend not to change their views of the world. You can either expand or limit your outlook, depending upon how you use language.

What other factors help to shape our perception of reality? How we perceive the world around us is influenced by more than vocabulary. Cultures may differ in many ways, and these differences influence how their members experience the world. The Japanese use paper walls as sound barriers and are not bothered by noise in adjacent rooms. Americans staying at hotels in Japan complain they are being bombarded with noise because Westerners have not been *conditioned* (mentally trained) to screen out sound.

Privacy is so important to most Germans that German executives generally have a "closed-door policy." Problems arise, as you might imagine, in American firms located in Germany because American executives leave their doors open.

In Japanese culture an emphasis on politeness has helped people learn to live harmoniously in close quarters.

Section 2 Assessment

1. What are symbols?
2. How does language affect culture?

Critical Thinking

3. **Understanding Cause and Effect** Describe some specific ways you see language affecting social behavior among students in your school.
4. **Drawing Conclusions** Some experts believe that without language there is no thought. Do you agree? Why or why not?

SOCIOLOGY *Online*

Student Web Activity
Visit the *Sociology and You* Web site at soc.glencoe.com and click on **Chapter 3—Student Web Activities** for an activity on language.

Sociology Today

Cultural Relativism

Different behaviors, traditions, and expectations can often result in misunderstandings between people of different cultures. Learning to look at things from a point of view different from your own, and not making value judgments based on your beliefs and norms, is called *cultural relativism*. Having mutual respect and understanding for other cultures is sometimes more effective than modern technology and money in producing change and goodwill between nations.

Cultural relativism is illustrated in the true story of a young Peace Corps volunteer who was sent to a remote village to help build a well. The stream that was near the village was used for everything from watering goats to bathing to washing clothes to cooking and drinking. It was obvious that clean drinking water would benefit the village and improve health. Armed with plans, equipment, and budget and schedule, the hopeful volunteer arrived ready to begin.

At first, the village people were not very willing to help. After several weeks of lonely effort the volunteer met with the council to ask why nobody was helping her with this urgent project. "A well would be nice," the people agreed, "but what we really need is a good soccer field where we can play without getting hurt on the stones and uneven ground." So the volunteer agreed that some of the money and equipment could be used to build a good soccer field first.

After several weeks of effort, the soccer field was complete and a village soccer team was formed. Now work was able to start on the well, but once again the villagers seemed reluctant to help. Another council meeting was held,

and the volunteer was told, "Ah yes, the well would be nice, but what we really need is a bridge across the stream so other villages can easily come to play soccer on our field." Since she couldn't dig the well alone, the volunteer agreed that some more time and money would be used to build a bridge. Unfortunately, the bridge proved to be more difficult than expected, and by the time it was complete, the budget and schedule were both used up.

The volunteer went back to the capital, disappointed and resentful that she had not been able to improve the village. Some weeks later, she was invited back by the villagers for a festival to celebrate the success of the soccer tournament they had arranged. When she arrived she was astonished to find a new well in the very center of the village. She asked the village elders for an explanation.

"The soccer tournament is important to us," she was told, "because it gives us pride and importance and gives us a reason to meet with the people of the other villages. We really never wanted a well."

"Then why did you build it?" she asked.

"We didn't build it because we wanted it," was the answer. "We built it because YOU wanted it."

Doing Sociology

1. What assumptions did the volunteer make about the needs of the villagers? What were the actual needs? Who was more right about what the villagers needed? Why?

2. Describe a time when you made assumptions that turned out to be culturally based.

Section 3

Norms and Values

K e y   T e r m s

- norms
- folkways
- mores
- taboo
- law

- sanctions
- formal sanctions
- informal sanctions
- values

Norms: The Rules We Live By

If you wanted to describe your culture, what would you look for? How could you begin to classify the elements of the American way of life? Sociologists begin with the defining components of a culture: its norms, its values and beliefs, and its use of material objects.

Norms are rules defining appropriate and inappropriate behavior. A Hindu peasant in India can be found lying dead of starvation beside perfectly healthy cattle. In order to strengthen bonds between clans, a young Basarwa girl in Africa might become engaged to a man she has not met. Roman emperors routinely exiled relatives to small isolated islands for "disgracing" the family. Each of these instances reflects cultural norms—ways of behaving in specific situations. Norms help to explain why people in a society or group behave similarly in similar circumstances.

William Graham Sumner (1906) was an early sociologist who wrote about norms. Anything, he stated, can be considered appropriate when norms approve of it. This is because once norms are learned, members of a society

Section Preview

Two essential components of culture are norms and values. There are several types of norms—folkways, mores, and laws. Sanctions are used to encourage conformity to norms. Values, the broadest cultural ideas, form the basis for norms.

norms
rules defining appropriate and inappropriate behavior

All cultures have norms relating to marriage and family life; weddings are always important occasions. This Hindu couple is celebrating their marriage with a garland ritual.

Figure 3.2 Cultural Etiquette

It might prevent some embarrassing moments if you were aware of norms and customs before traveling to foreign places.

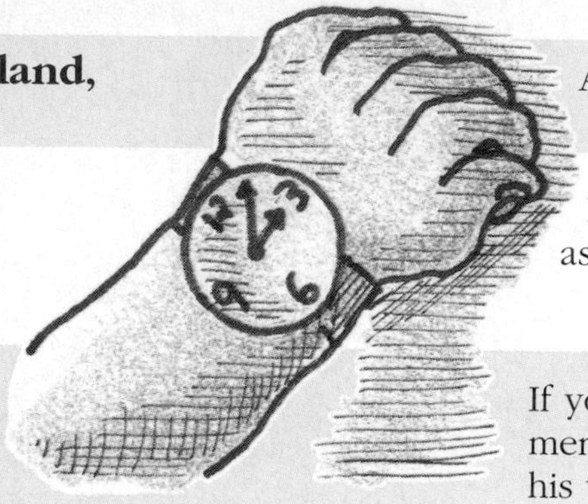

Country	Custom
England, Scotland, and Wales	Appointments are essential. You may be ten minutes late but not ten minutes early.
Greece	Be careful not to praise a specific object too enthusiastically or the host may insist on giving it to you.
Libya	If you are invited to a Libyan home for dinner, only men will be present. Take a gift for the host but not for his wife.
Senegal	Never eat food with the left hand, as this is considered offensive.
Zambia	Avoid direct eye contact with members of the opposite sex—it may suggest romantic overtures.
Saudi Arabia	It is an insult to sit in such a way as to face your host with the soles of your shoes showing. Do not place your feet on a desk, table, or chair.
Oman	If an Arab businessman takes your hand and holds it as you walk, do not be alarmed. He means it only as a sign of friendship.
China	A visit to a Chinese home is rare—unless the government has given prior approval.
Japan	If you are offered a gift, thank the person and wait for one or two more offers before accepting it. Receive the gift with both hands.
South Korea	Men go through doors first. Women help men with their coats.

Source: Roger E. Axtell, *Do's and Taboos Around the World*, 3rd ed. (New York: John Wiley & Sons, 1993).

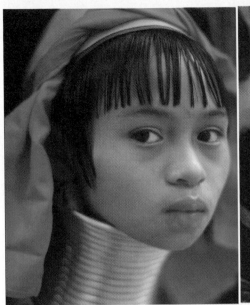

Norms help define a culture's perception of beauty for both males and females. What are some norms that shape the American ideal of beauty?

use them to guide their social behavior. Norms are so ingrained they guide behavior without our awareness. In fact, we may not be consciously aware of a norm until it has been broken. For instance, you may not think about standing in line for concert tickets as a norm until someone attempts to step in front of you. Then it immediately registers that waiting your turn in line is expected behavior. Cutting in front of someone violates that norm. Norms range from relatively minor rules, such as the idea that we should applaud after a performance, to extremely important ones, such as laws against stealing.

Folkways, Mores, and Laws

Sumner identified three basic types of norms: *folkways, mores,* and *laws.* These three types of norms vary in their importance within a society. Accordingly, their violation is tolerated to different degrees.

What are folkways?   Rules that cover customary ways of thinking, feeling, and behaving but lack moral overtones are called **folkways.** For example, sleeping in a bed versus sleeping on the floor is not a moral issue; it qualifies as a folkway. Folkways in the United States include supporting school activities, speaking to other students in the hall, and, if you are male, removing your hat in church.

Because folkways are not considered vital to group welfare, disapproval of those who break them is not very great. Those who consistently violate folkways—say, by talking loudly in quiet places, wearing shorts with a suit coat and tie, or wearing a different-colored sock on each foot—may appear odd. We may avoid these people, but we do not consider them wicked or immoral.

Some folkways are more important than others, and the social reaction to their violation is more intense. Failure to offer a woman a seat on a crowded bus draws little notice today. In contrast, obnoxious behavior at a party after excessive drinking may bring a strong negative reaction from others.

A knowledge of one other culture should sharpen our ability to scrutinize more steadily, to appreciate more lovingly, our own.

**Margaret Mead
U.S. anthropologist**

**folkways
norms that lack moral significance**

mores
norms that have moral dimensions and that should be followed by members of the society

taboo
a rule of behavior, the violation of which calls for strong punishment

What are mores?   The term **mores** (pronounced "MOR-ays") is based on the word *moral.* Morality deals with conduct related to right and wrong. Mores are norms of great moral significance. They are vital to the well-being of a society. Conformity to mores draws strong social approval; violation of this type of norm brings strong disapproval. For example, Americans believe that able-bodied men should work for a living. Able-bodied men who do not work are scorned.

Although following folkways is generally a matter of personal choice, conformity to mores is a social requirement. Still, some mores are more vital to a society than others. Failure to stand at attention while the national anthem is being played is not as serious a violation of American mores as using loud profanity during a religious service.

The most serious mores are taboos. A **taboo** is a norm so strong that its violation demands punishment by the group (or, some people think even the supernatural). In India, followers of Hinduism have a taboo forbidding the killing of cows. Other taboos are related to sexual behaviors. Although definitions of incest vary from society to society, the incest taboo (forbidding sexual contact with close relatives) is generally regarded as the only taboo that is present in all societies. The "mother-in-law" taboo existing in some societies prohibits or severely restricts social contact between a husband and his wife's mother.

What folkways, mores, or laws are being demonstrated (or broken) in these scenes?

World View

Patterns of Tourism

Although people often want to observe and experience cultures different from their own, exposure to cultural diversity can be uncomfortable. Most international tourist travel occurs among countries sharing common cultural traditions and languages.

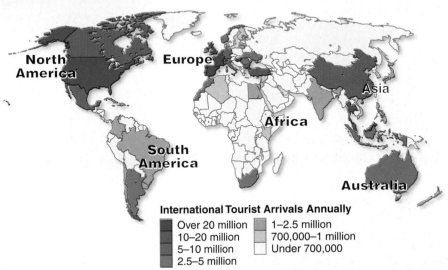

International Tourist Arrivals Annually

Over 20 million	1–2.5 million
10–20 million	700,000–1 million
5–10 million	Under 700,000
2.5–5 million	

Interpreting the Map

1. Identify the world regions that receive the highest and lowest number of tourists.
2. Are there any reasons to believe that these travel patterns might change in the near future? If so, what factors might bring about this change?

Adapted from the *Student Atlas:* DK Publishing, Inc.

How do laws differ from mores?   The third type of norm is **law.** Laws are norms that are formally defined and enforced by officials. Folkways and mores emerge slowly and are often unconsciously created, while laws are consciously created and enforced.

> **law**
> a norm that is formally defined and enforced by officials

Mores are an important source for laws. At one time, the norm against murder was not written down. But as civilization advanced, the norm against murder became formally defined and enforced by public officials.

Folkways can become mores or laws. Smoking, for example, was an acceptable behavior to most Americans until the late 1970s, when mounting health concerns convinced many that smoking should be limited or banned in public places. Today, many states have laws against smoking in airports, government buildings, restaurants, and other places open to the general public.

Not all mores become laws. For example, it is not against the law to cheat on an exam (although you may be suspended or punished by the teacher). Furthermore, not all laws started out as mores. Fines for overtime parking and laws against littering have never been mores.

Figure 3.3 Silly Laws Still on the Books

There are many laws throughout the country whose purposes and existence have long been forgotten. At the time, they may have been perfectly logical. As society changed, the need for them disappeared.

State	Law
Alabama	It is illegal for a driver to be blindfolded while operating a vehicle.
Arizona	Hunting camels is prohibited.
Florida	If an elephant is left tied to a parking meter, the fee has to be paid just as it would be for a vehicle.
Illinois	You must contact the police before entering the city in an automobile.
Iowa	Kisses may last for as much as, but no more than, five minutes.
Maine	You must not step out of a plane in flight.
Massachusetts	No gorilla is allowed in the back seat of any car.
Minnesota	A person may not cross state lines with a duck atop his or her head.
Vermont	Whistling underwater is illegal.
Washington	It is illegal to pretend that one's parents are rich.

Laws often remain on the books for a long time after the mores of a society have changed. It is illegal in Minnesota to hang male and female undergarments on the same clothesline. New York prohibits card playing on trains; elephants in Natchez, Mississippi, cannot legally drink beer; and it is against the law to wear roller skates in public bathrooms in Portland, Oregon. (For additional laws that seem strange to us today, see Figure 3.3.)

Enforcing the Rules

People do not automatically conform to norms. Norms must be learned and accepted. Groups teach norms, in part, through the use of *sanctions*. **Sanctions** are rewards and punishments used to encourage conformity to norms. They can be formal or informal.

What are formal sanctions? **Formal sanctions** are sanctions that may be applied only by officially designated persons, such as judges and teachers. Formal sanctions can take the form of positive as well as negative rewards. A soldier earns a Congressional Medal of Honor as a positive sanction for heroism. Teachers reward outstanding students with A's. Of course, formal sanctions can also take the form of punishments.

Formal punishments range widely in their severity. From the Middle Ages to the Protestant Reformation, it was an unpardonable sin for lenders to charge interest on money. (This practice was called *usury* and was condemned in the Bible.) This crime was punishable on the third offense by public humiliation and social and economic ruin. More recently, a few courts across the United States have handed down sentences involving public shaming. For example, some courts have required child molesters to display, in front of their homes, signs describing their crimes (El Nasser, 1996). In

sanctions
rewards and punishments used to encourage people to follow norms

formal sanctions
sanctions imposed by persons given special authority

A law's final justification is in the good it does or fails to do to the society of a given place and time.

Albert Camus
French philosopher

Formal sanctions often involve action in the criminal or civil judicial systems.

1997, Latrell Sprewell, star basketball player for the Golden State Warriors, physically attacked his coach, P. J. Carlesimo. The NBA revoked his $32 million, four-year contract and suspended him for one year before he joined the New York Knicks.

What are informal sanctions?   **Informal sanctions** are sanctions that can be applied by most members of a group. They, too, can be positive or negative. Informal sanctions include thanking someone for pushing a car out of a snowbank (positive) or staring at someone who is talking loudly during a movie (negative).

Sanctions are not used randomly or without reason. Specific sanctions are associated with specific norms. A high school student who violates his parents' curfew is not supposed to be locked in a closet, for example.

After we reach a certain age, most of us conform without the threat of sanctions. We may conform to norms because we believe that the behavior expected of us is appropriate, because we wish to avoid guilt feelings, or because we fear social disapproval. In other words, we sanction ourselves mentally.

informal sanctions
rewards or punishments that can be applied by most members of a group

THE FAR SIDE   By GARY LARSON

"Frank. ... Don't do that."

Frank seems to have forgotten that "real men" don't cross their legs.
This informal sanction will probably bring him into line.

Values—The Basis for Norms

Norms and sanctions are relatively specific. The next major component of culture—*values*—is much more general.

What are values?   **Values** are broad ideas about what most people in a society consider to be desirable. Values are so general that they do not dictate precise ways of thinking, feeling, and behaving. Thus, different societies or different groups within the same society can have quite different norms based on the same value.

For instance, consider the norms used to express the value of freedom in America and in the former Soviet Union. Soviet leaders said their people were free because the leaders claimed to provide full employment, medical care, and education. Americans have different norms based on the value of freedom. These norms include the right to free speech and assembly, the right to engage in private enterprise, and the right to a representative government. Identical values do not result in identical norms.

Why are values important?   Values have a tremendous influence on human social behavior because they form the basis for norms. A society that values democracy will have norms ensuring personal freedom. A society that values human welfare will have norms providing for its most unfortunate members. A society that values hard work will have norms against laziness.

Values are also important because they are so general that they are involved in most aspects of daily life. In America, for example, the influence of the value of freedom goes beyond political life. The value of freedom affects how family relationships are conducted, how people are treated within the legal system, how organizations are run, and how people worship.

values
broad ideas about what is good or desirable shared by people in a society

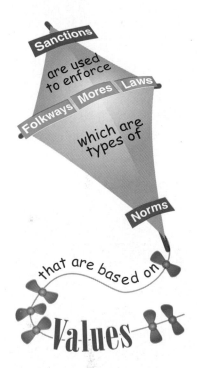

Figure 3.4 The Norm Kite. *If a society is to fly, it must have these basic elements of social structure. Sanctions (rewards and punishments) are needed to enforce norms (folkways, mores, laws). Guiding the Norm Kite are a society's values, the basis for norms.*

After winning the World Cup, members of the U.S. women's soccer team became role models for many girls. What strong cultural values do these young women demonstrate?

Basic Values in the United States

What cultural values are represented in these photos?

The United States is home to many different groups. No single set of values is likely to hold across the entire country. Despite this problem, sociologist Robin Williams (1970) identified important values that guide the daily lives of most people in the U.S. A partial list includes:

❖ *Achievement and success.* People emphasize achievement, especially in the world of work. Success is supposed to be based on effort and competition and is viewed as a reward for performance. Wealth is viewed as a symbol of success and personal worth.

❖ *Activity and work.* People tend to prefer action over inaction in almost every case. For most Americans, continuous and regular work is a goal in itself. Promotion should be for merit rather than favoritism. Finally, all citizens should have the opportunity to perform at their best.

❖ *Efficiency and practicality.* People pride themselves on getting things done by the most rational means. We search for better (faster) ways of doing things, praise good workmanship, and judge performance by the results. We love to rely on science and technology.

❖ *Equality.* From the very beginning of our history as a nation, we have declared a belief in equality for all citizens. As minority groups and women achieved citizenship, our concept of equality grew. We tend to treat one another as equals, defend everyone's legal rights, and favor equal opportunity—if not equal results—for everyone.

❖ *Democracy.* People emphasize that all citizens are entitled to equal rights and equal opportunity under the law. In a democracy, the people elect their government officials. Power is not in the hands of an elite few.

❖ *Group superiority.* Despite their concern for equality of opportunity, people in the U.S. tend to place a greater value on people of their own race, ethnic group, social class, or religious group.

These values are clearly interrelated. Achievement and success affect and are affected by efficiency and practicality, for example. But we can also see conflicts among some values. For instance, people in the U.S. value group superiority while at the same time stressing equality and democracy.

Do these values still prevail in the United States today?   Williams identified these major values approximately thirty years ago—about the time many of your parents were teenagers. Although these values have remained remarkably stable over the years, some have changed. Today there is less emphasis on group superiority in America than in the past. This can be seen in the decline of openly racist attitudes and behaviors (Farley, 1996; Rochen, 1998). In reality, however, it is usually norms and behavior rather than underlying values that change radically. It is probably because of the passage of civil rights laws that many Americans are now less likely to make overt racist statements. Racism (group superiority) remains part of the fabric of American culture.

The norms related to hard work and activity have also changed in recent years. Many Americans now work as hard at their leisure activities (for example, long-distance running and mountain climbing) as they do at their jobs.

Calvin and Hobbes   by Bill Watterson

Calvin's father is trying to transmit the cultural value of competition. As usual, Calvin has his own view. What is yours?

Although Williams's analysis of major American values remains basically sound today, some sociologists believe that his list is incomplete. They would add, for example, optimism, honesty, and friendliness to the list of major values in the United States.

Section 3 Assessment

1. Indicate whether these statements best reflect a folkway (F), a more (M), a law (L), or a value (V).
   a. norm against cursing aloud in church
   b. norm encouraging eating three meals daily
   c. idea of progress
   d. norm against burning a national flag
   e. norm encouraging sleeping in a bed
   f. norm prohibiting murder
   g. norm against overtime parking
   h. idea of freedom
2. Sociologists make a distinction between norms and values. How are these concepts different? Support your answer with examples.

Critical Thinking

3. **Analyzing Information**   Review the partial list of values identified by Robin Williams on the previous page. Is there a value not listed that you think should be included? What is it? Why would you include it?

> 66
> No written law has ever been more binding than unwritten custom supported by popular opinion.
>
> **Carrie Chapman Catt
> American reformer**
>
> 99

Section 4

Beliefs and Material Culture

Key Terms

- nonmaterial culture
- beliefs
- material culture
- ideal culture
- real culture

Section Preview

Besides norms and values, beliefs and physical objects make up culture. Ideal culture includes the guidelines we claim to accept, while real culture describes how we actually behave.

nonmaterial culture
ideas, knowledge and beliefs that influence people's behavior

beliefs
ideas about the nature of reality

material culture
the concrete, tangible objects of a culture

Beliefs and Physical Objects

The **nonmaterial culture** involves beliefs, ideas, and knowledge. The *material culture* is about how we relate to physical objects. Values, norms, knowledge, ideas (nonmaterial), and physical objects (material) make up a culture.

Why do beliefs matter? **Beliefs** are ideas about the nature of reality. Beliefs can be true or false. The Romans believed Caesar Augustus to be a god; the Tanala, a hill tribe of Madagascar, believed that the souls of their kings passed into snakes; and many Germans believed that pictures of Hitler on their walls would prevent the walls from crumbling during bombing raids. We would certainly consider these beliefs to be false. In contrast, other beliefs—such as the belief that the human eye can distinguish over seven million colors and the belief that no intelligent life exists on Mars—are supported by factual evidence. We consider these to be true. Beliefs are important because people base their behavior on what they believe, regardless of how true or false the beliefs are.

What is material culture? **Material culture** consists of the concrete, tangible objects within a culture—automobiles, basketballs, chairs, highways, art. These physical objects have no meaning or use apart from the meanings people give them.

Acres of discarded cars in a junkyard plainly show that the automobile is one of the most common objects of America's material culture.

Consider newspaper and pepper as physical objects. Each has some meaning for you, but can you think of a use for them in combination? Some Americans have used pepper and newspaper in a process known as "nettling." An elderly medical doctor tells the story of his first encounter with nettling:

The ink of my medical license was hardly dry, and as I was soon to find out, my ears would not be dry for some time. I had never delivered a baby on my own and faced my maiden voyage with some fear.

Upon entering Mrs. Williamson's house, I found a local midwife and several neighbors busily at work preparing for the delivery. My fear caused me to move rather slowly and my happiness over my reprieve prompted me to tell the women that they were doing just fine and to proceed without my services.

Having gotten myself off the hook, I watched the ladies with a fascination that soon turned to horror.

At the height of Mrs. Williamson's labor pains, one of the neighbors rolled a piece of newspaper into a funnel shape. Holding the bottom end of the cone she poured a liberal amount of pepper into it. Her next move was to insert the sharp end of the cone into Mrs. Williamson's nose. With the cone in its "proper" place, the neighbor inhaled deeply and blew the pepper from the cone into the inner recesses of Mrs. Williamson's nose—if not her mind.

Suddenly alert, Mrs. Williamson's eyes widened as her senses rebelled against the pepper. With a mighty sneeze, I was introduced to nettling. The violence of that sneeze reverberated through her body to force the baby from her womb in a skittering flight across the bed. An appropriately positioned assistant fielded the baby in midflight and only minor details of Orville's rite of birth remained.

Before this doctor was introduced to nettling, this particular combination of newspaper and pepper had no meaning for him. And until nettling was devised, the combination was without meaning for anyone, even though the separate physical objects existed as part of the culture.

For this country doctor, the physical objects of newspaper and pepper took on new meaning.

How is material culture related to nonmaterial culture?   The uses and meanings of physical objects can vary among societies. Although it is conventional to use a 747 jet for traveling, it is possible that a 747 downed in a remote jungle region of the world could be used as a place of worship, a storage bin, or a home. In the United States, out-of-service buses, trains, and trolley cars have been converted to restaurants.

Clearly, the cultural meaning of physical objects is not determined by the physical characteristics of the objects. The meanings of physical objects are based on the beliefs, norms, and values people hold with regard to them. This is obvious when new meanings of a physical object are considered. At one time, only pianos and organs were used in church services. Guitars, drums, and trumpets were not "holy" enough to accompany a choir. Yet many churches today use these "worldly" instruments regularly in their worship activities. The instruments have not changed, but the cultural meanings placed on them have.

Though American ideal culture values natural athletic ability, in reality, some professional and amateur athletes use drugs or steroids to improve their performances.

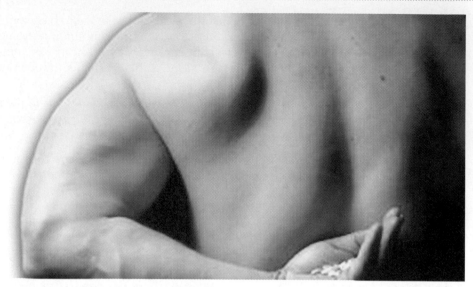

Ideal and Real Culture

A gap sometimes exists between cultural guidelines and actual behavior. This gap is captured in the concepts of ideal and real culture. **Ideal culture** refers to cultural guidelines publicly embraced by members of a society. **Real culture** refers to actual behavior patterns, which often conflict with these guidelines.

One value of America's ideal culture is honesty. Yet in real culture, honesty is not always practiced. Some taxpayers annually violate both the letter and spirit of existing tax laws. Some businesspeople engage in dishonest business practices. Some students cheat on exams. Some college athletes do the "high $500" handshake, during which a team booster leaves illegal money in their palms. These are not isolated instances. They are real cultural patterns passed on from generation to generation.

It is important to remember that we are not referring here to individuals whose violations of norms include murder, rape, and robbery. These types of antisocial behavior violate even real culture.

Does the fact that we sometimes ignore cultural guidelines make ideal culture meaningless? Absolutely not. In an imperfect world, ideal culture provides high standards. These ideals are targets that most people attempt to reach most of the time. Ideal culture also permits the detection of deviant behavior. Individuals who deviate too far from the ideal pattern are sanctioned. This helps to preserve the ideal culture.

ideal culture
cultural guidelines that group members claim to accept

real culture
actual behavior patterns of members of a group

Section 4 Assessment

1. How is the material culture influenced by the nonmaterial culture?
2. How is real culture different from ideal culture?

Critical Thinking

3. **Drawing Conclusions**   Think of an example of real and ideal culture in your school. Should the aspect of ideal culture be abandoned? Why or why not?

Section 5

Cultural Diversity and Similarity

Key Terms

- **social categories**
- **subculture**
- **counterculture**

- **ethnocentrism**
- **cultural universals**
- **cultural particulars**

Cultural Change

So far we have talked about culture as if it did not change. Actually the processes that govern cultural change are so important they are discussed in Chapter 17 on social movements and collective behavior. Briefly, however, you should realize that all cultures experience change. Norms, values, and beliefs are relatively stable, but they do change over time. For example, many of your grandparents never went to college; as teenagers, your parents never e-mailed friends or made last-minute dates on their cell phones. It was not that long ago that middle-class women with young children were discouraged from working outside the home. Interracial dating, while still relatively uncommon, is becoming more acceptable in the United States. These are aspects of culture that are changing in response to certain processes.

Why does culture change?   Culture changes for three reasons. One cause is *discovery*, the process of finding something that already exists. The United States is currently discovering the generally unrecognized athletic abilities of females. This is changing the perception of women and the relationship between males and females.

Culture is also changed through *invention*, the creation of something new. Science has led to inventions that have changed the world since the fifteenth century, from the creation of the steam engine to the cellular phone. Such inventions have greatly altered our way of life.

A third cause of cultural change is *diffusion*, the borrowing of aspects of culture from other cultures. One aspect of culture that diffuses rapidly is food. Tacos, pizza, and hamburgers can be found on menus all over the world. Christmas trees and piñatas are part of celebrations in many countries. Ideas are also diffused. Japanese society has been fundamentally transformed as a result of the adoption of democracy and capitalism after World War II. As stated earlier, these three processes will be examined more closely in a later chapter.

Section Preview

Cultures change according to three major processes. Cultures contain groups within them called *subcultures* and *countercultures* that differ in important ways from the main culture. People tend to make judgments based on the values of their own cultures. While apparently very different on the surface, all cultures have common traits or elements that sociologists call *cultural universals*.

The Scottish kilt is an essential part of this South African traditional dance that tells the story of a historic battle with the British in the 1800s.

Focus on Research

Survey Research: How Do Schools and Parents Fail Teens?

Adolescence is often marked with drama and difficulty. Jacquelynne Eccles (1993) investigated the experience of American teenagers entering a midwestern junior high school and discovered that some teenage troubles are more than hormonal—they are cultural as well.

Eccles studied 1,500 early adolescents moving from sixth-grade elementary schools to seventh-grade junior high schools. The junior high schools were located in twelve school districts in middle-class Michigan communities. Students filled out questionnaires at school for two consecutive years—the sixth and seventh grades. This procedure permitted Eccles to document changes the teenagers experienced after the first year of their transition.

The findings were not encouraging. The relationships between students and teachers tended to worsen over the year. At the very time when the young adolescents especially needed supportive relationships outside of their homes, personal and positive relationships with teachers were strained by cultural and organizational changes in junior high school.

There was more grouping based on academic achievement and more comparing of students with one another. This increased emphasis on student ranking comes just when young adolescents are most insecure about their status relative to their peers. In addition, in the junior high culture, the students experienced less opportunity to participate in classroom decision making.

As a result, student motivation and self-confidence declined. Eccles concluded that junior high school culture denies adolescents the emotionally supportive environment they need for proper social development.

Junior high students who are in supportive environments are more likely to have higher motivation and self-esteem than students in less supportive schools and families.

Eccles's news was no better on the home front. Changes in family paralleled those of the school system. Parental control over teenagers went up during the year, often to excessive levels. At the same time, school motivation and self-esteem of the junior high students went down.

As a check on these general findings, Eccles compared students in more supportive schools and families with those in less supportive ones. In both the school and the family settings, she found more positive results in supportive environments. Students who were able to participate in school and family decision making showed higher levels of academic motivation and self-esteem than their peers with less opportunity to participate.

The solution to this problem, Eccles concludes, lies in a change in the norms and values of the schools and families. Schools and families need to develop balanced cultural expectations of young adolescents based on their developmental needs. Adolescents, Eccles points out, have a growing need for independence that is rarely encouraged in the culture of the public school system. Neither cracking down on them nor giving up control strikes the proper balance. The task is for the family and school to provide "an environment that changes in the right way and at the right pace" (Eccles, 1993:99).

Working with the Research

1. Do you recall your junior high experience? Was your situation similar to the one described by Eccles? Did you feel the same pressures?
2. Which of the three theoretical perspectives do you think is most helpful in understanding the social relationships Eccles describes? Apply this perspective to explain her findings.

Cultural Diversity

social categories
groupings of persons who share a social characteristic

subculture
a group that is part of the dominant culture but that differs from it in some important respects

counterculture
a subculture deliberately and consciously opposed to certain central beliefs or attitudes of the dominant culture

ethnocentrism
judging others in terms of one's own cultural standards

Cultural diversity exists in all societies. Some diversity is a result of **social categories**—groups that share a social characteristic such as age, gender, or religion. Certain behaviors are associated with particular ages, genders, or religions. For example, devout Catholics are expected to attend Mass regularly.

What are subcultures and countercultures? Cultural diversity also comes from groups that differ in particular ways from the larger culture. These groups participate in the larger culture. They may speak the language, work regular jobs, eat and dress like most others, and attend recognized houses of worship. But despite sharing in the broader culture, these groups have some ways of thinking, feeling, and behaving that set them apart. Such groups—known as *subcultures* and *countercultures*—are usually found in large, complex societies.

Subculture is part of the dominant culture but differs from it in some important respects. The subculture of San Francisco's Chinatown is a good example. Early Chinese immigrants brought much of their native culture with them to America and have attempted to retain it by passing it from generation to generation. Although Chinese residents of Chinatown have been greatly affected by American culture, they have kept many cultural patterns of their own, such as language, diet, and family structure. Other examples of subcultures are those formed by circus people, musicians, and mental patients (Fine, 1996; Redhead, 1997; Kephart and Zellner, 1998).

Counterculture is a subculture deliberately and consciously opposed to certain central beliefs or attitudes of the dominant culture. A counterculture can be understood only within the context of this opposition.

Examples of primarily teenage countercultures include the "goth" and the "punk" scenes. Goth is a shortening of the term *gothic*, meaning dark, strangely mysterious, and remote. Punk is a philosophy of rebellion and sexual revolution popularized by the lyrics and music of punk-rock bands.

Prison counterculture surfaced at the trial of John King, a man convicted of the gruesome truck-dragging murder of James Byrd, Jr. During an earlier prison stretch, King had become a member of a white supremacist gang that promoted many forms of violence. The gang's motto was "blood in, blood out," meaning that entry into the gang demanded a violent act, and leaving the gang would result in violence as well (Galloway, 1999). Delinquent gangs, motorcycle gangs, certain types of drug groups, and revolutionary or religious groups may also form countercultures (Zellner, 1999).

The punk movement began in Britain and quickly developed into an American counterculture.

Ethnocentrism

Once people learn their culture, they tend to become strongly committed to it. In fact, they often cannot imagine any other way of life. They may judge others in terms of their own cultural standards—a practice referred to as **ethnocentrism.**

Tech Trends

Star Wars and the Internet

When *Star Wars* first appeared in theaters in the late 1970s, director George Lucas probably did not realize that he had almost single-handedly created a full-fledged cultural phenomenon. Virtually everyone in the United States now recognizes Luke Skywalker, Darth Vader, and Yoda. Most Americans know what "May the Force be with you" means.

The movies in the *Star Wars* series have certainly been extremely popular in their own right, but the Internet has also been important in their penetration into popular culture. In 1999, *Star Wars* fans kept in touch over the Internet as they eagerly awaited *The Phantom Menace*, the first new *Star Wars* film in sixteen years. Anticipation of the first "prequel" was incredibly intense, and pirated footage spread to more than sixty web sites within hours of first being posted. In response, Lucasfilm's official web site posted the film's trailer and was promptly overwhelmed with 340 "hits" per second. The impact of the Internet on this bit of American culture is undeniable.

"Everyone said this was the most top-secret movie ever made, that it was tighter than Fort Knox, no leaks whatsoever," says Scott Chitwood, aged twenty-five, who's the emperor of TheForce.net. "Well, most web site operators knew the plot a year ago. That's all because of the Internet."

Of course, the cultural effects of *Star Wars* are not limited to the box office. *Star Wars* is much more than a movie. It is a mini-culture, or subculture, unto itself. It has its own icons, symbols, and language. And elements of this subculture have entered the larger culture. Merchandise related to the first three *Star Wars* movies totaled over $4.5 billion in sales between 1977 and 1999. That alone amounts to more than four times the revenues generated from the films themselves. These items include toys, soundtracks, costumes, and licensing fees. With the increased popularity of e-commerce, the Internet has become a cultural force to be reckoned with.

Analyzing the Trends

1. What other recent events are now part of popular culture in the United States? Tell what aspects of these events have made their way into our thinking, feeling, and behaving.

2. Predict ways in which the increasing popularity of the Internet may alter our understanding of culture.

What are some examples of ethnocentrism?   Examples of ethnocentrism are plentiful. The Olympic Games are much more than an arena of competition for young men and women. In addition to competition, the games are an expression of ethnocentrism. Political and nationalistic undercurrents run through the Olympics. A country's final ranking in this athletic competition for gold, silver, and bronze medals is frequently taken as a reflection of the country's worth and status on the world stage.

Ethnocentrism also exists within societies. Regional rivalries in the United States are a source of many humorous stories, but these jokes reflect an underlying ethnocentrism. Boston is said by some (mostly Bostonians) to be the hub of the universe. Texans often claim to have the biggest and best of everything. New Yorkers bemoan the lack of culture in Los Angeles. Finally, members of churches, schools, and country clubs all over America feel that their particular ways of living should be adopted by others.

Does ethnocentrism help or hurt society?   Ethnocentrism has two faces—it offers both advantages and disadvantages. People feel good about themselves and about others in their group when they believe that what they are doing is right and superior to what other groups do. Stability is promoted because traditions and behaviors are highly valued. If a society is too rigid, however, it becomes inflexible. Extreme ethnocentrism can prevent change for the better. Societies whose members are firmly convinced of their superiority tend not to create anything new. The ancient Chinese built a wall to keep both invaders and new ideas out. The civil rights movement was born to combat racial ethnocentrism. Hitler's Final Solution was ethnocentrism at its worst. Today many states are passing laws that increase the penalties against people who commit violent acts against others based on their race, origin, or religion. (Civil rights and hate crimes are discussed in more detail in Chapter 9.)

Ethnocentrism is still a divisive force in Germany. A riot erupts when members of the ultraright National Democratic Party march in support of their racist policies.

Cultural Universals

Although it may seem that different cultures have little in common, researchers have identified more than seventy common cultural traits. These **cultural universals** are traits that exist in all cultures. They include such things as sports, cooking, courtship, division of labor, education, etiquette, funeral rites, family, government, hospitality, housing, inheritance rules, joking, language, medicine, marriage, mourning, music, property rights, religious rituals, sexual restrictions, status differences, and tool making (Murdock, 1945). Because all societies have these cultural universals, they are more similar than you think. (See Figure 3.5 on page 102 for a more detailed list of cultural universals.)

cultural universals
general cultural traits that exist in all cultures

How are cultural universals expressed?   Cultural universals are not always carried out in the same way. In fact, different cultures have developed quite different ways to express universals. These are called **cultural particulars.** One cultural universal is caring for children. In the United States, women have traditionally worked within the home caring for children, and men have worked outside the home. (Although this is changing, women in this country are still largely responsible for child care.) Among the

cultural particulars
the ways in which a culture expresses universal traits

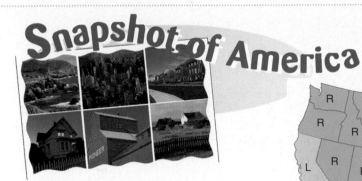

Snapshot of America

Gun Control

Some observers believe groups that promote gun ownership form a subculture. For example, the National Rifle Association (NRA) brings together people who share an interest in guns and the right to own them. The map displays the states that permit citizens to carry concealed guns.

Concealed Carry Codes:

R Right-to-carry permitted: Less restrictive discretionary permit system.

L Right-to-carry permitted: Limited by local authority's discretion over permit issuance.

D Right-to-carry denied: No permit system exists; concealed carry is prohibited.

Source: *NRA Institute for Legislative Action*

Interpreting the Map

1. What code marks the states with the most liberal gun control laws?
2. Can you find a pattern between gun control and regions in the U.S.?
3. How might regional differences in gun control laws reflect variations in socialization patterns?

Manus of New Guinea, in contrast, the man is completely in charge of child rearing. Among the Mbuti pygmies, the Lovedu of Africa, and the Navajo and Iroquois Indians, men and women share equally in domestic and economic tasks (Little, 1975).

Why do cultural universals exist? The biological similarity shared by all human beings helps to account for many cultural universals. If a society is to survive, children must be born and cared for, and some type of family structure must exist. (Groups that deliberately eliminate the family—such as the Shakers religious sect of New England—disappear.) Because people become ill, there must be some sort of medical care. Because people die, there must be funeral rites, mourning, and inheritance rules. Because food is necessary, cooking must be done.

The physical environment provides another reason why cultural universals exist. Because humans cannot survive without protection from the environment, some form of shelter must be created. Armies were formed to settle disputes over boundaries and important waterways.

Finally, cultural universals exist because societies face many of the same social problems. If a society is to survive, new members must be taught the

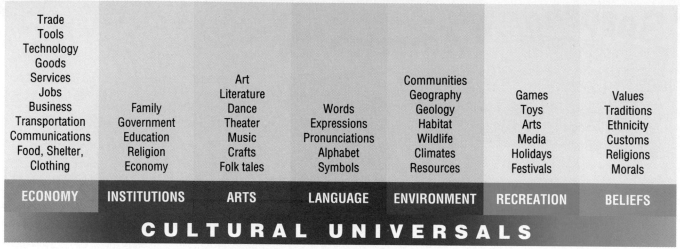

ECONOMY	INSTITUTIONS	ARTS	LANGUAGE	ENVIRONMENT	RECREATION	BELIEFS
Trade Tools Technology Goods Services Jobs Business Transportation Communications Food, Shelter, Clothing	Family Government Education Religion Economy	Art Literature Dance Theater Music Crafts Folk tales	Words Expressions Pronunciations Alphabet Symbols	Communities Geography Geology Habitat Wildlife Climates Resources	Games Toys Arts Media Holidays Festivals	Values Traditions Ethnicity Customs Religions Morals

CULTURAL UNIVERSALS

Figure 3.5 Cultural Universals. *Researchers have identified more than seventy traits that appear to one degree or another in all cultures.*

culture. Goods and services must be produced and distributed. Tasks must be assigned, and work must be accomplished. Cultures develop similar methods of solving these problems.

Section 5 Assessment

If we cannot end now our differences, at least we can help make the world safe for diversity.

John F. Kennedy
U.S. president

1. Identify each of the following as a social category (SC), subculture (S), or counterculture (C).
    a. Chinatown in New York City
    b. motorcycle gang
    c. Catholics
    d. females
    e. revolutionary political group
    f. the super rich
2. Define ethnocentrism.
3. What are cultural universals? Why do they exist?

Critical Thinking

4. **Analyzing Information** Are you and your friends members of a subculture? If so, describe some specific elements of that subculture.
5. **Making Comparisons** From the chart above, choose a cultural universal. Compare or contrast how this cultural universal is addressed by two different cultures. For example, how do the United States and Mexico differ in recreational activities?

Summary

Section 1: The Basis Of Culture

Main Idea: Culture defines how people in a society behave in relation to others and to physical objects. Although most behavior among animals is instinctual, human behavior is learned. Even reflexes and drives do not completely determine how humans will behave, because people are heavily influenced by culture.

Section 2: Language and Culture

Main Idea: Humans can create and transmit culture. The symbols of language play a role in determining people's view of reality.

Section 3: Norms and Values

Main Idea: Two essential components of culture are norms and values. There are several types of norms—folkways, mores, and laws. Sanctions are used to encourage conformity to norms. Values, the broadest cultural ideas, form the basis for norms.

Section 4: Beliefs and Material Culture

Main Idea: Besides norms and values, beliefs and physical objects make up culture. Ideal culture includes the guidelines we claim to accept, while real culture describes how we actually behave.

Section 5: Cultural Diversity and Similarity

Main Idea: Cultures change according to three major processes. Cultures contain groups within them called subcultures and countercultures.

SOCIOLOGY Online

Self-Check Quiz
Visit the *Sociology and You* Web site at soc.glencoe.com and click on **Chapter 3—Self-Check Quizzes** to prepare for the chapter test.

Reviewing Vocabulary

Complete each sentence using each term once.

a. sociobiology

b. sanctions

c. real culture

d. beliefs

e. society

f. laws

g. mores

h. subculture

i. ethnocentrism

j. informal sanctions

1. _____ are the ideas about the nature of reality.

2. A group that belongs to the larger culture but differs from it in some significant way is called _____.

3. _____ is the study of the biological basis of human behavior.

4. Formally defined norms enforced by officials are called _____.

5. _____ are rewards and punishments that can be applied by most members of a group.

6. Actual behavior patterns of the members of a group are called _____.

7. _____ are rewards and punishments used to encourage desired behaviors.

8. Norms with moral dimensions are called _____.

9. A specific territory composed of people who share a common culture are called _____.

10. Judging others in terms of one's own cultural standards is called _____.

Reviewing the Facts

1. According to sociobiology, how is human behavior influenced?

2. What are the differences between reflexes and drives?

3. What are folkways? Give three examples of folkways in the United States.
4. Explain the Sapir-Whorf hypothesis.
5. What are the three basic types of norms?
6. Define formal and informal sanctions.
7. Describe the relationship between norms and sanctions.
8. How does a social category differ from a subculture?
9. Ethnocentrism offers both advantages and disadvantages. Give an example of a positive role that ethnocentrism can play in a society. When is ethnocentrism a negative force in a society?
10. What are cultural universals?

Thinking Critically

1. **Making Inferences** More than any other symbol of our country, the American flag provokes emotional responses. Some people are willing to give their lives for it, while others have burned it in protest. In groups, discuss why this symbol is so powerful.
2. **Applying Concepts** All societies have cultural universals, as discussed in this chapter. Why, then, are so many groups in conflict? Think of examples of groups in this country that seem to be in conflict (such as animal rights activists and fur shop owners), and examine the reasons for these conflicts.
3. **Making Comparisons** Discuss how you think a functionalist would look at the topic of culture. How do you think a conflict theorist would view it?
4. **Evaluating Information** Some Amish parents have gone to jail rather than enroll their children in public schools. Even though you might wish that your parents had taken this stand on your behalf, what does it say about Amish cultural values?
5. **Categorizing Information** We have created a whole new language as a result of computers. A mouse is no longer necessarily an animal; another definition would be a device for navigating through electronic files. Make a list of the words in your school that are unique to your community (or school group) and that would take an "outsider" a while to learn.

6. **Understanding Cause and Effect**
   Use the diagram below to illustrate three causes of cultural change.

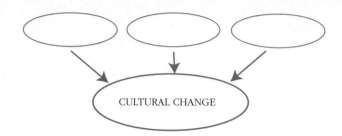

Sociology Projects

1. **Cultural Universals** Using the cultural universals diagram in your text (Figure 3.5 on page 102), create your own culture. Your culture must include all the components of the second level: an economy, institutions, arts, language, environment, recreation, and beliefs. Make sure that elements of the third level on the cultural universal diagram are part of your culture. For example, how will your culture entertain itself? What types of music will you listen to? How old are the members of your culture? You must also name this culture and locate it on a world map. Present your culture to the class with a detailed poster.
2. **Culture** You are an archaeologist and you have just uncovered a civilization called "America." Find at least one item from each of these aspects of culture: economy, religion, sports, science/technology, education, families, and politics/ government. For example, you might uncover a checkbook, a small cross, a baseball card, a mouse (not the animal), a piece of chalk, pictures, and campaign buttons. As you find these items around your house or school, try to imagine what they might mean to this American culture by answering the following questions.

a. Is this item culturally universal? Can it be found in other cultures?

b. What uses might someone from another culture find for this item? Be creative.

c. What does this item tell us about this culture?

3. **Popular Culture** T-shirts are a great example of popular culture. Everyone wears them, and they are very symbolic; they say a lot about our culture and about the people that wear them. Find a public place where you can discreetly observe people. Look for individuals wearing T-shirts, and jot down your observations of those shirts. Do the shirts make a statement about the people wearing them? Do they carry messages related to any different aspects of culture such as family, politics, or religion? Do they reflect social values? Are any of them inappropriate? If so, what does it say about the wearer's values compared to yours? Did you see similarities in T-shirts, such as a lot of black T-shirts or sports T-shirts? Use standard grammar, spelling, sentence structure and punctuation to write a brief report on your observations.

4. **Handshakes in U.S. Culture** Handshakes are also symbolic representations of cultures. List some situations in which people shake hands in U.S. culture. For example, do boyfriends and girlfriends shake hands in the hallway when they meet? Do some students use special handshakes when they greet other students? As a class, determine all the ways in which handshakes are used in U.S. culture, and explain how the social situation can change the meaning of a handshake.

5. **American Values** Based on the section on American values in your text (see pages 89–91), find ads in several magazines that reflect aspects of American values. For example, many ads for fast-food restaurants emphasize efficiency. These businesses pride themselves on their ability to get your meal out fast. The value of efficiency is seen as very American. Look for ads that reflect each one of the American values listed in your text. Put the ads together in a booklet with a title page and conclusions drawn from what you discovered.

6. **Cultural Lag** Material tools of a culture, such as computers, change faster than nonmaterial tools, such as norms and values. This difference creates what has been called *cultural lag*. (You will learn more about this topic in Chapter 17.) Computers have been around for some time. Still, many Americans lag behind in their proficiency with the technology. Interview people you know of varying ages: someone under age twelve, some fellow teens, some young adults, and some elderly adults. Ask them how computer literate they are. Do they know how to use Windows? The Internet? Does cultural lag exist in your sample? If so, try to find reasons or explanations for the lag. Does everyone have equal access to computers? Do certain populations tend to avoid computers? Is fear of technology or change involved?

7. **Cultural Norms** Create a chart comparing cultural norms among U.S. subculture groups such as ethnic, socioeconomic strata, and gender groups.

Technology Activities

1. Compare the use of language between two social categories within your culture (e.g., teenagers and parents). Make a list of ten examples of words or phrases that differ in meaning between the members of each social category. Using the Internet and your school or local library, find the original derivation of the word or phrase. Record your information in a database.

Chapter 3

Enrichment Reading
Cultural Explanations for Teen Violence

from an article by James Gilbert

Every social crisis generates its share of easy explanations, but adolescent crime wins the contest for pat answers. Not only is everyone an expert, but out-of-control children are often already the focus of uneasiness about social change, general anxiety, and just plain undisguised dislike. The tragic shootings at Columbine High School in Littleton, Colorado, have generated more than the usual number of theories. Few of these are original, and, in fact, many of them repeat a formula tried out almost 45 years ago, during the national panic over juvenile delinquency. True, the supposed cultural influences have changed, with blame pointed now at the dark lyrics of Marilyn Manson or virtual-reality, murder-and-mayhem computer games, but the ultimate message is pretty much the same: our children's behavior is out of control because our culture is out of control. The only solution is to find a form of censorship that can block adolescents' access to the violent images that impel them to behave violently.

One problem with the cultural explanation for teen violence is that, notwithstanding numerous scientific attempts to do so, it is impossible to prove—there are simply too many other possible causes to factor into the equation. Not that this should necessarily deter critics of our current teen culture. But it is one thing to regard what young people listen to, play, or consume as strange or vulgar or even mildly threatening, and another to argue that it incites specific behavior. Teenagers might be persuaded by advertising to buy a Big Mac or smoke a Camel, but that doesn't mean that song lyrics can make them commit mass murder.

Another problem with the cultural explanation is that we have been there before and ought to recognize from our experience some of the outcomes and implications of the argument. In the mid-'50s, especially between 1954 and 1956, Americans worried as deeply about juvenile delinquency as they did about the cold war, atomic **annihilation,** unemployment, and other social ills. The reason for this is not hard to figure out. Government commissions, the FBI . . . , and a number of leading psychologists and social critics were all warning of a terrible **scourge** of juvenile crime. Cities and towns rushed to pass new ordinances . . . . The favorites of these were local curfews, naming the hour when children under 18 had to be home. Quite naturally, this led to some increased incidence of lawbreaking by youths. But, overall, during the '50s juvenile crime was no higher than the decade that preceded it. Yet fears of juvenile delinquency continued to soar.

While there were many explanations offered for delinquency, the one most printed in the pages of popular magazines and voiced during congressional hearings convened to examine the problem was the **malevolent** influence of crime and horror comic books. No one could accuse "Howdy Doody" or "I Love Lucy" of inciting teen violence, although there were cop-and-gangster TV shows and scores of films that might have been blamed. . . . Comic books, on the other hand, particularly violent and horror comics, . . . became the focus of a **concerted** effort to censor youth culture. The effort was led by liberal Senator Estes Kefauver of Tennessee and was founded on the psychological theories of Fredric Wertham, whose 1954 best-seller, *Seduction of the Innocent*, inspired a vast outcry against the comics. Wertham's theory was based on asking teenage criminals if they read comic books—not much different from the logic behind today's blaming of computer games or music. Kefauver and Wertham's movement ultimately persuaded the publishing industry to impose self-censorship. Juvenile crime didn't fall, but the comics changed; and some of the most violent ones disappeared altogether.

If the anti–comic-book agitation did nothing much to end juvenile crime . . . what explains this panic? Clearly, something was happening in the '50s, just as it appears to be happening in our own time. The postwar era was a revolutionary time, the first generation in American history wherein children had substantial amounts of spending money. The result was the explosion of a youth culture designed to appeal specifically and exclusively to young people. The teenage market expanded rapidly, from clothing to automobiles to movies and fast food. . . . Children were growing up faster; they acted more like adults or at least demanded adult privileges. All of this looked immensely threatening to parents and parenting experts in the '50s. Parents and parenting experts in our age are also confronting a major new development. In this case, it's the advent of the Internet—which has exponentially increased the amount and scope of influences to which American kids are exposed.

So what can we learn from the experience of the '50s . . . ? First, we should be wary of the attempt to link behavior directly and precisely to culture. There is no clear evidence to support this, and, besides, we can probably never develop a form of acceptable censorship any-

way. It is also important to separate things that we don't like (or understand) from those social problems that might, in fact, cause teenage alienation and criminal behavior. Banning Marilyn Manson, hip-hop clothes, and rap music will certainly have an effect, but not the desired one. And, finally, we need to remind ourselves that youth culture is something that modern society has invented and celebrated. By extending affluence to children, by giving them computers and spending money, by making them consumers and therefore members of the marketplace, we have given them access to an adult world and an adult culture. We will have to learn to live with the consequences of that.

Source: Excerpted from James Gilbert, "Juvenilia," *The New Republic* (June 14, 1999), 54. Reprinted by permission of *The New Republic*, © 1999, The New Republic, Inc.

What Does it Mean?

annihilation
total destruction

concerted
organized; mutually arranged

malevolent
vicious or harmful

scourge
a cause of widespread distress

Read and React

1. What common assumption about juvenile crime is the author questioning?

2. Why does Gilbert think it is not possible to scientifically prove how culture affects a particular behavior?

3. What does Gilbert say about the power of advertising to affect teenage behavior?

4. What modern day invention does Gilbert compare to the influence of comic books in the 1950s?

5. In two or three sentences, state the main point that the author makes in this article. Do you agree or disagree with his assessment? Why or why not?

to her toilet needs, and dress herself (except for handling buttons and snaps). At this point, she had acquired the speech level of a two-year-old. By the time of her death at age ten, she had made some additional progress. She could carry out instructions, identify a few colors, build with blocks, wash her hands, brush her teeth, and try to help other children. Her developing capacity for emotional attachment was reflected in the love she had developed for a doll.

Who was Isabelle?   Nine months after Anna was found, Isabelle was discovered. She, too, had been hidden away because her mother was unmarried. Isabelle's mother had been deaf since the age of two and did not speak. She stayed with her child in a dark room, secluded from the rest of the family. When found at the age of six and a half, Isabelle was physically ill from an inadequate diet and lack of sunshine. Her legs were so bowed that when she stood the soles of her shoes rested against each other, and her walk was a skittering movement. Some of her actions were like those of a six-month-old infant. Unable to talk except for a strange croaking sound, Isabelle communicated with her mother by means of gestures. Like an animal in the wild, she reacted with fear and hostility to strangers, especially men.

At first, Isabelle was thought to be severely learning disabled. (Her initial IQ score was near the zero point.) Nevertheless, an intensive program of rehabilitation was begun. After a slow start, Isabelle progressed through the usual stages of learning and development at a faster pace than normal. It took her only two years to acquire the skills mastered by a normal six-year-old. By the time she was eight and a half, Isabelle was on an educational par with children her age. By outward appearances, she was an intelligent, happy, energetic child. At age fourteen, she participated in all the school activities normal for other children in her grade.

To Isabelle's good fortune, she, unlike Anna, benefited from intensive instruction at the hands of trained professionals. Her ability to progress may also have been because she was confined with her mother for company and comforting.

What can we learn from these case studies?   The implication of the cases of Anna, Isabelle, and Genie is unmistakable. The personal and social development associated with being human is acquired through intensive and prolonged social contact with others.

Section 1 Assessment

1. Define the term *socialization*.
2. What did Harlow's research on rhesus monkeys reveal?
3. Did the case studies on Anna, Isabelle and Genie support Harlow's conclusions? Why or why not?

Critical Thinking

4. **Analyzing Information**   Do you think sociologists have overemphasized the importance of social contact in learning? What are some legal and moral implications for the government in this kind of child abuse? Should the state protect children from their parents?

Section 2

Socialization and the Self

Key Terms

- self-concept
- looking-glass self
- significant others
- role taking
- imitation stage

- play stage
- game stage
- generalized other
- "me"
- "I"

The Functionalist and Conflict Perspectives on Socialization

Each of the three major theoretical perspectives provides insights into socialization. However, the symbolic interactionist perspective allows a more complete understanding than the other two.

How does the functionalist perspective explain socialization? Functionalism stresses the ways in which groups work together to create a stable society. Schools and families, for example, socialize children by teaching the same basic norms, beliefs, and values. If it were otherwise, society could not exist as a whole. It would be fragmented and chaotic.

How does the conflict perspective explain socialization? The conflict perspective views socialization as a way of perpetuating the status quo. When people are socialized to accept their family's social class, for example,

Section Preview

All three theoretical perspectives agree that socialization is needed if cultural and societal values are to be learned. Symbolic interactionism offers the most fully developed perspective for studying socialization. In this approach, the self-concept is developed by using other people as mirrors for learning about ourselves.

According to the conflict theory, these young boys are being socialized to accept their social class.

they help preserve the current class system. People learn to accept their social status before they have enough self-awareness to realize what is happening. Because they do not challenge their position in life, they do not upset the existing class structure. Consequently, socialization maintains the social, political, and economic advantages of the higher social classes.

Symbolic Interactionism and Socialization

In the early part of the twentieth century, Charles Horton Cooley and George Herbert Mead developed the symbolic interactionist perspective. They challenged the once widely held belief that human nature is biologically determined (that you are a certain way because you were born that way). For them, human nature is a product of society.

How does symbolic interactionism help us understand socialization? Symbolic interactionism uses a number of key concepts to explain socialization. These concepts include

- ❖ the self-concept
- ❖ the looking-glass self
- ❖ significant others
- ❖ role taking (the imitation stage, the play stage, the game stage)
- ❖ the generalized other.

self-concept
an image of yourself as having an identity separate from other people

looking-glass self
an image of yourself based on what you believe others think of you

Where does the self-concept come from? Charles Horton Cooley developed the idea of the **self-concept** from watching his own children at play. Your self-concept is your image of yourself as having an identity separate from other people.

Cooley (1902) realized that children interpreted how others reacted to them in many ways. For example, young children learn quickly that causing some disturbance when adult visitors are present turns attention from the guests to themselves. From such insights, children learn to judge themselves in terms of how they imagine others *will* react to them. Thus, other people serve as mirrors for the development of the self. Cooley called this way of learning the **looking-glass self**—a self-concept based on our idea of others' judgments of us.

How does the looking-glass process work? According to Cooley, we use other people as mirrors to reflect back what we imagine they think of us. In this view, the looking-glass self is the product of a three-stage process that is constantly taking place.

1. First, we imagine how we appear to others. (What is our perception of how others see us?)
2. Next, we imagine the reaction of others to our (imagined) appearance.
3. Finally, we evaluate ourselves according to how we imagine others have judged us.

This is not a conscious process, and the three stages can occur in very rapid succession. The result of the process is a positive or negative self-evaluation.

Consider this example of the looking-glass process. Suppose you have a new teacher you want to impress. You prepare hard for the next day's class.

Figure 4.1 Focus on Theoretical Perspectives

Socialization and Mass Media. Each theoretical perspective has a unique view of the socialization process. This table identifies these views and illustrates the unique interpretation of each view with respect to the influence of the mass media on the socialization process.

Theoretical Perspective	View of Socialization	How the Media Influence Socialization
Functionalism	Stresses how socialization contributes to a stable society	Network television programs encourage social integration by exposing the entire society to shared beliefs, values, and norms.
Conflict Theory	Views socialization as a way for the powerful to keep things the same	Newspaper owners and editors exercise power by setting the political agenda for a community.
Symbolic Interactionism	Holds that socialization is the major determinant of human nature	Through words and pictures, children's books expose the young to the meaning of love, manners, and motherhood.

In class, as you are making a comment on the assignment, you have an image of your performance (stage 1). After finishing your comments, you think your teacher is disappointed (stage 2). Because you wanted your teacher to be impressed, you feel bad about yourself (stage 3).

Can the looking glass be distorted?   Because the looking glass we use comes from our imaginations, it may be distorted. The mirror may not accurately reflect others' opinions of us. The teacher in the above example may not have been disappointed at all.

Unfortunately, the looking-glass process works even if we are mistaken about others' perceptions of us. If we incorrectly believe that a teacher, or a date, or our parents dislike us, the consequences to us are just as real as if it were true.

Do we use some people as mirrors more than others?   George Herbert Mead pointed out that some people are more important to us than others (Mead, 1934). The people whose judgments are most important to our self-concepts are called **significant others.** For a child, significant others are likely to include mother, father, grandparent, teachers, and playmates. Teenagers place heavy reliance on their peers. The variety of significant others is greater for adults, ranging from spouses, parents, and friends to ministers and employers.

significant others
those people whose reactions are most important to your self-concept

What is role taking?   As humans, we carry on silent conversations. That is, we think something to ourselves and respond internally to it. All of us do this when we predict the behavior of others. Through internal conversation, we can imagine the thoughts, emotions, and behavior of others in any social situation. **Role taking** allows us to see ourselves through the eyes of someone else. It allows us to take the viewpoint of another person and then respond to ourselves from that imagined viewpoint.

With role taking, we can play out scenes in our minds and anticipate what others will say or do. For example, you might want to ask your employer for a raise. If you could not mentally put yourself in your boss's place, you would have no idea of the objections that she might raise. But by role-playing her reaction mentally, you can prepare for those objections and be ready to justify your raise.

How does the ability for role taking develop? According to Mead, the ability for role taking is the product of a three-stage process. He called these the imitation stage, the play stage, and the game stage.

In the **imitation stage,** which begins at around one and a half to two years, the child imitates (without understanding) the physical and verbal behavior of a significant other. This is the first step in developing the capacity for role taking.

At the age of three or four, a young child can be seen playing at being mother, father, police officer, teacher, or astronaut. This play involves acting and thinking as a child imagines another person would. This is what Mead called the **play stage**—the stage during which children take on roles of others one at a time.

The third phase in the development of role taking Mead labeled the **game stage.** In this stage, children learn to engage in more sophisticated role taking as they become able to consider the roles of several people simultaneously. Games they play involve several participants, and there are specific rules designed to ensure that the behaviors of the participants fit together. All participants in a game must know what they are supposed to do and what is expected of others in the game. Imagine the confusion in a baseball game if young first-base players have not yet mastered the idea that the ball hit to a teammate will usually be thrown to them. In the second stage of role taking (the play stage) a child may pretend to be a first-base player one moment and pretend to be a base runner the next. In the game stage, however, first-base players who drop their gloves and run to second base when the other team hits the ball will not remain in the game for very long. It is during the game stage that children learn to gear their behavior to the norms of the group.

When do we start acting out of principle?   During the game stage, a child's self-concept, attitudes, beliefs, and values gradually come to depend less on individuals and more on general concepts. For example, being an honest person is no longer merely a matter of pleasing significant others such

---

role taking
assuming the viewpoint of another person and using that viewpoint to shape the self-concept

imitation stage
Mead's first stage in the development of role taking; children begin to imitate behaviors without understanding why

play stage
Mead's second stage in the development of role taking; children act in ways they imagine other people would

game stage
Mead's third stage in the development of role taking; children anticipate the actions of others based on social rules

as one's mother, father, or minister. Rather, it begins to seem wrong *in principle* to be dishonest. As this change takes place, a **generalized other**—an integrated conception of the norms, values, and beliefs of one's community or society—emerges.

What is the self?

According to Mead, we can think of the self as being composed of two parts: the *"me"* and the *"I."* The **"me"** is the part of the self created through socialization. The "me" accounts for predictability and conformity. Yet much human behavior is spontaneous and unpredictable. An angry child may, for example, unexpectedly yell hurtful words at the parent whom he loves. To account for this spontaneous, unpredictable, often creative part of the self, Mead proposed the **"I."**

The "I" does not operate only in extreme situations of rage or excitement. It interacts constantly with the "me" as we conduct ourselves in social situations. According to Mead, the first reaction of the self comes from the "I." Before we act, however, this reaction is directed into socially acceptable channels by the socialized "me." When the "I" wants a piece of a friend's candy bar, the "me" reflects on the consequences of taking the candy without permission. Thus, the "I" normally takes the "me" into account before acting. However, the unpredictability of much human behavior demonstrates that the "me" is not always in control!

What do you think is the developmental level of the "generalized other" in each of these two shoplifters?

generalized other
integrated conception of the norms, values, and beliefs of one's community or society

"me"
the part of the self formed through socialization

"I"
the part of the self that accounts for unlearned, spontaneous acts

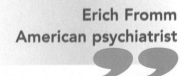

Man can be defined as the animal that can say I, that can be aware of himself as a separate entity.

Erich Fromm
American psychiatrist

Section 2 Assessment

1. What is the looking-glass self?
2. What are the consequences of having a distorted looking glass?
3. Which "self" is the first to react to a situation, the "me" or the "I"?

Critical Thinking

4. **Applying Concepts** Describe an experience you have had with the looking-glass process. How did this experience touch or change your self-concept?

Another Time

Surviving a Prisoner-of-War Camp

By learning the culture around them—whatever that culture is—human beings can and do adapt to almost any situation. This learning process is a type of socialization. The following description of adaptation in a German prison camp during World War II was written by Bruno Bettelheim, a noted American scholar who survived imprisonment.

When a prisoner had reached the final stage of adjustment to the camp situation, he had changed his personality so as to accept various values of the SS [Hitler's elite troops] as his own. A few examples may illustrate how this acceptance expressed itself.

Slowly prisoners accepted, as the expression of their verbal aggressions, terms which definitely did not originate in their previous vocabularies, but were taken over from the very different vocabulary of the SS. From copying the verbal aggressions of the SS to copying its form of bodily aggressions was one more step, but it took several years to make this step. It was not unusual to find old prisoners, when in charge of others, behaving worse than the SS.

Old prisoners who identified themselves with the SS did so not only in respect to aggressive be-

havior. They would try to acquire old pieces of SS uniforms. If that was not possible, they tried to sew and mend their uniforms so that they would resemble those of the guards. The length to which prisoners would go in these efforts seemed unbelievable, particularly since the SS punished them for their efforts to copy SS uniforms. When asked why they did it, the old prisoners admitted that they loved to look like the guards.

The old prisoners' identification with the SS did not stop with the copying of their outer appearance and behavior. Old prisoners accepted Nazi goals and values, too, even when these seemed opposed to their own interests. It was appalling to see how far even politically well-educated prisoners would go with this identification. At one time American and English newspapers were full of stories about the cruelties committed in these camps. The SS punished prisoners for the appearance of these stories, true to its policy of punishing the group for whatever a member or a former member did, since the stories must have originated in reports from former prisoners. In discussions of this event, old prisoners would insist that it was not the business of foreign correspondents or newspapers to bother with German institutions, expressing their hatred of the journalists who tried to help them.

After so much has been said about the old prisoners' tendency to conform and to identify with the SS, it ought to be stressed that this was only part of the picture. The author has tried to concentrate on interesting psychological mechanisms in group behavior rather than on reporting types of behavior which are either well known or could reasonably be expected. These same old prisoners who identified with the SS defied it at other moments, demonstrating extraordinary courage in doing so.

Source: From *Surviving and Other Essays,* by Bruno Bettelheim. © 1979 by Bruno Bettelheim and Trude Bettelheim as Trustees.

Thinking It Over

1. Describe an experience you have had in which you or someone you know, as a new member of a group, imitated the ways of the group.

2. How does gang affiliation (such as wearing gang colors or using their slogans) demonstrate the tendency to conform?

Agents of Socialization

Key Terms

- **hidden curriculum**
- **peer group**
- **mass media**

The Family and Socialization

The child's first exposure to the world occurs within the family. Some essential developments occur through close interaction with a small number of people—none of whom the child has selected. Within the family the child learns to

❖ think and speak

❖ internalize norms, beliefs, and values

❖ form some basic attitudes

❖ develop a capacity for intimate and personal relationships

❖ acquire a self-image (Handel, 1990).

The impact of the family reaches far beyond its direct effects on the child. Our family's social class shapes what we think of ourselves and how others treat us, even far into adulthood. Author Jean Evans offers an illustration of this in the case of Johnny Rocco, a twenty-year-old living in a city slum.

Johnny hadn't been running the streets long when the knowledge was borne in on him that being a Rocco made him "something special"; the reputation of the notorious Roccos, known to neighbors, schools, police, and welfare agencies as "chiselers, thieves, and trouble-makers" preceded him. The cop on the beat, Johnny says, always had some cynical smart crack to make. . . . Certain children were not permitted to play with him. Wherever he went—on the streets, in the neighborhood, settlement house, at the welfare agency's penny milk station, at school, where other Roccos had been before him—he recognized himself by a gesture, an oblique remark, a wrong laugh. (Evans, 1954:11)

Section Preview

During childhood and adolescence, the major agents of socialization are the family, school, peer group, and mass media. The family's role is critical in forming basic values. Schools introduce children to life beyond the family. In peer groups, young people learn to relate as equals. The mass media provide role models for full integration into society.

The infant in the photo on the left is likely to be socialized in a very different way from the two children above. What are some differences in attitudes that will probably be formed by these children because of their different family life?

And then when I was talking to him he took the clicker and tried to turn me off.

Parents are no longer the only significant socializing force.

Socialization in Schools

In school, children are under the care and supervision of adults who are not relatives. For the first time, many of the child's relationships with other people are impersonal. Rewards and punishments are based on performance rather than affection. Although a mother may cherish any picture that her child creates, a teacher evaluates her students by more objective standards. Slowly, children are taught to be less dependent emotionally on their parents. The school also creates feelings of loyalty and allegiance to something beyond the family.

How do schools socialize students?   The socialization process in school involves more than reading, writing, and arithmetic. Underlying the formal goals of the school is the **hidden curriculum**—the informal and unofficial aspects of culture that children are taught in preparation for life. The hidden curriculum teaches children discipline, order, cooperation, and conformity—characteristics required for success in the adult world of work. (You will learn more about the hidden curriculum in Chapter 12.)

School also teaches children the reality of how we experience time in the real world. According to education critic John Holt (1967), life in schools is run by the clock, as it is in the working world. A bell signals when children must move to the next scheduled event, whether or not they understand what they have been working on and whether or not they are ready to switch to a different subject. Getting through a preset number of activities within a given time period often becomes more important than learning.

hidden curriculum
the informal and unofficial aspects of culture that children are taught in school

Schools have rules and regulations to cover almost all activities—how to dress, how to wear one's hair, which side of the hall to walk on, when to speak in class. Teachers reward children with praise and acceptance when they recite the "right" answers, behave "properly," or exhibit "desirable" attitudes.

Children are isolated from the working adult society by being set apart in school for most of their preadult lives. Because they are separated from the adult world for such a long time, young people must depend on one another for much of their social life.

peer group
set of individuals of roughly the same age and interests

Peer Group Socialization

The family and the school are both agencies of socialization organized and operated by adults. The child's **peer group**—composed of individuals of roughly the same age and interests—is the only agency of socialization that is not controlled primarily by adults. Children usually belong to several peer groups. A child may belong to a play group in the neighborhood, a clique at school, an after-school club or sports team.

How do peer groups contribute to socialization? In the family and at school, children are subordinated to adults. In the peer group, young people have an opportunity to engage in give-and-take relationships. Children experience conflict, competition, and cooperation in such groups. The peer group also gives children experience in self-direction. They can begin to make their own decisions; experiment with new ways of thinking, feeling, and behaving; and engage in activities that involve self-expression.

Socialization is occurring in each of the peer groups pictured here, perhaps with far different consequences for the larger society.

Independence from adults is also promoted by the peer group, because often the norms of the peer group conflict with those of the adult world. Children learn to be different from their parents in ways that help to develop self-sufficiency.

The peer group also provides an opportunity for children to develop close ties with friends outside the family, including members of the opposite sex. At the same time, they are learning to get along with large numbers of people, many of whom are quite different from themselves. This helps develop the social flexibility needed in a mobile, rapidly changing society.

Do friends or family have more influence on young people? The majority of Americans now live in either urban or suburban areas. In both two-income families and single-parent families, parents may commute many miles to work and spend much of their time away from home. Consequently, once children reach the upper levels of grade school, they may spend more time with their peers than they do with their parents.

According to psychologist Judith Harris (1998), peers are more important than parents in socializing children. Even though most sociologists do not agree with this extreme conclusion, many do believe that the peer group is having a growing effect on social development.

mass media
means of communication designed to reach the general population

The mass media are a relatively new source of socialization. How does television advertising influence the dating behavior of teenagers?

The Mass Media and Socialization

Mass media are means of communication designed to reach the general population. They include such things as television, radio, newspapers, magazines, movies, books, the Internet, tapes, and discs. Many popular images presented in the mass media are highly distorted. For example, detective and police work are not as exciting and glamorous as depicted in books, in movies, and on television. Nevertheless, it is often through the mass media that children are first introduced to numerous aspects of their culture (Fishman and Cavender, 1998).

What role do the mass media play in socialization? The mass media display role models for children to imitate. Learning these role models helps to integrate the young into society.

The mass media, by their content alone, teach many of the ways of the society. This is evident in the behavior we take for granted—the duties of the detective, waitress, or sheriff; the functions of the hospital, advertising agency, and police court; behavior in hotel, airplane, or cruise ship; the language of the prison, army, or courtroom; the relationship between nurses and doctors or secretaries and their bosses. Such settings and relationships are portrayed time and again in films, television

World View

Availability of Television

The mass media play a key role in the socialization process. Since nearly every U.S. home has at least one television (the majority have more), this medium is one of the most influential in the United States. This map shows that ownership of televisions varies widely around the world.

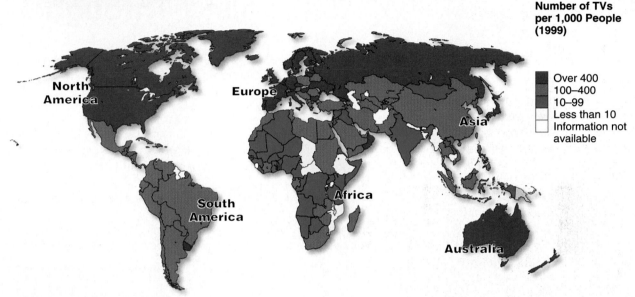

Number of TVs per 1,000 People (1999)

- Over 400
- 100–400
- 10–99
- Less than 10
- Information not available

North America · Europe · Asia · Africa · South America · Australia

Interpreting the Map

1. What geographical factor(s) might contribute to the density of TV households in South America?
2. Do you think the attitudes of members of societies with more televisions are influenced more by government advertising than members of societies with fewer televisions? Why or why not?

Adapted from World Development Indicators, *The World Book,* 2001.

---

shows, and comic strips; and all "teach"—however misleadingly—norms, status positions, and institutional functions (Elkin and Handel, 1991:189).

The mass media also offer children ideas about the values in their society. They provide children with images of achievement and success, activity and work, equality and democracy.

What about violence in the mass media? On the negative side, consider the relationship between violence on television and real-life violence. By age sixteen, the average American child will have seen twenty thousand homicides on television (Leonard, 1998). Social scientists have been reluctant in the past to recognize a causal connection between television violence and real-life violence. However, based on hundreds of studies involving over ten thousand children, most now conclude that watching aggressive behavior on television significantly increases aggression (Hepburn, 1993; Strasburger, 1995; Dudley, 1999).

SOCIOLOGY Online

Student Web Activity
Visit the *Sociology and You* Web site at soc.glencoe.com and click on **Chapter 4—Student Web Activities** for an activity on mass media and socialization.

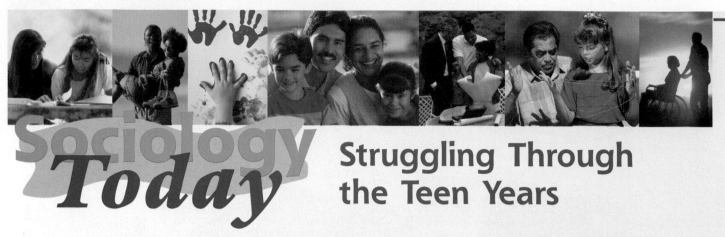

Sociology Today

Struggling Through the Teen Years

Adolescents do not get good press. They are often portrayed by the media as awkward, unreasonable, strong-willed, and overconfident. Some parents, taking their cue from comedian Bill Cosby, jokingly attribute teen behavior to temporary "brain damage." Researcher David Elkind (1981) offers another explanation for much troublesome adolescent behavior. Teens' problem, he concludes, is not brain damage. They are simply struggling through the emotional and physiological changes of the teen years as best they can.

Teenagers may appear to behave irrationally (by adult standards) because of new thinking capabilities not yet under their control. Contrary to the long-accepted belief that the human brain is fully developed by the age of 8 or 12, startling new research reveals that the brain remains a construction site even into the 20s (Begley, 2000). And the part of the brain that undergoes the greatest change between puberty and young adulthood is responsible for such activities as judgment, emotional control, and organization and planning.

Whereas adults are accustomed to looking at situations from several different viewpoints, teens are not. Confusion can result when inexperienced young people attempt to move from making simple, one-factor decisions to consideration of several factors simultaneously. For example, a teen who wants to join friends in a ride from a night football game may consider that the driver has a license, but may fail to consider the driver's experience, driving habits, or drinking behavior.

Teens assume that other people have as much interest in them as they have in themselves. Consequently, they surround themselves with an

Consider a few examples. A two-year-old girl died when her older brother, age five, set the house on fire with matches while imitating behavior he had seen on the cartoon program *Beavis and Butt-Head*. Just on the basis of televised *reports* of violence, a rash of would-be copycat crimes followed the shooting massacre of thirteen students and one teacher at Columbine High School by two students who then shot themselves. Television's effects, of course, are usually more hidden, subtle, and long term:

> . . . [N]ot every child who watched a lot of violence or plays a lot of violent games will grow up to be violent. Other forces must converge, as they did [at Columbine]. . . . But just as every cigarette increases the chance that someday you will get lung cancer, every exposure to violence increases the chances that some day a child will behave more violently than they would otherwise (*To Establish Justice, 1999:vi*).

"imaginary audience." Since teenagers believe that everyone is watching and evaluating them, they are extremely self-conscious. In groups, adolescents often play to this imaginary audience by engaging in loud and provocative behavior. Yet they fail to understand why adults become annoyed with them. Gradually, they begin to realize that others have their own pre-occupations, and the imaginary-audience behavior lessens.

Teenagers frequently have the feeling of invulnerability. For example, they may think that drug addiction, cancer from smoking, pregnancy, and death happen only to others. Their reckless behavior must be seen within this context.

Young people tend to assume that fairly common adolescent experiences are unique. Common complaints include "Mom, you just don't know how much it hurt for Carlos to take out Maria," and "Dad, you don't know what it's like not to have my own bike." At the other extreme, adolescents may feel that their own perceptions are shared by everyone. A young boy, for example, may believe that others find him unattractive because of what he thinks is a large nose. No amount of talking can convince him that he is exaggerating the size of his nose or that others pay little attention to it. This self-centered view of reality begins to decrease as teens discover that others are having similar feelings and experiences.

Doing Sociology

Identify three ways in which adults and adolescents could use this developmental awareness to ease the struggle of the teen years.

Section 3 Assessment

1. Why does the family have such strong influence on a child's socialization?
2. What aspect of socialization does the child first encounter in school that he or she does not meet in the family?
3. What is the hidden curriculum?
4. Besides family and school, identify two other socializing agents.

Critical Thinking

5. **Evaluating Information** Some pyschologists believe that peer groups have more influence on later socialization than the family group. Give reasons why you agree or disagree with that premise.

Section 4 Processes of Socialization

Key Terms

- total institutions
- desocialization
- resocialization
- anticipatory socialization
- reference group

Section Preview

Symbolic interactionism views socialization as a lifelong process. Desocialization is the process of having to give up old norms. Resocialization begins as people adopt new norms and values. Anticipatory socialization and reference groups are concerned with voluntary change as when moving from one life stage to another.

total institutions
places in which people are separated from the rest of society and controlled by officials in charge

desocialization
the process of giving up old norms, values, attitudes, and behaviors

resocialization
the process of adopting new norms, values, attitudes, and behaviors

Desocialization and Resocialization

Whenever change occurs over the course of your life, you will learn new behaviors and skills. This learning is important to socialization. Symbolic interactionism describes four processes associated with socialization after childhood: *desocialization, resocialization, anticipatory socialization,* and *reference groups.*

How does desocialization prepare people for new learning? Mental hospitals, cults, and prisons are **total institutions**—places where residents are separated from the rest of society. These residents are not free to manage their own lives, but are controlled and manipulated by those in charge. The end purpose of this control and manipulation is to permanently change the residents. The first step is **desocialization**—the process by which people give up old norms, values, attitudes, and behaviors. For those in total institutions, desocialization often means the destruction of old self-concepts of personal identity.

Desocialization in institutions is accomplished in many ways. Replacing personal possessions with standard-issue items promotes sameness among the residents. It deprives them of the personal items (long hair, hair brushes, ball caps, T-shirts) they have used to present themselves as unique individuals. The use of serial numbers to identify people and the loss of privacy also contribute to the breakdown of past identity. Cult members, for example, may even be denied use of their given names.

How does resocialization begin? Once the self-concept has been broken down, **resocialization**—the process in which people adopt new norms, values, attitudes, and behaviors—can begin. Those in control of total institutions, using an elaborate system of rewards and punishments, attempt to give residents new self-

The starkness of this prison cell with its lack of individual possessions aids in the desocialization process.

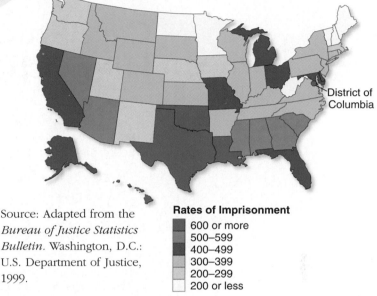

The U.S. has one of the highest rates of imprisonment in the industrialized world—over four times that of any Western European country. Justice officials worry that some prisons function as "schools for crime." If prisons do first desocialize and then resocialize inmates toward a criminal identity, then the U.S. prison system is unintentionally increasing the criminal portion of the population. This map shows the number of prisoners with sentences of more than one year per 100,000 U.S. residents.

Source: Adapted from the *Bureau of Justice Statistics Bulletin*. Washington, D.C.: U.S. Department of Justice, 1999.

Rates of Imprisonment
- 600 or more
- 500–599
- 400–499
- 300–399
- 200–299
- 200 or less

Interpreting the Map

1. Where does your state rank in terms of imprisonment rate? Can you relate the extent of imprisonment in your state to the nature of the socialization that occurs in your state?
2. Do the states adjoining your state have imprisonment rates that are similar or dissimilar to your state?

Online **UPDATE**
Visit soc.glencoe.com and click on **Textbook Updates–Chapter 4** for an update of the data.

concepts. Rewards for taking on a new "identity" can include extra food, special responsibilities, or periods of privacy. Punishments for nonconformity involve shaming, loss of special privileges, physical punishment, and physical isolation.

The concepts of desocialization and resocialization were developed to analyze social processes in extreme situations. They still apply to other social settings, including basic training in the U.S. Marine Corps and plebe (freshman) year at the United States Military Academy. In much less extreme form, these concepts illuminate changes in our normal life course. Desocialization and resocialization occur as a child becomes a teenager, when young adults begin careers, and as the elderly move into retirement or widowhood.

Anticipatory Socialization

Anticipatory socialization is the process of preparing (in advance) for new norms, values, attitudes, and behaviors. It does not generally occur in prisons or mental hospitals because it involves *voluntary change*.

anticipatory socialization the voluntary process of preparing to accept new norms, values, attitudes, and behaviors

Focus on Research

Case Study: High School Reunions

Socialization occurs throughout life. Even high school reunions play a part. If you asked most Americans to talk about their experiences at a recent high school reunion, what would they say?

"It was great seeing old friends."

"I was curious about how things turned out for people I loved and hated as a teenager."

"I plan to get together with some old friends in the near future."

High school reunions are generally thought to be a time to recapture fond memories of youth.

One researcher wished to investigate the meaning of high school reunions. Keiko Ikeda (1998) studied eight reunions in the American Midwest. He observed these reunions armed with a camera, a tape recorder, and a notebook. After each reunion, he also conducted in-depth, life-story interviews with samples of participants.

Ikeda's results are too complex and varied to easily summarize. (This is typical of in-depth observational studies.) One aspect of the study, however, reveals the socializing aspect of high school reunions. Ikeda compared several reunions of one high school—tenth, fifteenth, twentieth, thirtieth, fortieth, and fiftieth. He focused on the relative emphasis on the past and the present. As you can see from the passage below, the past becomes more important as age increases.

> It is thus with most of us; we are what other people say we are. We are ourselves chiefly by hearsay.
>
> **Eric Hoffer**
> **American author**

In the earlier reunions (the tenth and fifteenth years), a concern with relative status and a sense of competitiveness is expressed, often blatantly, through award-giving ceremonies. . . . The hall was decorated in the school colors, and images of the high school mascot were present, but beyond this no high school memorabilia were displayed. The music, too, was current, and not the rock 'n' roll of the late sixties and early seventies.

The twentieth-year reunion of the Class of '62 is typical of a transitional phase in which elements from the past begin to assume an important role. The past is expressed in high school memorabilia . . . in . . . films and slides taken during high school, and in . . . high school anecdotes that are playfully interwoven throughout the ceremonial events.

In the thirtieth-year reunion of the Class of '52, the past firmly occupied center stage. A carefully crafted, chronological narrative of the senior year, entitled "The Way We Were," was read, in which major class activities were recalled month by month. . . .

In the fiftieth-year reunion, we find a dramatic disappearance of all ritual activities. According to the president of the Class of '32, his class had held reunions every ten years since graduation, and in earlier ceremonies they had given awards, but this time, "none of the folks in the reunion committee felt like doing that kind of thing." It seemed that attendees at the fiftieth-year reunion, for the most part, had risen above concerns of past and present and were content to celebrate together the simple fact that they all still had the vigor to attend a reunion.

Source: Keiko Ikeda, *A Room Full of Mirrors.* Stanford, CA: Stanford University Press, 1998, pp. 143–145.

Working with the Research

1. Ask an adult to describe the activities at one or more high school reunions that he or she has attended. Compare the description with Ikeda's findings.
2. Suppose you had a class assignment to study an upcoming reunion at your school. Select a research question you would want to ask. Identify the research methods you would use.

The dress on these young people indicates they are preparing for entry into the adult world of work or higher education. How does a peer group act as a tool for anticipatory socialization?

reference group
group whose norms and values are used to guide behavior; group with whom you identify

Anticipatory socialization may occur in people who are moving from one stage in their lives to another. Consider teenagers, for example. Because they want to resemble those their own age, they may willingly abandon many of the norms, values, attitudes, and behaviors learned previously. This process generally begins in the preteen years. Preteens begin early to observe the ways of teenagers. Teens become their new **reference group**—the group they use to evaluate themselves and from which they acquire attitudes, values, beliefs, and norms. In this situation, the new reference group is a tool for anticipatory socialization.

Seniors in college, normally seen on campus only in jeans and oversized sweatshirts, suddenly, as graduation nears, are wearing tailored suits and much more serious expressions. In preparing for entry into the business world, they are talking with friends who have graduated as well as company recruiters. In effect, they are preparing themselves for the resocialization they know awaits them (Atchley, 1999).

Section 4 Assessment

1. Identify the following actions as desocialization (D), resocialization (R), or anticipatory socialization (A).
   a. First-year students acquire a new identity during their freshman year at a military academy.
   b. Prison personnel deliberately attempt to destroy the self-concepts of inmates.
   c. High school students identify with college students.
2. Which of the following is *not* an example of a reference group?
   a. Rock-star subculture   c. Terrorists
   b. United States Military Academy d. Mass media

Critical Thinking

3. **Applying Concepts** Which group do you feel is the most influential in the present stage of your socialization—family, peers, school, or the media? Why?

Summary

Section 1: The Importance of Socialization

Main Idea: Socialization is the cultural process of learning to participate in group life. Without it, we would not develop many of the characteristics we associate with being human. Studies have shown that animals and human infants who are deprived of intensive and prolonged social contact with others are stunted in their emotional and social growth.

Section 2: Socialization and the Self

Main Idea: All three theoretical perspectives agree that socialization is needed if cultural and societal values are to be learned. Symbolic interactionism offers the most fully developed perspective for studying socialization. In this approach, the self-concept is developed by using other people as mirrors for learning about ourselves.

Section 3: Agents of Socialization

Main Idea: During childhood and adolescence, the major agents of socialization are the family, school, peer group, and mass media. The family's role is critical in forming basic values. Schools introduce children to life beyond the family. In peer groups, young people learn to relate as equals. The mass media provide role models for full integration into society.

Section 4: Processes of Socialization

Main Idea: Symbolic interactionism views socialization as a lifelong process. Desocialization is the process of having to give up old norms. Resocialization begins as people adopt new norms and values. Anticipatory socialization and reference groups are concerned with voluntary change as when moving from one life stage to another.

SOCIOLOGY Online

Self-Check Quiz
Visit the *Sociology and You* Web site at soc.glencoe.com and click on **Chapter 4—Self-Check Quizzes** to prepare for the chapter test.

Reviewing Vocabulary

Complete each sentence using each term once.

a. socialization
b. personality
c. anticipatory socialization
d. looking-glass self
e. role taking
f. generalized other
g. total institutions
h. resocialization

1. _____ is the attitudes, beliefs, values, and behaviors associated with an individual.

2. The cultural process of learning to participate in group life is called _____.

3. _____ allows us to assume the viewpoint of another person and use that viewpoint to shape our self-concept.

4. _____ are places in which people are separated from the rest of society and controlled by officials in charge.

5. The process of adopting new norms, values, attitudes, and behaviors is known as

    _____.

6. An image of yourself based on what you believe others think of you is called

    _____.

7. _____ is the voluntary process of preparing to accept new norms, values, attitudes, and behaviors.

8. The integrated conception of the norms, values, and beliefs of one's society is called the

    _____.

Reviewing the Facts

1. What does the study involving rhesus monkeys suggest about the choices that human infants would make in the same situation?

2. What is socialization from the viewpoint of symbolic interactionism?

3. What are the three major theoretical perspectives of sociology?

4. What concept discussed in this chapter relates to the song lyric: "Walk a Mile in My Shoes"?

5. What are the four major agents of socialization? Use a ladder as your diagram and list the agents on the steps of the ladder.

1.	
2.	
3.	
4.	

6. What is a distinguishing characteristic of total institutions?
7. How does resocialization differ from anticipatory socialization?

Thinking Critically

1. **Making Predictions** You read in this chapter about the concern that extensive computer use stunts social development. Another growing concern is that some people (and groups of people) are being "left behind" because they don't have equal access to technology. How might this become a problem for your generation?

2. **Evaluating Information** This chapter discusses the socializing influences of mass media. Our perceptions of the ideal body types seem to be largely a product of media socialization. In a later chapter, you will have an opportunity to look at how the media idealizes body types. Girls feel the need to be thin and boys tend to measure how muscular they are. Discuss how television, magazines, CDs, and video games reinforce these images. Give examples from your experience of how the media has socialized Americans to admire certain figure and body types.

3. **Analyzing Information** Your daily life includes many social networks, or groups that regularly contribute to your socialization. They include family, friends, teachers, people at work, teammates, and so forth. Identify one of these groups, and imagine your day if you suddenly lost contact with those people. What support would you be missing? What key elements are provided by this particular social network?

4. **Interpreting Information** Sociologists claim the average American watches television seven hours a day, yet some students say they never watch TV. How could you account for this fact? Remember to refer to what you learned from the chapter in discussing this question.

5. **Making Generalizations** Total institutions, such as prisons, presume that desocialization and resocialization occur, since one of their goals is to make prisoners law abiding. Yet nearly half of the inmates released in the United States return to prison. If desocialization and resocialization really do take place, why is the recidivism rate (the number of prisoners who return to prison) so high? Propose a theory for what might be happening, using the concept of resocialization.

Sociology Projects

1. **Socialization** As you read in the chapter, children are socialized in many ways. Some books that you read when you were a child probably had a lasting impact on you. Your task is to analyze children's books armed with your newfound sociological knowledge. Read three children's books or re-read three of your favorites. Use the following questions to help you in your analysis.

   a. What was the socializing message of the book? (In other words, what lesson did it teach?)

   b. How are females/males portrayed in the book?

   c. Are any values dealt with? Do you agree or disagree with those values?

   d. What ethnic groups are portrayed in the book? How are they portrayed?

   e. Are any other concepts from the chapter presented in the books (resocialization, anticipatory socialization, looking-glass self, and so forth)?

2. **Socialization and Music** Create the "Song of Your Life." From several different songs, select the lyrics that best describe your life. Try to create a flow, as your life represents a continuous flow of events and circumstances. Prepare a written summary of each song's significance to you, using the socialization concepts presented in the text. Do you think music is a socializing agent?

3. **TV and Real Life** The text mentioned the impact of TV on our daily lives. This activity asks you to assess how "real" TV is compared with what we see and do every day. You are to watch two hours of TV. Watch shows that fictionally portray real life (sporting events, the news, and documentaries are not appropriate for this activity). Take detailed notes on the characters, commenting on their clothing, body types, occupations, social class, race, ethnic group, age, and so forth. Then venture out into the real world, to a public place such as a park, laundromat, mall, bus terminal, or airport, and observe for two hours. (It might be easier to do this one hour at a time.) Concentrate on several people, and note the same features that you did for the TV characters. You might want to focus on shows that portray teens or the elderly and then observe members of that group. (Remember the ethics of doing research, and do not invade a subject's privacy without permission.) Write a paragraph comparing the characters on television with those you observed in real life.

4. **Violence on TV and in Film** Select a classmate to debate the issue of violence on TV and in film. Take the position that violence on TV and in film promotes real-life violence and propose a solution to this problem. Your classmate should try to persuade the audience that violence on TV does not encourage people to become more violent in real-life. Base your arguments on research.

5. **Major Agents of Socialization** Some children without parents or close family find themselves being moved from one foster home to another for the greater part of their childhood. Write an essay of at least one page in length, using standard grammar, proper spelling, and good sentence structure, in which you examine the role of each major agent of socialization in the development of an individual growing up in this environment.

HINT: Family is a major agent of socialization. Family exists in the traditional sense and in variations of all kinds.

Technology Activities

1. As indicated in this chapter, the process of socialization occurs throughout a person's life. The Internet has assumed a significant role in the socialization of Americans. It actually aids television in the process.

   1. What are the most popular television shows among your friends?
   2. Use a search engine to see if these shows have a web site on the Internet.
   3. Describe the kinds of information available on the web sites.
   4. What benefits do the web sites provide to the viewers? To the television show?

2. Using the Internet and your school or local library, research the role the following technological inventions of their time played in the socialization of Americans: the popularity of the radio during 1940–1950; the growing popularity of color television from 1960 to the present; and the popularity of the Internet over the last five years. Consider the positive and negative effects, analyzing how norms and behaviors were changed by the available programming and/or advertising.

Chapter 4
Enrichment Reading
National Television Violence

Key Findings

Today, violence is not only seen on the streets but also in the schools. During the last five years of the twentieth century, there were over 120 people shot in schools. We now hear stories in the news about young people participating in violent shootings on school grounds and killing innocent bystanders. In a Michigan school in 2000, one six-year-old shot and killed a classmate at school. These violent acts raise questions: Why is there an increase in violence, especially among today's youth? Does television have a negative effect on individuals? Does television encourage violent behaviors?

In 1994, the National Television Violence Study initiated the first part of its three-year project to assess violence on television. This study, which is the largest study of media content ever undertaken, was funded by the National Cable Television Association. The project examined approximately 2,500 hours of television programming that included 2,693 programs.

The first of the three studies analyzes violent content in television programming. The second study examines children's reactions to ratings and viewer advisories. The final study analyzes the content of antiviolence public service announcements (PSAs).

Following is a summary of the first study conducted in 1994–1995. Collectively, these findings establish the norms that exist in the overall television environment. Many of the patterns observed cause some concern.

Overall Conclusions about Violence on Television

❖ **Violence predominates on television, often including large numbers of violent interactions per program.**

The majority (57 percent) of programs on television contain violence, and roughly one third of violent programs contain nine or more violent interactions. The frequency of violence on television can contribute to **desensitization** and fear, as well as provide ample opportunities to learn violent attitudes and behaviors.

This man is holding up the V-chip used to control television viewing by children.

- **In the majority of the episodes of violence, the perpetrator engages in repeated violent acts.**

  The perpetrator engages in repeated acts of violence in more than half (58 percent) of all violent interactions. This increases the amount of violence to which viewers are exposed.

- **In one-quarter of the violent interactions, a gun is used.**

  Certain visual cues, such as weapons, tend to activate aggressive thoughts in viewers. Later, these thoughts cause individuals to interpret neutral events as possibly threatening or aggressive.

- **In about three-quarters of all violent scenes, perpetrators go unpunished.**

  The portrayal of rewards and punishments is probably the most important of all contextual factors for viewers as they interpret the meaning of what they see on television. Viewers who would otherwise think of a class of behaviors such as violence as bad may eventually learn that those behaviors are good (useful, successful, or desirable) if they are repeatedly and consistently portrayed as rewarded or unpunished. Across all channel types, this study discovered a common pattern that the majority of violent scenes lack any form of punishment for the perpetrators.

- **In a high proportion of violent episodes, the consequences are not realistically portrayed.**

  Less than half of violent interactions show the victims experiencing any signs of pain. Furthermore, only about one in six programs depict any long-term negative consequences, such as physical suffering or financial or emotional harm. All of these patterns increase the risk that viewers will believe that violence is not a particularly painful or harmful behavior.

- **Violence is often presented as humorous.**

  More than one third of all violent scenes involve a humorous context. Humor tends to trivialize or undermine the seriousness with which violence is regarded. Humorous violence can serve to desensitize viewers to the serious or harmful effects of violence.

- **Violent programs rarely employ a strong antiviolence theme.**

  Only 4 percent of all television programs emphasize a strong anti-violence theme. *Touched by an Angel, Little House on the Prairie,* and *Mr. Rogers* are among the exceptions.

Source: Adapted from "National Television Violence Study: Executive Summary." Studio City, CA: Mediascope, Inc., 1998.

What Does it Mean?

contextual
meaning that is derived from the setting or the environment; not stated, but implied

desensitization
the process of preventing an emotional response; make less sensitive

perpetrator
someone who carries out or brings about an action; in law, one who commits a crime

predominate
to exert control over; to hold an advantage in numbers

trivialize
to make something less important or serious than it is

Read and React

1. What was the stated purpose of the first study?
2. Why does the report state that the contextual factors for viewing violence are the most important?
3. Do you think the report reaches its stated purpose (see Question #1)? Why or why not?

CHAPTER 5
Social Structure and Society

USING Your Sociological Imagination

Because we are deeply involved in our own social world, we forget that our ability to participate in daily life is based on years of socialization. In the play, *As You Like It,* William Shakespeare wrote a line reminding us of the place of social learning in our lives: "All the world's a stage. And all the men and women merely players; They have their exits and their entrances; And one man in his time plays many parts."

All members of a group (including you) have parts they are expected to play. Students are expected to attend class, listen to the instructor, and participate in class activities. Teachers are expected to be in the classroom when students arrive, hold class, teach and guide the class, and make assignments. In any American high school, you will find similar relationships between students and staff. Interactions are orderly and predictable. In most cases, the teacher knows what the student expects of her and the student knows what the teacher expects of him.

If, however, you suddenly found yourself in a class where the teacher raised his hand to talk and brought his dog to class; where students played frisbee and took naps on the floor, you might wonder what planet you had beamed down to. Missing the order and predictability you expected, you would wonder how you should act in this unfamiliar setting. To fit in, what you would need is some awareness of the underlying *social structure.* This chapter will discuss concepts that underlie social structure.

Sections

1. **Social Structure and Status**
2. **Social Structure and Roles**
3. **Preindustrial Societies**
4. **Industrial and Postindustrial Societies**

Learning Objectives

After reading this chapter, you will be able to

❖ explain what sociologists mean by *social structure.*

❖ discuss how statuses and roles are related to social structure.

❖ identify and illustrate the concepts of social structure.

❖ explain how culture and social structures are related.

❖ describe the means of subsistence in preindustrial societies.

❖ discuss the characteristics of industrial society.

❖ compare and contrast preindustrial, industrial, and postindustrial societies.

SOCIOLOGY *Online*

Chapter Overview
Visit the *Sociology and You* Web site at soc.glencoe.com and click on **Chapter 5— Chapter Overviews** to preview chapter information.

Section 1

Social Structure and Status

Key Terms

- social structure
- status
- ascribed status
- achieved status
- status set
- master status

Section Preview

The underlying pattern of social relationships in a group is called social structure. Status is one very important element of social structure. Ascribed statuses are assigned at birth; achieved statuses are earned or chosen.

social structure
the underlying patterns of relationships in a group

status
a position a person occupies within a social structure

Social Structure Is All Around You

You learned in Chapter 4 that culture shapes human social behavior. In the absence of biological pre-programming, culture guides us in our thinking, feeling, and behaving. Without culture, humans would have no blueprint for social living. This chapter helps explain the relationship between culture and social structure.

So, what is social structure?   The chapter opening described a situation in which unexpected classroom behavior resulted in confusion for a newcomer. We are usually spared such confusion when entering a new group because we bring some knowledge of how people will normally relate to one another. In our minds, we carry a "social map" for various group situations. We have mental images of the new group with its patterns of social relationships. This underlying pattern is called **social structure.**

Everyone Has Status

We are not born with mental maps of social structure; we must learn them from others. In the process, we learn about *statuses* and *roles*—major elements of social structure.

What do sociologists mean by status?   People may refer to themselves as students, doctors, welders, secretaries, mothers, or sons. Each of these labels refers to a **status**—a position a person occupies within a social structure. Status helps us define who and what we are in relation to others within the same social structure. Some social statuses are acquired at birth. For example, a newborn female instantly becomes a child and a daughter. From then on, she assumes an increasingly larger number and variety of statuses.

Sociologists are interested in the relationships among social statuses. A sociologist investigating delinquency, for example, may focus on the status of social worker in relation to the statuses of the police officer, judge, and teacher. Figure 5.1 illustrates the status of a high

The two different status people in this photograph are behaving exactly as most people would expect.

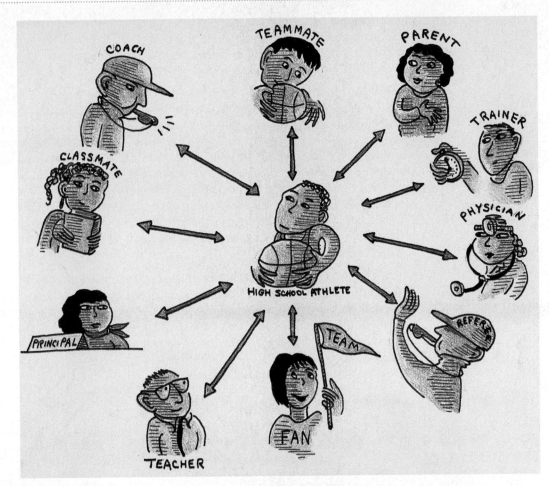

Figure 5.1 The Interrelationships of Social Statuses. *Social statuses do not exist in isolation. All statuses are interrelated with other statuses.*

school athlete related to various other statuses. There are two basic types of social statuses—*ascribed* and *achieved*.

What is an ascribed status? An **ascribed status** is neither earned nor chosen; it is assigned to us. At birth, an infant is either a male or a female. We do not choose our gender. Age is another example of an ascribed social status. In some societies, religion and social class are ascribed by the family of birth. If you were born into a lower-class home in India, for example, you would not be permitted to rise to a higher social class.

How is status achieved? An **achieved status** is earned or chosen. Achieving statuses is possible where people have some degree of control and choice. In most modern societies, for

Pictured is an African Masai man in traditional clothes. Do you think that his clothing reflects an ascribed or an achieved status?

ascribed status
a position that is neither earned nor chosen but assigned

achieved status
a position that is earned or chosen

example, an individual can decide to become a spouse or a parent. Occupations are also achieved statuses in modern societies where people have freedom to choose their work. Plumber, electrician, sales representative, nurse, executive, lawyer, and doctor are examples of achieved statuses.

What is a status set?   A person who is a social worker does not occupy only one status. This person holds various other statuses that may be totally unrelated to that of social worker. A **status set** is all of the statuses that a person occupies at any particular time. One social worker may be a wife, mother, author, and church choir director. Another may be a single parent, service club leader, and jazz musician. Another status set might be that of a student, a brother, a tennis player, a tutor, and a store clerk. Each of these statuses is part of another network of statuses. Assume, for example, that in addition to being a social worker, an individual is also a part-time jazz musician. In this status, she might interact with the statuses of nightclub owner, dancer, and fellow musician, among others.

Are all of a person's statuses equal?   Among the statuses held by an individual, some are more important than others. **Master statuses** are important because they influence most other aspects of the person's life. Master statuses may be achieved or ascribed. In industrial societies, occupations—achieved statuses for the most part—are master statuses. Your occupation strongly influences such matters as where you live, how well you live, and how long you live. "Criminal" is an achieved master status, since it affects the rest of your life.

status set
all of the statuses that a person occupies at any particular time

master status
a position that strongly affects most other aspects of a person's life

"I hunt and she gathers—otherwise, we couldn't make ends meet."

Expected behavior is often based on master statuses such as gender.

Explain why the status of a lawyer is a master status.

Student Web Activity
Visit the *Sociology and You* Web site at soc.glencoe.com and click on **Chapter 5—Student Web Activities** for an activity on social status.

Age, gender, race, and ethnicity are examples of ascribed master statuses. These statuses are master statuses because they significantly affect the likelihood of achieving other social statuses. When will the United States have a female president? Would you let a nineteen-year-old or a ninety-year-old handle your case in court? Or remove your appendix?

Section 1 Assessment

1. Briefly define the term *social structure*.

Match the definition with the type of status (a–d) it best describes.

2. wife, mother, author, church choir director
3. electrician, spouse
4. the presidency of the United States, professional athlete
5. sex, gender, race
6. daughter, son
7. quarterback, coach, fan, trainer

   a. ascribed status
   b. achieved status
   c. master status
   d. status set

Critical Thinking

8. **Categorizing Information** On a separate piece of paper, make a diagram of your life—the statuses you possess and the responsibilities or role expectations for each. Examples of statuses include son/daughter, student, band member, etc.

9. **Applying Concepts** What is the most important master status you have held? Has the master status helped or hindered you? What master status would you like to achieve? Why?

Our individual lives cannot generally be works of art unless the social order is also.

**Charles Horton Cooley
American sociologist**

Focus on Research

Experiment: Adopting Statuses in a Simulated Prison

Social psychologist Philip Zimbardo and his colleagues designed an experiment to observe the behavior of people without criminal records in a mock "prison." They were amazed at the rapidity with which statuses were adopted and roles fulfilled by the college students playing "prisoners" and "guards." This experiment reveals the ease with which people can be socialized to statuses and roles. Zimbardo's own words describe the design and results of this experiment.

In an attempt to understand just what it means . . . to be a prisoner or a prison guard, Craig Haney, Curt Banks, Dave Jaffe and I created our own prison. We carefully screened over 70 volunteers who answered an ad in a Palo Alto city newspaper and ended up with about two dozen young men who were selected to be part of this study. They were mature, emotionally stable, normal, intelligent college students from middle-class homes. . . . They appeared to represent the cream of the crop of this generation. None had any criminal record. . . .

Half were arbitrarily designated as prisoners by a flip of a coin, the others as guards. These were the roles they were to play in our simulated prison. The guards . . . made up their own formal rules for maintaining law, order and respect, and were generally free to improvise new ones during their eight-hour, three-man shifts. The prisoners were unexpectedly picked up at their homes by a city policeman in a squad car, searched, handcuffed, fingerprinted, booked at the Palo Alto station house and taken

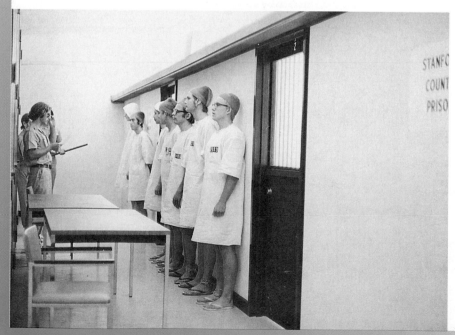

Students on the right in Zimbardo's mock prison experiment held very low statuses.

blindfolded to our jail. There they were stripped, deloused, put into a uniform, given a number and put into a cell with two other prisoners where they expected to live for the next two weeks. . . .

At the end of only six days we had to close down our mock prison because what we saw was frightening. It was no longer apparent to most of the subjects (or to us) where reality ended and their roles began. The majority had indeed become prisoners or guards, no longer able to clearly differentiate between role playing and self. There were dramatic changes in virtually every aspect of their behavior, thinking and feeling. . . . We were horrified because we saw some boys (guards) treat others as if they were despicable animals, taking pleasure in cruelty, while other boys (prisoners) became servile, dehumanized robots who thought only of escape, of their own individual survival and of their mounting hatred for the guards. We had to release three prisoners in the first four days because they had such acute situational traumatic reactions as hysterical crying, confusion in thinking, and severe depression. Others begged to be paroled, and all but three were willing to forfeit all the money they had earned [$15 per day] if they could be paroled. By then (the fifth day) they had been so programmed to think of themselves as prisoners that when their request for parole was denied they returned docilely to their cells. . . .

About a third of the guards became tyrannical in their arbitrary use of power, in enjoying their control over other people. They were corrupted by the power of their roles and became quite inventive in their techniques of breaking the spirit of the prisoners and making them feel they were worthless. . . . By the end of the week the experiment had become a reality. . . .

Excerpted with permission of Transaction, Inc., from *Society,* Vol. 9, No. 6. Copyright © 1972 by Transaction, Inc.

Working with the Research

1. If you were asked to discuss Zimbardo's experiment in light of one of the three major theoretical perspectives, which would you choose? Why?

2. One of Zimbardo's conclusions, not stated in the above account, is that the brutal behavior found in real-life prisons is not due to the antisocial characteristics or personality defects of guards and prisoners. Can you argue, sociologically, that he is right in this conclusion? How?

3. There was some controversy over the ethics of this experiment. Do you think this experiment could be carried out today under the ASA Code of Ethics? Why or why not?

Section 2

Social Structure and Roles

Key Terms

- role
- rights
- obligations
- role performance

- social interaction
- role conflict
- role strain

Section Preview

People interact according to prescribed roles. These roles carry certain rights and obligations. Sometimes conflict or strain occurs when an individual has too many roles to play.

Rights and Obligations

An expected behavior associated with a particular status is a **role.** Any status carries with it a variety of roles. The roles of a modern doctor, for example, include keeping informed about new medical developments, scheduling office appointments, diagnosing illnesses, and prescribing treatments.

Roles can be thought of as statuses "in action." Whereas statuses describe positions, roles describe behaviors. These behaviors are based on the rights and obligations attached to various statuses. **Rights** are behaviors that individuals expect from others. **Obligations** are behaviors that individuals are expected to perform toward others. The rights of one status correspond to the obligations of another. Doctors, for example, are obligated to diagnose

role
an expected behavior associated with a particular status

right
a behavior that individuals can expect from others

obligation
a behavior that individuals are expected to perform toward others

"No, Hoskins, you're not going to do it just because I'm telling you to do it. You're going to do it because you believe in it."

Hoskins is being forced to follow roles whether he wants to or not. Are such cues ever sent your way?

their patients' illnesses. Correspondingly, patients have the right to expect their doctors to diagnose to the best of their ability. Teachers have an obligation to be prepared to teach the daily lesson. Students have a right to expect that teachers will be adequately prepared to explain the material. Correspondingly, teachers have a right to expect that students will make the attempt to learn. Students have the obligation to make that effort.

Recall that this chapter began with a quotation from Shakespeare's play *As You Like It*. In terms of a play, roles are the part of the script that tells the actors (status holders) what beliefs, feelings, and actions are expected of them. A playwright or screenwriter specifies the content of a performer's part. In the same way, culture underlies the parts played in real life. Mothers, for instance, have different maternal "scripts" in different cultures. Most American mothers emphasize independence more than most Iranian mothers.

It is never too late to be what you might have been.

George Eliot
English author

Role Performance and Social Interaction

Statuses and roles provide the basis for group life. It is primarily when people interact with each other socially that they "perform" in the roles attached to their statuses.

Role performance is the actual conduct, or behavior, involved in carrying out (or performing) a role. Role performance can occur without an audience (as when a student studies alone for a test). Most role performance, though, involves social interaction.

Social interaction is the process of influencing each other as people relate. For example, before two boys begin to fight, they have probably gone through a process of insulting and challenging each other. Fortunately, most social interaction is not as negative and violent, but the same process of influence and reaction to others is involved.

Think again of the analogy of the play. If statuses are like the parts in a play and roles are like the script, then social interaction represents the way actors respond to cues given by other actors. Role performance is the performance itself.

role performance
the actual behavior of an individual in a role

social interaction
the process of influencing each other as people relate

These students each have particular roles and statuses within their group.

How does play-acting differ from social interactions? The play analogy is a valid one, but it is dangerous to take it too far. For one thing, "delivery of the lines" in real life is not the conscious process used by actors. Unlike stage performances, most real-life role performance occurs without planning.

Second, although actors may sometimes ad-lib, change lines to suit themselves, and so forth, overall they stick pretty closely to the script. Departures are fairly easy to detect and control. This is not the case with differences between a role and a role performance.

Third, on the stage, there is a programmed and predictable relationship between cues and responses. One performer's line is a cue for a specific response from another actor. In life, we can choose our own cues and responses. A student may decide to tell a teacher that her tests are the worst he has ever encountered. On hearing this, the teacher may tell the student that it is not his place to judge, or the teacher may ask for further explanation so that improvement may be made. In effect, the teacher can choose from several roles to play at that time. Likewise, the student can choose from a variety of responses to the teacher's behavior. If the teacher tells the student he is out of line, the student may report the matter to a counselor, or he may decide to forget it altogether. The process of choosing the role and then acting it out occurs in nearly all instances of social interaction.

Keep in mind, however, that the range of responses is not limitless. Only certain responses are culturally acceptable. It is not an appropriate response for the teacher to bodily eject the student from her classroom, and the student would be very foolish to pound the teacher's desk in protest.

Figure 5.2 outlines the connection between culture and social structure. As you can see at the top of the figure, the first link between culture and social structure is the concept of role (behavior associated with a status). Roles are in turn attached to statuses (a position a person occupies within a group). Yet people do not always follow roles exactly. The manner in which roles are actually carried out is role performance, the third link in the conceptual chain. Role performance occurs through social interaction. This is the fourth link between culture and social structure. Social interaction based on roles is observable as patterned relationships, which make up social structure. In turn, existing social structure affects the creation of and changes in culture.

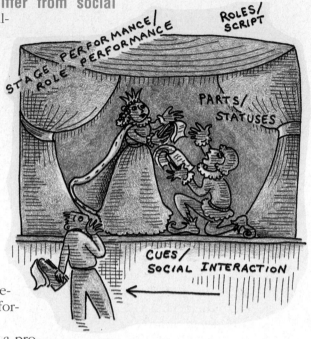

This illustration draws an analogy between rehearsed behavior on the stage and real social behavior. How do community cultural standards affect the role behavior of students and teachers?

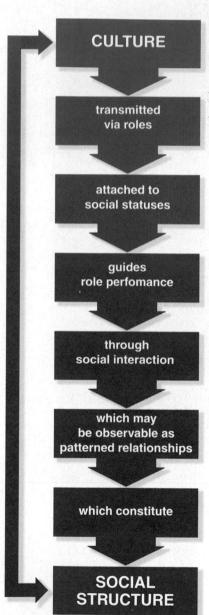

Figure 5.2 The Links Between Culture and Social Structure.
Sociologists concentrate on the study of social structure. They have developed a set of concepts and an understanding of their relationships in order to examine the basic nature of social structure.

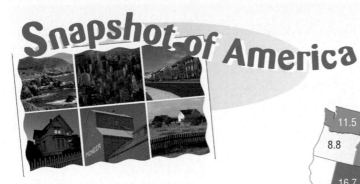

Snapshot of America

Guns in School

Bringing firearms to school is a major violation of the student role. Teachers have a right to expect students to come to school unarmed. Students are obligated not to bring weapons to school. This map gives us some idea of the relative extent to which this role is being violated and punished in various states. In total, 3,523 students were expelled during the 1998–99 school year for carrying guns to school. The good news—this number represents a substantial drop over the two previous survey years.

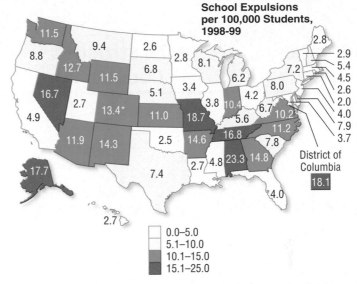

Number of Gun-related School Expulsions per 100,000 Students, 1998-99

0.0–5.0
5.1–10.0
10.1–15.0
15.1–25.0

Source: U.S. Dept. of Education, 2000.   *Includes all weapons, not just firearms.

Interpreting the Map

1. Which states reported the most expulsions per 100,000 students in the 1998–1999 school year? (Which states fall in the over 15.0 range?)
2. Explain why violation of a law can also be a role violation.

Online **UPDATE**
Visit soc.glencoe.com and click on **Textbook Updates–Chapter 5** for an update of the data.

Source: U.S. Dept. of Education

Role Conflict and Role Strain

The existence of statuses and roles permits social life to be predictable and orderly. At the same time, each status involves many roles, and each individual holds many statuses. This diversity invites conflict and strain.

What are role conflict and role strain?   **Role conflict** exists when the performance of a role in one status clashes with the performance of a role in another. Many teenagers, for example, hold the statuses of student and employee. Those who do often find it difficult to balance study and work demands.

role conflict
condition in which the performance of a role in one status interferes with the performance of a role in another status

Figure 5.3 Focus on Theoretical Perspectives

Illustrating Social Structure Concepts. This table illustrates how each theoretical perspective might approach the study of social structures. The concepts could be switched to any other theoretical perspective and illustrated from that perspective. Associate each concept with a different theoretical perspective and provide your own example.

Theoretical Perspective	Social Structure Concept	Example
Functionalism	Role	Social integration is promoted by culturally defined rights and obligations honored by group members.
Conflict Theory	Ascribed Master Status	Ascribed master statuses such as gender and race empower some to subjugate others.
Symbolic Interactionism	Social Interaction	Roles are carried out by individuals on the basis of the symbols and meanings they share.

role strain
condition in which the roles of a single status are inconsistent or conflicting

Role strain occurs when a person has trouble meeting the many roles connected with a single status. College basketball coaches, for example, have to recruit for next year's season while trying to win games in the current season. Besides preparing daily lessons, high school teachers often are required to sponsor social clubs. Each of these roles (coach and recruiter or teacher and advisor) is time consuming, and the fulfillment of one role may interfere with the performance of the others. If your expectations as a high school student require you to perform well academically, join a social organization, pursue a sport, date, and participate in other school activities, you will probably experience some degree of role strain as a result of these expectations.

How do we manage role conflict and strain?   Role conflict and strain may lead to discomfort and confusion. To feel better and to have smoother relationships with others, we often solve role dilemmas by setting priorities. When roles clash, we decide which role is most important to us and act accordingly. For example, a student who frequently misses school-related activities because of work demands will have to assess her priorities. She can eliminate the role conflict completely by quitting work and putting a priority on school activities. If she remains in both statuses, she can reduce work hours or cut down on extracurricular school activities.

We also segregate roles. That is, we separate our behavior in one role from our behavior in another. This is especially effective for reducing the negative effects of conflicting roles. A college coach experiencing the role strain associated with coaching and recruiting simultaneously can decide to give priority to one over the other. He may, for example, let his assistant coach do most of the recruiting until the season ends. Ranking incompatible roles in terms of their importance is a good way to reduce role conflict and strain. An organized-crime member may reduce role conflict by segregating his criminal activities from his role as a loving father.

Because of role conflict and role strain, meeting the goals and expectations of all our roles is impossible. This poses no problem as long as role performance occurs within accepted limits. Professors at research-oriented universities may be permitted to emphasize teaching over research. Coaches may accent fair play, character building, and scholarship rather than a winning record. Professors at research universities who do too little publishing or coaches who win too few games, however, usually will not be rewarded for very long. At some point they will be judged as failing to meet expected role performance. (For more on handling role conflict, see Sociology Today on the next page.)

Do you think this young man is suffering from role conflict or role strain?

Section 2 Assessment

Match each situation below with the key term (a–e) it illustrates.

1. A husband and wife discuss the disciplining of one of their children.
2. A mother is expected to take care of her children.
3. A businessman has no time for his children.
4. A school principal hands out diplomas at a graduation ceremony.
5. A corporate chief executive officer is economically forced to terminate employees who are his friends.

   a. role
   b. role conflict
   c. role performance
   d. role strain
   e. social interaction

6. Which of the following is *not* one of the differences between a play and social life?
   a. There is considerably more difference between roles and role performance in social life than between a script and a stage performance.
   b. Unlike the stage, there are no cues and responses in real life.
   c. Role performance in real life is not the conscious process that actors go through on the stage.
   d. In social life, the cues and responses are not as programmed and predictable as on the stage.

Critical Thinking

7. **Applying Concepts** Are you presently experiencing role conflict or role strain? If you are, analyze the source. If not, explain why at this time you are free from role conflict and role strain, making clear the meaning of the concepts.

Sociology Today

Reducing Conflict in Two-Career Families

Families with two working adults have special strains. While in 1960, less than 20 percent of married women with young children worked outside of the home, by 2000, the figure was about 65 percent (U.S. Bureau of the Census). This increase has resulted in added role conflict for women. In a two-career family, the woman is more likely to suffer from conflict because she is still generally expected to balance her traditional homemaker roles with her career roles. The women are not the only ones who suffer, however. The effects of this conflict are felt by husbands and children, as well. Since you will likely be faced with the stress associated with dual-career families, you would be wise to learn now some techniques for reducing role conflict.

1. Focus on the Positive

Conflict can be reduced when couples define their situation positively. If both partners are working from choice rather than necessity, it can be helpful to remember some of the reasons why they first made the choice for both to work. These reasons might include additional income or personal satisfaction.

2. Put Family Needs First

Role conflict can be most effectively managed when family roles are placed ahead of working roles. When a baby-sitter fails to show up, when a child is sick, or when a parent-teacher conference is called, one of the parents can place these demands above work-related demands. Placing a higher priority on family needs will help keep the family support structure intact.

3. Assume One Role at a Time

Conflict can be reduced if a person focuses on only one role at a time. Leaving job-related problems at work and family issues at home is often difficult but is very effective in reducing role conflict.

4. Find the Compromise Balance

Although many men take active roles in child care today in order to meet family obligations, women still make the most compromises in their careers. With the increasing number of women in better-paying professional careers, we should expect more equality in career compromises between husbands and wives.

Doing Sociology

Identify three ways that you believe would help reduce role conflict in dual-career families. Provide specific examples not given in the text.

Preindustrial Societies

Key Terms

- society
- hunting and gathering society
- horticultural society
- pastoral societies
- agricultural society

Through mostly grunts and exaggerated gestures, two fishermen/gatherers attempt to communicate.

Even the earliest societies had patterned and predictable social relationships.

Types of Society

The culture and social structure of a society are greatly affected by the way the society provides for basic needs. A **society,** as you may remember from Chapter 3, is composed of people living within defined territorial borders who share a common culture. Societies meet their members' basic needs, such as the needs for food and shelter, in diffferent ways. These differences form the basis of a system anthropologists often use to classify societies. In this system, societies are classified as preindustrial, industrial, or postindustrial. We will look at preindustrial societies in this section and examine industrial and postindustrial societies in the following sections.

In theory, a society is independent of outsiders. It contains enough smaller social structures—family, economy, and so forth—to meet the needs of its members. As you will see, preindustrial societies actually could be independent and self-sufficient. Modern societies, although capable of caring for most members' needs, must have political, military, economic, cultural, and technological ties with other societies. In fact, modern societies are rapidly moving toward the creation of a global society.

In the next few pages, several basic types of societies will be distinguished. Each type of society is unique in important ways. All societies, however, are comprised of social structures. Members in each type of society know what is expected of them and what they can expect from others. Members of a particular type of society engage in the same basic social patterns time after time because they share patterned and predictable social relationships that are passed from generation to generation.

Section Preview

The way a society provides for basic needs greatly affects its culture and social structure. Preindustrial, industrial, and postindustrial societies meet basic needs in different ways. Preindustrial societies include hunting and gathering, horticultural, pastoral, and agricultural societies.

society
people living within defined territorial borders and sharing a common culture

Preindustrial

| Hunting and gathering 2 million to 10,000 years ago | Horticultural gardening 12,000 to 10,000 years ago | Pastoral herding 12,000 to 10,000 years ago |

Hunting and Gathering Societies

hunting and gathering society
a society that survives by hunting animals and gathering edible plants

The **hunting and gathering society** survives by hunting animals and gathering edible foods such as wild fruits and vegetables. This is the oldest solution to the problem of providing for the basic need for food, or subsistence. In fact, it was only about nine thousand years ago that other methods of solving the subsistence problem emerged.

Hunting and gathering societies are usually nomadic—they move from place to place as the food supply and seasons change. Because nomads must carry all their possessions with them, they have few material goods. Hunting and gathering societies also tend to be very small—usually fewer than fifty people—with members scattered over a wide area. Because the family is the only institution in hunting and gathering societies, it tends to all the needs of its members. Most members are related by blood or marriage, although marriage is usually limited to those outside the family or band.

Economic relationships within hunting and gathering societies are based on cooperation—members share what they have with other members. Members of hunting and gathering societies seem simply to give things to one another without worrying about how "payment" will be made. In fact, the more scarce something is, the more freely it is shared. Generosity and hospitality are valued. Thrift is considered a reflection of selfishness. Because the obligation to share goods is one of the most binding aspects of their culture, members of hunting and gathering societies have little or no conception of private property or ownership.

Without a sense of private ownership and with few possessions for anyone to own, hunting and gathering societies have no social classes, no rich or poor. These societies lack status differences based on political authority because they have no political institutions; there is no one to organize and control activities. When the traditional Inuit in Canada and Alaska, for example, want to settle disputes, they use dueling songs. The people involved in the dispute prepare and sing songs to express their sides of the issue. Their families, as choruses, accompany them. Those listening to the duel applaud their choice for the victor (Hoebel, 1983).

Judging from this photograph, to what type of society do these Navajo women belong?

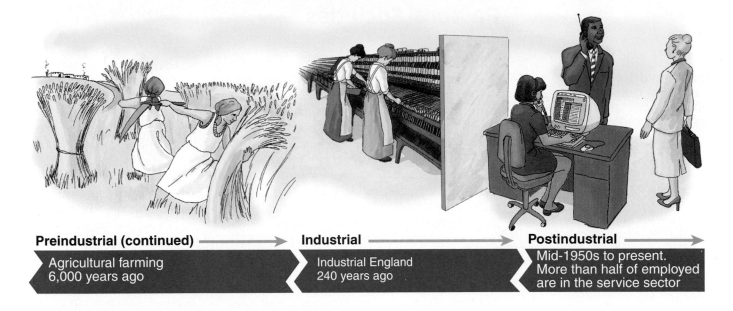

Preindustrial (continued)
Agricultural farming
6,000 years ago

Industrial
Industrial England
240 years ago

Postindustrial
Mid-1950s to present.
More than half of employed
are in the service sector

The division of labor in hunting and gathering societies is limited to the sex and age distinctions found in most families, since the family is the only institution. Men and women are assigned separate tasks, and certain tasks are given to the old, the young, and young adults. There is more leisure time in hunting and gathering societies than in any other. Today, few true hunting and gathering societies remain other than the Khoi-San (Bushmen) in Southern Africa, the Kaska Indians in Canada, and the Yanomamö of Brazil. (See Another Place on page 158.)

Horticultural Societies

A **horticultural society** solves the subsistence problem primarily through the growing of plants. This type of society came into being about ten to twelve thousand years ago, when people learned they could grow and harvest certain plants instead of simply gathering them. The gradual change from hunting and gathering to horticultural societies occurred over several centuries (Nolan and Lenski, 1999).

The shift from hunting and gathering to horticulture, or gardening, led to more permanent settlements. People no longer needed to move frequently to find food. Even without plows and animals to pull them, they could work a piece of land for extended periods of time before moving on to more fertile soil. This relative stability permitted the growth of multicommunity societies averaging one thousand to two thousand people each.

The family is even more basic to social life in horticultural societies than in hunting and gathering societies. In hunting and gathering societies, the survival of the group usually has top priority. In horticultural societies, primary emphasis is on providing for household members. This is because producing food in horticultural societies can be handled through the labor of family members. With the labor necessary for survival, households depend more on themselves and less on others outside the family unit for their subsistence.

horticultural society
a society that survives primarily through the growing of plants

Pastoral Societies

pastoral society
a society in which food is obtained primarily by raising and taking care of animals

Most horticultural societies keep domesticated animals such as pigs and chickens. They do not, however, depend economically on the products of these animals the way *pastoralists*, or herders, do. In **pastoral societies,** food is obtained primarily by raising and taking care of animals. For the most part, these are herd animals such as cattle, camels, goats, and sheep, all of which provide both milk and meat. Since grains are needed to feed the animals, pastoralists must also either farm or trade with people who do (Nanda and Warms, 1998; Peoples and Bailey, 2000).

There is more migration in pastoral societies than in those based more fully on cultivation of land. However, permanent (or at least long-term) villages can be maintained if, as seasons change, herd animals are simply moved to different pastures within a given area. In such societies, the women remain at home while the men take the herds to different pastures. With men being responsible for providing food, the status of women in pastoral societies is low. These societies are male dominated.

Because both horticultural and pastoral societies can produce a surplus of food, they usher in important social changes unknown in hunting and gathering societies. With a surplus food supply, some members of the community are free to create a more complex division of labor. People can become political and religious leaders or make goods such as pottery, spears, and clothing. Because nonedible goods are produced, an incentive to trade with other peoples emerges.

agricultural society
a society that uses plows and draft animals in growing food

The creation of a surplus also permits the development of social inequality (class or caste), although it is limited. Even a relatively small surplus, however, means that some families, villages, or clans have more wealth than others.

Agricultural Societies

An **agricultural society,** like a horticultural society, subsists by growing food. The difference is that agricultural societies use plows and animals. In fact, the transition from horticultural to agricultural society was made possible largely through the invention of the plow (Nolan and Lenski, 1999).

The plow not only allows the farmer to control weeds but also turns the weeds into fertilizer by burying them under the soil. By digging more deeply into the ground than was possible with sticks, hoes, and spades, the plow is able to reach nutrient-rich dirt that had sunk below root level. The result is more productivity—more food per unit of land.

This Bali farmer lives in an agricultural society. How does his society differ technologically from a horticultural society?

This medieval manuscript shows a noble instructing villeins on crop harvesting. Why would this type of superior-subordinate behavior first appear in an agricultural society?

Using animals also increases productivity, because larger areas can be cultivated with fewer people. As a result, more people are free to engage in noneconomic activities such as formal education, concerts, and political rallies. Cities can be built, and occupations appear that are not directly tied to farming, such as politician, blacksmith, and hat maker. New political, economic, and religious institutions emerge. Although family ties remain important, government replaces the family group as the guiding force for agricultural societies.

In the past, agricultural societies were headed by a king or an emperor. Distinct social classes appeared for the first time. Wealth and power were based on land ownership, which was controlled by the governing upper class. These elites enjoyed the benefits of the work done by the peasants. Urban merchants were better off than peasants, but they, too, worked hard for their livings. An economy based on trade began to emerge as an identifiable institution during this time. Monetary systems, which use money rather than goods for payment, began to be used as well. Increasingly, religion and government became separate as institutions. Rulers were believed to be divinely chosen, but few of them were also religious leaders.

Section 3 Assessment

1. Briefly restate the chief traits of each type of society: hunting and gathering, horticultural, pastoral, and agricultural.
2. In which type of society did a marked class system first appear? Explain why.

Critical Thinking

3. **Synthesizing Information** Using information from this section, develop a theory that would explain why conflict increases as society becomes more complex.

Money is the most egalitarian force in society. It confers power on whoever holds it.

Roger Starr
American economist

Another Place

The Chest-Pounding Duel

A description of the "chest-pounding" ritual that takes place among the Yanomamö tribe in Southern Venezuela was recorded by anthropologist Napoleon Chagnon. It provides a good example of social structure in a preindustrial society. All of the participants in this activity—even those merely observing—know exactly what is expected of them and what to expect of the others. This is what sociologists mean by *social structure*.

. . . There were about sixty adult men on each side in the fight divided into two arenas, each comprised of hosts and guests. Two men, one from each side, would step into the center of the milling, belligerent crowd of weapon-wielding partisans, urged on by their comrades. One would step up, spread his legs apart, bare his chest, and hold his arms behind his back, daring the other to hit him. The opponent would size him up, adjust the man's chest or arms so as to give himself the greatest advantage when he struck and then step back to deliver his close-fisted blow. The striker would painstakingly adjust his own distance from his victim by measuring his arm length to the man's chest, taking several dry runs before delivering his blow. He would then wind up like a baseball pitcher, but keeping both feet on the ground, and deliver a tremendous wallop with his fist to the man's left pectoral muscle, putting all of his weight into the blow. The victim's knees would often buckle and he would stagger around a few moments, shaking his head to clear the stars, but remain silent. The blow invariably raised a "frog" on the recipient's pectoral muscle where the striker's knuckles bit into his flesh. After each blow, the comrades of the deliverer would cheer and bounce up and down from the knees, waving and clacking their weapons over their heads. The victim's supporters, meanwhile, would urge their champion on frantically, insisting that he take another blow. If the delivery were made with sufficient force to knock the recipient to the ground, the man who delivered it would throw his arms above his head, roll his eyes back, and prance victoriously in a circle around his victim, growling and screaming, his feet almost a blur from his excited dance. The recipient would stand poised and take as many as four blows before demanding to hit his adversary. He would be permitted to strike his opponent as many times as the latter struck him, provided that the opponent could take it. If not, he would be forced to retire, much to the dismay of his comrades and the delirious joy of their opponents. No fighter could retire after delivering a blow. If he attempted to do so, his adversary would plunge into the crowd and roughly haul him back out, sometimes being aided by the man's own supporters. Only after having received his just dues could he retire. If he had delivered three blows, he had to receive three or else be proven a poor fighter. He could retire with less than three only if he were injured. Then, one of his comrades would replace him and demand to hit the victorious opponent. The injured man's two remaining blows would be canceled and the man who delivered the victorious blow would have to receive more blows than he delivered. Thus, good fighters are at a disadvantage, since they receive disproportionately more punishment than they deliver. Their only reward is . . . [prestige]: they earn the reputation of being fierce.

Source: Excerpted from Napoleon A. Chagnon, *Yanomamö: The Fierce People* (New York: Holt, Rinehart and Winston, 1977), pp. 113–115.

Thinking It Over

Describe an activity in your culture that illustrates patterned social relationships. Explain the statuses and roles involved.

Section 4

Industrial and Postindustrial Societies

Key Terms

- industrial society
- mechanization
- urbanization
- Gemeinschaft
- Gesellschaft

- social solidarity
- mechanical solidarity
- organic solidarity
- postindustrial society

Basic Features of Industrial Societies

The Industrial Revolution created a society that is dependent upon science and technology to produce its basic goods and services. Sociologists call this an **industrial society.**

What happens when agricultural societies become industrial societies? Neil Smelser (1976) has identified some basic structural changes that occur in societies shifting from an agricultural to an industrial base. Industrialism brings with it a change—*away* from simple, traditional technology (plows, hammers, harnesses) *toward* the application of scientific knowledge to create more complex technological devices. Early examples of

Section Preview

The Industrial Revolution created a new type of society, called industrial society. Characteristics that distinguish this society from all earlier ones include the growth of large cities and a wide-spread dependence on machines and technology. Postindustrial society has a predominately white-collar labor force that is concentrated in service industries. Social instability has been linked to the transition from an industrial to a postindustrial society.

industrial society
a society that depends on science and technology to produce its basic goods and services

Ford Motor Company employees work on the Model T assembly line. What technology underlies industrial society?

mechanization
the process of replacing animal and human power with machine power

urbanization
the shifting of population from farms and villages to large cities

industrial technology include the steam engine and the use of electrical power in manufacturing. More recent technological developments include nuclear energy, aerospace-related inventions, and the computer.

In industrial societies, intensive animal and human labor is replaced by power-driven machines, a process known as **mechanization.** These machines are operated by wage earners who produce goods for sale on the market. With the help of machinery, farmers are able to produce enough food to support themselves and many others. This surplus allows people to move away from farms and villages, adding to the growing population in large cities. **Urbanization,** then, is also a basic feature of industrial societies.

How does the role of the family change? With industrialization, family functions change in many ways. Economic activities, once carried out in the home, move to the factory. Similarly, the education of the young, which in agricultural societies centered on teaching farming, moves from the home to the formal school. An industrial society requires a more broadly educated and trained labor force, so young people can no longer be prepared for the work force by their families. Blood relationships decline in importance as families begin to separate socially and physically due to urbanization and the necessity of taking jobs in distant locations where factories have been built. Personal choice and love replace arranged marriages. Women, through their entrance into the work force, become less subordinate to their husbands. Individual mobility increases dramatically, and social class is based more on occupational achievement than the social class of one's parents. Because the United States has been an industrial society for so long, its characteristics are taken as a given. The effects of industrialization are easier to observe in societies currently moving from an agricultural to an industrial economic base. For example, Vietnam and Malaysia are experiencing mechanization and urbanization at the beginning of the twenty-first century (Singh, 1998; Phu, 1998).

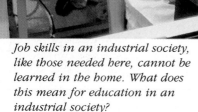

Job skills in an industrial society, like those needed here, cannot be learned in the home. What does this mean for education in an industrial society?

Gemeinschaft
preindustrial society based on tradition, kinship, and close social ties

Gesellschaft
industrial society characterized by weak family ties, competition, and impersonal social relationships

social solidarity
the degree to which a society is unified

A Conversation with Two Sociologists

Ferdinand Tönnies and Emile Durkheim were two early sociologists who wrote about preindustrial and industrial societies. Sociologists today still study their writings.

What did Tönnies write? Ferdinand Tönnies (1957, originally published in 1887), was an early German sociologist. In his writing, he distinguished between *gemeinschaft* (ga MINE shoft) and *gesellschaft* (ga ZELL shoft). **Gemeinschaft** is German for "community." It describes a society based on tradition, kinship, and intimate social relationships. These are the types of communities found in preindustrial societies. **Gesellschaft** is the German word for "society." This concept represents industrial society and is characterized by weak family ties, competition, and less personal social relationships.

What were Durkheim's views? Shortly after Tönnies published his theory, Emile Durkheim (1964a, originally published in 1893) made a similar observation. He distinguished the two types of societies by the nature of their social *solidarity*. **Social solidarity** is the degree to which a society is unified or can hold itself together in the face of obstacles.

World View

Agricultural Employment

As societies move from the preindustrial to the postindustrial stage, fewer people are required to raise food to feed the population. This map shows the percentage of each country's population involved in the production of agricultural products.

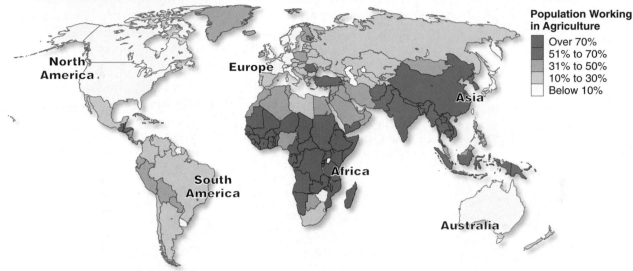

Population Working in Agriculture
- Over 70%
- 51% to 70%
- 31% to 50%
- 10% to 30%
- Below 10%

Interpreting the Map

1. After examining this map, what generalizations about types of societies around the world would you make? Explain.
2. Which countries do you think could be ready to move from one type of society to another? Be specific about countries and types of societies.
3. What parts of the world are least likely to change in the near future? Explain your answer.

Adapted from *Compact Peters Atlas of the World*. Essex, England: Longman Group UK Limited.

Social solidarity, Durkheim contended, is a result of society's division of labor. In societies in which the division of labor is simple—in which most people are doing the same type of work—**mechanical solidarity** is the foundation for social unity. A society based on mechanical solidarity achieves social unity through a consensus of beliefs, values, and norms; strong social pressures for conformity; and dependence on tradition and family. In this type of society, which is best observed in small, nonliterate societies, people tend to behave, think, and feel in much the same ways, to place the group above the individual, and to emphasize tradition and family.

In contrast, in an industrial society, members depend on a variety of people to fulfill their needs—barbers, bakers, manufacturers, and other suppliers of services. This modern industrial society is based on **organic solidarity.** It achieves social unity through a complex of specialized statuses that make members of the society interdependent.

mechanical solidarity
a type of social unity achieved by people doing the same type of work and holding similar values

organic solidarity
a type of social unity in which members' interdependence is based on specialized functions and statuses

The term *organic solidarity* is based on an analogy with biological organisms. If a biological organism composed of highly specialized parts is to survive, its parts must work together. Similarly, the parts of a society based on organic solidarity must cooperate if the society is to survive.

Major Features of Postindustrial Society

postindustrial society
a society in which the economic emphasis is on providing services and information

Some societies, such as the United States, have passed beyond industrial society into **postindustrial society.** In this type of society, the economic emphasis is on providing services and information rather than on producing goods through basic manufacturing.

Sociologist Daniel Bell (1999) identifies five major features of a postindustrial society, a society based on a service economy.

1. *For the first time, the majority of the labor force are employed in services rather than in agriculture or manufacturing.* These industries emphasize services (banking, medical care, fast food, entertainment) rather than producing tangible goods, such as oil or steel. They include organizations in the areas of trade, finance, transportation, health, recreation, research, and government. In 2000, about 75 percent of all employed workers in the United States were in service jobs.

2. *White-collar employment replaces much blue-collar work.* White-collar workers outnumbered blue-collar workers in the United States for the first time in 1956, and the gap is still increasing. The most rapid growth has been in professional and technical employment.

3. *Technical knowledge is the key organizing feature in postindustrial society.* Knowledge is used for the creation of innovations as well as for making government policy. As technical knowledge becomes more important, so do educational and research institutions.

4. *Technological change is planned and assessed.* In an industrial society, the effects of a technology are not assessed before its introduction. When the automobile engine was invented, no one asked whether it would have an effect on the environment. In postindustrial societies, the effects—good and bad—of an innovation can be considered before it is introduced.

5. *Reliance on computer modeling in all areas.* With modern computers, it is possible to consider a large number of interacting variables simultaneously. This "intellectual technology" allows us to manage complex organizations—including government at national, state, and local levels.

The New York Stock Exchange symbolizes the shift from production-based work to knowledge-based work in postindustrial society.

Social Instability in Postindustrial Society

Historian Francis Fukuyama (1990) believes that the transition to a service economy has increased social instability in nations undergoing this change. He writes the following about deteriorating social conditions that began in the mid-1960s.

Crime and social disorder began to rise, making inner-city areas of the wealthiest societies on earth almost uninhabitable. The decline of kinship as a social institution, which has been going on for more than 200 years, accelerated sharply in the second half of the twentieth century. Marriages and births declined and divorce soared; and one out of every three children in the United States and more than half of all children in Scandinavia were born out of wedlock. Finally, trust and confidence in institutions went into a forty-year decline (Fukuyama, 1999:55).

Will social instability continue? According to Fukuyama, this social instability is now lessening. He sees current indications of a return to social stability. The establishment of new social norms, he believes, is reflected in the slowing down of increases in divorce, crime, distrust, and illegitimacy. In the 1990s, Fukuyama notes, many societies have even seen a reversal of these rates—crime, divorce, illegitimacy, and distrust have actually declined.

This is particularly true in the United States, where levels of crime are down a good 15 percent from their peaks in the early 1990s. Divorce rates peaked in the early 1980s, and births to single mothers appear to have stopped increasing. Welfare rolls have diminished almost as dramatically as crime rates, in response both to the 1996 welfare-reform measures and to opportunities provided by a nearly full-employment economy in the 1990s. Levels of trust in both institutions and individuals have also recovered significantly since the early 1990s (Fukuyama, 1999:80).

What has caused the return to social stability? Fukuyama believes that humans find it difficult to live without values and norms:

The situation of normlessness . . . is intensely uncomfortable for us, and we will seek to create new rules to replace the old ones that have been undercut (Fukuyama, 1999:76).

Because culture can be changed, it can be used to create new social structures better adapted to changing social and economic circumstances.

Section 4 Assessment

1. Explain why blood relationships are less important in an industrial society than in a preindustrial society.
2. State whether each of the following is or is not a major feature of a postindustrial society.
   a. emphasis on technical knowledge
   b. employment of the majority of the labor force in service industries
   c. reliance on advanced technology
   d. increased dependence on skilled blue-collar workers
   e. shift toward the employment of white-collar workers

Critical Thinking

3. **Analyzing Information** Explain from your own observation why family relationships would probably weaken in an industrial society.
4. **Making Predictions** As the United States becomes a more complete information society, how may life for you change?

We live in a moment of history where change is so speeded up that we begin to see the present only when it is disappearing.

R.D. Laing
Scottish psychiatrist

coercion
interaction in which individuals or groups are forced to behave in a particular way

What type of social interaction is involved in city curfews?

conformity
behavior that matches group expectations

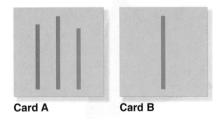

Card A   Card B

Figure 6.1   Cards for Asch's Experiments. *Which of the lines on Card A matches the line on Card B? You may be surprised to learn that in a group setting many people associated the first and the third lines with the longer line on Card B. Read about Asch's experiment in the text.*

Coercion

Coercion is social interaction in which individuals or groups are forced to give in to the will of other individuals or groups. Prisoners of war can be forced to reveal information to enemies, governments can enforce laws through legalized punishment, and parents can control the behavior of young children by threatening to withdraw privileges.

Coercion is the opposite of social exchange. Whereas social exchange involves voluntary conformity for mutual benefit, coercion is a one-way street. The central element in coercion, then, is domination. This domination may occur through physical force, such as imprisonment, torture, or death. More often, however, coercion is expressed more subtly through social pressure— ridicule, rejection, withdrawal of affection, or denial of recognition.

Conflict theory best describes this type of social interaction. When parents coerce children with a curfew, guards coerce prisoners with force, and governments coerce drivers with fines, obvious power differentials are at work.

Conformity

Conformity is behavior that matches group expectations. When we conform, we adapt our behavior to fit the behavior of those around us. Social life—with all its uniformity, predictability, and orderliness—simply could not exist without this type of social interaction. Without conformity, there could be no churches, families, universities, or governments. Without conformity, there could be no culture or social structure.

Do most people conform to group pressures?   The tendency to conform to group pressure has been dramatically illustrated in a classic experiment by Solomon Asch (1955). In this experiment, many participants publicly denied their own senses because they wanted to avoid disagreeing with majority opinion.

Asch asked groups of male college students to compare lines printed on two cards. (See Figure 6.1.) The students were asked to identify the line on the second card that matched, in length, one of the lines on the first card. In each group, all but one of the subjects had been instructed by Asch to choose a line that obviously did not match. The *naive* subject—the only member of each group unaware of the real nature of the experiment—was forced either to select the line he actually thought matched the standard line or to yield to the unanimous opinion of the group.

In earlier tests of individuals in isolation, Asch had found that the error rate in matching the lines was only 1 percent. Under group pressure, however, the naive subjects went along with the majority's wrong opinion over one-third of the time. If this large a proportion of naive subjects yielded to group pressure in a group of strangers, it is not difficult to imagine the conformity rate in groups where people are emotionally committed to the welfare of the group (Myers, 1999).

What is groupthink?   Because of the difficulty of going against decisions made by the group, Irving Janis (1982) has argued that many decisions are likely to be the product of *groupthink*. **Groupthink** exists when thinking in a group is self-deceptive, based on conformity to group beliefs, and created by group pressure. In groupthink, pressures toward uniformity discourage members from expressing their concerns about group decisions.

During the administration of President John F. Kennedy in the early 1960s, for example, the president and his advisers decided to launch an invasion of Cuba at the Bay of Pigs. The invasion failed. Analysis by Janis revealed that during the decision process, because of group pressure, several top advisers failed to admit that they thought the plan would probably not succeed.

Research indicates that groupthink can be avoided when leaders or group members make a conscious effort to see that all group members participate actively in a multisided discussion. In addition, members must know that points of disagreement and conflict will be tolerated (Moorhead, Neck, and West, 1998; Myers, 1999).

groupthink
self-deceptive thinking that is based on conformity to group beliefs, and created by group pressure to conform

How is groupthink promoted?

Figure 6.2 Focus on Theoretical Perspectives

Illustrating Types of Social Interaction. A type of social interaction is illustrated below from the viewpoint of a particular theoretical perspective. Each concept can be viewed from either of the other two perspectives. Associate a type of social interaction with a different theoretical perspective and make up your own example.

Theoretical Perspective	Type of Social Interaction	Example	
Functionalism	Conformity	Team integration is promoted when basketball players accept their roles on the floor.	
Conflict Theory	Coercion 	Conflict in prisons is kept in check by the superior power of the guards.	
Symbolic Interactionism	Social Exchange	Two neightbors share recipes and ideas so each benefits.	

Section 3 Assessment

Match terms a–e with the appropriate numbered example.

1. Blood donors expect payment.
2. Students read what a teacher assigns.
3. Saddam Hussein invades Kuwait.
4. Flood victims help each other.
5. Employees are forced to work overtime or be fired.

     a. cooperation
     b. conflict
     c. social exchange
     d. coercion
     e. conformity

6. Solomon Asch's experiment demonstrates the positive consequences of group pressure. *T* or *F*?
7. Why is conformity essential for the development of social structures?

Critical Thinking

8. **Analyzing Information** Describe an example of groupthink in your school. Analyze this situation in terms of its positive or negative consequences.

Tech Trends
Working in the Virtual Office

Vanishing are the traditional offices [in formal organizations] that occupy a common, fixed space, and employ a totally permanent workforce. Numerous companies are now utilizing what have come to be called "virtual offices." For the most part, these offices are staffed by at-home employees who telecommute, use Internet resources, and are frequently temporary employees.

Virtual offices offer many benefits in today's climate of global competition. For those workers who previously found it difficult to work outside the home (the elderly, [disabled], or parents with child-care responsibilities), telecommuting can be a vehicle into the workforce. What's more, corporate executives and managers enjoy advantages of the Internet: It provides rich resources of both people and information; it improves operations; it markets products. In fact, telecommuting has been shown to result in productivity gains of between 15–20%. Finally, virtual offices afford companies dramatic savings in the costs of employees and facilities.

But what of the problems associated with telecommuting? Notable is the telecommuters' sense of alienation. They may feel isolated from fellow workers and the larger organization. This alienation can be minimized by bringing telecommuters together for periodic meetings. Ostensibly established to allow telecommuters to report to their supervisors, such get-togethers serve to reinforce the telecommuters' membership in, and loyalty to, the organization for which they work.

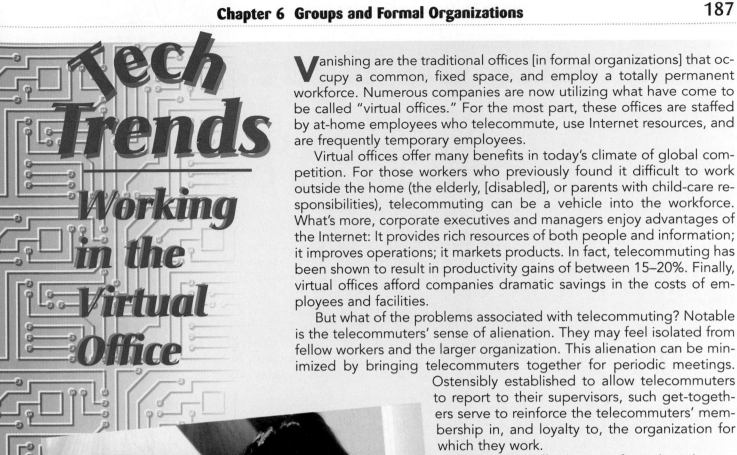

Two other difficulties confront the telecommuter. The first is low wages. In most instances, wages paid for work done by home telecommuters lag noticeably behind wages paid to office workers. This is unlikely to change given the difficulties that trade unions face in unionizing such workers. The second difficulty is the family tension stemming from the home/office merger. Until traditional views about appropriate work locations become more enlightened, home telecommuters are likely to be perceived by other family members as "not really working."

Source: William E. Snizek, "Virtual Offices: Some Neglected Considerations," *Communications of the ACM*, 38 (September 1995):15, 16. Reprinted by permission of the author.

Analyzing the Trends

Do you think the trend toward the virtual office is a good thing? Defend your answer from a functionalist viewpoint.

Focus on Research

Experiment: Group Pressure and Obedience

Can a group cause a person to physically punish a victim with increasing severity despite the victim's pleas for mercy? Researcher Stanley Milgram (1963, 1974) has shown that this could happen.

As noted in the text, Solomon Asch demonstrated that group pressure can influence people to make false claims about what they see. Specifically, experimental subjects can be pressured to claim that two lines (drawn on a card) match in length even though they originally perceived these same two lines as different in length. Milgram wanted to know if group pressure can have the same effect on behavior. Can group pressure cause people to treat others in ways they otherwise would not?

To test this question, Milgram could have chosen a desired behavior relatively easy to induce, such as sharing food with a stranger or damaging someone else's property. Choosing a much harder case, Milgram asked research participants to administer increasingly stronger electric shocks to people who appeared to be in pain. And these research participants were people just like you and me!

Milgram placed eighty males in an experimental situation in which a team of three individuals (two "confederates" who knew the nature of the experiment and one "subject" who did not) tested a fourth person (who was also in on the experiment) on a learning task. Each mistake by the fourth party brought an apparent electric shock from the subject. The two confederates (participants cooperating with Milgram) on each team suggested increasingly higher shock levels for successive mistakes made by the "learner" (the third confederate in the electric chair). The researcher recorded the degree to which the "operator" (the subject of the experiment) resisted or went along with group pressure to increase the voltage levels.

After explaining to the subject that the purpose of the experiment was to determine the effects of punishment (electric shocks) on memory, the learner was strapped into an electric-chair apparatus in full view of the other three team members. These three were seated in front of a large shock generator whose switches were labeled from 15 to 450 volts in 15-volt increments. The lowest-level group of switches was labeled "Slight Shock"; the highest-level group of switches read "Danger: Severe Shock."

The "operator" controlled the maximum shock that could be administered. He could keep the shock level at 15 volts throughout or increase the shock level in line with the group's recommendation. It was his decision. (Remember—he was the only one not in on the real purpose.)

The learner was primed to not only answer questions incorrectly. As the shocks become stronger, he grunted, protested, and finally demanded that the experiment stop. Each of these complaints was actually prerecorded and played in coordination with a given shock level. No discomfort was indicated until a 75-volt shock was administered. At 120 volts, the learner shouted that the shocks were becoming painful. Groans followed a 135-volt shock, and at 150 volts the learner cried out to be released from the experiment, complaining of a heart condition. At 180 volts, the learner cried out, "I can't stand the pain," and 285 volts was followed by an agonized scream. From 300 to 450 volts, the learner continuously shouted desperately that he would no longer answer questions.

Milgram first needed to know how far the operator would go in administering shocks *without* group influence. To accomplish this, an identical experiment was run minus the two confederates in the punishing group. Response to group pressure was measured by the difference in the operator's behavior in the two situations.

Group pressure heavily affected the level of shock administered by the operator. That is, the average shock level in the three-person situation was significantly higher than in the one-person situation. Perhaps most interesting are the results on *maximum* shock levels. When alone, only two operators went beyond the point where the learner first vehemently protested. Under group pressure, twenty-seven of the operators went beyond this point. Nineteen of the operators went above 255 volts ("Intense Shock"), and ten went into the group of voltages labeled "Danger: Severe Shock." Seven even reached 450 volts (the highest shock level possible).

The research by Milgrim and Asch reveal the power of group pressure to create conformity in thought and behavior. Clearly, conformity must occur for social structure and society to exist. What worries many scholars is the extent to which social pressure can determine how humans think and act.

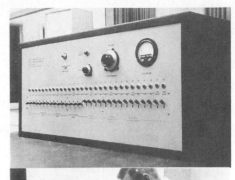

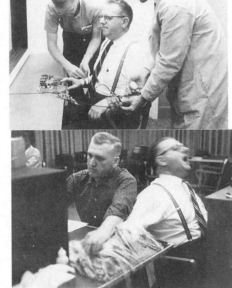

Photographs from Stanley Milgram's experiment show participants ordering higher and higher level shocks for the actor pretending to be shocked.

Working with the Research

1. Discuss the ethical implications of Milgram's experiment. (You may want to refer to Chapter 2, pp. 59–61, for a discussion about ethics in social research.)

2. If the researcher had not been present as an authority figure during the experiment to approve the use of all shock levels, do you think group pressure would have been as effective? Explain.

3. Discuss some implications of this experiment for democratic government. Can you relate it to George Orwell's novel *1984*?

4. Do you think society would be possible without this tendency to conform? Explain your position.

Section 4

Formal Organizations

Key Terms

- formal organization
- bureaucracy
- power
- authority

- rationalization
- informal organization
- iron law of oligarchy

Section Preview

A formal organization is created to achieve some goal. Most are bureaucratic. The existence of primary groups and primary relationships within formal organizations can either help or hinder the achievement of goals.

formal organization
a group deliberately created to achieve one or more long-term goals

bureaucracy
a formal organization based on rationality and efficiency

The Nature of Formal Organizations

Until the 1920s, the majority of Americans lived on farms or in small towns and villages. Nearly all of their daily lives were spent in primary groups such as families, neighborhoods, and churches. As industrialization and urbanization have advanced, however, Americans have become more involved in secondary groups. Born in hospitals, educated in large schools, employed by huge corporations, regulated by government agencies, cared for in nursing homes, and buried by funeral establishments, Americans, like members of other industrialized societies, now often find themselves within *formal organizations* (Pfeffer, 1997).

How are formal organizations and bureaucracies related? A **formal organization** is deliberately created to achieve one or more long-term goals. Examples of formal organizations are high schools, colleges, corporations, government agencies, and hospitals.

Most formal organizations today are also **bureaucracies**—formal organizations based on rationality and efficiency. Although bureaucracies are popularly thought of as "monuments to inefficiency," they have proven to be effective in industrial societies.

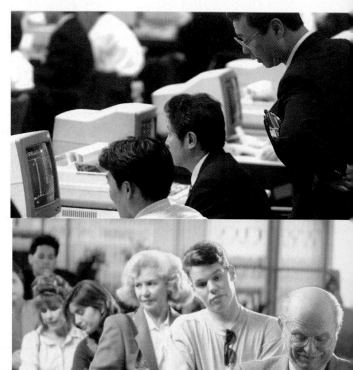

Both these Japanese workers and these bank customers in the U.S. feel the effects of the formal organization structure. Do you think most organizations are bureaucratic in nature?

Major Characteristics of Bureaucracies

All bureaucracies possess certain characteristics. The most important of these are listed below.

❖ **A division of labor based on the principle of specialization.** Each person in a bureaucracy is responsible for certain functions or tasks. (See Figure 6.3 for an organizational chart outlining the division of labor in a public school district.) This specialization allows an individual to become an expert in a limited area.

❖ **A hierarchy of authority.** Before discussing authority, it is necessary to define power. **Power** refers to the ability to control the behavior of others, even against their will. **Authority** is the exercise of legitimate power—power that derives from a recognized or approved source.

power
the ability to control the behavior of others

authority
the legitimate or socially approved use of power

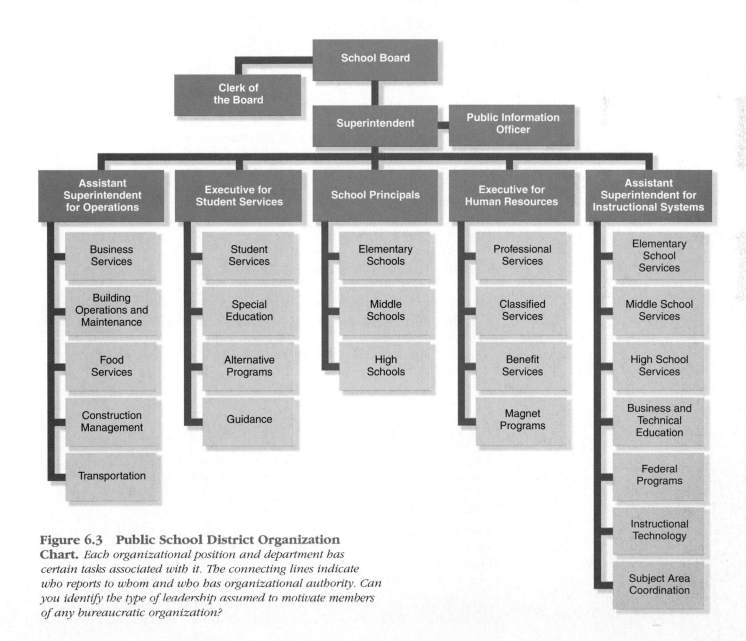

Figure 6.3 Public School District Organization Chart. *Each organizational position and department has certain tasks associated with it. The connecting lines indicate who reports to whom and who has organizational authority. Can you identify the type of leadership assumed to motivate members of any bureaucratic organization?*

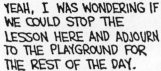

Calvin doesn't think that bureaucratic rules should apply to him if they interfere with his wishes.

People submit to authority because they believe it is the right thing to do. With respect to authority, bureaucratic organizations are like pyramids. The greatest amount of authority is concentrated in a few positions at the top, with decreasing amounts of authority in a larger number of lower positions. This is what is meant by "hierarchy of authority."

❖ **A system of rules and procedures.** Rules and procedures direct how work is to be done and provide a framework for decision making. They stabilize the organization because they coordinate activities and provide guidelines to follow in most situations.

❖ **Written records of work and activities.** Written records of work and activities are made and then kept in files. This organizational "memory" is essential to smooth functioning, stability, and continuity.

❖ **Promotion on the basis of merit and qualifications.** Jobs are filled on the basis of technical and professional qualifications. Promotions are given on the basis of merit, not favoritism. The norm in a bureaucracy is equal treatment for all.

Max Weber and Bureaucracy

Max Weber was the first to analyze the nature of bureaucracy. Although he recognized there were problems with this type of organization, overall he believed that bureaucracies were very efficient in dealing with the needs of industrial societies.

What are the advantages of bureaucracy? In Chapter 1, you read how Weber feared the dehumanizing effects of bureaucracies. As the values of preindustrial societies began to weaken, however, Weber also saw advantages to bureaucracy. On these advantages, he wrote the following:

The decisive reason for the advance of bureaucratic organization has always been its purely technical superiority over any other form of or-

ganization. The fully developed bureaucratic mechanism compares with other organizations exactly as does the machine with the nonmechanical modes of production (Gerth and Mills, 1958:214).

Earlier kinds of organizations, where the decision makers were chosen on the basis of family or wealth, were just not capable of dealing with an industrial economy. The fast-moving industrial economy required steadiness, precision, continuity, speed, efficiency, and minimum cost—advantages bureaucracy could offer. **Rationalization**—the mindset emphasizing knowledge, reason, and planning rather than tradition and superstition—was on the rise. (See pages 17–18 for a review of this concept.)

rationalization
the mind-set emphasizing knowledge, reason, and planning

Snapshot of America

Membership in Fraternal Orders

You may not realize it, but fraternal orders, such as Moose, Elk, Eagles, and Shriners, are bureaucracies. They have a division of labor, hierarchy of authority, system of rules and procedures, written records, and promotion based on merit within the organization. This map shows fraternal organization membership by region in relation to the national average.

Fraternal Order Membership Compared to U.S. Average
- High
- Above average
- Below average
- Low

Interpreting the Map

Look back at the map of population densities in the United States on page 57. Do you see any patterns common to that map and this one? Explain.

Adapted from *Latitudes and Attitudes: An Atlas of American Tastes, Trends, Politics, and Passions.* Boston: Little Brown.

World View

Military Might

In preindustrial societies, military groups are loosely organized and informal in nature. They are composed of group members who live nonmilitary lives except during defense emergencies. In industrial societies, bureaucratic principles are applied to military organizations.

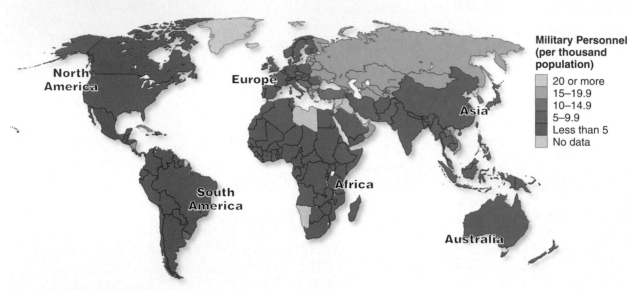

Military Personnel (per thousand population)

- 20 or more
- 15–19.9
- 10–14.9
- 5–9.9
- Less than 5
- No data

Interpreting the Map

Does this map show a relationship between the type of political leadership and the extent of citizen participation in the military? If so, describe this relationship.

Adapted from *Atlas of the World Today.* New York: Harper & Row.

Do bureaucracies undervalue people?   As strange as it might sound, bureaucracy is designed to protect individuals. People often complain about the rules, procedures, and impersonal treatment that characterize bureaucracy. Without them, though, decision making would be arbitrary and without reason. It might sound great, for example, to abolish final exams, but then grading would not be objective. For example, a teacher might give higher grades to males. This is not to say that favoritism never occurs in bureaucratic organizations. Nevertheless, the presence of rules guarantees at least a measure of equal treatment.

informal organization
groups within a formal organization in which personal relationships are guided by norms, rituals, and sentiments that are not part of the formal organization

Informal Structure within Organizations

Bureaucracies are designed to act as secondary groups. As anyone who has worked in a bureaucratic organization knows, though, there are primary relationships as well. Primary relationships emerge as part of the **informal organization**—groups within a formal organization in which personal relationships are guided by norms, rituals, and sentiments that are not part of the formal organization. Based on common interests and personal relationships, informal groups are usually formed spontaneously.

When were informal organizations first studied?   The existence of informal organizations within bureaucracies was first documented in the mid-1920s, when a group of Harvard researchers was studying the Hawthorne plant of the Western Electric Company in Chicago. In a study of fourteen male machine operators in the Bank Wiring Observation Room, F. J. Roethlisberger and William Dickson (1964, originally published in 1939) observed that work activities and job relationships were based on norms and social sanctions of that particular group of male operators. Group norms prohibited "rate busting" (doing too much work), "chiseling" (doing too little work), and "squealing" (telling group secrets to supervisors). Conformity to these norms was maintained through ridicule, sarcasm, criticism, and hostility.

Why do informal organizations develop?   Informal groups exist to meet needs ignored by the formal organization. Modern organizations tend to be impersonal, and informal groups offer personal affection, support, humor, and protection. The study mentioned above pointed out that informal organizations encourage conformity, but the resulting solidarity protects group members from mistreatment by those outside the group.

Despite working in a bureaucratic organization, these construction workers seem to be on very personal terms. How do sociologists explain this?

Iron Law of Oligarchy

If an organization's goals are to be achieved, power must be exercised. Sometimes this power may be grabbed by individuals for their own purposes. This process is described by the *iron law of oligarchy* (Michels, 1949; originally published in 1911).

iron law of oligarchy
theory that power increasingly becomes concentrated in the hands of a few members of any organization

What is the iron law of oligarchy?   According to the **iron law of oligarchy,** formulated by German sociologist Robert Michels, power increasingly tends to become more and more concentrated in the hands of fewer members of any organization. Michels observed that, even in organizations intended to be democratic, a few leaders eventually gain control, and other members become virtually powerless. He concluded that this increased concentration of power occurs because those in power want to remain in power.

The government in communist China is a prime example of Michels's principle. Not subject to popular election, the aging individuals at the top have been able to consolidate, or strengthen, their power over a long period of time. Each of the leaders is able to build a loyal staff, control money, offer jobs, and give favors.

Why does organization lead to oligarchy?   According to Michels, three organizational factors encourage oligarchy. First, organizations need a hierarchy of authority to delegate decision making. Second, the advantages held by those at the top allow them to consolidate their powers. They can create a staff that is loyal to them, control the channels of communication, and use organizational resources to increase their power. Finally, other members of the organization tend to defer to leaders—to give in to those who take charge.

Section 4 Assessment

1. Define the term *formal organization.*
2. List the major characteristics of bureaucracy, according to Max Weber.
3. Identify whether the following are advantages (A) or disadvantages (D) of a bureaucracy:
   a. its use of appropriate criteria in hiring employees
   b. its use of rules to provide definite guidelines for behavior within the organization
   c. its ability to hide the true nature of authority relationships
   d. its encouragement of administrative competence in managers
4. Can you describe the form of leadership most suited to the operation of the iron law of oligarchy? Explain your answer.

Critical Thinking

5. **Synthesizing Information** Analyze your school as a bureaucracy. Give an example of the following characteristics of bureaucracy: (1) system of rules and procedures; (2) impersonality and impartiality (lack of favoritism). Discuss a positive and negative consequence of each characteristic.

Guidelines for
Bureaucrats:
(1) When in charge—
    ponder.
(2) When in trouble—
    delegate.
(3) When in doubt—
    mumble.

James H. Boren
business author

Summary

Section 1: Primary and Secondary Groups

Main Idea: Groups are classified by how they develop and function. Primary groups meet emotional and support needs, while secondary groups are task focused.

Section 2: Other Groups and Networks

Main Idea: Reference groups help us evaluate ourselves and form identities. In-groups and out-groups divide people into "we" and "they." Social networks extend our contacts and let us form links to many other people.

Section 3: Types of Social Interaction

Main Idea: Five types of social interaction are basic to group life: cooperation, conflict, social exchange, coercion, and conformity.

Section 4: Formal Organizations

Main Idea: A formal organization is created to achieve some goal. Most are bureaucratic. The existence of primary groups and primary relationships within formal organizations can either help or hinder the achievement of goals.

Self-Check Quiz

Visit the *Sociology and You* Web site at soc.glencoe.com and click on **Chapter 6—Self-Check Quizzes** to prepare for the chapter test.

Reviewing Vocabulary

Complete each sentence using each term once.

a. social category
b. social aggregate
c. primary group
d. secondary group
e. reference group
f. social network
g. social exchange
h. conformity
i. groupthink
j. formal organization
k. bureaucracy
l. rationalism

1. A _____ is an impersonal and goal-oriented group that involves only a segment of one's life.

2. A group of people who are in the same place at the same time is called _____.

3. A _____ is a web of social relationships that join a person to other people and groups.

4. A _____ is composed of people who are emotionally close, know one another well, and seek one another's company.

5. A situation in which pressures toward uniformity discourage members from expressing their reservations about group decisions is called _____.

6. A type of social interaction in which one person voluntarily does something for another, expecting a reward in return, is called _____.

7. _____ is behavior that goes according to group expectations.

8. A _____ is a group used for self-evaluation.

9. _____ are deliberately created to achieve one or more long-term goals.

10. A _____ is a formal organization based on efficiency and rationality.

11. The solution of problems on the basis of logic, data, and planning is called _____.

12. People who share a social characteristic are called a _____.

Reviewing the Facts

1. Use the diagram below to list the basic societal functions of primary groups.

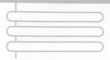

BASIC SOCIETAL FUNCTION OF PRIMARY GROUPS

2. List the major characteristics of primary and secondary groups.
3. What is the difference between a reference group and a social network?
4. What is the main difference between cooperation and social exchange?
5. Explain the relationship between in-groups and out-groups.

Thinking Critically

1. **Applying Concepts** Your high school is probably made up of many diverse in-groups. Identify some of these groups with their own labels, and then list common links joining all of the groups. Look for characteristics that the groups share, not for what separates them. For example, all members of the various groups might need to take two math classes in order to graduate. See how many items you can list that all the different groups share.
2. **Making Generalizations** Social networks are an important component of group interactions. Are there any people in your sociology class you would consider part of your social network? Are there any classmates who are part of your family, work, church, team, or neighborhood groups? Are the people that you sit next to closely related to your social network? Do these people have strong or weak ties to you? Are any of them among your best friends?
3. **Evaluating Information** Some high school administrators and educators have expressed concern that school violence is an indication that many high school groups are in conflict. Do you believe conflicts exist between the in-groups in your school? Have these conflicts ever erupted or are they just below the surface? How could your school work to lessen any potential group conflicts?
4. **Analyzing Information** You read about social exchange, the type of interaction in which someone does something for another person and expects a reward in return. This might also be described as the "I'll scratch your back if you'll scratch mine" expectation. Do you think that this expectation is always present? Is it possible to perform truly random acts of kindness? If you have ever done volunteer work, haven't you done something with no reward expected?
5. **Making Inferences** The text discusses the issue of groupthink in the Kennedy administration. Have you ever been in a situation in which you disagreed with the majority opinion or felt that something that was about to happen was wrong? Did you speak up? If not, did the power of the group influence you? When might failing to speak up lead to harm?
6. **Making Comparisons** You are a member of a variety of informal groups—church, school clubs, work, sports, band, and so forth. Compare and contrast the roles of group membership in two of these groups.

Sociology Projects

1. **Formal and Informal Groups** Places such as teen centers, homeless shelters, food pantries, and crisis centers are all formal organizations established to help people. Sometimes these organizations are less bureaucratic than more official government aid agencies. Informal groups are often more apparent. Create a brochure that describes such social agencies in your neighborhood, city, or town. Identify as many agencies as you can, and list an address, phone number, and contact person for each. Then select one agency to call. Ask if you can interview someone who works there to get an idea of what the agency does. Ask him or her to describe the organization in terms of formality or informality. Ask about regulations, rules, and procedures. Does he or she think the procedures are gener-

ally helpful or a barrier to providing service? Create a special brochure on this organization alone. Share the results of your work with the social agency.

2. **Social Categories** In this activity, you will look at generations as social categories. Write down some of the things that you believe define your generation—for example, skateboarding, extreme sports, rap music, Gap clothes. Then find adults in their forties or early fifties and ask them to define their own generation. What were the things that identified their generation? What are the things that define them now? Each list should include about ten cultural items of that generation. Share your findings with the class. If possible, bring in some items that represent the two generations.

3. **Promotions According to Merit** The text discusses the major characteristics of a bureaucracy. One of these involves the principle of promoting people according to merit. Another principle, however, is that people are treated equally and not given special consideration or shown favoritism. In many organizations, merit is sometimes synonymous with seniority so that the length of time on the job becomes just as important or more important than the skill exercised in the job. Do an informal interview of six people who work for relatively large corporations or businesses to determine what role they think seniority should play in promotion decisions. Should a mediocre—but satisfactory—employee who has been with a company for many years be skipped over for a position in favor of an employee with much less time on the job, but who has demonstrated superior skill? Summarize the results of your interviews and be prepared to share your feelings with the class.

4. **Sexual Harassment in Schools** As you know, individual actions are linked to group and organizational norms. One of the emerging norms in all grades of school involves behaviors that could be interpreted as sexual harassment. Even very young children are being cautioned about comments and actions that could be interpreted as being sexist or being intimidating to one gender. Check with your school administration or guidance office to find out about the formal policy about sexual harassment in schools. What constitutes harassing behavior? Do you think your school has an effective policy to help prevent sexual harassment? Or do you think that sometimes the bureaucracy misinterprets behavior and assigns motivations that may not be intended?

5. **Reference Groups** Reread the section on reference groups. Then take a quick survey of ten or fifteen of your schoolmates. Ask them to identify their three most important reference groups. Compare the lists to see what groups show up most frequently. What are the norms and objectives of these most commonly cited groups?

6. **Groupthink** Using articles from the newspaper and magazines, find an article that is an example of groupthink. Using the article as a starting point, write a brief report that describes a model of group system in which the interactive roles of the individuals would have brought about a better outcome.

Technology Activities

1. *Dilbert* is a popular cartoon strip that makes fun of the bureaucratic structures in American corporations. Go to the *Dilbert* web site at http://www.unitedmedia.com/comics/dilbert and read several of the comic strips.

   1. Find a few cartoons that illustrate some important ideas presented in this chapter. Explain the cartoons in terms of knowledge gained in this chapter.

   2. Discuss some of the strips with an adult who works in a corporation. What does that person think about the accuracy of the situations portrayed in *Dilbert?*

   3. Prepare a brief report describing what you learned about formal organizations and bureaucracies from your review of *Dilbert.*

Chapter 6

Enrichment Reading
The McDonaldization of Society

by George Ritzer

George Ritzer defines McDonaldization as "the process by which the principles of the fast-food restaurant are coming to dominate more and more sectors of American society as well as of the rest of the world" (Ritzer, 1996:1). Ritzer sees McDonaldization as an extension of Max Weber's theory of rationalization. (See p. 17 in Chapter 1.) For Weber, the industrial West was becoming increasingly rational—dominated by efficiency, predictability, calculability, and nonhuman technology. These features, in his view, were beginning to control human social behaviors.

W hy has the McDonald's model proven so irresistible? Four **alluring** dimensions lie at the heart of the success of this model and, more generally, of McDonaldization. In short, McDonald's has succeeded because it offers consumers, workers, and managers efficiency, **calculability,** predictability, and control.

Efficiency First, McDonald's offers *efficiency,* or the optimum method for getting from one point to another. For consumers, this means that McDonald's offers the best available way to get from being hungry to being satisfied. . . . Other institutions, fashioned on the McDonald's model, offer similar efficiency in losing weight, lubricating cars, getting new glasses or contacts, or completing income-tax forms. In a society where both parents are likely to work, or where there may be only a single parent, efficiently satisfying the hunger and many other needs of people is very attractive. In a society where people rush, usually by car, from one spot to another, the efficiency of a fast-food meal, perhaps even without leaving their cars by **wending** their way along the drive-through lane, often proves im-

possible to resist. The fast-food model offers people, or at least appears to offer them, an efficient method for satisfying many needs.

Calculability Second, McDonald's offers *calculability,* or an emphasis on the quantitative aspects of products sold (portion size, cost) and service offered (the time it takes to get the product). Quantity has become equivalent to quality; a lot of something, or the quick delivery of it, means it must be good. As two observers of contemporary American culture put it, "As a culture, we tend to believe deeply that in general 'bigger is better.'"

Predictability Third, McDonald's offers *predictability,* the assurance that their products and services will be the same over time and in all locales. The Egg McMuffin in New York will be, for all intents and purposes, identical to those in Chicago and Los Angeles. Also, those eaten next week or next year will be identical to those eaten today. There is great comfort in knowing that McDonald's offers no surprises. People know that the next Egg McMuffin they eat will taste about the same as the others they have eaten; it will not be awful, but it will not be exceptionally delicious, either. The success of the McDonald's

What Does it Mean?

albeit
even though; although

alluring
attractive or fascinating

calculability
bring about by deliberate intent by controlling quantities

wending
traveling; proceeding on your way

Explain why you would expect service at this McDonald's restaurant in Guang Zhou, China, except for language, to be the same as the one in your neighborhood. Use sociological terms in your response.

model suggests that many people have come to prefer a world in which there are few surprises.

Control   Fourth, *control,* especially through the *substitution of nonhuman for human technology,* is exerted over the people who enter the world of McDonald's. A *human technology* (a screwdriver, for example) is controlled by people; a *nonhuman technology* (the assembly line, for instance) controls people. The people who eat in fast-food restaurants are controlled, **albeit** (usually) subtly. Lines, limited menus, few options, and uncomfortable seats all lead diners to do what management wishes them to do—eat quickly and leave. Further, the drive-through (in some cases walk-through) window leads diners to leave before they eat.

Source: Adapted from George Ritzer, *McDonaldization of Society,* rev. ed., Thousand Oaks, CA: Pine Forge Press, 1996.

Read and React

1. State what Ritzer means by *McDonaldization.*

2. Since Ritzer contends that McDonaldization is spreading throughout modern society, he thinks you are affected by it. Describe a part of your social life, aside from eating at fast-food restaurants, that has been McDonaldized.

3. Describe your feelings about the McDonaldization you are experiencing.

4. Do you think McDonaldization is a rational or an irrational process? That is, does McDonaldization produce results that work for or against an organization's goal? Defend your answer.

CHAPTER 7
Deviance and Social Control

USING Your Sociological Imagination

U S I N G

What would a Martian, after watching an evening of prime-time television, think about American culture? If the impression of our culture were formed solely from these programs, the Martian likely would conclude that the inhabitants of Earth are an exceptionally violent people. If the Martian then began to display violent behavior, could we conclude that he or she had been watching too much television?

Before answering this question, think for a moment about these statistics: Children aged two to eleven spend an average of twenty-eight hours per week watching television (compared to thirty hours in school). Fifty-seven percent of television programming contains violence. In one-quarter of the violent interactions, a gun is used. Finally, in about three-quarters of all violent scenes, the persons committing the violent acts go unpunished (National Television Violence Study, 1998).

In the past sociologists have hesitated to link violent behavior with exposure to television violence. But after hundreds of studies, researchers now confirm a link between televised aggression and personal aggressiveness. This link between imagined and actual violence is an example of culturally transmitted social behavior.

As humans learn the culture around them, they adopt certain patterns of behavior. In this chapter we will examine the learned behavior called *deviance*.

Sections

1. **Deviance and Social Control**
2. **Functionalism and Deviance**
3. **Symbolic Interactionism and Deviance**
4. **Conflict Theory and Deviance**
5. **Crime and Punishment**

Learning Objectives

After reading this chapter, you will be able to

❖ define deviance.

❖ define social control and identify the major types of social control.

❖ discuss the positive and negative consequences of deviance.

❖ differentiate the major functional theories of deviance.

❖ discuss the conflict theory view of deviance.

❖ describe four approaches to crime control.

SOCIOLOGY *Online*

Chapter Overview
Visit the *Sociology and You* Web site at soc.glencoe.com and click on **Chapter 7—Chapter Overviews** to preview chapter information.

Section 1

Deviance and Social Control

Key Terms

- deviance
- negative deviance
- positive deviance

- deviant
- social control
- social sanctions

Section Preview

Deviance is the violation of social norms. It is difficult to define because not everyone agrees on what should be considered deviant behavior.

deviance
behavior that departs from societal or group norms

The Nature of Deviance

Deviance refers to behavior that departs from societal or group norms. It can range from criminal behavior (recognized by almost all members of a society as deviant) to wearing heavy makeup (considered deviant by some religious groups). Some people violate norms by robbing banks or committing assault or murder. Incidents of deviance sometimes receive a great deal of attention because they involve prominent figures whose behavior is captured on national television. Former heavyweight boxing champion Mike Tyson, in a bout with the current champion, Evander Holyfield, actually bit off the tip of Holyfield's right ear and spat it onto the ring mat. Figure 7.1 illustrates the frequency of two types of juvenile deviance.

These examples appear clear-cut, but deviance is not always so easy to identify. Because deviance is a matter of social definition, it can vary from group to group and society to society. In a diverse society like that of the United States, it is often difficult to agree on what is or is not deviant behavior. In a groundbreaking study, Simmons (1969) polled people on this issue:

The sheer range of responses [to the question "What constitutes deviant behavior?"] predictably included homosexuals, prostitutes, drug addicts, radicals, and criminals. But it also included liars, career women, Democrats, reckless drivers, atheists, Christians, suburbanites, the retired, young folks, card players, bearded men, artists, pacifists, priests, prudes, hippies, straights, girls who wear makeup, the President of the United States, conservatives, integrationists, executives, divorcees, perverts, motorcycle gangs, smart-alec students, know-it-all professors, modern people, and Americans.

To this list, one researcher would add obese people. For a week, she wore a "fat suit," adding 150 pounds to her normal body weight, in order to experience firsthand what it feels like to be

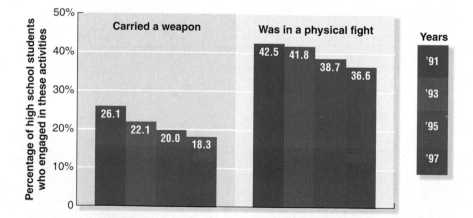

Figure 7.1 Two Types of Youth Deviance.
What does the graph say about the trend in youth violence?

Source: *Journal of the American Medical Association* 282 (August, 1999): 440–446.

an overweight woman in American society. She concluded that American "society not only hates fat people, it feels entitled to participate in a prejudice that at many levels parallels racism and religious bigotry" (Lampert, 1993:154).

Deviance may be either *positive* or *negative*. **Negative deviance** involves behavior that fails to meet accepted norms. People expressing negative deviance either reject the norms, misinterpret the norms, or are unaware of the norms. This is the kind of behavior popularly associated with the idea of deviance. There is, however, another type of deviance. **Positive deviance** involves overconformity to norms—leading to imbalance and extremes of perfectionism. Positive deviants idealize group norms. In its own way, positive deviance can be as disruptive and hard to manage as negative deviance. Think about the norms related to personal appearance in American society. The mass media are constantly telling young people that "lean is mean." Negative deviants will miss the mark on the obese side. Positive deviants may push themselves to the point of anorexia. Most young people will weigh somewhere between these two extremes.

Singapore political opposition leader Chee Soon Juan is selling his book without a license, an example of negative deviance in that culture.

Minor instances of behavior that some might consider deviant occur frequently in modern societies. For that reason, sociologists generally reserve the term *deviance* for violations of significant social norms. Significant norms are those that are highly important either to most members of a society or to the members with the most power. For a sociologist, a **deviant** is a person who has violated one or more of society's most highly valued norms. Reactions to deviants are usually negative and involve attempts to change or control the deviant behavior.

negative deviance
involves behavior that underconforms to accepted norms

positive deviance
involves behavior that overconforms to social expectations

deviant
a person who breaks significant societal or group norms

This anorexic teenager in a made-for-television movie is displaying positive deviance. How would you explain to her mother that her child's behavior is "positive"?

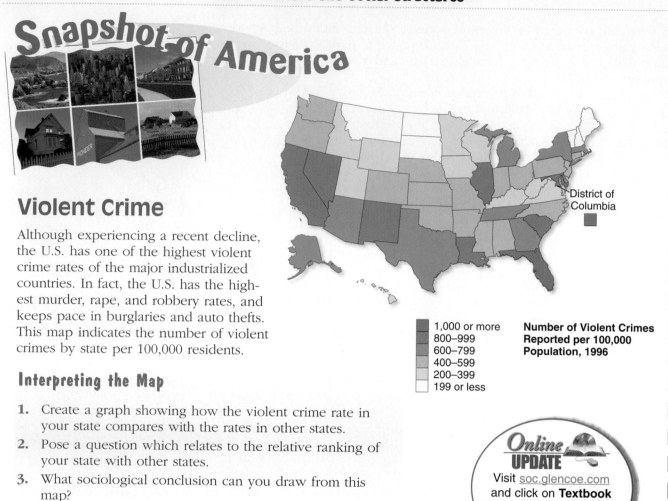

Snapshot of America

Violent Crime

Although experiencing a recent decline, the U.S. has one of the highest violent crime rates of the major industrialized countries. In fact, the U.S. has the highest murder, rape, and robbery rates, and keeps pace in burglaries and auto thefts. This map indicates the number of violent crimes by state per 100,000 residents.

District of Columbia

1,000 or more
800–999
600–799
400–599
200–399
199 or less

Number of Violent Crimes Reported per 100,000 Population, 1996

Interpreting the Map

1. Create a graph showing how the violent crime rate in your state compares with the rates in other states.
2. Pose a question which relates to the relative ranking of your state with other states.
3. What sociological conclusion can you draw from this map?

Adapted from *The World Almanac of the U.S.A.*, Mahwah, NJ, 1998.

Online **UPDATE**
Visit soc.glencoe.com and click on **Textbook Updates–Chapter 7** for an update of the data.

Social Control

All societies have ways to promote order, stability, and predictability in social life. We feel confident that drivers will stop for red lights, that waiters will not pour soup in our laps, and that store clerks will give us the correct change. Without **social control**—ways to promote conformity to norms—social life would be unpredictable, even chaotic. There are two broad types of social control: internal and external.

social control
ways to encourage conformity to society's norms

What is internal social control?   Internal social control lies within the individual. It is developed during the socialization process. You are practicing internal social control when you do something because you know it is the right thing to do or when you don't do something because you know it would be wrong. For example, most people most of the time do not steal. They act this way not just because they fear arrest or lack the opportunity to steal but because they consider theft to be wrong. The norm against stealing has become a part of them. This is known as the *internalization* of social norms.

What is external social control? Unfortunately for society, the process of socialization does not ensure that all people will conform all of the time. For this reason, external social control must also be present. External social control is based on **social sanctions**—rewards and punishments designed to encourage desired behavior. Positive sanctions, such as awards, increases in allowances, promotions, and smiles of approval, are used to encourage conformity. Negative sanctions, such as criticism, fines, and imprisonment, are intended to stop socially unacceptable behavior.

Sanctions may be formal or informal. Ridicule, gossip and smiles are examples of informal sanctions. Imprisonment, low grades, and official awards are formal sanctions.

social sanctions
rewards or punishments that encourage conformity to social norms

Because of its hurtful nature, gossip can be a very effective informal sanction.

Section 1 Assessment

1. What is the term sociologists use for behavior that significantly violates societal or group norms?
2. State a major problem sociologists have in defining deviance.
3. What is the purpose of a social sanction?

Critical Thinking

4. **Applying Concepts** At some point in growing up, nearly everyone displays some minor deviant behaviors, such as cutting class or telling a lie. Getting "caught" in such behaviors generally results in attempts at social control. Recall such an instance for yourself. How successful were these controls in changing your behavior? (Be specific as to the types of social control and their precise application to you.)

No crime is rational.

Livy
Roman historian

Another Time

Murder among the Cheyenne

Historically, the Cheyenne believed that when a member of the tribe committed murder, the whole tribe suffered the consequences. The punishment for this terrible crime was banishment from the tribe. The Cheyenne way of dealing with murders illustrates both deviance and social control.

[The Cheyenne have] specific concepts related to the killing of a fellow tribesman and specific mechanisms for dealing with homicide when it does occur.

The first of these is purely mystical and relates to the major tribal fetish, the Four Sacred Arrows. A murderer becomes personally polluted, and specks of blood contaminate the feathers of the Arrows. The very word for murder is *he'joxones,* "putrid." A Cheyenne who kills a fellow Cheyenne rots internally. His body gives off a fetid odor, a symbolic stigma of personal disintegration, which contrition may stay, but for which there is no cure. The smell is offensive to other Cheyennes, who will never again take food from a bowl used by the killer. Nor will they smoke a pipe that has touched his lips. They fear personal contamination with his "leprous" affliction. This means that the person who has become so un-Cheyenne as to fly in the face of the greatest of Cheyenne injunctions is cut off from participation in the symbolic acts of mutuality—eating from a common bowl and smoking the ritual pipe. With this alienation goes the loss of many civil privileges and the cooperative assistance of one's fellows outside of one's own family. The basic penalty for murder is therefore a lifetime of partial social ostracism [forced isolation from society].

On the legal level, the ostracism takes the form of immediate exile imposed by the Tribal Council sitting as a judicial body. The sentence of exile is enforced, if need be, by the military societies. The rationalization of the banishment is that the murderer's stink is noisome to the buffalo. As long as an unatoned murderer is with the tribe, "game shuns the territory; it makes the tribe lonesome." Therefore, the murderer must leave.

Banishment is not in itself enough, however. His act has disrupted the fabric of tribal life. Symbolically, this is expressed in the soiling of the Arrows, the allegorical identity of the tribe itself. As long as the Arrows remain polluted, bad luck is believed to dog the tribe. Not only does the spectre of starvation threaten, but there can be no success in war or any other enterprise. The earth is disjointed and the tribe out of harmony with it. The Arrow Renewal is the means of righting the situation. The oneness of the tribe is reasserted in the required presence at the ceremony of every family—save those of murderers. The renewed earth, effected by the rites in the Lone Tipi, is fresh and unsullied, once again free of the stain of killing.

Source: Excerpted from E. Adamson Hoebel, *The Cheyennes: Indians of the Great Plains* (New York: Holt, Rinehart and Winston, 1960), pp. 50–52. © 1960 by Holt, Rinehart and Winston, Inc. Reprinted by permission.

Thinking It Over

Many societies, both in the past and today, placed responsibility for the behavior of an individual on the family or tribe. Would you favor similar laws in the U.S., such as those making parents accountable for their children's actions? Why or why not?

Section 2

Functionalism and Deviance

Key Terms

- anomie
- strain theory
- control theory

Costs and Benefits of Deviance

As you probably remember from earlier chapters, the functionalist perspective emphasizes social stability and the way the different parts of society contribute to the whole. It may surprise you to know that functionalists believe that some deviance can contribute to the smooth operation of society. Deviance, therefore, has both positive and negative consequences for society.

What are some of the negative effects of deviance? Deviance erodes trust. If bus drivers do not follow planned routes, if television stations constantly change their schedules, if parents are not consistent in their discipline, trust will be undermined. A society with widespread suspicion and distrust cannot function smoothly.

If not punished or corrected, deviance can also cause nonconforming behavior in others. If bus drivers regularly pass students waiting for the bus, the students may begin to heave rocks at the bus. If television stations offer random programming, customers may picket the stations in protest. If parents neglect their children, more teenagers may turn to delinquency. Deviance stimulates more deviance in others.

Deviant behavior is also expensive. It diverts resources, both human and monetary. Police may have to spend their time dealing with wayward bus drivers and angry students rather than performing more serious duties.

How does deviance benefit society? Society can sometimes benefit from deviance in spite of its negative effects. Emile Durkheim observed that deviance clarifies norms by exercising social control to defend its values; society defines, adjusts, and reaffirms norms. When parents are taken to court or lose their children because of neglect, for example, society shows other parents and children how it expects parents to act.

Deviance can be a temporary safety valve. Teens listen to music, watch television programs, and wear clothes that adults may view as deviating from expected behavior. This relatively minor deviance may act to relieve some of the pressure teens feel from the many authority figures in their lives, including parents, relatives, teachers, and clergy.

Deviance increases unity within a society or group. When deviance reminds people of something they value, it strengthens their commitment to that value. Consider

Section Preview

According to functionalists, deviance has both negative and positive consequences for society. Functionalism also forms the basis for two important theories of deviance: strain theory and control theory.

How did the Reverend King's use of nonviolent deviance benefit American society?

spies who sell government secrets to an enemy, for example. When they are discovered, citizens who read or hear about them experience stronger feelings of patriotism.

Deviance promotes needed social change. Suffragettes who took to the streets in the early 1900s scandalized the nation but helped bring women the right to vote. Prison riots in the past have led to the reform of inhuman conditions.

anomie
a social condition in which norms are weak, conflicting, or absent

strain theory
theory that deviance is more likely to occur when a gap exists between cultural goals and the ability to achieve these goals by legitimate means

Strain Theory

According to Emile Durkheim, **anomie** (*AN-uh-me*) is a social condition in which norms are weak, conflicting, or absent. Without shared norms, individuals are uncertain about how they should think and act. Societies become disorganized. In 1968, sociologist Robert Merton adapted Durkheim's concept of anomie to deviant behavior and called his hypothesis the **strain theory.** Deviance, said Merton, is most likely to occur when there is a gap between culturally desirable goals, such as money and prestige, and a legitimate way of obtaining them. Every society establishes some goals and socially approved ways of reaching them. In the United States, an important goal is success and the material possessions that go with it. Education and hard work are two of the approved means for being successful. This is when people accept the goal and the means to achieve it; Merton calls this *conformity.* Wealthy people conform, but so do poor people who continue to work hard in low-paying jobs in the hope of improving life for themselves or their children.

According to strain theory, what kind of deviance is homelessness?

How do people respond to strain?   By definition, conformity is not deviant behavior. Each of the remaining four responses to strain are considered deviant, however. (See Figure 7.2.)

❖ In *innovation,* the individual accepts the goal of success but uses illegal means to achieve it. People engaging in this response may use robbery, drug dealing, or other lucrative criminal behavior to be successful. Innovation is the most widespread and obvious type of deviant response.

❖ In *ritualism,* the individual rejects the goal (success) but continues to use the legitimate means. Here people go through the motions without really believing in the process. An example is the teacher who goes about the daily routines of work without any concern for students or the quality of his or her teaching.

❖ *Retreatism* is a deviant response in which both the legitimate means and the approved goals are rejected. Skid-row alcoholics, drug addicts, and bag ladies are retreatists; they have dropped out. They are not successful by either legitimate or illegitimate means and they do not seek success.

❖ In *rebellion,* people reject both success and the approved means for achieving it. At the same time, they substitute a new set of goals and means. Some militia group members in the United States illustrate this response. They may live in near isolation as they pursue the goal of changing society through deviant means: creating their own currency, deliberately violating gun laws, and threatening (or engaging in) violent behavior against law enforcement officers.

Figure 7.2 Merton's Strain Theory

Culturally Approved Goal: Success	Socially Accepted Way to Succeed: Hard Work	Conformity Response	Deviant Responses	Examples
Accepts goal of success	Accepts hard work as the appropriate way to succeed	**Conformity**—works hard to succeed		Business executive
Accepts goal of success	Rejects hard work as the appropriate way to succeed		**Innovation**—finds illegal ways to succeed	Criminal
Rejects goal of success	Accepts hard work as the appropriate way to succeed		**Ritualism**—acts as if he wants to succeed but does not exert much effort	Unmotivated teacher
Rejects goal of success	Rejects hard work as the appropriate way to succeed		**Retreatism**—drops out of the race for success	Skid row alcoholic
Rejects goal of success	Rejects hard work as the appropriate way to succeed		**Rebellion**—substitutes new way to achieve new goal	Militia group member

Adapted from Robert K. Merton, *Social Theory and Social Structure*, rev. ed. New York: Free Press.

Control Theory

Travis Hirschi's control theory (1972) is also based on Durkheim's views. According to **control theory**, conformity to social norms depends on the presence of strong bonds between individuals and society. If those bonds are weak—if anomie is present—deviance occurs.

In this theory, social bonds *control* the behavior of people, thus preventing deviant acts. People conform because they don't want to "lose face" with family members, friends, or classmates.

control theory
theory that compliance with social norms requires strong bonds between individuals and society

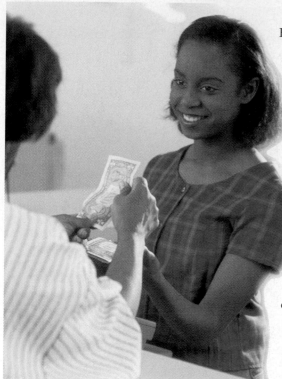

This young woman is completing her purchase in a clothing store. Relate this transaction to control theory and anomie.

A loving person lives in a loving world. A hostile person lives in a hostile world. Everyone you meet is your mirror.

Ken Keys
U.S. author

What are the basic elements of social bonds?   According to Hirschi, the social bond has four basic components:

1. *Attachment.* The stronger your attachment to groups or individuals, the more likely you are to conform. In other words, the likelihood of conformity varies with the strength of ties with parents, friends, and institutions such as schools and churches.

2. *Commitment.* The greater your commitment to social goals, the more likely you are to conform. The commitment of individuals who believe their hard work will be rewarded is greater than the commitment of people who do not believe they can compete within the system.

3. *Involvement.* Participation in approved social activities increases the probability of conformity. Besides positively focusing your time and energy, participation puts you in contact with people whose opinions you value.

4. *Belief.* Belief in the norms and values of society promotes conformity. A belief in the appropriateness of the rules of social life strengthens people's resolve not to deviate from those norms.

In short, when social bonds are weak, the chances for deviance increase. Individuals who lack attachment, commitment, involvement, and belief have little incentive to follow the rules of society.

Section 2 Assessment

1. Which of the following is *NOT* one of the benefits of deviance for society?
    a. It decreases suspicion and mistrust among members of a society.
    b. It promotes social change.
    c. It increases social unity.
    d. It provides a safety valve.
    e. It promotes clarification of norms.
2. Briefly describe the main idea of Merton's strain theory.
3. A high school teacher who simply goes through the motions of teaching classes without any thought of success is an example of which response in strain theory?
4. What are the four basic elements needed to create strong social bonds?

Critical Thinking

5. **Applying Concepts**   Describe someone you know (anonymously, of course) who falls into one of the four deviant response categories identified by strain theory. Use specific characteristics of this person to show the influence of different aspirations on economic decisions.

Is Teen Smoking a Deviant Behavior?

Sociologist Philip Hilts believes that tobacco companies target young people in their advertisements and that the strategy has a sociological basis.

[C]hildren are just beginning to shape their image of themselves, elbowing out a niche in the world, and must somehow differentiate themselves from parents and other adults, and get out from under what the authorities in life want from them. They dress differently, sometimes shockingly. They listen to different, sometimes shocking, music. In this quest, the children are worried, insecure, seeking to make choices and have them supported by their friends or others they respect. Most obviously, their choices are supported by each other. They have learned to lean on each other for aid and assent. Sometimes older siblings lend support. But because the insecurity is great, as many supports as possible are needed (Hilts, 1997:33).

Cigarette advertising, claims Hilts, portrays smoking as another ally in teenagers' attempts to find their own identities. Smoking is portrayed as a pleasurable, cool way for them to declare their successful transition into adulthood. In other words, tobacco corporations assume correctly that teenagers are at a time in their lives when deviant behavior can serve a developmental need. To teens, smoking (like their choice of clothing, music, and slang) begins as simply a form of deviance.

Doing Sociology

Do you agree with Hilts's analysis? State your arguments for or against it. Search magazines and newspapers for examples of advertising that emphasizes "young adult smokers" moving into adult activities. Or, see if you can find any advertisements that picture middle-aged or older people smoking. Why do you think these ads are virtually unknown?

This mural advertising a brand of cigarettes is designed to attract the attention and admiration of teenagers.

Focus on Research

Case Study: Saints and Roughnecks

In this classic study, William Chambliss (1973) observed the behavior of two white teenage gangs at "Hanibal High School" over a two-year period. In addition to gang activity, Chambliss documented the responses of parents, teachers, and police to the delinquent behavior.

The Saints On weekends the automobile was even more critical than during the week, for on weekends the Saints [a delinquent high school gang] went to Big Town—a large city with a population of over a million. . . . Every Friday and Saturday night most of the Saints would meet between 8:00 and 8:30 and would go into Big Town. Big Town activities included drinking heavily in taverns or nightclubs, driving drunkenly through the streets, and committing acts of vandalism and playing pranks. . . .

Searching for "fair game" for a prank was the boys' principal activity after they left the tavern. The boys would drive alongside a foot patrolman and ask directions to some street. If the policeman leaned on the car in the course of answering the question, the driver would speed away, causing him to lose his balance. The Saints were careful to play this prank only in an area where they were not going to spend much time and where they could quickly disappear around a corner to avoid having their license plate number taken.

Construction sites and road repair areas were the special province of the Saints' mischief. A soon-to-be-repaired hole in the road inevitably invited the Saints to remove lanterns and wooden barricades and put them in the car, leaving the hole unprotected. The boys would find a safe vantage point and wait for an unsuspecting motorist to drive into the hole. Often, though not always, the boys would go up to the motorist and commiserate [sympathize] with him about the dreadful way the city protected its citizenry.

Leaving the scene of the open hole and the motorist, the boys would then go searching for an appropriate place to erect the stolen barricade. An "appropriate place" was often a spot on a highway near a curve in the road where the barricade would not be seen by an oncoming motorist. The boys would wait to watch an unsuspecting motorist attempt to stop and (usually) crash into the wooden barricade.

A stolen lantern might well find its way onto the back of a police car or hang from a street lamp. Once a lantern served as a prop for a reenactment of the "midnight ride of Paul Revere" until the "play," which was taking place at 2:00 A.M. in the center of a main street of Big Town, was interrupted by a police car several blocks away. The boys ran, leaving the lanterns on the street . . . .

The Roughnecks   [T]ownspeople never perceived the Saints' . . . delinquency. The Saints were good boys who just went in for an occasional prank. After all, they were well dressed, well mannered and had nice cars. The Roughnecks [a delinquent gang at the same high school] were a different story. Although the two gangs of boys were the same age, and both groups engaged in an equal amount of wild-oat sowing, everyone agreed that the not-so-well-dressed, not-so-well-mannered, not-so-rich boys were heading for trouble. . . .

From the community's viewpoint, the real indication that these kids were in for trouble was that they were constantly involved with the police. Some of them had been picked up for stealing, mostly small stuff, of course, "but still it's stealing small stuff that leads to big time crimes." "Too bad," people said. "Too bad that these boys couldn't behave like the other kids in town; stay out of trouble, be polite to adults, and look to their future." . . .

The fighting activities of the group were fairly readily and accurately perceived by almost everyone. At least once a month, the boys would get into some sort of fight, although most fights were scraps between members of the group or involved only one member of the group and some peripheral hanger-on. Only three times in the period of observation did the group fight together: once against a gang from across town, once against two blacks and once against a group of boys from another school. For the first two fights the group went out "looking for trouble"—and they found it both times. The third fight followed a football game and began spontaneously with an argument on the football field between one of the Roughnecks and a member of the opposition's football team.

More serious than fighting, had the community been aware of it, was theft. Although almost everyone was aware that the boys occasionally stole things, they did not realize the extent of the activity. Petty stealing was a frequent event for the Roughnecks. Sometimes they stole as a group and coordinated their efforts; other times they stole in pairs. Rarely did they steal alone. . . . Types of thievery varied with the whim of the gang. Some forms of thievery were more profitable than others, but all thefts were for profit, not for thrills.

Roughnecks siphoned gasoline from cars as often as they had access to an automobile, which was not very often. Unlike the Saints, who owned their own cars, the Roughnecks would have to borrow their parents' cars, an event which occurred only eight or nine times a year. The boys claimed to have stolen cars for joy rides from time to time.

Source: Excerpted from William J. Chambliss, "The Saints and the Roughnecks," *Society* 11 (November/December, 1973):24–31.

Working with the Research

1. From your understanding of Chambliss's study, is deviance socially created? Explain.
2. Which of the three major theoretical perspectives best explains Chambliss's findings? Support your choice.

Section 5

Crime and Punishment

Key Terms

- crime
- criminal justice system
- deterrence
- retribution
- incarceration
- rehabilitation
- recidivism

Section Preview

Crime statistics in the U.S. come from two major sources: the FBI and the Census Bureau. Differences in statistics between the two agencies are due to differences in methods of collecting data. Four approaches to crime control are deterrence, retribution, incarceration, and rehabilitation.

crime
acts committed in violation of the law

Measurement of Crime

Most Americans think of **crime**—acts in violation of statute law—as including a narrow range of behavior. On the contrary, more than 2,800 acts are classified as federal crimes. Many more acts violate state and local statutes.

How much crime is there in the United States today? Crime increased sharply between the 1960s and the 1990s. For example, the FBI Index of violent crime has increased from a big city offense rate per 100,000 of 860 in 1969 to 1207 in 1999. Violent crime rates are considerably higher in the U.S. than in most other industrialized countries.

Today the rate of homicide death for a young man is 23 times higher in the U.S. than in England. In 1995, handguns were used to kill 2 people in New Zealand, 15 in Japan, 30 in Great Britain, 106 in Canada, 213 in Germany, and 9,390 in the United States (To Establish Justice, 1999:iv).

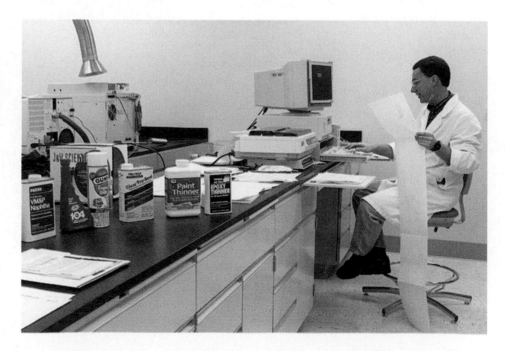

The job of this forensic scientist is to examine evidence—fingerprints, DNA, handwriting, firearms—for indications that a crime has occurred.

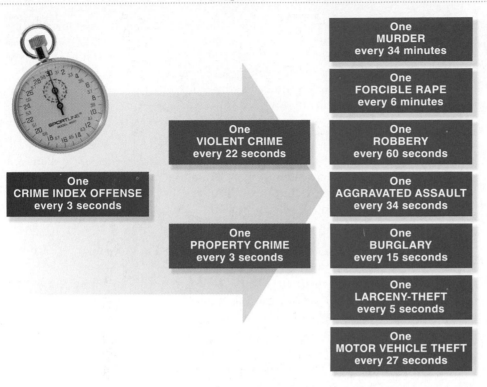

Visit soc.glencoe.com
and click on **Textbook Updates–Chapter 7** for an
update of the data.

Figure 7.4 FBI's Crime Clock: 1999. How often do Americans commit crimes? *The number to the far left, of course, does not mean that one Crime Index offense actually occurs every three seconds. It does mean that* when *all Crime Index offenses for 1999 are divided by the total number of seconds in a year there are enough of them to be spaced out every three seconds.*

Source: Federal Bureau of Investigation, *Uniform Crime Reports,* 1999.

How are crime statistics collected? The major source of American crime statistics is the Federal Bureau of Investigation's *Uniform Crime Reports* (UCR). These official statistics are gathered from police departments across the country. Reports are submitted voluntarily by law enforcement agencies.

What do UCR statistics cover? Nine types of crimes (called crime index offenses) are tracked: murder, forcible rape, robbery, aggravated assault, burglary, larceny–theft, motor vehicle theft, arson, and hate crimes.

Figure 7.4 shows UCR statistics on the frequency of seven of these crimes in the United States in 1999. Figure 7.5 presents another view of the 1998 statistics. Crimes known to the police totaled 11,635,900 (total violent crime plus total property crime). As the table shows, both violent crime and property crime have declined since 1990. Since murder receives the most publicity, it can be used to highlight this general, across-the-board reduction in

Types of crime	Number of crimes	Crime rate per 100,000 residents	1990–1999	
			Percent change in crime rate	Percent change in number of crimes
Violent crime	**1,430,690**	**524.7**	**-28.3**	**-21.4**
Murder	15,530	5.7	-39.4	-33.7
Forcible rape	89,110	32.7	-20.6	-13.1
Robbery	409,670	150.2	-41.6	-35.9
Aggravated assault	916,380	336.1	-20.7	-13.1
Property crime	**10,284,500**	**3,742.1**	**-26.5**	**-19.4**
Burglary	2,099,700	770.0	-37.7	-31.7
Larceny-theft	6,957,400	2,551.4	-20.1	-12.4
Motor vehicle theft	1,147,300	420.7	-36.0	-29.9

Figure 7.5 Crimes in the United States, 1999. *If you were a law enforcement officer, would you be encouraged or discouraged by this data? Why?*

Source: Federal Bureau of Investigation, *Uniform Crime Reports,* 1999.

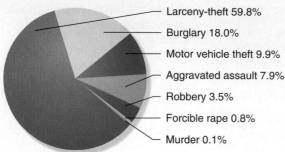

Larceny-theft 59.8%

Burglary 18.0%

Motor vehicle theft 9.9%

Aggravated assault 7.9%

Robbery 3.5%

Forcible rape 0.8%

Murder 0.1%

Figure 7.6 Types of Crimes Americans Commit. *This figure shows the contribution each major type of crime makes to the total of U.S. crime.*

Source: Federal Bureau of Investigation, *Uniform Crime Reports,* 1999.

SOCIOLOGY *Online*

Student Web Activity
Visit the *Sociology and You* Web site at soc.glencoe.com for an activity on juvenile crime.

crime. The murder rate in the United States has declined more than 39 percent since the late 1980s. This decline has gained momentum since the mid-1990s. One major reason for this new downward crime trend is a recent reduction in juvenile crime.

Figure 7.6 indicates that violent crime—murder, forcible rape, aggravated assault, and robbery—made up 12.3 percent of the known crimes. Property crime—burglary, larceny-theft, motor vehicle theft—accounted for 87.7 percent.

How reliable are UCR statistics? The UCR statistics provide considerable information about crime. A major strength of this reporting system lies in the fact that experienced police officers decide if an incident should be reported as a crime. The UCR statistics also have serious limitations, however:

❖ The UCR tends to overrepresent the lower classes and undercount the middle and upper classes.

❖ Some crimes (amateur thefts, minor assaults) are not as likely to be reported to the police as murder and auto thefts.

❖ Prostitutes and intoxicated persons are subject to arrest in public places, but are fairly safe in private settings where the police cannot enter without a warrant.

❖ About two-thirds of U.S. crimes are not reported at all.

❖ Crime reporting varies from place to place and crime to crime, and white-collar offenders are seldom included.

Are any other crime statistics available? In response to these criticisms, the *National Crime Victimization Survey* (NCVS) was launched in the early 1970s. This survey is conducted semiannually for the Bureau of Justice Statistics by the U.S. Census Bureau.

The NCVS has two advantages. First, it helps make up for the underreporting of crime. Second, its surveys are more scientifically sound than methods used in the UCR. At the very least, the NCVS is an increasingly important supplement to the FBI's official statistics. Together they provide a more complete account of the extent and nature of crime in the United States (Wright, 1987; U.S. Department of Justice, 1999).

Juvenile Crime

Juvenile crime refers to legal violations among those under 18 years of age. Juvenile offenders are the third largest category of criminals in the United States. Teenage criminal activity includes theft, murder, rape, robbery, assault, and the sale of illegal substances. Juvenile delinquent behavior includes deviance that only the young can commit, such as failing to attend school, fighting in school, and underage drinking and smoking.

What is the trend in juvenile crime? Violent juvenile crime reached its lowest level in a decade in 1999, a fall of 36 percent since 1994 (Office of Justice Programs, 2000). During the 1990s

❖ the juvenile murder arrest rate dropped by 68 percent.

❖ juvenile arrests for weapons violations declined by a third.

❖ the juvenile rape arrest rate went down by 31 percent.

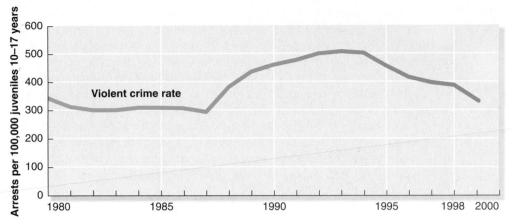

Figure 7.7 Juvenile Violent Crime Declines. *Why is the juvenile violent crime rate in the U.S. dropping?*

Source: U.S. Bureau of the Census, *Juvenile Offenders and Victims,* 1999, and Office of Justice Programs, 2000.

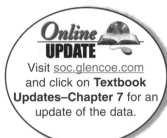

Visit soc.glencoe.com and click on **Textbook Updates–Chapter 7** for an update of the data.

There were also fewer juvenile victims of murder—down from almost 3,000 to about 2,000. Juvenile crime, in short, returned to the rates typical of the years prior to the crack epidemic of the late 1980s.

Why has juvenile crime gone down?   Several factors are said to account for this decline in juvenile crime. For one, there has been a decline in the demand for crack cocaine. Remaining crack gangs that provided guns to juveniles have reached truces. Repeat violent juvenile offenders have been given stiffer sentences. Finally, police are cracking down on illegal guns on the street.

Approaches to Crime Control

The **criminal justice system** is made up of the institutions and processes responsible for enforcing criminal statutes. It includes the police, courts, and correctional system. A criminal justice system may draw on four approaches to control and punish lawbreakers—*deterrence, retribution, incarceration,* and *rehabilitation.*

Does punishment discourage crime?   The **deterrence** approach uses the threat of punishment to discourage criminal actions. A basic idea of this approach is that punishment of convicted criminals will serve as an example to keep other people from committing crimes. There is considerable debate on the effectiveness of deterrence (DiIulio and Piehl, 1991). Research indicates that the threat of punishment *does* deter crime if potential lawbreakers know two things: that they are likely to get caught and that the punishment will be severe. In the U.S., however, the punishment for crime is usually not certain, swift, or severe. Consequently, punishment does not have the deterrent effect that it could have (Pontell, 1984).

Capital punishment (the death penalty) is a special case. Over four thousand people have been executed in the United States since 1930, the year the federal government began gathering statistics on capital punishment. Unless

criminal justice system
system comprising institutions and processes responsible for enforcing criminal statutes

deterrence
discouraging criminal acts by threatening punishment

Tech Trends

Look Out for Identity Thieves!

One of the newest forms of deviance is "identity theft." An identity thief "steals" credit information belonging to another person, then commits fraud with it. The results for victims can be devastating.

In testimony before the Maryland legislature, one couple reported that a thief used their credit cards to purchase five automobiles. Graciela has been a victim of identity theft for more than ten years. A thief gained access to her Social Security number, birth certificate, and driver's license. With this information, the imposter has obtained credit cards, purchased furniture, bought cars, and obtained welfare. (All of these examples, and more, are available through the Privacy Rights Clearinghouse, http://www.privacyrights.org, a nonprofit group for consumers' privacy rights.)

Beth Givens of the Privacy Rights Clearinghouse explains that identity theft can occur in many ways. A thief can steal a wallet or purse, get copies of credit card slips from trash, or steal someone's mail. There are also high-tech methods of identity theft. The most common method is to illegally gain access to credit rating company computers. These companies maintain credit reports that provide valuable information about a consumer—Social Security number, birth date, credit card numbers, and address. Although credit rating companies try to prevent high-tech identity theft, the very nature of their service makes this information accessible through computer terminals. This access is an open invitation to criminals.

The victims of identity theft obviously suffer great damage. Unless the thief is caught in the act, there seems to be little the police can do to stop this kind of crime. Many victims also have to deal with abusive collection agencies. It has taken some people ten years or more to clean up the mess the thieves have created. Victims are often scarred emotionally and report feelings of violation, hopelessness, and great anger.

The goal of today's identity thieves is to get items at no cost, not to take over the victims' identities. But what if identity theft also involved losing one's identity? What would happen if a person's identity were actually "stolen"? This was the topic of a film called *The Net*. In this movie, a woman's entire identity is erased. The villains in the movie steal the documents that would prove her identity and destroy all of her existing computer records. Using her photograph and Social Security number, they create a whole new identity for her, including a new name, a bad credit report, and a criminal record. As the woman in the movie says, "They knew everything about me. It was all on the Internet."

Analyzing the Trends

Which theoretical perspective would be most useful in analyzing identity theft? Explain your choice, and apply that perspective to the issue of identity theft.

it is premeditated, a murder is an extremely emotional and irrational act. Under such circumstances, you would not expect the threat of capital punishment to be a deterrent, and research shows that it is not. If the death penalty were a deterrent to murder, a decline in its use should be followed by an increase in the murder rate. Research indicates, however, that the murder rate remains constant, or even drops, following a decline in the use of the death penalty (Sellin, 1991; Lester, 1998; Sarat, 1998).

Do Americans believe capital punishment deters criminals?

Despite those findings, about three-fourths of Americans believe that the death penalty acts as a deterrent to murder. Actually, attitudes regarding the ability of the death penalty to prevent crime do not seem to affect attitudes toward the death penalty itself. Of those Americans who favor the death penalty, over three-fourths indicate they would continue to favor it even if confronted with conclusive evidence that the death penalty does not act as a deterrent to murder and that it does not lower the murder rate. Feelings of revenge and a desire for retribution, then, appear to contribute more to the support of capital punishment than do its deterrent effects. When asked to choose, a significantly higher proportion of the American population support the death penalty for murder (66 percent) than oppose it (26 percent; Gallup, 2001).

Why does the attitude toward the death penalty vary?

Attitudes toward the death penalty in the United States vary according to race and ethnicity. Over three-fourths of whites favor the death penalty compared with 40 percent of African Americans and 52 percent of Latinos. This racial and ethnic variation in attitude toward the death penalty is not surprising. The less favorable African American and Latino attitude is due, in part, to the fact that, when convicted, they are more likely than whites to receive the death penalty (Spohn, 1995). While African Americans comprise only about 13 percent of the U.S. population, they make up 43 percent of death row inmates. Racial minorities constitute half of all inmates in U.S. prisons.

Demonstrators protest in support of and in opposition to the death penalty. Based on the evidence, do you think support for the death penalty is motivated by deterrence or retribution?

What is retribution?

Retribution is a type of punishment intended to make criminals pay compensation for their acts. It comes from the idea of "an eye for an eye and a tooth for a tooth." The law allows designated officials to exact retribution. However, it does not allow individuals to take personal vengeance. If a mother "takes the law into her own hands" by shooting her son's killer, she must also answer to society for her action.

retribution
punishment intended to make criminals pay compensation for their acts

Why does society keep criminals in prisons?

The basic idea behind **incarceration**—keeping criminals in prisons—is that criminals who are not on the street cannot commit crimes. Recently, the United States has taken a tougher stance in favor of the incarceration approach with such bills as the *three strikes law*. As a result, the number of local, state, and federal prisoners increased by almost 700,000 between 1990 and 2000, and is expected to exceed 2 million very shortly. In more repressive societies, such as the former Soviet Union and present-day Nationalist China, people may spend their entire lives in prison camps for crimes ranging from political opposition to murder.

incarceration
a method of protecting society from criminals by keeping them in prisons

World View

Death Penalty Policy

Countries vary in their approach to the control of crime. The most extreme form of social control, the death penalty, is utilized in many countries, while some countries have abolished capital punishment completely. This map shows variations in national policy regarding the death penalty.

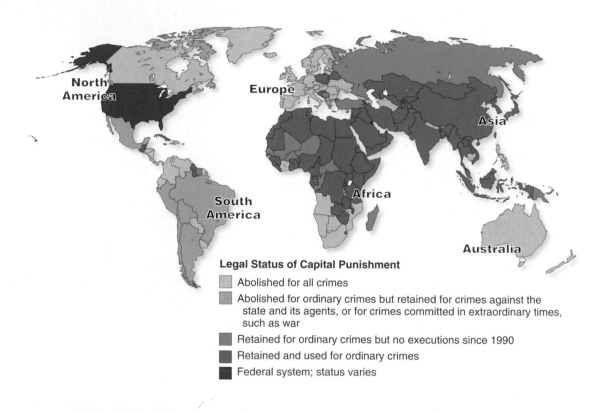

Legal Status of Capital Punishment

- Abolished for all crimes
- Abolished for ordinary crimes but retained for crimes against the state and its agents, or for crimes committed in extraordinary times, such as war
- Retained for ordinary crimes but no executions since 1990
- Retained and used for ordinary crimes
- Federal system; status varies

Interpreting the Map

1. Do you notice any pattern in the use of the death penalty? Describe it.
2. What additional information would you need to determine if capital punishment is an effective deterrent to crime? Explain.

Source: Amnesty International Online

---

rehabilitation
process of changing or reforming a criminal through socialization

Do prisons rehabilitate criminals?   **Rehabilitation** is an approach to crime control that attempts to resocialize criminals. Most prisons have programs aimed at giving prisoners both social and work skills that will help them adjust to normal society after their release. Unfortunately, 30 to 60 percent of those released from penal institutions are sent back to prison in two to five years. This return to criminal behavior is called **recidivism.** The relatively high rate of recidivism makes it seem unlikely that prison rehabilitation programs are working (Elikann, 1996; Zamble and Quinsey, 1997). Reasons for the high rate of recidivism include

❖ the basic nature of the offenders
❖ influences of more hardened criminals
❖ the stigma of being an ex-convict.

recidivism
a repetition of or return to criminal behavior

It is difficult to change attitudes and behavior within the prison subculture. Conformity with the "inmate code" stresses loyalty among inmates as well as opposition to correctional authorities. Also, a released prisoner is likely to bring the toughness reinforced in prison life to the workplace. This transfer of prison norms does not work because most jobs in the service economy require interpersonal skills (Hagan, 1994b).

What are some alternatives to prisons? If prisons do not rehabilitate, what are some alternatives? Several are being considered.

1. *A combination of prison and probation.* A mixed or split sentence, known as *shock probation,* is designed to shock offenders into recognizing the realities of prison life. Prisoners serve part of their sentences in an institution and the rest on probation.

2. *Community-based programs.* These programs are designed to reintroduce criminals into society. By getting convicts out of prison for at least part of the day, community-based programs help break the inmate code. At the same time, prisoners have a chance to become part of society— participating in the community but under professional guidance and supervision.

3. *Diversion strategy.* Diversion is aimed at preventing, or greatly reducing, the offender's involvement in the criminal justice system. Diversion involves a referral to a community-based treatment program rather than a prison or a probationary program. Because offenders are handled outside the formal system of criminal law, authorities believe the offenders will not acquire stigmatizing labels and other liabilities (Morris and Tonry, 1990; Lanier and Henry, 1997).

These juveniles are in the Texas-based Del Valle Correctional Boot Camp. What is the reasoning behind this alternative to imprisonment?

Will any of these alternatives work? Most of the alternative programs have not been sufficiently evaluated to determine how well they work. Continued use of these alternatives will depend on what American voters believe are the appropriate functions of prisons. These programs can exist only so long as rehabilitation has a high priority. Recently, Americans have taken a harsher view toward criminals, so support for alternatives may be eroding.

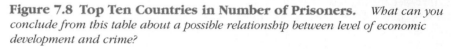

Rank	Country	Prisoners*	Population (in millions)	Incarceration rate per 1,000
1	United States	1,726,000	267.5	6.45
2	China	1,410,000	1,243.7	1.15
3	Russia	1,010,000	147.0	6.85
4	India	231,000	960.2	.25
5	Ukraine	212,000	51.2	4.15
6	Brazil	167,000	157.1	1.05
7	South Africa	142,000	44.3	3.20
8	Thailand	131,000	59.3	2.20
9	Mexico	103,000	94.9	1.10
10	Iran	102,000	65.0	1.55

*Approximate figures for latest year available.

Figure 7.8 Top Ten Countries in Number of Prisoners.   *What can you conclude from this table about a possible relationship between level of economic development and crime?*

Source: British Home Office Online Research and Development Statistics.

Section 5 Assessment

1. Indicate whether the approaches to punishment listed below are rehabilitation (R), deterrence (D), retribution (Rb), or incarceration (I).
    a. imprisonment without parole
    b. longer prison sentences
    c. extremely harsh prison conditions
    d. psychological counseling in prison
    e. swift justice

2. According to the FBI's *Uniform Crime Reports,* has crime in the United States increased or decreased since 1989?

3. Do you believe that the cultural values of American society affect the policies of government regarding approaches to crime control? Why or why not?

4. Has research supported the position that the death penalty deters crime?

Critical Thinking

5. **Synthesizing Information** The text outlines several distinct approaches to crime control. Choose one approach, and explain why you believe it is or is not successful. Use functionalism, conflict theory, or symbolic interactionism as a reference point.

6. **Evaluating Information** What are your beliefs on capital punishment? Defend your viewpoint.

Violence is the last refuge of the incompetent.

Isaac Asimov
author

Summary

Section 1: Deviance and Social Control

Main Idea: Deviance is the violation of social norms. It is difficult to define because not everyone agrees on what should be considered deviant behavior.

Section 2: Functionalism and Deviance

Main Idea: According to functionalists, deviance has both negative and positive consequences for society. Functionalism also forms the basis for two important theories of deviance: strain theory and control theory.

Section 3: Symbolic Interactionism and Deviance

Main Idea: The symbolic interactionist perspective yields two theories of deviance. We read in Chapter 3 that culture is learned. Sociologists believe that deviance is a learned behavior that is culturally transmitted. Labeling theory holds that an act is deviant only if other people name it so.

Section 4: Conflict Theory and Deviance

Main Idea: The conflict perspective looks at deviance in terms of social inequality and power. The most powerful members of a society determine who will be regarded as deviant. Conflict theorists point to some disproportional statistical relationships between minorities and crime.

Section 5: Crime and Punishment

Main Idea: Crime statistics in the U.S. come from two major sources: the FBI and the Census Bureau.

SOCIOLOGY Online

Self-Check Quiz
Visit the *Sociology and You* Web site at soc.glencoe.com and click on **Chapter 7—Self-Check Quizzes** to prepare for the chapter test.

Reviewing Vocabulary

Complete each sentence using each term once.

a. deviance
b. stigma
c. social control
d. white-collar crimes
e. social sanctions
f. anomie
g. Uniform Crime Reports
h. strain theory
i. deterrence
j. control theory
k. recidivism
l. rehabilitation
m. differential association theory
n. retribution
o. labeling theory

1. The tactic that uses intimidation to prevent crime is called _____.

2. _____ is the approach to crime control that attempts to resocialize criminals.

3. _____ is an undesirable characteristic or label used to deny the deviant acceptance.

4. A violation of social norms is called _____.

5. _____ are crimes committed by high-status people in the course of their occupation.

6. _____ is a theory that states that people are defined by those in power as deviant.

7. The theory that states that deviance exists when there is a gap between culturally desirable goals and means is called _____.

8. The theory that conformity to social norms depends on a strong bond between individuals and society is known as the _____.

9. _____ are rewards or punishments designed to encourage desired behavior.

10. _____ is a theory that states that deviance is learned in proportion to exposure to deviant acts.

11. When past offenders return to prison, such an occurrence is called _____.

12. _____ are ways for promoting conformity to norms.

13. _____ is the social condition in which norms are weak, conflicting or absent.

14. The major source of American statistics on crime gathered from police departments is known as _____.

15. _____ is the practice in which criminals pay compensation equal to their offenses.

Reviewing the Facts

1. In a famous study known as the Minneapolis Domestic Violence Study, sociologists discovered that arresting someone for hitting his wife did not necessarily stop him from hitting her again. What is the name of the theory upon which they based their hypothesis that arrest would stop the behavior?

2. A group of lower-class youths are accused of a crime for behavior that higher-status teens have engaged in without punishment. What sociological term describes this process?

3. When a high school student admits to cheating on a test, this behavior is labeled as primary deviance. Explain why.

4. Give two reasons why the crime statistics reported by the Uniform Crime Reports differ from those statistics reported by the National Crime Victimization Survey. Which report would you consider more reliable and why?

5. What is the strain theory?

6. Robert Merton's strain theory of deviance is based on four types of responses. Using the chart below, list each response. Then, from the perspective of means and goals explain each response and give an example.

MERTON'S DEVIANT RESPONSES TO STRAIN

Response	Explanation	Example
Innovation	Individual accepts success as a goal but uses illegal means to achieve it.	Shoplifter

Thinking Critically

1. **Interpreting Information** Use the information in this chapter to explain the following statement: "Deviance, like beauty, is in the eye of the beholder."

2. **Applying Concepts** There is a chain of restaurants in this country known for the outrageous behavior of its servers. At these restaurants, servers might purposely spill drinks and food on the patrons. Despite this apparently deviant behavior, patrons seem to love the restaurants and recommend them to friends. How do these restaurants, which clearly violate concepts of social control, continue to attract customers?

3. **Making Inferences** If a person is rarely deviant, people come to expect that behavior. If a person is often deviant, people expect *that* behavior. What do you think happens when people are deviant occasionally? How might unpredictability of behavior be more alarming or disturbing?

4. **Drawing Conclusions** Some states are considering life imprisonment with no chance of parole as an alternative to the death penalty. The states argue that the capital punishment process is more costly than imprisonment over time. Proponents also claim that offenders given life-time sentences are more likely to develop remorse for their crimes. Do you think this argument has merit? Why or why not?

5. **Evaluating Information** The conflict perspective says that the capitalistic society of the United States—with its emphasis on gaining wealth—is really responsible for crime. Find examples to support or to refute the hypothesis that crime is the result of society's materialistic values.

6. **Analyzing Information** The chapter case study "Saints and Roughnecks" describes how social class contributed to people's perceptions of the level of deviance of two groups of boys. Some students complain that there are special groups in their schools (athletes, honor students, and so forth) that never seem to be held responsible for their actions. Is this true of your school? If so, why? If not, what do you credit for the even-handed discipline?

Sociology Projects

1. **Random Acts of Kindness and Positive Deviance** Go out of your way to help a stranger (not a friend or family member). You might give someone directions, help someone to carry parcels, or even smile and say a friendly hello. (*Important note:* Remember to keep safety and sensitivity to others' feelings in mind when you approach people you don't know.) Write answers to the following questions to help you evaluate the stranger's reactions to your act.

   a. How do you think the traits of the individual you helped (race, age, gender) affected the situation?

   b. Why did you choose your particular act of kindness?

   c. How did you feel while performing the random act of kindness?

   d. What surprised or impressed you the most about the individual's reaction?

2. **Categorizing Deviance** As you read in the quotation on page 204, in a diverse society such as that of the United States, many groups of people may be categorized as deviant by someone. List the groups named in the quotation on a piece of paper. For each group, assign a number from 1 to 7, with 1 being the most deviant and 7 the least deviant. Afterward, compare your list with those of two or three of your classmates to see if there was any agreement. Discuss possible reasons for major differences.

3. **Deviant Crimes** What crimes today do people consider the most severe? Working individually, make a list of the five crimes you consider the most deviant, with the first item on the list the most deviant, the second item the next most deviant, and so forth. Next, assign a punishment for each crime. Does the crime warrant the death penalty? Life imprisonment? After you have completed your list, work with two or three classmates until you agree on a new list. You must reach consensus on the crimes included on the list, their rankings, and the punishment assigned to each. Finally, compare your group's results with the results of other groups in your class. What have you learned about the difficulty of reaching agreement on this sensitive topic?

4. **The Role of the Media** The text discussed how race is an important factor in understanding deviance. Another factor you might wish to consider is the role of the media in shaping our perceptions of crime and criminals. Your task is to collect one crime-related newspaper article per day for one week. Analyze the article for information such as the race, age, gender, and status, of the accused. Also consider the geographic location of the crime. How does the newspaper describe the area where the crime took place? Do you detect any bias in the type of words used to report these incidents?

5. **Preparing a News Broadcast** As an extension of the project above (i.e., number 4), imagine yourself as a news anchor on the local news. Choose one of the stories that you have collected. Limiting yourself to one paragraph, prepare your news broadcast using the facts as reported in the newspaper. Now, evaluate your broadcast and write another version that is neutral (i.e., gives no indication of race, gender or age). Which version do you feel the program producer would choose to put on the air? Why?

Technology Activity

1. Using the Internet, your school or local library, find a murder case from the year 1900. Find a similar type of murder case from the year 2000. Consider how each murder was reported and punished (i.e., the type of approach to crime control that was used). Design a database to illustrate similarities and differences between the two deviant acts. What can you conclude about society's view of deviance at the time the crime was committed?

Chapter 7

Enrichment Reading
The Police and the Black Male

by Elijah Anderson

The police, in the Village-Northton [neighborhood] as elsewhere, represent society's formal, legitimate means of social control. Their role includes protecting law-abiding citizens from those who are not law-abiding by preventing crime and by apprehending likely criminals. Precisely how the police fulfill the public's expectations is strongly related to how they view the neighborhood and the people who live there. On the streets, color-coding often works to confuse race, age, class, gender, incivility, and criminality, and it expresses itself most concretely in the person of the **anonymous** black male. In doing their job, the police often become willing parties to this general color-coding of the public environment, and related distinctions, particularly those of skin color and gender, come to convey definite meanings. Although such coding may make the work of the police more manageable, it may also fit well with their own **presuppositions** regarding race and class relations, thus shaping officers' perceptions of crime "in the city." Moreover, the anonymous black male is usually an **ambiguous** figure who arouses the utmost caution and is generally considered dangerous until he proves he is not. . . .

To be white is to be seen by the police—at least superficially—as an ally, eligible for consideration and for much more deferential treatment than that accorded to blacks in general. This attitude may be grounded in the backgrounds of the police themselves. Many have grown up in . . . "ethnic" neighborhoods. They may serve what they perceive as their own class and neighbor-hood interests, which often translates as keeping blacks "in their place"—away from neighborhoods that are socially defined as "white." In trying to do their job, the police appear to engage in an informal policy of monitoring young black men as a means of controlling crime, and often they seem to go beyond the bounds of duty. . . .

On the streets late at night, the average young black man is suspicious of others he encounters, and he is particularly wary of the police. If he is dressed in the uniform of the "gangster," such as a black leather jacket, sneakers, and a "gangster cap," if he is carrying a radio or a suspicious bag (which may be confiscated), or if he is moving too fast or too slow, the police may stop him. As part of the routine, they search him and make him sit in the police car while they run a check to see whether there is a "detainer" on him. If there is nothing, he is allowed to go on his way. After this ordeal the youth is often left afraid, sometimes shaking, and uncertain about the area he had previously taken for granted. He is upset in part because he is painfully aware of how close he has come to being in "big trouble." He knows of other youths who have gotten into a "world of trouble" simply by being on the streets at the wrong time or when the police were pursuing a criminal. In these circumstances, particularly at night, it is relatively easy for one black man to be mistaken for another. Over the years, while walking through the neighborhood I have on occasion been stopped and questioned by police chasing a mugger, but after explaining myself I was released.

Many youths, however, have reason to fear such mistaken identity or harassment, since they might be jailed, if only for a short time, and would have to post bail money and pay legal fees to **extricate** themselves from the mess. . . . When law-abiding blacks are ensnared by the criminal justice system, the scenario may proceed as follows. A young man is **arbitrarily** stopped by the police and questioned. If he cannot effectively negotiate with the officer(s), he may be accused of a crime and arrested. To resolve this situation he needs financial resources, which for him are in short supply. If he does not have money for any attorney, which often happens, he is left to a public defender who may be more interested in going along with the court system than in fighting for a poor black person. Without legal support, he may well wind up "doing time" even if he is innocent of the charges brought against him. The next time he is stopped for questioning he will have a record, which will make detention all the more likely.

Because the young black man is aware of many cases when an "innocent" black person was wrongly accused and detained, he develops an "attitude" toward the police. The street word for police is "the man," signifying a certain machismo, power, and authority. He becomes concerned when he notices "the man" in the community or when the police focus on him because he is outside his own neighborhood. The youth knows, or soon finds out, that he exists in a legally precarious state. Hence he is motivated to avoid the police, and his public life becomes severely **circumscribed**. . . .

To avoid encounters with the man, some streetwise young men camouflage themselves, giving up the urban uniform and emblems that identify them as "legitimate" objects of police attention. They may adopt a more conventional presentation of self, wearing chinos, sweat suits, and generally more conservative dress. Some youths have been known to "ditch" a favorite jacket if they see others wearing one like it, because wearing it increases their chances of being mistaken for someone else who may have committed a crime.

But such strategies do not always work over the long run and must be constantly modified. For instance, because so many young ghetto blacks have begun to wear Fila and Adidas sweat suits as status symbols, such dress has become incorporated into the public image generally associated with young black males. These athletic suits, particularly the more expensive and colorful ones, along with high-priced sneakers, have become the leisure dress of successful drug dealers. . . .

What Does it Mean?

ambiguous
capable of being understood in two or more ways

anonymous
lacking individuality, distinction, or recognition

arbitrarily
without meaning; resulting from the unrestrained exercise of power

circumscribe
to reduce the range or scope of action

extricate
to remove from an entanglement

presuppositions
assumed knowledge

Ed. note: This article is based on the author's field research on two city neighborhoods he calls Village-Northton.

From: Elijah Anderson, *Streetwise* (Chicago: University of Chicago Press, 1990), pp. 190–206. © 1990 University of Chicago Press. Reprinted by permission of the publisher and author.

Read and React

1. According to the article, what are some consequences to black youth of being arrested, innocent or not?

2. What presuppositions regarding race and class exist in your neighborhood?

3. Do you think color-coding exists in your town or city? Why or why not?

CHAPTER 8
Social Stratification

Jane Smith, aged forty and reeling from a bitter divorce, was discouraged. A serious back injury meant she could no longer work at her nursing aide job. Without a high school diploma, she found that no one was willing to hire her. Reluctantly, she applied for welfare and was enrolled in a program designed to develop job skills. She completed an eighteen-month course and was hired by an engineering firm. After two years, Jane has moved up in the company and now thinks of herself as an intelligent, capable person.

A different type of welfare story involves Mary, the "welfare queen." Many politicians have used her as a typical example of how the social welfare system is abused. Mary managed to register for government aid under dozens of assumed names and collected thousands of dollars from food stamps and other federally subsidized programs. With this money, she supported her drug and alcohol habits while her children were left cold and underfed.

Which welfare case do you believe is typical? Your answer depends a lot on your social class and such characteristics as age, education, politics, and income. Sociologists know that most Americans seriously overestimate both the amount of welfare fraud and the amount of money spent on welfare. At the same time, negative attitudes about welfare recipients have become part of the American culture. This chapter will look at attitudes and behaviors of different social classes.

Sections

1. **Dimensions of Stratification**
2. **Explanations of Stratification**
3. **Social Classes in America**
4. **Poverty in America**
5. **Social Mobility**

Learning Objectives

After reading this chapter, you will be able to

- ❖ explain the relationship between stratification and social class.
- ❖ compare and contrast the three dimensions of stratification.
- ❖ state the differences among the three major perspectives on social stratification.
- ❖ identify the distinguishing characteristics of the major social classes in America.
- ❖ describe the measurement and extent of poverty in the United States.
- ❖ discuss social mobility in the United States.

SOCIOLOGY Online

Chapter Overview
Visit the *Sociology and You* Web site at soc.glencoe.com and click on **Chapter 8— Chapter Overviews** to preview chapter information.

Section 1

Dimensions of Stratification

Key Terms

- social stratification
- social class
- bourgeoisie
- proletariat

- income
- wealth
- power
- prestige

Section Preview

Stratification is the division of society into classes that have unequal amounts of wealth, power, and prestige. Karl Marx and Max Weber studied these dimensions of stratification in great detail.

social stratification
ranking of people or groups according to their unequal access to scarce resources

social class
segment of society whose members hold similar amounts of resources and share values, norms, and an identifiable lifestyle

Social Stratification and Social Class

In one of his best-known children's books, Dr. Seuss writes of the Sneetches, birds whose rank depends on whether or not they have a large star on their stomachs. Star-bellied Sneetches have high status, and plain-bellied Sneetches have low status. In the classic novel

In George Orwell's Animal Farm, *the animals overthrew their human master to form their own soon-to-be stratified society.*

Animal Farm, George Orwell creates a barnyard society where the pigs ultimately take over the previously classless animal society. The animals' motto changes from "All animals are equal" to "All animals are equal—but some animals are more equal than others." Both books mock the tendency of humans to form ranks. **Social stratification** is the creation of layers (or strata) of people who possess unequal shares of scarce resources. The most important of these resources are income, wealth, power, and prestige (Levine, 1998).

How is social stratification related to social class?   Each of the layers in a stratification system is a **social class**—a segment of a population whose members hold similar amounts of scarce resources and share values, norms, and an identifiable lifestyle. The number of social classes in a society varies. Technologically developed countries generally have three broad classes—upper, middle, and lower—subdivided into smaller categories. In some developing countries, there might only be an upper class and a lower class.

Karl Marx and Max Weber made the most significant early contributions to the study of social stratification. (See Chapter 1, pages 16–18 for an introduction to these two pioneers of sociology.) Marx explained the importance of the economic foundations of social classes, while Weber emphasized the prestige and power aspects of stratification.

World View

Poverty and Death

Receiving basic nutrition and medical care is critical to survival in the early years of human life. Because wealth and income have a significant impact on a family's ability to provide these necessities of life, extreme poverty matters a great deal. This map shows the number of deaths of children less than five years old per 1,000 live births in each country.

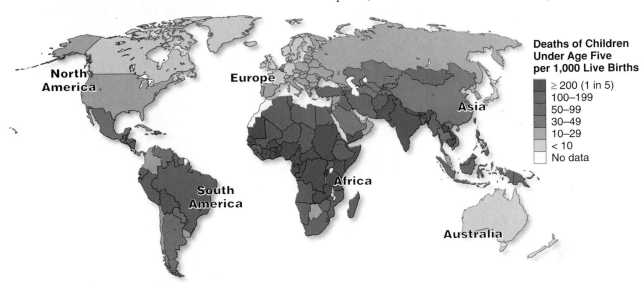

Deaths of Children Under Age Five per 1,000 Live Births

- ≥ 200 (1 in 5)
- 100–199
- 50–99
- 30–49
- 10–29
- < 10
- No data

Interpreting the Map

1. Do you see a pattern in the death rates for children under five years old? Explain.
2. Why do you think the U.S. ranks higher than some countries in Europe?
3. Imagine you have the job of reducing the world's death rate among children under age five. What programs would you introduce?

Adapted from *The State of the World Atlas,* 5th ed.

The Economic Dimension

Marx identified several social classes in nineteenth-century industrial society, including laborers, servants, factory workers, craftspeople, proprietors of small businesses, and moneyed capitalists. He predicted, however, that capitalist societies would ultimately be reduced to two social classes. He thought that those who owned the means of production—the **bourgeoisie**—would be the rulers. Those who worked for wages—the **proletariat**—would be the ruled. Marx predicted that because the capitalists owned the means of production (factories, land, and so forth), they would both rule and exploit the working class. The working class would have nothing to sell but its labor.

bourgeoisie
class that owns the means of production

proletariat
class that labors without owning the means of production

income
amount of money received
by an individual or group
over a specific time period

wealth
total economic resources
held by a person or group

Marx believed that control of the economy gave the capitalists control over the legal, educational, and government systems as well. For Karl Marx, the economy determined the nature of society.

Are there extremes of income and poverty in the United States?   In his writings, Marx emphasized the unequal distribution of economic resources. How unequally are these resources distributed in the United States? When discussing this issue, economists often make a distinction between income and wealth. **Income** is the amount of money received within a given time period by an individual or group. **Wealth** refers to all the economic resources possessed by an individual or group. In brief, your income is your paycheck, and your wealth is what you own.

In 1999, over 32 million Americans were living in poverty. (In 2000, the poverty level was set at $17,603 for a family of four.) At the other extreme, there were about 5 million millionaire households and around 260 billionaires in the United States. The economist Paul Samuelson described income inequality in America in these words: "If we made an income pyramid out of a child's blocks, with each layer portraying $500 of income, the peak would be far higher than Mt. Everest, but most people would be within a few feet of the ground" (Samuelson and Nordhaus, 1995). The truth in Samuelson's statement is supported by government figures on the distribution of income. In 1999, the richest 20 percent of American households received over 49 percent of the nation's income. The poorest 20 percent received under 4 percent (U.S. Bureau of the Census).

Income inequality exists and is growing. Figure 8.1 charts percentage changes in after-tax income in the United States over a twenty-two year period. During this period, the income

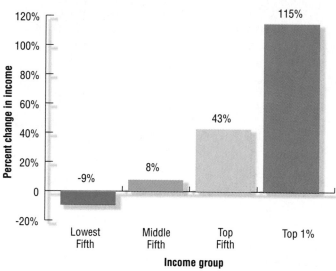

Figure 8.1 Percentage Change in After-Tax Income 1977 to 1999. *To what percentages do the labels Lowest, Middle, and Top Fifth refer?*

Sources: Washington, DC: Center on Budget and Policy Priorities, 1999.

Online
UPDATE
Visit soc.glencoe.com
and click on **Textbook Updates–Chapter 8** for an update of the data.

"*Actually, Lou, I think it was more than just my being in the right place at the right time. I think it was my being the right race, the right religion, the right sex, the right socioeconomic group, having the right accent, the right clothes, going to the right schools...*"

This cartoon is illustrating what sociologists have confirmed—usually, those who have, get.

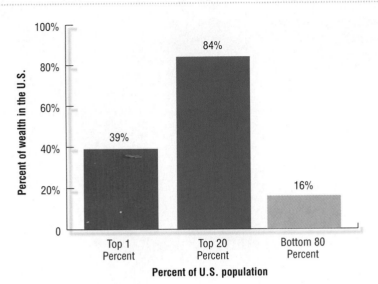

Figure 8.2 Shares of Wealth.
Is this picture of the distribution of wealth different from what you would expect? Explain.

Source: Washington, DC: Center on Budget and Policy Priorities, 1999.

of the top 1 percent of the population increased by 115 percent. Compare this to a 9 percent decline for the lowest fifth of the population. How much inequality in wealth exists in the United States?

Income distribution figures reveal economic inequality, but they do not show the full extent of inequality. For that, inequality in wealth (what you own) must be considered. In the United States, there is a high concentration of wealth. The richest 20 percent of the population holds 84 percent of the wealth. The top 1 percent alone has 39 percent of the total wealth in the United States. (See Figure 8.2)

The Power Dimension

You will recall from Chapter 1 that **power** is the ability to control the behavior of others, even against their will. Individuals or groups who possess power are able to use it to enhance their own interests, often—but not necessarily—at the expense of society.

Can you exercise power without being wealthy? According to Marx, those who own and control capital have the power in a society. Weber, on the other hand, argued that while having money certainly helps, economic success and power are not the same. Money and ownership of the means of production are not the only resources that can be used as a basis for power. Expert knowledge can be used to expand power, too. For example, many lawyers convert their expertise into substantial amounts of political power. Fame is another basis for power. In 1952, for example, Albert Einstein was offered the presidency of Israel. (He refused, saying, "I know a little about nature, and hardly anything about men.")

Power is also attached to the social positions we hold. Elected officers in organizations have more power than rank-and-file members. People in top executive positions in the mass media are powerful, even if they themselves do not have great wealth. People who are wealthy and powerful also are assumed to have characteristics they may not have. Not all of these people are as intelligent and wise as is usually assumed. Still, these attributed characteristics help them gain prestige.

power
the ability to control the behavior of others, even against their will

Jesse Jackson has channeled his intense interest in civil rights into the exercise of power on behalf of the poor and disadvantaged.

Finally, we can overcome a lack of wealth if we have large numbers of people on our side or if we are skillful at organizing our resources. Hitler, for example, was able to turn the problem of limited resources into a mass political movement. He gained absolute power by promising to deliver Germany from economic hardship following World War I.

The Prestige Dimension

prestige
recognition, respect, and admiration attached to social positions

A third dimension of social stratification is **prestige**—recognition, respect, and admiration attached to social positions. Prestige is defined by your culture and society. Honor, admiration, respect, and deference are extended to dons within the Mafia, for example; but outside their own circles Mafia chiefs do not have high prestige.

Popular actors such as Julia Roberts and Will Smith have considerable wealth. Their prestige rating is stronger in some circles than others, however.

Occupations	Prestige Score	Occupations	Prestige Score	Occupations	Prestige Score
Surgeon	87	Police officer	61	Automobile dealer	43
Astronaut	80	Actor	60	Deep-sea diver	43
Lawyer	75	Journalist	60	Landlord	41
College professor	74	TV anchorman	60	Prison guard	40
Airline pilot	73	Businessperson	60	Auto mechanic	40
Dentist	72	Actress	59	Roofer	37
Priest	71	Nursery school teacher	55	Barber	36
Engineer	71	Fashion designer	55	Sales clerk in a store	36
TV anchorwoman	70	Firefighter	53	Bus driver	32
Secret Service agent	70	Airplane mechanic	53	Dry cleaner	32
School principal	69	Commercial artist	52	Waitress	29
Medical technician	68	Housewife	51	Taxicab driver	28
Optometrist	67	Funeral director	49	Used car salesperson	25
Registered nurse	66	Jazz musician	48	Bill collector	24
High school teacher	66	Mail carrier	47	Janitor	22
Air traffic controller	65	Insurance agent	46	Grocery bagger	18
Professional athlete	65	Mechanic	46	Street-corner drug dealer	13
Paramedic	64	Disc jockey	45	Fortune teller	13
Public grade school teacher	64	Photographer	45	Panhandler	11
Advertising executive	63	Plumber	45		
Veterinarian	62	Bank teller	43		

Figure 8.3 Prestige Rankings of Selected Occupations in the United States. *Why do you think the highest listed prestige score is 87? What occupations might rate a higher score?*

Prestige must be voluntarily given, not claimed. Scientists cannot proclaim themselves Nobel Prize winners; journalists cannot award themselves Pulitzer Prizes; and corporate executives cannot grant themselves honorary doctorates. Recognition must come from others.

People with similar levels of prestige share identifiable lifestyles. The offspring of upper-class families are more likely to attend private universities and Episcopalian churches. Children from lower-class homes are less likely to attend college at all and tend to belong to fundamentalist religious groups. In fact, some sociologists view social classes as subcultures because their members participate in distinctive ways of life.

How is prestige distributed?   The social positions that are considered the most important, or are valued the most highly, have the most prestige. Because Americans value the acquisition of wealth and power, they tend to assign higher prestige to persons in positions of wealth and power.

In America, most people achieve prestige because of their occupations. (See Figure 8.3.) White-collar occupations (doctors, ministers, schoolteachers) have higher prestige than blue-collar jobs (carpenters, plumbers, mechanics). Even though wealth and power usually determine prestige, that is not always the case. You may find it somewhat surprising, for example, that priests and college professors have more prestige than bankers.

All wealth is power, so power must infallibly draw wealth to itself by some means or other.

Edmund Burke
British statesman

Associate each of these people with a prestige level. If an occupation is not obvious, choose a likely one for that person. Can the young girl even be ranked?

Section 1 Assessment

1. What is social stratification?
2. Match the dimensions of stratifications with the examples below. Use (W) for wealth, (Po) for power, and (Pr) for prestige.
   a. the respect accorded doctors
   b. a politician considering the interests of a lobby
   c. the Nobel Peace Prize
   d. stock market holdings
   e. a Supreme Court ruling
   f. real estate assets
3. The top 20 percent of U.S. households receive approximately what percent of the total income?
4. What are the most common sources of prestige in U.S. society?

Critical Thinking

5. **Analyzing Information** Social class level influences the likelihood of gaining political power. Can you analyze the relationship between social class level and political power?

Another Time

You Are What You Wear

Social rank in Europe in the Middle Ages was reflected, as it is today, in clothing and accessories. The following excerpt describes some of the norms associated with dress and status.

Clothing [in medieval Europe] served as a kind of uniform, designating status. Lepers were required to wear gray coats and red hats, the skirts of prostitutes had to be scarlet, released heretics carried crosses sewn on both sides of their chests—you were expected to pray as you passed them—and the breast of every Jew, as [required] by law, bore a huge yellow circle.

The rest of society belonged to one of the three great classes: the nobility, the clergy, and the commons. Establishing one's social identity was important. Each man knew his place, believed it had been [determined] in heaven, and was aware that what he wore must reflect it.

To be sure, certain fashions were shared by all. Styles had changed since Greece and Rome shimmered in their glory; then garments had been wrapped on; now all classes put them on and fastened them. Most clothing—except the leather gauntlets and leggings of hunters, and the crude animal skins worn by the very poor—was now woven of wool. (Since few Europeans possessed a change of clothes, the same [dress] was worn daily; as a consequence, skin diseases were astonishingly prevalent.) But there was no mistaking the distinctions between the parson in his vestments; the toiler in his dirty cloth tunic, loose trousers, and heavy boots; and the aristocrat with his jewelry, his hairdress, and his extravagant finery. Every knight wore a signet ring, and wearing fur was as much a sign of knighthood as wearing a sword or carrying a falcon. Indeed, in some European states it was illegal for anyone not nobly born to adorn himself with fur. "Many a petty noble," wrote historian W. S. Davis, "will cling to his frayed tippet of black lambskin, even in the hottest weather, merely to prove that he is not a villein [a type of serf]."

Source: Excerpted from *A World Lit Only by Fire,* © 1992 by William Manchester. By permission of Little, Brown and Company. Reprinted by permission of Don Congdon Associates, Inc. © 1993 by William Manchester.

Clothing in medieval society was strictly regulated.

Thinking It Over

Think about how you and your classmates dress. Identify some ways in which differences in dress reflect social status in your school.

Section 2

Explanations of Stratification

Key Term

- false consciousness

Section Preview

Each of the three perspectives—functionalism, conflict theory, and symbolic interactionism—explains stratification in society in a different way.

false consciousness
adoption of the ideas of the dominant class by the less powerful class

Functionalist Theory of Stratification

According to the functionalists, stratification assures that the most qualified people fill the most important positions, that these qualified people perform their tasks competently, and that they are rewarded for their efforts. The functionalist theory recognizes that inequality exists because certain jobs are more important than others and that these jobs often involve special talent and training. To encourage people to make the sacrifices necessary to fill these jobs (such as acquiring the necessary education), society attaches special monetary rewards and prestige to the positions. That is why, for example, doctors make more money and have more prestige than bus drivers. A higher level of skill is required in the medical profession, and our society's need for highly qualified doctors is great.

Conflict Theory of Stratification

According to the conflict theory of stratification, inequality exists because some people are willing to exploit others. Stratification, from this perspective, is based on force rather than on people voluntarily agreeing to it.

The conflict theory of stratification is based on Marx's ideas regarding class conflict. For Marx, all of history has been a class struggle between the powerful and the powerless, the exploiters and the exploited. Capitalist society is the final stage of the class struggle. Although the capitalists are outnumbered, they are able to control the workers. This is because the capitalists use a belief system that legitimizes the way things are. For example, the powerful contend that income and wealth are based on ability, hard work, and individual effort. Those who own the means of production are able to spread their ideas, beliefs, and values through the schools, the media, the churches, and the government. (More will be said about how this might happen in the next section.) Marx used the term **false consciousness** to refer to working-class acceptance of capitalist ideas and values.

How would functionalists explain the different places of these people on the stratification structure?

Later conflict sociologists have proposed that stratification is based more on power than on property ownership. America's legal system, for example, is used by the wealthy for their benefit, and the political system is skewed toward the interests of the powerful. For followers of the conflict perspective, stratification occurs through the struggle for scarce resources.

Symbolic Interactionism and Stratification

Symbolic interactionism helps us understand how people are socialized to accept the existing stratification structure. According to this perspective, American children are taught that a person's social class is the result of talent and effort. Those "on top" have worked hard and used their abilities, whereas those "on the bottom" lack the talent or the motivation to succeed. Hence, it is not fair to challenge the system. In this way, people come to accept the existing system.

Understandably, people in the lower social classes or social strata tend to suffer from lower self-esteem. How could it be otherwise when messages from all sides tell them they are inferior? Remember that, in the symbolic interactionist view, self-esteem is based on how we think others see us. In other words, the looking-glass process is at work. Those at the top blame the victims; the victims blame themselves. (See pages 116–117 for an explanation of the looking-glass self.)

The reverse is true for the higher classes. Those profiting most from the stratification structure tend to have higher self-esteem. This, in turn, fuels their conviction that the present arrangement is just. In short, people's self-concepts also help preserve the status quo.

These South Dakotans are protesting the unequal treatment of Native Americans in the criminal justice system. How could the protestors use conflict theory to support their viewpoint?

It isn't always easy being out of the "in–group."

Figure 8.4 | Focus on Theoretical Perspectives

Social Stratification. This table summarizes what issues of social stratification might be of interest to each of the major perspectives and predictions that they would make. Why would the symbolic interactionists be more likely than the functionalists to look at issues of self-esteem?

Theoretical Perspective	Research Topic	Expected Result	
Functionalism	Relationship between job performance and pay	Pay levels increase with job performance.	
Conflict Theory	Relationship between social class and the likelihood of punishment for a crime	The chances for prosecution decrease as the level of social class increases.	
Symbolic Interactionism	Link between social class and self-esteem	Self-esteem is higher among the upper class than the lower class.	

Section 2 Assessment

1. Identify which of the major perspectives describes the examples below.
   a. Corporate executives make more money because they decide who gets what in their organizations.
   b. Engineers make more money than butlers because of their education.
   c. Poor children tend to have low self-esteem.
2. How did Marx explain the stratification of society?
3. According to the symbolic interactionists, people are socialized to accept the existing stratification structure through _____.
   a. the "I"
   b. evolution
   c. conflict
   d. the self-concept

Critical Thinking

4. **Making Comparisons** Compare and contrast the explanations given by functionalism, conflict theory, and symbolic interactionism for the existence of poor people in the United States.

Focus on Research

Field Research: Who's Popular, Who's Not?

In 1995, sociologist Donna Eder and her research team studied popularity among middle-schoolers. They observed lunchtime interactions and attended extracurricular activities. After several months of observation, informal interviews were conducted with individuals and groups. To capture interaction for closer study, the researchers received student and parental permission for audio and video recordings.

For adolescent males, playing sports is a way to become popular.

Eder and her colleagues found that in the sixth grade, there were no elite groups. Seventh and eighth graders, however, did not see each other as equals; popular seventh graders were divided along gender lines. By the eighth grade, the two groups intermingled. In both grades, popularity was based on how many others knew who you were and wanted to talk with you.

Status differences could arise in the seventh and eighth grades because cheerleading and team sports existed as a way to become highly visible. Realizing the source of their prestige, male athletes took every opportunity to display symbols of their team affiliation. Team uniforms, jerseys, and athletic shoes were among the most important items of dress. Bandages, casts, and crutches were worn with pride.

Girls could not use sports to gain visibility because female athletics were not as valued by faculty, administrators, or students. Girls, therefore, used cheerleading to make themselves widely known. In addition to performing at basketball and football games, cheerleaders appeared in front of the entire student body at pep rallies and other school events.

Boys made fun of this high-status female activity by mockingly imitating cheers. One male coach joined the mockery by telling football players that either they must practice harder or he would get them cheerleading skirts. He then pretended to cheer in a falsetto voice.

Girls, in contrast, regarded cheerleaders highly. Popular girls in the seventh and eighth grades were either cheerleaders or friends of cheerleaders. Flaunting their status (just as the male athletes did), cheerleaders put on their uniforms as far ahead of games as possible and wore their cheerleading skirts for extracurricular school activities.

Working with the Research

Which of the three major theoretical perspectives best explains the stratification structure described in this feature? Give reasons for your choice.

Section 3

Social Classes in America

Key Terms

- class consciousness
- working poor
- underclass

Section Preview

Sociologists have identified several social classes in the United States. They include the upper class, the middle class, the working class and the working poor, and the underclass.

class consciousness
identification with the goals and interests of a social class

Class Consciousness

Americans have always been aware of inequality, but they have never developed a sense of **class consciousness**—a sense of identification with the goals and interests of the members of a particular social class. In part because the American public has shown relatively little interest in class differences, sociologists began to investigate inequality rather late. It was not until the 1920s that sociologists in the United States began systematically to identify social classes. Since that time, however, research on this subject has been plentiful. Early efforts to study stratification were mostly case studies of specific communities. Only in relatively recent times have attempts been made to describe the stratification structure of America as a whole.

Since social classes are changeable and full of exceptions, any attempt to identify the social-class structure of American society is hazardous. Nevertheless, sociologists have described some of the major classifications. (See Figure 8.5.)

Figure 8.5 American Class Structure. *What does this chart of the American class structure indicate about stratification in the U.S.?*

Source: Adapted from Dennis Gilbert, *The American Class Structure*, 1998.

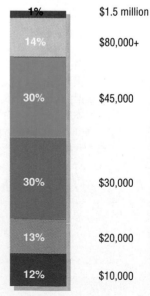

Typical Occupations

Upper Class	Investors, heirs, chief executive officers
Upper Middle Class	Upper-level managers, professionals, owners of medium-sized businesses
Middle Class	Lower-level managers, semiprofessionals, craftspeople, foremen, non-retail salespeople, clerical
Working Class	Low-skill manual, clerical, and retail sales workers
Working Poor	Lowest-paid manual, retail, and service workers
Underclass	Unemployed people, people in part-time menial jobs, people receiving public assistance

Typical Incomes

%	Income
1%	$1.5 million
14%	$80,000+
30%	$45,000
30%	$30,000
13%	$20,000
12%	$10,000

The Upper Class

The upper class includes only 1 percent of the population (Gilbert, 1998) and may be divided into the upper-upper class and the lower-upper class. At the top is the "aristocracy." Its members represent the old-money families whose names appear in high society—Ford, Rockefeller, Vanderbilt, and du Pont, among others. The basis for membership in this most elite of clubs is blood rather than sweat and tears. Parents in this class send their children to the best private schools and universities. People in this group seldom marry outside their class.

People are in the lower-upper class more often because of achievement and earned income than because of birth and inherited wealth. Some have made fortunes running large corporations or investing in the stock market. Members of this class may actually be better off financially than members of the upper-upper class. However, they often are not accepted into the most exclusive social circles.

Upper-class people tend to shop at upscale stores such as Saks and Company.

The Middle Classes

Most Americans think of themselves as middle class. In reality, though, only about 40 to 50 percent of Americans fit this description. And most of these people are not in the upper-middle class.

The upper-middle class (14 percent of the population) is composed of those who have been successful in business, the professions, politics, and the military. Basically, this class is made up of individuals and families who benefited

Student Web Activity
Visit the *Sociology and You Web* site at soc.glencoe.com and click on **Chapter 8—Student Web Activities** for an activity on social class.

This family fulfills the American image of comfortable middle-class living.

from the tremendous corporate and professional expansion following World War II. Members of this class earn enough to live well and to save money. They are typically college educated and have high educational and career goals for their children. They do not have national or international power, but they tend to be active in voluntary and political organizations in their communities.

The middle-middle class (30 percent of the population) is a very mixed bag. Its members include owners of small businesses and farms; independent professionals (small-town doctors and lawyers); other professionals (clergy, teachers, nurses, firefighters, social workers, police officers); lower-level managers; and some sales and clerical workers. Their income level, which is at about the national average ($21,181 in 1999), does not permit them to live as well as the upper-middle class. Many have only a high school education, although many have some college, and some have college degrees. Members of this class are interested in civic affairs. They participate in political activities less than the classes above them but more than either the working class or the lower class.

The Working Class

The working class (often referred to as the lower-middle class) comprises almost one-third of the population. Working class people include roofers, delivery truck drivers, machine operators, and salespeople and clerical workers (Rubin, 1994). Although some of these workers may earn more than some middle-class people, in general the economic resources of the working class are lower than those of the middle class.

Members of the working class have below-average income and unstable employment. They generally lack hospital insurance and retirement benefits. The threat of unemployment or illness is real and haunting. Outside of union activities, members of the working class have little opportunity to exercise power or participate in organizations. Members of the working class—even those with higher incomes—are not likely to enter the middle class.

The Working Poor

The **working poor** (13 percent of the population) consists of people employed in low-skill jobs with the lowest pay. Its members are typically the lowest-level clerical workers, manual workers (laborers), and service workers (fast-food servers). Lacking steady employment, the working poor do not earn enough to rise above the poverty line ($17,603 for a family of four in 2000). The working poor tend not to belong to organizations or to participate in the political process. (See also Enrichment Reading: No Shame in My Game on page 460 in Chapter 13.)

The Underclass

The **underclass** (12 percent of the population) is composed of people who are usually unemployed and who come from families with a history of unemployment for generations. They either work in part-time menial jobs (unloading trucks, picking up litter) or are on public assistance. In addition

> The upper class is a nation's past; the middle class is its future.
>
> **Ayn Rand**
> **novelist**

working poor
people employed in low-skill jobs with the lowest pay who do not earn enough to rise out of poverty

underclass
people typically unemployed who came from families that have been poor for generations

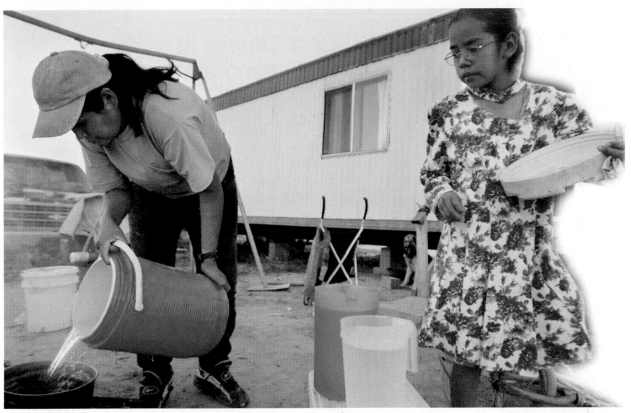

This Navajo single mother belongs to the underclass, America's poorest.

to a lack of education and skills, many members of the underclass have other problems. Physical or mental disabilities are common, and many are single mothers with little or no income.

The most common shared characteristic of the working poor and the underclass is a lack of skills to obtain jobs that pay enough to meet basic needs. There are many routes into these classes—birth, old age, loss of a marriage partner, lack of education or training, alcoholism, physical or mental disability. There are, however, very few paths out. Poverty in the United States, another way to discuss the working poor and the underclass, is the topic of the next section.

Section 3 Assessment

1. Statistically, out of 500 people, how many would belong to the upper class?
2. What is a major distinction between members of the upper-middle and the middle-middle classes?
3. Which class is the largest segment of society?

Critical Thinking

4. **Summarizing Information** Chapter 5 discussed the concept of status. How does ascribed status relate to social class? How does achieved status relate to social class?

World View

Social Classes in World Perspective

The World Bank, whose business it is to dispense economic advice and loans to low- and middle-income countries, continuously monitors income levels around the world. The map below displays the World Bank's classification of countries in terms of per capita income. For example, the United States is one of the few nations with a "high-income" economy—one that has a gross national product (GNP) per capita of over $9,655.

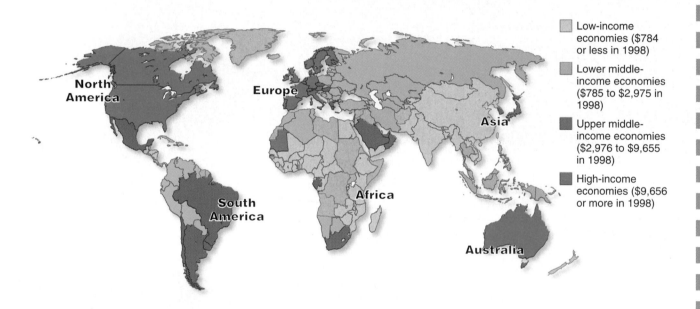

Low-income economies ($784 or less in 1998)

Lower middle-income economies ($785 to $2,975 in 1998)

Upper middle-income economies ($2,976 to $9,655 in 1998)

High-income economies ($9,656 or more in 1998)

Interpreting the Map

1. Explain the definitions of the four income groups.
2. Identify two countries within each of the four income categories.
3. Why do you think the U.S. is one of the few countries to fall within the high-income category?
4. Compare poverty in the United States to poverty in low-income economies.

Source: World Bank, 1999.

Section 4

Poverty in America

Key Terms

- absolute poverty
- relative poverty
- feminization of poverty

Measuring Poverty

Absolute poverty is the absence of enough money to secure life's necessities—enough food, a safe place to live, and so forth. It is possible, however, to have the things required to remain alive and still be poor. We measure **relative poverty** by comparing the economic condition of those at the bottom of a society with the economic conditions of other members of that society. According to this measure, the definition of poverty can vary. It would not, for example, be the same in India as in the United States.

How is poverty measured in the United States?   Historically, the United States government has measured poverty by setting an annual income level and considering people poor if their income is below that level. As noted earlier, in 2000 that figure was $17,603 for a family of four.

How many Americans are poor?   Poverty is widespread throughout the United States. According to 2000 U.S. Census Bureau reports, the poor comprise 11.8 percent of the American population, or more than 32.2 million people. Great poverty existed when it became a national political and social issue in the 1960s. Forty years later, poverty in America is still a problem (Newman, 1999). (See Figure 8.6 on page 260.)

Section Preview

Poverty can be measured in absolute or relative terms. The poor in the U.S. are disproportionately represented by African Americans, Latinos, women, and children.

absolute poverty
the absence of enough money to secure life's necessities

relative poverty
a measure of poverty based on the economic disparity between those at the bottom of a society and the rest of the society

From the slums of Calcutta to a project in the United States, what do these photos say about the relativity of poverty?

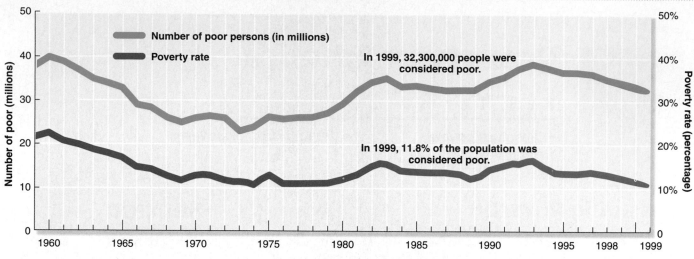

Source: U.S. Bureau of the Census, *Poverty in the United States: 1999,* 2000.

Figure 8.6 Number of Poor and Poverty Rate: 1959–1999. *This graph shows two types of information: (1) the number of poor in the total population and (2) the poverty rate as a percentage of the total population. Why is it often helpful to have related information plotted on the same graph?*

Source: U.S. Bureau of the Census, *Poverty in the United States: 1999,* 2000.

Identifying the Poor

Minorities, female-headed households, children under eighteen years of age, elderly people, people with disabilities, and people who live alone or with nonrelatives make up the most disadvantaged groups in the United States.

How are race and ethnicity related to poverty? About 47 percent of the poor in America today are non-Latino white. The poverty rate for African Americans and Latinos is much higher than that for whites, however. The poverty rate for whites is 7.5 percent; for African Americans and Latinos about 23 percent. African Americans and Latinos together account for only about one-fourth of the total population, but they make up nearly half of the poor population. (See Figure 8.7.)

How are gender and age related to poverty? Another large segment of the poor population is made up of female-headed households. We can look at this issue in two different ways. We can look at all poor households as a group and determine what proportion of them are headed by females. When we do this, we find that nearly one-half of poor households are female headed. In contrast, when we look at nonpoor households, we find that only about 14 percent are headed by females. Another approach would be to look at all female-headed households as a group and determine what proportion of them are poor. We find that the poverty rate for these households is about 25 percent, compared with just under 10 percent for all families.

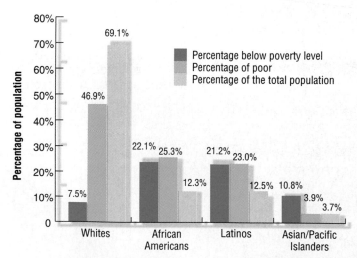

Figure 8.7 The Distribution of Poverty in the U.S. *What are the most important conclusions you would reach from this figure?*

Source: U.S. Bureau of the Census, 2000.

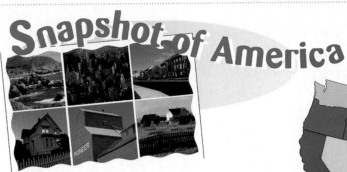

Snapshot of America

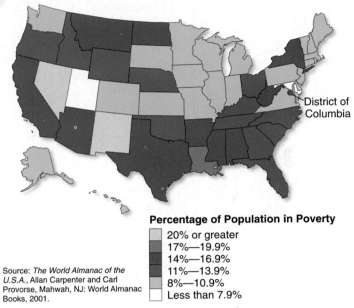

District of Columbia

Percentage of Population in Poverty

Although the U.S. economy is booming, some people are concerned that many have not benefited from this prosperity. In fact, many people still live in poverty. This map shows the percentage of the poor by state.

Percentage of Population in Poverty
- 20% or greater
- 17%—19.9%
- 14%—16.9%
- 11%—13.9%
- 8%—10.9%
- Less than 7.9%

Source: *The World Almanac of the U.S.A.*, Allan Carpenter and Carl Provorse, Mahwah, NJ: World Almanac Books, 2001.

Interpreting the Map

1. Can you make any generalization about poverty from this map?
2. If you were the governor of your state, what would your platform on poverty be? Be specific.

Adapted from *The World Almanac of the U.S.A.*, 2001.

By either measure, then, households headed by females are poorer than those headed by males. A related factor is the poverty rate for children under six years of age. The current rate for this group is about 22 percent—the highest rate for any age group in the United States (U.S. Bureau of the Census, 1999a). The high poverty rates for women and children reflect a trend in U.S. society. Between 1960 and today, women and children make up a larger proportion of the poor. Sociologists refer to this trend as the **feminization of poverty** (*The State of America's Children*, 1998).

There are several reasons why women have a higher risk of being poor. As we discuss in more detail in Chapter 10 (see pages 323–324), women earn only about $.72 for every dollar earned by men. Women with children find it more difficult to find and keep regular, long-term employment. A lack of good child-care facilities adds to the likelihood that they will not be able to continue working.

Older Americans account for another large segment of the poor. About 9 percent of people aged sixty-five or older live in poverty (U.S. Bureau of the Census, 2000b). Another large segment of the poor are people with disabilities—those who are blind, deaf, or otherwise disabled. This group accounts for some 12 percent of America's poor. Finally, more than one out of every four poor persons lives either alone or with nonrelatives.

feminization of poverty
a trend in U.S. society in which women and children make up an increasing proportion of the poor

Blaming the victim is easy. Accepting blame is harder.

Responses to the Problem of Poverty

Before the mid-1960s, fighting poverty was not a major goal of the federal government. Some programs, such as Social Security and Aid to Families with Dependent Children, had been enacted during the Great Depression. These measures did not usually reach the lowest levels of needy citizens, however. Finally in 1964, President Lyndon Johnson marshalled the forces of the federal government to begin a War on Poverty.

What were the goals of the War on Poverty?   The philosophy behind the War on Poverty was to help poor people help themselves (Patterson, 1986; Jacoby, 1997; Barry, 1999). President Johnson's predecessor, President John F. Kennedy, believed that if the chains of poverty were to be broken, it had to be through self-improvement, not temporary relief. Accordingly, almost 60 percent of the first poverty budget was earmarked for youth opportunity programs and the work experience program (work and job training designed primarily for welfare recipients and unemployed fathers).

Hopes for positive results from the War on Poverty were high. However, not all of the programs were as successful as predicted. Indeed, some have come under severe criticism. These criticisms center around supposed widespread abuses and the fear that the system encourages people to become dependent upon the government longer than is necessary. "Fixing" the way social welfare should be provided and payments should be distributed has been the focus of many hot political debates.

Wealth is conspicuous, but poverty hides.

James Reston
American journalist

Welfare Reform

In 1999, actual spending for education, training, employment, and social services was $56 billion, or 3 percent of total U.S. government expenditures. Payments for Temporary Assistance for Needy Families (TANF) was less than 1 percent of the federal budget.

What is the nature of welfare reform?

The most recent legislation on welfare reform, enacted in 1996, limits the amount of time those able to work can receive welfare payments. The bill has three major elements: it reduces welfare spending, it increases state and local power to oversee welfare rules, and it adds new restrictions on welfare eligibility. For example, benefits to children of unwed teenage mothers are denied unless the mothers remain in school and live with an adult. Cash aid to able-bodied adults will be terminated if they fail to get a job after two years.

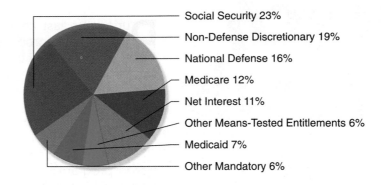

- Social Security 23%
- Non-Defense Discretionary 19%
- National Defense 16%
- Medicare 12%
- Net Interest 11%
- Other Means-Tested Entitlements 6%
- Medicaid 7%
- Other Mandatory 6%

Has welfare reform worked?

It is too early to give a final evaluation of this latest attempt at welfare reform. But a recent major study indicates that the welfare rolls have decreased more dramatically than most predicted (Loprest, 1999). Just over seven million people were on welfare in 1999, down from over twelve million in 1996 when the welfare bill was signed. Well over half of those leaving the welfare rolls report finding jobs. Only a small percentage of recipients have been removed from the rolls because of the new time limits on benefits.

There is a darker side, however. Most of those leaving the rolls since 1996 hold entry-level jobs—in restaurants, cleaning services, and retail stores—earning less than $7 per hour. Despite extraordinary national economic prosperity, most of those leaving public assistance are at the bottom of the economy with little hope of advancing. One-fourth work at night, and over half report child-care problems. Most have jobs without health insurance. A substantial minority report a food shortage and difficulty paying rent. In short, many of those leaving welfare still live in poverty. The true test of the success of welfare reform will come in a few years when the economy weakens, when we get down to the harder cases still on the rolls, and when the last time limits take effect for the more difficult cases (Rosin and Harris, 1999).

Figure 8.8 The Federal Government Dollar—Where It Goes. *Where is the largest share of the federal dollar spent?*

Source: "A Citizen's Guide to the Federal Budget," Washington, D.C., 2001.

Section 4 Assessment

1. Discuss the difference between absolute and relative measures of poverty.
2. Which of the following is *not* one of the major categories of poor people in the United States?
   a. children under age eighteen
   b. able-bodied men who refuse to work
   c. elderly people
   d. people with disabilities
   e. people who live alone or with nonrelatives
3. Do government welfare programs affect the poor's decision to work? Explain.

Critical Thinking

4. **Understanding Cause and Effect** Describe the feminization of poverty. How does this trend affect the motivation to have children?

the economic conditions of others is called _____.

13. The creation of layers, or strata, of people who possess unequal shares of scarce resources is called _____.

14. _____ is the absence of enough money to secure life's necessities.

15. A segment of the population whose members hold similar amounts of resources and share values, norms, and an identifiable lifestyle is called _____.

16. The mobility that occurs from one generation to the next is known as _____.

Reviewing the Facts

1. Examine the graph in Figure 8.7 on page 260 of your text. The graph illustrates that just over 46 percent of all poor people in the United States are white, while only 12% of the population is poor. What can you conclude from the graph about the representation of white people in terms of the total population of poor people?

2. According to Figure 8.8 on page 263, where does the federal government spend the largest share of the federal budget?

3. Describe false consciousness.

4. Explain how a sociologist determines relative poverty.

5. A man who has worked at a factory for twenty years loses his job because of layoffs. After several months, he ends up homeless. What type of social mobility is illustrated in this scenario?

6. Bill Gates has an estimated net worth of $90 billion. How would sociologists label Gates in terms of social class?

Thinking Critically

1. **Analyzing Information** As implied in "Using Your Sociological Imagination" on page 241, attitudes about welfare spending are partially shaped by politicians and the media. Why do you think the media portray welfare spending as such a serious problem when it represents such a small portion of federal spending? Why do Americans seem to complain less about the money spent on military or science projects?

2. **Applying Concepts** At least a hundred members of Congress are millionaires, which suggests that power and wealth do go hand in hand. Why is it unlikely that a poor person would become a member of Congress? Why do many poor people not participate in voting and political parties? What implications does this have for democratic government?

3. **Interpreting Graphs** In Figure 8.3, "Prestige Rankings of Selected Occupations in the United States," surgeons are rated as having the most prestigious job. In your view, what jobs on this list are essential? What jobs could society do without? Are there high-prestige jobs that are really not essential? What does this say about prestige rankings?

Create a diagram similar to the one below to record your answer.

JOBS—ESSENTIAL AND NOT ESSENTIAL TO SOCIETY

Essential	Prestige Rank	Not Essential	Prestige Rank
Surgeon	87	Disc Jockey	45

4. **Analyzing Information** Herbert Gans (1971), a noted sociologist, has written about the functions of poverty. He says that poverty serves many useful purposes in society. For example, the poor act as dishwashers, maids, and parking attendants. What are some other ways in which poverty might benefit society? What are some conflicts that poverty causes?

5. **Summarizing Information** Can you describe the cultural values underlying the federal government's philosophy in the War on Poverty in the 1960s?

6. **Making Inferences** The sinking of the luxury liner *Titanic* offers some insights into social class. Among first-class passengers, only 3 percent of the women died, and none of the children died. Among third-class passengers, 45 percent of the women died, and 70 percent of

the children died. In all, 76 percent of the third-class passengers died, compared with 40 percent of the first-class passengers. What implications would you draw from these numbers? Is it important to know that the third-class passengers were restricted to the lower decks and thus farther away from the lifeboats?

Sociology Projects

1. **Understanding Disadvantaged Families** This activity may provide some insight into the difficulties faced by disadvantaged families every day. Work on the task with three or four of your classmates. Tear a sheet of paper into six pieces. On each piece, write one of the following: health care, education for my children, car maintenance, food, and housing. Now, imagine that because of an unexpected financial setback, you do not have enough money to take care of all these necessities and will need to eliminate one. Reach consensus to decide which category to eliminate.

2. **Researching Employment** Using the employment section from your local newspaper, look for job ads in the following categories: jobs that require postgraduate degrees (highly skilled), jobs that require college or special training, and unskilled jobs. Which category has the most jobs available? What assumptions could you make about the job market based on analyzing these ads? What factors might influence how and where employers advertise certain kinds of jobs?

3. **Perception and Reality** One of the themes of sociology is the difference between perception and reality. Write down five perceptions that you have heard people say about others based on their social class. Next to each, describe the reality based on information in this text or additional research. If not sure, write "unknown–needs further research." For example, a common perception of wealthy people is that they consider themselves superior to other people (snobbery). The reality is that no one has ever found a correlation between how much money you have and how nice you are.

4. **Social Class** From magazines and newspapers, cut out as many pictures as you can find of different classes to make a montage. Label or circle traits that led you to determine that a person was in a particular class. (For example, the person may be driving a luxury car or working with hand tools.)

Technology Activity

1. The National Center for Children in Poverty measures poverty rates for children in the United States. Visit its web site at http://cpmcnet.columbia.edu/dept/nccp/.

   a. What is the Young Child Poverty Rate (YCPR) in the United States?

   b. How does the YCPR in the United States compare to that of other industrialized Western nations?

   c. Now click on "Child Poverty Facts" and select "Young Child Poverty in the States—Wide Variation and Significant Change." Scroll down to the map of the United States. How does your state compare to the other states?

   d. Now scroll further down the page to the table entitled "Change in the percentage and number of children under age six in poverty, by state, 1979–1983 to 1992–1996." What is your state's most recent YCPR? Has the percentage increased or decreased from the earlier YCPR?

   e. Go back to the "Child Poverty Facts" page and select "Poverty and Brain Development in Early Childhood." According to this page, when is the period for a child's optimal brain development? What are some of the pathways through which a child in poverty is put at risk for poor brain development? How do you think poverty affects these pathways?

271

Chapter 8

Enrichment Reading
The Lives of
Homeless Women

by Elliot Liebow

On the street or in a shelter, homelessness is hard living. . . . How do they manage to slog through day after day, with no end in sight? How, in a world of **unremitting** grimness, do they manage to laugh, love, enjoy friends, even dance and play the fool? How, in short, do they stay fully human while body and soul are under continuous and grievous assault?

Simple physical survival is within the grasp of almost everyone willing and able to reach out for it. As the women thrash about, awash in a sea of need, emergency shelters, along with public assistance in the form of cash, food stamps, and medical assistance, make it just possible for many of the women to keep their heads above water. Through the use of shelters, soup kitchens, and hospital emergency rooms, it is even possible for most homeless people who do not get public assistance to survive at some minimal level without benefit of a structured assistance program.

At their very best, however, these bare-boned elements of a life-support system merely make life possible, not necessarily tolerable or livable. Serious problems remain. Homelessness can transform what for others are little things into **insurmountable hurdles.** Indeed, homelessness in general puts a premium on "little things." Just as some homeless women seem to have learned (more than most of us, perhaps) to value a small gesture of friendship, a nice day, a bus token, or a little courtesy that others might take for granted or not notice at all, so too can events or circumstances that would be trivial irritants to others approach **catastrophic proportions** for the homeless person.

For homeless women on the street, the struggle for **subsistence** begins at the animal level—for food, water, shelter, security, and safe sleep. In contrast, homeless women in shelters usually have these things; their struggle begins at the level of human rather than animal needs—protection of one's property, health care, and avoidance of boredom. The struggle then moves rapidly to the search for companionship, modest measures of independence, dignity, and self-respect, and some hope and faith in the future. . . .

For some of the women, day-by-day hardships begin with the problem of getting enough sleep. A few women complained they could never get any sleep in a shelter. Grace was one of them. "There's no getting sleep in a shelter," she said. "Only rest. . . ."

There was indeed much night noise and movement. There was snoring, coughing, sneezing, wheezing, retching, . . . cries from bad dreams, occasional weeping or seizures, talking aloud to oneself or to someone else who may or may not have been present, and always movement to and from the bathroom. Grace was complaining about noise, and she found a partial remedy in ear plugs. But ear plugs could not help those women like Kathleen who were kept awake not by noise but by questions: Is this for me? How did I end up here? How will I get out? But eventually, as the night wore on, there was a lot of snoring, and that meant that, Grace and Kathleen notwithstanding, there was a lot of sleeping, too.

Having to get up at 5:30 A.M., and be out of the shelter by 7:00 was a major hardship of shelter life. It was not simply the fact of having to get up and out, but rather that the women had to do this every day of the week, every day of the year (Thanksgiving and Christmas Day excepted), no matter what the weather or how they felt. On any given morning, as the women drifted onto the street, one might see two or three ailing women—this one with a fever or cough or a headache, that one with a limp or stomach ache or other ailment—pick up their bags and walk silently into the weather. . . .

Along with **perennial** fatigue, boredom was one of the great trials of homelessness. Killing time was not a major problem for everyone but it was high on most women's lists of hardships. Betty could have been speaking for most of them when she talked about the problem. On a social visit to the state psychiatric hospital where, four years earlier, she had been an inpatient in an alcoholic program, Betty sought out a nurse named Lou. They embraced and Lou asked Betty what she was doing these days. Betty said she was living in a shelter. Lou said that was a shame, and asked Betty how she spent her time.

"I walk the streets," said Betty. "Twelve hours and 15 minutes a day, every day, I walk the streets. Is that what I got sober for? To walk the streets?" Betty went on to say that she sits on a lot of park benches looking for someone to talk to. Many times there is no one, so she talks to the birds. She and the birds have done a lot of talking in her day, she said. . . .

Some of the women with jobs also had trouble killing time. Like the others, Grace had to leave the shelter by 7:00 A.M. but she couldn't report to work much before 9:00, and her job was less than a 10-minute drive away. "Have you ever tried to kill two hours in the morning, every morning, with nowhere to go and nothing to do?" she asked. "I have some tapes I can listen to in the car—some Christmas carols and some Bible readings. But two hours? Every day?"

. . . It is all too easy to think of homeless people as having few or no possessions . . . , but one of the major and most talked-about problems was storage—how to keep one's clothing, essential documents, and other belongings secure and **accessible.** . . . Stealing was believed to be common: "You've got to expect these things in shelters" was heard from staff and women alike. The end result was that many homeless women who would have left their belongings behind had they had a safe place to store them were forced to take most of their belongings with them. Some wore them in layers. Others carried them. They had become, in short, bag ladies.

During a discussion of Luther Place, one of the best-run shelters in downtown Washington, one of the women said Luther Place was OK but she didn't like the women there—they were all bag ladies. One of the other women objected that the women at Luther Place were no different from women in other shelters. They were bag ladies, she said, because Luther Place had no storage space. . . .

Past and future . . . and even one's self were **embedded** in one's belongings. When Louise could no longer pay for storage and lost her belongings to auction, she was surprised at her own reaction to the loss. Her belongings had been so much a part of her, she said, that now that she's lost them, she's not sure who she is.

Source: Excerpted from Elliot Liebow, *Tell Them Who I Am: The Lives of Homeless Women.* New York: Penguin Books, 1995.

Read and React

1. What are the two major problems related to homelessness discussed in this writing?

2. What attitude or belief about the homeless that you had before reading this article has been changed? If none, what did you learn that you didn't know before?

What Does it Mean?

accessible
available; easy to reach

catastrophic proportions
a size approaching disaster; too large to deal with individually

embedded
made a part of; surrounded by

insurmountable hurdles
obstacles or barriers that cannot be overcome

perennial
regularly repeated; enduring and persistent

subsistence
meeting basic needs

unremitting
constant; never ending

CHAPTER 9
Inequalities of Race and Ethnicity

USING Your Sociological Imagination

"The Four Americas" is a report published by a major think tank, a national newspaper, and a prestigious university (Brodie, 1995). These organizations used an extensive national survey to investigate race in the United States. The survey asked people to respond to such questions as "Do you think the average African American is better off, worse off, or as well off as the average white person in terms of jobs, education, housing, and health care?"

Most Asians and Latinos answered that African Americans are doing less well than whites. But most whites thought blacks were doing about equally well.

The evidence shows that the average income of African American households is considerably less than that of white households. Moreover, at each level of education—the gateway to good jobs—African American males earn less than white males. On average, for example, white high school graduates can expect to earn annually nearly as much as African American college graduates with associate degrees. The report concluded that while most minorities understand each other's real-life difficulties, "whites stand alone in their misperceptions of the problems facing minorities in America today."

Whites, of course, are not the only group of people who would benefit from a better understanding of the issues facing all Americans. This chapter will take a close look at how race and ethnicity have affected the ability of people to achieve the American dream.

Sections

1. **Minority, Race, and Ethnicity**
2. **Racial and Ethnic Relations**
3. **Theories of Prejudice and Discrimination**
4. **Minority Groups in the United States**

Learning Objectives

After reading this chapter, you will be able to

❖ describe what sociologists mean by the terms *minority, race,* and *ethnicity.*

❖ discuss patterns of racial and ethnic relations.

❖ discuss the difference between prejudice and discrimination.

❖ explain how functionalists, conflict theorists, and symbolic interactionists view racial inequalities.

❖ compare the condition of American minorities with that of the white majority.

SOCIOLOGY Online

Chapter Overview
Visit the *Sociology and You* Web site at soc.glencoe.com and click on **Chapter 9— Chapter Overviews** to preview chapter information.

Section 1

Minority, Race, and Ethnicity

Key Terms

- minority
- race
- ethnic minority

Section Preview

Sociologists have specific definitions particular to their field of study for *minority, race,* and *ethnicity*. Ethnic minorities have historically been subjected to prejudice and discrimination.

---

minority
a group of people with physical or cultural traits different from those of the dominant group in the society

Minorities

Imagine that one evening, you and eight friends are unable to decide whether to go bowling or to the movies. Being a democratic group, you decide to put the question to a vote. If only three of you vote for the show, the movie fans—being fewer in number—will make up a minority.

But numbers alone are not the basis of the sociological definition of minority. Women in the United States outnumber males, and yet they are still referred to as a minority. Blacks in South Africa and in many large cities in the United States are minority populations even though they outnumber the white population. For sociologists, then, a minority population is defined by something more than size or number.

What are the characteristics of a minority?   In 1945, sociologist Louis Wirth offered the following definition of **minority:**

> We may define a minority as a group of people who, because of their physical or cultural characteristics, are singled out from the others in the society in which they live for differential and unequal treatment, and who therefore regard themselves as objects of collective discrimination. The existence of a minority in a society implies the existence of a corresponding dominant group with higher social status and greater privileges. Minority carries with it the exclusion from full participation in the life of the society.

A minority, then, has several key features.

Which of these teens are members of a minority group? Explain why.

1. *A minority has distinctive physical or cultural characteristics which can be used to separate it from the majority.* Physical characteristics may include such things as skin color, facial features, and disabilities. Cultural characteristics may include accent, religion, language, and parentage. In the past, some people have been forced to carry papers or wear badges that marked them as members of a minority. For example, during the Nazi regime, Jews in German-occupied countries were forced to wear yellow stars to separate them from non-Jewish citizens.

2. *The minority is dominated by the majority.* Because the majority is the dominating group, it holds an unequal share of the desired goods, services, and privileges. Further, minority members have fewer opportunities to get these goods and services. The best jobs are hard for minorities to get because of a lack of education or unfair hiring practices.

3. *Minority traits are often believed by the dominant majority to be inferior.* This presumed inferiority can be used to justify unequal treatment. For example, a majority may justify job discrimination by depicting a minority as shiftless or lazy.

4. *Members of the minority have a common sense of identity, with strong group loyalty.* Efforts to keep the minority isolated create empathy among those suffering discrimination. Within the minority, there is a "consciousness of kind." Because of this sense of common identity, members of the minority accept a "we" and "they" vocabulary.

5. *The majority determines who belongs to the minority through ascribed status.* People become members of the minority at birth. Thus, membership is an ascribed status and is not easily changed. This is especially true when physical characteristics such as *race* are involved.

Defining Race

Members of a **race** share certain biologically inherited physical characteristics that are considered equally important within a society. Biologists use characteristics such as skin color, hair color, hair texture, facial features, head form, eye color, and height to determine race. The most common system classifies races into three major divisions—Negroid, Mongoloid, and Caucasian.

How many races are represented in this photo? On what basis did you make that determination?

race
people sharing certain inherited physical characteristics that are considered important within a society

Is there a scientific basis for race? Although certain physical features have been associated with particular races, scientists have known for a long time that there is no such thing as a "pure" race. Features, or markers, typical of one race show up in other races quite frequently. For example, some people born into African American families are assumed to be white because of their facial features and light skin color. Most scientists consider racial classifications arbitrary and misleading. For students of sociology, social attitudes and characteristics that relate to race are more important than physical differences.

But aren't some physical characteristics superior? It has sometimes been argued that certain physical characteristics often associated with race are superior and others are inferior. In fact, physical characteristics are superior only in the sense that they provide advantages for living in particular environments. For example, a narrow opening between eyelids protects against bright light and driving cold such as found in Siberia or Alaska. A darker skin is better able to withstand a hot sun. But these physical differences are controlled by a very few genes. In fact, geneticists claim that there may be more genetic difference between a tall person and a short person than between two people of different races who are the same height. Only about six genes in the human cell control skin color, while a person's height is affected by dozens of genes. Thus a six-foot white male may be closer genetically to a black male of the same height than to a five-foot white male. What is important to remember is that there is no scientific evidence that connects any racial characteristic with innate superiority or inferiority (Hurley, 1998). There is, for example, no evidence of *innate* differences in athleticism or intelligence among the various races.

Ethnicity

The term *ethnicity* comes from the Greek word *ethnos*, originally meaning "people" or "nation." Thus, the Greek word referred to cultural and national identity. Today, an **ethnic minority** is socially identified by unique characteristics related to culture or nationality. Just as physical characteristics define racial minorities, cultural differences define ethnic minorities.

An ethnic minority is a subculture defined by its own language, religion, values, beliefs, norms, and customs. (See page 98 in Chapter 3 for an introduction to subcultures.) Like any subculture, it is part of the larger culture—its members work in the majority, or host, economy, send their children through the host educational system, and are subject to the laws of the land. Ethnic minorities are also separate from the larger culture. The separation may continue because the ethnic minority wishes to maintain its cultural and national origins or because the majority erects barriers that prevent the ethnic group from blending in with the larger culture. For example, Michael Novak (1996) makes a case that members of white ethnic minorities from southern and eastern Europe—Poles, Slavs, Italians, Greeks—have not been able to blend completely into American society. Compared with other white European immigrant groups, such as German immigrants, groups from southern and eastern Europe were more culturally different from the white Anglo-Saxon Protestant (WASP) majority and thus mixed less easily with the majority culture.

Why are ethnic minorities seen as inferior?   Negative attitudes toward ethnic minorities exist in part because of *ethnocentrism*. As you read in Chapter 3, ethnocentrism involves judging others in terms of one's own cultural standards. Ethnocentrism creates the feeling of "us," the group one belongs to, versus "them," the other groups that are out there.

People in the majority, out of loyalty to and preference for their own values, beliefs, and norms, may consider other views to be inferior. Because members of ethnic minorities do not measure up to the majority's conception of appropriate ways of behaving, it may be assumed that something is wrong with them. Ethnocentric judgments are often expressed as prejudice and discrimination. Figure 9.1 shows American attitudes toward specific immigrant groups. In general, European immigrants are viewed more positively than non-European immigrants.

> **ethnic minority**
> group identified by cultural, religious, or national characteristics

Figure 9.1. Attitudes of Americans Toward Immigrant Minorities.   *The results of a Gallup poll are displayed in this graph of attitudes toward various immigrant groups in the United States. What pattern is reflected in this graph among the groups that are most favored as helping the country?*

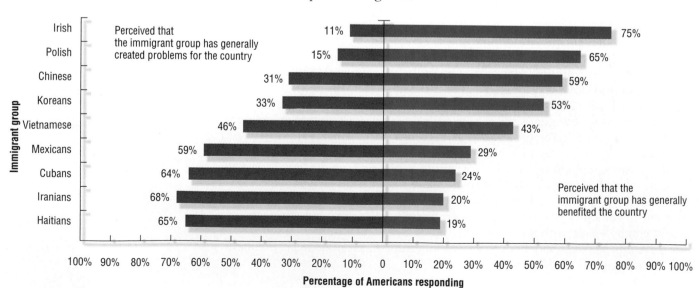

Another Place

The Travelling People

The following excerpt describes the Irish "Travelling People," who are viewed by mainstream Irish as inferior.

They are Ireland's unrecognized minority—homeless and ostracized. Despite public disapproval, their family groups wander the Irish countryside. Other than a limited number of official halting sites they have no place to stop. Most live by the side of the road. They bathe, eat, and sleep in public. They live without electricity or permanent running water, bathing facilities, or toilets. Their child-mortality rate is similar to those in Third World countries, and there is a 98 percent illiteracy rate among adults. According to the Economic and Social Research Institute's 1985 report, "The circumstances of the Irish Travelling People are intolerable. No humane and decent society once made aware of such circumstances could permit them to persist."

But although local political groups and organizations have expressed the need to create permanent housing for the Travellers (most commonly described as "gypsies" or "tinkers"), the settled community prefers what Traveller Nell McDonaugh calls an "unspoken segregation." Travellers are evicted from areas not designated as official halting sites, and grassy lanes that Traveller groups have frequented for years are blocked and barred. Most official halting sites are located in undesirable, often industrial, areas.

Most settled people want nothing to do with Travellers. Popular belief has it that Travellers draw the dole [welfare] in more than one county at a time, are troublemakers, and leave piles of garbage in their wake. Many local people are opposed to having halting sites in their vicinity. Why should "respectable" people support itinerants?

But these "homeless" outcasts have filled a social niche in Ireland for centuries. Theirs may be a distinct lifestyle, and their traditions are unlike those of other Irish, but they are, nonetheless, Irish. In a traditionally rural society, Travellers served acceptable social purposes as itinerant farm workers, metal craftsmen, lace makers, and storytellers. But in today's settled urban society, this integrated group of nomads are a people displaced by and at odds with contemporary expectations. They are a community without a place in its own homeland and a cultural group in danger of losing its identity.

Source: Excerpted and reprinted with permission from *The World & I,* Amy Seidman, June 1993, *The Washington Times Corporation,* © 1993, pp. 250, 252.

Thinking It Over

Use either functionalism or conflict theory to explain this attitude toward the Travellers.

Section 1 Assessment

1. Summarize the five main characteristics of a minority.
2. What is the difference between race and ethnicity? Between race and nationality?

Critical Thinking

3. **Summarizing Information** Identify the main racial or ethnic minorities in your area. Are you a member of any minority groups? What are they?

I know of no rights of race superior to the rights of man.

Frederick Douglas
American abolitionist

Section 2

Racial and Ethnic Relations

Key Terms

- assimilation
- cultural pluralism
- genocide

- subjugation
- de jure segregation
- de facto segregation

Section Preview

Patterns of racial and ethnic relations take two forms: assimilation and conflict. Patterns of assimilation include Anglo-conformity, melting pot, cultural pluralism, and accommodation. Conflict patterns include genocide, population transfer, and subjugation.

assimilation
the blending or fusing of minority groups into the dominant society

Patterns of Assimilation

Generally, minority groups are either accepted—which leads to *assimilation*—or rejected—which leads to *conflict*. Within these two broad approaches, however, is a wide range of outcomes.

Anglo-conformity has been the most common form of assimilation in U.S. society.

Assimilation refers to the blending or fusing of minority groups into the dominant society. When a racial or ethnic minority is integrated into a society, its members are given full participation in all aspects of the society. Assimilation has taken several forms in the United States: *Anglo-conformity, melting pot, cultural pluralism,* and *accommodation.*

What is the most common pattern of assimilation? Anglo-conformity has been the most prevalent pattern of assimilation in America. *Anglo* is a prefix used to indicate an American of English descent. In Anglo-conformity, traditional American institutions are maintained. Immigrants are accepted as long as they conform to the "accepted standards" of the society. Anglo-conformity is the least egalitarian pattern of assimilation because the immigrant minority is required to conform. By implication, it must either give up or suppress its own values.

Is America more like a melting pot or a tossed salad? A second pattern of assimilation is the *melting pot,* in which all ethnic and racial minorities voluntarily blend together. Older history textbooks, in describing the immigrant experience in the United States, often referred to a melting pot of cultures. However, there is some question about how much fusing of cultures has really taken place. Instead of a melting pot, many sociologists are now using the idea of a "tossed salad," in which traditions and cultures exist side by side. The cultures of the Tejanos in Texas and the Creoles of New

Orleans are examples. This pattern of assimilation is called **cultural pluralism.** It recognizes immigrants' desire to maintain at least a remnant of their "old" ways. In so doing, however, the immigrants have an impact on institutions in the United States. Because of the large numbers of Hispanic immigrants, for example, many states have instituted bilingual education programs in public schools. The government now routinely makes official forms available in both English and Spanish, many churches throughout the country conduct services in both languages, and cable television stations offer English and Spanish audio tracks.

Accommodation is an extreme form of cultural pluralism. It occurs when a minority maintains its own culturally unique way of life. The minority learns to deal with, or accommodate, the dominant culture when necessary but remains independent in language and culture. The Cubans in Miami and the Amish in Pennsylvania are examples of distinct groups within larger communities that have kept separate identities.

cultural pluralism
desire of a group to maintain some sense of identity separate from the dominant group

Patterns of Conflict

In looking for broad patterns of conflict, sociologists examine historical records and analyze current events. Three basic patterns have emerged that describe approaches that dominant cultures take in their rejection of minority groups. These are *genocide, population transfer,* and *subjugation* (Mason, 1970).

What is the most extreme pattern of conflict? At the extreme, conflict takes the form of **genocide,** the systematic effort to destroy an entire population. One of the best-known examples is the Holocaust, Adolf Hitler's attempt to destroy all European Jews during the 1930s and 1940s. (See Figure 9.2 below.) Less well known is the "Rape of Nanking," begun in

genocide
the systematic effort to destroy an entire population

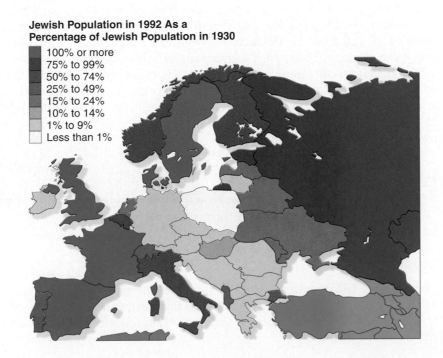

Jewish Population in 1992 As a Percentage of Jewish Population in 1930

- 100% or more
- 75% to 99%
- 50% to 74%
- 25% to 49%
- 15% to 24%
- 10% to 14%
- 1% to 9%
- Less than 1%

Figure 9.2. Impact of the Holocaust. *One of the worst examples of genocide was the Nazis' attempt, in the 1930s and 1940s, to exterminate the European Jewish population. This map shows the decline in Jewish population in European countries as a result of the Holocaust.*

The Cherokees were not the only Native American population transferred from their homes. The Creeks and the Seminoles were also forcibly removed by U.S. troops.

subjugation
process by which a minority group is denied equal access to the benefits of a society

de jure segregation
denial of equal access based on the law

de facto segregation
denial of equal access based on everyday practice

We're not where we want to be. And we're not where we're going to be. But we are sure a long way from where we were.

**Rev. M. L. King, Jr.
civil rights leader**

1937, during which the Japanese massacred an estimated 260,000 to 350,000 Chinese men, women, and children (Chang, 1998).

Tragically, genocide campaigns are more common in world history than might be supposed. Recently, the Serbians have been accused of conducting campaigns of "ethnic cleansing" against the Muslims in Bosnia and Kosovo. In 1994, the Tutsi tribe of Rwanda slaughtered 500,000 to 800,000 of the minority Hutu tribe.

What is population transfer? In *population transfer*, a minority is forced either to move to a remote location or to leave entirely the territory controlled by the majority. This was the policy most often used against Native Americans. For example, in 1838, sixteen thousand Cherokees from the southeastern United States were set on a forced march along the "Trail of Tears" to Oklahoma reservations, where they became dependent on the U.S. government. An estimated four thousand Cherokees (nearly a fourth of the tribes) died because of harsh conditions along the Trail of Tears.

What conflict pattern appears most often? **Subjugation** is the most common pattern of conflict. A subjugated minority is denied equal access to the culture and lifestyle of the larger society. Subjugation may be based on the law, or *de jure*. An example was the **de jure segregation** of public schools in the United States during the latter part of the nineteenth century and the first half of the twentieth century. In *Brown vs. Board of Education of Topeka* (1954) the Supreme Court overturned previous case law that had made racial segregation legal in the U.S.

Subjugation may also arise from the everyday practices of people, even when specific laws do not exist to deny opportunities to minority groups. *De facto* is a term used in case law that describes the actual, or real, situation regardless of what the law is. **De facto segregation** is operating when, for example, neighboring homeowners agree among themselves not to sell to members of certain ethnic groups or races. De facto discrimination exists when people of certain backgrounds are not promoted to important positions in local government or in businesses because of widely held stereotypes. Although illegal, the difficulty of proving bias can make this type of subjugation a very effective tool for controlling a minority.

Section 2 Assessment

1. Identify and define four patterns of assimilation.
2. What is the difference between de jure and de facto segregation?

Critical Thinking

3. **Evaluating Information** Work with one or more of your classmates to research and evaluate the impact that the assimilation of Latinos is having on American institutions such as public schools, churches, and government agencies.

Sociology Today

Bridging the Digital Divide

In 2000, Delta Airlines and Ford Motor Company both publicly announced their multimillion-dollar (hundreds of millions, in fact) bet they are placing on their employees (Miller and Silverstein, 2000). Each intends to provide home computers and Internet access to all of their 422,000 workers. It is a new company benefit costing each employee as little as $5 per month.

The bet is that employees become more efficient and effective when they are proficient with computers. Expected payoffs for the companies is improved communication with their workforces, heightened employee morale, and increased employee loyalty. Employees at Ford and Delta enthusiastically welcomed the new benefit.

There is a possible downside for employees. When workers can be reached instantaneously at home day or night, the traditional boundaries between the home and the workplace could erode. And Ford and Delta do have plans to communicate with workers at home. According to sociologist Arlie Hochschild, this apparent gift could be a Trojan horse by extending the "long arm of the workplace." Even worse, some workers fear that companies might intrude on their private lives by monitoring their Internet activities.

There could also be a social upside to wide-scale on-line access. Sociologists have recognized computer literacy as a key to social mobility in the twenty-first century. (See the *Enrichment Reading* entitled "Falling Through the Net" in Chapter 17.) Since those nearer the bottom of the social class structure lack the resources necessary to be computer literate, sociologists fear they will be hopelessly left behind.

Given this situation, widespread exposure of less-skilled workers to computer technology could have benefits Ford and Delta employees may not have considered. Since both companies are encouraging workers' families to use the technology, the spouses and children of a significant number of individuals will have access to an indispensable tool for occupational advancement. While Ford and Delta may be concerned only about keeping their employees out of the digital divide, their action may unintentionally enable many more Americans to cross this divide. Company-provided computer technology at home may become a staple in most future corporate benefit packages.

Doing Sociology

1. Do you believe that computer literacy is a key element in today's job market? Tomorrow's?
2. Evaluate your own capabilities regarding computer technology.
3. Go to your library and examine the employment page of the Sunday edition of a major newspaper. Write a brief report on the extent to which computer literacy appears to be an important qualification in today's urban marketplace.

Section 3

Theories of Prejudice and Discrimination

Key Terms

- prejudice
- racism
- discrimination

- hate crime
- stereotype
- self-fulfilling prophecy

Section Preview

Prejudice involves attitudes, while discrimination is about behavior. Prejudice usually leads to discrimination. Conversely, in some instances, discrimination creates prejudiced attitudes through stereotyping. Each of the three major perspectives looks at different aspects of prejudice.

prejudice
widely held negative attitudes toward a group (minority or majority) and its individual members

racism
an extreme form of prejudice that assumes superiority of one group over others

Prejudice, Racism, and Discrimination

Individuals hold prejudices of many types. To a sociologist, though, **prejudice** has a very particular meaning. It refers to widely held preconceptions of a group (minority or majority) and its individual members. Prejudice involves a generalization based on biased or insufficient information. Prejudiced attitudes are based on strong emotions, so they are often difficult to change, even in the face of overwhelming evidence. It is easier to explain individuals who don't fit the stereotype as exceptions than

it is to reexamine a whole set of established beliefs. For example, many people believe that Asian students have a particular "gift" for mathematics. Suppose that Susie is one of these people. In algebra class, she sits next to an Asian student who is not doing well. Will Susie change her idea about the mathematical abilities of Asian people as a result of this? Probably not. It will be less trouble for her to think that this one Asian student is the exception to the rule.

Racism is an extreme form of prejudice, because it not only involves judging people unfairly, but it assumes that a person's own race or ethnic group is superior. Racists believe that discrimination or exclusion is morally justified because of their own natural superiority.

When prejudice is used as a basis for making decisions—as in denying minorities advancement—then it becomes discrimination.

How is discrimination different from prejudice? While prejudice involves holding biased opinions, **discrimination** involves acting upon those opinions by treating people unfairly. Prejudice does not always result in discrimination, but it often does.

Discrimination takes many forms, including avoiding social contact with members of minority groups, denying them positions that carry authority, and blocking their access to the more exclusive neighborhoods. It can also involve such extremes as attacking or killing minority members.

> **discrimination**
> treating people differently based on ethnicity, race, religion, or culture

Hate Crimes

In 1998, James Byrd, Jr., an African American from Texas, was chained to a pickup truck, then dragged to death. That same year saw Matthew Shepard, a gay college student, tied to a fence and beaten to death. Both incidents fell under a special kind of crime called *hate crimes*.

How are hate crimes different? A **hate crime** is a criminal act that is motivated by extreme prejudice (Lawrence, 1999). Hate crimes involve bias related to race, religion, sexual orientation, national origin, or ancestry (Levin and McDevitt, 1993). Victims include, but are not limited to, African Americans, Native Americans, Latinos, Asian Americans, Jews, gay men, lesbian women, and people with disabilities. While the term *hate crime* is relatively new, the behavior is not. The federal government has kept statistics since 1900. Hate crimes still occur in relatively small numbers, but the frequency is increasing. Just under 8,000 cases were reported to the FBI in 1999. By 2000, forty-three states had passed hate-crime laws.

These federal agency employees are searching through the ashes of an African American church in Mississippi. What would make this case of arson a hate crime?

How does sociology interpret hate crimes? Each of the theoretical perspectives discussed below can help us understand hate crimes. The functionalist might notice that members of a group are bolstering their sense of unity against a common enemy. Some hate crimes, consistent with conflict theory, are based on the belief that the victim is somehow threatening the person's livelihood or self-interest. This is the case when immigrants are attacked out of fear that they will take the jobs of the white majority. Finally, hate crimes always involve labeling. People who commit hate crimes have vocabularies filled with demeaning stereotypes that attempt to justify violence directed against the victims.

> **hate crime**
> a criminal act motivated by prejudice

Stereotypes

A **stereotype** is a set of ideas—based on distortion, exaggeration, and oversimplification—that is applied to all members of a group. Stereotypes appear throughout any society. In the United States, examples of stereotypes include that athletes are "all brawn and no brain" and that politicians are corrupt.

Stereotypes are sometimes created to justify unethical behavior against minority groups. For example, very early relationships between the colonists and

> **stereotype**
> a distorted, exaggerated, or oversimplified image applied to a category of people

Native Americans in early colonial times were relatively peaceful and cooperative. As the population of the colonies grew, however, conflicts over land and resources became more frequent and intense. To justify expansion onto Indian territory, the colonists began perceiving Native Americans as "lying, thieving, un-Christian savages" who did not deserve the rights accorded to white settlers. This image helped the colonists defend their otherwise unjustifiable treatment of the Native American population.

Even marching band members suffer from stereotyping.

Student Web Activity
Visit the *Sociology and You* Web site at soc.glencoe.com and click on **Chapter 9—Student Web Activities** for an activity on examples of stereotypes.

The Functionalist Perspective

In studying prejudice and discrimination, functionalists focus on the dysfunctions caused by these practices. (We will look at this topic in greater detail in Section 4.) When minorities are exploited or oppressed, the social, political, educational, and economic costs to society are extremely high. Furthermore, the safety and stability of the larger society are at risk, because violence periodically erupts between the groups.

Functionalists recognize, however, that by fostering prejudice, a dominant group can create a feeling of superiority over minority groups. This feeling can strengthen its members' own self-concepts. Strangely, then, for the majority culture, functionalists can see a positive aspect to discrimination.

The Conflict Perspective

According to conflict theory, a majority uses prejudice and discrimination as weapons of power to control a minority. The majority does this to increase its control over property, goods, and other resources. The example about stereotypes used by colonists to portray Native Americans is based on the conflict perspective.

In the conflict perspective, despite being common targets, different minorities tend to view one another as competitors rather than as allies in their struggle against the majority (Olzak and Nagel, 1986). Conflict among minorities, particularly African Americans and Latinos, is increasing in the United States as whites leave cities and African Americans assume political power. To many urban blacks, Latinos appear to be benefiting from the civil rights movement waged by African Americans. Many Latinos, on the other hand, believe that African Americans are using their political clout to push an agenda that favors their own community at the expense of others. It remains to be seen if urban African Americans and Latinos will become allies for their mutual welfare or if they will engage in fierce conflict over the scarce resources available to them.

Prejudice is what fools use for reason.

Voltaire
French philosopher

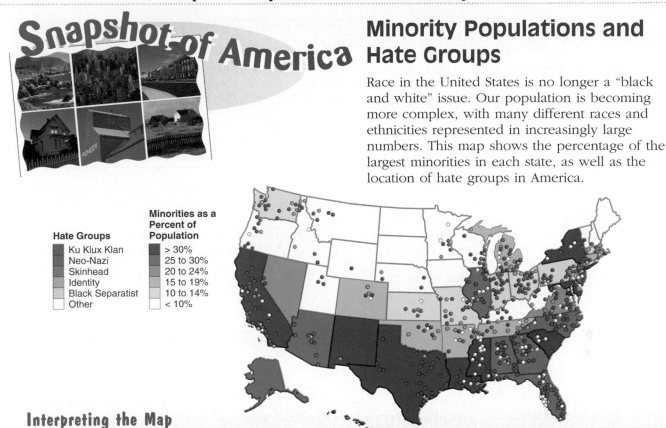

Snapshot of America

Minority Populations and Hate Groups

Race in the United States is no longer a "black and white" issue. Our population is becoming more complex, with many different races and ethnicities represented in increasingly large numbers. This map shows the percentage of the largest minorities in each state, as well as the location of hate groups in America.

Hate Groups
- Ku Klux Klan
- Neo-Nazi
- Skinhead
- Identity
- Black Separatist
- Other

Minorities as a Percent of Population
- > 30%
- 25 to 30%
- 20 to 24%
- 15 to 19%
- 10 to 14%
- < 10%

Interpreting the Map

1. Do you see any relationship between the location of hate groups and the location of minority populations? Explain.

2. Do you see a pattern in the location of U.S. minority populations? Why might U.S. minority populations be distributed as they are?

3. Create a question for your classmates to answer regarding the geographic distribution of U.S. minority populations.

Adapted from the *The State of the U.S.A. Atlas,* New York and Southern Poverty Law Center.

The Symbolic Interactionist Perspective

According to the symbolic interactionist perspective, members of a society learn to be prejudiced in much the same way they learn to be patriotic. Sociologist Gordon Allport (1958) described two stages in the learning of prejudice. In the *pregeneralized learning period,* children may overhear parents make racist or prejudiced statements, but they have not yet learned to separate people by race or ethnic group. By the time children reach the *total rejection stage,* however, they are able to use physical clues to sort people into groups. If children repeatedly hear parents malign a minority, they will reject all members of the group, on all counts and in all situations.

Symbolic interactionists also point out that language itself can reflect prejudices. For example, in Anglo culture, many terms that include *black* are negative. Such terms as *blackball, blacklist, black mark,* and *black eye* illustrate the negative slant associated with the word *black.*

Figure 9.3 Focus on Theoretical Perspectives

Prejudice and Discrimination. This table illustrates how a particular theoretical perspective views a central sociological concept. Switch the concepts around and illustrate how each theoretical perspective would view a different concept. For example, discuss some functions and dysfunctions of the self-fulfilling prophecy.

Theoretical Perspective	Concept	Example
Functionalism	Ethnocentrism	White colonists used negative sterotypes as a justification for taking Native American land.
Conflict Theory	Competition for power	African Americans accuse Latinos of using their political clout to win advantages for themselves.
Symbolic Interactionism	Self-fulfilling prophecy	Members of a minority fail because of the low expectations they have for their own success.

self-fulfilling prophecy an expectation that leads to behavior that causes the expectation to become reality

Symbolic interactionism underlies the concept of the **self-fulfilling prophecy**—an expectation that leads to behavior that then causes the expectation to become a reality. For example, if a student is continually encouraged and told that she is capable of succeeding at a task, she will likely act as if she can succeed. If, however, she is discouraged from trying and told she will probably fail, that same student will likely act in a manner that will cause her to fail. Similarly, if members of any minority are continually treated as if they are less intelligent or less competent than the majority, they may eventually accept this limitation. This acceptance, in turn, may lead them to place less emphasis on education as a way of succeeding. Given this negative interaction, and the lack of opportunity to develop their abilities, members of minorities may become locked in low-level jobs.

Section 3 Assessment

1. Can you hold a prejudice about a group without discriminating against that group? Why or why not?
2. Why do you think most stereotypes are negative? Can you think of any positive stereotypes?
3. Why does conflict exist between African Americans and Latinos?

Critical Thinking

4. **Evaluating Information** Discuss specific ways in which African Americans and Latinos have attempted to resolve their role conflicts.

Tech Trends

Spinning a Web of Hate

White supremacists, neo-Nazis, and other hate groups have discovered the Internet as a channel to spread hatred of Jews, African Americans, homosexuals, and fundamentalist Christians, among others (Sandberg, 1999). From one hate site in 1995, the Anti-Defamation League estimates that there are now thousands of web sites advocating racism, anti-Semitism, and violence. Aryan Nation identifies Jews as the natural enemy of whites; White Pride Network offers a racist joke center; Posse Comitatus defends alleged abortion-clinic bomber Eric Robert Rudolph; World Church of the Creator is violently anti-Christian.

Organized racists use high technology to deliver their message to a mass audience. While members of hate groups used to be recognized by their white hoods or neo-Nazi swastikas, they can now just as easily be wearing business suits instead of brown shirts. The Southern Poverty Law Center is especially concerned about the repackaging of hate-based ideologies to make them appear more respectable to mainstream America. To reach the young, hate web sites offer such child-friendly attractions as crossword puzzles, jokes, cartoons, coloring books, contests, games, and interactive comic strips.

Not all hate-group activity comes from white supremacists who target African Americans. The Southern Poverty Law Center also tracks the activities of Black Separatists and documents several recent hate crimes committed by blacks against whites. In addition, the continued immigration of Asians and Central and South Americans is drawing the angry attention of hate groups of all types. More information on hate group activities can be found at the Southern Poverty Law Center web site, http://www.splcenter.org.

Analyzing the Trends

When the economy is not performing well, membership in hate groups rises, and membership declines when the economy is doing well. Relate this fluctuating membership pattern to scapegoating and conflict theory.

How is propaganda used by hate groups to deliver their message?

Young people today may grow up to be "Internet policemen." This software company CEO designs and markets programs that prevent children from accessing web sites their parents think unsuitable.

Section 4

Minority Groups in the United States

Key Terms

- institutionalized discrimination
- hidden unemployment
- underclass

Section Preview

Discrimination in the United States has caused some ethnic and racial groups to lag behind the white majority in jobs, income, and education. Progress is being made, but gains remain fragile. African American, Latino, Asian American, Native American, and white ethnics are the largest minority groups in this country.

institutionalized discrimination unfair practices that grow out of common behaviors and attitudes and that are a part of the structure of a society

Institutionalized Discrimination

Many people believe that discrimination in the United States ended when civil rights legislation was passed in the 1960s. These laws did stop many discriminatory practices. Nevertheless, minorities in this country still suffer from what sociologists call **institutionalized discrimination.** This type of discrimination results from unfair practices that are part of the structure of society and that have grown out of traditional, accepted behaviors.

Seniority systems, in which promotion and pay increase with years of service, for example, can discriminate against minority workers. Because they were shut out of jobs in the past, members of minorities are just now beginning to enter seniority systems. Having fewer years of service than majority members who have been in the system for years, minority members' chances for quick promotion are slight, even though the seniority systems may not have been intentionally designed to obstruct their progress.

Another example of institutionalized discrimination exists in public education. Schools with large numbers of minority students are more likely to be located in large urban areas than in wealthier suburbs. This is the case in part

Institutionalized discrimination has contributed to the deterioration of some inner-city public schools.

because of white flight to the suburbs. As a result, minority children in many states are more concentrated in school districts with a tax base too low to provide resources equal to those in the suburbs. This lack of funding means that teachers in minority schools receive fewer opportunities for training. Textbooks, when students have them, are outdated. Parental and community support is generally not as strong. There is little, if any, money for new technology, and buildings are badly in need of repair.

Institutionalized discrimination in the United States is reflected in the experiences of minorities—African Americans, Latinos, Native Americans, Asian Americans, white ethnics, and Jewish Americans. For each minority, the social and economic costs of discrimination have been enormous.

African Americans

African Americans make up the largest racial minority group in the United States, numbering almost 34 million, or about 12 percent of the total population. (See Figure 9.4.) They are also one of the oldest minorities, first brought to America as indentured servants and slaves in the early 1600s.

What are the barriers to African American assimilation? There are many reasons for the lack of acceptance of African Americans into the mainstream of U.S. society. Skin color and physical features make it possible to identify at a glance people of African American lineage. This makes it easy for the dominant white ethnic group to create negative stereotypes based on physical characteristics.

A second reason for the continuing minority status of African Americans has its roots in early American history. Brought into the country to labor on plantations, African Americans were immediately assigned to the lowest class status. Even when freed, ex-slaves and their descendants in the United States

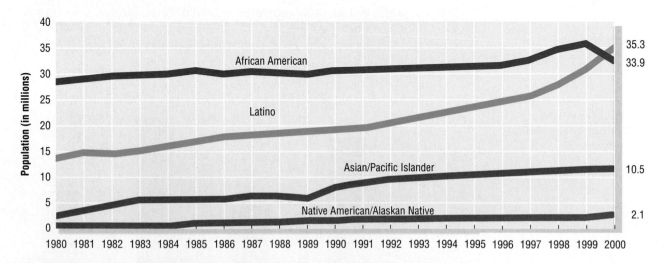

Figure 9.4 U.S. Resident Minority Populations, 1980–2000. *This graph shows the increase in the larger minority populations in the United States since 1980. Are you surprised by the growth of any group?*

Source: U.S. Bureau of the Census, 2000.

Could institutionalized discrimination help to account for the near absence of African Americans in this corporate merger meeting?

were rarely accepted as equal to free whites. Upward social mobility for freed slaves (or any African Americans) was virtually impossible.

Slavery was legally abolished by the Thirteenth Amendment (1865), but the legacy of prejudice and discrimination that grew out of slavery affects African Americans to this day. Practices and laws that segregated the races became institutionalized, especially in the South, but also throughout the country. Such practices continued until the late 1960s, when they were made illegal by the passage of civil rights legislation and by key Supreme Court decisions. In a very real sense, then, African Americans have experienced barely forty years of constitutional equality. The gap between African Americans and whites in education, income, and employment represents the legacy of centuries of prejudice and discrimination.

What are average income levels for African Americans?   As noted in the Sociological Imagination feature opening this chapter, average African American income in the United States is far from equal to the average income for whites. Specifically, African American income is approximately 64 percent that of whites. This means that for every $100 an average white family earns, an average African American family earns $64. Figure 9.5 shows differences in household income for various minority groups.

Not surprisingly, African Americans and whites also differ in wealth (home and car, business assets, and the like). The average African American family holds less than one-quarter of the wealth of the average white family (U.S. Bureau of the Census, 1999e).

How do African Americans fare in the job market?   Part of the reason for the economic differences can be traced to employment patterns. Compared with white men and women, a lower percentage of African American men and women are employed in professional, managerial, technical, and administrative occupations. African Americans are almost twice as likely as whites to work in low-level service jobs (U.S. Department of Labor, 1997).

Figure 9.5 Majority and Minority Median Household Incomes. *Explain why sociologists consider Asian Americans a minority group despite their relatively high annual income.*

Source: U.S. Bureau of the Census, 2000.

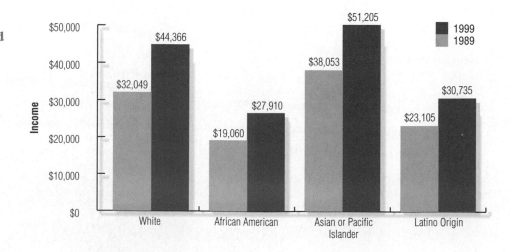

New long-term economic trends threaten to make matters even worse. These trends include a shift from higher-paying manufacturing jobs to lower-paying service jobs and replacement of workers because of the transfer of high-wage jobs to low-wage countries.

Patterns of unemployment also affect the economic status of African Americans. Jobless rates among African Americans are double those of whites, and these rates do not account for all unemployed persons. Traditional unemployment rates are based on the number of unemployed people who are looking for jobs. They do not include so-called **hidden unemployment**— discouraged workers who have stopped looking or part-time workers who would prefer to have full-time jobs. When hidden unemployment is considered, the jobless rate for African Americans exceeds one in four workers, the national unemployment rate during the Great Depression of the 1930s (Swinton, 1989; Wilson, 1997).

hidden unemployment
unemployment that includes people not counted in the traditional unemployment categories

The greatest unemployment problem exists among African American teenagers. According to official statistics, about one out of every three African American teenagers is unsuccessfully looking for work. With hidden unemployment taken into account, it is estimated that over 40 percent of all African American teenagers are unemployed. Consequently, thousands of African American youths are becoming adults without the job experience vital to securing good employment in the future (*World Without Work*, 1999).

Have African Americans made advances? Education is the traditional American path to economic gain and occupational prestige. The educational story for African Americans is mixed. As of 1999, 84 percent of whites had finished high school, compared with 77 percent of African Americans. Similarly, where 25 percent of whites had completed college, only 15 percent of African Americans had done so.

Moreover, higher educational attainment doesn't pay off for African Americans as it does for whites. Although income tends to rise with educational level for all races, it increases much less for African American men (and for women of both races) than for white men. White male high school graduates, on the average, earn nearly as much each year as African American men with college associate degrees. At each level of schooling, black men tend to gain less than their white peers.

While these figures may seem discouraging, real gains have been made. Since the 1960s, the number of African Americans in professional and technical occupations—doctors, engineers, lawyers, teachers, writers—has increased by 128 percent. The number of African American managers or officials is more than twice as high as in 1960. As a result of the recent upward mobility of educated African Americans, some sociologists predict the emergence of two black Americas—a growing black middle class and a black **underclass** composed of unemployed people who come from families that have been poor for generations (Wilson, 1984; Landry, 1988; Kilson, 1998).

This African American congressman has made providing quality education a top priority.

underclass
people typically unemployed who come from families that have been poor for generations

African Americans have seen their political power grow since 1970. More than 5,300 African Americans are serving as city and county officials, up from 715 in 1970. There are nearly 9,000 African American elected officials in the United States, a sixfold increase since 1970 (Yorke, 2000). The emergence of "biracial politics"—election of African Americans in predominantly white areas—is a hopeful sign. African Americans, though still vastly under-represented, have entered the "power elite" of America:

> *Although the power elite is still composed primarily of Christian white men, there are now . . . blacks . . . on the boards of the country's largest corporations; presidential cabinets are far more diverse than was the case forty years ago; and the highest ranks of the military are no longer filled solely by white men (Zweigenhaft and Domhoff, 1998:176).*

Latinos

Latino is a term that refers to ethnic minorities from Latin America, a region that includes Mexico, Central America, South America, and the islands of the Caribbean. High birth rates and immigration rates make Latinos (along with Asian Americans) one of the fastest-growing minorities in the United States. In fact, early in the twenty-first century, Latinos overtook African Americans as America's largest minority group (U.S. Bureau of the Census, 2000). By the time you retire—about the year 2050—it is predicted that nearly one out of every four Americans will be Latino. (See Figure 9.6.)

What are the largest Latino groups in the United States? Nearly 60 percent of Latinos today are of Mexican descent. Puerto Ricans make up a little less than one-tenth of the total Latino population. Most Puerto Ricans are concentrated in or near New York City, although the population is beginning to shift to the outlying areas. Cubans make up the third most populous group of Latinos, with about one million people. Most Cuban Americans are located in the Miami, Florida, area (U.S. Bureau of the Census, 1998a).

Like Anglos, Native Americans, and African Americans, Latino peoples are diverse. Each group came to the United States under different circumstances and retains a sense of its own identity and separateness. In addition, there are significant internal differences within individual Latino minorities. For example, the first large group of Cuban immigrants to enter the United States were successful middle- and upper-class people who fled from Cuba when Fidel

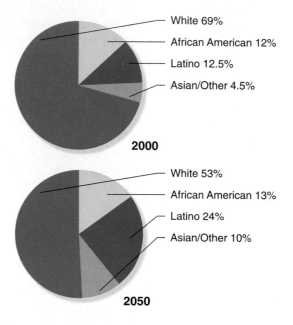

White 69%
African American 12%
Latino 12.5%
Asian/Other 4.5%

2000

White 53%
African American 13%
Latino 24%
Asian/Other 10%

2050

Percentages do not total 100% due to rounding.
Note: The White, African American, and Asian/Other categories exclude Latinos, who may be of any race.

Figure 9.6 The U.S. Population by Race and Ethnicity, 2000 and 2050. *The racial and ethnic composition in the U.S. is expected to look very different by 2050. Discuss some social consequences of this changing composition.*

Source: U.S. Bureau of the Census, 2000.

Castro instituted a communist government there in the late 1950s. These Cuban Americans differ substantially from later Cuban immigrants, who were relatively uneducated members of the lower class.

What is the general level of education among Latinos? Latinos fall behind white Americans in formal education. Just over half of adult Latinos have completed high school, compared with 84 percent of non-Latinos. Mexican Americans have the lowest levels of educational attainment. Cubans have the highest, owing to the fact that many Cuban immigrants to the United States were middle- and upper-class people, as explained earlier (Stefancic and Delgado, 1998).

The meager wages earned by migrant farm laborers still keep many Latino children in the fields and out of schools where they could receive an education.

How much money do Latinos earn? Average income for Latinos ($30,735) is higher than that of African Americans but significantly lower than that of non-Latino whites ($44,366). Cubans are the most affluent Latinos, but their median income is only about 75 percent that of whites. The poorest among the large Latino groups are the Puerto Ricans, whose income is only half that of whites. Almost one-fourth of Latino families live below the poverty level, compared with about one-tenth of white non-Latinos (U.S. Bureau of the Census, 1999).

From the data above, it should come as no surprise that many Latinos work in low-paying and low-status jobs as semiskilled workers and unskilled laborers. Mexican Americans make up the majority of migrant workers in the country. Cuban men belong to the only Latino minority with occupations similar to those of the white Anglo majority (Moore and Pachon, 1985). The numbers of Latino-owned homes and businesses are increasing rapidly, but they still fall far behind the national averages.

How do Latinos stand politically? Politically, Latinos are becoming a force in shaping American politics. As of 2000, there were no Latino U.S. senators, but seventeen seats in the U.S. House of Representatives were held by Latinos. Of these members of Congress, thirteen were Mexican Americans, three were of Cuban descent, and one was of Puerto Rican ancestry. Issues of education and immigration, as well as income and the quality of life, promise to keep Latinos politically active.

No one can make you feel inferior without your consent.

Eleanor Roosevelt
American humanitarian

Native Americans

Today, Native Americans number just over two million. About five hundred separate tribes and bands have been identified in the United States. This great diversity is generally unrecognized because of stereotyped images of Native Americans based on old Hollywood films and paperback adventures of the Old West. In fact, however, tribal groups such as the Navajo and Sioux are as different from one another as Anglo Americans are from Italians or Brazilians.

Some Native American tribes are becoming more economically independent through the gaming industry. Not everyone agrees that this will result in long-term gains.

What is the current situation of Native Americans?   Native Americans, perhaps more than any other minority, are suffering today from the effects of hundreds of years of discrimination. Abject poverty remains a major fact of life among Native Americans, especially on reservations. Just over one-fourth of the Native American population live below the poverty line. Fewer Native Americans graduate from high school than any other major minority group.

Native Americans have the lowest annual income of any minority group in the United States ($21,619). Only 20 percent of all employed Native American men and women hold professional, managerial, or administrative positions. One-third are in blue-collar jobs (craftworkers, supervisors, machine operators, and nonfarm laborers). In 2001 there were two Native Americans in Congress—one in the Senate and one in the House of Representatives.

Are conditions on reservations better or worse?   About one-fourth of Native Americans live on reservations. For these Native Americans, the situation is considerably worse than for those living off the reservations. Fully 50 percent of those on reservations live below the poverty level, compared with over 25 percent of the total Native American population. Reservation dwellers earn only $16,000 per year on average. The rate of college education for Native Americans living on reservations is only about half that for those living off reservations—5 percent versus 9.3 percent (U.S. Bureau of the Census, 1993e, 1993i).

A recent development on reservations is the introduction of casino-type gaming establishments. Native American gaming both on and off reservations has grown unexpectedly into an enormous, rapidly expanding industry. In 1999, over 184 tribes were operating more than 300 gaming facilities. Gaming revenues had exceeded $10 billion. Most tribal governments use this revenue to promote services and to promote economic and community development. Over half the tribal revenues, however, had gone to only ten of the tribes. Given the poor social and economic conditions on reservations, it is not surprising that the gaming industry has been embraced by many Native Americans as a source of money. The long-term effects, however, are yet to be seen.

Asian Americans

More than 10 million Asians live in the United States, comprising 4 percent of the total population. Like Latinos, Asians come from many different national and ethnic backgrounds. The largest groups are from China, the Philippines, Japan, India, Korea, and Vietnam.

If a success story can be told for any minority group in America, those groups are Chinese and Japanese Americans. Even for them, however, the road has not been smooth.

How have Chinese Americans fared over the years?   Attracted at first by the California gold rush, Chinese immigrants arrived in large numbers during the 1850s. They worked as agricultural laborers, on railroad crews, and in low-paying industrial jobs. When hard times hit in the 1870s, unemployed European Americans began to compete for jobs that the Chinese had held. Race riots erupted, and the children of Chinese immigrants were barred from attending schools in San Francisco. Chinese Americans were driven into large urban ghettos known as Chinatowns, where they are still concentrated today. Pressure by congressmen from California led to the Chinese Exclusion Act of 1882, which virtually ended Chinese immigration to the United States for nearly a hundred years.

Although Chinese Americans, in many ways, remain isolated from American life, their situation began to improve after 1940. American-born Chinese college graduates began to enter professional occupations, and Chinese American scholars and scientists began to make publicly recognized contributions to science and the arts. Most Americans today recognize Chinese Americans' willingness to work hard, their dedication to education, and their contributions to American society.

What has been the history of Japanese Americans in the United States?   Early diplomatic relations between the United States and Japan were warm and cordial. But beginning in 1885, large numbers of Japanese men immigrated to the West Coast of the United States. Their arrival coincided with the attempt described above to exclude Chinese immigrants. The Japanese suffered prejudice and discrimination during these early years. Nevertheless, they moved from being laborers in certain industries (railroads, canning, logging, mining, meat packing) to being successful farmers.

When the Japanese began to compete with white farmers, however, anti-Japanese legislation was passed. The California Alien Land Bill of 1913, for example, permitted Japanese to lease farmland for a maximum of three years; it did not allow land they owned to be inherited by their families. In 1924, the U.S. Congress halted all Japanese immigration, and the 126,000 Japanese already in the United States became targets for still more prejudice, discrimination, stereotyping, and scapegoating.

In 1941, Japan attacked the Pearl Harbor naval base in Hawaii, an act that brought the United States into World War II. Wartime hysteria generated a fear of a possible Japanese invasion that led President Franklin Roosevelt to issue Executive Order 9066. This emergency law moved more than 110,000 Japanese people into internment camps away from the West Coast. Historians later agreed that the Japanese Americans had posed no security threat during World War II. (Immigrants from Germany and Italy were not relocated, even though their countries were also at war with the United States.) Eventually, in the 1980s, the U.S. government formally apologized to Japanese American internees and paid them $20,000 each in compensation.

Over 100,000 Japanese residents in America were sent to internment camps during World War II. Many lost homes and businesses as a result.

Focus on Research

Survey Research: The Legacy of Racism

According to many scholars, African Americans today suffer more from low economic class than from racism. In a well-known study of the early 1990s, one sociologist, Joe Feagin, challenged this line of argument. Feagin set up a study that looked at African Americans' access to public accommodations, including restaurants, hotels, and motels.

Feagin interviewed middle-class African Americans in several cities. He wished to study African Americans in the middle class because they would have the economic resources needed to take advantage of public accommodations. His research was guided by several questions:

Do middle-class African Americans still experience racism in public accommodations?

If so, how is it manifested?

What means do middle-class African Americans use to handle discrimination?

What are the effects of discrimination on its victims?

Feagin conducted 37 in-depth interviews. Those interviewed were drawn from a larger group of 135 middle-class African Americans in several large cities.

The interviewees were representative of the larger sample based on such characteristics as occupation, age, income, education, sex, and location. The initial participants in the study were identified as middle class by city-based consultants. Names of additional participants were suggested by the first people interviewed. (This is known as "snowball" sampling.) Middle class was defined as "those holding a white-collar job (including those in professional, managerial, and clerical jobs), college students preparing for white-collar jobs, and owners of successful businesses."

Middle-class African Americans, Feagin concluded, still experience discrimination based on race. Several types of discrimination were reported by the respondents, including avoidance, verbal attack, physical abuse, and subtle slights. Rejection and poor service were the most common forms of discrimination, however.

According to Feagin, the most tragic cost of this continuing discrimination is the ongoing physical and psychological drain felt by the victims. Isolated discriminatory acts may appear insignificant to whites, but years of being the target of discriminatory actions have a cumulative effect. Many African Americans report having developed a "second eye" to analyze interracial situations. As one respondent said:

> I think that it causes you to have to look at things from two different perspectives. You have to decide whether things that are done or slights that are made are made because you are black or they are made because the person is just rude, or unconcerned and uncaring. So it's kind of a situation where you're always kind of looking to see with a second eye or a second antenna just what's going on (Feagin, 1991:115).

Feagin concluded that what may appear to American whites as "black paranoia," then, is actually a developed sensitivity to continuous discriminatory encounters. Despite decades of legal protection, Feagin says, African Americans have not attained the full promise of the American dream. Although middle-class African Americans work hard for their success, it is too often overshadowed by the legacy of past racist actions.

Because of decades of racism and discrimination, this obviously successful African American couple may still have trouble getting a cab driver to stop for them.

Working with the Research

1. Do you agree that disadvantages related to economic class are currently more harmful to African Americans than racism and discrimination? Why or why not?
2. Do you believe that Feagin adequately tested his hypothesis? Explain your conclusion.
3. Which of the three major theoretical perspectives best fits Feagin's research study? Defend your choice.

Figure 9.7 Socioeconomic Characteristics of Minorities

This figure presents some important social and economic characteristics of the majority and larger minorities in the U.S. Can you make sociological generalizations about income level and education based on these data?

	Whites	African Americans	Latinos	Native Americans	Asian Americans
Percent of Families in Poverty	7.7%	23.6%	22.8%	25.9%	10.7%
Median Income	$44,366	$27,910	$30,735	$21,619	$51,205
Percent with High School Diploma	84.3%	77.0%	56.1%	66%	84.7%
Percent with College Degree	25.9%	15.4%	10.9%	9.4%	42.4%

Source: U.S. Bureau of the Census, 2000.

Online **UPDATE**
Visit soc.glencoe.com and click on **Textbook Updates–Chapter 9** for an update of the data.

Japanese Americans have not had to deal with the centuries of prejudice and discrimination endured by African Americans and Native Americans. Nevertheless, they have overcome great hardship and have become one of the most successful racial minorities in the United States (Zwiegenhaft and Domhoff, 1998).

Why have so many Asian Americans been successful? In large part, Asian Americans have been successful because they have used the educational system for upward mobility. This is reflected in the academic achievement of school-aged Asian Americans, whose average SAT scores are 45 points higher than the general high school population. Furthermore, over 42 percent of Asian Americans have completed four years of college, compared with about 26 percent of whites and 11 percent of Latinos (U.S. Bureau of the Census, 2000c).

White Ethnics

White ethnics are the descendants of immigrants from Eastern and Southern European nations, particularly Italy and Poland. They also include Greek, Irish, and Slavic peoples. The majority are blue-collar workers living in small communities surrounding large cities in the eastern half of the United States.

During the 1960s, white ethnics gained the undeserved reputation of being conservative, racist, pro-war "hardhats." In fact, surveys conducted during the 1960s showed white ethnics to be more against the Vietnam War than white Anglo-Saxon Protestants. Catholic blue-collar workers were found to be more liberal than either Protestant blue-collar workers or the country as a whole. They were more likely to favor a guaranteed annual wage, more likely to vote for an African American presidential candidate, and more concerned about the environment. Finally, white ethnics tended to be more sympathetic to government help for the poor and more in favor of integration.

White ethnics have not traditionally been the victims of occupational or income discrimination. Despite their relative success, many white ethnics have in recent years become very conscious of their cultural and national origins. There is, in fact, a white ethnic "roots" movement. The new trend toward white ethnic identity began with the black power movement of the 1960s. Just as many African Americans decided that they wanted to preserve their cultural and racial identities, many white ethnics now believe that "white ethnicity is beautiful." Many think that the price of completely abandoning one's cultural and national roots is simply too high.

Lillian Rubin (1994) links the continuing accent on white ethnicity to the rising demands of ethnic minorities. White ethnics, she believes, are attempting to establish a public identity that enables them to take a seat at the "multicultural table."

Why do many of these descendants of European immigrants wish to be identified as a minority group?

Section 4 Assessment

1. How are general discrimination and institutionalized discrimination different?
2. In what ways have white ethnics influenced American culture?
3. What does the level of Latino participation at the top of the American political structure suggest about the relationship between cultural group membership and political power in the United States?
4. Does the economic situation of Native Americans today help or hurt the economy?

Critical Thinking

5. **Drawing Conclusions** Do you think that affirmative action has affected American culture positively or negatively? Explain.

Choose your friends by their character and your socks by their color. Choosing your socks by their character makes no sense, and choosing your friends by their color is unthinkable.

Anonymous

Summary

Section 1: Minority, Race, and Ethnicity

Main Idea: Sociologists have specific definitions particular to their field of study for minority, race, and ethnicity. Ethnic minorities have historically been subjected to prejudice and discrimination.

Section 2: Racial and Ethnic Relations

Main Idea: Patterns of racial and ethnic relations take two forms: assimilation and conflict. Patterns of assimilation include Anglo-conformity, melting pot, cultural pluralism, and accommodation. Conflict patterns include genocide, population transfer, and subjugation.

Section 3: Theories of Prejudice and Discrimination

Main Idea: Prejudice involves attitudes, while discrimination is about behavior. Prejudice usually leads to discrimination. Conversely, in some instances, discrimination creates prejudiced attitudes through stereotyping. Each of the three major perspectives looks at different aspects of prejudice.

Section 4: Minority Groups in the United States

Main Idea: Discrimination in the United States has caused some ethnic and racial groups to lag behind the white majority in jobs, income, and education. Progress is being made, but gains remain fragile. African American, Latino, Asian American, Native American, and white ethnics are the largest minority groups in this country.

SOCIOLOGY Online

Self-Check Quiz
Visit the *Sociology and You* Web site at soc.glencoe.com and click on **Chapter 9—Self-Check Quizzes** to prepare for the chapter test.

Reviewing Vocabulary

Complete each sentence, using each term once.

a. minority
b. stereotype
c. hate crime
d. self-fulfilling prophecy
e. race
f. institutionalized discrimination
g. ethnic minority
h. underclass
i. subjugation
j. assimilation
k. de jure segregation
l. de facto segregation
m. prejudice
n. discrimination
o. cultural pluralism
p. racism
q. genocide
r. hidden unemployment

1. An expectation that leads to behavior that causes the expectation to become a reality is called _____.
2. _____ is a group identified by cultural, religious, or national characteristics.
3. A set of ideas based on distortion, exaggeration, and oversimplification is called _____.
4. _____ is a group of people with physical or cultural characteristics different from the dominant group.
5. People living in poverty and either continuously unemployed or underemployed are known as _____.
6. The denial of equal access based on law is called _____.
7. A criminal act that is motivated by prejudice is called _____.
8. _____ is a type of subjugation that takes place outside the law.
9. People who share certain inherited physical characteristics are known as _____.
10. _____ are unfair practices that are part of the structure of a society.
11. Treating people differently because of their ethnicity, race, religion, or culture is called _____.

12. _____ is the denial of equal access based on everyday practice.

13. _____ is best described as negative attitudes toward some minority and its individual members.

14. _____ is the blending or fusing of minority groups into the dominant society.

15. Extreme prejudice is called _____.

16. _____ is assimilation that maintains element of ethnic roots.

17. _____ is unemployment that includes people who are not counted in traditional work categories.

18. The systematic effort to destroy a population is known as _____.

Reviewing the Facts

1. What is the name given to people who have some distinctive characteristic, are dominated by the majority, and are denied equal treatment?

2. What is a feature that is characteristic of a minority group?

3. Name the three patterns of assimilation.

4. What is the name of the process that occurred throughout American history when waves of immigrants came to this country and eventually became full members of the dominant class?

5. What does the lyric of the following song suggest about prejudice? "You've got to be taught to hate and fear, it's got to be drummed in your dear little ear."

6. How would sociologists explain the fact that on average, African Americans earn $64 for every $100 earned by whites?

7. What sociological perspective focuses on the majority's subjugation of minorities as a weapon of power and domination?

8. Examine Figure 9.7 on page 300. Which racial minority has come the closest to achieving mainstream white status?

9. How have white ethnics affected business in American society?

10. From what part of the world did the ancestors of white ethnics emigrate?

Thinking Critically

1. **Making Inferences** Several years ago, a high school principal canceled his school's senior prom when it was brought to his attention that perhaps a dozen students were planning to bring dates from other races. A reaction this extreme is rare, but strong cultural norms about interracial dating do exist. These norms vary by class and region. Recent studies have shown that over half of all teens in the United States have dated someone of another race, but interracial marriages are not common. Why do you think people might be willing to date but not marry outside their race?

2. **Applying Concepts** Recently, the students and administration at a largely Latino high school wanted to change the name of the school to honor a deceased Hispanic community leader. When the school had been built, the neighborhood had been primarily Anglo. Many of the old graduates protested the name change, and the original name was kept. Can you use what you have learned in this chapter about the relationship between cultural group membership and political power to explain why the decision was made to keep the school's old name?

3. **Drawing Conclusions** A recent documentary examined a suburb in the Midwest where the racial balance had gradually changed from mostly white to mostly African American. Even though statistics proved that school scores had not dropped and that the quality of government services remained the same, the perception was that property values had declined. What do you think was responsible for this perception? What can be done to avoid this type of thinking?

4. **Applying Concepts** Many businesses, colleges, and schools have banned "hate speech" and "fighting words" that express views based on bigotry or racism. Some people believe that this ban is the same as censorship and that it vio-

lates First Amendment rights to freedom of speech. Others say that the right to free speech ends when speech causes psychological or emotional harm, or when society may be endangered. What is your opinion on hate speech? How would you handle an individual who was routinely offensive about your race, gender, or nationality?

5. **Implementing Solutions** Read the following scenario, and then answer the questions that follow based on your best instincts and reasoning: Two people are in a twenty-mile race. The winner will receive a prize of $100,000. Two of the competitors—Lynn and Tony—are very good runners, and both are in good physical condition. At the beginning of the race Tony is told to put a set of ten-pound ankle weights on each leg, but Lynn is not. In fact, Lynn does not even know about the weights. When Lynn reaches the thirteen-mile marker, Tony is two miles behind. He is not only exhausted but is also experiencing a shortened running stride and is off-rhythm because of the weights. The judges decide to remove the ankle weights from Tony.

a. Is it fair to continue the race with each runner finishing from his or her present position, or should Tony be moved forward in the race?

b. What is fair to both parties?

c. Assume that the race cannot be restarted. How do we compensate the runner who had to carry extra weights for over half of the race?

d. Are there solutions to the problem?

e. Since the problem is difficult to solve, would it be fair simply to ignore it and conclude that things will eventually work out?

6. **Analyzing Information** Suppose there was a third competitor in the race described above. Ayesha is almost as good a runner as Tony and Lynn. Ayesha does not have to wear ankle weights, but both Tony and Lynn have high-quality professional running shoes, and Ayesha has to run in cheap "tennies." At the time the

race is stopped, Ayesha has run twelve miles. If you compensate Tony by moving him forward, Ayesha is likely to feel that the race is still not fair.

a. Is there a way to make the race fair for all three runners? Remember, you cannot restart the race.

b. How is institutional discrimination similar to the race described in these questions? What are the issues in both?

7. **Evaluating Information** Explain how the experiences of various Native American tribes have been different from other racial and ethnic minority groups in the United States. Discuss whether you think allowing gaming on Indian reservations is a long-term benefit or disadvantage for Native Americans.

8. **Making Comparisons** How has the African American experience in the United States been different from that of other racial and ethnic minority groups?

9. **Understanding Cause and Effect** Use the diagram below to show the cause-and-effect relationship between discrimination and poverty. Incorporate the elements of unequal educational opportunity, unfair hiring practices, and low-level jobs to complete your diagram.

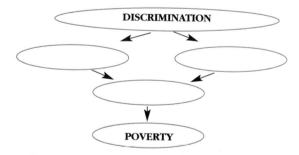

10. **Evaluating Information** Have any of the methods of role conflict resolution used by African Americans and Latinos worked?

Sociology Projects

1. **Race and Ethnicity** Write a brief answer to each of the following questions.

a. How would you describe yourself racially or ethnically?

b. How do you think others would describe you?

c. How important is your race or ethnicity to you personally?

d. Do you believe that race or ethnicity is a factor in how your friends relate to you?

e. Is your community (neighborhood) a reflection of your race or ethnicity?

f. Do you place much importance on race or ethnicity?

g. Do you think others put a lot of importance on your race or ethnicity?

h. Is race an important issue in society, or do we make too much of it? Is ethnicity an important issue?

After you have answered these questions, form a group with two or three of your classmates and share your responses to questions a–h. Do you believe their assessments were accurate?

2. **Ethnic and Racial Heritage** This project will give you an opportunity to create a family tree. Ask parents and other relatives about your ethnic/racial heritage, going back as far as you can. Chances are you have relatives who have old photos with dates and other pieces of information. As you trace your family tree, note when new cultures, races, or ethnicities join the family. If this has happened several times in your family, consider how it complicates assigning yourself to a specific racial and ethnic category. You might want to turn this project into an album that your whole family can enjoy and pass on.

3. **Native Americans and Immigrant Cultures** This chapter deals extensively with the effects of American culture on various racial and ethnic groups. Minorities, of course, also affect American culture. For example, Mexican Americans play a pivotal role throughout the Southwest, including in Texas, where Mexican restaurants serving enchiladas and fajitas compete with those serving traditional Texas barbecue. In many parts of the nation, Native Americans have opened tourist-based businesses. The profits from these businesses have benefited the economies of the surrounding areas as well. Asian Americans have a significant presence in California, where sushi bars serve fresh fish and Chinese groceries cater to a large clientele. Businesses, in attempts to win new customers among these many ethnic groups, often tailor their print, radio, and television advertising to cater to immigrant tastes. To do so, advertising companies often employ ethnic Americans as models and consultants. Work with one or two of your classmates to find information about immigrant and Native American cultures in your community. Analyze changes such as those in advertising, food, and business in your local culture that have resulted from adaptations to various immigrant or Native American cultures.

4. **Native Americans and White Ethnics** This chapter deals extensively with the effects of American culture on various racial and ethnic groups. Minorities, of course, also affect American culture. How have Native Americans and white ethnics influenced American advertising and food? Which of the two minorities has had the greatest influence on each of these two aspects of American culture? Information may be found in print, online, in documentaries, and through interviews with a Native American and a white ethnic.

Technology Activity

1. The textbook describes a stereotype as a set of ideas based on distortion, exaggeration, and oversimplification that is applied to all members of a social category. Popular media often use stereotypes to convey assumed meanings about characters and situations. The Movies Cliché List at http://www.moviecliches.com/ provides an abundant list of stereotypes used in films.

a. Select "Women" from the Cliché Topics. Name some of the stereotypes about women suggested by the list.

b. Do the same for "Men" and "Minorities."

c. Based on what you have read in the text and on these lists, do you think stereotypes are helpful in understanding social categories?

Chapter 9

Enrichment Reading
The Skin Color Tax

Patricia J. Williams

◆

Several years ago, at a moment when I was particularly tired of the unstable lifestyle that academic careers sometimes require, I surprised myself and bought a real house. Because the house was in a state other than the one where I was living at the time, I obtained my mortgage by telephone. I am a prudent little squirrel when it comes to things financial, always tucking away stores of nuts for the winter, and so I meet the **criteria** of a quite good credit risk. My loan was approved almost immediately.

A little while later, the contract came in the mail. Among the papers the bank forwarded were forms documenting **compliance** with the Fair Housing Act, which outlaws racial discrimination in the housing market. The act monitors lending practices to prevent banks from redlining—redlining being the phenomenon whereby banks circle certain neighborhoods on the map and refuse to lend in those areas. It is a practice for which the bank with which I was dealing, **unbeknownst** to me, had been cited previously—as well as since. In any event, the act tracks the race of all banking customers to prevent such discrimination. Unfortunately, and with the **creative variability of all illegality,** some banks also use the racial information disclosed on the fair housing forms to engage in precisely the discrimination the law seeks to prevent.

I should repeat that to this point my entire mortgage transaction had been conducted by telephone. I should also note that I speak a Received Standard English, regionally marked as Northeastern perhaps, but not easily identifiable as black. With my credit history, my job as a law professor and, no doubt, with my accent, I am not only middle class but apparently match the cultural stereotype of a good white person. It is thus, perhaps, that the loan officer of the bank, whom I had never met, had checked off the box on the fair housing form indicating that I *was* white.

Race shouldn't matter, I suppose, but it seemed to in this case, so I took a deep breath, crossed out "white" and sent the contract back. That will teach them to presume too much, I thought. A done deal, I assumed. But suddenly the transaction came to a screeching halt. The bank wanted more money, more points, a higher rate of interest. Suddenly I found myself facing great resistance and much more debt. To make a long story short, I threatened to sue under the act in question, the bank quickly backed down and I **procured** the loan on the original terms.

What was interesting about all this was that the reason the bank gave for its new-found **recalcitrance** was not race, heaven forbid. No, it was all about economics and increased risk: The reason they gave was that property values in that neighborhood were suddenly falling. They wanted more money to buffer themselves against the snappy winds of projected misfortune.

The bank's response was driven by demographic data that show that any time black people move into a neighborhood, whites are overwhelmingly likely to move out. In droves. In panic. In concert. Pulling every imaginable resource with them, from school funding to garbage collection to social workers who don't want to work in black neighborhoods. The imagery is awfully catchy, you had to admit: the neighborhood just tipping on over like a terrible accident, whoops! Like a pitcher, I suppose. All that fresh wholesome milk spilling out running away . . .

leaving the dark echoing, upended urn of the inner city.

In retrospect, what has remained so fascinating to me about this experience was the way it so exemplified the problems of the new rhetoric of racism. For starters, the new rhetoric of race never mentions race. It wasn't race but risk with which the bank was so concerned.

Second, since financial risk is all about economics, my exclusion got reclassified as just a consideration of class. There's no law against class discrimination, goes the argument, because that would represent a restraint on that basic American freedom, the ability to contract or not. If schools, trains, buses, swimming pools and neighborhoods remain segregated, it's no longer a racial problem if someone who just happens to be white keeps hiking up the price for someone who accidentally and purely by the way happens to be black. Black people end up paying higher prices for the attempt to integrate, even as the integration of oneself threatens to lower the value of one's investment.

By this measure of mortgage-worthiness, the ingredient of blackness is cast not just as a social toll but as an actual tax. A fee, an extra contribution at the door, an admission charge for the high costs of handling my dangerous propensities, my inherently unsavory properties. I was not judged based on my independent attributes or financial worth; not even was I judged by statistical profiles of what my group actually does. (For in fact,

anxiety-stricken, middle-class black people make grovelingly good cake-baking neighbors when not made to feel defensive by the unfortunate historical strategies of bombs, burnings or abandonment.) Rather, I was being evaluated based on what an abstraction of White Society writ large thinks we—or I—do, and that imagined "doing" was treated and thus established as a self-fulfilling prophecy. It is a dispiriting message: that some in society apparently not only devalue black people but devalue *themselves* and their homes just for having us as part of their landscape.

"I bet you'll keep your mouth shut the next time they plug you into the computer as white," laughed a friend when he heard my story. It took me aback, this postmodern pressure to "pass," even as it highlighted the intolerable logic of it all. For by "rational" economic measures, an investment in my property suggests the selling of myself.

Source: Patricia J. Williams, "Of Race and Risk," *The Nation* (December 29, 1997):10.

"Let's just forget for a moment that you're black."

© 1996 *The New Yorker Collection*, Mick Stevens. (Reprinted with permission.)

What Does it Mean?

compliance
agreement with; following the terms of

creative variability of all illegality
cleverness of wrongdoers to get what they want

criteria
standards on which judgments or decisions are made

procured
obtained

recalcitrance
reluctance; unwillingness

unbeknownst
not knowing; unaware

Read and React

1. What does the author mean when she writes "All that fresh wholesome milk spilling out running away . . . leaving the dark echoing, upended urn of the inner city"?

2. What are the main issues of what the author calls the "problems of the new rhetoric of racism"?

3. Why has the author titled this article *The Skin Color Tax*?

CHAPTER 10
Inequalities of Gender and Age

USING Your Sociological Imagination

True or false? Women in the United States lead the world in efforts to achieve job equality with men.

Did you answer "true" to this statement? If so, you may be interested in the following facts. Among industrialized nations, America is surprisingly near the bottom of the list in ranking male/female income equality. Only Luxembourg and Japan have wider gaps than the United States between what men and women earn for doing the same work. Swedish women in manufacturing jobs, for example, earn about 90 percent of the wages paid men, while females in the United States earn only 72 percent of the wages paid men for the same work (U.S. Bureau of the Census, 2000a).

Throughout history, men have dominated the social, political, and economic spheres outside the home. Traditionally, women have assumed responsibility for child care and household tasks. These domestic tasks are generally undervalued in industrial societies, where a person's contributions to society are pegged to monetary rewards. Women—thought to be dependent, passive, and deferring—have usually been considered subordinate to independent, aggressive, and strong men. This division of labor based on sex has almost always led to gender inequality.

This chapter examines how various cultures view gender roles and also how America looks at its aged population.

Sections

Learning Objectives

After reading this chapter, you will be able to

❖ distinguish the concepts of sex, gender, and gender identity.

❖ summarize the perspectives on gender taken by functionalists, conflict theorists, and symbolic interactionists.

❖ describe the status of women in the United States.

❖ compare and contrast the ways in which functionalism, conflict theory, and symbolic interactionism approach ageism.

❖ discuss the inequality experienced by America's elderly.

SOCIOLOGY Online

Chapter Overview
Visit the *Sociology and You* Web site at soc.glencoe.com and click on **Chapter 10— Chapter Overviews** to preview chapter information.

Section 1

Sex and Gender Identity

Key Terms

- sex
- biological determinism
- gender identity

Section Preview

All societies expect people to behave in certain ways based on their sex. Through socialization, members of a society acquire an awareness of themselves as masculine or feminine. Behavioral differences between men and women are culturally conditioned.

sex
classification of people as male or female based on biological characteristics

Defining Male and Female

> What are little girls made of?
> Sugar and spice
> And everything nice
> That's what little girls are made of.
>
> What are little boys made of?
> Snips and snails
> And puppy dog tails
> That's what little boys are made of.

As the above well-known nursery rhyme indicates, when it comes to males and females, most Americans believe that anatomy is destiny. If men and women behave differently, it is assumed to be because of their **sex**— the biological distinction between male and female. Males are assumed to be naturally more aggressive than women and to be built for providing and protecting. Thought of as being naturally more passive, females are believed to be designed for domestic work. If this popular conception were true, men

Many Americans believe that infant boys are just naturally more active than infant girls. Would you agree or not?

and women in all societies would behave uniformly in their unique ways because of inborn biological forces beyond their control. This way of thinking is called **biological determinism**—the belief that behavioral differences are the result of inherited physical characteristics.

The theory of biological determinism lacks scientific proof. Significant behavioral differences between men and women have not been causally linked to biological characteristics. Although biology may create some behavioral tendencies in the sexes, such tendencies are so weak that they are easily overridden by cultural and social influences (Ridley, 1996; Sapolsky, 1997).

From the moment of birth—on the basis of obvious external biological characteristics—males and females are treated differently. Few parents in American society point with pride to the muscular legs and broad shoulders of their baby girls or to the long eyelashes, rosebud mouth, and delicate curly hair of their baby boys. Rather, parents stress the characteristics and behaviors that fit the society's image of the ideal male or female, including modes of dress, ways of walking, manner of talking, play activities, and life aspirations.

Girls and boys gradually learn to behave as their parents expect. From this process comes **gender identity**—an awareness of being masculine or feminine, based on culture. Sociologist Margaret Andersen succinctly captured the difference between sex and gender.

The terms sex and gender have particular definitions in sociological work. Sex refers to the biological identity of the person and is meant to signify the fact that one is either male or female. . . . Gender refers to the socially learned behaviors and expectations that are associated with the two sexes. Thus, whereas "maleness" and "femaleness" are biological facts, becoming a woman or becoming a man is a cultural process. Like race and class, gender is a social category that establishes, in large measure, our life chances and directs our social relations with others. Sociologists distinguish sex and gender to emphasize that gender is a cultural, not a biological, phenomenon (Andersen, 1997).

Sociologists are part of an ongoing debate concerning the reasons for gender differences. At the heart of the debate is the so-called nature versus nurture issue: Does biology or socialization play a greater role in gender differences? Today, research by sociologists and other investigators

Gender identities go way back.

biological determinism
principle that behavioral differences are the result of inherited physical characteristics

gender identity
a sense of being male or female based on learned cultural values

How did family structures develop?   As discussed in Chapter 5, the development of agriculture and industry shaped society. These developments also shaped family structure.

In the earliest societies, hunting and gathering were the primary family activities. Small bands of nuclear families followed herds of animals and changing seasons, moving around constantly, never staying long in any one place.

When humans domesticated animals to help with tilling the soil and cultivating crops (about ten thousand years ago), they no longer needed to be mobile to maintain a food supply. Families began to farm, settle down, and establish roots. Large families were needed to plow and harvest. The growth of family farms encouraged the development of the extended family. Agriculture became the basis of the economy, and the extended family was essential for successful farming.

As societies moved from agricultural economies to industrialized ones, the extended family was slowly replaced by the nuclear family. Large families were no longer needed to work on the farm. Industrial and postindustrial economies favor the nuclear family that has fewer mouths to feed and that is easier to move (Goode, 1970; Nydeggar, 1985).

Patterns of Family Structure

Whether nuclear or extended, families behave in similar ways across cultures. These patterns of behavior relate to inheritance, authority, and place of residence.

Who inherits?   Determining who becomes head of the family—for purpose of descent—and who owns the family property—for inheritance—are extremely important to families. Three arrangements are used.

patrilineal
descent and inheritance is passed through the male line

matrilineal
descent and inheritance is passed through the female line

bilateral
descent and inheritance are passed equally through both parents

patriarchy
the pattern in which the oldest man living in the household has authority over the rest of the family members

matriarchy
the pattern in which the oldest woman living in the household has authority over all other family members

❖ In a **patrilineal** arrangement, descent and inheritance are passed from the father to his male descendants. The people of Iran and Iraq and the Tikopia in the western Pacific live in patrilineal societies.

❖ In a **matrilineal** arrangement, descent and inheritance are transmitted from the mother to her female descendants. Some Native American tribes, such as the Pueblo peoples of the Southwest, are matrilineal.

❖ In some societies, descent and inheritance are **bilateral**—they are passed equally through both parents. Thus both the father's and mother's relatives are accepted equally as part of the kinship structure. Most families in the United States today are bilateral.

Who is in authority?   Similar patterns govern authority in a family.

❖ In a **patriarchy,** the oldest man living in the household has authority over the rest of the family members. We see this in many countries around the world, such as Iraq and China. In its purest form, the father is the absolute ruler.

❖ In a **matriarchy,** the oldest woman living in the household holds the authority. So rare is matriarchal control that controversy exists over whether any society has ever had a genuinely matriarchal family structure.

❖ With **equalitarian** control, authority is split evenly between husband and wife. Many families in the Scandinavian countries and in the United States follow the equalitarian model.

Where do couples live? Where newly married couples set up their households also varies from culture to culture.

❖ The **patrilocal** pattern, such as in premodern China, calls for living with or near the husband's parents.

❖ Residing with or near the wife's parents is expected under a **matrilocal** pattern. The Nayar caste of Kerala in southern India is an illustration of this type of arrangement.

❖ In the **neolocal** pattern (if finances allow) married couples establish residences of their own. This is the Euro-American model. Extended families, of course, have different norms.

Marriage Arrangements

Mention a wedding and Americans commonly think of a bride walking down the aisle in a long white gown. She and the groom make vows that involve some form of loving, honoring, and (until recently, in some cases) obeying. In other cultures, the wedding ceremony looks very different. This is part of the ceremony among the Reindeer Tungus of Siberia:

After the groom's gifts have been presented, the bride's dowry is loaded onto the reindeer and carried to the groom's lodge. There, the rest of the ceremony takes place. The bride takes the wife's place—that is, at the right side of the entrance of the lodge—and members of both families sit around in a circle. The groom enters and follows the bride around the circle, greeting each guest, while the guests, in their turn, kiss the bride on the mouth and hands. Finally, the go-betweens spit three times on the bride's hands, and the couple is formally "husband and wife." More feasting and revelry bring the day to a close (Ember and Ember, 1999:310–311).

Whatever form it takes, the marriage ceremony is an important ritual announcing that a man and woman have become husband and wife, that a new family has been formed, and that any children born to the couple can legitimately inherit the family name and property.

What forms do marriage take? **Monogamy**—the marriage of one man to one woman —is the most widely practiced form of marriage in the world today. In fact, it is the only form of marriage that is legally

equalitarian
family structure in which authority is evenly shared between the husband and wife

patrilocal
refers to the pattern in which married couples live with or near the husbands' parents

matrilocal
refers to the pattern in which married couples live with or near the wives' parents

neolocal
refers to the pattern in which newly married couples set up their own households

monogamy
a marriage consisting of one man and one woman

Although wedding ceremonies may vary, the basic social structures of marriage are common to all societies.

acceptable in the United States and in most Western societies. Some often-married people practice *serial* monogamy—having several husbands or wives, but being married to only one at a time.

In contrast to monogamy, **polygamy** involves the marriage of a male or female to more than one person at a time. It takes two forms: polygyny and polyandry.

Polygyny is the marriage of one man to two or more women at the same time. An obvious example of polygyny is found in the Old Testament. King Solomon is reported to have had seven hundred wives and three hundred concubines. Although common in earlier societies and still legal in India, parts of Africa, and much of the Middle East, polygyny is not practiced widely in any society today. However, in 1999 the Muslim Russian republic of Ingushetia legalized the practice of polygyny.

Polyandry—the marriage of one woman to two or more men at the same time—is an even rarer form of marriage. It is known to have been common in only three societies: in Tibet, in parts of Polynesia, and among the Todas and other hill peoples of India (Queen et al., 1985). Where polyandry has existed, it usually has consisted of several brothers sharing a wife.

You have been introduced to a lot of new terms that relate to family structure and marriage arrangements. Figure 11.1 illustrates several of the characteristics of these family and marriage forms to help you understand and remember them.

polygamy
the marriage of a male or female to more than one person at a time

polygyny
the marriage of one man to two or more women at the same time

polyandry
the marriage of one woman to two or more men at the same time

Figure 11.1   Families/Marriages

This chart summarizes possible variations in family and marriage forms. Describe the general nature of the American family using terms from this table.

Nuclear Family Composition	parents and children
Extended Family Composition	parents, children, and other relatives
Inheritance	patrilineal (inherit through the father) or matrilineal (inherit through the mother) or bilateral (inherit through both)
Authority	patriarchal (father rules the family) or matriarchal (mother rules the family) or equalitarian (parents share authority)
Residence	patrilocal (couple lives with or near husband's parents) or matrilocal (couple lives with or near wife's parents) or neolocal (couple lives apart from both sets of parents)
Marriage Composition	polygyny (one husband, many wives) or polyandry (one wife, many husbands) or monogamy (one husband, one wife)

World View

Types of Marriages

Monogamy—the marriage of one man and one woman—is the only legal form of marriage in all industrial and postindustrial societies. It is also the only form of marriage allowed by law in the Western Hemisphere. However, in many African and southern Asian nations, where Islam is the predominant religion, polygyny—the marriage of one man to two or more women at the same time—is legal. This map shows the countries where monogamy and polygyny are legal forms of marriage.

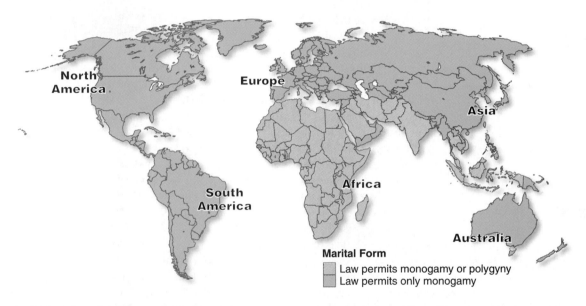

Marital Form

Law permits monogamy or polygyny
Law permits only monogamy

Interpreting the Map

1. Suggest one or more reasons for the widespread presence of polygyny in Africa, Southwest Asia (the Middle East), India, and Southeast Asia.
2. Why do you think the caption explains that the map shows only the countries where polygyny and monogamy are legal forms of marriage?

Choosing a Mate

Suppose you came home from school one afternoon and your parents asked you to come into the living room to meet your future husband or wife. You might wonder if you had somehow been beamed to another planet. Similarly, you will probably never enroll in a college course entitled "Negotiating Dowries with Prospective In-laws," this being a skill not much in demand today. If, however, you assume that you have complete freedom of choice in the selection of a marriage partner, you are mistaken. All cultures and societies, including the United States, have norms and laws about who may marry whom.

exogamy
the practice of marrying outside one's group

incest taboo
a norm forbidding marriage between close relatives

endogamy
marriage within one's own group as required by social norms

homogamy
the tendency to marry someone similar to oneself

Exogamy refers to mate-selection norms requiring individuals to marry someone outside their kind or group. (*Exo* is a prefix meaning "outside.") The most important norms relating to exogamy are called **incest taboos,** which forbid marriage between certain kinds of relatives. In the traditional Chinese culture, for example, two people with identical family names could not marry unless their family lines were known to have diverged at least five generations previously (Queen et al., 1985). In the United States, you are not legally permitted to marry a son or daughter, a brother or sister, a mother or a father, a niece or nephew, or an aunt or uncle. In twenty-nine states, marriage to a first cousin is prohibited. Furthermore, it is illegal to marry a former mother-in-law or father-in-law. Incest is almost universally prohibited, although exceptions were common among the royalty of ancient Europe, Hawaii, Egypt, and Peru. Even in these instances, most members of the royal families chose partners to whom they were not related by blood.

Endogamy involves mate-selection norms that require individuals to marry within their own kind. (*Endo* is a prefix that means "inside.") In the United States, for example, norms have required that marriage partners be of the same race. These norms are not as strong as they once were. Although they represent only five percent of all marriages in the United States, mixed marriages have quadrupled since 1980. Figure 11.2 shows the racial and ethnic breakdown of intergroup marriages today. Also, class lines are crossed with greater frequency because more Americans of all social classes are attending college together. Finally, norms separating age groups have weakened.

Norms encouraging (rather than requiring) marriage within a group usually exist. And people are most likely to know and prefer to marry others like themselves. For these reasons, people tend to marry those with social characteristics similar to their own. This tendency, the result of the rather free exercise of personal choice, is known as **homogamy.**

For example, in spite of what fairy tales and movies often tell us, it is rare for the son or daughter of a multimillionaire to marry someone from a lower

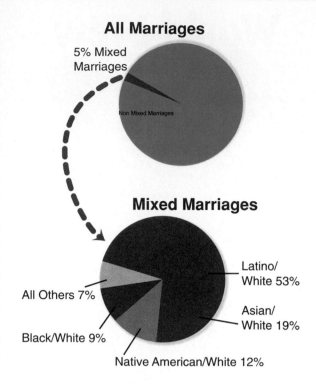

All Marriages

5% Mixed Marriages

Non Mixed Marriages

Mixed Marriages

All Others 7%

Black/White 9%

Native American/White 12%

Latino/White 53%

Asian/White 19%

Figure 11.2 Mixed Marriages and Intergroup Married Couples in the United States.
Although only 5 percent of marriages in the U.S. are mixed, the number has quadrupled since 1980.

Source: American Demographics, Population Reference Bureau, 1998; Miliken Institute, 2001.

class. Furthermore, most marriages in the United States occur between individuals who are about the same age. Most people who are marrying for the first time marry someone who also has not been married before. Divorced people tend to marry others who have been previously married. Finally, people tend to choose marriage partners from their own communities or neighborhoods.

Although it is still the exception in the United States, **heterogamy** is rising. In heterogamous marriages, partners are dissimilar in some important characteristics. More American marriages, for instance, are crossing traditional barriers of age, race, social class, and ethnicity. This trend results from several factors. America has become more racially and ethnically integrated, so that people have an opportunity to mix more freely. The television and film industries help foster heterogamy by the sympathetic portrayal of couples and families from

> Success in marriage is not so much finding the right person as it is being the right person.
>
> **Anonymous**

heterogamy
marriage between people with differing social characteristics

Are these two individuals in a homogenous or heterogamous relationship? Explain.

different racial and social backgrounds. In addition, class lines are crossed with greater frequency, and norms separating age groups have weakened.

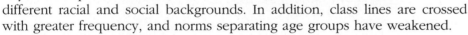

Section 1 Assessment

1. What is the difference between a nuclear and an extended family? Which type represents your household?
2. Why are nuclear families more common in industrial societies?
3. What is another term for the family of birth?
4. Indicate whether exogamy (Ex), endogamy (En), or homogamy (H) is reflected in each of the following situations.
   a. Catholics are supposed to marry Catholics.
   b. A father is not permitted to marry his daughter.
   c. Members of the same social class marry.
   d. A brother and sister are legally prohibited from marrying.
   e. People tend to marry others of the same age.
   f. Rich people marry other wealthy people.

Critical Thinking

5. **Synthesizing Information** Write a paragraph based on personal knowledge or experience that supports or refutes the idea that homogamy dominates American society.

Another Time

Courtship and Marriage Among the Hopi

Courtship and marriage customs among the Hopi Indians of the southwestern United States are quite different from those of the dominant U.S. culture.

Once the decision to marry is made by the young couple, the boy goes in the evening after supper to the girl's house and there states his intentions to her parents. If he is acceptable, he is told to go home and tell his parents about it. The girl then grinds cornmeal or makes bread, and carries it to the house of her prospective groom. At this time the mother of the boy may refuse the bread or meal, in which case the match is usually broken off. If, however, the food is accepted, it is given by the mother to her brothers and to her husband's clansmen, and the wedding plans go forward.

After this event the girl returns home to grind more meal with the help of her kinswomen, while the boy fetches water and chops wood for his mother. In the evening after these chores are completed, the bride dresses in her manta beads and her wedding blanket. Accompanied by the boy, who carries the meal she has ground, she walks barefoot to his house. There she presents the meal to her prospective mother-in-law and settles down for a temporary three-day stay before the wedding. During this period the young couple may see each other, but they [do not become intimate].

At some time during the three-day period the groom's house is visited, or "attacked," by his paternal aunts, who break in on the bride and shower her with [abusive language] and often with mud. They accuse her of laziness, inefficiency, and stupidity. The boy's mother and her clanswomen protect the girl and insist that the accusations are unfounded. In spite of appearances all this is carried off in a good-humored way, and finally the aunts leave, having stolen the wood their nephew had brought his mother. The wood is used to bake piki, which is given to the mother, and thus all damages are paid for.

On the morning of the fourth day the marriage is consummated. On this occasion the girl's relatives wash the boy's hair and bathe him, while the boy's relatives do the same for the girl. The couple may now sleep together as man and wife, but they remain at the boy's mother's house until the girl's wedding garments are complete. These garments are woven by the groom, his male relatives, and any men in the village who wish to participate.

Source: Stuart A. Queen and Robert W. Habenstein, *The Family in Various Cultures,* 4th ed. (Philadelphia: Lippincott, 1974, pp. 54–55, 56–58. Copyright 1952, © 1961, 1967, 1974 by J.B. Lippincott Company.) Reprinted by permission of Harper & Row, Publishers.

Thinking It Over

1. What do you think the staged "fight" with the groom's aunts signifies?
2. What are some of the advantages Hopi society gains by following these wedding customs?

Contemporary Hopi Indians play traditional roles during a formal ceremony.

Section 2

Theoretical Perspectives and the Family

Key Term

- socioemotional maintenance

Functionalism

For the functionalists, the family plays many roles, including socializing the young, providing social and emotional support, managing reproduction, regulating sexual activity, transmitting social status, and serving as an economic center. Let's look more closely at each of these functions.

How does the family socialize children? In addition to caring for an infant's physical needs, parents begin the vital process of teaching the child what he or she must learn to learn to participate in society. During the first year, the infant begins to mimic words and, later, sentences. During the second and third years, parents begin to teach the child values and norms of behavior. By being role models and through training and education, the family continues the process of socialization in each new stage of development.

What do functionalists believe about the roles associated with this father and daughter?

What is the socioemotional function of the family? Another major function of the family is **socioemotional maintenance.** Generally, the family is the one place in society where an individual is unconditionally accepted and loved. Family members accept one another as they are; every member is special and unique. Without this care and affection, children will not develop normally. (See Chapter 4, pages 109–114, on children raised in isolation.) They may have low self-esteem, fear rejection, feel insecure, and eventually find it difficult to adjust to marriage or to express affection to their own children. Even individuals who are well integrated into society require support when adjusting to changing norms and in developing and continuing healthy relationships. Here again, the family can provide socioemotional maintenance.

Section Preview

The family is the very core of human social life. It is not surprising that each of the major perspectives focuses on the family. Functionalism emphasizes the benefits of the family for society. The conflict perspective looks at the reasons males dominate in the family structure. Symbolic interactionism studies the way the family socializes children and promotes the development of self-concept.

socioemotional maintenance provision of acceptance and support

Figure 11.3 American Youths Grade Their Parents

In a national survey, Americans in the seventh through the twelfth grades were asked to "grade" their mothers and fathers. The results are shown below. The left-hand column lists various aspects of child rearing, and the remaining columns indicate the percentage of students who assigned each grade. For example, on the dimension "Raising me with good values," 69 percent gave their fathers an A, 17 percent a B, and so forth.

Grading Dad

Aspect of Child Rearing	A	B	C	D	F
Raising me with good values	69%	17%	8%	4%	2%
Appreciating me for who I am	58	21	11	8	2
Encouraging me to enjoy learning	58	24	12	4	2
Making me feel important and loved	57	22	13	6	2
Being able to go to important events	55	22	13	5	5
Being there for me when I am sick	52	20	16	8	4
Spending time talking with me	43	24	19	10	4
Establishing traditions with me	41	26	15	11	7
Being involved in school life	38	24	19	12	7
Being someone to go to when upset	38	22	15	12	13
Controlling his temper	31	27	20	10	12
Knowing what goes on with me	31	30	17	12	10

Assigned Grade

Grading Mom

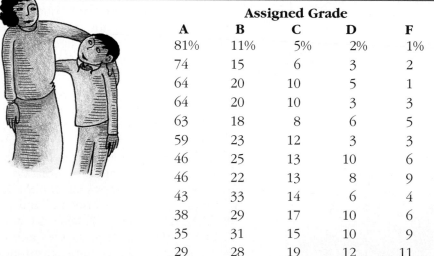

Aspect of Child Rearing	A	B	C	D	F
Being there for me when I am sick	81%	11%	5%	2%	1%
Raising me with good values	74	15	6	3	2
Making me feel important and loved	64	20	10	5	1
Being able to go to important events	64	20	10	3	3
Appreciating me for who I am	63	18	8	6	5
Encouraging me to enjoy learning	59	23	12	3	3
Being involved in school life	46	25	13	10	6
Being someone to go to when upset	46	22	13	8	9
Spending time talking with me	43	33	14	6	4
Establishing traditions with me	38	29	17	10	6
Knowing what goes on with me	35	31	15	10	9
Controlling her temper	29	28	19	12	11

Assigned Grade

1. Based on this data, what conclusions would you draw about the closeness of families in America?
2. Select the three aspects of child rearing you think are most important, and compare the grade you would give your parent or parents on these aspects with the grades in this national sample.

Source: Ellen Galinsky, *Ask the Children* (New York: William Morrow & Co., Inc., 1999).

What is the reproductive function of the family?

Society cannot survive without new members. The family provides an orderly means for producing new members, generation after generation. So important is this function that for many cultures and religions, it is the primary purpose for sexual relations. In many societies in developing nations the failure of a wife to bear children can lead to divorce. Residents of places such as the Punjab region of North India, for example, view children as an economic necessity. The significance of having children is also seen in the hundreds of rituals, customs, and traditions that are associated with pregnancy and birth in virtually all cultures around the world. (Later in the chapter, we look at the rise of marriages without children in the United States.)

What important functions are being fulfilled by this family?

How does the family regulate sexual activity?

In no known society are people given total sexual freedom. Even in sexually permissive societies, such as the Hopi Indians, there are rules about mating and marrying. Norms regarding sexual activities vary from place to place. Families in a few cultures, such as in the Trobriand Islands, encourage premarital sex. Other societies, like those in Iran and Afghanistan, go to great lengths to prevent any contact between nonrelated single males and females. The United States has traditionally fallen somewhere between these two extremes. In the ideal culture in the United States, adolescents would abstain from sexual activity. In real culture, however, the abundance of sexual references directed at teens by the advertising and entertainment industries make abstinence very difficult and even seem undesirable. Clearly, we are sending a mixed message to young people today. One of the consequences of this cultural confusion is the increase in teenage pregnancies and the number of teenagers having abortions. But whatever the norms, it is almost always up to the family to enforce them.

How does the family transmit social status?

Families provide economic resources that open and close occupational doors. The sons and daughters of high-income professionals, for example, are more likely to attend college and graduate school than are the children of blue-collar workers. Consequently, the children of professionals are more likely as adults to enter professional occupations. The family also passes on values that affect social status. The children of professionals, for example, tend to feel a greater need to pursue a college degree than their counterparts from blue-collar families. In these and many other ways, the family affects the placement of children in the stratification structure.

What is the economic function of the family?

At one time, families were self-sufficient economic units whose members all contributed to the production of needed goods. Every family member would join in such tasks as growing food, making cloth, and taking care of livestock. The modern American family is a unit of consumption rather than production. Adult members—increasingly including working mothers—are employed outside the home and pool their resources to buy what they need. But the end result is the same. The family provides what is needed to survive.

Home is the place where, when you have to go there, they have to take you in.

**Robert Frost
American poet**

Conflict Theory

Conflict theorists focus on the way family members compete and cooperate. Most family structure throughout history has been patriarchal and patrilineal. Women have historically and traditionally been considered the property of men, and the control of family members and property has typically passed through male bloodlines. This male dominance has been considered "natural" and "legitimate." Thus, most family systems have had built-in gender inequality.

How does conflict theory explain gender relationships in the family? According to conflict theorists, males are dominant and in control; females have traditionally been expected to be submissive helpers. In the traditional division of labor, males work outside the home for finances to support the family. Women remain at home to prepare meals, keep house, and care for the children. Women are unpaid laborers who make it possible for men to earn wages. With men having control over the money, the wives and mothers are kept in a dependent and powerless role. According to the conflict perspective, families in the past, then, have fostered social inequality.

How do the ideas of feminist writers fit with conflict theory? Writers and activists who organize on behalf of women's rights and interests have come to be called feminists. Many feminists today view the family from the conflict perspective. They believe that family structure is the source of the inequality between men and women in society. They point out that men have had control over women since before private property and capitalism existed. Women's contributions in the home (mother and homemaker) are not paid and are therefore undervalued in a capitalist society. Attempts by women to gain more power within the family structure can result in conflict.

Feminist Betty Friedan is the godmother of the American women's movement. Many conflict theorists study her writings.

Symbolic Interactionism

According to symbolic interactionism, a key to understanding behavior within the family lies in the interactions among family members and the meanings that members assign to these interactions.

How does the family help develop a person's self-concept? Socialization begins within the family. As family members share meanings and feelings, children develop self-concepts and learn to put themselves mentally in the place of others. Interactions with adults help children acquire human personality and social characteristics. Children develop further as they meet others outside the home.

According to symbolic interactionists, relationships within the family are constantly changing. A newly married couple will spend many months (perhaps years) testing their new relationship. As time passes, the initial relationship changes, along with some aspects of the partners' personalities, including self-concepts. These changes occur as the partners struggle with such problem issues as chores and responsibilities, personality clashes, and in-laws.

With the arrival of children comes a new set of adjustments. Parental views may differ on child-rearing practices, number of children desired, and education for the children. The situation is made even more complex by the new member of the family, who must also become part of the interaction patterns.

Children have more need of models than of critics.

Carolyn Coats
author for young adults

Section 2 Assessment

1. Match the following examples with the major theoretical perspectives: functionalism (F), conflict theory (C), symbolic interactionism (SI)
   a. fathers "giving away" brides
   b. having children
   c. development of self-concept
   d. newly married partners adjusting to each other
   e. child abuse
   f. social class being passed from one generation to another

Critical Thinking

2. **Finding the Main Idea** Select a memorable family experience (such as the Thanksgiving holiday) and interpret it from the viewpoint of one of the three major perspectives.

Figure 11.4 Focus on Theoretical Perspectives

Perspectives on the Family. Both functionalism and conflict theory are concerned with the ways social norms affect the nature of the family. Symbolic interactionism tends to examine the relationship of the self to the family. How might functionalism and conflict theory focus on the self?

Theory	Topic	Example
Functionalism	Sex norms	Children are taught that sexual activity should be reserved for married couples.
Conflict Theory	Male dominance	Husbands use their economic power to control the ways money is spent.
Symbolic Interactionism	Developing self-esteem	A child abused by her parents learns to dislike herself.

Sociology Today

Looking for Mr. or Ms. Right

This activity will give you some ideas for evaluating whether a current boyfriend or girlfriend is a good candidate for a successful long-term relationship.

From the list on the right, (and on a separate sheet of paper), list the ten most important qualities to you. (Number 1 as the most important, number 2 the next most important, and so forth.) Then fold your paper in half. In the right-hand column, either have your partner fill out the questionnaire or rank the characteristics yourself according to how you think your partner would.

Evaluating Your Responses. Which of the items listed on the right do you think are the most important in predicting marital success? According to research, the last seven items (17–23) are the most important. High compatibility between you and your partner on these seven characteristics would probably increase your chances of marital success. A low degree of matching does not, of course, ensure an unhappy marriage or a divorce, but it does suggest areas that may cause problems in the future.

Adapted from the Department of Human Development and Family Studies, Colorado State University.

I am looking for a partner who . . .

Partner   Self

1. _____ is honest and truthful.
2. _____ is fun to be with.
3. _____ is of the same educational background.
4. _____ will take care of me.
5. _____ wants to have children.
6. _____ communicates well with me.
7. _____ will share household jobs and tasks.
8. _____ is a good friend with whom I can talk.
9. _____ is of the same religious background.
10. _____ makes decisions.
11. _____ earns good money.
12. _____ is physically attractive.
13. _____ is in love with me and I with him/her.
14. _____ encourages me to be my own person.
15. _____ has interests like mine in making money and having fun.
16. _____ makes me feel important.
17. _____ is faithful.
18. _____ shares mutual interests in home, children, romantic love, and religion.
19. _____ has had a happy childhood with happily married parents.
20. _____ is emotionally mature.
21. _____ is prepared to support a family.
22. _____ is interested in waiting to marry until age twenty-two or older.
23. _____ wants a six-month to two-year engagement period.

Doing Sociology

Do you think that the qualities listed in the questionnaire are relevant to you in choosing a wife or a husband? Why or why not? Are there characteristics more important to you and your friends? Explain.

Section 3

Family and Marriage in the United States

Key Terms

- divorce rate
- marriage rate

The Nature of the American Family

The United States is a large, diverse society. Describing the "typical" family might be impossible. There are, however, more similarities than differences among American families. As the various ethnic groups blend into life in the United States, their families tend to follow the American pattern described below.

❖ Families are nuclear (a household contains only a set of parents and their children).

❖ Families are bilateral (they trace lineage and pass inheritance equally through both parents).

❖ Families are democratic (partners share decision making equally).

❖ Families are neolocal (each family lives apart from other families).

❖ Families are monogamous (each includes only one husband and one wife at a time).

Romantic Love and Marriage

To Americans, it's like the old song—"Love and marriage go together like a horse and carriage." In a recent poll of the American public, 83 percent of both men and women rated "being in love" as the most vital reason to marry.

The relationship between love and marriage is not always viewed in this way. Among the British feudal aristocracy, romantic love was a game of pursuit played outside of marriage. Marriage was not thought to be compatible with deeply romantic feelings. In ancient Japan, love was considered a barrier to the arrangement of marriages by parents. Among Hindus in India today, parents or other relatives

Section Preview

Modern marriages are based primarily on love, but there are many reasons for marrying—and as many reasons for divorce. Although the American family provides social and emotional support, violence in this setting is not uncommon. Child abuse and spousal abuse are serious problems in too many American families.

In the United States today, the norm is for love to precede the marriage vows. Not all societies share this norm.

Figure 11.5 Divorce and Marriage Rates: 1940–1998.
Can you apply what you learned in history to interpret this chart?
(a) What happened in the mid-1940s that caused the dramatic rise in marriage rates during this period?
(b) Why do you think the marriage rate dropped so low in the 1950s?
(c) What are some possible reasons that the divorce rate peaked in 1980?

Source: National Vital Statistics Reports 47, 1999.

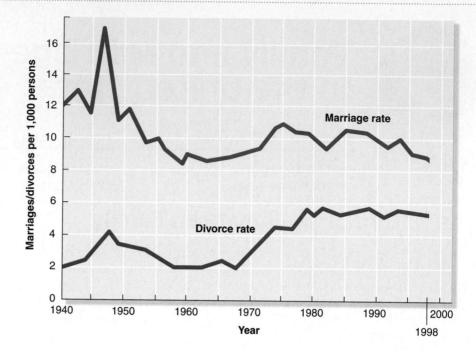

are expected to find suitable mates for the young. Criteria for mate selection include caste, wealth, family reputation, and appearance. Love is not absent in Hindu marriages, but love follows marriage rather than the other way around (Cox, 1999).

While romantic love is almost always stated as a condition for marriage in modern societies, it is seldom the only condition. People marry for many reasons, and romantic love may be only one of many reasons. A person may marry to enter a powerful family or to advance a career. One of the strongest motivations for marriage is conformity. Parents expect their children to marry after a certain age and worry about them—perhaps even pressure them—if their children remain single very long. Peers are another source of pressure. Since well over 90 percent of all adults in the United States do marry, conformity must certainly be a motivating factor.

Americans typically believe that a marriage that is not based on romantic love cannot last. It is more accurate to say that a marriage based only on romantic love is almost sure to fail. While love may be a good start, it is only the beginning. For a marriage to last, a couple must build a relationship that goes beyond romantic love (Crosby, 1985).

marriage rate
the number of marriages per year for every one thousand members of a population

The **marriage rate**—the number of marriages per year for every thousand members of the population—has fluctuated, in the United States, since 1940. As shown in Figure 11.5, the marriage rate peaked at over 16.0 immediately following World War II. Since then, the marriage rate, with ups and downs, has been cut in half.

Divorce

divorce rate
the number of divorces per year for every one thousand members of the population

The **divorce rate** is the number of divorces per year for every one thousand members of the population. Except for a peak and decline after World War II, the divorce rate in the United States increased slowly between 1860 and the early 1960s. A dramatic increase occurred over the next twenty years, when

Snapshot of America

Marriage Rates

As noted in the text, the U.S. marriage rate overall has declined dramatically since 1940. Variation in the marriage rate among individual states is interesting. The lowest marriage rate occurs in New Jersey. Nevada has far and away the highest marriage rate.

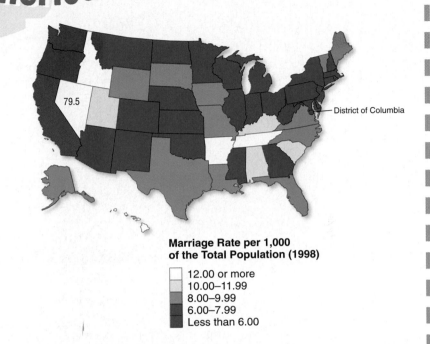

District of Columbia

Marriage Rate per 1,000 of the Total Population (1998)

- 12.00 or more
- 10.00–11.99
- 8.00–9.99
- 6.00–7.99
- Less than 6.00

Interpreting the Map

1. Create a chart comparing the marriage rate in your state with other states, keeping in mind that the national average is just over 8.0. Pose a question for your classmates to answer describing their reaction to your state's position in the marriage rate ranking.

2. Would you expect the divorce rates of states to be correlated with their marriage rates? Make a prediction before looking up the divorce rates for comparison. Report your findings to the class.

Source: PRIMEDIA Reference Inc., 1998.

---

the divorce rate more than doubled (from 2.2 percent in 1960 to 5.3 percent in 1981). Since then, the rate has leveled off. In fact, it has declined slightly since 1985. (See Figure 11.5 on page 364.)

What are the causes of divorce? Both personal and societal factors influence why people divorce. At the individual level, these factors include:

❖ the age of the people when they married. The later the age upon marriage, the lower the chance of divorce.

❖ how many years the partners have been married. The longer the marriage, the lower the chance of divorce.

❖ the nature and quality of the relationship. The more respect and flexibility exists between the partners, the lower the chance of divorce.

Sociologists are most concerned with how larger forces in society affect marriages. There are four main factors. First, the divorce rate rises during economic prosperity and goes down when times are hard. This is probably

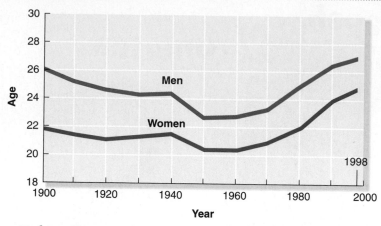

Figure 11.6 Median Age at First Marriage. *This figure shows changes in the median age at first marriage in the U.S. since 1900. The marrying age for both men and women has been on the increase since the 1960s. How might this trend affect the future divorce rate?*

Source: U.S. Bureau of the Census, March 1998.

No matter how many communes anybody invents, the family always creeps back.

Margaret Mead anthropologist

because people are more likely to make changes and take chances when they are not worried about basic survival.

Second, the rise in the divorce rate after 1960 followed the growing up of the baby-boom generation. Baby boomers did not attach a stigma to divorce the way earlier generations did and so were more likely to leave unhappy marriages than to stay.

Third, the increasing financial independence of women means they are more willing to end bad marriages. They are not as dependent (especially if there are no children) upon the husband's willingness to support an ex.

Fourth, American values and attitudes about marriage and divorce are changing. Society is much more forgiving of divorce and remarriage. Women, especially, are no longer "punished," as they were in the past, for leaving a marriage.

What does the future for marriage look like?   For several reasons, there is a good chance that the recent decline in the U.S. divorce rate may continue:

❖ The average age at first marriage in the United States is increasing. (See Figure 11.6.) We know that the later people marry, the less likely they are to divorce. (Mature individuals have more realistic expectations about their mates and have fewer economic and career problems.) This trend is likely to continue well into the twenty-first century.

❖ The average age of the population of the United States is increasing as baby boomers grow older. This exceptionally large generation set records for divorce in the late 1960s and 1970s. Baby boomers now range in age from the mid thirties to the early fifties, which removes them from the age bracket that produces the highest divorce rates.

❖ American couples are having fewer children, and the children are spaced farther apart. This reduces pressure on marriages.

Tragically, violence has been a pattern of some family relationships throughout history.

Family Violence

Americans have traditionally denied the existence of widespread violence in the family setting. Violent behavior has in the past mistakenly been associated mostly with lower-class families. Part of the reason for this attitude was the fact that the first research in this area used law enforcement and public medical records. Because the police and hospitals dealt mostly with the lower classes (middle and upper classes had lawyers and private doctors), the statistics were skewed toward the lower class. We are learning that domestic violence occurs at all class levels.

Is violence in the family common?   Although the family provides a safe and warm emotional haven, it can in some cases be a hostile environment. Family violence, or domestic violence, affects all members of the family—children, spouses, and older people. Celebrated trials during the 1990s brought increased public attention to the issue of domestic violence. For more than a year, media focus was centered on the trial of football superstar O. J. Simpson, accused of the murder of his former wife Nicole Brown Simpson and Ronald Goldman. Evidence presented during the trial indicated that Simpson had abused her when they were married. In another high-profile case, the wealthy Menendez brothers were convicted of the murder of their parents. (Trial evidence indicated that the brothers had been abused as children.)

According to a national survey, almost one-quarter of adults in the United States report having been physically abused as children. In most cases, physical violence involves a slap, a shove, or a severe spanking. However, kicking, biting, punching, beating, and threatening with a weapon are part of abusive violence as well. Furthermore, according to estimates, one of every four girls and one in ten boys are victims of sexual aggression, either within the home

Country	Reported Abuse
Industrialized Countries	
Canada	**29%** of ever-married/common law–partnered women report being physically assaulted by a current or former partner since the age of sixteen.
New Zealand	**20%** of women report being hit or physically abused by a male partner.
Switzerland	**20%** of women report being physically assaulted.
United Kingdom	**25%** of women had been punched or slapped by a partner or ex-partner in their lifetimes.
United States	**28%** of women report at least one episode of physical violence from their partner.
Asia and the Pacific	
Korea	**38%** of wives report being physically abused by their spouses in the last year.
Thailand	**20%** of husbands acknowledge physically abusing their wives at least once in their marriage.
Middle East	
Egypt	**35%** of women report being beaten by their husbands at some point in their marriage.
Israel	**32%** of women report at least one episode of physical abuse by their partners during the last twelve months; 30% report sexual coercion by their husbands in the last year.
Africa	
Kenya	**42%** of women report ever being beaten by a partner; of those, 58% report that they were beaten often or sometimes.
Uganda	**41%** of women report being beaten or physically harmed by a partner; 41% of men report beating their partners.
Latin America and the Caribbean	
Chile	**26%** report at least one episode of violence by a partner, 11% report at least one episode of severe violence, and 15% of women report at least one episode of less severe violence.
Columbia	**19%** of women have been physically assaulted by their partners in their lifetimes.
Mexico	**30%** report at least one episode of physical violence by a partner; 13% report physical violence within the last year.

Figure 11.7 Events of Domestic Violence against Women in Selected Countries. *Levels of domestic violence against women clearly vary from country to country.*

Source: World Health Organization, 1997.

or outside (Heller, Kempe, and Krugman, 1999; Pryor, 1999). Reported child sexual abuse in the United States has skyrocketed in recent years. Between 1976 and 1997, the number of reported child abuse cases rose from 662,000 to over 3 million. Statistics collected nationally indicate that 47 out of every 1,000 children are reported annually as victims of child maltreatment (Wang and Daro, 1998). Child sexual abuse goes beyond physical contact. Some children are forced into pornography or are made to view pornography in the presence of the abuser. What's worse, the abuser is usually someone the child trusts—a parent, friend of the family, child-care giver, brother.

At least four million women are battered by their husbands annually, probably many more. Over four thousand women each year are beaten to death. The extent of physical abuse is underestimated in part because three-fourths of spousal violence occurs during separation or after divorce, and most research is conducted among married couples.

Is abuse always directed against women? Husband abuse is frequently overlooked in studies of physical abuse. Although marriages in the United States are generally male dominated, it seems there is equality in the use of physical violence. One set of researchers found that almost one-third of the husbands in their survey had acted violently against their wives and that wives were almost as likely to have used physical violence against their husbands. Other studies also show that husbands and wives assault each other at about the same rate. Much of the violence committed by women, however, involves self-protection or retaliation, and as a category, females are not as violent as males (Gelles, 1997).

Is abuse always physical?   Family violence is not limited to physical abuse. Verbal and psychological abuse are also a part of many families. Psychologists report that the feelings of self-hate and worthlessness that are often the effects of abuse can be as damaging as physical wounds. And more than nine million children in the United States suffer from neglect, a condition of being ignored rather than abused.

What is the most common form of family violence?   Probably the most frequent and most tolerated violence in the family occurs between children. This *sibling violence* appears to be prevalent and on the rise. Abuse among siblings may be based on rivalry, jealousy, disagreements over personal possessions, or incest. Although it declines somewhat as children get older, it does not disappear.

Little is known about abuse of elderly people, because less research has been done in this area. Abuse of older people usually takes the form of physical violence, psychological mistreatment, economic manipulation, or neglect. Estimates of elder abuse range from 500,000 to 2.5 million cases annually (Gelles, 1997). Some observers fear that abuse of older people will increase as baby boomers age and the population grows older.

Abuse directed against the elderly in nursing homes has been a recent concern of social activists.

Section 3 Assessment

1. Choose the word from each pair that best describes the typical American family.
   a. nuclear or extended
   b. patrilineal or bilateral
   c. neolocal or matrilocal
   d. polygynous or monogamous
2. Identify three factors discussed in the text that are associated with divorce.

Critical Thinking

3. **Making Predictions** What is your prediction for the divorce trend in the United States in 2050? Use information in this section to support your answer.

> All happy families resemble each other; each unhappy family is unhappy in its own way.
>
> **Count Leo Tolstoy**
> **Russian writer**

Tech Trends

Technology and the Family

According to many experts, the influence of technology is just as far-reaching in the home as in the office. Activities in the home are changing dramatically because of recent technological innovations.

Because more American families are living farther from relatives, more are using the Internet to stay in touch with each other. Birth announcements, reunion plans, gift registries for weddings, and funeral arrangements are now being shared with families and friends on-line (Bulkeley, 1997). Although somewhat impersonal, these social connections may reduce social isolation and friction in families.

Many, however, see a darker side to new technology for the family. For example, one critic offers this concern: "If we wish to raise our children as androids who respond to Internet packets rather than parental guidance, I can't think of a better way to do that than to put computer networks in homes" (Wingfield, 1998:R23).

Another critic believes that high-tech home equipment like cable television, the Internet, and video games increasingly rules the lives of American families. Children who spend a great deal of time alone with these technological wonders are deprived of frequent and intense social contact with other children, their parents, and other adults in the neighborhood. Consequently, the current generation of children could very well be the first to grow up with highly deficient social skills. Offering indirect support for this conclusion is the fact that almost three-fourths of Americans say they do not know their neighbors. The number of Americans who admit they have spent no time with the people living next to them has doubled in the last twenty years (Quintanilla, 1996).

Technology can also separate, socially, those family members who use the new technology from those who do not. For example, some couples who depend on web pages to inform their relatives of family news have found that some family members cannot share in this information. Older members of the family who do not have access to the Internet often feel cut off from the rest of the family (Bulkeley, 1997).

Analyzing the Trends

A dark picture of the Internet has been presented in this feature. Think of some positive consequences of this technology for the family. Discuss two of them.

The computer, to an even greater degree than the television, is being credited with isolating family members.

Section 4

Changes in Marriage and Family

Key Terms

- blended family
- adolescents
- dual-employed marriages
- cohabitation
- boomerang kids

Blended Families

The relatively high divorce rate in the United States has created the **blended family**—a family formed when at least one of the partners in a marriage has been married before and has a child or children from the previous marriage. This type of family can become extremely complicated (Ganong and Coleman, 1994; Barnes, 1998). Here's an example: A former husband (with two children in the custody of their biological mother) marries a new wife with two children in her custody. They have two children of their own. The former wife also remarries a man with two children, one in his custody and one in the custody of his former wife. That former wife has remarried and has had a child with her second husband, who has custody of one child from his previous marriage. The former husband's parents are divorced, and both have remarried. Thus, when he remarries, his children have two complete sets of grandparents on his side, plus one set on the mother's side, plus perhaps more on the stepfather's side (Cox, 1999).

Blended families create a new type of extended family, a family that is not based strictly on blood relationships. As the example above shows, it is possible for a child in a blended family to have eight grandparents. Of

Section Preview

Many new patterns of marriage and family living have emerged in the United States. They include blended families, single-parent families, child-free families, cohabitation, same-sex domestic partners, and families with boomerang children. In spite of these new arrangements, the traditional nuclear family is not going to be replaced on any broad scale.

blended family
a family formed when at least one of the partners in a marriage has been married before and has a child or children from a previous marriage

Americans knew the "Brady Bunch" family long before the term blended families became common.

course, not all blended families are this complicated. But about 40 percent of households in the United States contain biologically unrelated individuals.

Many blended families are successful, especially if they make adjustments during the first few years. Children from previous marriages, however, are one factor in the higher divorce rates among second marriages (Baca Zinn and Eitzen, 1998).

What major problems face blended families?   Sociologists point to three major problems facing blended families—a lack of money, stepchildren's dislike of the new spouse, and uncertainty about roles played by stepparents.

❖ **Money difficulties.** Financial demands from both the former and present families generally result in lower incomes in stepfamilies. Remarried husbands are often legally obligated to support children from their previous marriages. Second wives may resent losing the income spent on children from a previous marriage.

❖ **Stepchildren's antagonism.** Hoping for a reunion of their original parents, stepchildren may try to derail the new marriage. Even five years after divorce, about a third of stepchildren continue to strongly disapprove of their original parents' divorce. This is especially true for teenagers, who can be very critical of their stepparents' values and personalities.

❖ **Unclear roles.** The roles of stepparents are often vague and ambiguous. A stepchild often doesn't consider a parent's new spouse as a "real" father or mother. It is also not clear to stepparents or stepchildren how much power the new spouse really has. Issues involving control and discipline reflect power struggles within the family, especially with teenagers involved.

Student Web Activity
Visit the *Sociology and You* Web site at soc.glencoe.com and click on **Chapter 11—Student Web Activities** for an activity on blended families.

Single-Parent Families

Over one out of four American families is a single-parent family. By far the greatest proportion of these households are headed by women. Only 10 percent of children living with one parent are in a male-headed household.

Why do women head the vast majority of single-parent households?   Although courts today are more sensitive to the fathers' claims, women in all social classes are still more likely to win custody of their children in cases of separation and divorce. Unwed mothers or women

A debate exists over the appropriateness of celebrities choosing to be single mothers.

abandoned by their husbands and/or the fathers of their children make up a large part of poor single-parent households. Finally, poor women marry (or re-marry) at a very low rate.

Though significantly fewer, there is an increasing number of well-educated, professional women who head single-parent households. With the stigma of unwed motherhood declining, more affluent unmarried women are *choosing* to have children and to care for them alone. These women have the economic resources to support an independent family. Finally, well-educated women are adopting higher standards for selecting husbands (Seligmann, 1999).

What are the effects of single-parent families on children?
Approximately 30 percent of America's children (defined as people under the age of eighteen) live in households with one parent. African American and Latino children are more likely than white children to live with only their mothers because of high divorce and out-of-wedlock birth rates, and lower rates of marriage and remarriage (U.S. Bureau of the Census, 1998a). Figure 11.8 shows how the number of never-married and single parents increased among African Americans and Latinos from 1970 to 1998. In general, the chances are increasing that American children will live at least part of their youth in a fatherless home.

Adolescents (persons from the ages of twelve to seventeen) who live with one parent or with a stepparent have much higher rates of deviant behavior, including delinquency, drug and alcohol abuse, and teenage pregnancy, than adolescents living with both natural parents (Dornbush et al., 1985; Popenoe, 1999). A national sample of twelve- to seventeen-year-olds indicates that arrests, school discipline, truancy, running away, and smoking occur more often in single-parent and stepparent families, regardless of income, race, or ethnic background.

These figures do not point to a lack of concern in single parents as much as they show the built-in problems of single parenting. Single working parents must struggle to provide their children with the time, attention, and guidance that two parents can give. Because the single mother typically makes little money, she has added financial problems. Finding good child care and adequate housing in a suitable neighborhood is often very difficult.

adolescents
youths from the ages of twelve to seventeen

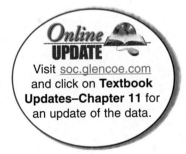

Online **UPDATE**
Visit soc.glencoe.com and click on **Textbook Updates–Chapter 11** for an update of the data.

Figure 11.8 Percentage of Single-Parent Families: 1970–1998. *This graph compares the percentage of African American, Latino, and white families that have never married or have one parent. What generalization can you make from this data?*

*Note: Latino data not available for 1970.

Source: U.S. Bureau of the Census, 1998.

Percentage of single-family homes

African American: 62% (1998), 61% (1990), 52% (1980), 36% (1970)
Latino*: 36% (1998), 33% (1990), 26% (1980)
White: 27% (1998), 23% (1990), 17% (1980), 10% (1970)

Legend: 1998, 1990, 1980, 1970

Childless Marriages

About one-fifth of couples today remain childless. In this an upward or downward trend?

In the past, married women without children were seen as failing to fulfill their "duty" as wives. In fact, in many religions, the inability to have children is still one of the few allowed reasons for divorcing a woman. Historically, married childless women were pitied and looked down upon, and single women rarely achieved respectability outside the role of "spinster aunt."

Why are some married women now choosing not to have children?   Around 19 percent of American women who have ever been married do not have children in 2000, compared with about 15 percent in 1970 (U.S. Bureau of the Census, 2000d). It is unclear if this upward trend will continue. Today, the reasons married women give for choosing not to have children are varied. Social stigmas against childless married women are disappearing. It is no longer automatically accepted that having children is the primary reason for marriage. Some women have elected to pursue personal or career goals instead. Other people, both men and women, have basic moral issues about raising children in what they consider to be an immoral world. Sometimes, having children is put off so long that it becomes hard for couples to make the adjustment to raising a family. Finally, it is important to remember that not all couples without children have chosen to be that way. Physical or psychological problems keep some couples from having children.

Are marriages happier with or without children?   The answer to this question generally depends upon the couple's decision about having children. Among childless couples who want children, marital happiness is generally lower than for married couples with children. However, research shows that couples who by choice have no children appear to be happier and more satisfied with their marriages and lives than couples with children (Cox, 1999).

Dual-Employed Marriages

dual-employed marriages marriages in which both spouses work outside the home

In families where both parents are working outside the home, special strains are put on the marriage. Women in these **dual-employed marriages** are apparently expected to handle most of the household and child-care responsibilities in addition to their full-time jobs.

What are drawbacks to the dual-employed family?   Because they must combine employment with child care and household tasks, married working women work about fifteen hours more a week than men. Sociologist Arlie Hochschild calls this home- and child-based work "the second shift." Although men spend an average of four to six hours per week in household and child-care duties, women bear the larger burden.

In addition to this greater workload, women in dual-employed marriages must cope with role conflict. They are torn between the time requirements of their jobs and their desire to spend more time with their children and husbands. Feelings of guilt may arise from not being able to meet all expectations of wife, mother, and breadwinner.

Men in dual-employed marriages are generally unwilling to assume household responsibilities equal to those of their wives. Even so, they feel the negative effects of role conflict and excessive demands on their time. In addition, having an employed wife, particularly if she earns more, may not fit with men's images of themselves as providers.

Is there a positive side to dual employment? Dual employment offers advantages as well as disadvantages. On balance, the effects of employment on the psychological well-being of women have been beneficial (Moen, 1992; Crosby, 1993; Cox, 1999). Working outside the home provides a wider set of social relationships and greater feelings of control, independence, and self-esteem. Employment also appears to provide a social and emotional cushion for women when their children leave home. Compared with women who do not work outside the home, employed women tend to have more outlets for self-expression (Adelmann et al., 1989; Wolfe, 1998). If a mother prefers working outside the home, other family members often benefit from her employment. With two incomes, there is more money to spend for purchases that raise the standard of living. Sons and daughters of working mothers also benefit in noneconomic ways. Daughters of working mothers are more likely to see themselves as working adults, as capable of being economically independent, and as benefiting from further education. Sons are more likely to choose wives with similar attitudes toward education and employment.

For men, benefits of a dual-employed marriage include freedom from the responsibility of being the sole provider, increased opportunity for job changes, and opportunities to continue education. Men with employed wives can share the triumphs and defeats of the day with someone who is in the same situation. If their wives are happier working outside the home, husbands enjoy a better marital relationship. Those husbands who take advantage of the opportunity can form a closer relationship with their children by being more active parents (Booth and Crouter, 1998).

A functionalist might suggest that this mother's economic function is clashing with her socioemotional function.

Cohabitation

Cohabitation—living with someone in a marriagelike arrangement without the legal obligations and responsibilities of formal marriage—has been a widely discussed alternative to traditional monogamy for some time. In fact, the number of American adults cohabiting increased from about one-half million to over seven million between 1970 and 2000. According to a nationwide

cohabitation
a marriagelike living arrangement without the legal obligations and responsibilities of formal marriage

Focus on Research

Survey Research: Spanking and Antisocial Behavior

Like many children in the United States, you probably experienced spanking and other legal forms of physical corporal punishment from your parents. In the mid-1980s, research revealed that over 90 percent of parents used corporal punishment on young children, and more than half continued its use during the early teen years. Although high, this rate of corporal punishment was less than in the 1950s (99 percent) and the mid-1970s (97 percent). The rate has declined further since 1985, but nearly all American children still experience some form of corporal punishment.

The use of corporal punishment to correct or control the behavior of children is widely accepted in American culture. "Spare the rod and spoil the child" is a warning deep in our national consciousness. However, Straus and his colleagues (1997) present evidence contradicting the notion that corporal punishment improves children's behavior.

These researchers used data from interviews with a sample of over eight-hundred mothers of children aged six to nine years in a national study. (This was a longitudinal study, one that follows respondents over a period of time.) This study compared parents' use of corporal punishment with antisocial behavior in children. The study defined corporal punishment as "the use of physical force with the intention of causing a child to experience pain, but not injury, for the purpose of correction or control of the child's behavior" (Straus, Sugarman, and Giles-Sims, 1997:761). Slapping a child's hand or buttocks and squeezing a child's arm are examples. A measure of antisocial behavior was based on the mothers' reports of their children's behavior: "cheats or tells lies," "bullies or is cruel or mean to others," "does not feel sorry after misbehaving," "breaks things deliberately," "is disobedient at school," and "has trouble getting along with teachers."

Since this was a longitudinal study, information on the frequency of parents' use of corporal punishment was collected *before* reports on subsequent antisocial behavior. Contrary to common expectations, Straus found that the higher the use of corporal punishment, the higher the level of antisocial behavior two years later.

At the end of their report, the authors move from being strictly social scientists to making a practical child-rearing recommendation. Straus and his colleagues suggest that the reduction or elimination of corporal punishment could lower antisocial behavior in children. In addition, given research indicating a relationship between antisocial behavior in childhood and violence and other crime in adulthood, society at large could benefit from abandoning the use of corporal punishment in child rearing. They state it this way:

> *Thus, because almost all American children experience [corporal punishment] in varying degrees, our findings suggest that almost all American children could benefit from a reduction or elimination of [corporal punishment]. Moreover, considering research showing that [antisocial behavior] in childhood is associated with violence and other crime as an adult, society as a whole, not just children, could benefit from ending the system of violent child-rearing that goes under the euphemism of spanking (Straus, Sugarman, and Giles-Sims, 1997).*

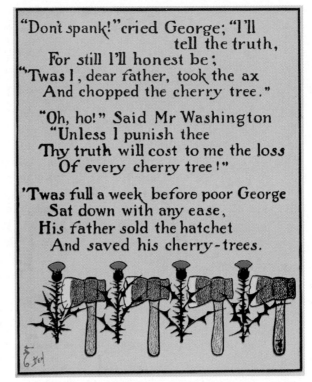

Spanking as a corrective for bad behavior was a norm in the past, as evidenced by this popular 1899 woodcut.

Working with the Research

1. Does a link between childhood corporal punishment and antisocial behavior surprise you? Explain.

2. Suppose that you are on a panel reporting on child rearing to the President of the United States. Using the Straus study as a model, describe the study you would conduct on a possible relationship between childhood corporal punishment and adult crime.

3. How do you anticipate these children will discipline their children later in life?

4. Describe what you think would be more effective means of discipline.

5. Do you think that social science evidence such as this has affected teacher disciplining behavior in schools? Will it? Should it? Explain.

survey, over one-fourth of adults in the United States have cohabited (U.S. Bureau of the Census, 1998a).

Cohabitation has risen among people of all ages and marital statuses, particularly among the young and the divorced. By 2000, about 53 percent of all unmarried-couple households were maintained by someone under thirty-five years of age and about forty-one percent involved at least one child under age fifteen.

Is cohabitation a workable alternative to marriage?   Research reports on cohabitation are not encouraging. Only about 25 percent of cohabiting couples stay together more than four years, reflecting a lower level of certainty about commitment than is true in married couples. This lack of commitment is probably an important reason for the lower satisfaction among cohabiting couples than among married couples (Nock, 1995). Another factor is the higher rate of abuse among cohabiting women than among married, divorced, or separated women.

Cohabitation has not fulfilled the promise of providing good experience for future marriage (Cox, 1999). Cohabitation does not appear to improve the quality of later marriage. Couples who cohabited have shown lower marital adjustment than couples who had not lived together. Finally, premarital cohabitation is associated with a higher risk of divorce (Brown and Booth, 1996).

Same-Sex Domestic Partners

Because of the social stigma that surrounds homosexuality, it is impossible to know precisely what proportion of the American population is homosexual. The Institute of Sex Research, founded by Alfred Kinsey, estimates that homosexuals constitute about 10 percent of the U.S. population (13 percent of the males, 5 percent of the females). Although estimating the number of cohabiting same-sex couples is difficult, the number is known to be increasing, both on college campuses and in the general public. It may have been in recognition of that increase that Vermont passed a bill in April of 2000 recognizing "civil unions" for same-sex partners. Same-sex couples united in civil unions would qualify for the same state benefits as married couples (and be held to the same burdens upon breakup). Same-sex unions are certain to remain a controversial issue confronting U.S. culture for many years to come.

Single Life

An increasing number of Americans are choosing to remain single rather than to marry. More than 26 million Americans over the age of fifteen now live alone, an increase of nearly 150 percent since 1970. Although many of these people will eventually marry, an increasing percentage will remain single all their lives (U.S. Bureau of the Census, 2000d).

Why are more Americans choosing to live alone?   Remaining single has always been a choice that has carried a stigma in the United States. Historically, society frowned on men and women who did not marry. It was seen as a form of deviance. England started taxing bachelors at the end of the seventeenth century and Missouri followed suit in 1820. The stigma attached to remaining single has faded over the past two decades, however. More single Americans are choosing to remain unmarried, pursuing careers or raising children from a former marriage.

While marriage is still a thriving institution, more people today are embracing the single life.

Will the current trend toward remaining single continue? It is too early to predict whether the increase in singlehood will lead to a decline in marriage at all ages. Although singlehood is an increasingly popular alternative to traditional marriage, people are not necessarily rejecting marriage. The implication is that many young adults wish to expand the period of "freedom" after leaving home and are unwilling to rush into the responsibilities of early marriage and parenthood.

Boomerang Kids

The boomerang is a weapon that, when thrown, returns in a wide arc to its point of origin. The term **boomerang kids** is being applied to young adults who either leave home and return or stay at home and live with parents. American adults aged eighteen to thirty-four have a much higher probability of living in their parents' home than Americans of the same age thirty years ago. More than one-fourth of adults eighteen to thirty-four years old now live with their parents (U.S. Bureau of the Census, 1996a).

Why are more adult children returning home? Increasing numbers of adult children are living with their parents for several reasons. Because young adults are marrying later, more stay at home longer. In addition, more are continuing their education and find living at home the best solution to the problem of supporting themselves and paying school expenses. Many young adults return home even after completing their education because the high cost of living outstrips their earning capacity. Also, since parents tend to give their children a home after a failed marriage, the high divorce rate is increasing the proportion of young adults living at home.

What are some consequences of the boomerang effect? Costs associated with education, day-to-day living, and perhaps even a grandchild or two can create financial strain for older parents whose adult children live with them. Many parents complain that their adult children do not share in expenses or help around the house. The children's presence robs their parents of privacy and may prevent them from developing relationships with spouses and friends. It is not surprising that higher marital dissatisfaction among middle-aged parents is associated with adult children living at home.

Adult children who find themselves in this situation suffer as well. Adult children who have returned home have normally been forced by circumstances to do so. They are likely to be having difficulties balancing school and work, making their way economically, forming a family, or surviving the aftermath of a divorce. They know the burden they represent. In addition, returning home usually means giving up some freedom.

In spite of these problems, most families appear to adjust well to the return of older children (Mitchell and Gee, 1996). This is especially true when the returning older child is able to help with expenses and household duties.

> A majority of colonial Americans probably spent some time in a stepfamily.
>
> **Stephanie Coontz
> social historian**

boomerang kids
adult children who return to the home of origin or who continue to live with parents

"Can't I just stay here with you and Mom? I don't like what I've seen of the real world."

The thoughts of a boomerang kid. Mom and Dad are not buying it, are they?

3. How would conflict theorists describe the family?

4. What is the most widely practiced form of marriage around the world today?

5. Who are the victims of family violence?

Thinking Critically

1. **Analyzing Information** According to Hochschild's *second shift* explanation, gender equity in the home does not exist. Why do men, on average, still do less housework than women? Do attitudes about masculinity have anything to do with this? Do women naturally feel inclined to do the housework, given their role as nurturers and caretakers? How might gender stereotypes contribute to inequality in the household?

2. **Making Inferences** One of the characteristics of families is that family members spend time together. As people grow busier and busier, however, spending time together becomes more difficult. Predict the future: twenty years down the road, what do you think will be a typical amount of family time? Do you believe family time will disappear, or do you think family members will always make time for each other, no matter what? Explain your views.

3. **Making Inferences** A prominent sociologist who studies marital relationships says that he can predict with 95 percent accuracy whether a newly married couple will fail or succeed in their marriage. He has newlyweds attend a retreat and perform a series of tasks, videotaping each couple's interactions as they work on projects together. At the end of the weekend, he tells the couples what he observed and what it could mean for the future of their marriages. Remember, his accuracy rating is 95 percent.

    a. What do you think he looks for while he watches couples' interactions?

    b. Do you believe his approach is ethical?

    c. If you had the opportunity as a newlywed, would you attend this retreat? Why or why not?

4. **Analyzing Information** Research on never-married individuals shows that they believe their marriages will be ideal. However, research on married couples suggests that their expectations of marital bliss don't last very long. Why do you think people have expectations of marriage that do not seem to reflect what marriage is really like? Areas to explore might include portrayals of marriage in movies and on TV.

5. **Summarizing Information** Use a chart like the one below to summarize the view of the family as proposed by the three theoretical perspectives.

Sociological Perspective	View of the Family
Functionalism	
Conflict Theory	
Symbolic Interactionism	

Sociology Projects

1. **Family Characteristics** On a piece of paper, rate your family members based on the following characteristics. Use a scale of 1 to 5, with 1 being the lowest (weakest) and 5 being the highest (strongest).
    - spending time together
    - expressing appreciation for each other
    - dealing with conflict
    - communicating with one another
    - spiritual wellness
    - commitment and follow-through

    You can total your scores and divide by 6 to come up with a mean value for your family. After completing the activity, you may want to discuss your results with family members to see if they agree with your evaluation or share your perspectives. Are there other characteristics that are more important to your family than the ones on this list?

2. **Divorce** The text listed several reasons why couples divorce. Working with a classmate, brainstorm several additional factors contributing to divorce (for example, no-fault divorce laws in some states). Give at least one reason why each of these factors has caused an increase in divorce over time. After you have come up with a list of at least five factors, discuss with your partner what would happen if the factors were eliminated (for example, if conditions allowing divorce were made stricter). Do you think these changes would improve society? Why or why not? Be prepared to present your findings to the class and to argue your position.

3. **Research Project** Divide a sheet of paper into three columns, labeled A, B, and C. In column A, write the number of children in your immediate family. In column B, write the number of children in your father's immediate family (include siblings that are no longer living). In column C, write the number of children in your mother's immediate family. One student should collect all the papers and tabulate the results. Has the number of children in the families represented in your class decreased since your parents' generation? Prepare a graph of the similarities or differences.

4. **The Second Shift** To see whether the second-shift explanation applies to your family, conduct the following experiment over the course of one week. Write down the number of hours you see your mother (or stepmother) doing housework each day. Then write down the number of hours your father (or stepfather) spends working in or around the house. In class, compile the numbers logged by all your classmates. Is the second-shift explanation valid for your class? (If you are living in a single-parent family, keep track of the number of hours of housework performed by that parent, but not by any children in the household.)

Technology Activity

1. Using your school or local library and the Internet, research family violence over the last 30 years—1970 to 1980; 1980 to 1990; 1990 to Present. Create a graph to show statistically the frequency of reported incidents of violence. In your own words, using correct grammar, spelling, punctuation, and terms learned in this chapter, write an essay that summarizes your graph. In the essay, consider reasons or changes in society that you believe influence the frequency of reported incidents of family violence. Consider the impact, if any, of hotlines and Public Service Announcements regarding family violence. Determine whether the information that you have found on reported incidents is correct and complete. Support your decision with at least two reasons.

Chapter 11
Enrichment Reading
Life Without Father
by David Popenoe

◆

"Fathers should be neither seen nor heard," Oscar Wilde once wrote. "That is the only proper basis for family life." With each passing year, American society has increasingly become an immense social testing ground for this proposition. Unfortunately for Wilde's reputation as a social analyst, to say nothing about the health of our society, the results have proved highly unsupportive. American fathers are today more removed from family life than ever before in our history. And according to a growing body of evidence, this **massive erosion of fatherhood** contributes mightily to many of the major social problems of our time. . . .

The print pages and airwaves have been filled with discussions of fatherhood in recent decades. Yet most discussions have focused on just one issue—how to get fathers to share their traditional breadwinner role and take up a new (for them) child-care-provider role. The call from younger women has been loud and clear: We need a new conception of fatherhood, a "new father," one who will help equally in the home just as women now strive to help equally in the workplace; one who will share the **"second shift"** with his mate.

The father's role—what society expects of fathers—has indeed changed enormously in recent years. Fathers are expected to be more engaged with their children and involved with housework—if not nearly as much as most women would like, certainly far more than the past generation of fathers would have thought possible.

This role change has been highly positive in most respects. But with all the concentration on "role equality" in the home, the larger and more **ominous** trend of modern fatherhood has been mostly overlooked. We have been through

many social revolutions in the past three decades—sex, women's liberation, divorce—but none more significant for society than the startling emergence of the absent father, a kind of **pathological counterpart** to the new father.

While the new father has been emerging gradually for most of this century, it is only in the past thirty years that we have witnessed the enormous increase in absent fathers. In times past, many children were left fatherless through his premature death. Today, the fathers are still alive and out there somewhere; the problem is that they seldom see much, if anything, of their children.

The main reason for contemporary father absence is the dramatic decline of marriage. . . . What this means, in human terms, is that about half of today's children will spend at least a portion of their growing-up years living apart from their fathers.

As a society, we can respond to this new fatherlessness in several ways. We can, as more and more of us seem to be doing, simply declare fathers to be unnecessary, superfluous. This is the response of "single parents by choice." It is the response of those who say that if daddies and mommies are expected to do precisely the same things in the home, why do we need both? It is the response of those who declare that unwed motherhood is a woman's right, or that single-parent families are every bit as good as two-parent families, or that divorce is generally beneficial for children.

In my view, these responses represent a human tragedy—for children, for women, for men, and for our society as a whole. . . . Fathering is different from mothering; involved fathers are **indispensable** for the good of children and society; and our growing [trend in] national fatherlessness is a disaster in the making. . . .

No one predicted this trend, few researchers or government agencies have monitored it, and it is not widely discussed, even today. But its importance to society is second to none. Father absence is a major force lying behind many of the attention-grabbing issues that dominate the news: crime and delinquency; premature sexuality and out-of-wedlock teen births; deteriorating educational achievement; depression, substance abuse, and alienation among teenagers; and the growing number of women and children in poverty. These issues all point to a **profound deterioration** in the well-being of children. Some experts have suggested, in fact, that the current generation of children and youth is the first in our nation's history to be less well-off—psychologically, socially, economically, and morally—than their parents were at the same age. Or as Senator Daniel Patrick Moynihan has observed, "the United States . . . may be the first society in history in which children are distinctly worse off than adults."

Along with the growing father absence, our cultural view of fatherhood is changing. Few people have doubts about the fundamental importance of mothers. But fathers? More and more the question is being raised, are fathers really necessary? Many would answer no, or maybe not. And to the degree that fathers are still thought necessary, fatherhood is said by many to be merely a social role, as if men had no inherent biological predisposition whatsoever to acknowledge and to invest in their own offspring. If merely a social role, then perhaps anyone is capable of playing it. . . .

The decline of fatherhood and of marriage cuts at the heart of the kind of environment considered ideal for childrearing. Such an environment, according to a substantial body of knowledge, consists of an enduring two-parent family that engages regularly in activities together, has many of its own routines and traditions, and provides a great deal of quality contact with their parents' world of work. In addition, there is little concern on the part of children that their parents will break up. Finally, each of these ingredients comes together in the development of a rich family subculture that has last-ing meaning and strongly **promulgates** such family values as responsibility, cooperation, and sharing. . . .

What the decline of fatherhood and marriage in America really means, then, is that slowly, insidiously, and relentlessly our society has been moving in an ominous direction—toward the devaluation of children. There has been an alarming weakening of the fundamental assumption, long at the center of our culture, that children are to be loved and valued at the highest level of priority. Nothing could be more serious for our children or our future.

Source: Excerpted from David Popenoe, *Life Without Father* (New York: The Free Press, 1996), pp. 1–2, 14.

What Does it Mean?

indispensable
absolutely necessary

massive erosion of fatherhood
great numbers of fathers not present in the home

ominous
dangerous; darkly threatening

pathological counterpart
diseased opposite

profound deterioration
very great decline

promulgates
teaches

second shift
work to be done at home

Read and React

1. Briefly state the main point of Popenoe's reading. Is he correct? Is he too pessimistic? Explain.

2. Explain why Popenoe thinks that Oscar Wilde's statement that "fathers should be neither seen nor heard" is wrong. Do you think Wilde was wrong? Why or why not?

3. Discuss the reasons Popenoe gives for the decline of the father's presence in the contemporary American family.

4. According to Popenoe, nothing could be more serious for children than the trend he sees toward "life without father." Why do you agree or disagree?

CHAPTER 12
Education

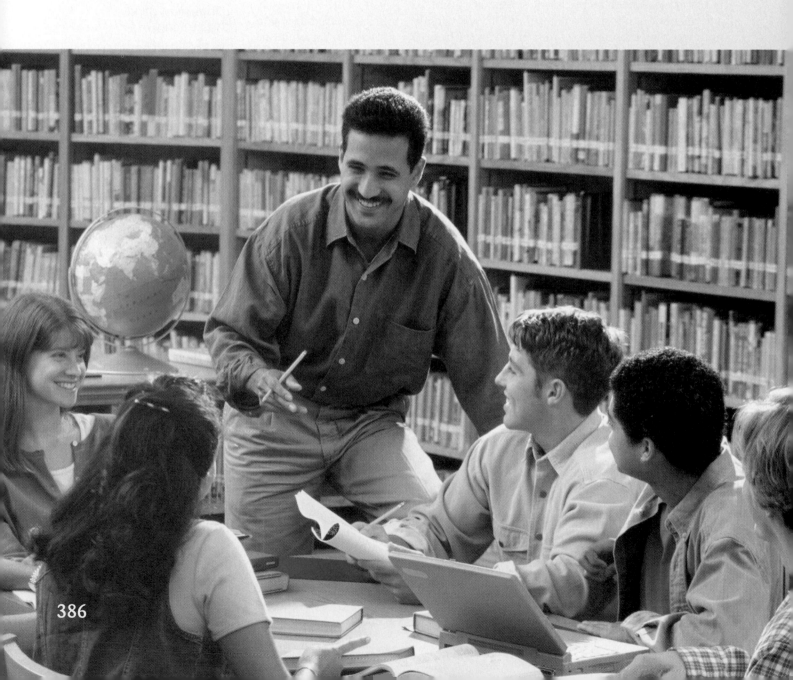

Your Sociological Imagination

Columnist Ann Landers published this letter from a teacher about the hidden realities of teaching in America. Let me see if I have this right. . . . I am also to instill a sense of pride in their ethnicity, modify disruptive behavior and observe them for signs of abuse.

I am to fight the war on drugs and sexually transmitted diseases, check their backpacks for guns and knives, and raise their self-esteem. I am to teach them patriotism, good citizenship, sportsmanship and fair play . . . I am to . . . maintain a safe environment, write letters of recommendation for student employment and scholarships, encourage respect for the cultural diversity of others, always making sure I give the girls in my class 50% of my attention.

I am required to work . . . toward additional certification and a master's degree, to sponsor the cheerleaders or the sophomore class (my choice); and after school, I am to attend committee and faculty meetings. . . .

I am to be a paragon of virtue, such that my presence will awe my students into being obedient and respectful of authority. I am to do all of this with just a piece of chalk, a bulletin board and a few books (some of which I may have to purchase myself). And for doing this, I am to be paid a starting salary that, in some states, qualifies my family for food stamps.

Is that all?

(Excerpted from "A Lesson on the Realities of Teaching," *The Los Angeles Times*, January 28, 2000).

Sections

1. **Development and Structure of Education**
2. **Functionalist Perspective**
3. **Conflict Perspective**
4. **Symbolic Interactionism**

Learning Objectives

After reading this chapter, you will be able to

❖ discuss schools as bureaucracies.
❖ outline the basic functions of education.
❖ evaluate the merit-based nature of public education.
❖ describe the ways in which schools socialize students.
❖ discuss educational inequality.

SOCIOLOGY *Online*

Chapter Overview
Visit the *Sociology and You* Web site at soc.glencoe.com and click on **Chapter 12— Chapter Overviews** to preview chapter information.

Section 1

Development and Structure of Education

Key Terms

- formal schooling
- open classroom
- cooperative learning
- integrative curriculum
- voucher system
- charter schools
- magnet schools
- for-profit schools

Section Preview

Schools are becoming more bureaucratic. Advocates of open classrooms and cooperative learning contend that bureaucratically run schools fail to take into account the emotional and creative needs of individual children.

Bureaucracy in Education

School administration in the early 1900s was based on a factory model of education. Educators believed that children could be and should be educated in much the same way as cars were mass produced.

Schooling came to be seen as work or the preparation for work; schools were pictured as factories, educators as industrial managers, and students as the raw materials to be inducted into the production process. The ideology of school management was recast in the mold of the business corporation, and the character of education was shaped after the image of industrial production (Cohen and Lazerson, 1972:47).

Although teachers and administrators work hard today to personalize the time you spend in school, public education in this country remains very much an impersonal bureaucratic process. Schools today are still based on specialization, rules and procedures, and impersonality.

The 1954 classroom on the left clearly reflects the traditional mass production approach to education. Recently, as seen in the photo at the right, there has been more of an attempt to personalize education.

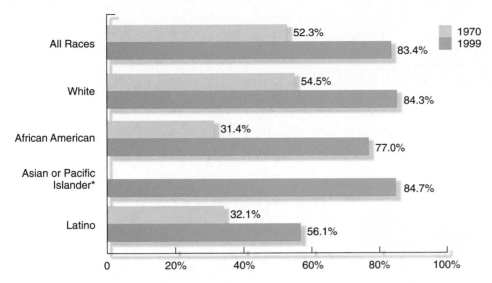

Figure 12.1 High School Graduates by Race (1970 and 1999).   *Displayed in this figure are the percentages, by racial and ethnic category, of persons 25 years old and older who have completed high school. Note that the proportion of high school graduates in each group has increased sharply between 1970 and 1999. As a result, each of these groups is placing more pressure on public schools to accommodate their members.*

*Note: No data available for Asian or Pacific Islander for 1970.
Source: U.S. Census Bureau, *Statistical Abstract of the United States: 2001.*

Why should schools be standardized?   For administrators, there are many advantages to following a bureaucratic model. For instance, in the discussion of formal organizations in Chapter 6, you read that one of the characteristics of a bureaucracy is the tendency to specialize. Professional educators are specialists—administrators, classroom teachers, librarians, curriculum specialists who decide on courses and content, and so forth.

In the bureaucratic model, education can be accomplished most efficiently for large numbers of students when they are at similar stages in their ability and development. (There were, in fact, approximately 60 million students in the public school system in 2000. Figure 12.1 shows the increasing percentage of young people from all races and ethnic groups who are completing high school.) In this way, a teacher can develop one lesson plan for a number of students. Age-based classrooms, in which all students receive the same instruction, reflect the impersonal, bureaucratic nature of schools.

Efficiency, the ultimate goal of a bureaucracy, is also increased when teachers teach the same, or at least similar, content. Materials can be approved and purchased in bulk, and testing can be standardized. This practice also allows students to transfer from one school to another and continue studying approximately the same things. Rules and procedures exist to ensure that all of this happens.

Schools are also part of a much larger bureaucratic system. This system begins with the federal government and progresses layer by layer through state and local governments. (See page 191 in Chapter 6 for an organizational chart of a public school district.)

Bureaucracy is a challenge to be confronted with a righteous attitude, a tolerance for stupidity, and a bulldozer when necessary.

Anonymous

What do critics of the bureaucratic model say?   Critics claim that the old factory, or bureaucratic, model is not appropriate for schooling. Children, they point out, are not inorganic materials to be processed on an assembly line. Children are human beings who come into school with previous knowledge and who interact socially and emotionally with other students. According to critics of **formal schooling,** education that is provided and regulated by society, the school's bureaucratic nature is unable to respond to the expressive, creative, and emotional needs of all children. These critics prefer several less rigid, more democratic alternatives.

formal schooling
education that is provided and regulated by society

Working cooperatively in groups is one of the more democratic school reforms of the twentieth century.

Democratic Reforms in the Classroom

Since colonial times, providing citizens with a good education has been an important value in the United States. The Puritans in Massachusetts in 1647 required towns with more than fifty families to hire a schoolmaster. The Land Ordinance of 1785 required that some of the income from land north of the Ohio River be used to support public schools. The first public schools were quite authoritarian, with firm rules and sharp lines drawn between students and teacher.

The American progressive education movement of the 1920s and 1930s was a reaction to the strict Victorian authoritarianism of early nineteenth-century schools. Educational philosopher John Dewey (1859–1952) led the progressive education movement, which emphasized knowledge related to work and to individual student interests. The progressive movement, with its child-centered focus, almost disappeared in the 1950s but reappeared in the 1960s as the humanistic movement. The humanistic movement supported the elimination of restrictive rules and codes and the involvement of students in the educational process. The aim of the humanistic movement was to create a more democratic, student-focused learning environment (Ballantine, 1993). It has proven to be an influential forerunner of classroom reform. Three ways to express the humanistic educational impulse are the *open classroom, cooperative learning,* and the *integrative curriculum.*

What is the open classroom?   The **open classroom** is a nonbureaucratic approach to education based on democratic relationships, flexibility, and noncompetitiveness. Here educators avoid the sharp authoritarian line traditionally drawn between teachers and students. The open classroom drops the idea that all children of a given age should follow a standardized curriculum. On the belief that competition is not a good motivator for children, the open classroom abandons the use of graded report cards based on comparison of student performance.

The open classroom, introduced in the 1960s, has resurfaced in the 1990s. Cooperative learning and the integrative curriculum are two important extensions of the open-classroom approach.

open classroom
a nonbureaucratic approach to education based on democracy, flexibility, and noncompetitiveness

What is cooperative learning? **Cooperative learning** takes place in a nonbureaucratic classroom structure in which students study in groups, with teachers as guides rather than as the controlling agents (the "guide on the side" versus the "sage on the stage" approach). According to the cooperative learning method, students learn more if they are actively involved with others in the classroom (Sizer, 1996). The traditional teacher-centered approach rewards students for being passive recipients of information and requires them to compete with others for grades and teacher recognition. Cooperative learning, with its accent on teamwork rather than individual performance, is designed to encourage students to concentrate more on the process of getting results than how their answers compare to those of other students. Cooperation replaces competition. Students typically work in small groups on specific tasks. Credit for completion of a task is given only if all group members do their parts.

> **cooperative learning**
> instructional method that relies on cooperation among students

Using this approach successfully requires some expertise on the part of the teacher and can initially discourage students who are motivated by letter grades based on individual work. Nevertheless, some benefits of the cooperative learning approach have been documented (Children's Defense Fund, 1991). For example,

❖ uncooperativeness and stress among students is reduced.
❖ academic performance increases.
❖ students have more positive attitudes toward school.
❖ racial and ethnic antagonism decreases.
❖ self-esteem increases.

What is the integrative curriculum? As you have seen, the curriculum is predetermined for students in the traditional classroom. In the **integrative curriculum,** however, the curriculum is created by students and teachers working together. Since students are asked to participate in curriculum design and content, the integrative curriculum is democratic in nature. Giving students such power obviously deviates from the traditional subject-centered curriculum. Students and teachers become collaborators (Barr, 1995).

> **integrative curriculum**
> an approach to education based on student-teacher collaboration

Subject matter is selected and organized around certain real-world themes or concepts. An example is a sixth-grade unit of study on water quality in Washington State.

In an integrative curriculum, students apply teachings from many disciplines at the same time. Students shown here are on a field trip to explore mineral production in a local community.

Another Time

Understanding Freedom and Education in America

One hundred years ago, Russian immigrant Marie Antin wrote about her first days at school in the United States. Reading about her reactions might make Americans more appreciative of the public school system they often criticize.

Education was free. That subject my father had written about repeatedly, as comprising his chief hope for us children, the essence of American opportunity, the treasure that no thief could touch, not even misfortune or poverty. It was the one thing that he was able to promise us when he sent for us; surer, safer, than bread or shelter.

In the past, schools played an important role in transmitting American culture to many immigrant children. Are schools today still carrying on that function?

On our second day I was thrilled with the realization of what this freedom of education meant. A little girl from across the alley came and offered to conduct us to school. My father was out, but we five between us had a few words of English by this time. We knew the word school. We understood. This child, who had never seen us till yesterday, who could not pronounce our names, who was not much better dressed than we, was able to offer us the freedom of the schools of Boston! No application made, no question asked, no examinations, rulings, exclusions; no machinations, no fees. The doors stood open for every one of us. The smallest child could show us the way.

This incident impressed me more than anything I had heard in advance of the freedom of education in America. It was a concrete proof—almost the thing itself. One had to experience it to understand it.

Source: Excerpted from Marie Antin, *The Promised Land* (New York: Houghton Mifflin Company, 1912).

Thinking It Over

1. Describe your thoughts and feelings about your school experiences as you think about Antin's perspective.

2. Do you agree with the author that education is the chief hope for children? Explain.

The unit became a part of an actual water quality project that originated in the Great Lakes region of the United States but now spans the globe. Lessons were organized around the actual work of determining water quality in Puget Sound. These lessons culminated in students' reporting to community groups about the quality of the water. In this way learning was relevant to a real-world problem that the students contributed to solving (Simmons and El-Hindi, 1998:33).

Instruction in this unit emphasized hands-on experience and utilized the multiple intelligences of various students. The latter idea recognizes that not all students in a classroom learn in identical ways. Students bring to any unit of study a variety of learning styles, interests, and abilities. Different units of study will engage students in varying ways.

Back-to-Basics Movement

In the 1990s, the "back-to-basics" movement emerged alongside cooperative learning and the integrative curriculum. Worried by low scores on achievement tests, supporters of this movement pushed for a return to a traditional curriculum ("reading, writing, and arithmetic") based on more bureaucratic methods.

What started the back-to-basics movement? In 1983, America received an educational wake-up call. The National Commission on Excellence in Education issued a report dramatically entitled *A Nation at Risk.* Catching the attention of politicians and the general public, it warned of a "rising tide of mediocrity" in America's schools. Because of deficiencies in its educational system, the report claimed, America was at risk of being overtaken by some of its world economic competitors (Gardner, 1983).

Unlike the recommendations of the progressive and humanistic reform movements, most of the solutions offered by the commission were bureaucratic in nature. The report urged a return to more teaching of basic skills such as reading and mathematics. High school graduation requirements should be strengthened to include four years of English, three years of mathematics, three years of science, three years of social studies, and a half year of computer science. School days, the school year, or both should be lengthened. Standardized achievement tests should be administered as students move from one level of schooling to another. High school students should be given significantly more homework. Discipline should be tightened through the development and enforcement of codes for student conduct.

voucher system
system in which public school funds may be used to support public, private, or religious schools

Alternatives to the Public School System

The debate over the most effective classroom methods continues. Meanwhile, educators and politicians are looking beyond the classroom to how schools are organized, funded, and administered. A new debate has arisen over school choice. The school choice movement promotes the idea that the best way to improve schools is by using the free enterprise model and creating some competition for the public school system. Supporters of school choice believe that parents and students should be able to select the school that best fits their needs and provides the greatest educational benefit. Methods used to accomplish this goal include the *voucher system, charter schools, magnet,* and *for-profit* schools.

What is a voucher system? People in favor of a **voucher system** say that the government should make the money spent per child on public education available to families to use for public, private, or religious schools. Families who chose a public school would pay nothing, just as in the current system. Parents who chose a religious or other private school would receive a government voucher to be used to pay a portion of the tuition equal to the amount the government spends per child in the public school system. Any additional tuition would be paid by the parents. A voucher plan in Cleveland, for example, provided publicly funded scholarships of

This charter school in Harlem is one alternative to the public school system.

about $2,000 annually to around four thousand city children in the 2001 school year. Most parents have chosen to spend the money at private schools rather than keep their children in public schools. The basic idea is that public schools would have to compete for the students and thus would improve their services. If parents were not happy with a school, they would have the freedom to remove their children and place them elsewhere.

Public reaction to the voucher approach has been mixed. So far, public vouchers affect only about one-tenth of 1 percent of American school children. Large-scale public programs exist in only two cities—Cleveland and Milwaukee. In 1999, Florida initiated the first statewide public voucher program. African American and Latino parents tend to prefer a voucher system because it provides some financial help to remove their children from public schools that they believe have let their children down. Because most whites seem to be satisfied with the public schools, they have not embraced the voucher system in large numbers (Thomas and Clemetson, 1999).

Courts have generally treated voucher systems as unconstitutional because they may contradict the principle of separation of church and state. On the other hand, in 1998 the U.S. Supreme Court let stand a ruling by the Wisconsin Supreme Court that allowed state money to go to low-income students for either private or parochial education schools. As of early 2002, the U.S. Supreme Court has not ruled directly on the constitutionality of school vouchers, but some state and federal judges have. Vouchers have been declared unconstitutional by lower court judges in Florida, Ohio, Vermont, Maine, and Pennsylvania. The Supreme Court is expected to rule on this issue before the end of 2002.

Up to now the evidence on the effectiveness of the voucher system is inconsistent. Although compared to public schools, some voucher programs have improved student test scores, other programs have produced no improvement (Toch and Cohen, 1998).

Critics fear that if this system were implemented, inner-city schools would suffer even more, since few inner-city parents could afford to make up the difference between the amount of the voucher and the cost of the highest-quality private schools. They also fear that national and local commitment to public education would decline, leaving the public school system in worse shape than it is now. Furthermore, the need to regulate private and religious schools would increase bureaucracy.

What are charter schools and magnet schools?
Charter schools are publicly funded schools operated like private schools by public school teachers and administrators. Freed of answering to local school boards, charter schools have the latitude to shape their own curriculum and to use nontraditional or traditional teaching methods.

The Mosaica Academy (now called School Lane), which opened in 1998 in Pennsylvania, is deliberately not organized along public school lines. The school day is about two hours longer than at public school and the school year is also longer. This school created its own curriculum with the goal of immersing students in the development of civilizations over 4,000 years (Symonds, 2000). In 2002 there were approximately 2,400 charter schools across the United States. The success of these schools is tied to the commitment of the teachers, principals, and parents.

Magnet schools are public schools that attempt to achieve high standards by specializing in a certain area. One school may emphasize the

> Education makes people easy to lead, but difficult to drive; easy to govern, but impossible to enslave.
>
> **Lord Brougham**
> **Scottish statesman**

charter schools
public schools that are operated like private schools by public school teachers and administrators

magnet schools
public schools that focus on particular disciplines or areas, such as fine arts or science

performing arts while another might stress science. Magnet schools are designed to enhance school quality and to promote desegregation. They have become a significant factor in improving urban education.

What is the nature of for-profit schools? Some reformers do not believe local or federal government is capable of improving the educational system. Government, they say, is too wasteful and ineffective. Why not look to business and market forces to solve the problems facing schools today? **For-profit schools** would be supported by government funds but run by private companies. By borrowing from modern business practices, the argument goes, these schools could be efficient, productive, and cost effective. Marketplace forces would ensure that the best schools will survive.

The most comprehensive for-profit organization is Edison, which launched a $40-million, three-year campaign in 1992 to develop its program. Edison schools feature challenging curriculums, along with a schedule that has children in school almost a third longer than the average public school. Beginning in the third grade, students are equipped with a computer and modem to take home, in order to access Edison's intranet system (Symonds, 2000).

Critics of this approach are bothered by the idea of mixing profit and public service. What would happen to the students when their needs were weighed against the profit margin? Would for-profit schools skimp on equipment, services, and training? Another problem involves oversight. That is, with a for-profit system, voters would lose the power to influence officials and educational policy.

Calvin expects to reap the rewards of education, but has a problem with the effort of getting educated.

for-profit schools
schools run by private companies on government funds

Section 1 Assessment

1. State three ways in which schools in the United States follow the bureaucratic model.
2. Identify three specific types of reform in public education.

Critical Thinking

3. **Analyzing Information** Explain why such reforms as open classrooms and integrative learning are characterized as more democratic than the traditional or bureaucratic approach.
4. **Summarizing Information** First briefly summarize the ideas about school choice presented in this section. Then evaluate them. Do you favor one approach over another? Give reasons for your choice.

succeed academically. Conservative political efforts have led twenty-four states to adopt English as their official language. The creation of a similar law for the nation is being discussed in Congress.

How do schools select and screen students?   For over fifty years, scores on intelligence and achievement tests have been used for grouping children in school. The stated purpose of testing is to identify an individual's talents and aptitudes. Test scores have also been used for **tracking**—placing students in curricula consistent with expectations for the students' eventual occupations. (Tracking is discussed further in Section 3 when we look at inequalities in education.) Counselors use test scores and early performance records to predict careers for which individuals may be best suited.

tracking
placement of students in programs according to academic ability levels

How do schools promote personal growth and development? Schools expose students to a wide variety of perspectives and experiences that encourage them to develop creativity, verbal skills, artistic expression, intellectual accomplishment, and cultural tolerance. In this way, education provides an environment in which individuals can improve the quality of their lives. In addition, schools attempt to prepare students for the world of work.

Latent Functions of Education

The educational institution has latent functions as well. Some are positive; others are not. Educators do not usually think of schools as day-care facilities for dual-employed couples or single parents. Nor do parents vote for additional school taxes so that their sons and daughters can find dates or marriage partners. Also, schools are not consciously designed to prevent delinquency by holding juveniles indoors during the daytime. Nor are schools intended as training grounds for athletes. Nonetheless, all of these activities are latent functions of the school system.

Each of the latent functions just mentioned is considered a positive contribution to society. But some consequences are negative, or dysfunctional. Tracking, for example, can perpetuate an unequal social-class structure from generation to generation. In addition, evidence suggests that tracking is harmful to those placed on "slower" tracks (Hurn, 1993).

Do you consider the opportunity to flirt a positive or negative latent function of schools?

Section 2 Assessment

1. List the essential functions of education described in the text.
2. What is the difference between a manifest and a latent function in education?
3. What type of function do schools perform when they keep children for their working parents?

Critical Thinking

4. **Making Comparisons** What do you think is the most significant latent function schools perform? Consider the advantages and disadvantages.

Sociology Today

Educating Yourself for the Future

By the time you graduate from high school, the competition for well-paying entry-level jobs will be stiffer than ever before. Here are some tips to keep you in demand—whether you are college bound or going directly into the job market.

Career counselors urge job seekers to think in terms of *lifelong learning*. Never think of your education as coming to an end. The excerpt below is as true today as it was a generation ago.

> *For education the lesson is clear: its prime objective must be to increase the individual's "cope-ability"—the speed and economy with which he can adapt to continual change. . . . It is not even enough for him to understand the present, for the here-and-now environment will soon vanish. Johnny must learn to anticipate the directions and rate of change. He must, to put it technically, learn to make repeated, probabilistic, increasingly long-range assumptions about the future (Toffler, 1970:403).*

Preparation for the future involves attempting to predict the future demand for particular occupations. The *Occupational Outlook Handbook* and the *Occupational Outlook Handbook for College Graduates* can be very helpful in this regard. Each year in these volumes, the U.S. Department of Labor publishes detailed predictions for specific occupations.

Educating yourself for the future also means being prepared to enter an occupation for which you have no specific training. You must remain willing to retrain and to enter an entirely new occupation—for example, to move from bank teller to computer programmer.

In spite of the fact that you will probably change occupations over the course of your work life, you should try to determine your true job preference before you spend a great deal of time learning a job that turns out not to be the one you want. Over half of all young people entering a chosen field quit their jobs within one year. This fact has led some observers to argue that few young people really understand the nature of the work for which they are preparing. How do you find out what jobs you would really enjoy? Volunteering time in a specific work situation can help. For example, hospitals usually have volunteer programs in which medical practitioners can be observed. If you think you would like to be a physician, nurse, or other health-care worker, get involved in one of these programs. You will not only help others but will help yourself, as well.

Finally, educating yourself for the future includes preparing for leisure choices. Careers have become so specialized that they satisfy only a small part of people's interests. Many high schools, colleges, and universities sponsor noncredit courses and seminars on such topics as personal development, photography, fine arts, and alternative lifestyles. These courses permit you to either pursue long-standing interests or develop new ones.

Doing Sociology

Make an informal survey of as many working adults as possible. Ask them what additional training, if any, they have undergone since taking their first jobs. Then ask them what plans they have for future training. Summarize your results, and bring the report to class to share.

Section 3

Conflict Perspective

Key Terms

- meritocracy
- competition
- educational equality
- cognitive ability
- cultural bias
- school desegregation
- multicultural education
- compensatory education

Section Preview

In theory, America is a meritocracy in which social status is achieved. Proponents of the conflict perspective identify flaws in this model by pointing to inequality in our schools. Methods and programs aimed at promoting educational equality have been developed.

meritocracy
a society in which social status is based on ability and achievement

competition
system in which rewards are based on relative performance

Participating in academic contests, such as building rockets, is one way teachers can find those students who merit special recognition.

Meritocracy

Conflict theorists attempt to show that popular conceptions about the relationship between schools and society are not entirely accurate. Schools and society often touch each other in complicated and unobvious ways.

In a **meritocracy,** social status is based on ability and achievement rather than social-class background or parental status. In theory, all individuals in a meritocracy have an equal chance to develop their abilities for the benefit of themselves and their society. A meritocracy, then, gives everyone an equal chance to succeed. It is free of barriers that prevent individuals from developing their talents.

Meritocracy is based on competition. For this reason, sport is seen as the ultimate meritocracy. Although some sports have glaring shortcomings in this regard (see Chapter 15), sport does fit very closely with the definition of competition. For sociologists, **competition** is a social process that occurs when rewards are given to people on the basis of how their performance compares with the performance of others doing the same task or participating in the same event (Coakley, 1998).

Is America really a meritocracy? Although America claims to be a meritocracy, sociologists have identified barriers to true merit-based achievement, such as gender, race, and ethnicity. An example (greatly simplified) is how the education system favors the wealthy. Schools in wealthy neighborhoods are significantly better than schools in economically disadvantaged areas. It follows, then, that students attending wealthier schools get a better education than students attending poorer schools. Furthermore, students attending poorer schools do not learn the values, manners, language, and dress of people in more affluent schools. Because the majority of students in poorer schools are members of racial and ethnic minorities, they find themselves at a disadvantage when applying for higher-level jobs that lead to higher incomes. (See Figure 12.2.)

How do minorities perform on college entrance exams?   There are related barriers to achievement faced by racial and ethnic minorities. An important one of these is lower performance on college entrance examinations. African Americans, Latinos, and Native Americans have lower average scores on the Scholastic Aptitude Test (SAT) than whites. (See Figure 12.3 on page 402.) Sociologists attribute this fact, in part, to the differences in school quality noted above. And both school quality and SAT performance are related to social class. Children from upper-class and upper-middle-class families attend more affluent schools. These children also have higher SAT scores. Social class clearly affects SAT performance.

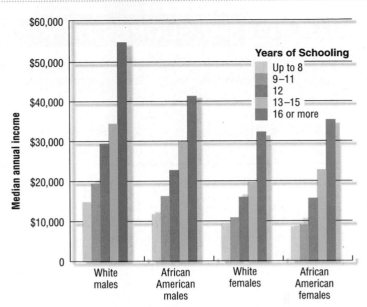

Figure 12.2 Median Annual Income by Gender, Race, and Education.   *Clearly, this graph documents the income advantage that white males in the U.S. have over white females and African Americans of both sexes. Explain how this data challenges the existence of a true meritocracy.*

Visit soc.glencoe.com and click on **Textbook Updates–Chapter 12** for an update of the data.

Source: U.S. Bureau of the Census, *Income 2000.*

Social class is a strong predictor of success on the SATs. How is race related to social class?

Figure 12.3 SAT SCORES BY RACE AND ETHNICITY

An examination of this table reveals the gap in average SAT scores for whites and Asian Americans versus African Americans, Latinos, and Native Americans. Interpret these data as a conflict theorist would in the context of the U.S. as a meritocracy.

Racial/Ethnic Category	SAT Verbal Mean Scores	SAT Math Mean Scores	Totals
Native American or Alaskan Native	482	481	963
Asian, Asian American, or Pacific Islander	499	565	1064
African American	434	426	860
Latino Background			
Mexican or Mexican American	453	460	913
Puerto Rican	456	451	907
Latin American, South American, Central American, or Other Latino	461	467	928
White (excluding Latino origin)	528	530	1058

Source: The College Board, 2001.

Why are SAT scores considered vital to a meritocratic American society?

How do SAT scores influence economic achievement? The SAT, created in 1926, was originally used to identify talented youth, regardless of social class background, so they could attend elite colleges and universities (Lemann, 1991). Ironically, as we have just seen, social class is a major factor in SAT performance. Consequently, social class (through SAT performance) still influences who will attend the institutions that are the gateway to America's higher social classes.

Don't the rewards tied to high SAT scores mean that America is a meritocracy? On the surface it does seem that merit is being rewarded in the system just outlined. After all, it is those who do better academically who enjoy higher levels of success.

There are two problems with this conclusion. The first is the advantage some people have because their parents' social class creates an unlevel playing field. Talent in the lower social classes often does not get recognized and developed. Second is the assumption that SAT performance measures academic ability and the likelihood of success in both college and life. For example, African American students who attend the most prestigious schools—including those students with lower SAT scores (below 1000)—complete college at a higher rate than black students attending less rigorous institutions. They are also more likely to go on to graduate or professional schools (Bowen and Bok, 2000). Apparently these students are succeeding because they attended better schools, even if they don't have high SAT scores.

At the least, these findings raise doubts about the ability of the SAT to achieve a level playing field. Recognizing this, an official at the Educational Testing Service (ETS)—developer and marketer of the SAT—announced in 1999 that ETS was creating a "strivers" score. The idea was to adjust a student's SAT score to factor in social class as well as racial and ethnic characteristics thought to place him or her at a competitive disadvantage. Any student whose original score exceeded by 200 points the score predicted for their social class, racial, or ethnic category would be considered a "striver." The strivers score would be made available to colleges and universities to use, if they desired, in their admissions decisions (Glazer, 1999; Wildavsky, 1999). The proposal was quickly withdrawn after a firestorm of criticism from both privileged and disadvantaged sources.

Equality and Inequality in Education

The situation for those disadvantaged by social class, racial, and ethnic background is actually even more complicated. As already implied, it is tied to the larger issue of educational equality and inequality. **Educational equality** exists when schooling produces the same results, in terms of achievement and attitudes, for lower-class and minority children as it does for less disadvantaged children. Results, not resources, are the test of educational equality (Coleman et al., 1966).

Do schools provide educational equality?
Research has shown that even the best teachers often evaluate students on the basis of their social class and their racial and ethnic characteristics. This tendency to judge students on nonacademic criteria is especially apparent in the practice of tracking. Researchers report that social class and race heavily influence student placement in college preparatory, vocational, or basic tracks regardless of their intelligence or past academic achievement (Oakes and Lipton, 1996; Taylor et al., 1997). Once students are placed, their grades and test scores are

It is no longer correct to regard higher education solely as a privilege. It is a basic right in today's world.

**Norman Cousins
American essayist**

educational equality condition in which schooling produces the same results for lower-class and minority children as it does for other children

Would you expect to find educational equality in these two schools?

Snapshot of America

School Expenditures

Everyone has heard "You get what you pay for." Because of this idea, many people use the amount of money spent on public schools as a measure of the quality of education. The accompanying map shows that some states spend more than twice as much per student as other states.

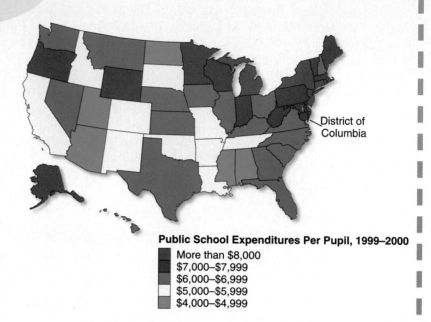

District of Columbia

Public School Expenditures Per Pupil, 1999–2000

- More than $8,000
- $7,000–$7,999
- $6,000–$6,999
- $5,000–$5,999
- $4,000–$4,999

Interpreting the Map

1. How does your state compare with other states in school expenditures?
2. Do you see a regional pattern in public school funding? Explain.
3. What other factors might you want to know to determine if the amount of money spent affected the quality of education delivered?

Source: U.S. Bureau of the Census, 2000.

influenced more by the track they are on than by their current performance. Regardless of earlier school performance or intelligence, the academic performance of college-bound students increases, whereas the performance of those on a noncollege track decreases. In other words, schools are not successfully providing educational equality for their students.

Cognitive Ability

cognitive ability
capacity for thinking abstractly

The technical term for intelligence is **cognitive ability**—the capacity for thinking abstractly. Dating back to the turn of the twentieth century, there has been a tradition in schools to attempt to measure cognitive ability.

Because cognitive ability testing is an important element in sorting and tracking students, it contributes to educational inequality. Whenever cognitive ability tests are discussed, the question of inherited intelligence always arises.

Is intelligence inherited? In the past, some people assumed that individual and group differences in measured intellectual ability were due to genetic differences. This assumption, of course, underlies Social Darwinism. (See pages 15–16 for a brief explanation of these assumptions.)

A few researchers still take this viewpoint. More than thirty years ago Arthur Jensen (1969), an educational psychologist, contended that the lower average intelligence score among African American children may be due to heredity. A recent book by Richard Herrnstein and Charles Murray (1994), entitled *The Bell Curve,* is also in the tradition of linking intelligence to heredity. According to these authors, humans inherit 60 to 70 percent of their intelligence level. Herrnstein and Murray further contend that the fact of inherited intelligence makes largely futile the efforts to help the disadvantaged through programs such as Head Start and affirmative action.

What are arguments against the inherited intelligence theory? Most social scientists oppose the genetic explanation of intelligence differences between races because it fails to consider the effects of the social, psychological, and economic environment on intelligence. Even those social scientists who believe that genetics plays an important role in intelligence criticize both the interpretations of the evidence and the public policy conclusions contained in *The Bell Curve.* They point to the body of research that runs counter to Herrnstein's and Murray's thesis. More specifically, they see intelligence not as an issue of nature *versus* nurture but as a matter of genetics *and* environment (Morganthau, 1994; Wright, 1996). We know, for example, that city dwellers usually score higher on intelligence tests than do people in rural areas, that higher-status African Americans score higher than lower-status African Americans, and that middle-class African American children score about as high as middle-class white children. We also have discovered that as people get older, they usually score higher on intelligence tests. These findings, and others like them, have led researchers to conclude that environmental factors affected test performance at least as much as genetic factors (Samuda, 1975; Schiff and Lewontin, 1987; Jencks and Phillips, 1998). One of these environmental factors is a *cultural bias* in the measurement of cognitive ability.

What are culturally biased intelligence tests? Many early social scientists have argued that intelligence tests have a **cultural bias**—that is, the wording used in questions may be more familiar to people of one social group than to those of another group. Tests with cultural bias unfairly measure the cognitive abilities of people in some social categories. Specifically, intelligence tests are said to be culturally biased because they are designed for middle-class children. The tests measure learning and environment as much as intellectual ability. Consider this intelligence test item cited by Daniel Levine and Rayna Levine:

A symphony is to a composer as a book is to what?

> *a. paper*
> *b. a musician*
> *c. a sculptor*
> *d. a man*
> *e. an author*

According to critics, higher-income children find this question easier to answer correctly than lower-income children because they are more likely to have been exposed to information about classical music. The same charge was made by critics of a recent SAT question that used a Bentley (a luxury-model

Do you think heredity or environment will have a greater effect on these boys' intelligence?

cultural bias
the unfair measurement of the cognitive abilities of people in some social categories

automobile) as its illustration. Several studies have indicated that because most intelligence tests assume fluency in English, minorities cannot do as well on intelligence tests. Some researchers have suggested that many urban African American students are superior to their white classmates on several dimensions of verbal capacity, but this ability is not recognized, because intelligence tests do not measure those specific areas (Gould, 1981; Goleman, 1988; Hurn, 1993).

Some researchers have shown that the testing situation itself affects performance. Low-income and minority students, for example, score higher on intelligence tests when tested by adult members of their own race or income group. Apparently children can feel threatened when tested in a strange environment by someone dissimilar to them. Middle-class children are frequently eager to take the tests because they have been taught the importance both of test results and of academic competitiveness. Because low-income children do not recognize the importance of tests and have not been taught to be academically competitive, they ignore some of the questions or look for something more interesting to do. Other researchers report that nutrition seems to play a role in test performance. Low-income children with poor diets may do less than their best when they are hungry or when they lack particular types of food over long periods of time.

school desegregation
the achievement of a racial balance in the classroom

Promoting Educational Equality

Although it is difficult to completely overcome the barriers of economic and social class, policy makers and educators are exploring ways to promote educational equality. Two methods are *school desegregation* and *compensatory education.*

The governor of Nebraska, Mike Johanns, is part of a program to educate school students on the culture of minority groups in their state.

Does desegregation always promote equality?   In this discussion, **school desegregation** refers to the achievement of a racial balance in the classroom. Desegregated classrooms can have either positive or negative effects on the academic achievement of minority children. Mere physical desegregation without adequate support may actually harm both white and African American children. However, desegregated classrooms with an atmosphere of respect and acceptance improve academic performance (Orfield et al., 1992).

Minority students who attend desegregated public schools get better jobs and earn higher incomes than minority students who attend segregated schools. The formal education they receive is only part of the reason. Middle-class students become models for the behavior, dress, and language often required by employers in the middle-class hiring world.

In addition, exposure to people of different backgrounds can lead to better racial and ethnic relations (Hawley and Smylie, 1988). On this evidence rests the promise of **multicultural education**—an educational curriculum that accents the viewpoints, experiences, and contributions of minorities (women as well as ethnic and racial minorities).

multicultural education
an educational curriculum that emphasizes differences among gender, ethnic, and racial categories

What is the purpose of multicultural education?   Among minorities, school attendance and academic performance appear to increase with multicultural education. Multicultural education attempts to dispel stereotypes and to make the traditions of minorities valuable assets for the broader culture (McLaren, 1997; Ladson-Billings, 1998).

Multicultural education has its critics, however. According to some opponents, encouraging people to think of themselves as culturally separate and unique divides rather than unites American society. Some critics point to instances in which multicultural programs, such as African American studies programs, actually promote feelings of racial separation in schools.

Does compensatory education work?   The term **compensatory education** refers to specific curricular programs designed to overcome deficiency. Special compensatory programs provided during early childhood, it appears, can improve the school achievement of disadvantaged children (Zigler and Styfco, 1993; Campbell and Ramey, 1994).

compensatory education
specific curricular programs designed to overcome a deficiency

The best-known attempt at compensatory education is Head Start. This federally supported program prepares disadvantaged preschoolers for public school. Its goal is to provide disadvantaged children an equal opportunity to develop their potential. Follow-up studies report positive long-term results. Low-income youngsters between the ages of nine and nineteen who had been in preschool compensatory programs performed better in school. They had higher achievement test scores and were more motivated academically than low-income youths who had not been in compensatory education programs (Bruner, 1982; Etzioni, 1982). Later research also supports the benefits of Head Start (Mills, 1998). For example, compared to their peers, a group of children who scored lower on intelligence tests when they entered a Head Start program later had better school attendance, completed high school at a higher rate, and entered the workforce in greater proportion.

Section 3 Assessment

1. Do you think the United States is a meritocracy, as stated in the text?
2. What is meant by the term *educational equality?*
3. What role conflicts does multicultural education pose for teachers?

Critical Thinking

4. **Finding the Main Idea** Students from higher social classes are more likely to go to college than students from the lower classes. How does this fit with the idea of meritocracy?
5. **Evaluating Information** If schools fail to provide educational quality, what do you think will be the consequences in terms of role conflict?

Education is what survives when what has been learned has been forgotten.

B.F. Skinner
American psychologist

Tech Trends

School's Out . . . Forever?

In a recent book, *The Age of Spiritual Machines,* author Ray Kurzweil makes forecasts concerning life in the twenty-first century. He claims that, by the end of the century, computers will be the most intelligent "beings" on the planet. Specific predictions on education in 2009 include the following scenarios.

The majority of reading is done on displays, although the "installed base" of paper documents is still formidable. The generation of paper documents is dwindling, however, as the books and other papers of largely twentieth-century vintage are being rapidly scanned and stored. Documents circa 2009 routinely include embedded moving images and sounds.

Students of all ages typically have a computer of their own, which is a thin tabletlike device weighing under a pound with a very high resolution display suitable for reading. Students interact with their computers primarily by voice and by pointing with a device that looks like a pencil. Keyboards still exist, but most textual language is created by speaking. Learning materials are accessed through wireless communication.

Preschool and elementary school children routinely read at their intellectual level using print-to-speech reading software until their reading skill level catches up. These print-to-speech reading systems display the full image of documents, and can read the print aloud while highlighting what is being read. Synthetic voices sound fully human. Although some educators expressed concern in the early '00 years that students would rely unduly on reading software, such systems have been readily accepted by children and their parents. Studies have shown that students improve their reading skills by being exposed to synchronized visual and auditory presentations of text.

Learning at a distance (for example, lectures and seminars in which the participants are geographically scattered) is commonplace. This also helps to relieve congested campuses and cut back on the burning of gasoline in city limits.

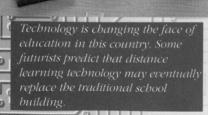

Technology is changing the face of education in this country. Some futurists predict that distance learning technology may eventually replace the traditional school building.

Analyzing the Trends

1. If Kurzweil's predictions came true, how would education's role in the socialization of students change?
2. If Kurzweil's predictions came true, would social stratification play a more or less important role in education than it does now? Use information from the chapter to support your answer.
3. If the predictions in the article came to pass, would we still need schools? Why or why not?

Section 4

Symbolic Interactionism

Key Terms

- hidden curriculum
- self-fulfilling prophecy

The Hidden Curriculum

Symbolic interactionists are very interested in how schools transmit culture through the socialization process. Besides teachers and textbooks, which we will discuss later, the most important agent of this socialization process is the *hidden curriculum*. Modern society places considerable emphasis on the verbal, mathematical, and writing skills an adult needs to obtain a job, read a newspaper, balance a checkbook, and compute income taxes. However, schools teach much more than these basic academic skills. They also transmit to children a variety of values, norms, beliefs, and attitudes.

Fire drills teach safety procedures, but they also reinforce the importance of obedience and cooperation, part of the school system's hidden agenda.

What is the hidden curriculum?

The **hidden curriculum** is the nonacademic agenda that teaches children norms and values such as discipline, order, cooperativeness, and conformity. These citizenship skills are thought to be necessary for success in modern bureaucratic society, whether one becomes a doctor, a college president, a computer programmer, or an assembly-line worker. Over the years, schools, for example, socialize children for the transition from their closely knit, cooperative families to the loosely knit, competitive adult occupational world. The school provides systematic practice for children to operate independently in the pursuit of personal and academic achievement. The values of conformity and achievement are emphasized through individual testing and grading. Because teachers evaluate young people as students, not as relatives, friends, or equals, students participate in a model for future secondary relationships—employer-employee; salesperson-customer; lawyer-client.

Section Preview

Symbolic interactionists emphasize the socialization that occurs in schools. Through the hidden curriculum, children are taught values, norms, beliefs, and attitudes. Much of this socialization helps young people make the transition from home to the larger society.

hidden curriculum
the nonacademic agenda that teaches discipline, order, cooperativeness, and conformity

What, in addition to academic content, do textbooks teach students?

Textbooks

A critical part of the hidden curriculum is the development of patriotism and a sense of civic duty in future adults. For this reason, courses such as history and government generally present a view of history that favors the nation. Accounts of the American Revolution, for example, are not the same in British and American textbooks. Because few societies are willing to admit to their imperfections, schools tend to resist teaching critical accounts of history. For example, for many years U.S. history textbooks failed to portray the U.S. government's harsh treatment of Native American peoples.

Textbooks convey values and beliefs as much by what they omit as by what they include. While today's textbooks present a more balanced picture, surveys of primary school textbooks written before the 1980s found they almost always presented men in challenging and aggressive activities while portraying women as homemakers, mothers, nurses, and secretaries. Women were not only placed in traditional roles but also appeared far less frequently in the books than men did. When women did appear, they were not initiators of action, but played passive roles. Minority groups were rarely present in textbooks, and when they were it was often in a negative context.

Similarly, textbooks tended to portray all students as living in "little white houses with white picket fences." That image may have been part of the worldview of middle-class Americans, but parents of low-income or inner-city children complained that such pictures of middle-class life harmed their children. Poor children who compared their homes with middle-class homes felt out of place (Trimble, 1988; Gibson and Ogbu, 1991).

Today, active parent groups, minority special interest groups, and state boards of education work with textbook publishers to ensure that a more balanced picture of society is presented to students. Problems arise, however, when conflicts occur over whose view of society is the most accurate.

Teachers and Socialization

Classroom teachers have a unique and important role in socializing children. Teachers are usually a child's first authority figures outside the family, and children spend a lot of time in school. In addition, most parents urge their children to obey teachers, in part because their children's futures are affected by school performance.

How do teachers affect students' performance?   All teachers set academic tasks for their students, but teachers affect children unintentionally as well. In a classic 1989 study, Robert Rosenthal and Lenore Jacobson explored the **self-fulfilling prophecy**—a prediction that results in behavior that makes the prediction come true. In their study, elementary school teachers were given a list of children in their classrooms who, according to the researchers, were soon to blossom intellectually. Actually, these children were

self-fulfilling prophecy
a prediction that results in behavior that makes the prediction come true

3. What are the three agents t
   transmit culture through th
   process?
4. What is the hidden curricul
   pose does it serve?
5. What is compensatory edu
   ample.
6. What is the difference betw
   and a magnet school?

Thinking Critically

1. **Drawing Conclusions** M
   situations involve a high d
   Still, much of our educatio
   competitive. ACT and SAT
   cooperatively, for example
   chapter, cooperative learni
   as an alternative to individ
   on your experience with c
   do you agree that it is a be
   Why or why not?
2. **Analyzing Information** I
   society benefits more from
   tions or cooperative situati
   proaches be beneficial to s
   instances might one appro
   the other?
3. **Applying Concepts** On p
   Chapter 1, you read about
   of higher education. Using
   ciency, calculability, predi
   ogy, discuss how high sch
   McDonaldized.
4. **Making Inferences** In th
   of student scores on the A
   come. What might explain
   higher family incomes also
   scores? Could intervening
   might an understanding of
   discrepancy in scores relat
5. **Drawing Conclusions** In
   4, notice that 15 percent o
   not answer the question al

Figure 12.4 | Focus on Theoretical Perspectives

Investigating education. This table illustrates differences in the ways the major theoretical perspectives investigate education as a social institution. It is, of course, possible for a theoretical perspective to study education using one of the concepts associated in this table with another perspective. Explain, for example, how conflict theory would interpret the hidden curriculum and tracking.

Theoretical Perspective	Concept	Example
Functionalism	Tracking	Schools shape the occupational future of children by placing them in educational programs based on test scores and early school performance.
Conflict Theory	Meritocracy	Students attending better schools have an occupational advantage over students from poorer schools.
Symbolic Interactionism	Hidden curriculum	Schools teach children the values of conformity and achievement.

picked at random from the school roster and were no different from other children in the school. At the end of the year, this randomly selected group of children significantly improved their scores on intelligence tests, while their classmates as a group did not. According to Rosenthal and Jacobson, the teachers expected the "late bloomers" to spurt academically. Consequently, the teachers treated these students as if they were special. This behavior on the part of the teachers encouraged the students to become higher academic achievers. (See Focus on Research on page 298. Also see Chapter 9, page 288, for a more general discussion of the self-fulfilling prophecy.)

Another early study by sociologist Eleanor Leacock (1969) found the self-fulfilling prophecy at work in a study of second and fifth graders in black and white low- and middle-income schools. And both studies demonstrate that self-fulfilling prophecies can transmit negative self-impressions as well as positive ones.

Do teachers foster sexism? As described in Chapter 10, children are taught to adopt the "appropriate" gender identity in school (Martin, 1998). Following a long line of earlier researchers, Myra Sadker and David Sadker (1995) have contended that America's teachers are often unfair to girls because they treat girls differently than boys based on assumptions and stereotypes of what is appropriate behavior. Well-meaning teachers unconsciously transmit sexist expectations of how male and female students should behave.

SOCIOLOGY Online

Student Web Activity
Visit the *Sociology and You* Web site at soc.glencoe.com and click on **Chapter 12—Student Web Activities** for an activity on sexism in schools.

Summary

Section 1: Development and St... Education

Main Idea: Schools are becomi... cratic. Advocates of open classroo... ative learning contend that bure... schools fail to take into accoun... and creative needs of individual ...

Section 2: Functionalist Perspe...

Main Idea: Functionalists see th... the educational institution as a r... ety's needs. The manifest functio... include transmission of culture... common identity, selection and ... ent, and promotion of personal ... velopment. Schools also serve lat...

Section 3: Conflict Perspective

Main Idea: In theory, America is ... which social status is achieved. P... conflict perspective identify flaws ... pointing to inequality in our s... and programs aimed at promo... equality have been developed.

Section 4: Symbolic Interaction...

Main Idea: Symbolic interactic... the socialization that occurs in s... the hidden curriculum, children a... norms, beliefs, ... and attitudes. Much of this so-... cialization helps young people make the transi-... tion from home to a larger society.

SOCIOLO...
Onl...

Self-Check...
Visit the *Soc...* site at soc.g... click on **Cha...** **Check Quiz...** the chapter ...

---

this story is true or not, it is a good example of the self-fulfilling prophecy (or the Pygmalion effect). What might have happened if the numbers next to the students' names had been 94 or 97? Do you think that teachers in your school do the same thing this teacher did?

8. **Analyzing Information** To ensure that all students have a minimum standard of knowledge before leaving school, several states now require high school seniors to pass a comprehensive exam. Passing the test would give employers and colleges some assurance that a certain standard of achievement was met. Some parents are challenging the exam, claiming that students with passing grades could fail to get into a good college if they failed the exam. Others contend that students who have failed to pass classes could pass the exam and get credit. They argue that many students are unmotivated learners but could pass such an exam. From a societal viewpoint, what position would you take? Would you favor the examination? Could you propose a compromise solution that would satisfy both sides?

Sociology Projects

1. **School Board Meetings** Attend a school board meeting in your community. Obtain a copy of the agenda from the board of education several days before the meeting. Choose one controversial or proposed issue to research. After the meeting, approach one of the board members to interview on this issue and find out his or her position. Report back to your class about the issue, giving an objective view from various perspectives. (As an alternative, you might want to visit a PTO or PTA meeting and find out how parents and teachers view one particular issue.)

2. **Mock School Board Meeting** Organize a mock school board meeting at your school. First, attend a regular school board meeting to become familiar with the procedures. (Many communities broadcast school board meetings on local cable channels.) Select an issue that is of interest to you or that will affect your high school.

Work with classmates to fill these roles: school board president (to act as a neutral moderator), several school board members, several community members, and several students (to function as observers and take notes on what they see and hear). It would be a good idea for students to spend some time researching the chosen issue. Each school board member will be allowed a few minutes for opening remarks. Community members must be allowed to express their views, and then a vote should be taken on the issue.

3. **School Issues** Contact a student or students from another high school in your area. (These might be students you have met through church, sports, or other activities.) Compare how your schools function. Look at such issues as discipline and detention, attendance policy, making up work, extra credit, and support for extracurricular activities. Identify two areas in which your schools differ. Discuss these differences with a counselor, your principal, or an assistant principal to see if you can explain why the policy differences exist. (Are the differences a result of the bureaucracy, or do they have physical or geographical causes? Does anyone really know why things are done in a particular way?) Offer explanations for the differences, and arrange to present your findings to the class.

4. **The Ideal School of the Future** You are an architect who has been hired by your school district to design the ideal school of the future. Money is no object, and property owners who pay taxes have stated that they will spare no expense to keep the project going. Your task is to create a draft of the floor plan for the building, outside space, ball fields, bathrooms, cafeteria, and so forth. Identify the purpose of all the rooms (classrooms, labs, resource areas, exercise rooms, saunas, and so on). Submit your plan to your class (which will act as the community). Be prepared to redo the plan based on class members' recommendations. Remember, you are working for them.

5. **School Handbooks** Form a committee with some of your classmates to reevaluate your student handbook. If your school prints such a handbook, look at it and make recommendations for change. If your school does not have a handbook, formulate one. In either case, consider such issues as the following: description of the school day, length of class periods, attendance policies, discipline policies, requirements for graduation, required courses for specific subjects (the guidance office should have this information), extracurricular activities, student rights, and map of the building. If your school's handbook is missing any of these, make a recommendation that it be added. Research other schools to see what their policies are. Ask your teacher if your committee can present its findings to a school administrator.

6. **Observing Classrooms** This mock experiment will you give some experience in recording data and formulating a conclusion. You should conduct the experiment for at least five days. As you sit in your classes throughout the day, discreetly keep track of what happens when students raise their hands. Can you determine a pattern for who is called upon? Do the teachers tend to call on boys more than girls? On noisy students more than quiet ones? On conservative dressers more than radical dressers? Summarize your findings. Remember to remain objective and to respect individuals' privacy at all times. (Don't feel bad if you can't seem to identify a pattern—it just means your teacher is sensitive to his or her students. This is still good research.)

7. **Schools in 2020** Design a school that will function in the year 2020, taking into account predicted advances in technology and presumed changes in social relationships and social roles.

8. **School Culture** Do a study of your school culture, including norms, roles, statuses, groups and subcultures. Include information about where people gather, common symbols and traditions, educational rites of passage, etc.

9. **Stakeholders** Stakeholders are people who have a vested interest in a process, or who are directly affected by a process. Identify the stakeholders of American education: the students, parents, colleges, technical schools, the military, employers, etc. What are their competing perceptions of the functions of education?

Technology Activity

1. The Center for Education Reform maintains a web site devoted to information about charter schools. Visit this site at http://www. edreform.com/charter_schools/. Select "Reform FAQS" and then click on "Charter Schools" that is colored blue.

   a. What are the three principles that govern charter schools?

   b. Be prepared to discuss the advantages and disadvantages of charter schools.

   c. Based on your review of this web site, do you feel that the Center for Education Reform presents an unbiased picture of charter schools?

   d. Now use your favorite search engine and see if there are any charter schools in your area with web sites. If there are, visit the site and find out about them. Do any of them sound attractive to you?

Chapter 12

Enrichment Reading
Savage Inequalities
by Jonathan Kozol

Jonathan Kozol is sociology's best known and most consistent advocate of educational reform. Kozol (1992) sees the roots of educational inequality in social inequality: Poor neighborhoods have poor schools. In the passage below, Kozol describes East St. Louis High School, an African American school located in "the most distressed small city in America." There are few jobs, no regular trash collection, and little protection from the pollution spewed from two chemical plants.

East St. Louis, says the chairman of the state board [of education], "is simply the worst possible place I can imagine to have a child brought up. . . . The community is in desperate circumstances." Sports and music, he observes, are, for many children here, "the only avenues of success." Sadly enough, no matter how it ratifies the stereotype, this is the truth; and there is a **poignant** aspect to the fact that, even with class size soaring and one quarter of the system's teachers being given their dismissal, the state board of education demonstrates its genuine but **skewed** compassion by attempting to leave sports and music untouched by the overall **austerity.**

Even sports facilities, however, are degrading by comparison with those found and expected at most high schools in America. The football field at East St. Louis High is missing almost everything—including goalposts. There are a couple of metal pipes—no crossbar, just the pipes. Bob Shannon, the football coach, who has to use his personal funds to purchase footballs and has had to cut and rake the football field himself, has dreams of having goalposts someday. He'd also like to let his students have new uniforms. The ones they wear are nine years old and held together somehow by a patchwork of repairs. Keeping them clean is a problem, too. The school cannot afford a washing machine. The uniforms are carted to a corner laundromat with fifteen dollars' worth of quarters. . . .

In the wing of the school that holds vocational classes, a damp, unpleasant odor fills the halls. The school has a machine shop, which cannot be used for lack of staff, and a woodworking shop. The only shop that's occupied this morning is the auto-body class. A man with long blond hair and wearing a white sweat suit swings a paddle to get children in their chairs. "What we need the most is new equipment," he reports. "I have equipment for alignment, for example, but we don't have money to install it. We also need a better form of **egress.** We bring the cars in through two other classes." Computerized equipment used in most repair shops, he reports, is far beyond the high school's budget. It looks like a very old gas station in an isolated rural town. . . .

The science labs at East St. Louis High are 30 to 50 years outdated. John McMillan, a soft-spoken man, teaches physics at the school. He shows me his lab. The six lab stations in the room have empty holes where pipes were once attached. "It would be great if we had water," says McMillan. . . .

In a seventh grade social studies class, the only book that bears some relevance to black concerns—its title is *The American Negro*—bears a publication date of 1967. The teacher invites me to ask the class some questions. Uncertain where to start, I ask the students what they've learned about the civil rights campaigns of recent decades.

A 14-year-old girl with short black curly hair says this: "Every year in February we are told to read the same old speech of Martin Luther King. We read it every year. 'I have a dream. . . .' It does begin to seem—what is the word?" She hesitates and then she finds the word: **"perfunctory."**

I ask her what she means.

"We have a school in East St. Louis named for Dr. King," she says. "The school is full of sewer water and the doors are locked with chains. Every student in that school is black. It's like a terrible joke on history."

It startles me to hear her words, but I am startled even more to think how seldom any press reporter has observed the irony of naming segregated schools for Martin Luther King. Children reach the heart of these hypocrisies much quicker than the grown-ups and the experts do.

Source: Excerpted from Jonathan Kozol, *Savage Inequalities* (New York: Harper Collins, 1992), p. 35.

What Does it Mean ?

austerity
hardship; severity

egress
act of coming out; exiting

perfunctory
routine; without enthusiasm

poignant
deeply affecting; touching

skewed
slanted; distorted

Jonathan Kozol, a long-time social activist, is author of seven award-winning books which focus on the plight of the disadvantaged children of our nation. Savage Inequalities: Children in America's Schools, *shows the disparities in America's public school system.*

Read and React

1. What does Kozol mean by "educational inequality"? Do you agree or disagree with his view? Why?

2. Does Kozol believe there is a link between economic resources and educational inequality? Explain. Discuss why you agree or disagree.

3. If Kozol were going to speak to your local school board, what would you like to say to him regarding educational inequality?

4. Is educational inequality a problem in your school? In other schools in your community? Elaborate.

5. Imagine yourself in the school Kozol describes. How would it affect your education, view of life, and future?

CHAPTER 13
Political and Economic Institutions

USING Your Sociological Imagination

Not so long ago, Americans looked at workers in Japan with "half-horrified awe." Rumors of workers slaving away ten hours a day, six days a week, made the rounds of corporate America. "You're so lucky to be working here," crowed U.S. bosses. "If you worked in Japan, you wouldn't be taking long lunches or two-week vacations. You'd sleep at the office and see your family on Sunday."

Management theorists likened the relationship between Japanese workers and supervisors to that of the family. A new management style based on the Japanese model was proposed. Where Type X was a worker needing close supervision and Type Y was a creative, self-directed worker, the new Type Z was an individual whose culture was focused entirely on work.

Today the reality is that Americans put in more hours than workers in any other industrialized country, including Japan. Between 1977 and 1997, the average work week among salaried American workers lengthened from forty-three to forty-seven hours. In that same period, the number of workers putting in more than fifty hours per week went from 24 percent to 37 percent. In fact, Americans work an equivalent of eight weeks longer every year than Western Europeans. Given these figures, it is even more surprising that over 80 percent of people at work say they are satisfied with their jobs. Where, why, and how Americans work are just some of the issues examined in this chapter on political and economic institutions in the United States.

Sections

1. **Power and Authority**
2. **Political Power in American Society**
3. **Economic Systems**
4. **The Modern Corporation**
5. **Work in the Modern Economy**

Learning Objectives

After reading this chapter, you will be able to

❖ distinguish among power, coercion, and authority.

❖ identify three forms of authority.

❖ discuss differences among democracy, totalitarianism, and authoritarianism.

❖ explain how voting is an exercise of power.

❖ list characteristics of capitalism and socialism.

❖ describe America's changing workforce.

❖ discuss the consequences of corporate downsizing.

SOCIOLOGY Online

Chapter Overview
Visit the *Sociology and You* Web site at soc.glencoe.com and click on **Chapter 13— Chapter Overviews** to preview chapter information.

Types of Interest Groups

Organization	Membership	Objectives
Business		
U.S. Chamber of Commerce	3,000,000 businesses	Lobby for businesses
National Association of Home Builders	205,000 members	Represent the housing and building industry
Agricultural		
National Farmers Union	300,000 farm and ranch families	Represent family farms and ranches
American Farm Bureau Federation	Over 5 million members	Lobby for agribusiness and farm owners
Professional		
American Medical Association (AMA)	Over 750,000 members	Represent physicians and improve the medical system
American Bar Association (ABA)	Over 400,000 members	Improve the legal system
Labor		
AFL–CIO	Over 64 affiliated unions (Over 13 million members)	Protect members from unfair labor practices
United Mine Workers	130,000 members	Represent mine workers and others
Public Interest		
League of Women Voters (LWV)	About 1,000 local leagues; 130,000 members and supporters	Promote voter registration and election reform
Common Cause	Over 200,000 members	Advocate political reform
Public Citizen	100,000 members	Focus on consumer issues
Single-Issue		
Sierra Club	Over 700,000 members	Protect the natural environment
National Audubon Society	550,000 members	Conserve and restore natural ecosystems
Greenpeace USA	250,000 members	Expose global environmental issues
Ideological		
Americans for Democratic Action (ADA)	65,000 members	Support liberal social, economic, and foreign policies
Christian Coalition	Over 1,000,000 members	Promote Christian values
National Organization for Women (NOW)	Over 500,000 members	Eliminate discrimination and protect the rights of women

*(Rows from U.S. Chamber of Commerce through United Mine Workers are grouped as **ECONOMIC GROUPS**; rows from League of Women Voters through National Organization for Women are grouped as **NON-ECONOMIC GROUPS**.)*

Figure 13.4 Types of Interest Groups.   *The United States government is influenced by a wide variety of interest groups. This figure provides some examples of the most important types. Do you believe that the influence of all these interest groups promotes or hinders democracy? Explain your answers, using conflict theory or functionalism.*

New interest groups are born all the time. The environmental lobby is a good example. There were relatively few environmental interest groups before the passage of major environmental legislation (such as the Clean Water Act) in the 1960s. The success of this legislation spawned additional groups, now numbering three times the original total. This added clout produced additional environmental legislation—for example, the 1990 Clean Air Act Amendments—that subsequently led to the creation of other interest groups (Schmidt, Shelley, and Bardes, 1999).

Conflict Perspective: The Power Elite

Sociologist C. Wright Mills was a leading proponent of the elitist perspective. In the 1950s, he claimed that the United States no longer had separate economic, political, and military leaders. Rather, the key people in each area overlapped to form a unified group that he labeled the **power elite.**

According to Mills, members of the power elite share common interests and similar social and economic backgrounds. Elites are educated in select boarding schools, military academies, and Ivy League schools; belong to the Episcopalian and Presbyterian churches; and come from upper-class families. Members of the power elite have known each other for a long time, have mutual acquaintances of long standing, share many values and attitudes, and intermarry. All this makes it easier for them to coordinate their actions to obtain what they want.

power elite
a unified group of military, corporate, and government leaders

Section 2 Assessment

1. What are the major agents of political socialization?
2. How do elitists differ from pluralists in explaining the relationship between racial membership and political power in the U.S.?
3. According to C. Wright Mills, which of the following is NOT part of the power elite?
   a. military organizations
   b. educational leaders
   c. large corporations
   d. executive branch of the government

Critical Thinking

4. **Analyzing Information** On page 435, the author writes: "Members of minorities, people with little education, and people with smaller incomes are less likely to vote in both congressional and presidential elections." Do you think that pluralists or elitists are more likely to use advertising to change the political attitudes of individuals in these social categories? Explain.
5. **Drawing Conclusions** Is America a pluralist society, or is it controlled by a power elite? Support your conclusion with information from this text and other classes.

The ballot is stronger than the bullet.

Abraham Lincoln
U. S. president

Economic Systems

Key Terms

- capitalism
- monopolies

- oligopolies
- socialism

Section Preview

Capitalist economies are based on private property and the pursuit of profit, and government, in theory, plays a minor role in regulating industry. In socialist economies, the means of production are owned collectively, and government has an active role in planning and controlling the economy.

capitalism
an economic system based on private ownership of property and the pursuit of profit

monopolies
companies that have control over the production or distribution of a product or service

oligopolies
combinations of companies that control the production or distribution of a product or service

Capitalism

Economic systems, as suggested earlier, involve the production and distribution of goods and services. **Capitalism** is an economic system founded on two basic premises: the sanctity of private property and the right of individuals to profit from their labors.

Capitalists believe that individuals, not government, deserve to own and to control land, factories, raw materials, and the tools of production. They argue that private ownership benefits society. Capitalists also believe in unrestricted competition with minimum government interference.

How is capitalism thought to benefit society?   According to Adam Smith, an eighteenth-century Scottish social philosopher and founder of economics, a combination of the private ownership of property and the pursuit of profit brings advantages to society. Because of competition, Smith stated, individual capitalists will always be motivated to provide the goods and services desired by the public at prices the public is willing and able to pay. Capitalists who produce inferior goods or who charge too much will soon be out of business because the public will turn to their competitors. The public, Smith reasoned, will benefit through economic competition. Not only will the public receive high-quality goods and services at reasonable prices, but also capitalists will always be searching for new products and new technologies to reduce their costs. As a result, capitalist societies will use resources efficiently.

Actually, no pure capitalist economy exists in the world. In practice, there are important deviations from Smith's ideal model. One of these deviations involves the tendency to form *monopolies* and *oligopolies*.

What are monopolies and oligopolies?   When capitalist organizations experience success, they tend to grow until they become giants within their particular industries. In this way, capitalism fosters the rise of **monopolies,** companies that control a particular market, and **oligopolies,** combinations of companies working together to control a market. New organizations find it difficult to enter these markets, where they have little hope of competing on an equal basis. Thus, competition is stifled.

Among other problems, the creation of monopolies and oligopolies permits price fixing. Consumers must choose between buying at the "going price" set by the sellers or not buying at all.

A recent example of alleged monopolistic practices in the U.S. economy involves the Microsoft Corporation. Microsoft manufactures, among other products, the Windows operating system—by far the most popular operating system for personal computers. Computer manufacturers typically include Windows on the machines they sell. In the 1990s, Microsoft began to insist that manufacturers include its Internet browser, Explorer, on their computers as well. The manufacturers were also instructed not to install another browser in addition to Explorer. If they refused, Microsoft would withhold their license to sell Windows on the machines. Because Microsoft had so much power over computer manufacturers, other makers of Internet browsers, such as Netscape, were essentially excluded from the market (Chandbasekaran, 1999). Eventually, the federal government took Microsoft to court, where it was ruled that Microsoft did indeed engage in monopolistic practices. The case is not resolved, however, and the corporation had some success in its 2001 appeal of this decision.

The Role of Government in Capitalism

Adam Smith is often misinterpreted as saying that government should have a strictly hands-off approach where the economy is concerned. While Smith strongly opposed overregulation by government, he reserved a place for some regulation. Because one of the legitimate roles of government was to protect its citizens from injustice, Smith knew that the state might have to "step in" to prevent abuses by businesses. In fact, the U.S. government has always been involved in the workings of the economy.

How does the government contribute to the U.S. economy? The Constitution expressly provided a role for the national government in the promotion of a sound economy. Government functions include the regulation of

The enormous success of Bill Gates and Microsoft led to a federal investigation of the software giant's business practices.

The Federal Aviation Administration (FAA) conducts jetliner crash tests as part of the federal government's authority over private business. In what way might cultural values promote such government involvement?

Figure 13.5 Examples of Government and Regulatory Assistance

The government is extensively involved in the U.S. economy. What would Adam Smith say about this?

Public utilities are often owned and operated by state or local governments.

The agricultural industry feels the influence of government through price controls and embargoes on exports to other countries.

Antitrust legislation exists to control the growth of corporations.

The federal government is heavily involved in the defense industry.

Business could not survive without publicly financed roadways, airports, and waterways.

Publicly funded public schools, colleges, and universities supply business with a skilled workforce and provide basic research for product development.

The U.S. military protects American international business interests.

Government supports business through tax breaks.

Legislation requires labor and business to obey labor laws.

commerce, development of a strong currency, creation of uniform standards for commerce, and the provision of a stable system of credit. In 1789, Congress supported our shipping industry through a tariff on goods imported by foreign ships. Since this initial move into the economy, the federal government has continued to help business, labor, and agriculture. For example, the federal government aids private industry through loan guarantees—as in the 1979 government guarantee (up to $1.2 billion) to bail out the Chrysler Corporation. Also, U.S. labor is supported by the government through regulations on such matters as minimum wages, maximum working hours, health and safety conditions, and unemployment support. Then there are the small farmers and agribusinesses that receive financial assistance amounting to billions of dollars each year (Patterson, 1999). See Figure 13.5 for additional examples of government economic and regulatory assistance.

Socialism

socialism
an economic system founded on the belief that the means of production should be controlled by the people as a whole

Socialism is an economic system founded on the belief that the means of production should be controlled by the people as a whole. The state, as the people's representative, should own and control property. Under a socialist system, government directs and controls the economy. The state is expected to ensure all members of society a share in the monetary benefits.

How is socialism thought to benefit society?   Socialist theory points to important benefits for workers. Workers under capitalism receive wages below the value their labor produces and have little control over their work. In theory, workers under socialism should profit because both the state and the workplace exist for their benefit. As a result, workers should be able to exert significant control over both their work organizations and the policy directions of the society as a whole.

Does socialism work this perfectly?   Cases of pure socialism are as rare as cases of pure capitalism. Strict socialist systems have not been successful in eliminating income inequalities nor have they been able to develop overall economic plans that guarantee sustained economic growth. In the socialistic economy of the former Soviet Union, for example, some agricultural and professional work was performed privately by individuals who worked for a profit. Significant portions of housing were privately owned as well. Managers received salaries that were considerably higher than those received by workers, and managers were eligible for bonuses such as automobiles and housing. Private enterprise existed in Poland under Russian communist rule. Service businesses, such as restaurants and hotels, had a significant degree of private ownership. Hotels, in fact, were typically built and managed by multinational chains. Because Poles could travel abroad, they formed business relationships, learned about capitalist methods, imported goods to fill demand, and brought back hard currency. They then used the hard currency earned abroad to create private businesses (Schnitzer, 2000).

> Socialism works, but nowhere as efficiently as in the beehive and the anthill.
>
> **Laurence Peter**
> **U. S. business writer**

Sweden has a socialist government. What types of market relationships would you expect to find there?

Mixed Economic Systems

As this Shanghai Kentucky Fried Chicken restaurant reflects, elements of capitalism are being introduced into China.

Most nations fall between the extremes of capitalism and socialism and include elements of both economic systems. Countries in Western Europe, for example, have developed capitalist economic systems in which both public and private ownership play important roles. In these nations, highly strategic industries (banks, transportation, communications, and some others) are owned and operated by the state. Other industries are privately owned but are more closely regulated than in the United States (Harris, 1997; Ollman, 1998).

As the former Soviet Union lost control over its republics and Eastern Europe, many of these formerly socialist countries began to move toward capitalism. Czechoslovakia, in several ways, has shifted from public to private ownership of businesses. Private property nationalized after the Russians took over in 1948 has been returned to the original owners or their heirs. These assets moved from the public to the private sector are valued at about $5 billion. Many small shops and businesses have been sold in public auctions. In 1992, Czechoslovakia sold over 1,000 of its bigger state enterprises to its citizens. During 1992–93 as it broke into the Czech Republic and Slovakia, 25 percent of the nations' assets were privatized. In Hungary, state-owned enterprises have been allowed to become privately owned companies. Over one million Hungarians have been given the right to buy land, businesses, buildings, or other property taken over by the Russians in 1949. Nearly all of the state-owned small businesses are now in the hands of private owners. Agricultural cooperatives have also been privatized (Schnitzer, 2000).

In 1993, Cuba's communist party allowed some degree of capitalism by permitting plumbers, carpenters, and other tradespeople to work for profit. China has been incorporating moderate free market reforms into its economy since the late 1970s (Muldavin, 1999).

Section 3 Assessment

1. Government policies are usually based on cultural values. Can you identify important differences in the cultural values underlying governmental policies that promote either capitalism or socialism?
2. How successful has socialism been as an economic system? Defend your answer.
3. What is meant by a mixed economic system?

Critical Thinking

4. **Making Comparisons** Briefly compare and contrast the advantages of capitalism and socialism.

Tech Trends

Cybernews and Democracy

Reporting the news has been part of the United States since its founding. Indeed, freedom of the press is one of the basic guarantees of the Bill of Rights. During the twentieth century, television displaced newspapers as the primary source of news for most Americans. Now, the Internet is promising to make much greater changes in the way news is gathered and delivered.

Central to the changes is the fact that today anyone with access to the Internet is free to "report" the news. Internet journalist Matt Drudge says that now, "any citizen can be a reporter" (Trigaboff, 1998:55). Drudge portrays the Internet as a democratizing institution eliminating differences between reporters and readers.

Many journalists, however, worry about the negative effects of instant reporting via the Internet. Sources for stories often go unchecked as reporters sacrifice accuracy for speed. Reporters on the Internet generally do not have editors reviewing their stories, in-house attorneys worrying about lawsuits, or publishers making judgment calls about the appropriateness of news stories. Joseph C. Goulden, former director of media analysis for Accuracy in Media, a nonprofit, grassroots citizens watchdog of the news media, describes the reporting style on the Internet as "Ready, fire, aim" (Rust and Danitz, 1998:23).

In the United States, one of the justifications for the freedom of the press is its role in delivering accurate information to voters. If Internet reporting represents a trend toward greater inaccuracy, this traditional contribution of a free press to American democracy could be weakened. What if voters grew to distrust even more the information they received and thus became increasingly cynical about the political process?

At this time no one can be sure what the future holds for Internet journalism. One thing, though, is certain: Internet journalism will have a profound impact on the way news is reported (Kinsley, 1998).

Matt Drudge became the symbol of Internet news reporting in the late 1990s. Is Internet journalism good or bad for democracy?

Analyzing the Trends

There is no question that the Internet will affect how democracy is practiced in the U.S. Discuss some ways in which the federal government currently uses the Internet to affect group behavior.

Section 4

The Modern Corporation

Key Terms

- corporation
- interlocking directorates
- conglomerates
- multinationals

Section Preview

Corporations, especially those with multinational connections, have grown very powerful. Corporate managers affect domestic political decision making and influence the political and economic institutions of countries around the world.

corporation
an organization owned by shareholders, who have limited liability and limited control

The Nature of Corporations

Sociologists study corporations because of their great importance in modern economic systems. U.S. corporations, for example, not only dominate the American economic system but also influence the economies of nations around the world. Corporations represent massive concentrations of wealth. And because of their economic muscle, corporations such as Microsoft, IBM, and General Electric command the attention of government decision makers. As a result, government policies regarding such matters as consumer safety, tax laws, and relationships with other nations usually reflect corporate influence.

What are corporations, anyway?   A **corporation** is an organization owned by shareholders. These shareholders have *limited liability* and *limited control*. Limited liability means they cannot be held financially responsible for actions of the corporation. For example, shareholders are not expected to pay debts the corporation owes. At the same time, they do not have a direct voice in the day-to-day operations of the firm. Shareholders are formally entitled to vote regularly for members of the board of directors. But in practice candidates are routinely approved as recommended by the existing board. The real control of a corporation rests with the board of directors and management.

Corporate Influence

Top corporate officials have tremendous influence on government decisions. This is true for several reasons. Because of their personal wealth and organizational connections, corporate officials are able to reward or punish elected government officials through investment decisions. For example, suppose a town depends on a single large corporation for jobs and other economic advantages. Corporate officials are deciding whether to increase their operation in this town or move some of the facilities to another town, which would endanger local jobs. Town officials are likely to do what they can to make corporate officials happy so that new investment will be made locally.

This agricultural worker is paid by a large corporation rather than a small business/farmer. Which employer would be more secure?

In what other ways do corporations wield power? Such political clout by large corporations is multiplied through **interlocking directorates.** A directorate is another name for the board of directors. Directorates interlock when the heads of corporations sit on one another's boards. Although by law competing corporations may not have interlocking directorates, such directorates are legal for noncompeting corporations. For example, various members of the General Motors board of directors also sit on the boards of many other corporations, including Sony, Sara Lee, and Marriott International. It is not difficult to imagine the political power created by a web of interlocks among already powerful corporations.

The political power of corporations is also enhanced through **conglomerates**—networks of unrelated businesses operating under a single corporate umbrella. RJR Nabisco, Inc., for example, holds companies in such different areas as tobacco, pet foods, candy, cigarettes, food products, bubble gum, research, and technology. A listing of the company's North American subsidiaries covers nearly an entire page in *Who Owns Whom* (1998).

> **interlocking directorates**
> directorates that result when heads of corporations sit on one another's boards

> **conglomerates**
> networks of unrelated businesses operating under one corporate umbrella

> **multinationals**
> firms based in highly industrialized societies with operating facilities throughout the world

Multinational Corporations

The political influence of corporations is not confined to their countries of origin. The world is increasingly being influenced by **multinationals**—firms based in highly industrialized societies with operating facilities throughout the world. Improvements in communication and transportation technology have allowed these companies to exert wide control over their global operations.

How powerful are multinational corporations? Suppose we combined all the political and economic units in the world and then chose the hundred largest units. Of these hundred units, fifty-one would be multinational corporations rather than countries. Several corporations based in the United States—ExxonMobil, IBM, General Motors, Ford Motor Company, AT&T, Wal-Mart Stores, and General Electric—have sales volumes exceeding the annual economic output of some industrialized nations. Figure 13.6 compares some multinational corporations with selected nations.

What are the effects of multinational corporations? Defenders of multinationals argue that the corporations provide developing countries with technology, capital, foreign markets, and products that would otherwise be unavailable to them. Critics claim that multinationals actually harm the economies of the foreign nations in which they locate by exploiting natural resources, disrupting local economies, introducing inappropriate technologies and products, and increasing the

Corporation		Country	
Wal-Mart Stores, Inc. $119.3 Billion	vs.	Greece $119.1 Billion	
Volkswagen AG $65.3 Billion	vs.	New Zealand $65 Billion	
IBM International Business Machines Corp. $78.5 Billion	vs.	Egypt $75.5 Billion	
Mitsubishi Corporation $128.9 Billion	vs.	South Africa $129.1 Billion	
Sony Corporation $55 Billion	vs.	Czech Republic $54.9 Billion	
General Electric Company $90.8 Billion	vs.	Israel $92 Billion	

Figure 13.6 Total Revenue of Multinational Corporations versus National Gross Domestic Products. *This table compares the revenue of selected multinational corporations to the gross domestic product (value of all goods produced and consumed domestically) of some countries in 1998. Were you surprised by any of the information?*

Source: John Stopford, "Think Again: Multinational Corporations," *Foreign Policy,* 113 (Winter, 1998–99).

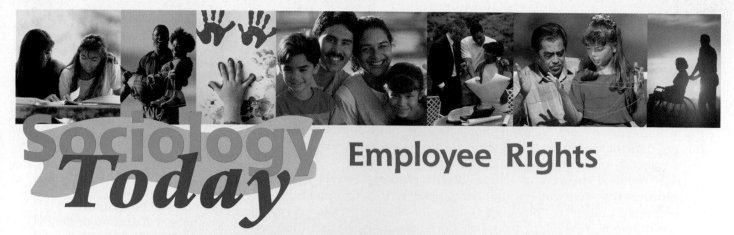

Employee Rights

The Supreme Court of the United States has historically granted employers a great deal of power over their employees. In 1878, a New York company posted a list of rules that told employees, among other things, "On the Sabbath, everyone is expected to be in the Lord's House" and "All employees are expected to be in bed by 10:00 P.M." At the turn of the nineteenth century, Henry Ford's automobile workers were carefully watched by management for signs of bad character. Many Ford Motor Company employees lost their jobs for smoking, drinking, or criticizing the firm.

Even today, some employee rights are curtailed at work. The Constitution, for example, protects free speech for all citizens. Employees, however, can be prevented from printing and distributing a critical newsletter to customers of their companies. Of recent concern is the right of employers to track workers' movements on the Internet and to read personal e-mails.

Today, a growing employee rights movement is pushing for greater political and legal protection on the job. Here is a partial list of the rights that many workers feel should be theirs today.

❖ the right to a job

❖ the right to protection from arbitrary or sudden termination

❖ the right to privacy of possessions and person in the workplace, including freedom from arbitrary searches, use of polygraphs, surreptitious surveillance, and intrusive psychological or medical testing

❖ the right to a clean, healthy, and safe environment on the job, including freedom from undue stress, sexual harassment, cigarette smoke, and exposure to toxic substances

❖ the right to be informed of records and information kept and to have access to personnel files

❖ the right to freedom of action, association, and lifestyle when off duty

❖ the right to freedom of conscience and to inform government or media about illegal or socially harmful corporate actions

❖ the right to due process for grievances against the employer

Many of these rights already exist; others need to be discussed with employers. There is one thing most employees and employers agree on, however. If employees take a balanced approach to pursuing their rights on the job, both individuals and organizations will benefit.

Doing Sociology

1. Some observers believe that violations of employee rights contradict the rational-legal basis of organizational authority. Do you agree? Why or why not?

2. Discuss the above list of workers' rights with your parents or other adults who work outside the home. Ask them if they know whether or not these rights exist in their workplaces. Are there any rights not on the list that they believe should be added?

Some multinationals are so successful that their products are widely (and illegally) copied. Here, a "faked" Nike athletic shoe is readied for sale in Shanghai, China.

amount of income inequality. Multinationals, these critics note, rely on inexpensive labor or abundant raw materials in developing nations while returning their profits to corporate headquarters and shareholders in rich nations. Multinationals' domination of their industries has made it difficult for the economically developing nations to establish new companies that can compete with the multinationals. As a result, multinationals may slow rather than promote economic development in these nations.

" The modern corporation is a political institution; its purpose is the creation of legitimate power in the industrial hemisphere.

**Peter Drucker
management author**

Section 4 Assessment

1. Discuss limited liability and limited control in relation to the modern corporation.
2. Describe the influence of the corporation in the world today. Identify some of the benefits and negative consequences for society.

Critical Thinking

3. **Drawing Conclusions** Would you rather work for a large, multinational corporation or for yourself as an independent businessperson? Explain your choice.

Section 5

Work in the Modern Economy

Key Terms

- primary sector
- secondary sector
- tertiary sector
- occupations
- core tier
- peripheral tier
- downsizing
- contingent employment

Section Preview

Workers today face a changing job structure. More corporations are downsizing and replacing full-time employees with consultants or temporary workers. Evidence indicates that this trend is having some negative consequences.

primary sector
that part of the economy producing goods from the natural environment

secondary sector
that part of the economy engaged in manufacturing goods

tertiary sector
that part of the economy providing services

The Changing Nature of Work

To understand work in modern society you need to be familiar with the three basic economic sectors. They are *primary, secondary,* and *tertiary.*

How do the economic sectors differ?   The **primary sector** of an economy depends on the natural environment to produce economic goods. The types of jobs in this sector vary widely—farmer, miner, fisherman, timber worker, rancher. In the **secondary sector,** manufactured products are made from raw materials. Occupations in this sector include factory workers of all types, from those who produce computers to those who turn out Pokémon cards. Those in the secondary sector are popularly known as blue-collar workers. Employees in the **tertiary sector** provide services. If today you went to school, filled your car with gas, stopped by the bank, and visited your doctor, you spent most of your time and someone's money in the tertiary (service) sector. Other service industries include insurance, real estate, retail sales, and entertainment. More and more people in these industries are white-collar workers.

To which sector of the economy does this California logger belong?

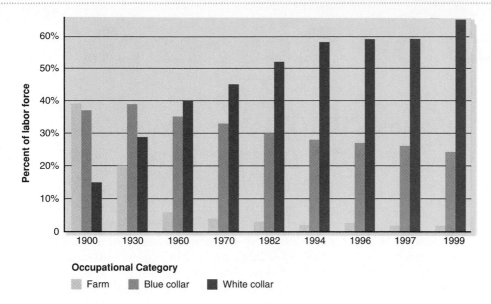

Figure 13.7 Changes in Labor Force by Occupational Category. *This figure tracks changes in the U.S. labor force from 1900 to 1999. Which labor division is growing the fastest?*

Source: U.S. Department of Labor, Bureau of Labor Statistics, 1999.

How have the three sectors changed historically?

Obviously, the primary sector dominated the preindustrial economy. At that stage of economic development, physical goods were made by hand. This balance began to change with the mechanization of farming in the agricultural economy. Mechanical inventions (cotton gin, plow, tractor), along with the application of new scientific methods (seed production, fertilization, and crop rotation), drastically increased production. During the 1800s, the average farmer could feed five workers or so. Today, the figure is eighty. At the same time production increased, labor demands decreased. Primary sector workers have declined from almost 40 percent of the labor pool in 1900 to about 2 percent today.

With other technological advancements in industry (power looms, motors of all types, electrical power) came the shift of agricultural workers from farms to factories, ushering in the secondary sector. As Figure 13.7 indicates, the percentage of the U.S. labor force engaged in blue-collar jobs reached almost 40 percent in 1900.

Just as in agriculture, technological developments permitted greater production with fewer workers. Since World War II, the fastest-growing occupations in the secondary sector have been white-collar—managers, professionals, sales workers, clerical workers. In 1956, white-collar workers for the first time accounted for a larger proportion of the U.S. labor force than blue-collar workers. In manufacturing industries, the number of white-collar workers is now three times the number of blue-collar workers.

Technological progress did not stop with the secondary sector. As relative growth in the proportion of workers in goods-producing jobs was decreasing, the demand for labor in the tertiary section was increasing. Fueled by computer technology, the United States economy moved from a manufacturing base to a knowledge, or information, base. The current demand is for people who can manage information and deliver services. Today, the proportion of white-collar workers in the U.S. is about 70 percent, up from just below 30 percent in 1930. (See Figure 13.7.)

Blue-collar workers, such as the longshore workers pictured here, may be an endangered species.

Focus on Research

Case Study: The End of the Line

Because she grew up near Chrysler's auto plant in Kenosha, Wisconsin, researcher Kathryn Marie Dudley had a special interest in studying the cultural fallout from the plant's closing in 1988. Dudley's research is a case study of a large plant in a one-industry community experiencing relocations, downsizings, and job eliminations. She offers Kenosha as a typical example of the effect of changing work patterns on midsize towns. As indicated in the excerpt below, the plant changes over the past few decades are seen as part of the shift from an industrial to a postindustrial society:

What was once a fundamental segment of the American economic structure—heavy industry and durable goods manufacturing—has now become a marginal part of the national portfolio. As this sector of the economy gives way to the new "knowledge industries," workers in this sector are being superseded as well. In America's new image of itself as a postindustrial society, individuals still employed in basic manufacturing industries look like global benchwarmers in the competitive markets of the modern world (Dudley, 1994:161).

When the auto plant was finally shut down, Dudley did in-depth follow-up interviews with autoworkers and with a wide variety of professionals in the Kenosha area. Interview questions were open-ended to give informants freedom to roam where their thoughts and feelings took them. Dudley's only restriction was that the interviews be geared to the cultural meaning of what was happening to the community because of its declining employment base.

For Dudley, the demolition of the auto plant was a metaphor for the dismantling of the way of life created since the early 1950s among U.S. blue-collar workers in core manufacturing industries. These increasingly displaced blue-collar workers, contends Dudley, find themselves caught between two interpretations of success in America. On the one hand, middle-class professionals justify their place in society by reference to their educational credentials and "thinking" jobs. Blue-collar workers, on the other hand, legitimize their place in society on the basis of the high market value society has traditionally placed on their hard labor. One ex-auto worker, whom Dudley calls Al Tirpak, captured the idea beautifully:

We're worth fifteen dollars an hour because we're producing a product that can be sold on the market that'll produce that fifteen dollars an hour. . . . I don't know if you want to [base a person's value] strictly on education. You can send someone to school for twelve years and they can still be doing something that's socially undesirable and not very worthwhile for society. I don't know if they should get paid *just* because they had an education. In my mind, yuppie means *young unproductive parasite.* We're gonna have an awful lot of yuppies here in Kenosha that say they are doing something worthwhile when, really, they aren't (Dudley, 1994:169).

Due to the massive loss of high-paying factory jobs, Dudley contends that the blue-collar vision of success is coming to "the end of the line." These workers have lost their cultural niche to a postindustrial world where work is based on education and the application of knowledge.

Dudley documents the blue-collar workers' view of this new reality. From her extensive interviews, she constructs a portrait of their struggle to preserve their cultural traditions in a world in which the type of employment on which these traditions were built is decreasing. The penalty for not creating new cultural supports for a sense of social worth, Dudley concludes, will be life in a state of confusion with a sense of failure.

The shift from an industrial to a postindustrial economy will necessarily result in plant shutdowns and layoffs.

Working with the Research

1. What is the focus of Dudley's research?
2. What does Dudley's conclusion mean for blue-collar workers in terms of their way of life?
3. Do you think Dudley's research methods are strong enough to support her conclusion?
4. Do you believe that Dudley can be objective in this study of her hometown? Explain your answer.

Occupational Structure

To what tier of America's occupational structure do these California aircraft workers belong?

Occupations are categories of jobs that involve similar activities at different work locations. For example, teacher, dental assistant, film producer, and electrician are all occupations because each position requires similar training and involves some standard operations. The United States Department of Labor has identified over 500 occupations with more than 21,000 various specialties within the broader occupation categories.

What is the shape of the U.S. occupational structure? A two-tier occupational structure has developed in the U.S. One tier—the **core**—includes jobs with large firms holding dominant positions within their industries. Computer technology, pharmaceutical, and aerospace firms are prime examples. About 35 percent of U.S. workers are in the core. The other level—the **peripheral tier**—is composed of jobs in smaller firms that either are competing for business left over from core firms or are engaged in less profitable industries such as agriculture, textiles, and small-scale retail trade. Most U.S. workers—around 65 percent—are employed in the peripheral tier.

What is the nature of core and peripheral jobs? Historically, jobs in the core paid more, offered better benefits, and provided longer-term employment. This is not surprising since the firms involved are large and highly profitable. Peripheral jobs are characterized by low pay, little or no benefits, and short-term employment. These features follow from the weaker competitive position and the smaller size of the employing firms.

How are the core and peripheral tiers changing? The industries that have supplied most of the core jobs in the U.S. have been scaling back during the last 20 years, laying off experienced workers and not hiring new ones. As early as 1983, for example, a steel mill in Hibbing, Minnesota, that once employed 4,400 people had a payroll of only 650 ("Left Out," 1983). Since 1983, the Weirton Steele Company continued to cut its production capacity by another 30 percent and has laid off more than half of its workforce (Riederer, 1999). In fact, more than 43 million jobs have been eliminated in the United States since 1979. Over 570,000 job cuts were announced in the United States in 1998, more than half of which occurred in manufacturing plants (McNamee and Muller, 1998; Riederer, 1999). Of course, as these top-tier jobs have been disappearing, peripheral jobs have become a larger share of the total jobs.

The good economic news, fueled by microchip technology, is that the U.S. economy continues its healthy growth and unemployment remains low. The bad economic news is that the new jobs are not as good as the manufacturing jobs they are replacing. The newer industries provide few jobs suited to the skills and backgrounds of laid-off manufacturing workers. Moreover, most jobs in high-tech industries pay minimal wages and offer few chances for promotion. Responsible positions with high pay are held by a very small proportion of high-tech employees.

occupations
categories of jobs that involve similar activities at different work locations

core tier
an occupational structure composed of large firms dominating their industries

peripheral tier
an occupational structure composed of smaller, less profitable firms

Thus, reemployment of laid-off workers is a significant problem. While the overwhelming majority of the over five million U.S. workers laid off between 1979 and 1992 had held full-time jobs, only half reported taking new full-time jobs. Another third were either unemployed or were no longer in the labor force. The rest were working part-time, running their own businesses, or occupied as unpaid family workers (Uchitelle and Kleinfield, 1996).

What difference does this make to U.S. workers? As has probably already crossed your mind, this trend makes a huge difference. The U.S. economy has been losing higher-paying jobs and gaining lower-paying jobs. This helps explain why, since the 1970s, the majority of workers have been losing economic ground. While thirty years ago one American worker alone could support a family, the dual-employed married couple has become the norm today.

This process, known as *downwaging,* is expected to continue in the twenty-first century. Of the top ten job categories projected to grow between 1998 and 2008, four pay below the poverty level for a family of four. Only two of the top ten shrinking job categories fall below the poverty threshold (U.S. Bureau of the Census, 2000d). Many sociologists believe that the job loss and downwaging trends threaten the American dream (Newman, 1993; Barlett and Steel, 1996).

downsizing
the process by which companies reduce their workforces

Downsizing and Contingent Employment

Clearly, the occupational structure in the United States has changed dramatically over the last few decades. *Downsizing* and *contingent employment,* two strategies used by top management, reduce employment in core industries. A discussion of these related practices will help explain why the U.S. occupational structure is changing.

contingent employment
the hiring of part-time, short-term workers

Downsizing is the process by which companies reduce the size of their full-time workforces. **Contingent employment** involves hiring people on a part-time or short-term basis. Although corporate downsizing had been going on since the late 1970s, it accelerated during the 1980s and 1990s. Since 1985, an estimated four million people have lost their jobs to downsizing alone. This trend is expected to continue (Sloan, 1996; Belton, 1999).

Why are downsizing and contingent employment taking place on such a large scale? Part of the motivation for downsizing is based on top management's belief that their companies employ a surplus of people and that, thanks to computers and other labor-saving technology, work can be done by fewer employees without reductions in efficiency and effectiveness. Top management also points to lower profits caused by increasing foreign competition. And it is true that about 20 percent of all U.S. workers are directly exposed to foreign competition (McNamee and Muller, 1998). Companies have responded to increased foreign competition by moving

Corporate downsizing is
associated with lower pay.

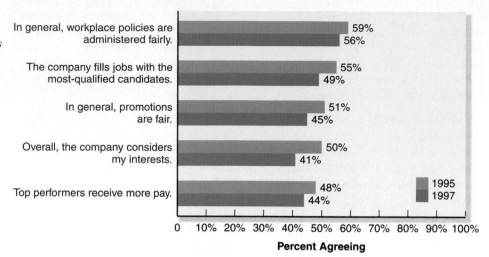

Figure 13.8 Evidence of Declining Trust In Management. *According to this graph, employee trust in management declined between 1995 and 1997. Are any of these factors affecting trust more important to you than others?*

Source: *Towers Perrin Workplace Index* (Boston, MA), 1998.

This unhappy worker has been caught in a corporate downsizing. What negative effects is this experience likely to have on him?

operations overseas and by replacing full-time employees with part-time workers hired to do a limited amount of work for a specified time period.

Contingent employment is a cost-cutting device. Unlike full-time employees, contingent workers receive lower pay and are not entitled to expensive benefits such as vacation time, health insurance, and retirement benefits.

Does downsizing and contingent employment have a downside? According to Robert Reich, former secretary of the U.S. Department of Labor, downsizing and contingent employment will create greater polarization between those who control capital and those who do not. Some critics believe the "disposable" workforce is the most important trend in business today. They contend that it is fundamentally changing the relationship between Americans and their employers.

A survey of 2,500 employees across the United States confirms that employees' attitudes toward their employers are changing. Although employees express high job satisfaction, their trust in management appears to be eroding. Workers seem to be losing some faith in management's commitment to them. (See Figure 13.8.)

Trust and loyalty are difficult to maintain when employees do not believe company policies treat them fairly. As time passes, additional research will help to focus attention on the full effects of corporate downsizing and contingent employment.

Section 5 Assessment

1. Why have white-collar jobs increased faster than jobs in other sectors of the workforce since the 1930s?
2. What are some immediate benefits of downsizing? Some long-term drawbacks?

Critical Thinking

3. **Drawing Conclusions** Would you like to spend your work life as a contingent employee? Why or why not?

Summary

Section 1: Power and Authority

Main Idea: Authority is the sanctioned use of power. Political systems can be based on three types of authority: charismatic, traditional, and rational-legal. Democratic, totalitarian, and authoritarian are types of political systems.

Section 2: Political Power in American Society

Main Idea: The two major models of political power are elitism and pluralism. Advocates of the conflict perspective believe American society is controlled by elites. Pluralists, whose view is associated with functionalism, depict power as widely distributed among interest groups. Voting does not seem to be an effective means for nonelites to influence political decisions in the U.S.

Section 3: Economic Systems

Main Idea: Capitalist economies are based on private property and the pursuit of profit, and government, in theory, plays a minor role in regulating industry. In socialist economies, the means of production are owned collectively, and government has an active role in planning and controlling the economy.

Section 4: The Modern Corporation

Main Idea: Corporations, especially those with multinational connections, have grown very powerful. Corporate managers affect domestic political decision making and influence the political and economic institutions of countries around the world.

Section 5: Work in the Modern Economy

Main Idea: Workers today face a changing job structure. More corporations are downsizing and replacing full-time employees with consultants or temporary workers. Evidence indicates that this trend is having some negative consequences.

SOCIOLOGY Online

Self-Check Quiz
Visit the *Sociology and You* Web site at soc.glencoe.com and click on **Chapter 13—Self-Check Quizzes** to prepare for the chapter test.

Reviewing Vocabulary

Complete each sentence using each term once.

a. charismatic authority
b. monopoly
c. downsizing
d. traditional authority
e. power elite
f. pluralism
g. elitism
h. primary sector
i. interest group
j. corporation
k. rational-legal authority
l. power

1. The ability to control the behavior of others is called _____.

2. _____ is the authority that arises from the personality of an individual.

3. The form of authority in which the power of government officials is based on their offices is called _____.

4. _____ is the form of authority in which the legitimacy of a leader is rooted in custom.

5. A group organized to influence political decision making is called _____.

6. _____ is a system in which a community or society is controlled from the top by a few individuals or organizations.

7. The process in which political decisions are made as a result of competition and compromise among special interest groups is called _____.

8. A coalition of top military, corporate, and government leaders is called the _____.

9. _____ is an organization owned by shareholders who have limited liability and limited control.

10. The reduction of a corporation's workforce is called _____.

11. A company that has control over the production or distribution of a product or service is called a _____.

12. Economic activities such as farming, fishing, or mining are known as the _____.

CHAPTER 13 ASSESSMENT

Reviewing the Facts

1. How did Max Weber define power?
2. What is elitism? Give an example.
3. According to C. Wright Mills, who controls the power in the United States? Use the diagram below to illustrate your answer.

**CONTROL OF POWER IN THE UNITED STATES
ACCORDING TO C. WRIGHT MILLS**

_____   _____   _____

POWER

4. What is socialism? Give an example.
5. The economic system of most nations most closely follows which system?
6. What is downsizing? In general, what can be said about the relationship between the disadvantages of downsizing and the advantages of downsizing?

Thinking Critically

1. **Making Inferences** Charismatic leaders such as Adolf Hitler and Branch Davidian cult leader David Koresh show us that the ability to exert control over people has little to do with issues of right and wrong. Why do people embrace men like Hitler or Koresh? What kind of training or education is essential in a democracy to counter the effects of dangerous yet charismatic leaders?
2. **Drawing Conclusions** The topic of enforced population control (see Another Place, page 432) is an intriguing one for many Americans. Only ten percent of American families in 2000 had more than two children. Does government ever have a right to legislate how many children couples are allowed to have? Should Americans be encouraged to have only two children for social reasons? Should income and educational levels be factors in how large families should be? Under what circumstances, if any, would government have a legitimate say in the size of families?
3. **Analyzing Information** The National Rifle Association (NRA) is one of the most powerful special interest groups in the country. Its membership is close to three million (slightly more than 1 percent of the U.S. population). Yet many people in the organization report that only a handful of the members are active and vocal. Why does the NRA get so much attention when only a small minority of its members express their opinions? How have these members influenced politicians?
4. **Analyzing Information** According to conflict theorists, members of the power elite control many aspects of not only politics but society at large. A recent book tried to examine the diversity of the power elite—that is, how many women and minorities are in its membership. Discuss the extent to which you think women and minorities are represented in the power elite.
5. **Evaluating Information** Many individuals in the history of the United States have been able to influence the political process because of their personal wealth. Examples include Andrew Carnegie, John D. Rockefeller, and—more recently—Microsoft founder Bill Gates. Capitalism encourages the accumulation of wealth. Do you think the government should put limits on how much wealth any one individual or organization can control? Why or why not?
6. **Evaluating Information** There is growing concern about the accuracy of the news reports that we receive daily, particularly from the Internet. Inaccuracies and sensationalized stories are becoming more and more common. What could this do to the credibility of news reporting? What does this say about the current state of American society?

Sociology Projects

1. **Political Influence** As an extension of question #5 above, instead of putting limits on how much wealth any one individual or organization could accumulate, consider the options that the government might use to limit the political influence of wealthy individuals and organizations. Using proper spelling, punctuation and grammar, write a brief essay listing and describing those options.

2. **Employee Rights** Review the list of employee rights in the Sociology Today feature on page 448. If you have a job, try to find out which of these rights your current employer recognizes. You might want to ask your manager if your company has a brochure that lists employee rights. If you don't have a job, discuss this activity with a friend who is working.

3. **Political Cartoons** Look in the newspaper or weekly newsmagazines for a political cartoon. Analyze the cartoon, and write a brief summary of the message you think the cartoonist is trying to get across. Does the cartoon have a political agenda? Does it reflect the viewpoint of a special interest group or a specific branch of government? Be sure to discuss the symbolism used by the artist in the cartoon. Be prepared to present your cartoon to the class for further discussion.

4. **Government at the Local Level** Visit or call your local city hall to find out the schedule for city council or school board meetings. Arrange to attend the next meeting. Review the agenda for the meeting, and record what happens at the meeting. Identify all the other social institutions that were affected by the decisions made at the meeting the night you attended. (In many towns, local city council or board meetings are televised on cable channels. Check with the city or your local cable carrier to see if this is the case for your location.)

5. **Political Beliefs** On a sheet of paper, write down your own political party affiliation and your parents' political party affiliations. Next, write down your views on some key issues that you feel strongly about, such as immigration or minority rights. Write down your parents' views on these topics. Do you and your parents share the same political beliefs? You might also want to try comparing your views with a friend's. Are your views and your friend's views similar? If so, do you think that this might explain why you are friends? Do you think that people tend to associate more with those who share similar political beliefs?

Technology Activities

1. One of the topics of debate about corporations in America is whether they have any responsibilities beyond making a profit for their shareholders. Some people say that corporations have a "social responsibility" to make their communities better places. Two companies that act on their social responsibilities are Ben & Jerry's and The Body Shop. Go to their web sites at http://www.benjerry.com/ and http://www.thebodyshop.ca/.

   a. Find their mission statements and read them. What do these companies believe about social responsibility?

   b. What specific actions do they take to make their communities better places?

2. Using your school or local library and the Internet, research and rank the 20 largest corporations in the United States according to their net worth. Also, research and rank the ten wealthiest individuals in the United States according to their net worth. Do you see any correlation or affiliation between the wealthy individuals and the powerful corporations (e.g., membership in one of the corporations, member on the directorate of one or more of the corporations, etc.)? Create a database to record your research. Summarize your research in a paragraph using proper spelling and grammar construction.

Chapter 13

Enrichment Reading
No Shame in My Game

by Katherine S. Newman

Katherine Newman has created a rich portrait of minimum-wage workers employed in four fast-food restaurants in central Harlem. These are the "working poor"—they hold jobs and pay taxes, but they do not earn enough money to buy the basic necessities of life. In the passage below, Newman argues that the working poor share the same basic values as the rest of American society. The shame referred to in the reading lies in society's view that employment in fast-food jobs is somehow degrading.

Swallowing ridicule would be a hardship for almost anyone in this culture, but it is particularly hard on minority youth in the inner city. They have already logged four or five years' worth of interracial and cross-class friction by the time they get behind a [Burger Barn] cash register. More likely than not, they have also learned from peers that self-respecting people don't allow themselves to be "dissed" without striking back. Yet this is precisely what they must do if they are going to survive in the workplace.

This is one of the main reasons why these [fast-food] jobs carry such a powerful stigma in American popular culture: they fly in the face of a national attraction to autonomy, independence, and the individual's "right" to respond in kind when dignity is threatened. In ghetto communities, this stigma is even more powerful because—ironically—it is in these **enclaves** that this mainstream value of independence is most vigorously elaborated and **embellished.** Film characters, rap stars, and local idols base their claim to notoriety on standing above the crowd, going their own way, being free of the ties that bind ordinary mortals. There are white parallels, to be sure, but this is a powerful **genre of icons** in the black community, not because it is a discon-nected subculture but because it is an intensified version of a perfectly recognizable American middle-class and working-class fixation.

It is therefore noteworthy that thousands upon thousands of minority teens, young adults, and even middle-aged adults line up for jobs that will subject them, at least potentially, to a kind of character assassination. They do so not because they start the job-seeking process with a different set of values, one that can withstand society's contempt for fast-food workers. They take these jobs because in so many inner-city communities, there is nothing better in the offing. In general, they have already tried to get better jobs and have failed, landing at the door of Burger Barn as a last resort. . . .

The stigma also stems from the low social status of the people who hold these jobs: minorities, teenagers, immigrants who often speak halting English, those with little education, and (increasingly in affluent communities afflicted with labor shortages) the elderly. To the extent that the prestige of a job refracts the social characteristic of its average **incumbents,** fast-food jobs are hobbled by the perception that people with better choices would never purposely opt for a "McJob." . . . There is no quicker way to indicate that a person is barely deserving of notice than to point out he or she holds a "chump change" job at Kentucky Fried Chicken or Burger King. . . .

Ghetto youth are particularly sensitive to the status degradation entailed in stigmatized employment. As Elijah Anderson . . . and others have pointed out, a high premium is placed on independence, autonomy, and respect among minority youth in inner-city communities—particularly by young men. No small amount of mayhem is committed every year in the name of injured pride. Hence jobs that routinely demand **displays of deference** force those who hold them to violate "macho" behavior codes that are central to the definition of teen culture. There are, therefore, considerable social risks involved in seeking a fast-food job in the first place, one that the employees and job-seekers are keenly aware of from the very beginning of their search for employment.

It is hard to know the extent to which this stigma discourages young people in places like central Harlem from knocking on the door of a fast-food restaurant. It is clear that the other choices aren't much better and that necessity drives thousands, if not millions, of teens and older job-seekers to ignore the stigma or learn to live with it. But no one enters the central Harlem job market without having to face this **gauntlet.**

Source: Excerpted from Katherine S. Newman, *No Shame in My Game,* New York: Alfred A. Knopf, 1999, pp. 93, 95.

What Does it Mean?

display of deference
acting in a humble or compliant way

embellish
to add to; to make more attractive

enclave
a territory or cultural unit within a foreign territory

gauntlet
ordeal or challenge

genre of icons
category or type of symbols

incumbent
occupant, job holder

Read and React

1. Who are the "working poor"? Give some examples of the types of jobs the working poor would hold.

2. According to Newman, the working poor share the same values as the rest of American society. Discuss the evidence she gives for this. Is she convincing?

3. Why did Newman select *No Shame in My Game* for her book title?

4. Do you think a stigma is attached to being a fast-food worker? Explain.

5. What do you think Newman means by "status degradation" in the context of her research?

CHAPTER 14
Religion

USING Your Sociological Imagination

More than thirty years after the Beatles' last recording session, the group's tapes and CDs are still being sold by the millions. But there was a moment—at the height of the Beatles' popularity—when radio stations around the United States banned their music and teenagers stomped on their records.

The angry reaction was the result of a comment made by John Lennon in a 1966 London interview:

Christianity will go. It will vanish and shrink. I needn't argue with that; I'm right and I will be proved right. We're more popular than Jesus now; I don't know which will go first—rock 'n 'roll or Christianity.

When the remark was printed in the United States, the resulting uproar caught many by surprise. Lennon's statement was quoted out of context. If the entire interview had been printed, the response might have been less extreme. Nevertheless, efforts to explain the remark failed, and Lennon was forced to apologize for saying something he hadn't really intended to say. Contrary to popular belief, it appeared that many young Americans took their religion seriously.

Today, many people fear that religious influence in the United States is declining. Evidence, however, reveals that America—compared with other industrialized nations—remains fairly religious. This chapter views religion within the context of sociology, defines religion as an institution, and explores the ways people express their religious beliefs.

Sections

1. **Religion and Sociology**
2. **Theoretical Perspectives**
3. **Religious Organization and Religiosity**
4. **Religion in the United States**

Learning Objectives

After reading this chapter, you will be able to

❖ explain the sociological meaning of religion.

❖ describe the different views of religion as seen by the major theoretical perspectives.

❖ distinguish the basic types of religious organization.

❖ discuss the meaning and nature of religiosity.

❖ define secularization and describe its relationship to religiosity in the United States.

❖ discuss religious fundamentalism in the United States from the sociological perspective.

SOCIOLOGY Online

Chapter Overview
Visit the *Sociology and You* Web site at soc.glencoe.com and click on **Chapter 14—Chapter Overviews** to preview chapter information.

Section 1

Religion and Sociology

Key Terms

- religion
- sacred
- profane

Section Preview

Religion is concerned with sacred things. Durkheim concluded that every religion separates the sacred from the profane. Sociologists studying religion face some unique problems. They do not judge the validity of various religions but rather look at those aspects of religion that can be measured and observed in society.

religion
a unified system of beliefs and practices concerned with sacred things

sacred
holy; set apart and given a special meaning that goes beyond, or transcends, immediate existence

profane
nonsacred

The Sociological Meaning of Religion

A **religion** is a unified system of beliefs and practices concerned with sacred things. This definition comes from Emile Durkheim, whose work was based on studies of the Australian aborigines in the late nineteenth century. According to Durkheim, every society distinguishes between the **sacred**—things and ideas that are set apart and given a special meaning that goes beyond, or transcends, immediate existence—and the **profane,** or nonsacred aspects of life. Profane in this context does not mean unholy. It simply means commonplace and not involving the supernatural. Another word for profane is *secular.*

Sacred things take on a public character that makes them appear important in themselves; profane things do not. The particular things considered sacred vary from culture to culture. For example, Bolivian tin miners attach sacred meaning to figures of the devil and of bulls. Because Americans do not share these religious beliefs, these cultural items are part of their nonsacred, or profane, world. Moreover, some nonreligious aspects of culture can assume a sacred character. Here, two sociologists illustrate the difference between the sacred and the profane:

When Babe Ruth was a living idol to baseball fans, the bat he used to slug his home runs was definitely a profane object. It was Ruth's personal instrument and had little social value in itself. Today, however, one of Ruth's bats is enshrined in

Buddhas, like this one in a Korean temple, are sacred objects in the Far East and Southeast Asia, and wherever Buddhists live. What makes an object sacred?

the Baseball Hall of Fame. It is no longer used by anyone. It stands, rather, as an object which in itself represents the values, sentiments, power, and beliefs of all members of the baseball community. What was formerly a profane object is now in the process of gaining some of the qualities of a sacred object (Cuzzort and King, 1976:27).

Babe Ruth's bat illustrates two particulars about the sociological study of religion. First, a profane object can become sacred, and vice versa. Second, sociologists can deal with religion without becoming involved in theological issues. By focusing on the cultural and social aspects of religion, sociologists avoid questions about the ultimate validity of any particular religion. This point is so important that it needs more explanation.

Is this Ford Mustang convertible a sacred or secular object? Why?

The Sociological Study of Religion

The sociological study of religion involves looking at a set of meanings attached to a world beyond human observation. Because this non-physical world cannot be directly observed, this task is particularly difficult. Sociologists have to ask themselves hard questions: How can we find evidence for something that can't be seen? How can we remain objective about such a value-laden subject, especially when we have our own beliefs? Is science really the proper tool to evaluate religion?

Obviously, sociologists cannot study the unobservable. Consequently, they avoid the strictly spiritual side of religion and focus on social aspects of religion that can be measured and observed. Sociologists, then, are not in the business of determining which religions people ought to follow. Sociologists keep their own faith personal while investigating the *social* dimensions of religion. Like people in any other occupation, sociologists themselves follow a variety of religions.

Sociologists study the social aspects of religion. One such aspect is the charitable work done by members of different religious organizations.

Section 1 Assessment

1. How does the sociological definition of religion differ from how you previously thought of religion?
2. How do sociologists manage to study religion if they can't see the spiritual world?

Critical Thinking

3. **Evaluating Information** Do you think religion can be studied scientifically? Using the material just presented, make an argument for or against this practice.

Another Place

Religion at War

As part of studying the effects of religion on society, sociologists note that throughout history, religion has both promoted social stability and led to social conflict. In this excerpt from the article *Religion at War,* the conflict aspect is highlighted.

In virtually every one of the world's 480 major wars since 1700, each side has imagined itself to be exclusively on the side of God, Gött, Allah, Dieu or other names for the deity.

Religion is often so closely linked with ethnic or national identity as to be seen as inseparable from them. Thus a struggle for expressions of ethnic or national identity is experienced as a religious war. This is so of the current unrest in the Punjab, created by Sikh demands for a separate Sikh state.

Religion evokes powerful emotions and commitments. It is capable of producing believers whose faith moves them to acts of great self-sacrifice and charity. At the same time it can produce believers who feel that their faith calls them to struggle violently in what they believe to be a just cause. One example is the Hindi/Muslim tension in India focused on Ayodhya. Here, a mosque built in the 15th century was destroyed in 1992 by militant Hindus because it is believed to have been built over the birthplace of the Hindu god Rama. While the majority of Hindis and Muslims have lived together peacefully for generations, extremists on both sides are capable of arousing violence through use of powerful religious symbols.

In many faiths, the issue of whether warfare is permissible has given rise to various theories of the just war. Such theories seek to define whether believers can ever engage in the use of violence. The usual conclusion is that violence—including warfare—is only acceptable in pursuit of a greater good. The problem, however, is who defines the greater good?

Source: Joanne O'Brien and Martin Palmer, *The State of Religion Atlas.* New York: Simon & Schuster, 1993, p. 117. Reprinted by permission.

Thinking It Over

Does functionalism or conflict theory best explain the link between strong religious conviction and war? Why?

Activists of a Hindu religious sect demand the right to build a temple on the site of a demolished mosque. Why are wars and conflicts often rooted in religious beliefs and values?

Section 2

Theoretical Perspectives

Key Terms

- legitimate
- spirit of capitalism

- Protestant ethic

Functionalism and Religion

Religion exists in some form in virtually all societies. (See Figure 14.1 on page 468 and World View on page 469 for a global distribution of major religions.) The earliest evidence of religion and religious customs and taboos has been traced as far back as 50,000 B.C. Humans had by then already begun to bury their dead, a practice based on the belief in existence after death. Evidence of religious practices appears in many ancient cultures. In Rome, there were specific gods for objects and events—a god of trees, a god of money, a goddess of fever. While the early Hebrews believed that pigs were unclean animals whose pollution would spread to all who touched or tasted them, the tribes of New Guinea considered pigs holy creatures worthy of ancestral sacrifice (Harris, 1974).

Emile Durkheim, the first sociologist to examine religion scientifically, wondered why it is that all societies

Section Preview

Religion has several functions. It legitimates the structure of society, promotes social unity, and provides a sense of meaning and belonging. Marx argued that religion is used to justify and maintain the group in power. Weber believed that religion could promote social change. He connected the Protestant ethic and the rise of capitalism.

We know that religion is an important part of almost all societies because of the religious symbols most have left behind.

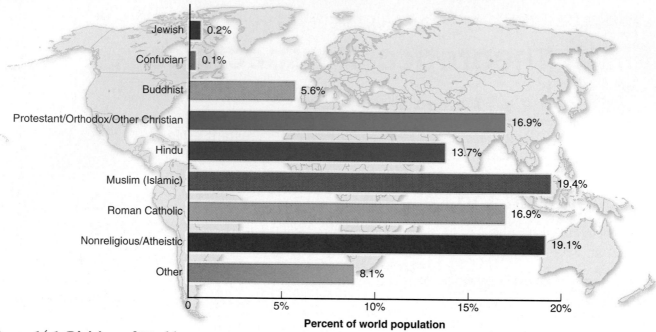

Figure 14.1 Division of World Population by Religions. *This graph compares the number of all religious believers belonging to a particular religion to the total estimated world population.*

legitimate
to justify or give official approval to

have some form of religion. In one of his books, *The Elementary Forms of Religious Life* (1915), Durkheim offered an explanation rooted in the function religion performs for society. The essential function of religion, he believed, was to provide through sacred symbols a mirror for members of society to see themselves. Through religious rituals, people worship their societies and thereby remind themselves of their shared past and future existence.

Following Durkheim's lead, sociologists have identified the following social functions of religion.

❖ *Religion gives formal approval to existing social arrangements.* Religious doctrine and scripture **legitimate** the status quo. Religion, then, justifies or gives authority to social norms and customs. A society's religion explains why the society is—and should be—the way it is. It tells us why some people have power and others do not, why some are rich and others poor, why some are common and others elite. Many social customs and rituals are based on religion. According to Durkheim, legitimation is the central function of religion.

❖ *Religion encourages a sense of unity.* Religion, according to Durkheim, is the glue that holds society together. Without religion, society would be chaotic. As Cuzzort and King have stated (1976), Durkheim "provided the greatest justification for religious doctrine ever formulated by a social scientist when he claimed that all societies must have religious commitments. Without religious dedication there is no social order."

In some cases, though, religion causes societies to fragment, even to the point of civil war. Religion divides Catholics and Protestants in Northern Ireland. Thus, while it is accurate to say that religion is usually a source of social unity, it can also divide a society. (See Another Place, page 466.)

❖ *Religion provides a sense of understanding.* Religion not only explains the nature of social life and encourages social unity, it also provides

World View

Religions of the World

This map displays the worldwide distribution of all religions. Emile Durkheim showed that suicide rates vary according to group characteristics. One of these characteristics was religious background. For example, Durkheim showed that the suicide rate is lower among Catholics than among Protestants.

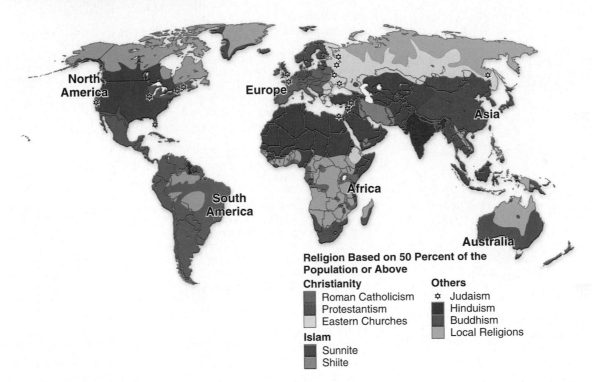

Religion Based on 50 Percent of the Population or Above

Christianity
- Roman Catholicism
- Protestantism
- Eastern Churches

Islam
- Sunnite
- Shiite

Others
- ✡ Judaism
- Hinduism
- Buddhism
- Local Religions

Interpreting the Map

1. Based on the information shown in this map, identify two countries where you would expect to find lower rates of suicide than in England.
2. What information on the map did you use in your analysis?

---

individuals meaning beyond day-to-day life. People mark important events in life—birth, sexual maturity, marriage, death—with religious ceremonies and explain such events in religious terms. Religion gives believers a sense of their place in the cosmos and gives eternal significance to a short and uncertain earthly existence.

❖ *Religion promotes a sense of belonging.* Religious organizations provide opportunities for people to share important ideas, ways of life, and ethnic or racial backgrounds. Religion supplies a kind of group identity. People usually join religious organizations freely and feel a

Religion	Origination	Key Figure	Beliefs	Main Geographic Areas	Number of Followers
Hinduism	Before 2000 B.C.	Unknown	Of many gods, Brahma is the creator of the universe. Life is determined by the law of karma (the spiritual force generated by one's own actions, which determines one's next reincarnation).	India	793,076,000
Judaism	Before 1200 B.C.	Abraham	The one true God has established a covenant with the people of Israel, who are called to lives of justice, mercy, and obedience to God.	Israel, Eastern Europe, USA	13,866,000
Buddhism	About 500 B.C.	Siddhartha Gautama	The existence of God is not assumed. Through adherence to the Eightfold Path (correct thought and behavior), one can escape from desire and suffering and achieve nirvana (a state of bliss reached through extreme denial of the self).	Far East, Southeast Asia	325,275,000
Confucianism	About 500 B.C.	Confucius	The *Analects* (sayings of Confucius) stress moral conduct and virtuous human relationships.	China	5,086,000
Christianity	About A.D. 1	Jesus Christ	Jesus is the Son of the one true God. Through God's grace and profession of faith, people have eternal life with God.	Europe, North America, South America	1,955,229,000
Islam	About A.D. 600	Muhammad	Muhammad received the Koran (holy scriptures) from the one true God. Believers go to an eternal Garden of Eden.	Africa, Middle East, Southeast Asia	1,126,325,000

Figure 14.2 Major World Religions. *This figure summarizes characteristics and beliefs of the major world religions being widely practiced today.*

degree of influence within these organizations. For many people in modern society, membership in a religious organization provides a sense of community. This feeling of belonging helps to counteract depersonalization, powerlessness, and rootlessness.

Conflict Theory and Religion

Conflict theory focuses on how religion works to either inhibit or encourge social change. Two early and important sociologists who looked at religion from these perspectives were Karl Marx and Max Weber.

What did Marx say about religion?   Marx believed that once people have created a unified system of sacred beliefs and practices, they act as if it were something beyond their control. They become "alienated" from the religious system they have set up. People have the power to change (or, better yet, in Marx's mind, to abandon) the religion they have created. They don't do so, however, because they see it as a binding force to which they must conform. Religion, Marx wrote, is used by the ruling class to justify its economic, political, and social advantages over the oppressed. Those in power justify poverty, degradation, and misery as God's will. To eliminate inequalities and injustices is to tamper with God's plan. Religion, then, gives people a sense that all is the way it should be.

Religions are many and diverse, but reason and goodness are one.

**Elbert Hubbard
American writer**

World View

Gender Inequality in Religion

Women have been fighting for equal rights in all aspects of society—religion as well as government and business. In some religions women have equal status within their orders. Other religions see feminism as a "Western" issue and irrelevant to their faiths. This map shows how major denominations in each country view the status of women.

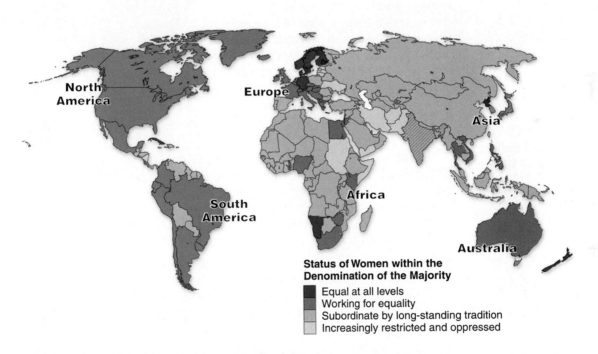

North America

Europe

Asia

South America

Africa

Australia

Status of Women within the Denomination of the Majority

- Equal at all levels
- Working for equality
- Subordinate by long-standing tradition
- Increasingly restricted and oppressed

Interpreting the Map

1. Do you see any patterns of inequality in women's rights in religion? Explain.
2. Where in the world would a woman be most likely to head an entire religious organization? Support your answer. Do some research to see if this has occurred. If it has not, explain why.
3. How does the United States compare with the Scandinavian countries in terms of gender equality? Why do you think this difference exists?
4. How would you explain the mixed status of women in India?

Adapted from *The State of Religion Atlas*. New York: Simon & Schuster, 1993.

How did Weber link Protestantism and capitalism? Whereas Marx believed that religion works against social change, Max Weber suggested that religion sometimes encourages social change. He pointed to the relationship between Protestantism and the rise of capitalism. Weber wondered why capitalism emerged in northwestern Europe and America and not in other parts of the world. A possible answer lay in what he termed the *spirit of capitalism* and the *Protestant ethic*. With capitalism, work became a moral obligation rather than a mere necessity. If businesses were to grow, money (capital) had to be put back into the business rather than spent. Investment for the future was more important than immediate consumption. All of this Weber called the **spirit of capitalism.**

Most major religions did not define hard work as an obligation or demand the reinvestment of capital for further profits (rather than for immediate enjoyment). But some Protestant sects did. Here, then, was a religion with a cluster of values, norms, beliefs, and attitudes that favored the emergence of modern capitalism. Weber referred to this cluster of values, norms, beliefs, and attitudes that stressed the virtue of hard work, thrift, and self-discipline as the **Protestant ethic.**

The theology of sixteenth-century theologian John Calvin formed the basis for the Protestant ethic.

spirit of capitalism
the obligation to reinvest money in business rather than to spend it

Protestant ethic
a set of values, norms, beliefs, and attitudes stressing hard work, thrift, and self-discipline

What is the nature of the Protestant ethic? The Protestant ethic is often associated with John Calvin (1509–1564), an early Protestant theologian. Calvin's followers were known as Calvinists. Calvinist beliefs illustrate several features of the Protestant ethic.

❖ According to Calvin, God identifies his chosen by rewarding them in this world. Therefore, the more successful people were in this life, the more sure they were of being a member of God's select few.

❖ Consumption beyond necessity was considered sinful; those who engaged in self-pleasure were agents of the devil.

❖ Calvinists believed there was an underlying purpose of life: glorification of God on earth through one's occupational calling. Because everyone's material rewards were actually God's, and the purpose of life was to glorify God, profits should be multiplied (through reinvestment) rather than used in the pursuit of personal pleasures.

Symbolic Interactionism and Religion

Sociologist Peter Berger (1990) captured the relationship between religion and symbolic interactionism in his book, *The Sacred Canopy*. In this book, Berger explored the idea that humans create from their religious traditions a canopy, or cover, of symbolic meanings, to "lay" over the secular world. These otherworldly symbolic meanings are used to guide everyday social interaction. Religious beliefs, rituals, and ideas tell people the difference between the sacred and the profane and provide stability and security in a changing and uncertain existence.

Symbolic interactionism, for example, helps us understand the expression "there are no atheists in foxholes." Insecurity and uncertainty, of course, are at a peak in the life-and-death situation of war, and the desire to regain

Figure 14.3 Focus on Theoretical Perspectives

Religion. This table shows that in examining religion the three major perspectives focus on different aspects. Discuss the conclusion of any one of the theories in light of your experience with the institution of religion.

Theoretical Perspective	Focus	Conclusion
Functionalist	Look at contributions of religion to society.	Religion legitimates social arrangements. It promotes social unity. It provides a sense of understanding. It encourages a sense of belonging.
Conflict Theory	Elites use religion to manipulate the masses.	Religion is used by the most powerful to justify their economic, political, and social advantages.
Symbolic Interactionism	People create symbolic meanings from their religious beliefs, rituals, and ideas.	People use their socially created symbolic meanings to guide everyday social interactions.

security and certainty is a natural human response. Religious meanings, especially those related to an afterlife, can offer some relief. Japanese kamikaze pilots in World War II and Middle Eastern terrorists infuse their sometimes suicidal behavior with ultimate meaning by focusing on their reward beyond life. Less dramatically, people enduring troubled marriages can be strengthened by their commitment to uphold their holy vows of matrimony spoken in a place of worship.

Each of the three major theoretical perspectives aids in the sociological study of religion. Figure 14.3 shows the unique light each perspective sheds.

Section 2 Assessment

1. How did Karl Marx view religion?
2. What was Weber's contribution to the sociological study of religion?
3. What did Berger mean by the phrase "the sacred canopy"?

Critical Thinking

4. **Analyzing Information** Does the Protestant ethic still exist in America today? Use Weber's analysis to justify your position.

You have not converted a man because you have silenced him.

John, Viscount Morley
English statesman

Tech Trends

Is Cloning Humans Ethical?

Aldous Huxley's 1932 novel *Brave New World* described a society in which babies were created scientifically. Another novel—*The Boys from Brazil,* written by Ira Levin and published in 1976—features a story about German Nazis cloning Adolf Hitler. Both of these books play on our fears about the effects and ethics of human cloning (a nonsexual creation of a genetically identical copy). Although no human has yet been cloned, the reproduction of a sheep called Dolly in February 1997, along with several subsequent clonings of mice, sheep, and pigs, have made the question much more pertinent today than it was a few years ago.

Even though the technology is not yet available to clone humans, companies and scientists are already beginning to offer their services to interested individuals. Dr. Richard Seed, an American physicist, announced in 1998 that he plans to clone humans, using his wife as the first subject. He also plans to open a for-profit clinic to assist childless couples in cloning themselves. A company called Valiant Venture has been formed to offer cloning services to humans—for as "little" as $200,000. Valiant Venture is owned by the Raelian Movement, an international cult whose members claim that life on earth was created in laboratories by extraterrestrials.

More traditional religious groups have expressed serious concerns about cloning. According to the general argument of Judaism and Christianity, human cloning allows the sacred process of generating life to enter the profane realm. A group of scientists sponsored by the Church of Scotland reached the following conclusions.

❖ If humans are cloned, people will be placing themselves in a position only God has occupied.
❖ The basic dignity and uniqueness of each individual will be violated.
❖ Political power could influence the creation of clones.
❖ Cloning will be limited to those who can afford it.

On the other hand, might it not be beneficial to clone Bill Gates, Mother Theresa, or Michael Jordan? What about the potential contributions from a new Christiaan Barnard, the South African physician who did the first heart transplant in 1967? Human cloning is just the latest in a long line of medical technologies that affect the length and quality of life. Society will have to decide if cloning is so different from other scientific advances that it should be legally prohibited.

Analyzing the Trends

What role, if any, should religion play in the debate over human cloning? Include some information from this chapter to support your answer.

Section 3 Religious Organization and Religiosity

Key Terms

- church
- denomination
- sect
- cult
- religiosity

Religious Organization

In Western societies, most people practice religion through some organizational structure. For this reason, the nature of religious organization is an important component of the sociological study of religion. Early scholars identified four basic types of religious organization: *church, denomination, sect,* and *cult.*

How do sociologists distinguish among the basic types of religious organization? To sociologists, a **church** is a life-encompassing religious organization to which all members of a society belong. This type of religious organization exists when religion and the state are closely intertwined. In Elizabethan England, for example, Archbishop Richard Hooker of the Church of England wrote that "there is not any man of the Church of England but the same man is also a member of the commonwealth; nor any man a member of the commonwealth which is not also of the Church of England." As you can see, the sociological definition of *church* is different from the one commonly used in American society. When Americans talk about "churches," they are actually referring to denominations.

A **denomination** is one of several religious organizations that most members of a society accept as legitimate. Because denominations are not tied to the state, membership in them is voluntary, and competition among them for

Section Preview

The major forms of religious organization are churches, denominations, sects, and cults. Religiosity—the ways people express their religious interests and convictions—can be analyzed in terms of five dimensions: belief, ritual, intellect, experience, and consequences.

church
a life-encompassing religious organization to which all members of a society belong

denomination
one of several religious organizations that most members of a society accept as legitimate

The Amish are a religious sect. How does a sect differ from a church, denomination, or cult?

Sociology Today

Understanding the Danger of Cults

In late November 1978, news began to arrive in the United States that a semireligious, socialistic colony in Guyana, South America, headed by the Reverend Jim Jones—founder of the California-based People's Temple—had been the scene of a shocking suicide-murder rite in which some nine hundred people died from cyanide poisoning. Many Americans wondered how people could have become involved in something like that.

Some dismissed the participants as ignorant or mentally unbalanced. But as more news came out, it became known that many of the members were fairly well-educated young people and that Jones was trusted and respected by some members of the California political establishment. We also learned that such events, although rare, have occurred before.

Why are people willing to join extremist religious groups? Sociology can help us understand the motivations.

❖ *Most converts to extremist religious groups seek friendship, companionship, acceptance, warmth, and recognition.* These groups can provide a supportive community that helps overcome past loneliness and isolation. They can provide emotional ties that converts have not found at home, school, church, or work. Many groups even adopt kinship terms to give recruits new identities to separate them from their former lives.

❖ *Most extremist religious groups emphasize immediate experience and emotional gratification.* Converts "feel" religion rather than merely think about it. Whether by meditation, speaking in tongues, or singing hymns, followers have frequent and intense emotional experiences they have not found elsewhere.

❖ *Extremist religious groups emphasize security through strict authority.* Under a firm authority structure and a clear, simple set of beliefs and rules, converts have something in which they can believe. Converts think they can exchange

The Reverend Jim Jones was the leader of a religious colony in Guyana, South America, where some nine hundred people were involved in a suicide-murder rite.

uncertainty, doubt, and confusion for trust and assurance through absolute obedience.

❖ *Extremist religious groups claim to offer authenticity and naturalness in an "artificial" world.* By emphasizing such things as natural foods, communal living apart from civilization, and a uniform dress code, these groups attempt to show they are not part of the flawed outside world.

Religious movements may not actually be able to meet their followers' needs any better than the outside world. Many of these religious groups lead to disillusionment, frustration, and bitterness when members realize that they cannot completely escape the outside world, which is full of uncertainty, confusion, fuzzy choices, and shades of gray. Moreover, many of these religious groups have joined the consumer society they profess to deplore, attractively packaging and selling themselves to the public. Not only may the new religious groups not solve the problems people in modern society must face, many are as inauthentic as they accuse society of being.

Some key questions exist to evaluate the authenticity of any religious group's claims. For purposes of self-protection, these questions should be answered carefully before committing to an extremist religious group.

❖ Does it require that you cut yourself off from family and friends?
❖ Does it consider drugs to be a major vehicle for true religious experiences?
❖ Is corporal punishment or intensive, hours-long psychological conditioning a part of its program?
❖ Does it claim to have special knowledge that can be revealed only to insiders?

Friends and family mourn the loss of loved ones who died in Jim Jones's People's Temple mass suicide.

If the answer to any *one* of these questions is yes, you stand a chance of getting "hooked." If the answers to *several* of these questions are positive, the chances of getting hooked increase dramatically.

Doing Sociology

1. Do you agree or disagree with the reasons given for why people join extremist religious groups? Discuss each reason and explain why you agree or disagree.
2. Can you think of other reasons why people may be attracted to such groups? Show that any reason you identify does not fit into one of the four reasons stated.
3. If you had a friend considering membership in an extremist religious group, how would you use the information in this Sociology Today to discourage him or her?

members is socially acceptable. Being one religious organization among many, a denomination generally accepts the values and norms of the secular society and the state, although it may at times oppose them. As mentioned, most American "churches"—Methodist, Episcopalian, Presbyterian, Baptist, Roman Catholic, and Reform Jew, for example—are actually denominations.

A **sect** is a religious organization formed when members of an existing religious organization break away in an attempt to reform the "parent" group. Generally, sect members believe that some valuable beliefs or traditions have been lost by the parent organization, and they form their own group to save these features. Thus, they see themselves not as establishing a new religious faith but as redeeming an existing one. The withdrawal of a sect from the parent group is usually psychological, but some sects go farther and form communal groups apart from the larger society. The Separatists, or Pilgrims, who landed at Plymouth in 1620, wished to reform the Church of England from which they had separated. Another example is the Amish, a sect formed in 1693 when a Swiss bishop named Jacob Amman broke from the Mennonite church in Europe (Kraybill and Olshan, 1994). Less extreme sects in the United States today include the Seventh-Day Adventists, the Quakers, and the Assemblies of God.

Unlike a sect, a **cult** is a religious organization whose characteristics are not drawn from existing religious traditions within a society. Whether imported from outside the society or created within the society, cults bring something new to the larger religious environment. We often think of cults as engaging in extreme behavior. The world has been shocked twice in recent years. In 1997, reports came of the ritualistic suicides of thirty-nine members of the Heaven's Gate cult in California (Thomas, 1997). Dwarfing this incident was the mass killing of ap-

sect
a religious organization that arises out of a desire to reform an existing religious organization

cult
a religious organization whose characteristics are not drawn from existing religious traditions within a society

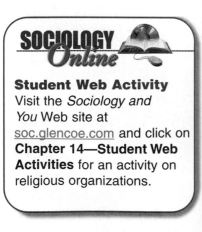

SOCIOLOGY Online

Student Web Activity
Visit the *Sociology and You* Web site at soc.glencoe.com and click on **Chapter 14—Student Web Activities** for an activity on religious organizations.

In 1997, thirty-nine members of the Heaven's Gate cult in California committed ritualistic suicide. Most cults are not this dangerous, however.

Calvin and Hobbes are engaged in a conversation about religiosity. Their beliefs are clashing.

proximately 1,000 members of the Ugandan cult called the Movement for the Restoration of the Ten Commandments of God in March 2000. Cults do not usually appear in such an extreme and bizarre form, however. More conventional examples of cults are the Unification Church, the Divine Light Mission, and the Church of Scientology (Clark, 1993).

Religiosity

Sociologists Charles Glock and Rodney Stark are two sociologists who have studied religion and society. Their work has focused on **religiosity**—the types of religious attitudes and behavior people display in their everyday lives.

religiosity
ways in which people express their religious interests and convictions

How do people display religiosity? Glock and Stark identify five dimensions of religiosity: belief, ritual, an intellectual dimension, experience, and consequences (Glock, 1965; Stark, 1968).

❖ *Belief* refers to what a person considers to be true. People may, for example, believe that Jesus is the son of God or that there is no God but Allah.

❖ A *ritual* is a religious practice that the members of a religion are expected to perform. A ritual may be private, such as personal prayer, or public, such as attending mass.

❖ The *intellectual dimension* of religiosity may involve knowledge of holy or sacred scripture or an interest in such religious aspects of human existence as evil, suffering, and death. Religious persons are expected to be knowledgeable about their faith.

The display of religious affiliation varies widely. Golfer Tiger Woods wears a Buddha image, and a Jewish boy reads from the Torah at his Bar Mitzvah.

Snapshot of America

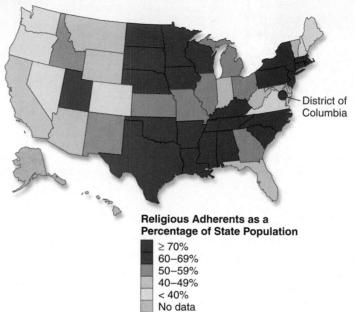

District of
Columbia

**Religious Adherents as a
Percentage of State Population**

≥ 70%
60–69%
50–59%
40–49%
< 40%
No data

Religious Believers

Religion is common to all societies.
Although the majority of Americans
are Christian, many other faiths are
represented in the United States. This
map shows the percentage of the population of each state who identify
themselves as members of a faith or
religion.

Interpreting the Map

1. Create a database comparing the number of religious believers in your state with other states in
    your region.
2. What do you think this map says about the state of religion in the U.S.? Explain.

Adapted from *The State of the U.S.A. Atlas.* New York: Simon & Schuster, 1994.

❖ *Experience* encompasses certain feelings attached to religious
   expression. This dimension is the hardest to measure. For example, a
   religious believer may feel "close" to the deity when praying.

❖ *Consequences* are the decisions and commitments people make as a
   result of religious beliefs, rituals, knowledge, or experiences.
   Consequences may be social, such as opposing or supporting capital
   punishment, or personal, as when practicing sexual abstinence before
   marriage or telling the truth regardless of the cost.

Section 3 Assessment

1. In your own words, describe the difference between a cult and a sect.
2. Give one example of each of the five dimensions of religiosity, using
    examples not given in the text.

Critical Thinking

3. **Summarizing Information** Of the dimensions of religiosity discussed
    in the text, which do you think is most important to denominations
    today? Give reasons for your answer.

Section 4

Religion in the United States

Key Terms

- secularization
- fundamentalism

The Development of Religion in America

The search for religious freedom was only one of many reasons Puritan colonists came to America—but it was an important one. From the outset, the Puritans viewed themselves as a religious example for the world to follow and admire. Sociologist Robert Bellah has described the American religious connection this way:

In the beginning, and to some extent ever since, Americans have interpreted their history as having religious meaning. They saw themselves as being a "people" in the classical and biblical sense of the word. They hoped they were a people of God (Bellah et al. 1991:2).

Section Preview

Through the process of secularization, the sacred and the profane tend to become intermixed. There has been a revival of religious fundamentalism in the United States. Religious faiths can be analyzed by major social characteristics such as class, and political tendencies.

The U.S. guarantees religious freedom. Pictured clockwise from the bottom left are a Hindu priest in Ohio, an Islamic prayer group in Maine, a Baptist congregation in Alabama, and a Jewish Chanukah celebration in Maryland.

The framers of the U.S. Constitution seldom raised arguments against religious faith. They were, however, sharply critical of any entanglement between religion and the state. Indeed, the ideas of separation of church and state and freedom of religious expression are cornerstones of American life. Despite this tradition, people in the United States have experienced incidents of religious persecution, including some directed at immigrant groups.

Religion has always been of great importance in American life; but historically, it has played a more active part in some periods than in others. There have been several "Awakenings" in U.S. history when religious principles have guided the development of culture and society. The 1830s, for example, saw new life come to many religious reform movements, including those against slavery and drinking alcohol. Later, the Protestant-led temperance movement resulted in the outlawing of alcohol for a short period during the 1920s.

Secularization in the United States

secularization
process through which the sacred loses influence over society

Countering the growth of religion in U.S. history is **secularization.** Through this process, the sacred loses influence over society, or aspects of the sacred enter into the secular (profane) world of everyday life. For example, formal education originally was a function of religion. Most early teachers and professors were clerics and church members. Over time in the United States, this function was taken over by the state, although many church-sponsored schools still exist.

Is secularization destroying religion in the United States?   Evidence is mixed concerning the relative importance of religion in the United States today. On the one hand, some findings indicate a decline in the importance of religion. The percentage of Americans claiming that religion is very important in their lives fell from 75 percent in 1952 to 57 percent in 2001. (See Figure 14.4.) Scores on the Princeton Religion Index, made up of eight leading indicators, have also declined since the 1940s. In 1957, 14 percent of the public indicated that they believed religion was losing influence on American life. In 2001, 55 percent of the public saw a loss of influence (Gallup, 2001).

On the other hand, some recent research has found Americans today to still be highly committed to religion. Whether measured by the number of churches per capita, the proportion of regular churchgoers, or financial support of the churches, sociologist Theodore Caplow observed a trend toward greater involvement in religious affairs (Caplow, 1998).

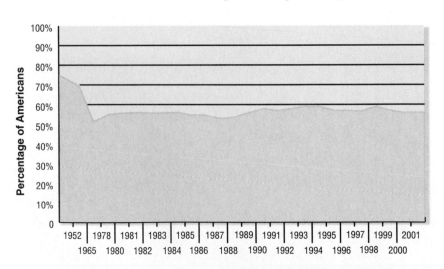

Figure 14.4 Percentage of Americans Saying Religion Is Very Important in Their Lives: 1952–2001.   *This figure tracks changes in the percentage of Americans who say that religion is very important in their lives. Why do you think the percentage was so high in the early 1950s? What prediction do you make for the next ten years?*

Source: The Gallup Organization, Gallup polls on religion.

Figure 14.5 Global Comparisons in Religiosity

This table compares the level of religiosity among selected industrialized countries. Which finding do you think is the most important? Which finding is the most surprising to you? Explain in both cases.

Consider Selves Religious Persons		Attend Church at Least Weekly		Average Ratings of Importance of God*	
Italy	83%	Ireland	82%	United States	8.2
United States	81	United States	43	Ireland	8.0
Ireland	64	Spain	41	Northern Ireland	7.5
Spain	63	Italy	36	Italy	6.9
Great Britain	58	West Germany	21	Spain	6.4
West Germany	58	Czechoslovakia	17	Finland	6.2
Hungary	56	Ethnic Lithuanians	15	Belgium	5.9
France	51	Non-ethnic Lithuanians	12	Great Britain	5.7
Non-ethnic Lithuanians	50	Great Britain	14	West Germany	5.7
Czechoslovaks	49	Hungary	13	Norway	5.4
Scandinavia	46	France	12	Netherlands	5.3
Ethnic Lithuanians	45	Scandinavia	5	Hungary	4.8
				France	4.7
				Denmark	4.4

*"10" is of highest importance.

Source: *Religion in America,* (Princeton, NJ: Princeton Religion Research Center).

In fact, as suggested in the Sociological Imagination opening this chapter, America still appears to be a religious nation when compared with other industrialized countries (see Figure 14.5). Only 8 percent of the American population is without a religious preference. About 88 percent identify themselves as Protestants, Catholics, Jews, or Mormons. There are now over three hundred recognized denominations and sects and thousands of independent congregations in the United States (Linder, 2000). About seven in ten Americans belong to some church, and over half of these claim to be active in their congregations. Four Americans in ten claim they have attended a church or synagogue in a typical week. (In England, for example, the average weekly church attendance is 14 percent.) Furthermore, although the proportion of Americans belonging to a church or synagogue has declined slightly from a high of 76 percent in 1947 to 69 percent in 1995, church attendance has changed very little over the years. Since 1939, weekly church or synagogue attendance in the United States has remained relatively stable—from 41 percent to 43 percent in 1995.

Americans also tend to support traditional religious beliefs. Ninety-six percent of the American population believe in God or a universal spirit, 65 percent believe in life after death, 90 percent believe in heaven, and 73 percent believe

Focus on Research

Survey Research: The Electronic Church

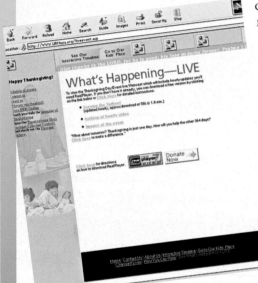

Along with the more "traditional" forms of radio and television, the Internet also offers remote religious services.

Old-time religious evangelists traveled from community to community and preached to the faithful in tents, open fields, or rented meeting halls. Modern-day communications technology has changed all that. To a great extent, radio, television, and the Internet are replacing the traditional meeting places.

Although the "electronic church" (church attendance through telecommunications) has attracted considerable attention, disagreement exists as to the actual size of its audience and the extent of its impact. Many television evangelists claim to have very large audiences, but most rating services estimate the total religious television audience to be of a rather modest size, approximately ten to thirteen million viewers.

William Stacey and Anson Shupe (1982) have advanced sociological understanding of the electronic church by examining the characteristics of its viewers. They surveyed residents of the Dallas–Fort Worth metropolitan area. This area is often referred to as the "buckle" of the southern Bible Belt.

Stacey and Shupe found regular viewers to have relatively low incomes and less than a high school education. Viewers also tended to be female, to be over thirty-five years of age, and to have large families. Blue-collar workers were more likely than white-collar workers to watch, but retired persons and homemakers were more likely to be viewers than people with jobs.

People who attended church regularly tended to watch, an important finding because it contradicted the claim that the electronic church was depriving local churches of members. Fundamentalists were more likely than reformed or moderate believers to tune in. The electronic church preaches to the converted who are already predisposed, or self-selected, to seek out its messages.

Working with the Research

1. According to Stacey and Shupe's research, what demographic groups are most likely to watch religious programming?
2. Would you predict that the electronic church will have greater social impact in the future? Why or why not?

in hell. Seventy-two percent believe in the existence of angels (Gallup, 1996).

Religious Preferences

What are the religious preferences in the U.S.? Although there are over three hundred denominations and sects in the United States, Americans in the mid-1990s were largely Protestant (58 percent) and belonged to a few major denominations—Baptist (20 percent), Methodist (10 percent), Lutheran (6 percent), Presbyterian (4 percent), and

Religious Organizations in the U.S.	Number of Members
Roman Catholic Church	60,280,454
Southern Baptist Convention	15,663,296
United Methodist Church	8,538,662
Jewish	6,840,000
Lutheran Church in America	5,190,489
Muslim	5,000,000
Presbyterian Church (U.S.A.)	3,669,489
Episcopal Church	2,536,550
Assembly of God	2,387,982
United Church of Christ	1,472,213
Jehovah's Witnesses	966,243
Christian Church (Disciples of Christ)	929,725
Seventh-Day Adventist	790,731
Church of the Nazarene	601,900
Salvation Army	453,150
Wisconsin Evangelical Lutheran Synod	412,478
Reformed Church in America	306,312

Episcopalian (4 percent). Fourteen percent prefer various other Protestant denominations. Catholics constitute a relatively large proportion of the American population (25 percent) and Jews a relatively small proportion (2 percent). As noted earlier, only 8 percent of Americans have no religious preference (Gallup, 1996). Figure 14.6 lists many of the religious organizations in the United States with memberships above 300,000.

Figure 14.6 Membership in Selected Religious Organizations in the United States. *On the basis of these data, how would you describe the religious composition of the U.S.?*

Sources: Gale Research and composite sources, 1995–1997.

Fundamentalism in America

Any careful observer of religion in the United States over the last twenty years or so will note the rise of religious *fundamentalism* in the country, especially among Protestant denominations. **Fundamentalism** is based on the desire to resist secularization and to adhere closely to traditional religious beliefs, rituals, and doctrines. It is, of course, inaccurate to limit fundamentalism to Protestants alone. Fundamentalism is found in all religions, including the Roman Catholic, Jewish, and Muslim faiths. This discussion, however, will focus on Protestant fundamentalism.

It is not surprising that most fundamentalists are politically conservative, given that the roots of contemporary religious fundamentalism are in the latter part of the nineteenth century. Two issues disturbed the early fundamentalists. First, fundamentalists were concerned about the spread of secularism. Science was challenging the Bible as a source of truth; Marxism was portraying religion as an opiate for the masses; Darwinism was challenging the biblical interpretation of creation; and religion in general was losing its traditionally strong influence on all social institutions. Second, fundamentalists rejected the movement away from emphasis on the traditional message of Christianity toward an emphasis on social service (Johnstone, 1996).

Since the late 1960s, many of the largest American Protestant denominations—Methodists, Lutherans, Presbyterians, Episcopalians—have either been declining in membership or fighting to hold their own. In contrast, contemporary

fundamentalism
the resistance of secularization and the rigid adherence to traditional religious beliefs, rituals, and doctrines

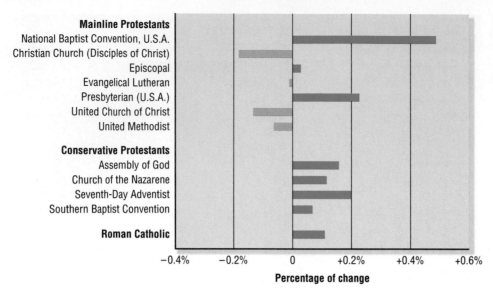

Mainline Protestants
National Baptist Convention, U.S.A.
Christian Church (Disciples of Christ)
Episcopal
Evangelical Lutheran
Presbyterian (U.S.A.)
United Church of Christ
United Methodist

Conservative Protestants
Assembly of God
Church of the Nazarene
Seventh-Day Adventist
Southern Baptist Convention

Roman Catholic

−0.4%   −0.2%   0   +0.2%   +0.4%   +0.6%

Percentage of change

Figure 14.7 American Church Membership Trends: 1990–1999. *Do you believe that this pattern will continue in the twenty-first century? Explain your conclusion using text materials.*

Source: *Yearbook of American and Canadian Churches, 1999.*

fundamentalist denominations have been growing. Fundamentalists exist in all Protestant organizations, but they are predominantly found in such religious bodies as the Mormons, the Assemblies of God, the Seventh-Day Adventists, the Baptists, and the Jehovah's Witnesses. (See Figure 14.7.)

What is the nature of fundamentalism today? The theological agenda of today's fundamentalists is very close to that of their forebears in the nineteenth century.

Fundamentalists believe in the literal truth of the Scriptures, or in taking the Bible at "face value." Protestant fundamentalism involves being "born again" through acceptance of Jesus Christ as the Son of God who was sent to redeem mankind through his sacrifice. Fundamentalist doctrine includes belief in the responsibility of all believers to give witness for God, the presence of Satan as an active force for evil, and the destruction of the world prior to the Messiah's return to establish His kingdom on earth.

Are all fundamentalists alike? Religious organizations that share in much of the fundamentalist theology have some unique beliefs and practices of their own. An example is neo-Pentacostalism—or the *charismatic movement,* as it is sometimes called—which has occurred for the most part within traditional religious organizations, particularly the Roman Catholic and Episcopal churches. Those involved in this movement often speak of receiving "the baptism of the Holy Spirit." But central to most neo-Pentecostal groups is the experience of "speaking in tongues," which believers claim is a direct gift of the Holy Spirit (Cox, 1992, 1996; Hunt, Hamilton, and Walter, 1998).

Why is fundamentalism so strong today? Several reasons for the growth of fundamentalism have been proposed.

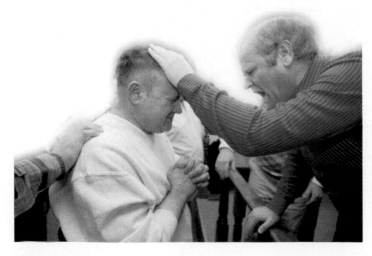

❖ Many Americans feel their world is out of control. The social order of the 1950s was shattered by a string of traumatic events beginning with the civil rights movement and progressing through campus violence, political assassinations, the Vietnam War, and Watergate. Increases in substance abuse, illegitimate births, divorce, and crime are taken as signs of moral decline. Fundamental religion, with its absolute answers and promise of eternal life, provides a strong anchor in a confusing, bewildering world.

This charismatic minister in Atlanta is engaged in faith healing.

❖ Fundamentalist churches, by emphasizing warmth, love, and caring, provide solace to people who are witnessing and experiencing the weakening of family and community ties. Mainline churches tend to be more formal and impersonal.

❖ Fundamentalist churches offer what they consider a more purely sacred environment, in contrast to mainline denominations that fundamentalists see as accommodating to secular society.

❖ The electronic church, in its role as part of the mass media, has been an important contributing factor in the growth of religious fundamentalism. (See Focus on Research on page 484.)

Religion, Class, and Politics

Religious affiliation is related to social class. There are marked differences in social class (as measured by education and income) among the various religions in the United States. Generally speaking, Presbyterians, Episcopalians, and Jews are at the top of the stratification structure. Below them are Lutherans, Catholics, and Methodists, followed by Baptists. Because these are average figures, there are, of course, many individual exceptions to these rankings.

Differences in religiosity exist between the upper and lower classes as well. Religion is important at both ends of the stratification structure, but the upper and lower classes express their beliefs in different ways. The upper classes display their religiosity through church membership, church attendance, and observance of ritual, whereas people in the lower classes more often pray privately and have emotional religious experiences.

Political affiliation, too, is related to religion. Followers of the Jewish faith are particularly aligned with the Democratic Party, followed in strength of support by Catholics and Protestants. This is predictable, because Protestants generally are more politically conservative than Catholics or Jews, and the Democratic Party is generally not associated with political conservatism in the United States today. Of the major Protestant denominations, the greatest support for the Republican Party is found among Episcopalians and Presbyterians. This is hardly surprising, because the upper classes are more likely to be identified with the Republican Party.

There are some contradictions in this general pattern. Despite their affiliation with the more conservative Republican Party, Episcopalians and Presbyterians are less conservative than Baptists, who are the strongest supporters of the Democratic Party of all Protestant denominations, especially in the South.

Religion, Science, and Society

Both science and religion examine humanity's relationship to the world, but they examine it in very different ways. Religion involves matters beyond human observation, while science is all about observation. These fields of study are not mutually exclusive. Many scientists are religious individuals, while many professional clergy appreciate and support the intellectual achievements of the field of science.

Sometimes, however, these two institutions can appear to be in conflict. Depending on the values and norms of the culture, society may favor religious

Religion and science sometimes come into heated conflict. One famous case was the 1925 "Monkey Trial" of John Thomas Scopes in Tennessee.

or scientific explanations. In the United States, following the principle of separation of state and church, it has been common to keep religion apart from government-sponsored institutions. Scientific explanations for natural phenomena, when commonly accepted, have been taught in the schools, leaving religious groups free to teach other interpretations within their organizations.

Strict fundamentalists do not believe that scientific theories such as the theory of evolution and the Big Bang theory of creation should be presented in public schools as facts, while Bible-based explanations such as creationism are not even discussed. In 1999, fundamentalists convinced the Kansas Board of Education to remove any questions about evolution from the state high school exit examination. Until the decision was repealed in 2001, Kansas teachers were not required to teach the theory of evolution.

Today, many people are questioning whether "pure science" can remain independent of cultural or social norms, as some scientists believe. Scientific discoveries and processes, such as cloning and gene therapy, are moving into ever more ethically debatable areas. The result appears obvious: the interface between science and religion is sure to increase. Society, in particular government, will need to learn how to deal constructively with apparent contradictions in these two areas.

Science without religion is lame; religion without science is blind.

Albert Einstein
Nobel Laureate physicist

Section 4 Assessment

1. What is secularization and why is it an important process to explore?
2. Describe the relationship between religion and political allegiance in the U.S.

Critical Thinking

3. **Analyzing Information** Analyze how progress in scientific research will affect religious beliefs and practices over the next twenty-five years.

Summary

Section 1: Religion and Sociology

Main Idea: Religion is concerned with sacred things. Sociologists studying religion face some unique problems. They do not judge the validity of various religions but rather look at those aspects of religion that can be measured and observed in society.

Section 2: Theoretical Perspectives

Main Idea: Religion has several functions. It legitimates the structure of society, promotes social unity, and provides a sense of meaning and belonging. Marx argued that religion is used to justify and maintain the group in power. Weber believed that religion could promote social change. He connected the Protestant ethic and the rise of capitalism.

Section 3: Religious Organization and Religiosity

Main Idea: The major forms of religious organization are churches, denominations, sects, and cults. Religiosity—the ways people express their religious interests and convictions—can be analyzed in terms of five dimensions: belief, ritual, intellect, experience, and consequences.

Section 4: Religion in the United States

Main Idea: Through the process of secularization, the sacred and the profane tend to become intermixed. Religious faiths can be analyzed by major social characteristics such as class and political tendencies.

Self-Check Quiz
Visit the *Sociology and You* Web site at soc.glencoe.com and click on **Chapter 14—Self-Check Quizzes** to prepare for the chapter test.

Reviewing Vocabulary

Complete each sentence using each term once.

a. religion
b. sacred
c. profane
d. legitimate
e. spirit of capitalism
f. Protestant ethic
g. church
h. denomination
i. sect
j. cult
k. religiosity
l. secularization
m. fundamentalism

1. _____ is the word used to describe things and ideas that are set apart and given a special meaning.

2. A religious movement based on the desire to adhere closely to traditional beliefs, rituals, and doctrines is called _____.

3. The _____ are the nonsacred aspects of life.

4. _____ is the name given to a cluster of values, norms, beliefs, and attitudes that favored the growth of capitalism.

5. _____ means to justify or give official approval to.

6. A religious organization arising out of a desire to reform another religious organization is called _____.

7. _____ is the obligation to reinvest money rather than spending it.

8. _____ is the name given to a life-encompassing religious organization to which all members of a society belong.

9. A unified system of beliefs and practices concerned with sacred things is called _____.

10. The ways in which people express their religious interests and convictions is called _____.

11. A _____ is a religious organization whose characteristics are not drawn from existing religious tradition within a society.

12. The process through which the sacred loses influence over society is known as _____.

13. A _____ is one of several religious organizations that most members of a society accept as legitimate.

Reviewing the Facts

1. Religious faiths can be analyzed by two major social characteristics. What are those characteristics?

2. Based on Figure 14.4 on page 482, has the percentage of Americans who claim that religion is very important in their lives decreased over time, increased over time, or showed no significant change?

3. How does the upper social class define its religiosity? Use the diagram below to record your answer.

RELIGIOSITY AS DEFINED BY THE UPPER CLASS

+   +   = **RELIGIOSITY**

4. In 1978, the Reverend Jim Jones led hundreds of people who belonged to his group in a mass suicide-murder. What term is used to describe Jones's religious organization?

5. Which sociologist published *The Elementary Forms of Religious Life* in 1915 and spoke of the functions of religion?

Thinking Critically

1. **Making Inferences** The crucifix is a widely known symbol even to non-Christians. How do the various meanings attached to this symbol relate to an understanding of Durkheim's concept of the sacred and profane? Could the crucifix easily represent other things if it was not for its relationship to Christ? Explain your answer.

2. **Drawing Conclusions** Current research says that religion often reflects conventional (traditional) norms. Accordingly, religious clergy tend to address their messages to the more tradi-

tional segments of society. Sermons, for example, are aimed at the typical married family arrangement (mother, father, two children). What effect, if any, do you think this could have on general attendance at gatherings?

3. **Analyzing Information** The United States has one of the highest standards of living in the world. It also has one of the most materialistic cultures and societies. Do you think this says anything about the religiosity of Americans?

4. **Making Inferences** About 96 percent of all Americans say they believe in God. Nevertheless, defining who is or is not religious is very difficult. Some people don't go to church yet claim to be religious, while others go to church but don't seem to be religious, for example. What dilemmas do all these issues present for sociologists who want to study religiosity? What variables could help to explain what religiosity is? Why do you think sociologists should research this issue at all?

5. **Analyzing Information** Do you think that economic decisions are influenced by religiously based motivations? Elaborate.

6. **Evaluating Information** Based on scales developed by sociologists, African Americans rate higher in religiosity than other racial or ethnic groups. Men like Martin Luther King, Jr., and Ralph Abernathy and women like Aretha Franklin have attributed their success to the role religion played in their lives. What events in this country's history might have contributed to the role that religion plays in the African American community?

7. **Applying Concepts** Many people appear to be less interested in religion during their teenage years. This might be seen in falling church attendance for this age group. Using your sociological imagination, suggest some reasons for this apparent lack of interest. Consider developmental (age) and social factors. Depending on your answers, what suggestions might you make to religious organizations looking for ideas on how to keep teenagers involved and active?

Sociology Projects

1. **Researching Religions** Choose a religion, denomination, sect, or cult to research. You can learn about the group by talking with some of its members. You can also find excellent material in libraries and on the Internet. (Be sure to consider the source of all information gathered from the Internet. Check it for bias, accuracy, and "hidden agendas.") In your research, focus on the following aspects of the group: its origin; fundamental beliefs, important rituals or ceremonies; internal social changes that occurred over time; and membership demographics (social class, ethnicity, and so forth). You may want to work with a classmate. Based on your research, prepare a report with visual aids that can be given orally. (You may want to use a computer presentation package such as PowerPoint.)

2. **Sacred and Profane** The chapter discusses the concepts of *sacred* and *profane*. Any object by itself is profane; people give it sacred meaning. Working with two of your classmates, select an object (profane), and create a skit in which you show how the profane object might become a sacred object.

3. **Defining and Analyzing Religion** This exercise will help you understand the difficulty social scientists have when it comes to defining and analyzing religion. Take out a piece of paper and answer the following questions:
   a. How do you define religion?
   b. What does it mean to you?
   c. Do you believe in the supernatural?
   d. If you do believe in the supernatural, how do you imagine it to be?

   After everyone in class has completed these questions, turn to your neighbor and compare your answers with his or her answers. Note the similarities and differences. Share your answers with as many of your classmates as possible.

4. **Charitable Organizations** Contact a religious organization in your neighborhood, and arrange to take part in some community service activity in which this organization is involved. Pay close attention to the various ways in which these groups conduct charitable work. Report to the class on the effectiveness of your service—both for the recipient and for yourself. Then consider how your community would be affected if the group stopped providing this service. Would some political or non-governmental organization continue it?

5. **Attitudes on Religion** Design a survey that would allow you to conduct an "unofficial" study of student attitudes toward religion. (You may want to refer back to the section on survey methods in Chapter 2.) Remember that your questions are directed at social practices and not at what or why individuals specifically believe. Some topics you may want to ask about include attendance at religious services, prayer, and belief in an afterlife. Information about respondents' ethnic and religious backgrounds would prove useful as well. Compare your survey with the surveys created by your classmates. Work with four or five students to combine your questions into the best survey possible, and ask twenty students to complete the survey for your group. Report your findings to the class. Do these results reflect the community you live in? Do you think that teens are more or less outwardly religious than adults?

Technology Activity

1. Using your school or local library and the Internet, research information on the clergy during the middle ages. Based on your research and the material you read in this chapter, how would you classify their religious organization? Some of the characteristics of the clergy might be regarded as a cult. Explain why the clergy in the middle ages were not a cult. Using proper grammar, sentence structure, spelling, and punctuation, write a paragraph defending your conclusion.

Chapter 14

Enrichment Reading
India's Sacred Cow

by Marvin Harris

People often take their own religion for granted, overlooking its connections with the rest of society. We are better able to see the link between religious beliefs and culture when we examine an unfamiliar setting. Marvin Harris's analysis of the place of the cow in Hinduism provides such a backdrop.

News photographs that came out of India during the famine of the late 1960s showed starving people stretching out bony hands to beg for food while sacred cattle strolled behind undisturbed. The Hindu, it seems, would rather starve to death than eat his cow or even deprive it of food. The cattle appear to browse unhindered through urban markets eating an orange here, a mango there, competing with people for meager supplies of food.

By Western standards, spiritual values seem more important to Indians than life itself. Specialists in food habits . . . consider Hinduism an irrational **ideology** that compels people to overlook abundant, nutritious foods for scarcer, less healthful foods.

Cow worship . . . carries over into politics. In 1966 a crowd of 120,000 people, led by holy men, demonstrated in front of the Indian House of Parliament in support of the All-Party Cow Protection Campaign Committee. In Nepal, the only **contemporary** Hindu kingdom, cow slaughter is severely punished. As one story goes, the car driven by an official of a United States agency struck and killed a cow. In order to avoid the international incident that would have occurred when the official was arrested for murder, the Nepalese magistrate concluded that the cow had committed suicide. . . .

The easy explanation for India's devotion to the cow, the one most Westerners and Indians would offer, is that cow worship is an integral part of Hinduism. Religion is somehow good for

the soul, even it if sometimes fails the body. Religion orders the cosmos and explains our place in the universe. Religious beliefs, many would claim, have existed for thousands of years and have a life of their own. They are not understandable in scientific terms.

But all this ignores history. There is more to be said for cow worship than is immediately apparent. The earliest Vedas, the Hindu sacred texts from the second millennium B.C., do not prohibit the slaughter of cattle. Instead, they ordain it as part of sacrificial rites. The early Hindus did not avoid the flesh of cows and bulls; they ate it at ceremonial feasts presided over by Brahman priests. Cow worship is a relatively recent development in India; it evolved as the Hindu religion developed and changed.

This evolution is recorded in royal **edicts** and religious texts written during the last 3,000 years of Indian history. The Vedas from the first millennium B.C. contain contradictory passages, some referring to ritual slaughter and others to a strict taboo on beef consumption. . . . [M]any of the sacred-cow passages were incorporated into the texts by priests of a later period.

By 200 A.D. the status of Indian cattle had undergone a spiritual transformation. The Brahman priesthood **exhorted** the population to **venerate** the cow and forbade them to abuse it or to feed on it. Religious feasts involving the ritual slaughter and consumption of livestock were eliminated and meat eating was restricted to the nobility.

Anthropologist Marvin Harris contends that science and culture can explain the reason cows are sacred to Hindus. How does he attempt to support his claim?

What Does it Mean?

ascertain
determine

contemporary
modern, current

edict
official proclamation or law

exhorted
strongly urged

ideology
a systematic body of thought about human culture or society

politically expedient
based on practical or advantageous reasons

venerate
worship or revere

By 1000 A.D., all Hindus were forbidden to eat beef. Ahimsa, the Hindu belief in the unity of all life, was the spiritual justification for this restriction. But it is difficult to **ascertain** exactly when this change occurred. An important event that helped to shape the modern complex was the Islamic invasion, which took place in the eighth century A.D. Hindus may have found it **politically expedient** to set themselves off from the invaders, who were beefeaters, by emphasizing the need to prevent the slaughter of their sacred animals. Thereafter, the cow taboo assumed its modern form and began to function much as it does today.

Source: Excerpted from James M. Henslin, *Down to Earth Sociology: Introductory Readings,* 10th ed., The Free Press, 1999.

Read and React

1. Summarize your understanding (prior to reading this article) of the Hindu religious belief about cows. Has your opinion changed after reading it? Why or why not?

2. How do non-Hindu people's reactions to the sacred cow relate to ethnocentrism and cultural relativism? Explain in each case, drawing on material in the reading.

CHAPTER 15
Sport

494

I haven't been the same since. I love it.
All of a sudden I find I'm stronger
than anyone else in the place—all
the girls and practically all of the guys. . . .
The boys respected me right away, and
that's important. They all act like they're
so tough, then you go in and lift more
than they can. They can't ignore that
there's a girl over in the corner doing
more than them, and they hang their
heads.

As this young female power lifter tells us,
playing sport can positively affect the self-
image of females, as well as improve gender
relations. The desire to achieve such benefits
was part of the motivation for the passage of
Title IX of the Educational Amendment Act
passed by the U.S. Congress in 1972. Title IX
makes gender discrimination illegal in any
educational institution receiving federal
funds. Thanks to Title IX an increasing number of females have joined school athletic
teams. Critics of Title IX fear that shifting
funds from men's sports places an unfair
strain on the most popular athletic programs,
but defenders of Title IX do not believe that
men's programs must suffer for women to
gain opportunities (Nixon and Frey, 1996).

Some sociologists refer to social institutions such as sport, health, and entertainment as *secondary institutions*. These
institutions are less pervasive than the family, education, politics, economics, or religion, but they also occur in every society.
This chapter will look at how sport contributes to the functioning and nature of society in the United States.

Sections

1. **The Nature of Sport**
2. **Theoretical Perspectives and Sport**
3. **Social Issues in Sport**

Learning Objectives

After reading this chapter, you will be able to

❖ justify sport as an American institution.

❖ compare and contrast sport in America from a functionalist, conflict, and symbolic interactionist perspective.

❖ understand the relationship between American sport and social mobility.

❖ cite evidence of sexism and racism in American sport.

Chapter Overview
Visit the *Sociology and You* Web site at
soc.glencoe.com and click on **Chapter 15—
Chapter Overviews** to preview chapter
information.

The Nature of Sport

Key Terms

- sport
- sport subculture

Section Preview

As a social institution, sport fulfills some important societal needs. One of these is helping individuals identify with other members of society. Sport subcultures have developed around both team and individual sports. For this reason, sport is a reflection of society.

sport
a set of competitive activities in which winners and losers are determined by physical performance within a set of established rules

A Definition of Sport

For most people, sport consists of certain leisure activities, exercise, and spectator events. It is actually more complex than that. Sociologists define **sport** as a set of competitive activities in which winners and losers are determined by physical performance within a set of established rules. While sport is an important aspect of recreation, many forms of recreation do not involve sport. Sport sociologist Jay J. Coakley (1998) sees a spontaneous race between two skiers as more of a contest than a sport. Although a contest between skiers involves physical activity and competition, it does not involve definite rules or standardized conditions.

Sport as a Social Institution

Institutions fulfill certain basic needs and reflect the most important aspects of a society. The five most commonly recognized social institutions have been examined in preceding chapters: family, education, government, economic systems, and religion. Although these social institutions take different forms in different societies, they appear in every society because they fulfill needs common to all societies.

What is the difference between a sport and a game?

Section 2

Theoretical Perspectives and Sport

Culture and Sport

Sport is a major social activity through which culture is created and re-inforced. As noted earlier, sociologists recognize this important aspect of sport.

> *American sport embodies American values—striving for excellence, winning, individual and team competition, and materialism. Parents want their children to participate in sport because participation teaches them the basic values of American society and builds character (Eitzen, 1999:3).*

Although sociologists agree that sport mirrors society, and that the relationship is complex, they disagree over the social implications of sport. Sport sociologist Stanley Eitzen has written a book on the paradoxes, or contradictions, of sport in America. (See Figure 15.1 on page 504.) Functionalists, who tend to concentrate on the benefits of sport, are represented in Eitzen's book. So are conflict theorists, who see a social downside to sport. Symbolic interactionists focus on personal meanings derived from sport.

Section Preview

Functionalists see sport positively, as a means for socializing young people, promoting social integration, providing a release for tensions, and developing sound character. Conflict theorists believe that organized sports can be harmful to character development. Symbolic interactionists focus on the self-concepts and relationships developed through sport activities.

"WE'RE IN BIG TROUBLE.. THEY PLAY LIKE GIRLS!"

Sport has long been an important basis for stratification in high schools.

Figure 15.1 Sport Paradoxes

Stanley Eitzen, a highly respected sport sociologist, argues that sport is inherently contradictory (Eitzen, 1999). Here are a few of the paradoxes Eitzen identifies. Do you agree with Eitzen that these paradoxes exist?

Social Integration
- Sport can unite different social classes and racial/ethnic groups
  but
- sport can heighten barriers that separate groups.

Fair Play
- Sport promotes fair play by teaching the importance of following the rules
  but
- sport's emphasis on winning tempts people to cheat.

Physical Fitness
- Sport promotes muscle strength, weight control, endurance, and coordination
  but
- sport can lead to the use of steroids and other drugs, excessive weight loss or gain, and injuries.

Academics
- Sport contributes to higher education through scholarships and fund raising
  but
- sport takes money away from academics and emphasizes athletic performance over learning and graduation.

Social Mobility
- Sport allows athletes who might otherwise not attend college to obtain an education
  but
- only a few can achieve the promise of fame and wealth in the professional ranks.

Source: D. Stanley Eitzen, *Fair and Foul* (Lanham, MD: Rowman & Littlefield Publishers, Inc. 1999), pp. 4–7.

Functionalism

How do functionalists view the role of sport in society?   Functionalists think sport is important primarily because it helps society work more smoothly. It does this by performing the following functions (Eitzen and Sage, 1997).

❖ *Sport teaches basic beliefs, norms, and values.* Sport readies us for adult roles. Games, for instance, prepare participating athletes for work in organizations. Young people who are exposed to competitive sport become more achievement motivated than those who are not. And the earlier the exposure occurs, the higher the orientation towards achievement. This is important because achievement-motivation is essential to productivity in the modern economy.

❖ *Sport promotes a sense of social identification.* A team binds people to their community and nation. Clevelanders are united in their love of the Browns, Indians, and Cavaliers. Around midcentury, the United States at times seemed to be divided into Dodger and Yankee fans. The Atlanta Braves are trying to be "America's team." Higher social integration results.

Cleveland Browns fans identified so strongly with their city's football team that the city brought suit to keep the team name and colors from leaving town.

❖ *Sport offers a safe release of aggressive feelings generated by the frustrations, anxieties, and strains of modern life.* It is socially acceptable to yell and scream for an athletic team. Similar behavior directed at a teacher, principal, parent, or employer can have negative consequences.

❖ *Sport encourages the development of character.* Coaches, school officials, and parents often draw a parallel between sport and "life." "When the going gets tough, the tough get going" is a sentiment expressed in most locker rooms. The hard work, discipline, and self-sacrifice demanded by team sports become part of an athlete's value system.

What are the social dysfunctions of sport?   Functionalists have identified some drawbacks to sport. Because sport reflects society, it draws on achievement-oriented values that can be intensified to an extreme degree (Kohn, 1992). When achievement and winning come to be seen as the primary goals of sport, any method of winning—including violence and cheating—may be encouraged.

We need not look far to see examples of violence in sport. Coaches and fans expect athletes to place their physical well-being on the line. Players in many sports are expected to resort to violence. In high school football, aggressive behavior is defended as preparation for "real-life" competition. Pressures are intensified at the professional level, where many sports have developed the informal role of *enforcer*—a team member whose major responsibility is to intimidate, provoke, and even injure opponents (Coakley, 1998). Boston Bruins hockey player Marty McSorley used his hockey stick to deliver a vicious blindside slash to the head of opposing player Donald

> You give 100 percent in the first half of the game, and if that isn't enough in the second half you give what's left.
>
> **Yogi Berra
> baseball coach**

World View

Olympic Success

Sport also plays an important role in today's global society. For some time, the winning of Olympic medals has been a source of regional and global prestige. This map shows the number of medals earned by each country in the 2000 Summer Olympic Games.

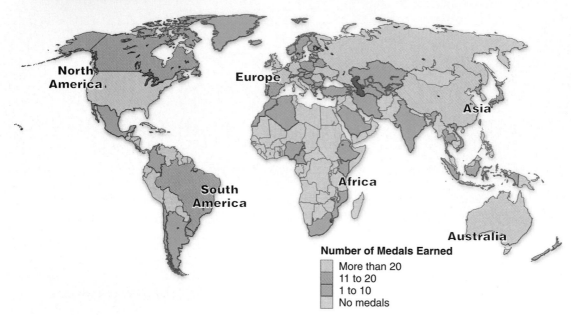

North America

Europe

Asia

Africa

South America

Australia

Number of Medals Earned

More than 20
11 to 20
1 to 10
No medals

Interpreting the Map

1. Why do you think there is such wide variation in the number of Olympic medals earned?
2. Do the Olympics illustrate a connection between sport and politics? Explain.

Source: Orbital Decisions, http://www.orbital.co.za/text/sydney2000/medals.htm.

Brashear in February of 2000. The attack was the culmination of a game marked by injuries and was the result of the long-standing rivalry between two "top enforcers."

Cheating may not be as easy as violent behavior to identify, but is often present, nonetheless. Cheating was no doubt involved when American Olympic skater Nancy Kerrigan was struck on the right leg with a metal rod by an assailant later linked to her competitor, Tonya Harding. In 2000, the Atlanta Braves were penalized for signing a player before his sixteenth birthday. They had followed the precedent of the Los Angeles Dodgers in 1999. Cheating can even extend beyond players, as when a Utah state committee used illegal inducements to attract the 2002 Winter Olympics.

Conflict Theory

Some sociologists have raised disturbing questions about the effects of sport on society. These questions are best understood through the conflict perspective. Conflict theorists are interested in who has the power and how elites use power to satisfy their own interests. To conflict theorists, sport is a social institution in which the most powerful oppress, manipulate, coerce, and exploit others. Conflict theorists highlight the ways in which sport mirrors the unequal distribution of power and money in society. They also emphasize the role of sport in maintaining inequality (Leonard, 1998).

While functionalists see sport as contributing to the unification of society, conflict theorists do not. While people from all major segments of a community or society may join in cheering for the same team, their union is only temporary.

When the game is over, the enthusiasm dies, the solidarity runs short, and disharmony in other relations reasserts itself. Much as one hour a week cannot answer to the religious impulse, one game a week cannot answer to the solidarity needs of a racist, sexist, or elitist society (Young, 1986).

Basic social class divisions, in other words, will continue to exist and to affect social relationships in a community even if the local team has just won the World Series or the Super Bowl.

The contribution sport makes in forming good character is also questioned by conflict theorists. Among college athletes, studies have shown that the degree of sportsmanship apparently declines as athletes become more involved in the sports system. As sociologist Stanley Eitzen (1993a) notes, nonscholarship athletes display greater sportsmanship than those with athletic scholarships, and those who have not earned letters exhibit more sportsmanship than letter winners.

Conflict theorists can point to any number of past and present scandals in both the college and professional ranks. Americans are constantly reading in the sports section of the daily newspaper about athletes, from high school to the professional level, who are taking drugs, cheating in school, or accepting illegitimate cash "gifts." One university after another is being investigated and penalized by the National Collegiate Athletic Association. Coaches as well as players are involved in misconduct.

Athletes may use performance-enhancing drugs such as steroids and amphetamines to achieve a "competitive edge." . . . Big-time college coaches in their zeal to win have been found guilty of exploiting athletes, falsifying transcripts, providing illegal payments, hiring surrogate test takers, paying athletes for nonexistent summer jobs, and illegally using government Pell grants and work study monies for athletes. So much, I would argue, for the myth that "sport builds character" (Eitzen, 1996:189).

In some cultures, sport is so important lives may depend on it. In 1994, Colombian soccer player Andres Escobar was gunned down, apparently for scoring against his own team in the World Cup soccer match against the U.S. (Colombia lost, 2–1.)

Symbolic Interactionism

Symbolic interactionism also contributes to our understanding of sport as a social institution. This theoretical perspective concentrates on personal meanings, social relationships, and self-identity processes. Symbolic interactionists are concerned with the symbols of sports. The meanings and interpretations of these symbols are important because they affect the self-concepts, as well as the relationships, of those involved.

The social context of Little League baseball illustrates this perspective. For three years, Gary Alan Fine (1987) studied American adolescent suburban males who played Little League baseball. He discovered and documented a variety of ways in which the boys assigned meanings to their team activities. In addition, he described how these meanings and interpretations influenced the boys' social interactions and affected their self-definitions.

What were these meanings?   Much of the activity of coaches and parents centered on teaching the rules of the game and teaching values, such as team play, hard work, fair play, competition, and winning. But these ten- to twelve-year-old boys formed their own interpretations of these messages. The boys misinterpreted the adult values of hard work, competition, and so forth as the "masculine" values of dominance, "toughness," and risky behavior.

How were social interaction and self-concepts affected?   In the first place, the boys' behavior convinced coaches and parents that the youngsters understood and accepted their values. For example, the aggressive behavior that the boys considered as evidence of their masculinity was seen by the coaches and parents as evidence of "hustle," dedication to competition, and the desire to win. The boys were praised for this behavior, which encouraged them to continue it. "Weaker" peers, younger children, and girls in general frequently experienced the disdain of these Little Leaguers. This disrespect often led to a loss of self-esteem for children who suffered the brunt of the Little Leaguers' scorn.

This young boy might be misinterpreting what his coach is trying to teach him about sportsmanship.

Figure 15.2 Focus on Theoretical Perspectives

Social Effects of Sport. This table illustrates how each theoretical perspective might study an issue involving sport. For each assumption, provide a specific example from your own experience or from a team you follow.

Theoretical Perspective	Concept	Assumption
Functionalism	Social integration	Athletic teams promote togetherness and belonging in a community.
Conflict Theory	Social conflict	Deep social conflict exists within a community and persists despite widespread attachment to athletic teams.
Symbolic Interactionism	Social concept	Participation in a team sport may promote or harm self-esteem depending upon factors such as emphasis on winning and fair play.

What are some limitations of each perspective? The functionalist perspective makes important points regarding the positive and negative role of sport in society. Its critics, however, contend that many sports have become so closely tied to elite interests that they contribute more to private profit than to the general well-being of society. To investigate this point, the conflict perspective concentrates on some major concerns of sport, such as racism and sexism (discussed in the next section). On the other hand, conflict theorists tend to overlook the positive contributions of sport to society. They are accused of placing too much emphasis on the extent to which sport is manipulated and controlled by the elite. Their critics also claim that conflict theorists underestimate the character-building benefit of team sports. Symbolic interactionism contributes greatly to understanding the socialization process in sport. But, because it concentrates on social interaction, it fails to include the broader social and cultural context. For example, symbolic interactionism does not address the functions of sport in society or explore sport within the context of power and social inequality.

Section 2 Assessment

1. What is the relationship between sport and achievement-oriented values?
2. Name three roles that sport plays in society, according to functionalists.
3. Summarize in one sentence the overall attitude of the conflict perspective toward sport.

Critical Thinking

4. **Finding the Main Idea** Has your self-concept been affected by sports? Explain the effects from the symbolic interactionist viewpoint.

> [Knute] Rockne wanted nothing but "bad losers." Good losers get into the habit of losing.
>
> George E. Allen
> American raconteur

Focus on Research

Case Study: Tough Guys, Wimps, and Weenies

SIDELINES

"When are you gonna learn when it's necessary to use unnecessary roughness?"

Remember Donna Eder's study of middle-school stratification? (See pages 66–67.) She also researched the nature of middle-school sports. Using the framework of symbolic interactionism, Eder assumes that the social world of teenagers is constructed through interaction with others. Thus, everyday exchanges—insults, greetings, gossip—give teenagers a sense of their social world.

Middle-school coaches accented the value of toughness. In the world of athletics, having a "mean" attitude is masculine, and being nice is effeminate. Wrestlers, for example, were told to make opponents "suffer." Football coaches did not tolerate fighting off the field, but as a means to handle conflict among athletes, these same coaches encouraged physical force on the field.

I said that I had heard that Coach Paulson wasn't pleased with the way the team played. Walter and Carl both agreed. Walter [the team manager] *said that the team didn't hit like they should have and that made the coach mad. Carl said, "Yeah, but I really socked that guy. Man, I threw him down on the concrete. Did you hear Coach James yelling, "Way to go, Orville"? (Eder, 1995:62)*

Evidence of weakness was greeted by derogatory names like "wuss," "wimp," and "girl." Ritual insults promoted stereotypically masculine behavior, particularly among higher-status boys. Stories of physical force in sports were repeated with pride. Even soccer players bragged about kicking opponents in the shins or throwing a ball into an opponent's face.

The most forcefully combative boys were the most respected. Although the coaches tried to curb physical violence outside of games and matches, many players considered fighting an appropriate way to handle all peer conflicts.

[The] importance of being tough extended to behavior off the playing field as well as on it. Boys were continually challenged to develop more aspects of toughness, including the ability to deny pain and suppress feelings as well as respond combatively to verbal and physical attacks. Boys who rejected these messages were

sometimes subject to ridicule by girls as well as boys, showing the difficulty boys faced when trying to escape the pressures of being masculine within this school setting (Eder, 1995:72).

Insult exchanges could be won by getting another boy to become angry. By losing his cool, the other boy lost his image of toughness. Some boys would insult another boy just to look good to others. An example is provided by one of the researcher's notes on Hank, the highest-status boy in the seventh grade, who had a reputation for verbal assault.

Future sociologists may study the effect that team sports plays on women's aggression.

Hank does seem to enjoy conflict or competition on a one-on-one basis. A couple of times today he left the table just to go down and abuse some kid at the end of the table, calling him a pud, a squirt, or a wimp. Then he would come back and tell the group how the guy had done nothing when he had said this. Hank would get a big smile on his face and was really pleased (Eder, 1995:73–74).

Insults and counter-insults delivered several messages. First, boys learned not to care about the feelings of others. Second, insulting, or even humiliating, their peers was a socially approved means of achieving or displaying higher status. Third, boys who humiliated low-status peers were rewarded with social recognition. This was true even if the target of ridicule was handicapped or overweight.

Working with the Research

1. Do you think this study describes sports at your school? Explain.
2. Do female athletes treat each other differently from the way boys treat each other? Explain.

Section 3

Social Issues in Sport

Key Term

* stacking

Section Preview

Sport contributes to upward mobility among collegiate athletes, but the opportunities are too few. Minorities still face discrimination in sport. Women in sport suffer from gender-based stereotypes. Intercollegiate female athletes do not receive treatment equal to the treatment received by males, although this situation is slowly improving.

Sport and Social Mobility

The autobiographies of star athletes often point to sport as their way out of poverty. One educator once predicted that "football would enable a whole generation of young men in the coal fields of Pennsylvania to turn their backs on the mines that employed their fathers" (Rudolph, 1962:378). Many athletes do use sport as a means out of their equivalent "coal fields," and many minority members work their way out of poverty through sport. It is also true that the average salaries of professionals are very high (Leonard, 1998). Even so, let's examine this alleged relationship between sport and social mobility.

Does sport really promote social mobility?   Participating in sport increases the likelihood of improving a person's place in the stratification structure. Whatever sport they play, college athletes tend to be better educated, earn more money, and have higher occupational prestige than their fathers. This is the very definition of upward social mobility. And in these terms, college athletes as a whole are more successful than college students who do not participate in sports (Leonard, 1998). Although this finding is meaningful, it has not settled the debate regarding how much sport promotes upward mobility for minorities.

Sports have long been an important basis for stratification in high schools.

Does sport promote upward mobility for minorities?   Some people argue that sport is a social class escalator for minorities. They point to Michael Jordan, Deion Sanders, and Sammy Sosa, among others. A different viewpoint argues that the emphasis on sport is harmful because it diverts attention away from learning the academic and business-related skills necessary for success in mainstream American society. Because of the lure of high salaries and prestige, many aspiring minority athletes fail to develop alternative career plans. Minority members who spend their youth sharpening their athletic skills at the expense of their general education will very likely be casualties of an unrealizable dream of wealth and glory (Lapchick and Matthews, 1999).

The phenomenal success of Michael Jordon is frequently used to prove that sport is a path of upward mobility for minorities. Is Jordon a typical example?

Some convincing evidence supports those who see sport as a barrier to upward mobility for minorities. Figure 15.3 shows that there are over one million high school football players. Just under 60,000 of these players become college football players. And 1,600 of these college players become professional players. Thus, the probability that a high school football player will make it to the pros is less than two-tenths of one percent. Similarly, a high school baseball player has a 0.2 percent chance of becoming a major leaguer. The odds are even worse for a high school basketball player, who has a 0.1 percent probability of making it to the National Basketball Association. Moreover, those who become professional athletes have short careers on the average: one to seven years for baseball players, four to six years for basketball players, and four and one-half years for football players.

Of course, this does not mean minority athletes should not enjoy the benefits of a collegiate sport. To be sure, some athletes have received good college educations who may otherwise not have had the chance. It does argue, however, that no high school athlete—minority or white, for that matter—should rely solely on sport as a ticket up the stratification structure.

	Number of Players in High School	Percentage Advancing from High School to College	Number of Players in College	Percentage Advancing from College to Professional Level	Number of Players at Professional Level	Percentage Advancing from High School to Professional Level
MALES						
Football	1,002,734	6%	57,593	3%	1,643	0.16%
Basketball	541,130	3%	15,874	2%	348	0.06%
Baseball	451,701	6%	25,938	3%	750	0.17%
Ice hockey	27,245	13%	3,647	18%	648	2.38%
Total	2,022,811	5%	103,052	3%	3,389	0.17%
FEMALES						
Basketball	451,600	3%	14,445	1%	132	0.03%
Golf	49,690	6%	3,108	2%	52	0.10%
Tennis	159,740	5%	8,314	2%	150	0.09%
Total	661,030	4%	25,867	1%	334	0.05%
Grand Total	2,683,841	5%	128,919	3%	3,723	0.14%

Figure 15.3 High School Athletes' Chances of Advancing to the Pros. *This table shows the slim chance that high school athletes have to play a professional sport. Does this surprise you?*

Sources: National Federation of State High School Associations, 1999–2000.

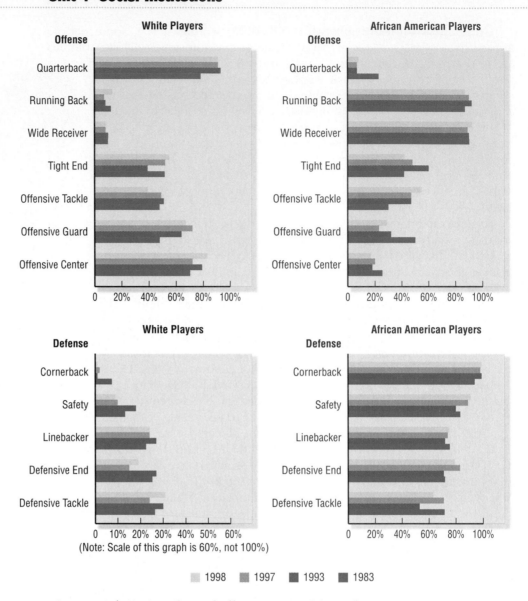

Figure 15.4 National Football League Positions, by Race.   *Do you think that these data support the presence of stacking in the NFL?*

Source: Northeastern University, Center for the Study of Sport in Society, 2001.

Sport and Racism

One sign of systematic discrimination shows up in what is called *stacking*. In **stacking,** players are assigned to less central positions on the basis of race or ethnicity. "Central" positions are those that involve leadership and decision-making responsibilities and thus offer a greater likelihood of influencing the outcome of the game. Historically, minorities have more often been assigned to positions requiring relatively little interaction and coordination with other players. In football, for example, African American quarterbacks are rare, while the proportions of African Americans in many defensive and other less central positions are high. (See Figure 15.4.)

stacking
assignment of players to less central positions on the basis of race or ethnicity

Such discrimination has important economic consequences, because the positions occupied by most African Americans have high injury rates that cut careers short. Both salaries and pension benefits are reduced as a result.

Is there salary fairness in professional sports?   Discrimination in salary at the professional level exists. African Americans in the major professional sports are, on the average, paid as much as or more than their white counterparts. It is only when level of performance is controlled that discrimination appears—African Americans have lower average salaries than whites for the same level of performance. In other words, African Americans must perform better than whites to avoid pay discrimination (Eitzen and Sage, 1997).

What other areas of discrimination have been found?   Minority former athletes profit much less than their white colleagues from personal appearances and commercial endorsements. They also lose out in sports-related careers when their playing days are over. While approximately 78 percent of players in the National Basketball Association (NBA) are black, only about 16 percent of radio and television NBA sports announcers are African American, and only about 3 percent of the announcers are Latino.

At the professional level, there are few minorities represented in the power structure—head coaches, general managers, owners, executives, commissioners. In 1989, Bill White became the first African American to head a major professional sports league. As of 2001, only one major sport franchise in the U.S. was owned by minorities. And no minorities in either the NFL or Major League Baseball were board chairs, presidents, or CEOs. In 2000, Michael Jordan became president of basketball operations for the NBA's Washington Wizards. In the following year, despite the fact that the deal would give him partial ownership of the team, Jordan resigned and signed a player's contract. There were only three African American head coaches in professional football in 2001, six African American baseball managers, and one Latino baseball manager. Only 21 percent of NBA head coaches were members of minority groups in 2001.

Student Web Activity
Visit the *Sociology and You* Web site at soc.glencoe.com and click on **Chapter 15—Student Web Activities** for an activity on sport and sexism.

Minorities are well represented as players in major U.S. sports. However, after their playing days are over, minorities are underrepresented in positions of power within their sport.

Snapshot of America

Who Are the Biggest Baseball Fans?

Baseball fans used to be young working-class white males. Today's fans are older and more affluent but still pre-dominantly white and male. The relative lack of African American fans might be traced to baseball's traditional racist policies on the field and in the front office.

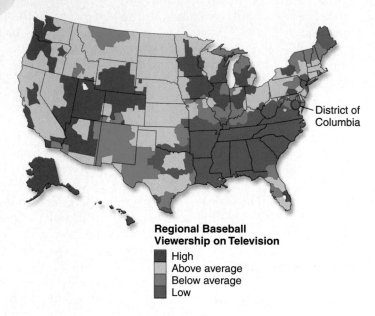

District of Columbia

Regional Baseball Viewership on Television

- High
- Above average
- Below average
- Low

Interpreting the Map

1. Do you see any regional patterns in the rates of baseball viewership? Describe.
2. How do you explain these patterns?
3. As a baseball fan, are you similar to or different from the general pattern in your state? Why?

Adapted from *Latitudes and Attitudes: An Atlas of American Tastes, Trends, Politics, and Passions*. Boston: Little, Brown.

Sexism in Sport

Racial and ethnic minorities have not been the only victims of prejudice and discrimination in sport. Women have experienced sexism in athletics. The cultural roots of sexism date back at least as far as the ancient Greeks. Greek gods were depicted as athletic, strong, powerful, competitive, rational, physical, and intellectual. Many Greek goddesses were passive, beautiful, physically weak, supportive, unathletic, and sexually attractive. (The few active, strong goddesses were usually not attractive to nor attracted by men. To Greek males, women who were physically or intellectually superior to them were unfeminine.) These gender definitions have survived in large part for the past 2,500 years. Their influence is felt in sport just as it is in other aspects of social life.

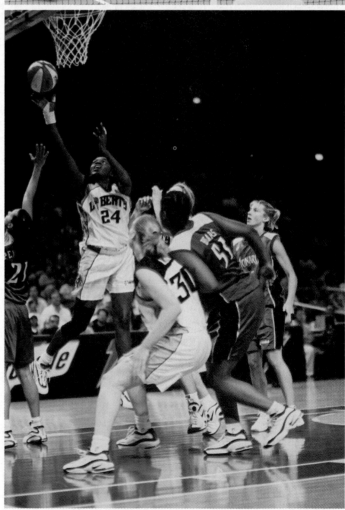

What are some of the consequences of sexism?   Stereotypes have traditionally discouraged females from playing sports. For centuries, the idea that playing sports makes females more masculine has been widespread. To be an athlete, females were told, is to be unfeminine. This stigma discouraged many females from participating in athletics and tyrannized many of those who did. Another barrier was the old, discredited argument that sports harm a woman's health, particularly her ability to have children.

Sexism has denied females equal access to organized sports. At the local level, resistance to female participation in sports continues to exist. It was not until the mid-1970s that, under legal threat, the national Little League organization ended its males-only policy. Only when the 1972 Educational Amendment Act (Title IX) was passed were public high schools and colleges required to offer females equal access to sports. Originally, Title IX was interpreted as providing equal opportunity in "all" sport programs of institutions receiving federal funds. Ambiguities in Title IX have led to many legal suits. Important issues remain unresolved. Currently, the courts favor matching the ratio of males and females in a school's athletic programs to their proportionate numbers in the student body of that school (Blum, 1993).

Why has the percentage of women coaching women's programs declined?   Women are still denied equal access to the power structure of sport (Lapchick and Matthews, 2001). What's more, although Title IX increased equality for female athletes, it led to a decrease in the number of coaching and administrative positions held by women. In the early 1970s, women's intercollegiate teams were headed almost entirely by women. As of 2000, more than half of the NCAA women's teams were coached by men. (See Figure 15.5 on page 518.) Less than 25 percent of all women's programs were headed by a female administrator, and females held

Although sexism in sports has been decreasing, women athletes continue to suffer from inequalities.

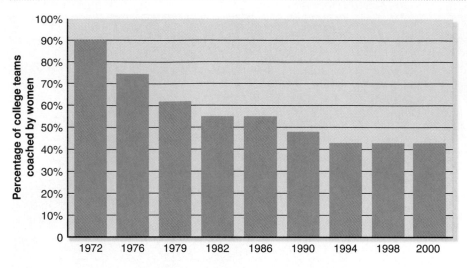

Figure 15.5 Percentage of College Women's Athletic Teams Coached by Women. *What is most interesting to you about these data?*

Source: Center for the Study of Sport in Society, 2001.

You don't save a pitcher for tomorrow. Tomorrow it may rain.

Leo Durocher
baseball coach

only one-third of all administrative jobs in women's programs (Acosta and Carpenter).

Ironically, Title IX may be one reason for this decline. As the money and prestige associated with women's programs have increased, men have found these coaching jobs much more attractive. And conflict theorists believe that men, who are overwhelmingly in charge of athletic programs and who have the power to make hiring decisions, are more likely to choose men as coaches (Nixon and Frey, 1996).

Are women represented at the national level? Currently, professional sports for women include a Women's National Basketball Association (WNBA), a volleyball league, a golf tour, and a tennis circuit. As we have already seen, few women athletes make it to the professional ranks. Even those women who become professionals earn significantly less than their male counterparts (Levin, 1996). Golf, for example, is one of the few professional sports offering significant opportunities for women. Still, the leading money winner on the men's tour typically earns more than twice as much as the leading money winner on the women's tour. This disparity is reflected in the total prize money for the Professional Golfers' Association (PGA) and the Ladies Professional Golf Association (LPGA) tours—$185 million for men in 2001; $43.5 million for women.

There are some positive, if small, signs of change. In addition to her Nike commercial, U.S. soccer star Mia Hamm has a lucrative deal with Gatorade. Chamique Holdsclaw, an extremely talented female professional basketball player for the Washington Mystics, obtained an unheard-of (for women athletes) five-year contract with Nike, plus her own signature Holdsclaw shoe (Hammel and Mulrine, 1999).

Section 3 Assessment

1. What advice would you give to a young man or woman planning to become a professional athlete? Use the information in this chapter in your response.
2. How did the Educational Amendment Act of 1972 (Title IX) affect women's sport programs?

Critical Thinking

3. **Analyzing Information** "American females experience more prejudice and discrimination in sport than males." Explain why you agree or disagree with this statement.

Sociology Today

How to Avoid Bigotry in Sport

Sports sociologist J. Coakley supports the concerns of many Native Americans on the issue of team names. He wrote the following article about this issue.

Most of us are not very concerned about the use of Native American names by many athletic teams. But to Native Americans, war whoops and tomahawk chopping portray negative stereotypes.

Using stereotypes to characterize Native Americans in the U.S. is so common that most people don't even realize they are doing it. . . . When these stereotypes are used as a basis for team names, mascots, and logos, sports become a way of perpetuating an ideology that exploits, trivializes, and demeans the history and cultural heritage of Native Americans.

If teachers, administrators, and students in U.S. schools had a deep knowledge of the rich and diverse cultures of Native Americans and realized the discrimination native peoples currently face, they would not use names such as Indians, Redskins, Chiefs, Braves, Savages, Tribe, and Redmen for their teams; they would not allow Anglo students to entertain fans by dressing up as caricatures of Native Americans; and they would not allow fans to mimic Native American chants or act out demeaning stereotypes of war-whooping, tomahawk-chopping Native Americans.

Schools should not use any Native American name or symbol in connection with sport teams unless they do the following:

1. Sponsor a special curriculum to inform students of the history, cultural heritage, and current living conditions of the native group after which their sport teams are named. Unless 70 percent of the students can pass annual tests on this information, schools should drop the names they say are used to "honor" native people.

2. Publish two press releases per year in which information about the heritage and current circumstances of the native peoples honored by their team names is described and analyzed; publish similar materials annually in school newspapers and yearbooks.

3. Once per year, during homecoming or a major sport event, sponsor a special ceremony designed by and for native peoples in the local area, with the purpose of informing students and parents about the people they say they honor with their team names.

Source: Jay J. Coakley, *Sport in Society*. 6th ed. Boston: Irwin McGraw-Hill, 1998, pp. 272–273.

Doing Sociology

Is there a sport symbol in your community or state that might be offensive to Native Americans? Has the existence of this offensive symbol hurt your community or state economically? Explain.

Summary

Section 1: The Nature of Sport

Main Idea: As a social institution, sport fulfills some important societal needs. One of these is helping individuals identify with others members of society. Sport subcultures have developed around both team and individual sports. For this reason, sport is a reflection of society.

Section 2: Theoretical Perspectives and Sport

Main Idea: Functionalists see sport positively, as a means for socializing young people, promoting social integration, providing a releaser for tensions, and developing sound character. Conflict theorists believe that organized sports can be harmful to character development. Symbolic interactionists focus on the self-concepts and relationships developed through sport activities.

Section 3: Social Issues in Sport

Main Idea: Sport contributes to upward mobility among collegiate athletes, but the opportunities are too few. Minorities still face discrimination in sport. Women in sport suffer from gender-based stereotypes. Intercollegiate female athletes do not receive treatment equal to the treatment received by males, although this situation is slowly improving.

SOCIOLOGY Online

Self-Check Quiz
Visit the *Sociology and You* Web site at soc.glencoe.com and click on **Chapter 15—Self-Check Quizzes** to prepare for the chapter test.

Reviewing Vocabulary

Complete each sentence using each term once.

a. sport
b. Title IX
c. sports subculture
d. functionalist perspective on sport
e. conflict perspective on sport
f. symbolic

interactionist perspective on sport
g. social mobility in sport
h. stacking
i. salary equity
j. sexism in sport

1. The assumption that all athletes are paid based on level of performance is known as _____.

2. The perspective that is most concerned with the relationships of those involved is called _____.

3. Using sport to improve a position in the stratification structure is known as _____.

4. _____ is the assigning of less central positions to minorities.

5. _____ is the perspective that emphasizes the positive contributions of sport to society.

6. A set of norms that surround a particular sport is called _____.

7. _____ is the perspective that sees sport as an institution in which the most powerful oppress, manipulate, coerce, and exploit others.

8. _____ is a set of competitive activities in which winners and losers are determined by physical performance within a set of established rules.

9. _____ was established with the intent of increasing opportunity for female athletes in school settings.

10. The defining of sport as a masculine activity is known as _____.

Reviewing the Facts

1. Why does sport play an important role in American society?

2. According to the functionalists, what is one purpose of sport?

3. What is the conflict theorists' view of sport as an institution?

4. Outline and summarize sport from the three sociological perspectives. Create a diagram similar to the one below to record your answer.

PERSPECTIVE	SUMMARY
Functionalist	
Conflict Theorist	
Symbolic Interactionist	

5. Identify the relationship between sport and social mobility.

Thinking Critically

1. **Drawing Conclusions** High school athletes with superior skills are often given extraordinary help in meeting college entrance requirements, including coaching for achievement and aptitude tests. Many students feel this is unfair to those who have higher grades but aren't accepted. Others justify the practice. They point out that athletics bring in lots of money for colleges. They also say that athletes have skills as rare as high intelligence and so deserve their sports scholarships every bit as much as others deserve academic scholarships. Do you think it is fair for athletes to be given help meeting college entrance requirements?

2. **Analyzing Information** The use of mascots is at the center of a current debate in sports. Some schools have made efforts to change their school nicknames and mascots so as not to offend various groups that might have been negatively portrayed by these mascots and nicknames. Do you think that schools and teams have an obligation to take such actions? Or should teams be allowed to retain their traditional nicknames and mascots?

3. **Making Generalizations** Typically, the rewards associated with a particular skill or occupation tell us how much society values that skill or occupation. Sports superstars are rewarded very highly. Relatively few "superstars" in the field of teaching or medicine make salaries comparable to those of successful professional athletes. Do you believe this indicates that U.S. society doesn't value education and health care as highly as sports? What other factors might influence compensation and salary?

4. **Making Inferences** Nearly 80 percent of the players in the National Basketball Association are African American, while over 90 percent of the members of the National Hockey League are white. Baseball and football are more evenly mixed. How would you explain the lack of African Americans in hockey and their apparent overrepresentation in basketball? (See also Activity 3 on the following page.)

5. **Evaluating Information** In the National Basketball Association draft, the best players go to the teams that completed the previous season with the worst records. Why do you think the NBA uses this approach instead of allowing the best players to go to the teams with the most prestige, status, and monetary resources?

6. **Applying Concepts** Here's a thought experiment to try. Using your answer to number 5 above, see if you can apply your reasoning to the institution of the family. Imagine that NBA teams are like families in various social classes and that each generation is like a season of professional basketball. Wouldn't it be fair to ask the winning families (those at the top of the social class ladder) not to pass on their advantages to their offspring? In other words, for the competition to be fair, wealthier families should not be allowed to go to the best schools but instead should be sent to the schools with the fewest resources. The logic used here is that the best and most talented succeed anywhere. What is the fallacy in this argument?

7. Drawing Conclusions In referring to the way a crowd of people can motivate a team of players, Emile Durkheim once said, "There are occasions when this strengthening and vivifying action of society is especially apparent. In the midst of an assembly animated by a common passion, we become susceptible of acts and sentiments of which we are incapable when reduced to our own forces." Do you believe that a home court or home field advantage really exists? Do players rise to the occasion when cheered on by the home crowd? Are there ever times when athletes might play better when not at home?

8. Evaluating Information Pretend that you are attending a professional tennis match with an economist, a political scientist, a psychologist, and a sociologist. Link each of the questions below to the discipline most likely to give a complete answer.

a. How did the hot dogs get to be five dollars?

b. Why do some athletes fall apart after a bad call?

c. What is the socioeconomic status of the players?

d. Does tennis reflect mainstream values?

e. How did Americans lose their dominance in this sport?

f. Why does it seem that all tennis courts are located in wealthy neighborhoods?

Sociology Projects

1. Sports and Statistics The sports section is a great place to examine how statistics are used. For one week follow a team in any sport that is currently in season. Track several team and individual statistics. Do dramatic changes occur in the statistics, or are the changes insignificant? Can you offer any reason for the change or lack of change? Compare your team's statistics with those of a classmate's team. Analyze the validity of the statistics. Do they accurately tell the story, or can statistics deceive us?

2. The Home Court Advantage Interview athletes who participate in several of your school's sports. Ask the following questions.

a. What are the advantages of playing at home?

b. What are the disadvantages of playing on the road?

c. What factors contribute to home court advantage?

d. What factors hinder better performances on the road?

e. Do you ever prefer to play at home?

f. Compare your notes with those of your classmates to see if there is consensus.

3. The Cost of Sports Research suggests that participation in sports reflects geographic location and economic conditions. For instance, basketball is an urban game that does not require a lot of money to play. All one needs is a ball and a place to shoot. Conduct research on other major sports—football, baseball, hockey, skiing, tennis, and golf. Try to determine where and by whom these sports tend to be played. How much does it cost an individual who is not professional to play these sports? Share your results with the class.

4. Minorities in Coaching and Management The text discusses underrepresentation of minorities in coaching and management positions. To find out whether this pattern still holds, conduct a quick survey of your own. (If your teacher allows, you may want to work in groups.) Concentrating on professional sports, what are the names of coaches and managers from all the teams in a national league? Use the Internet to find answers to these questions. (Most professional sports leagues include at least twenty-five teams.) Identify as many of the coaches and managers as possible by race and ethnicity. What is the proportion of minority coaches and managers in your sample?

5. Sports Apparel One way to see the impact of sports on U.S. society is to walk the halls of any American high school. (You may rather observe people at a mall or shopping center if your school does not allow clothes with commercial logos.) To get an idea how many people at your school wear clothes that represent sports teams or sports activities, sit in one place for fifteen minutes and simply count the number of students and teachers wearing sports clothing. Are many students wearing clothing representing their own high school teams? Or do most favor logos from local college or professional teams? Do you think wearing team clothes fosters a sense of identification with the team?

6. **Sports in Film** Numerous movie videos deal with sports themes. Select a video, and write a report on it using concepts discussed in the chapter. For example, the film *Jerry McGuire* touches on player salaries and issues of race, among other themes. Present your report to the class.

7. **Sports as a Social Institution** Imagine that you are a visitor from a planet where the institution of sport does not exist. The objective of your visit to Earth is to observe social interactions in sport in order to determine whether sport is an institution that should be established on your planet.

As a "visitor" you attend a game of basketball, football, volleyball and baseball. What conclusions would you make regarding the social interactions of those involved in the game?

Consider and list any perceived negative or positive interactions. Analyze those interactions as either being constructive or destructive to the development of desirable social interactions on your planet.

Write a one-page essay that summarizes your findings and supports your decision to recommend or to not recommend that sport be established as an institution on your planet.

Technology Activity

1. Using your favorite search engine, do a search for "sociology of sport."

   a. How many web page matches did your search find? What does that indicate to you about the importance of this subject?

   b. Go to the electronic journal *Sociology of Sport On-Line* (sosol) at http://physed.otago.ac.nz/sosol/. Review the table of contents of the most recent issue. What types of topics are covered by the authors?

   c. Click on Overview. Where is this journal published? Why was it started?

Chapter 15
Enrichment Reading
We Don't Like Football, Do We?

by D. Stanley Eitzen

◆

If you grew up female in America, you heard this: *Sports are unfeminine.* And this: *Girls who play sports are tomboys.* You got this message: *Real women don't spend their free time sliding feet-first into home plate or smacking their fists into soft leather gloves.*

So you didn't play or you did play and either way you didn't quite fit. You didn't fit in your body—didn't learn to live there, breathe there, feel dynamic and capable. Or maybe you fell madly, passionately in love with sports but didn't quite fit in society, never saw yourself—basketball player, cyclist, golfer—reflected in movies, billboards, magazines.

Or you took a middle ground, shying away at first but then later sprinting toward aerobics and weight lifting and in-line skating, **relishing** your increasing endurance and grace and strength. Even then, though, you sensed that something was wrong: all the ads and articles seemed to focus on weight loss and beauty. While those may have inspired you to get fit in the first place, there are more important things, you now know, than how you looked. No one seemed to be talking about pride, pleasure, power, possibility.

If you grew up male in America, you heard this: Boys who *don't* play sports are sissies or . . . [homosexuals]. And this: Don't throw like a girl. You got this message: Sports are a male initiation rite, as fundamental and natural as shaving and deep voices—a **prerequisite,** somehow, to becoming an American man. So you played football or soccer or baseball and felt competent, strong, and bonded with your male buddies. Or you didn't play and risked ridicule.

Whether we were inspired by Babe Ruth or Babe Didrikson or neither, and whether we played kickball with our brothers or sisters or both, all of us, female and male, learned to associate sports prowess and sports privilege with masculinity. Even if the best athlete in the neighborhood was a girl, we learned from newspapers, television, and from our own parents' prejudices that batting, catching, throwing, and jumping are not neutral, human activities, but somehow more naturally a male domain. **Insidiously** our culture's reverence for men's professional sports and its silence about women's athletic accomplishments shaped, defined, and limited how we felt about ourselves as women and men.

. . . You may have noticed that boys are no longer the only ones shooting baskets in public parks. One girl often joins the boys now, her hair dark with sweat, her body alert as a squirrel's. Maybe they don't pass her the ball. Maybe she grabs it anyway, squeezes mightily through the barricade of bodies, leaps skyward, feet flying.

Or she teams with other girls. Gyms fill these days with the rowdy sounds of women hard at play: basketballs seized by calloused hands, sneakers squealing like shocked mice. The players' high, urgent voices resonate, too—"Here!" "Go!"—and right then nothing exists for them except the ball, the shifting constellation of women, the chance to be fluid, smooth, alive.

What Does it Mean **?**

insidiously
developing in a stealthy and harmful manner so gradually as to become established before being apparent

prerequisite
required as a prior condition to something

relishing
being pleased with or gratified by

This West Virginia high school student is a starter on her school's only varsity basketball team.

What does this mean? What does it mean that everywhere, women are running, shooting baskets, getting sweaty and exhausted and euphoric? What changes when a woman becomes an athlete?

Everything.

On playing fields and in gyms across America, women are engaged in a contest with higher stakes than trophies or ribbons or even prize money. Through women's play, and through their huddles behind the scenes, they are deciding who American women will be. Not just what games they will play, but what role they will play in this still-young nation. Not only what their bodies will look like, but what their bodies can do.

Adapted from Mariah Burton Nelson. "We Don't Like Football, Do We?" in D. Stanley Eitzen, *Sport in Contemporary Society: An Anthology,* 5th ed., St. Martin's Press, Inc., 1996, pp. 25–26.

Read and React

1. State briefly the main point of this article.
2. What do you think is the author's viewpoint on the relationship between gender and sport? Do you agree with him?
3. Do you believe that attitudes in the United States regarding female participation in sport are changing? Explain.
4. From which theoretical perspective is the author writing? Use examples to illustrate that perspective.

CHAPTER 16
Population and Urbanization

USING Your Sociological Imagination

Suppose you read the following story in your local newspaper.

On October 12, 1999, the United Nations officially declared that the world's population had reached six billion. United Nations Secretary-General Kofi Annan was visiting Sarajevo, Bosnia, when the historic milestone was reached. To symbolize the event, he chose a baby boy born in a local clinic at two minutes after midnight to be named "Baby Six Billion."

How big is six billion? If you counted a hundred numbers every minute for eight hours a day, five days a week, it would take you five hundred years to reach six billion!

According to Zero Population Growth (ZPG), the world's population is currently growing at a rate of 78 million people per year. If asked about the reason for this rapid world population growth, what would you say? Like most people, you would probably refer to the high birth rate in developing countries. You could point out that every year, 94 million infants are born—equal to the population of Mexico—or that every time you watch a half-hour TV program, 4,860 infants are born.

This explanation, however, is only half of the story. It leaves out the other side of the equation—the death rate. The population in these countries is growing rapidly because their birth rates remain high while their death rates have dropped sharply, thanks to modern medicine, improved sanitation, and better hygiene. In this chapter, we look at demography and discuss why this issue is important to sociologists.

Sections

1. **The Dynamics of Demography**
2. **World Population**
3. **The Urban Transition**
4. **Urban Ecology**

Learning Objectives

After reading this chapter, you will be able to

❖ identify the three population processes.

❖ relate the ideas of Thomas Malthus to population changes.

❖ predict world population trends.

❖ trace the development of preindustrial and modern cities.

❖ compare and contrast four theories of city growth.

SOCIOLOGY Online

Chapter Overview
Visit the *Sociology and You* Web site at soc.glencoe.com and click on **Chapter 16— Chapter Overviews** to preview chapter information.

529

Section 1

The Dynamics of Demography

Key Terms

- population
- demography
- fertility
- fecundity
- crude birth rate

- fertility rate
- total fertility rate
- mortality
- life span
- life expectancy

- crude death rate
- infant mortality rate
- migration
- gross migration rate
- net migration rate

Section Preview

Demography is the scientific study of population. The collection of population data is very important today, in part because of its use by government and industry. Demographers consider three population processes when looking at population change: fertility, mortality, and migration.

population
a group of people living in a particular place at a specified time

demography
the scientific study of population

The Changing Population

Sociologists study population because it affects social structure, especially in crowded areas. They look for patterns that will help them understand and predict how groups of people will

Social structures reflect the ability of the land to support people.

behave. For example, they might examine the relationship between population growth and politics. We know that historically the growth of minorities in the United States has benefited Democrats more than Republicans (Tilove, 1999). But the situation today is different with respect to Latinos. Now the largest minority in the United States, Latinos are not firmly aligned with either political party. Regardless of political affiliation, the growth of minority populations affects how congressional districts are drawn and is one reason why census taking can be a controversial topic. Or sociologists might study trends in population shifts, such as the aging baby boomers, to help plan for hospitals and long-term nursing facilities.

How do sociologists define population?   A **population** is a group of people living in a particular place at a specified time. The scientific study of population is called **demography** (*demos* is a Greek word that means "people"). To study population, demographers look at many factors, including the number of people (size); how and where they are located (distribution); what groups make up the population (composition); and the ages represented in the population (age structure). Demographers also analyze three processes: birth *(fertility)*, death *(mortality)*, and movement from one place to another *(migration)*. Major changes in populations come from one or all of these three processes. In the following sections, we look at the factors and processes that affect populations.

How might fertility drugs affect the crude birth rate?

Fertility

Fertility measures the actual number of children born to a woman or to a population of women. **Fecundity** is the potential number of children that could be born if every woman reproduced as often as biology allowed. Obviously, fertility rates are much lower than fecundity rates. The highest realistic fecundity rate you could expect from a society would be about fifteen births per woman. The record fertility rate for a group probably is held by the Hutterites, who migrated a century ago from Switzerland to North and South Dakota and Canada. Hutterite women in the 1930s were giving birth to an average of more than twelve children each (Westoff and Westoff, 1971). The Hutterites give us a good estimate of fecundity, because they are the best example of *natural fertility*—the number of children born to women in the absence of conscious birth control (Weeks, 1999).

How is fertility measured?   The **crude birth rate** is the annual number of live births per one thousand members of a population. The crude birth rate varies considerably from one country to another. The crude birth rate for the United States is fifteen per one thousand. Niger, in West Africa, experiences a very high crude birth rate of fifty-three per one thousand; and Germany, a very low rate of nine per one thousand.

To calculate the crude birth rate, divide the annual number of live births by the total population and multiply that number by 1,000.

$$\text{Crude Birth Rate} = \frac{\text{Number of Live Births}}{\text{Total Population}} \times 1{,}000$$

The term *crude* in this case means rough, or approximate. The crude birth rate is approximate because it is based on the entire population rather than just women of child-bearing age. It also ignores the age structure of the population. Both sex and age affect the number of live births in any given year. Consequently, in addition to the crude birth rate, demographers use the **fertility rate**—the annual number of live births per one thousand women

fertility
a measure of the number of children born to a woman or a population of women

fecundity
the maximum rate at which women can physically produce children

crude birth rate
the annual number of live births per one thousand members of a population

fertility rate
the annual number of live births per one thousand women aged fifteen to forty-four

Snapshot of America

Percentage of Population 18 and Under

Many high school students feel that as members of society they are not given enough respect by society. One reason could be that there are too few people in this age bracket to influence policy makers. This map shows the percentage of each state's population aged eighteen years and under.

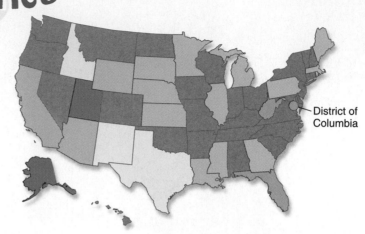

District of Columbia

Percentage of Population 18 and Under
- 29% or more
- 28%–28.9%
- 26%–27.9%
- 24%–25.9%
- 23%–23.9%
- < 23%

Interpreting the Map

1. Which states have the smallest concentrations of young people? Can you explain why?
2. From this map, can you make any generalization about the American population? What additional information would help you to further describe the age structure of the U.S. population? Get that information for your state.

Source: U.S. Bureau of the Census, 2001.

---

total fertility rate
average number of children born to a woman during her lifetime

aged fifteen to forty-four. The rate that is easiest to use is the **total fertility rate,** or the average number of children born to a woman during her lifetime. Currently, total fertility rates in the world range from 5.2 in Africa to 1.4 in Europe.

What other factors influence birth rate?   The birth rate of a population is influenced by both health and social factors. For example, widespread disease (especially rubella, or German measles) causes the birth rate to decline because many pregnancies end in miscarriages. Social factors affecting the birth rate include the average age at marriage, the level of economic development, the availability and use of contraceptives and abortion, the number of women in the labor force, the educational status of women, and social attitudes toward reproduction.

The U.S. birth rate in recent years has shown a steady decline. More couples today consider two children—or even one child—a desirable number. Work patterns have affected the birth rate as well. More American women today are postponing having children until their late twenties and early thirties. As a result, women are having fewer children.

Mortality

Mortality refers to death. To analyze patterns of mortality within a population, sociologists look at *life span* and *life expectancy*. **Life span** is the most advanced age to which humans can survive. We know for sure of a Japanese man who lived nearly 121 years, but few people even approach this age. **Life expectancy** is the average number of years that persons in a given population born at a particular time can expect to live. World life expectancy is sixty-seven years (*World Population Data Sheet,* 2001).

How is mortality measured? The **crude death rate** is figured by dividing the annual number of deaths by the total population and multiplying by 1,000. Like the crude birth rate, the crude death rate varies widely throughout the world. The worldwide average crude death rate is nine per one thousand persons. Looking at specific regions of the world, the death rate varies from a low of six per thousand in Latin America and the Caribbean to a high of fourteen per thousand in Africa and Hungary. The death rate in the United States is about nine per thousand (*World Population Data Sheet,* 2001).

Demographers are also interested in the variations in death rates for specific groups. They have devised *age-specific death rates* to measure the number of deaths per thousand persons in a specific age group, such as fifteen- to nineteen-year-olds or sixty- to sixty-four-year-olds. This allows them to compare the risk of death to members of different groups. Although death eventually comes to everyone, the rate at which it occurs depends on many factors, including age, sex, race, occupation, social class, standard of living, and health care.

The **infant mortality rate**—the number of deaths among infants under one year of age per one thousand live births—is considered a good indicator of the health status of any group. This is because infants are the first to suffer

mortality
deaths within a population

life span
the most advanced age to which humans can survive

life expectancy
the average number of years that persons in a given population born at a particular time can expect to live

crude death rate
the annual number of deaths per thousand members of a population

infant mortality rate
the annual number of deaths among infants under one year of age per one thousand live births

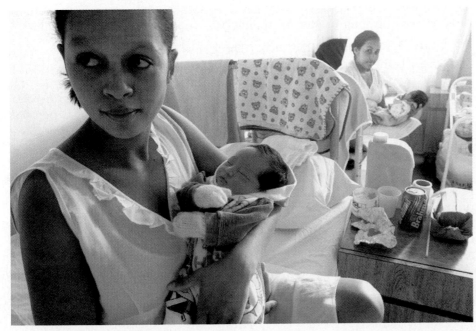

This Brazilian mother attends a local clinic to get health care for her infant.

Figure 16.1 World Population Growth. *This figure shows estimated world population growth to 2150. What factors do you think led to the sharp rise in population around 1850?*

Source: Washington, DC: Population Reference Bureau.

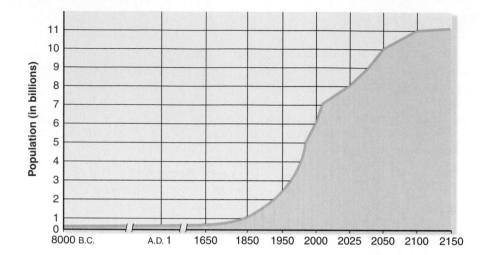

from a lack of good medical care and sanitation. Infants in developing countries are almost eight times more likely to die before their first birthday than infants in the developed nations. Working together, the birth rates, fertility rates, and mortality rates determine the world population growth. (See Figure 16.1.)

Migration

migration
the movement of people from one geographic area to another

Migration refers to the movement of people from one geographic area to another. Migration can occur within a country or between countries. An example of migration from country to country is the resettlement of Asian refugees from Vietnam and Cambodia in countries around the world. Many of the refugees who settle in the United States in one particular city or region later move to another region, thus becoming internal migrants. Anyone who moves from one part of the country to another—say, from New York to Arizona—is engaging in internal migration.

gross migration rate
the number of persons per year per one thousand members of a population who enter or leave a geographic area

How is migration measured?   The **gross migration rate** into or out of an area is the number of persons per one thousand members of a population who enter or leave a geographic area in a given year. *Net migration* is the difference between the number of people entering and leaving an area. Thus, the **net migration rate** is the annual increase or decrease per one thousand members of a population resulting from movement into and out of the population. In 1999, for example, the United States had a net migration rate of about 3.0 per one thousand population. That is, 3.0 more persons per one thousand population entered the country than left the country. It is also possible of course, to have a negative net migration rate showing more people overall left an area than entered it.

net migration rate
the annual increase or decrease per one thousand members of a population resulting from migration into and out of the population

When the U.S. Census Bureau reports migration rates, it refers only to the number of legal immigrants. Many people violate immigration laws to enter the United States. In the 1970s, the issue of illegal immigration—primarily from Latin American and Caribbean countries—became a major concern and continues to be controversial today. There are no precise statistics on either the illegal immigration rate or the total number of illegal aliens living in the United States. Estimates of the current number of illegal aliens range from three million to six million persons.

Another Place

The Graying of Japan

Birth rates and death rates have important social and cultural consequences. In Japan, elders have traditionally been held in high esteem. This tradition is threatened by a combination of two factors: People are generally living longer, and there are fewer young people to support the elders' existence. As they lose respect, many older Japanese now pray in their temples for a quick death.

The population of Japan is aging faster than any on earth, a result of declining birth and death rates. The situation of the elderly of Japan is like the proverbial glass of water that is either half full or half empty, depending on whether the positive or negative aspects of their lives are emphasized. In some ways, elderly Japanese are better off than the elderly of the other developed countries. They hold the position of "honorable elders," a reflection of the Confucian precept of duty owed to parents. Japan even has a national holiday, "Respect for the Aged Day," September 15th, when most offices and factories are closed. Furthermore, a relatively high proportion of elderly Japanese live with their adult children, which is often cited as evidence of the reverence this country pays to the aged.

However, it can also be argued that elderly Japanese are not really so well off and that the "ecstasy years" of old age are losing their rosy glow—if they truly ever had one. Among the more sensational evidence cited are the supposedly high rate of suicide among elderly Japanese and the existence of temples where the elderly go to pray for a quick death. Also, in recent years, the number of activities for or honoring the elderly on their special day have been few and far between. For most Japanese, September 15th is just another holiday.

The particularly rapid pace of aging in Japan and the potential consequences have captured the attention of policymakers and officials. [A major government report] listed population aging along with internationalization and maturation of the economy as the three major challenges for twenty-first-century Japan. Japanese prime ministers have regularly referred to aging as they have set the policy agenda, recognizing that population aging affects many aspects of the society and the economy.

Source: Linda G. Martin, "The Graying of Japan," *Population Bulletin* (Washington, DC).

Thinking It Over

Are the effects of the graying of Japan best explained by functionalism, conflict theory, or symbolic interactionism? Defend your choice.

Section 1 Assessment

1. What three major processes affect the way populations change?
2. How might data about age-specific death rates or population shifts be of use?
3. Why is the infant mortality rate a key statistic for health workers?

Critical Thinking

4. **Drawing Conclusions** Why is demography increasingly important? Think of a way in which the federal government could use some specific piece of demographic data. State how this information would help the government make a policy decision.

You have to enjoy getting older.

Clint Eastwood
actor and director

Section 2

World Population

Key Terms

- census
- doubling time
- exponential growth
- demographic transition theory
- zero population growth
- population momentum
- replacement level
- population control
- family planning
- population pyramid
- dependency ratio

Section Preview

Thomas Malthus (1798) predicted that population size would ultimately outstrip the food supply, resulting in mass starvation and death. The demographic transition theory looks at economic development to predict population patterns. While the rate of world population growth is slowing, the world's population will continue to increase for many years. Population control has become a concern of many governments worried about providing for their future citizens.

census
regularly occurring count of a particular population

The Problem of Population Growth

No organization has actually ever counted all the people in the world. World population figures are a composite of best estimates and national **census** figures where available. While many countries count and categorize people living in those countries, the quality of census data varies a great deal and can be very unreliable. Nevertheless, world population growth patterns can be identified.

If the counting of the population is a problem in developed societies, imagine the difficulty with obtaining accurate counts in developing societies.

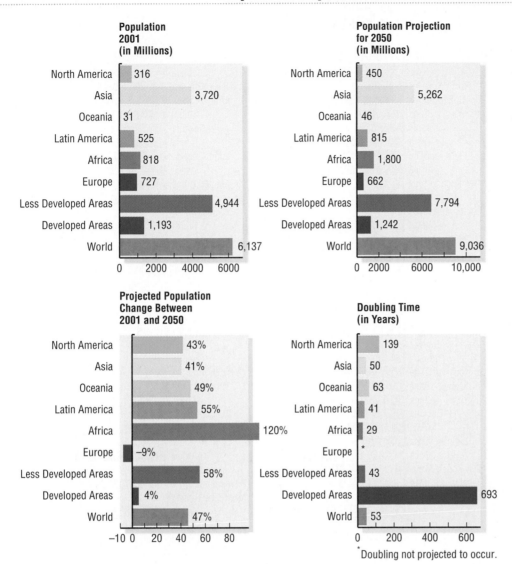

Population 2001 (in Millions)

Region	Population
North America	316
Asia	3,720
Oceania	31
Latin America	525
Africa	818
Europe	727
Less Developed Areas	4,944
Developed Areas	1,193
World	6,137

Population Projection for 2050 (in Millions)

North America	450
Asia	5,262
Oceania	46
Latin America	815
Africa	1,800
Europe	662
Less Developed Areas	7,794
Developed Areas	1,242
World	9,036

Projected Population Change Between 2001 and 2050

North America	43%
Asia	41%
Oceania	49%
Latin America	55%
Africa	120%
Europe	−9%
Less Developed Areas	58%
Developed Areas	4%
World	47%

Doubling Time (in Years)

Region	Years
North America	139
Asia	50
Oceania	63
Latin America	41
Africa	29
Europe	*
Less Developed Areas	43
Developed Areas	693
World	53

*Doubling not projected to occur.

Figure 16.2 Population Projections by Regions of the World. *This graph displays population projections, by regions of the world, from 2001 to 2050. Note the dramatic difference in population doubling time between less developed areas and developed areas.*

Source: Adapted from *World Population Data Sheet, 2001.*

Online **UPDATE**
Visit soc.glencoe.com and click on **Textbook Updates–Chapter 16** for an update of the data.

Rapid world population growth is a relatively recent phenomenon. In fact, your grandparents have seen more population growth during their lifetimes than occurred during the preceding four million years. An estimated 250 million people were on the earth in A.D. 1. (Refer back to Figure 16.1 on page 534.) It was not until 1650 that the world's population doubled, to half a billion. The second doubling occurred in 1800, bringing the world population to one billion. By 1930, another doubling had taken place. Less than fifty years after that, in 1976, a fourth doubling raised the world's population to four billion. At the current growth rate, the world's population is expected to double again in about fifty years and will approach eight billion persons by the year 2025. As you can see, the number of years between each doubling of the population—called, for obvious reasons, the **doubling time**—is getting shorter and shorter (*World Population Data Sheet,* 1999). Figure 16.2 breaks down world population projections by region. Figure 16.3 on the next page looks at key demographic statistics by world regions.

doubling time
number of years needed to double the base population size

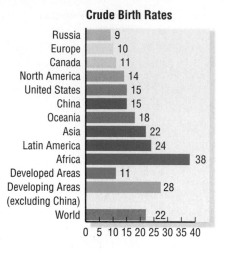

Crude Birth Rates

Russia	9
Europe	10
Canada	11
North America	14
United States	15
China	15
Oceania	18
Asia	22
Latin America	24
Africa	38
Developed Areas	11
Developing Areas (excluding China)	28
World	22

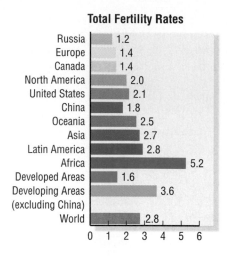

Total Fertility Rates

Russia	1.2
Europe	1.4
Canada	1.4
North America	2.0
United States	2.1
China	1.8
Oceania	2.5
Asia	2.7
Latin America	2.8
Africa	5.2
Developed Areas	1.6
Developing Areas (excluding China)	3.6
World	2.8

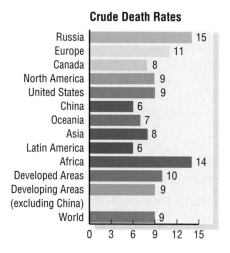

Crude Death Rates

Russia	15
Europe	11
Canada	8
North America	9
United States	9
China	6
Oceania	7
Asia	8
Latin America	6
Africa	14
Developed Areas	10
Developing Areas (excluding China)	9
World	9

Infant Mortality Rates

Russia	16
Europe	9
Canada	6
North America	7
United States	7
China	31
Oceania	28
Asia	55
Latin America	31
Africa	88
Developed Areas	8
Developing Areas (excluding China)	67
World	56

exponential growth
growth in which the amount
of increase is added to the
base figure each time period

Why is the world's population growing so fast?   The population has increased so dramatically in part because of the way population increases. We are accustomed to thinking in terms of *linear growth,* whereby amounts increase arithmetically (as in the progression 1, 2, 3, 4, 5 . . .). Population, however, does not grow linearly. It follows the principle of **exponential growth,** and increases geometrically (as in the progression 2, 4, 8, 16, 32). With exponential growth, the *amount* of increase is greater each time period even though the *rate* of increase remains the same. This is because each increase is added to the base amount and becomes part of the calculation for the next rise.

A classic example of exponential growth follows: The story tells of a clever minister who presented a beautiful chess set to his king. In return, he asked only that the king give one grain of rice for the first square on the chessboard; two grains, or double the amount, for the second square; four (doubling again) for the third; and so forth. The king, not being mathematically minded, agreed and ordered the rice brought forth. The eighth square required 128 grains, and the twelfth took more than a pound of rice. Long before reaching the sixty-fourth square, the king's coffers were depleted. Even today, the world's richest king could not produce enough rice to fill the final square. It would require more than 200 billion tons, or the equivalent of the world's current total production of rice for the next 653 years.

If a population is growing at 1 percent per year, it takes seventy years to double. For example, suppose the population of a city was 50,000 in 1800. At a growth rate of 1 percent, that population would grow to 100,000 in 1870. By 1940 it would reach 200,000; by 2010, 400,000. Recalling the chessboard example, you can see that even a 1 percent growth rate can have serious consequences. The number of people added each year becomes part of the total population, which then increases by another 1 percent in the following year.

Malthus and Population Growth

Concern about population is not new. In 1798, Thomas Robert Malthus, an English minister and economist, published *An Essay on the Principle of Population*. In his essay, Malthus described relationships between population growth and economic development. Here are the key concepts in his theory.

❖ Population, if left unchecked, will exceed the food supply. This is because population increases exponentially, while the food supply does not.

❖ Checks on population can be *positive* or *preventive*. Positive factors are events or conditions that increase mortality. They include famine, disease, and war. Preventive factors decrease fertility and include sexual abstinence and marrying at a later age. (Remember that at the time Malthus wrote there was no reliable birth control. For this conservative minister, sexual abstinence was the only acceptable way to reduce the number of births.)

❖ For the poor, any improvement in income is eaten up in additional births. This leads to lower per-person food consumption, lower standards of living, and eventually death.

❖ The wealthy and well educated already exercise preventive checks.

English minister and economist Thomas Malthus wrote about the ability of the food supply to keep up with population growth.

How did Malthus apply his theory to population control? Malthus believed that positive checks on population growth could be avoided through education of the poor. With education, he wrote, the poor would raise their standard of living and choose to have smaller families. That part of Malthus's theory is not generally known, however, because he is most remembered for his dire predictions that overpopulation would result in famine and poverty.

The Demographic Transition

Although wrong in some of his key assumptions, Malthus had a lasting impact on population study. His is not the only theory, however. Developed

Figure 16.4 Stages of the Demographic Transition.
This figure illustrates the demographic transition. Stage 1 begins with small population growth due to a balance between birth rates and death rates (both at high levels). In Stage 2, population grows dramatically because the death rate decreases so much faster than the birth rate. Population growth begins to slow in Stage 3, when the birth rate belatedly drops sharply. Stage 4 is again a condition of smaller population growth because birth rates and death rates come into balance (both at low levels).

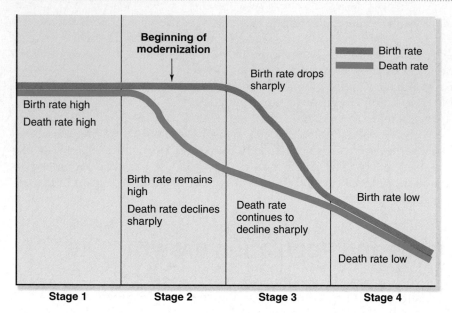

demographic transition theory theory that population growth is a function of the level of economic development in a country

nations have followed a pattern of population growth different from that predicted by Malthus's theory. The **demographic transition theory** looks at the stages of economic development in a country to make predictions about population growth. This theory takes into consideration two things Malthus did not predict—agricultural productivity and reliable methods of birth control. Demographic transition theory describes four stages of population growth. (See Figure 16.4 shown above.)

❖ Stage 1. Both the birth rate and the death rate are high. Population growth is slow. No countries are at this stage today.

❖ Stage 2. The birth rate remains high, but the death rate drops sharply because of modernizing factors such as sanitation, increased food production, and medical advances. The rate of population growth is very high. Most sub-Saharan African countries are presently at this stage.

❖ Stage 3. The birth rate declines sharply, but because the death rate continues to go down, population growth is still rapid. Many Latin American countries are currently at this stage.

❖ Stage 4. Both the birth rate and the death rate are low, and the population grows slowly if at all. Anglo America, Europe, and Japan are at this stage today.

Future World Population Growth

World population growth has reached a turning point. After more than two hundred years of increase, the annual population growth rate is declining. The current growth rate is 1.3 percent, compared with the peak of 2.04 percent in the late 1960s. Moreover, the rate is projected to drop to zero by the year 2100.

But as we have seen, despite the reduction in the annual growth rate and birth rate, the world's population will continue to increase. Nearly seven billion people are expected to inhabit the globe by 2010. Throughout the first half of the twenty-first century, the annual growth rate is expected to decline until world population stabilizes at about eleven billion people. (See Figure 16.5.) At this point, the world will have reached **zero population growth**—when deaths are balanced by births so that the population does not increase (*World Population Data Sheet,* 2001).

Contrary to popular belief, limiting the average family size to two children does not immediately produce zero population growth. There is a time lag of sixty to seventy years because of the high proportion of young women of childbearing age in the world's population. Even if each of these women had only two children, the world population would grow.

The time lag is what demographers call **population momentum.** The growth of the world's population, like a huge boulder rolling down a mountain, cannot be stopped immediately. But the sooner the momentum of current population growth is halted, the better. The sooner the world fertility rate reaches the **replacement level** (the rate at which people replace themselves without adding to the population) the sooner zero population growth will be reached. The ultimate size of the world's population, when it does stop growing, depends greatly on the timing of reaching replacement level. To state it another way, for each decade it takes to reach replacement level, the world's population will increase by 15 percent.

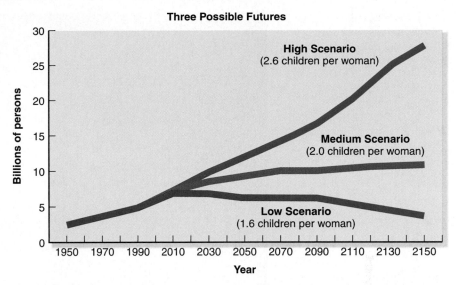

Figure 16.5 Long-Range Projections of World Population: 2000–2150.
The United Nations' estimate of future growth is based on three different assumptions. The high scenario would push world population growth to over 27 billion. The medium scenario would result in a world population of about 11 billion. The low scenario would leave the world population at about 4 billion.

Source: United Nations, *Long-Range World Population Projections,* 1999.

zero population growth
situation in which deaths are balanced by births so that the population does not increase

population momentum
inability to stop population growth immediately because of previous high rate of growth

replacement level
birth rate at which a couple replaces itself without adding to the population

population control
attempts by government to control birth rates

Population Control

As discussed earlier, death rates in both developing and developed nations have already dropped dramatically. Any significant progress in curbing world population growth must concentrate on lowering birth rates. **Population control** refers to the conscious attempt to regulate population size through national birth control programs.

Is government-sponsored population control new? Historically, most societies were more concerned with increasing the population than with overpopulation. Many births were needed to offset the high death rates from disease and poor hygiene. With surplus populations, aggressive nations were able to maintain larger armies. Agricultural societies needed large numbers of people to work the land. Aging parents wanted to be more secure in old age. High birth rates were also encouraged in countries with religious laws against birth control.

European countries, such as Germany, have been very successful in controlling population growth through family planning.

Since the middle of the twentieth century, however, more (but certainly not all) governments have come to view high birth rates as a threat to their national well being. By 1990, most countries had in place formal programs to reduce birth rates. Government policies for population control range from voluntary to compulsory.

What is voluntary population control?   The voluntary use of population control methods is generally known as **family planning.** Governments that support family planning provide information and services that help couples have only the number of children they want. Voluntary government policies range from indirect means such as family planning education to direct means such as distributing birth control materials at health clinics.

Even when effective, however, family planning programs merely enable families to achieve their *desired* family size. Unfortunately for effective population control, the desired family size in many nations is quite high. The average preferred family size (number of children) in African nations is 7.1; in Middle-Eastern nations, 5.1; in Latin American nations, 4.3; and in Asian Pacific nations, 4.0. In European countries, the average preferred family size ranges from 2.1 to 2.8.

How successful is voluntary population control?   Family planning has succeeded in Taiwan, where the birth rate had fallen below replacement level by 2000. Taiwan's family planning efforts were launched under very favorable conditions. When the Japanese withdrew from Taiwan after World War II, they left behind a labor force trained for industrial work. Consequently, the Taiwanese were able to use this advantage to build an expanding economy. With economic development came a decline in both birth and death rates. In short, the Taiwanese went through the demographic transition fairly rapidly.

India was a different story. Family planning there got off to a very slow start, and the country has been unable to reduce the rate of population growth through voluntary means. Family planning efforts failed because government officials and family planners did not take the broader social context

family planning
the voluntary use of population control methods

into account. For one thing, India did not have Taiwan's advantage of relatively rapid economic development. In addition, the Indian officials and planners did not make enough efforts to overcome cultural and religious opposition to birth control. Nor did they find enough ways to effectively communicate birth control information and technology. Finally, the national birth control program was left in the hands of individual state governments to implement.

Efforts to control population began to succeed in India only after the government turned to a sterilization program in 1976. Although the government did not use the force of law, a system of *disincentives* had the effect of compulsion. Those who could not produce official proof of a sterilization were denied such things as business permits, gun licenses, and ration cards for the purchase of basic goods (Weeks, 1999).

India's population control programs have been only moderately successful at best.

Have compulsory population control methods ever been used successfully? Both China and Singapore have forced population control policies that seem to achieve their goals. China has been successful in reducing its total fertility rate from 7.5 in 1963 to 1.8 in 2001 through a system of rewards and punishments that includes a "one-child" policy. One-child families receive a larger retirement pension and enjoy preference in housing, school admission for their children, and employment. Families with more than one child are subject to an escalating tax on each child, and they get no financial aid from the government for the medical and educational costs of their extra children.

The island city-state of Singapore began formally discouraging large families in 1969. The government passed laws that penalized parents with large families (Weeks, 1999). These measures included

❖ denial of a paid eight-week maternity leave.

❖ loss of an income tax allowance.

❖ diminished access to public housing.

❖ increased maternity costs for each additional child.

❖ a lower likelihood of children's entering good schools.

China's population control efforts have been very effective. This poster of a mother and baby was designed to promote small families.

These policies worked so well that the total fertility rate in Singapore dropped from 4.5 children per woman to 1.4 between 1966 and 1987. In fact, the government became worried about the reduction in population size and, in 1986, reversed some of its earlier policies. The government of Singapore now supports three or more children for people able to afford them (Yap, 1995). Despite this effort, Singapore's total fertility rate of 1.6 is still below replacement level.

Does one child make a difference?   The importance of limiting family size, even by one child, can be illustrated by population projections for the United States. Even though the United States is unlikely to increase to a three-child average in the future, the hypothetical American case can help us understand the importance of population control. Figure 16.6 contrasts the projected population of the United States in the year 2070 for an average family size of two children and an average family size of three children. When small decreases in the death rate and net migration at the present level are assumed, an average two-child family size would result in a population of 300 million in 2015. Taking the hypothetical average family size of three children, the U.S. population would grow to 400 million by 2015. As time passed, the difference of only one extra child per family would assume added significance. By 2070, the two-child family would produce a population of 350 million, but the three-child family would push the population close to one billion! To say it another way, with an average family of two children, the U.S. population would not quite double itself between 1970 and 2070. But should the three-child family have been the average, the population would have doubled itself twice during this same period.

The consequences of limiting population in developing regions becomes clearer when the effect of even one child added to the average number of children in a family is recognized. Moreover, the addition of one child per family has a greater effect as the population base gets larger; not only is one extra person added, but theoretically that one person will be involved with the reproduction of yet another three, and on it goes. The largest populations are found in developing countries, which also have the largest average number of children per family.

Figure 16.6 Projected Populations of the United States.   *This graph illustrates the importance of reaching the population replacement level (two children per family). Are you surprised at the difference in U.S. population growth caused by an average of three children per family versus two children?*

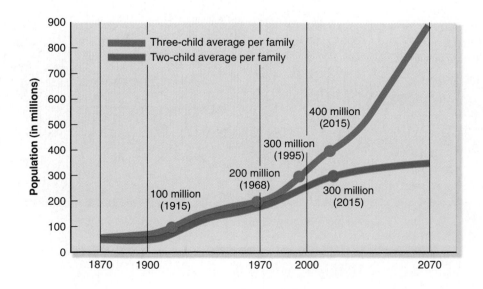

Population Pyramids

Population pyramids allow you to see at a glance the age and sex composition of a population. Age and sex are key indexes to fertility and mortality rates, which in turn are used to project school and housing needs, health resources, and other key social services. Population pyramids illustrate the *dependency ratio* that results from different rates of population growth. The **dependency ratio** is the ratio of persons in the dependent ages (under fifteen and over sixty-four) to those in the "economically active" ages (fifteen to sixty-four). The two aspects of the dependency ratio are *youth dependency* and *old-age dependency*. Developing nations have much higher youth dependency than developed nations. Developed nations have significantly higher old-age dependency. Figure 16.7 displays typical age-sex pyramids for developed and developing nations.

Why is the dependency ratio important? For developing countries such as Mexico, a high youth dependency means that national income must be diverted from economic development to provide food, housing, and education for its large young population. In developed countries such as the United States, rising old-age dependency creates a different set of problems. With a larger

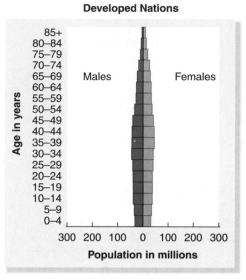
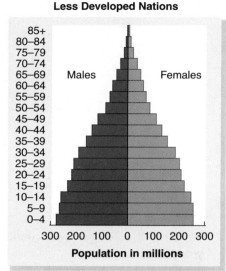

Figure 16.7 Age-Sex Pyramids in Developed and Less Developed Countries. *This figure shows general population patterns by age and sex in developed and developing countries. Using the dependency ratio, explain why children in developed countries are economically better off than those in the developing nations.*

Source: United Nations Population Division.

population pyramid
a graphic representative of the age and sex composition of a population

dependency ratio
the ratio of dependent persons to economically active persons

America's aging population is raising the dependency ratio. Why should that concern you?

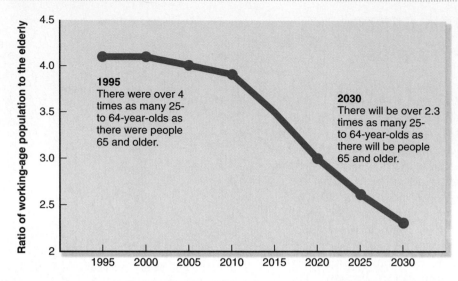

Figure 16.8 Ratio of Working-Age Population to the Elderly in the U.S. 25-to-64-Year-Olds vs 65 and Older. *This graph illustrates the rising old-age dependency occurring in the U.S.*

Source: Population Reference Bureau, Washington, D.C.

older population, there are fewer young people in the labor force to support the growing number of older people. For example, in the United States in 1995 there were just over four times as many people age 25 to 64 as people 65 and over. By 2030, there will be only 2.3 times as many. (See Figure 16.8.) This shift will increase the burden on the young to pay for Social Security and Medicare. Other problems will include the need for increasing health care services and institutional arrangements for the long-term care of elderly people.

Mankind owes to the child the best it has to give.

UN declaration

Section 2 Assessment

1. Briefly explain the difference between exponential and linear growth.
2. What are positive checks?
3. How does the demographic transition theory reflect the development of Western nations?
4. Which of the following figures is the world's population most likely to reach before it stops growing?
   a. four billion
   b. eight billion
   c. eleven billion
   d. twenty-five billion

Critical Thinking

5. **Evaluating Information** Given the exponential rate at which population grows, discuss the effect of zero population growth on the size of the world's population in 2020.

Sociology Today

Demography for Businesses

Businesses have discovered that they can grow bigger by targeting smaller groups of consumers. These groups, called generations, or cohorts, are defined by important life experiences. Events occurring when people first become economic adults (usually between ages 17 and 21) affect their life-long attitudes and values. These attitudes and values are unlikely to change as a person ages. So the kind of music that is popular during these formative years often remains the preferred type of music for life. Similarly, early lifetime experiences influence preferences in many other product and service categories.

Studies of the U.S. population have identified seven distinct groups described in the table below. Which cohort are you? Your parents?

Cohort	Description	Born	Popular Music Styles
The Depression cohort	The G.I. generation	1912–1921	Big band
The World War II cohort	The Depression generation	1922–1927	Swing
The Postwar cohort	The silent generation	1928–1945	Frank Sinatra/Rat Pack
The Boomers I cohort	The Woodstock generation	1946–1954	Rock and roll
The Boomers II cohort	The zoomer generation	1955–1965	Rock and roll, disco
The generation X cohort	The baby-buster generation	1966–1976	Grunge, rap, country western
The Boomlet cohort	The echo-boom generation	1977–	Retro-swing, Latin

Doing Sociology

Have short interviews with members of at least two of the demographic business cohorts profiled above. Identify a number of differences in preferences for products between the members of different cohorts.

Source: Berkowitz, Kerin, Hartley, and Rudelius, *Marketing,* 5th ed. Chicago: Irwin, 1997.

The products in this mall store have been selected by taking into account the buying preferences of teenagers.

Section 3

The Urban Transition

Key Terms

- city
- urbanization
- overurbanization
- suburbanization

- central-city dilemma
- gentrification
- edge city

Section Preview

The first preindustrial cities developed in fertile areas where surplus food could be grown. With the Industrial Revolution came a major increase in the rate of urbanization. The development of factories was an especially important influence on the location of cities. Urbanization in developed and developing nations has occurred at different speeds. The United States is now primarily a suburban nation.

city
dense and permanent concentration of people living in a specific area and working primarily in nonagricultural jobs

urbanization
process by which an increasingly larger portion of the world's population lives in cities

Defining a City

When does a village become a city? In Denmark and Sweden, an area with 200 inhabitants officially qualifies as a city. Populous Japan uses a much higher number—30,000. The cutoff point used by the U.S. Census Bureau to define a city is a population of 2,500. This number was set at a time when urbanization had just begun and population concentrations were small. It is obviously low for modern times.

A city is more than just a reasonably large number of people, however. Cities are also long-lasting. The periodic Woodstock rock festivals gather a large number of people in one place, but only for short periods of time. Clearly, large gatherings alone do not make a city. Cities also have a centralized economic focus. That is, they provide people with a chance to work in commerce, industry, or service. In summary, a **city** is a dense and permanent concentration of people living in a limited geographic area who earn their living primarily through nonagricultural activities.

Crowded inner cities and sprawling suburbs appear in all American cities.

Urbanization

The world has been greatly changed by **urbanization**—the process by which an increasingly larger portion of the world's population lives in or very near to cities. Urbanization has been so common that it is now taken for granted in many parts of the world. Today, almost as many people live in urban areas as in rural areas. This is a fairly recent development in human history.

What were early cities like?   The first cities appeared about five or six thousand years ago and were quite small by modern standards. One of the world's first major cities was Ur, located at the point where the Tigris and Euphrates Rivers meet (in modern-day Iraq). At its peak, Ur held only about 24,000 people. Later, during the time of the Roman Empire, only a few cities had populations over 100,000. The population of Rome itself was probably between 500,000 and 1 million.

In addition to their small size, the cities of ancient and medieval periods contained only a small portion of the world's population. As recently as 1800, less than 3 percent of the world's population lived in cities of 20,000 or more. By contrast, today, 46 percent of the world's population live in urban areas. In North America, 75 percent of the population live in cities (*World Population Data Sheet,* 2001). How did cities develop so quickly and why have cities replaced rural living for most people?

Preindustrial Cities

Many of the first urban settlements were located in Mesopotamia and were established around 3500 B.C. This was after people learned how to cultivate plants and domesticate animals, a period known as the *agricultural revolution.* The Mesopotamian region is among the world's most fertile areas and the farmers in the area were able to provide enough extra, or surplus, food to feed people in the cities. A surplus food supply is necessary for urbanization to occur.

Who lived in preindustrial cities?   Besides available food, people needed other reasons to gather in cities. Cities tended to attract four basic types of people: elites, functionaries, craftspeople, and the poor and destitute. For elites, the city provided a setting for consolidating political, military, or religious power. The functionaries were the political or religious officials who carried out the plans of the elites. Their lives were undoubtedly easier than those of the peasant-farmers in the countryside. Craftspeople, still lower in the stratification structure, came to the city to work and sell their products to the elites and functionaries. The poor came hoping to find work but were seldom able to improve their condition.

Do preindustrial cities still exist today?   Africa, Asia, and Latin America are only partly industrialized. For this reason, many of their cities still have some preindustrial characteristics. This is particularly true in capital cities because they are a magnet to the rural poor seeking a better life. Rural migrants are attracted to these cities because there are limited opportunities for making a living in the rural areas and the city promises a better life. Unfortunately, most of those who migrate to the cities are disappointed, because the expected employment opportunities do not exist. The migrants end up living in terrible slums.

In Calcutta, India, for example, over 13 million people are crowded into a city whose last major sewer line was built in 1896. Epidemics are frequent, and disease is commonplace. Calcutta's housing supply, waterworks, electrical system, and other facilities are not sufficient to cope with the city's rapid growth.

Calcutta, India, remains essentially a preindustrial city.

World View

Urban Population as a Proportion of Total Population

As discussed in the text, the Industrial Revolution encouraged the rapid growth of cities. The map below shows that many countries now have urban populations that comprise 60 percent or more of their total populations.

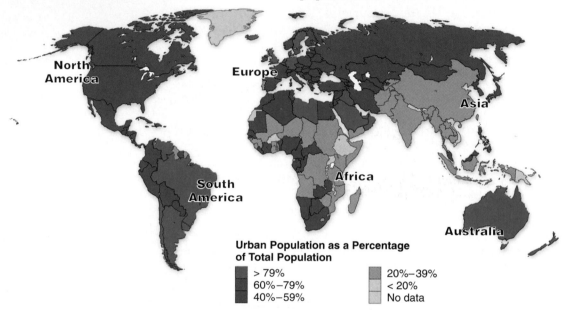

Urban Population as a Percentage of Total Population

> 79%	20%–39%
60%–79%	< 20%
40%–59%	No data

Interpreting the Map

1. The map shows that countries such as England, Germany, and Sweden have urban populations that make up over 80 percent of their total populations. This can be explained by the effects of the Industrial Revolution, since these countries' economies are highly developed. However, other countries, such as Venezuela, Argentina, and Libya, which are not highly developed, also have urban populations that comprise over 80 percent of their totals. Can you think of reasons why this is so? Explain.

2. What effects will increased urbanization have on countries and the world?

Adapted from *The State of the World Atlas,* 5th ed.

The Rise of the Modern City

Beginning in the 1700s, the Industrial Revolution created major changes in transportation, agriculture, commerce, and industry. Technological developments led to better agricultural productivity and more efficient transportation systems. Farm workers were free to leave rural areas and move into cities. More important, however, was the spread of factories.

Figure 16.9 Focus on Theoretical Perspectives

Urban Society. This table illustrates how functionalism and conflict theory might approach the study of urban society. Symbolic interactionism was not included. Why do you think it was excluded? Can you suggest a research topic in either population or urbanization for which symbolic interactionism would be appropriate?

Theoretical Perspective	Concept	Sample Research Topic	
Functionalism	Urbanization	Study of the relationship between population density and the suicide rate	
Conflict Theory	Overurbanization	Investigation of the relationship between the distribution of scarce resources and social class	

Factories were not established to encourage the growth of cities, but they had that effect. Factory owners tended to build in the same area to share raw materials and to take advantage of natural features such as water power and river transport. Machinery and equipment makers located their plants next to the factories they would be supplying. All these businesses in turn attracted retailers, innkeepers, entertainers, and a wide range of people offering services to city dwellers. The more services offered, the more people were attracted, maintaining the cycle of urban growth. The industrial world was becoming an urbanized world.

World Urbanization

Urbanization is a worldwide movement. From 1800 to the mid-1980s, the number of urban dwellers increased one hundred times, while the population increased only about fivefold. Over 2.8 billion people—nearly 46 percent of the world's population—now live in urban areas. In developed countries, 75 percent of the population lives in urban areas compared to 40 percent in developing countries. (See Figure 16.10 on page 553.)

What are the patterns for urbanization? Developed and developing countries have distinct patterns of urbanization. Most of the urban growth in developing countries before the turn of the century occurred through colonial expansion. Western countries, which had been involved in colonial expansion since the late fifteenth century, held half the world under colonial rule by the latter part of the nineteenth century. It has been only since World War II that many of these colonial countries have become independent nations (Bardo and Hartman, 1982).

Since gaining independence, these former colonies have been experiencing rapid urbanization and industrialization. In fact, urbanization in these areas is now proceeding nine times faster than it did in the West during its urban expansion period. The rate of urbanization for major industrial nations in the West was 15 percent each decade throughout the nineteenth century. In the 1960s, the rate of urbanization in major developing countries was 20 percent per decade (Light, 1983).

What are some other differences in the pattern of world urbanization? In the first place, industrialization in developing countries, unlike the Western experience, has not kept pace with urbanization. Cities of North America and Europe had jobs for all migrants from rural areas. In the cities of developing nations, the supply of labor from the countryside is greater than the demand for labor in the cities. A high rate of urban unemployment is the obvious result. The term **overurbanization** has been created to describe a situation in which a city is unable to supply adequate jobs and housing for its inhabitants.

Another difference between urbanization in developed and developing countries is the number and size of cities. When grouped by size, cities in developed countries form a pyramid: a few large cities at the top, many medium-sized cities in the middle, and a large base of small cities. In the developing world, in contrast, many countries have one tremendously big city that dwarfs a large number of villages. Calcutta, India, and Mexico City are examples. Of the world's ten largest cities, only three—Shanghai, Buenos Aires, and Calcutta—were in developing countries in 1950. By 2000, as you can see in Figure 16.10 on the opposite page, seven of the top ten largest urban areas were in developing countries. By the year 2015, it is predicted that there will be twenty-one "megacities" with populations of ten million or more. Seventeen of these will be in developing countries, including the most impoverished societies in the world.

What are "push" and "pull" factors? In explaining why people in developing countries move to large cities with inadequate jobs and housing, urban sociologists point to the operation of "push" and "pull" factors. People are pushed out of their villages because expanding rural populations cannot be supported by the existing agricultural economy. They are forced to migrate elsewhere, and cities are at least an alternative. Poor people are also attracted to cities in the belief there are opportunities for better education, employment, social welfare support, and good medical care. Unfortunately, they are likely to be disappointed.

overurbanization
situation in which a city cannot supply adequate jobs and housing for its inhabitants

Los Angeles drivers spend about 82 hours a year, two full weeks of work, waiting in traffic. Does this mean that Los Angeles is overurbanized?

suburbanization
loss of population of a city to surrounding areas

Suburbanization in the United States

Unlike cities in the developing world, cities in the United States have recently been losing population, not gaining. Since 1950, the proportion of the population living in suburbs has more than doubled. **Suburbanization** occurs when central cities lose population to the surrounding areas. The United States is now predominantly suburban.

What makes suburbanization possible? Suburbanization has become an important trend partly because of technological developments. Improvements in communication (such as telephones, radios, and television and later computers, fax machines, and the Internet) have allowed people to live away from the central city without losing touch with what is going on there. Developments in transportation (especially trains, highways, automobiles, and trucks) have made it possible both for people to commute to work and for many businesses to leave the central city for suburban locations.

Technology is not the only cause of suburbanization. Both cultural and economic pressures have encouraged the development of suburbs. Partly because of America's frontier heritage, American culture has always had a bias against urban living. Some Americans prefer urban life, but most report that they would rather live in a rural setting. Even those who choose to live in the city believe they are giving up some advantages. Suburbs, with their low-density housing, have allowed many people to escape the problems of urban living without leaving the urban areas completely. Suburbs are attractive because of decreased crowding and traffic congestion, lower taxes, better schools, less crime, and reduced pollution.

The scarcity and high cost of land in the central city also encourages suburbanization. Developers of new housing, retail, and industrial projects often find suburban locations far less expensive than those near the central city. Finally, government policy has often increased the impact of economic forces. Federal Housing Administration regulations, for example, have favored the financing of new houses (which can be built most cheaply in suburban locations) rather than the refurbishing of older houses in central cities. Among other things, this has led to the *central-city dilemma*.

What is the central-city dilemma? When suburbanization first became noticeable in the 1930s, only the upper and middle classes could afford to leave the central city. Not until the 1950s did the white working class follow them. Despite federal legislation prohibiting housing discrimination, the suburbs remained largely white until the 1970s. Since then, central-city minorities have moved to the suburbs in greater numbers. Still, the percentage of African Americans living in central cities has declined only slightly since 1970 (Farley, 1997; Palen, 1997).

The problem is not merely that minorities remain trapped in inner cities. Businesses have followed the more affluent people to the suburbs where they can find lower tax rates, less expensive land, less congestion, and their customers who have already left the city. Accompanying the exodus of the middle class, manufacturers, and retailers is the shrinking of the central-city tax base. As a result, the central city has become increasingly populated by the poor, the unskilled, and the uneducated. This has created the **central-city dilemma**—the concentration of a large population in need of public services (schools, transportation, health care) without the tax base to provide them.

Can the central-city dilemma be solved? Some countertrends exist. There are city governments now requiring certain public employees to live in

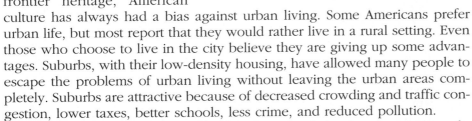

1950		**2000**	
New York	12.3	Tokyo	26.4
London	8.7	Mexico City	18.0
Tokyo	6.9	Sao Paulo	17.9
Paris	5.4	New York	16.7
Moscow	5.3	Bombay	16.0
Shanghai	5.3	Los Angeles	13.2
Rhein-Ruhr	5.3	Calcutta	13.0
Buenos Aires	5.0	Shanghai	12.8
Chicago	4.9	Dhaka	12.5
Calcutta	4.4	Delhi	12.4

Population (in millions)

Figure 16.10 World's Largest Urban Areas: 1950, 2000. *This figure compares the world's largest urban areas in 1950 and 2000. What is the most surprising aspect of these data to you?*

Source: Population Division of the UN Secretariat Estimate.

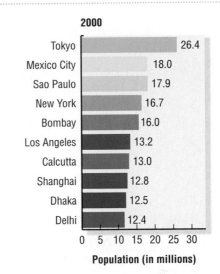

SOCIOLOGY Online

Student Web Activity
Visit the *Sociology and You* Web site at soc.glencoe.com and click on **Chapter 16—Student Web Activities** for an activity on suburbanization.

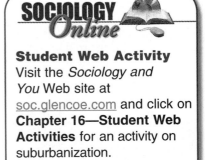

central-city dilemma concentration of people in need of public services without tax base–generated money to provide for them

This view of Dallas was taken from the rooftop pool area of an old garment factory converted into luxury apartments.

gentrification
the development of low-income areas by middle-class homebuyers, landlords, and professional developers

edge city
a suburban unit specializing in a particular economic activity

Our national flower is the concrete cloverleaf.

Lewis Mumford
U.S. novelist

the city. Some parts of inner cities are being restored through **gentrification**—the development of low-income areas by middle-class home buyers, landlords, and professional developers. Finally, there is a fairly significant movement of whites back to the central city. This movement is particularly evident among baby boomers who are remaining single or establishing childless or two-income families. Because these people are not as heavily involved in child rearing, they prefer central-city living more than the previous generation did (Palen, 1997). The importance of these countertrends for easing the central-city dilemma remains to be seen. They certainly have not been sufficiently important to stop the emergence of *edge cities*.

What are edge cities?   As stated, increasing numbers of businesses and jobs have followed people to the suburbs. In fact, "suburban downtowns" are changing the face of urban America. An **edge city** is a smaller, more focused, version of an urban downtown. It is a suburban unit that specializes in a particular economic activity (Garreau, 1991). Employment in one edge city may focus on computer technology; employment in another, on financial services or health care. A specialized edge city, of course, will have many other types of economic activities as well, such as industrial tracts, office parks, distribution and warehousing clusters, and home offices of national corporations. Edge cities are actually little cities in themselves with a full range of services, including schools, retail sales, restaurants, malls, recreational complexes, medical facilities, and hotels and motels.

Edge cities do not have legal and physical boundaries separating them from the larger urban area in which they are located. This has not prevented names from being attached to several of them. Tyson's Corner is located in northern Virginia near Washington, D.C., Los Colinas is close to the Dallas-Fort Worth airport, and King of Prussia is northwest of Philadelphia. Some edge cities bear the names of highways, such as Route 128 outside of Boston.

Section 3 Assessment

1. Give a brief definition of *urbanization*.
2. What are two conditions necessary for the development of modern cities?
3. Where are preindustrial cities located today?
4. What term do sociologists use to describe mass migration to the suburbs?

Critical Thinking

5. **Analyzing Information**   Do you think preindustrial cities can continue to exist? Why or why not?

Tech Trends

Virtual Communities

Some people find life in the big city so impersonal that they feel no sense of belonging to a community. Recently organizers in several locations have been trying to use the Internet to rebuild community relationships through electronic networks. These *dedicated*—specialized—virtual communities use communications technology to link people who live in the same area, city, or neighborhood.

Organizers of community networks share the goals of local participation, community building, and democracy. As with the New England colonies' town meetings, the ideal of the new community networks is to include everyone. Supporters of the new technology claim that electronic communications will allow people to reestablish more personal relationships.

As with all projects involving technology, though, the problem of "electronic stratification" arises. Because of the costs involved, access to technological advances is not equally distributed throughout the community. Low-income individuals and families cannot afford computers or Internet access, and public agencies are not ready to supply sufficient funding. Furthermore, as computers become more sophisticated, people who are not already computer literate (especially lower-income people) will have an increasingly difficult time catching up. The technologically poor will become technologically poorer.

The Boulder (Colorado) Community Network (BCN), established in the mid-1990s, experienced many of these problems. The founders of BCN trained many different Boulder groups to use community networks. They found that acceptance varied widely among the groups. For example, residents at a local senior citizens' home became avid users of the community computers placed in their facility. In contrast, a group of low-income single parents virtually ignored the existence of the computers and the Internet, even after extensive training (Virnoche, 1998).

If community networks do become firmly established, critics warn, the "human factor" will still be lacking. When people meet through the Internet, they have no social clues, such as body language and facial expressions, with which to learn about their new acquaintances. No matter how much you learn about another person on-line, critics say, you have not met someone for real until you meet in person (Herbert, 1999).

iVillage.com is a Web site offering a virtual community for women.

Analyzing the Trends

What do you think will be the most significant effects of virtual communities on social roles?

Section 4

Urban Ecology

Key Terms

- urban ecology
- concentric zone theory
- sector theory
- multiple nuclei theory
- peripheral theory

Section Preview

Urban ecologists have developed four major theories of city growth: concentric zone theory, sector theory, multiple nuclei theory, and peripheral theory. Combining insights from all four theories is useful to our understanding of how humans relate to city environments.

urban ecology
the study of the relationships between humans and city environments

concentric zone theory
theory that describes urban growth in terms of circular areas that grow from the central city outward

The Nature of Urban Ecology

Although every city is unique, patterns have been found in the way humans interact with the cities they inhabit. **Urban ecology** is the study of the relationships between humans and their city environments.

In the 1920s and 1930s, sociologists at the University of Chicago studied the effects of the city environment on city residents. They asked such questions as why there are differences between areas of a city, how do different areas affect one another, and what processes change an area. To answer these and other questions, the University of Chicago sociologists developed theories of urban ecology, including theories of city growth (Flanagan, 1993; Kleniewski, 1997; Micklin and Poston, 1998).

Theories of City Growth

Sociologists focus on four major theories of city growth. *Concentric zone theory* describes urban growth in terms of circular areas that grow from the central city outward. *Sector theory* emphasizes the importance of transportation routes in the process of urban growth. *Multiple nuclei theory* focuses on specific geographic or historical influences. *Peripheral theory* emphasizes the growth of suburbs around the central city. The four approaches lead to quite different images of urban space. (See Figure 16.11 on the facing page.) No city exactly fits any of these images, however. Indeed, the theories tell us more when considered together than they tell us separately. To understand why this is so, we must first examine each theory.

What is concentric zone theory?   Ernest Burgess (1925), like other early sociologists at the University of Chicago, was interested in the causes and consequences of Chicago's growth. His work led to the **concentric zone theory,** which describes city growth in terms of distinctive zones—zones that develop from the central city outward in a circular pattern. Many northern cities that experienced a great deal of immigration and rapid growth developed this way.

As illustrated in Figure 16.11, the innermost circle is the *central business district,* the heart of the city. This district contains major government and private office buildings, banks, retail and wholesale stores, and entertainment and cultural facilities. Because land values in the central city are high, space is at a premium. The central business district contains a large proportion of a city's important businesses partly because the less important

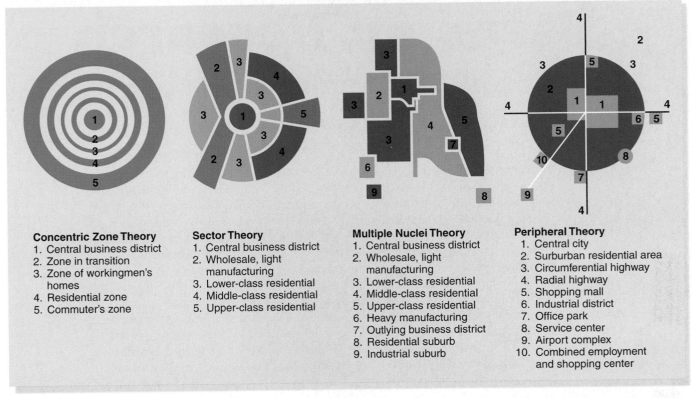

Concentric Zone Theory
1. Central business district
2. Zone in transition
3. Zone of workingmen's homes
4. Residential zone
5. Commuter's zone

Sector Theory
1. Central business district
2. Wholesale, light manufacturing
3. Lower-class residential
4. Middle-class residential
5. Upper-class residential

Multiple Nuclei Theory
1. Central business district
2. Wholesale, light manufacturing
3. Lower-class residential
4. Middle-class residential
5. Upper-class residential
6. Heavy manufacturing
7. Outlying business district
8. Residential suburb
9. Industrial suburb

Peripheral Theory
1. Central city
2. Surburban residential area
3. Circumferential highway
4. Radial highway
5. Shopping mall
6. Industrial district
7. Office park
8. Service center
9. Airport complex
10. Combined employment and shopping center

ones are unable to compete for the expensive space in the central business district.

The central business district strongly influences other parts of a city. Its influence is especially clear in the zone immediately surrounding it. Burgess called this the *zone in transition* because it is in the process of change. As new businesses and activities enter the central business district, the district expands by invading the next zone. This area may have been a residential area inhabited by middle- or upper-class families, who left because of the invasion of business activities. Most of the property in this zone is bought by those with little interest in the area. Rather than investing money in building maintenance, landowners simply extract rent from the property or sell it at a profit after the area has become more commercialized. Until the zone in transition is completely absorbed into the central business district (which may never occur), it is used for slum housing, warehouses, and marginal businesses that are unable to compete economically for space in the central business district itself. In short, the invasion of business activities creates deterioration for the zone in transition.

Surrounding the zone in transition are three zones devoted primarily to housing. The *zone of workingmen's homes* contains modest but stable neighborhoods populated largely by blue-collar workers. In the northern United States, the zone of workingmen's homes is often inhabited by second-generation immigrants who have had enough financial success to leave the deteriorating zone in transition. Next comes a *residential zone* containing mostly middle-class and upper-middle-class neighborhoods. Single-family dwellings dominate this zone, which is inhabited by managers, professionals, white-collar workers, and some well-paid factory workers. On the outskirts of

Figure 16.11 Theories of City Growth. *This figure diagrams the four major theories of city growth. Discuss one important contribution each theory makes to our understanding of urban growth.*

Source: Adapted from Chauncy D. Harris, *Urban Geography,* 1997.

The planner's problem is to find a way of creating, within the urban environment, the sense of belonging.

Leo Marx
philosopher and culturist

Focus on Research

Secondary Analysis: Gang Violence

Gangs have been a constant feature of the American urban landscape during most of the twentieth century. James Hagedorn's research (1998), however, led him to propose that postindustrial society has changed patterns of gang violence. Hagedorn's conclusions are based on a combination of three methods: a review of the research of others, secondary analysis of data collected by other researchers, and original data gathered himself.

Gangs (mostly male) in the industrial period were tied to specific neighborhoods and new immigrant groups. Gang violence primarily centered on "turf" battles among neighborhood peer groups. Pride in violence came from defending territory. Violence provided excitement and a sense of place in a group. Nevertheless, these working- and lower-class boys would eventually move on to hold decent jobs, have families, and live in better neighborhoods.

Gangs today still tend to form around racial and ethnic groups and neighborhoods. Currently, gangs tend to be African American, Latino, or Asian, just as earlier gangs were formed mostly by European immigrants, such as those from Ireland, Italy, or Eastern Europe. According to Hagedorn, however, postindustrial gangs are different in important ways. First, gang violence has significantly increased. Second, gang-related homicides have risen dramatically. Gang violence, he notes, skyrocketed at the same time American corporations were moving well-paying jobs away from the central city. As legitimate work disappeared in inner cities, gangs turned from their earlier territorial emphasis to participation in the illegitimate drug market. The common outlook of gang members today is expressed by this gang member:

I got out of high school and I didn't have a diploma, wasn't no jobs, wasn't no source of income, no nothing. That's basically the easy way for a . . . young man to be—selling some dope—you can get yourself some money real quick, you really don't have nothing to worry about, nothing but the feds. You know everybody in your neighborhood. Yeah, that's pretty safe just as long as you don't start smoking it yourself (Hagedorn, 1998:390).

Significantly, this gang member was not a teenager. While a minority of gang members remain committed to the drug economy, most seek "legit" jobs as they approach their thirties.

Working with the Research

1. Explain why urban gangs tend to form around minority groups.
2. Relate Hagedorn's findings on urban gang violence to Merton's strain theory, discussed in Chapter 7.

the city, often outside the official city limits, is the *commuter's zone,* which contains upper-class and upper-middle-class suburbs.

What is sector theory?

Not everyone agreed with Burgess's theory of how cities grow. The sociologist Homer Hoyt (1939) offered another model—**sector theory.** Hoyt's work indicated that growth patterns do not necessarily spread out in rings from the central business district. Instead, growth is more strongly affected by major transportation routes.

As Figure 16.11 shows, sectors tend to be pie-shaped, with wedges radiating from the central business district to the city's outskirts. Each sector is organized around a major transportation route. Once a given type of activity is organized around a transportation route, its nature tends to be set. Thus, some sectors will be predominantly industrial, others will contain stores and professional offices, others will be "neon strips" with motels and fast-food restaurants, and still others will be residential sectors, each with its own social class and ethnic composition.

As in concentric zone theory, cities are generally circular in shape. But because of the importance of transportation routes extending from the central business district, the boundaries of many cities form a starlike pattern, rather than a uniformly circular shape. The exact shape of a city, however, is not a major issue in sector theory. Emphasis here is on how patterns of growth are organized around transportation routes. Cities that follow this pattern include Seattle, Richmond, and San Francisco.

What is multiple nuclei theory?

Many cities have areas that cannot be explained by either concentric zone or sector theory. Chauncy Harris and Edward Ullman (1945) suggested that cities do not always follow a pattern dependent on a central district. The **multiple nuclei theory** states that a city may have several separate centers, some devoted to manufacturing, some to retail trade, some to residential use, and so on. These specialized centers can develop because of the availability of automobiles and highways. They reflect such factors as geography, history, and tradition. The city of Boston fits this model.

What is peripheral theory?

The three theories of urban growth just discussed were originally developed more than fifty years ago. Despite their age, the insights of each theory still help us to understand how cities have expanded from the center outward. This is especially the case for older cities such as Chicago and San Francisco. Many cities today, however, no longer have a central city core to which other parts of the metropolitan area are oriented all of the time.

Dependence on shipping, railroads, and heavy manufacturing has been replaced by more flexible means of transportation, such as cars and trucks. And large urban areas are now encircled by highways. New technologies (fax machines, cell phones, computers, the Internet) are also loosening the ties of most parts of the city to the central city core. As a result, many cities are now oriented *away* from the older urban core.

As noted earlier, many Americans have moved from the city to the suburbs. They have done so in part because many businesses—offices, factories, schools, retail stores, restaurants, health centers—are also in the suburbs. To describe changes in urban areas today, urban geographer Chauncy Harris (1997) has formulated the **peripheral theory.** The dominant feature of this model is the growth of suburbs (and edge cities) around

sector theory
theory that emphasizes the importance of transportation routes in the process of urban growth

multiple nuclei theory
theory that focuses on specific geographic or historical influences on urban growth

peripheral theory
theory that emphasizes the growth of suburbs around the central city

Explain which theory of urban growth best accounts for this suburban office building.

and away from the central cities. (See Figure 16.11.) Peripheral theory brings urban growth research up to date.

Which of these theories of city growth is correct?   As suggested earlier, no single theory covers the dynamics of city growth for all cities. But each theory emphasizes the importance of certain factors that cannot be overlooked by anyone interested in city growth.

❖ Concentric zone theory emphasizes the fact that growth in any one area of a city is largely influenced by politics and economics. According to this theory, the distribution of space is heavily influenced by those with the money to buy the land they want for the purposes they have in mind.

❖ Sector theorists have also contributed to an understanding of urban growth. As they have noted, transportation routes have a strong influence on cities. Decisions about the placement of railroad lines had important effects on the growth of cities in the nineteenth and early twentieth centuries. Highways and major streets have an even larger impact now.

❖ Although multiple nuclei theory is vague in its predictions, the types of geographic and historical factors it emphasizes are also important for understanding any specific city.

❖ Peripheral theory has brought urban growth research up to date by emphasizing the development of suburbs around the central city.

> Men come together in cities in order to live. They remain together in order to live the good life.
>
> Aristotle
> Greek philospher

Section 4 Assessment

1. Provide a brief description of each of the following zones.
   a. central business district
   b. commuter's zone
   c. residential zone
   d. zone in transition
   e. zone of workingmen's homes
2. What is the driving force behind the sector theory?
3. Why is the multiple nuclei theory considered more flexible than the concentric zone theory or the sector theory?

Critical Thinking

4. **Summarizing Information** Summarize the evolution of cities, focusing on the differences between life in preindustrial cities and life in industrial and suburban cities.
5. **Applying Concepts** Discuss the major contributions the four theories of city growth have made to our understanding of city growth.

Summary

Section 1: The Dynamics of Demography

Main Idea: Demography is the scientific study of population. The collection of population data is very important today, in part because of its use by government and industry. Demographers consider three population processes when looking at population change: fertility, mortality, and migration.

Section 2: World Population

Main Idea: Thomas Malthus (1798) predicted that population size would ultimately outstrip the food supply, resulting in mass starvation and death. The demographic transition theory looks at economic development to predict population patterns. While the rate of world population growth is slowing, the world's population will continue to increase for many years.

Section 3: The Urban Transition

Main Idea: The first preindustrial cities developed in fertile areas where surplus food could be growth. With the Industrial Revolution came a major increase in the rate of urbanization. The development of factories was an especially important influence on the location of cities. Urbanization in developed and developing nations has occurred at different speeds. The United States is now primarily a suburban nation.

Section 4: Urban Ecology

Main Idea: Urban ecologists have developed four major theories of city growth: concentric zone theory, sector theory, multiple nuclei theory, and peripheral theory.

SOCIOLOGY Online

Self-Check Quiz
Visit the *Sociology and You* Web site at soc.glencoe.com and click on **Chapter 16—Self-Check Quizzes** to prepare for the chapter test.

Reviewing Vocabulary

Complete each sentence using each term once.

a. demography
b. fertility
c. fecundity
d. crude birth rate
e. fertility rate
f. mortality
g. crude death rate
h. infant mortality rate
i. migration
j. doubling time
k. replacement level
l. urban ecology

1. _____ is the number of children born to a woman or a population of women.
2. The annual number of live births per one thousand women aged fifteen to forty-four is called _____.
3. _____ refers to the deaths within a population.
4. The annual number of deaths per one thousand members of a population is called _____.
5. _____ is the annual number of deaths among infants under the age of one per one thousand live births.
6. The number of years needed to double the base population is known as the _____.
7. _____ is the birth rate at which a couple replaces itself without adding to the population.
8. The scientific study of population is called _____.
9. The study of relationships between humans and their city environments is called _____.
10. _____ is the movement of people from one geographic area to another.
11. The annual number of live births per one thousand members of a population is called _____.
12. _____ is the maximum rate at which women can physically produce children.

CHAPTER 16 ASSESSMENT

Reviewing the Facts

1. Identify and describe the three population processes. Use a diagram similar to the one below to record your answers.

Process	Description
1.	
2.	
3.	

2. What is suburbanization?
3. What was Thomas Malthus' solution for over-population?
4. In your own words, explain population momentum.
5. What is the difference between replacement level and zero population growth?
6. List and explain the four major theories of city growth.

Thinking Critically

1. **Making Generalizations** The United States is actually nearing zero population growth—except for the influx of immigrants. Recall from your history or government classes as many of the benefits and disadvantages of open immigration as you can and discuss them in class. Do you think immigration should be a factor in considering methods of controlling population? Why or why not?
2. **Drawing Conclusions** Sometime in October 1999, the world population reached six billion. As you read in the chapter, the population is expected to reach seven billion by 2010. How are technological improvements contributing to this rapid growth?
3. **Analyzing Information** Technology has been credited with increasing population growth. In what ways might it be employed to slow down the rate of population growth?
4. **Making Inferences** One of the great debates concerning population growth is whether there is enough food to supply the world. Some argue that, each year, tons of food supplies sit in bins waiting to be used but are wasted because there is no way to get the supplies where they are needed. Others argue that we can raise agricultural productivity no higher and will soon be unable to feed the world. What factors affect the availability of food in developing nations? In industrial and postindustrial societies?
5. **Drawing Conclusions** Universal education, according to Thomas Malthus, could be the great equalizer in raising the quality of life for all human beings. As a budding sociologist, would you agree with Malthus that education is the only real solution to current world problems? Would universal education really level the playing field for all? Explain your views.
6. **Making Inferences** Emile Durkheim was concerned about the changes brought on by the Industrial Revolution. He studied suicide rates and found them to be higher in urban areas. What factors might contribute to higher suicide rates in urban areas that would not be factors in rural areas? Do you think Durkheim's findings hold today, or is the likelihood of suicide just as great in rural and suburban areas?
7. **Applying Concepts** By U.S. Census Bureau definition, a population of 2,500 qualifies a community to be called a city. What are some factors that clearly distinguish communities of 2,500 from places such as Los Angeles and New York? Do you consider your community to be a city in the modern sense? Why or why not?

Sociology Projects

1. **Doubling Time** Choose a country and find its doubling time. Then, using the library or multi-media sources, identify reasons for that country's doubling time. Consider some of the variables mentioned in the text, such as infant mortality rate, wars, and epidemics. Be prepared to give a brief oral report to the class on your findings.

2. **The Effects of Doubling Time** Review the analogy of the chessboard given on page 538 of the text. Now, get a calculator and draw a chessboard with sixty-four squares. Starting with one "person" on the first square, start doubling the number of people for each square. At what point do the numbers become unmanageable? How does this little demonstration illustrate the effects of doubling time?

3. **Demographic Transition** Pick another country. Of the four stages of demographic transition described on pages 539–540, which one best reflects the country you chose? What are the factors that caused you to place the country at this stage?

4. **Theories of Urban Growth** Obtain a map of a large city in your area. (If you live in a fairly large city, use a map of it.) By looking at the map, can you determine if patterns of growth in this city proceeded according to one of the theories of urban growth described in the chapter? If so, take a marker and illustrate the patterns on the map. You might also talk with people in the city who have some knowledge of how the city changed over time, such as the local historical society, city clerks, or a local sociologist. Try to find out what growth pattern the city followed.

5. **Social Institutions** By definition, all communities have the following social institutions: family, education, science/technology, politics, religion, sports, and economy. Locate a map of your community (city hall is a good source for these maps). With two or three classmates, pick a part of town for the focus of your project. In the part of town you chose, take a photograph of at least one example of each type of institution. For the family, for instance, you might take a picture of a house. Look to see how many of the institutions are in your chosen neighborhood, and then bring back some item or souvenir from each of the institutions, if possible. For example, if you select a restaurant (economic institution) you might bring back a menu. *Be sure to ask permission for everything you take.* Present your photos and souvenirs to the class on a poster board.

6. **World Population Growth** Talk with some older people in your family or neighborhood about how the growing world population has affected them. Ask them to identify some changes that have taken place since 1960 (when the world population was only three billion). Write down their comments in the form of a script, as if you were interviewing them for a magazine article.

7. **Urban Planning** Choose three classmates to join you as members of the Urban Planning Board of Betterville, USA. As members of the Urban Planning Board, it is your task to jointly design the city for redevelopment. Examine the four major theories of city growth. Determine which theory or combination of theories you would use to design Betterville. Create a visual representation of your city design (e.g., blueprint, chart, artist rendering, etc.). Write a one-page essay explaining the theory or combination of theories that you chose and the rationale for your choice.

Technology Activity

1. William Julius Wilson, a sociologist at Harvard University, has done extensive research on what the text calls the central-city dilemma. The Public Broadcasting System (PBS) sponsored an on-line forum with Dr. Wilson, called "A Look at the Truly Disadvantaged." Go to this web site at http://www.pbs.org/newshour/forum/november96/wilson10.html and select "Why is inner city education so poor?"

   a. What is to blame for the poor results often obtained in inner city schools, according to Dr. Wilson?

   b. Now select "How can inner cities be reconnected to the rest of American society?" What are Dr. Wilson's recommendations for solving the central-city dilemma?

   c. Read some of the "Viewer comments." Do you agree or disagree with any of the comments shown there? What do you think could be done to solve the problems in inner cities?

Chapter 16
Enrichment Reading
Life Expectancy: Surprising Demographic Trends
by David Stipp

Baby boomers have ushered in most every major trend over the past 50 years. But it was their grandparents who initiated the most radical demographic change of the past half-century—a dramatic decline in death rates at older ages. In fact, about the time boomers were rambunctiously burning draft cards, their elders quietly began **nullifying actuarial tables.** By 1990 there were more than 1.5 million Americans age 85 and over who wouldn't have been alive if death rates had stayed at the 1960 level.

Extrapolating this trend, demographer James Vaupel has made a bold prediction: Half of the girls and a third of the boys recently born in the developed world will live to be 100. Vaupel similarly expects millions of former flower children to defy federal population forecasts and make good on their old chant, "Hell no, we won't go!"—he has projected there could be nearly 37 million boomers age 85 and over by 2050, more than twice the government's best guess. That would mean a much higher proportion of senior citizens nationwide than Florida has today. . . .

Vaupel [is] no shallow visionary. A few years ago many of his colleagues scoffed when he challenged a grim **canon** about aging. It holds that death rates rise exponentially with age in adult animals, including humans—the older you are, the theory goes, the more likely you are to die. Aided by other researchers, he marshaled data on everything from Swedish women to Medflies to show it ain't so; for good measure, he threw in supporting data on the death rates of old cars. The team demonstrated that mortality can plateau and, strangely, even drop among the very old—as if the Fates were nodding off after a long wait.

Vaupel sees this "mortality deceleration" as a subplot of a grand mystery that has preoccupied demographers for over a decade: Why have the elderly been living longer than their forebears since about 1970? Some of the causes are obvious, such as the **averting** of millions of fatal heart attacks by blood-pressure drugs widely used since the 1960s. But many experts on aging feel that such well-known factors can't explain the trend's surprising speed and breadth. . . .

Casting about for explanations, some demographers theorize that deep, little-understood changes are afoot that will help sustain the trend for decades. Vaupel has stuck his neck out farther than most by proposing that the aging process may actually slow down in very old people, an idea based on his mortality-deceleration work. That particular idea remains highly controversial. But Vaupel's **bullish** view that longevity gains will continue apace is widely shared. Indeed, many demographers are now more bullish than the Social Security Administration, which projects that the decline in old-age death rates will slow to a crawl early in the next century.

The bulls' predictions raise a burning issue: If we receive a gift of extra years, will it turn out to be a **Pandora's box** filled with hobbling diseases? For most of this century death rates and the prevalence of chronic diseases among the elderly have dropped in tandem. But "we're balanced on a razor's edge," says Eric Stallard, a demography professor at Duke University. If medical advances make mortality fall faster than disease, we'll wind up spending costly extra years in nursing homes. Or worse: "We may face the gruesome prospect of poor, disabled, homeless older Americans living out the end of their lives on city streets and in parks," warns Edward L. Schneider, dean of gerontology at the University of South Carolina.

Source: Adapted from David Stipp, "Hell No, We Won't Go," *Fortune*, July 19, 1999: 102, 104.

What Does it Mean?

averting
turning aside; avoiding

bullish
optimistic; encouraging

canon
an accepted principle or rule

extrapolating
projecting known data into an area not known or experienced

nullifying actuarial tables
reversing current population trends

Pandora's box
source of many troubles (based on a Greek myth about a box of evils released by a curious woman who had been instructed not to open the box)

This active older couple is enjoying the increasing longevity in modern society. What are some of the most important consequences of this trend?

Read and React

1. What is the surprising demographic trend referred to in the title of this article?

2. What has happened to the death rates in the United States since 1960?

3. What is meant by the term *mortality deceleration?*

4. What are some positive and negative effects an aging population would have on the social structure of this country?

CHAPTER 17

Social Change and Collective Behavior

Using Your Sociological Imagination

When you see photos or films showing the Plains Indians of the Old West—Sioux, Crow, and so forth—what do you think about the culture of those Native Americans? If you're like most of us, you may assume that it had remained unchanged for many centuries—that these people dressed and acted in exactly the same way as their ancestors.

We often assume that nonindustrial societies such as these stand still over time. Actually, though, sociology teaches us that change comes to all societies. Whether by borrowing from other cultures, discovering new ways of doing things, or creating inventions that ripple through society, all peoples experience social change.

Let's return to the example of the Plains Indians. You may picture these tribes as fierce, buffalo-hunting warriors. Perhaps images of Sitting Bull and Crazy Horse astride fast horses attacking Custer come to mind, leading you to think that their ancestors for centuries had also ridden horses. In fact, horses were a relatively recent introduction to Plains Indian culture in the 1800s. The Spanish brought modern horses to North America, and not until the late 1600s and early 1700s were horses available in large numbers to the Plains Indians. Early Native American tribes on the Plains had been nomads living more off wild food plants than buffalo. This chapter will examine different ways change affects society.

Sections

1. **Social Change**
2. **Theoretical Perspectives on Social Change**
3. **Collective Behavior**
4. **Social Movements**

Learning Objectives

After reading this chapter, you will be able to

❖ illustrate the three social processes that contribute to social change.

❖ discuss how technology, population, natural environment, revolution, and war cause cultures to change.

❖ describe social change as viewed by the functionalist and conflict perspectives.

❖ discuss rumors, fads, and fashions.

❖ compare and contrast theories of crowd behavior.

❖ compare and contrast theories of social movements.

SOCIOLOGY *Online*

Chapter Overview
Visit the *Sociology and You* Web site at soc.glencoe.com and click on **Chapter 17— Chapter Overviews** to preview chapter information.

Section 1

Social Change

Key Terms

- social change
- social processes
- discovery
- invention

- diffusion
- technology
- revolution
- war

Section Preview

Social change refers to new behaviors that have long-term and relatively important consequences. Discovery, invention, and diffusion are the major social processes through which social change occurs. Important agents of social change are technology, population, the natural environment, revolution, and war.

---

social change
new societal behaviors with important long-term consequences

Defining Social Change

Change is one of the most constant features of American society. This is so true that it is almost a cliché. In fact, all societies change—some rapidly, others more slowly. For sociologists, **social change** occurs when many members of the society adopt new behaviors. The behaviors must have long-term and important consequences.

How fast has social change occurred? Scientists use an analogy to help people understand the pace of social change. Imagine for a moment the entire history of Earth as a 365-day period. Midnight of January 1 is the starting point. Today's date is December 31. Each Earth "day" represents about twelve million years. The first form of life, a simple bacterium, appeared in February. More complex life, such as fish, appeared about November 20. On December 10, the dinosaurs appeared; by Christmas they were extinct. The first recognizable human beings did not appear until the afternoon of December 31. Modern humans (*homo sapiens*) emerged shortly before midnight that day. All of recorded history occurred in the last sixty seconds of the year (Ornstein and Ehrlich, 1991). In the scheme of history, then, human social changes occur in the "blink of an eye." Only when we look at social change from the perspective of the human life span does it sometimes seem to be a slow process.

Can social change be predicted? It is difficult to predict how a society will change. This is partly because the course of change in a society depends on the nature of the existing culture. For example, two societies that adopt a democratic form of government may develop in very different ways. Both Britain and the United States are democracies. But their histories prior to becoming democracies were different, since Britain had a royal tradition. As a result, democratic government took different forms in these two nations.

Figure 17.1 Key Assumptions in Predicting Social Change in America

The most accurate predictor of trends in American society has been the Frenchman Alexis de Tocqueville. Tocqueville's *Democracy in America,* which was published in the 1830s, displayed an amazing grasp of American society. Tocqueville's success has been attributed to several key assumptions he made. Do you think that any of these assumptions are less important today in predicting social change than the others?

1. **Major social institutions would continue to exist.** Unlike many of his contemporaries—and many of ours—Tocqueville did not expect the family, religion, or the state to disappear or to be greatly changed.

2. **Human nature would remain the same.** Tocqueville did not expect men and women to become much better or worse or different from what history had shown them to be.

3. **Equality and the trend toward centralized government would continue.**

4. **The availability of material resources (such as land, minerals, and rich soils) limits and directs social change.**

5. **Change is affected by the past, but history does not strictly dictate the future.**

6. **There are no social forces aside from human actions.** Historical events are not foreordained by factors beyond human control.

Adapted from Theodore Caplow, *American Social Trends* (New York: Harcourt Brace Jovanovich, 1991), p. 216.

In addition, change does not merely "happen" to people. People in a society can consciously decide for themselves how change will occur. They can, for example, deliberately avoid a predicted state of affairs (Caplow, 1991).

These facts should not discourage people from attempting to understand changes in society. Alexis de Tocqueville was a Frenchman who published a remarkably penetrating study of American society after a tour in the early 1830s. The accuracy of his predictions was based upon sound assumptions he made about American society. Figure 17.1 discusses these basic premises.

Why do some societies change faster than others? Understanding why some societies change faster than others is another difficult task. Sociologists have identified several important social processes that influence the pace of social change. In addition, several specific factors play important roles. We turn first to the social processes and then to the specific agents, or factors, that affect rates of change.

The past is a foreign country. They do things differently there.

L.P. Hartley
short story author

Social Processes

A process is a series of steps that lead gradually to a result. As you get closer to graduation from high school, you may decide to continue your formal education. You will then begin a process of applying for acceptance to various colleges. If you follow all the steps in the necessary order and meet the colleges' criteria for entrance, the end result of your application process will be an acceptance letter.

Rapid social change means that generations do not share certain knowledge. Besides "snail-mail," what are some other products or technologies that might become obsolete?

Cultures and societies experience **social processes** that result in significant changes. Three important social processes are *discovery, invention,* and *diffusion.*

How does discovery promote social change?   In the **discovery** process, something is either learned or reinterpreted. When early ocean explorers did not fall off the end of the world, they changed what all but a few people believed about the shape of the earth. With this geographical knowledge came new patterns of migration, commerce, and colonization. Salt, another early discovery, was first used to flavor food. Because it was so highly valued, it also came to be used as money in Africa and as a religious offering among early Greeks and Romans. Fire was used at first by prehistoric peoples for warmth and cooking. Later, people discovered that fire could be used to clear fields, to create ash for fertilizer, and to melt ores to combine into new metals.

social processes
series of steps leading to change on a societal level

discovery
process by which something is learned or reinterpreted

invention
the creation of something new from previously existing items or processes

What is the role of invention in social change?   **Invention** is the creation of something new from items or processes that already exist. Examples of physical inventions come easily to mind. Consider the airplane. It was not so much the materials Orville and Wilbur Wright used—most of the parts were available—but the way the brothers combined these materials that enabled them to make their successful flight at Kitty Hawk.

The pace of social change through invention is closely tied to how complex the society or culture already is. The greater the number of existing items, or elements, the more ways they can be combined into inventions. Thus, the more complex and varied a society, the more rapidly it will change. This helps to explain why people reached the moon less than seventy years after the Wright brothers' first flight, even though scientists believe that several million years had passed between the appearance of the human species and the invention of the airplane. NASA was able to reach the moon relatively quickly because the United States had become advanced in such areas as physics, aerodynamics, and the manufacturing of specialized materials.

diffusion
process by which one culture or society borrows from another culture or society

How important is diffusion in social change?   When one group borrows something from another group—norms, values, foods, styles of architecture—change occurs through the process of **diffusion.** The extent and rate of diffusion depend on the degree of social contact. The more contact a group has with another group, the more likely it is that objects or ideas will be exchanged. In other words, social contact has the same effect on diffusion that complexity has on invention.

Borrowing may involve entire societies. The American colonists learned methods of growing cotton that were first developed in India. Potatoes from South America were transplanted across the Atlantic to become Ireland's most important food crop. Diffusion may also take place between groups within the same society. African American musicians were the creators of a jazz subculture that spread throughout white America (and into other countries as well).

By which social process did this image of Elvis reach Jerusalem, Israel?

Before it is widely accepted, a borrowed element must harmonize with the group culture. In spite of the fact that unisex fashion is popular in America today, wearing a Scottish kilt on the job could get a construction worker laughed off the top of a skyscraper. Wearing kilts still clashes with the American definition of manhood. If skirts are ever to become as acceptable for American men as pants are for women, either their form will have to be modified or the cultural concept of masculinity will have to change.

Diffusion may involve using only part of a borrowed characteristic or trait. The Japanese, for example, accept capitalism but resist the American form of democratic government, style of conducting business, and family structure. Diffusion almost always involves picking and choosing.

In modern society, most aspects of culture are borrowed rather than created. The processes of discovery and invention are important, but usually far more elements enter a society through cultural diffusion.

Technology

Besides the three processes for social change, sociologists have identified some major forces that lead to change. **Technology** includes knowledge and hardware (tools) that are used to achieve practical goals. The appearance of new technology is generally a sign that social change will soon follow (MacKenzie and Wajcman, 1998).

technology
knowledge and tools used to achieve practical goals

How important is technology to social change? Technology is a prime promoter of social change. *Time* magazine's selection of Albert Einstein as the person of the century reflected the magazine's conclusion that the twentieth century will be remembered most for its advances in science and technology (Golden, 1999).

The creation of the silicon chip, which led to the computer revolution, has brought about technological change at an astounding rate. It took more than a century for telephones to spread to 94 percent of the homes in the United States. In contrast, in less than five years the Internet had reached over 25 percent of Americans. (See page 29 for a comparison of the number of years it took for various technologies to be adopted in U.S. households.)

The changes that resulted from the use of computers are almost impossible to list. In 1999, social historian Francis Fukuyama described a workplace undergoing a transformation. The effects of these changes, he claims, will be as great as those of the Industrial Revolution. Telecommunications technology, for example, will allow many to work from their homes, but it will result in far less human interaction (McGinn and Raymond, 1997–98). In the field of medicine, computer technology has radically changed many surgical techniques. Microsurgeries and radio wave therapy are examples (Cowley and Underwood, 1997–98). Drivers in Germany can get real-time computer-generated information on traffic problems on the autobahn by using cell phones or electronic consoles in their cars.

These college students at a campus cyber café seem very comfortable with the fast pace of technological change in American society.

Population

Changing demographics are another important factor for creating social change. A classic example is the huge increase in the birth of babies following the return of American soldiers at the end of World War II (the so-called baby boom). Americans born between 1946 and 1964 caused the expansion of child healthcare facilities and created the need for more teachers and schools in the 1950s and 1960s. On the other hand, the generation following baby boomers now in their thirties and in the labor market are experiencing increased competition for jobs and fewer opportunities to move up the career ladder. As the baby boomers retire, problems of health care and Social Security loom large. Longer working hours, retraining programs, and reeducation for older people will probably become political issues for future elections. As America's population continues to age, more attention is being paid to our senior citizens. Already, there are more extended-care homes, an increase in geriatric emphasis in medicine, and more television advertising and programming targeting the aging elderly population.

The Natural Environment

Interaction with the natural environment has, from the earliest times, also transformed American life. The vast territory west of the thirteen colonies permitted the nation to expand, ultimately to the Pacific Ocean. This western movement helped shape our cultural identity and values. It also caused untold changes, most tragically the destruction of many Native American cultures.

The environment continued to shape historical events, especially when natural disasters occurred. The Great Depression of the 1930s was due in part to a long drought that hit the Midwestern plains states. Overplanting and plowing had upset the fragile ecosystem and turned the prairies into a giant "dust bowl."

In 1986, the Chernobyl nuclear plant in Ukraine had a meltdown. This event added to opposition in the U.S. to using nuclear power as an energy source.

Another Time

The Horse Among the Plains Indians

Diffusion is one of the social processes that creates social change. The society of the Plains Indians in the west central United States was altered drastically by the European introduction of the horse—an example of diffusion.

In the nineteenth century, horses were the primary means of transportation and as such were an integral part of Plains Indian culture. The modern horse, however, was not native to the Americas, but was first brought by the Spanish. It was not until the late 1600s and early 1700s that horses in any numbers became available to the tribes of the Great Plains. . . .

The horse truly revolutionized life among the Plains tribes. The horse drastically altered the economic base and changed the lifestyle of these peoples. On horseback a hunter armed with bow and arrow could find and kill enough bison within a few months to feed his family for the year. Not only could he kill larger numbers of game animals, but he could pack the meat onto horses and readily transport it vast distances. Horses also allowed for the transporting of increased quantities of material goods. Teepees increased in size, and clothing and other material items became increasingly abundant and elaborate in decoration. For the first time these widely scattered groups could gather together in large camps, sometimes numbering in the thousands, for at least a portion of the year. In short, the horse quickly elevated the Plains tribes to relative prosperity.

The horse also sharply altered the relationship between these peoples and the neighboring farming tribes. The once relatively inoffensive nomads were now transformed into aggressive, predatory raiders. The Plains tribes were now capable of quickly assembling large parties of horse-mounted warriors who could raid the sedentary farming villages with impunity. The military balance of power had shifted.

In the decades immediately after the acquisition of the horse, the original Plains tribes flourished. Attacks on the neighboring farming peoples had a devastating effect, and many villages were abandoned. It was not long, however, before many cultivators saw both the economic and the military advantages derived from being horse-mounted nomadic bison hunters. The Cheyenne and some of the Dakota abandoned the life of settled farmers and moved westward to the plains to become nomadic, teepee-dwelling, bison hunters themselves. As they moved onto the plains, they came to challenge directly the original Plains tribes for dominance over critical hunting resources, which intensified warfare. As a result, warfare and the warrior tradition became an integral part of Plains Indian values, social organization, and behavior.

Source: Adapted from James Peoples and Garrick Bailey, *Humanity,* 5th ed. Belmont, CA: Wadsworth, 2000, p. 284.

Thinking It Over

1. List at least five major changes that resulted from the introduction of the horse to the culture of the Plains Indians.

2. Identify an item that has been introduced to your culture from another place. (This item could be food, clothing, an invention, or even an idea.) What effect has it had on your life?

World View

Internet Connections

As this map shows, the number of people connected to the Internet varies widely from country to country. As of the late 1990s, nearly 60 percent of Internet connections were on the North American continent. This map shows the number of computers connected to the Internet per 100,000 people.

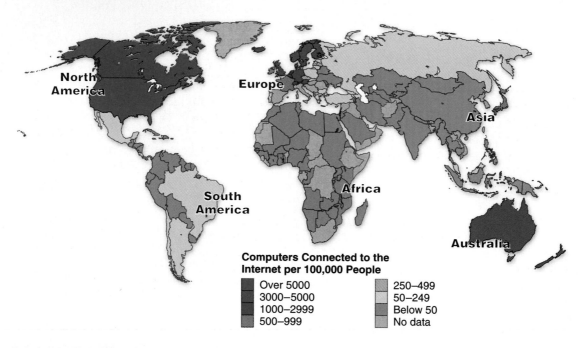

Computers Connected to the Internet per 100,000 People

Over 5000	250–499
3000–5000	50–249
1000–2999	Below 50
500–999	No data

Interpreting the Map

1. Do you see a pattern in the number of connections to the Internet? Explain.
2. What implications might this distribution have for future social change?

Adapted from *The Macmillan Atlas of the Future.* New York: Macmillan, 1998.

In the early 1970s, OPEC (an organization of oil-producing nations) launched an embargo, refusing to sell its oil to other countries. Because of the natural short supply of oil without the contribution of the oil-rich Mideastern countries, oil products became scarce and expensive, contributing to economic inflation in the United States in the 1970s and early 1980s. As a result, Americans began driving smaller, more fuel-efficient automobiles.

Revolution and War

revolution
sudden and complete overthrow of a social or political order

Revolution and war are related factors that lead to social change. A **revolution** involves the sudden and complete overthrow of an existing social or political order. A revolution is often, but not always, accompanied by violence. Most revolutionaries expect that the revolution will bring about fundamental changes. Marx, for example, expected workers' revolutions to eliminate class-based inequality and therefore to have a profound effect on the social and economic structures of the societies in which they occurred.

Wars often bring about social change because culturally dissimilar societies, such as the U.S. and Kuwait, come into increased contact.

Are revolutions normally followed by radical changes?
According to Charles Tilly, a revolution results in the replacement of one set of power holders by another (Tilly, 1978, 1997). In the view of another respected sociologist, a post-revolutionary society is eventually replaced by a society that looks much like the original one (Brinton, 1990). Radical changes are rarely permanent because people tend to revert to more familiar customs and behaviors. They do so in part because continuity with the past provides security and a blueprint for behavior.

What sorts of changes do follow revolutions?
In most cases, the new social order created by a successful revolution is likely to be a compromise between the new and the old. Consider the example of China, the site of a communist revolution in 1949. The revolution did not result in the wholesale changes promised by its leaders. One of the revolutionary reforms, for example, promised liberation from sexism. The situation for Chinese women has improved, but sexual equality is a far-distant dream in that country ("Closing the Gap," 1995).

How does war promote social change?
War is organized, armed conflict that occurs within a society or between nations. Sociologist Robert Nisbet (1988) described how war brings about social change through diffusion, discovery, and invention. Social change is created through diffusion because wars break down barriers between societies, bringing people from different societies together. This association leads to the adoption of new ways of thinking, feeling, and behaving.

war
organized, armed conflict that occurs within a society or between nations

Wars also promote invention and discovery. For example, during World War II (1939–1945), the pressure of war enabled the U.S. government to promote and finance the development of such technologies as the atomic bomb, synthetic rubber, and antibiotics. Each contributed to a cultural revolution after the war. And America's culture, both during and after World War I, was imported by societies all over the world.

Every generation revolts against its fathers and makes friends with its grandfathers.

**Lewis Mumford
American author**

Section 1 Assessment

1. Briefly describe three important processes for social change.
2. Provide one example each (not given in the text) of how population and interaction with the natural environment have caused social change.
3. Explain how war can be both a positive and a negative force for social change.

Critical Thinking

4. **Drawing Conclusions** Identify a major social change that has occurred in your lifetime. What do you think are the major sources of this change—discovery, diffusion, or invention? Be careful to relate the manner of change to the *nature* of the change itself.

Focus on Research

Case Study: Is the American Dream Dying?

Americans have long expected to achieve a higher standard of living than their parents. Instead, according to Katherine Newman (1994), social and economic change are placing the American Dream in jeopardy. The downscaling of jobs and pay that occurred during the 1980s and 1990s has replaced earlier optimism with anger, doubt, and fear.

Newman spent two years conducting personal interviews with 150 Americans living in "Pleasanton," a suburban community representative of much of America. Pleasanton is a mix of skilled blue-collar workers and white-collar professionals from a variety of ethnic and religious origins. Her respondents were schoolteachers, guidance counselors, and sixty families whose children were then grown.

The residents of Pleasanton believed that the promise of America had taken an unexpected wrong turn, and they were trying to make sense of it. Newman attempted to understand the residents' view of this downward mobility. The stresses associated with changing economic conditions, she believed, would bring cultural expectations, disappointments, and conflicts close enough to the surface for a trained social scientist to see. As the study progressed, she did, in fact, see conflict between parents and grown children, disagreements along lines of race and ethnicity, and unhappy marriages. The following statement reveals a baby boomer's shattered confidence in the American Dream.

I'll never have what my parents had. I can't even dream of that. I'm living a lifestyle that's way lower than it was when I was growing up and it's depressing. You know it's a rude awakening when you're out in the world on your own. . . . I took what was given to me and tried to use it the best way I could. Even if you are a hard worker and you never skipped a beat, you followed all the rules, did everything they told you you were supposed to do, it's still horrendous. They lied to me. You don't get where you were supposed to wind up. At the end of the road it isn't there. I worked all those years and then I didn't get to candy land. The prize wasn't there . . . (Newman, 1994:3).

After a detailed and often personal exploration of what Newman calls the "withering American Dream," she turns to the larger social and political implications for society. She explores the transition from a society of upward mobility based on effort and merit to a society in which social classes of birth increasingly dictate future social and economic positions.

According to Newman, the soul of America is at stake. She raises these questions: Will Americans turn to exclusive self-interest, or will they care for others as well as themselves? Will suburbanites turn a blind eye to the rapidly deteriorating inner cities? Will the generational, racial, and ethnic groups turn inward, or will they attempt to bridge the divides that threaten to separate them further?

A partial answer to these questions is reflected in public opinion about federal, state, and local tax revenues. If the residents of Pleasanton are any guide, Americans do not wish to invest in the common good. Public schools, colleges, universities, and inner cities, for example, are receiving a rapidly declining share of public economic support. In conclusion, Newman states:

A former G.E. worker stands in front of signs lamenting the move of a plant from North Carolina to Mexico. This thirty-year veteran of the closing plant would agree that the American dream is dying.

> *This does not augur well for the soul of the country in the twenty-first century. Every great nation draws its strength from a social contract, an unspoken agreement to provide for one another, to reach across the narrow self-interests of generations, ethnic groups, races, classes, and genders toward some vision of the common good. Taxes and budgets—the mundane preoccupations of city hall—express this commitment, or lack of it, in the bluntest fashion. Through these mechanistic devices, we are forced to confront some of the most searching philosophical questions that face any country: What do we owe one another as members of a society? Can we sustain a collective sense of purpose in the face of the declining fortunes that are tearing us apart, leaving those who are able to scramble for advantage and those who are not to suffer out of sight? (Newman, 1994:221)*

Working with the Research

1. Think about your past experiences at home and in other social institutions (such as schools and churches). What is your conception of the American dream, based on these experiences? Critically analyze the ways in which society shaped your conception.

2. Newman's research was done in the early 1990s. Do you believe that she is right about the fate of the American dream? Explain.

3. If the American dream is withering, many social changes are in store. Describe the major changes you foresee.

4. Suppose Katherine Newman had decided to place her study in the context of sociological theory. Write a conclusion to her book from the theoretical perspective—functionalist or conflict theorist—that you think is most appropriate.

Section 2

Theoretical Perspectives on Social Change

Key Terms

- equilibrium
- urbanism

Section Preview

The functionalist and conflict perspectives view social change in very different ways. The functionalist perspective depicts societies as relatively stable. Following a major change, these integrated systems seek a new equilibrium. According to the conflict perspective, societies are unstable systems that are constantly undergoing change. Symbolic interactionism identifies decreasing shared values as a source of social instability.

equilibrium
a state of functioning and balance, maintained by a society's tendency to make small adjustments to change

The Functionalist Perspective

Because functionalism emphasizes social stability and continuity, it may seem contradictory to refer to a functionalist theory of social change. There are, however, two functionalist theories of social change—proposed by William Ogburn and Talcott Parsons—that are especially interesting. Both of these theories are based on the concept of *equilibrium*.

Close your eyes and imagine a tightrope walker inching his way across a deep chasm on a narrow rope. If you have an active imagination, you will picture him continually shifting his body and using a pole to counterbalance the effects of the wind as well as the effects of his own motions. The tightrope walker is concerned with maintaining equilibrium. When used by sociologists, **equilibrium** describes a society's tendency to react to changes by making small adjustments to keep itself in a state of functioning and balance.

A society in change, then, moves from stability to temporary instability and back to stability. Sociologists refer to this as a dynamic, or moving, equilibrium. For example, in 1972, a broken dam led to the destruction of the community of Buffalo Creek, West Virginia. The physical destruction of the community was accompanied by death and the loss of the old way of life. Despite the ensuing chaos, residents of the community slowly pulled their lives together again. Although things were not the same as before, a new equilibrium was built out of the physical, social, and human wreckage (Erikson, 1976).

Social equilibrium was shaken for a while, after an earthquake caused the collapse of this Los Angeles area freeway.

led by Mao Zedong in China. As a result of Mao's revolutionary movement, a communist government was instituted.

Demonstrators, with banners in hand, ride a truck en route to Tiananmen Square to protest for democracy and human rights in Beijing, China, in 1989. Explain the type of social movement this demonstration best illustrates.

❖ A **reformative movement** aims to effect more limited changes in a society. The Women's Christian Temperance Union (an antialcohol organization founded in 1874) and the antiwar movement of the 1960s illustrate this type of social movement.

❖ A **redemptive movement** focuses on changing people completely. The religious cult of David Koresh (the Branch Davidians) was a redemptive movement.

❖ An **alternative movement** seeks only limited changes in people. Zero Population Growth, an organization that celebrated its thirtieth anniversary in 1998, illllustrates such a movement. It attempts to persuade people to limit the size of their families. It does not advocate sweeping lifestyle changes, however; nor does it advocate legal penalties for large families.

Theories of Social Movements

Because of the highly structured nature of social movements, sociologists have been able to analyze this form of collective behavior. Two major theories of social movements have evolved. One is *value-added theory,* and the other is *resource mobilization theory.*

What is value-added theory? Before discussing value-added theory, we need to understand the concept of adding value. In the value-added process, each step in the creation of a product contributes, or adds value, to the final entity. Neil Smelser, the sociologist who originated the value-added theory of social movements, gives an example involving automobile production.

> *An example of [the value-added process] is the conversion of iron ore into finished automobiles by a number of stages of processing. Relevant stages would be mining, smelting, tempering, shaping, and combining the steel with other parts, painting, delivering to retailer, and selling. Each stage "adds its value" to the final cost of the finished product. The key element in this example is that the earlier stages must combine according to a certain pattern before the next stage can contribute its particular value to the finished product, an automobile. Painting, in order to be effective as a "determinant" in shaping the product, has to "wait" for the completion of the earlier processes. Every stage in the value-added process, therefore, is a necessary condition for the appropriate and effective condition of value in the next stage (Smelser, 1971:13–14).*

Smelser used this process as a model to understand social movements. The **value-added theory** identifies six conditions that must exist in order for social movements to occur.

reformative movement a social movement that attempts to make limited changes in society

redemptive movement a social movement which seeks to change people completely

alternative movement a social movement that focuses on bringing about limited changes in people

value-added theory theory holding that certain conditions must exist for social movements to occur

1960s	**1970s**	**1980s**	**1990s**	**2000s**
Hot Topics Vietnam War Civil Rights	**Hot Topics** Clean Air and Water Female Empowerment	**Hot Topics** International Human Rights Endangered Species Sexual Harassment	**Hot Topics** Gay Rights Sweatshop Labor Medical Use of Marijuana	**Hot Topics** Globalization Corporate Dominance Immigration

Figure 17.4 Hot Buttons for College Activists. *According to Robert Merton, protest movements are reactions on structural strains of burning importance. College activists have been moved to action by different structural strains since the 1960s.*

Source: **U.** *The National College Magazine* (February, 2000).

1. *Structural conduciveness.* The environment must be social-movement friendly. The college student demonstrations in the 1960s and 1970s occurred because of the war in Vietnam, yes, but also because most college campuses had convenient sites for rallies and protest meetings.

2. *Structural strains.* A second condition promoting the emergence of a social movement is the presence of conflicts, ambiguities, and discrepancies within a society. Without some form of strain, there is no stimulus for change. A key discrepancy in the antiwar movement case was the government's continued stance that there was no war (no legal war had been declared), despite the vast resources being devoted to battle and the obvious combat casualties. (Figure 17.4 identifies major structural strains that have mobilized college students since the 1960s.)

3. *Generalized beliefs.* Generalized beliefs include a general recognition that there is a problem and agreement that something should be done to fix it. Two shared beliefs were crucial to the antiwar movement. One was the belief that the Johnson and Nixon administrations were not telling the truth about the war. Another was that the Vietnam War was so morally wrong that it had to be stopped.

This famous photograph of the tragic antiwar demonstrations at Kent State University in 1970 captured the attention of the nation.

4. *Precipitating factors.* One or more significant events must occur to galvanize people into action. On April 30, 1970, President Nixon ordered the invasion of the neutral country of Cambodia. This event was a show of force to the North Vietnamese government with which the United States government was negotiating to end the war.

5. *Mobilization of participants for action.* Once the first four conditions exist, the only remaining step is to get the people moving. Massive demonstrations were part of the political furor the Cambodian invasion provoked. More than 100,000 opponents of the Vietnam War marched on Washington, D.C. Hundreds of colleges were forced to close as a result of strikes by 1.5 million students.

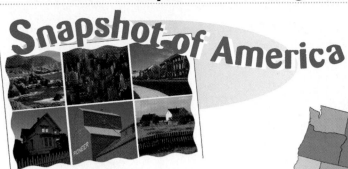

Snapshot of America

Women in the Workplace

The number of women in the U.S. work-place is related to social change and social movements. The U.S. female workforce shot up during World War II. Once the soldiers returned home, however, a large percentage of those working women quit work to raise families. Owing in part to the women's movement, the U.S. has seen a peacetime resurgence of women entering the workforce. This map shows the percentage of women in each state who are active in the labor force.

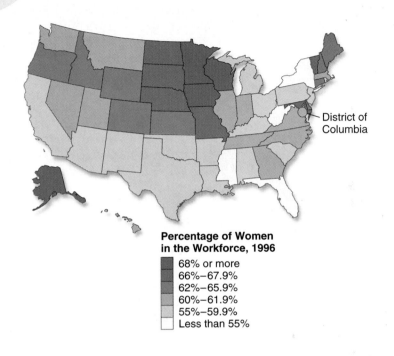

— District of Columbia

Percentage of Women in the Workforce, 1996

- 68% or more
- 66%–67.9%
- 62%–65.9%
- 60%–61.9%
- 55%–59.9%
- Less than 55%

Interpreting the Map

1. Relate strain theory, the women's movement, and increased female labor force participation.
2. How does your state compare with other states in terms of female employment? Describe.

Adapted from *The World Almanac of the U.S.A.* 1998.

6. *Social control.* The sixth determinant of a social movement is ineffective social control. Actions of the media, police, courts, community leaders, and political officials can lead to the success or failure of a social movement. If the right kind of force is applied, a potential social movement may be prevented, even though the first five determinants are present. Efforts to control the situation may block the social movement, minimize its effects, or make matters worse. Efforts to control the antiwar movement, for example, were actually counterproductive. During the student antiwar protests following the Cambodian invasion, the Ohio National Guard, mobilized by the governor of Ohio, killed four students and wounded at least nine others on the Kent State University campus. Two African American students were killed during an antiwar protest at Jackson State University in Mississippi. Such heavy-handedness on the part of politicians and law enforcement officials only stimulated further protest that hastened the ending of the war.

resource mobilization theory theory of social movements that focuses on the use of resources to achieve goals

What is resource mobilization theory? **Resource mobilization theory** focuses on the process through which members of a social movement secure and use the resources needed to advance their cause. Resources include human skills such as leadership, organizational ability, and labor power, as well as material goods such as money, property, and equipment (Cress and Snow, 1996; McCarthy and Wolfson, 1996).

The civil rights movement of the 1960s succeeded in part because of the commitment of African Americans and in part because people of other races contributed the money, energy, and skills necessary to stage repeated protests. In contrast, the gay movement in the United States has experienced difficulty partly because of a relative shortage of money, foot soldiers, and affluent supporters.

Muslim worshippers donate money to aid the relief effort for Turkey, which was devastated by a tremendous earthquake in 1999. Relate this behavior to resource mobilization theory.

Section 4 Assessment

1. How would a sociologist define the term *social movement?*
2. Which of the following is an example of a reformative social movement?
   a. the French Revolution
   b. Zero Population Growth
   c. the Branch Davidians
   d. Women's Christian Temperance Union
3. How is Smelser's theory of social movements an example of the value-added process?
4. Briefly explain the resource mobilization theory of social movements.

Critical Thinking

5. **Synthesizing Information** If you wished to mount a social movement to change some U.S. policy (i.e., air pollution limits), which theory of social change would most likely guide your strategy? Explain why you would select a particular theory and how it would guide your approach.

One hundred and eighty-one years ago, our forefathers started a revolution that still goes on.

Dwight D. Eisenhower
U.S. president

Summary

Section 1: Social Change

Main Idea: Social change refers to new behaviors that have long-term and relatively important consequences. Discovery, invention, and diffusion are the major social processes through which social change occurs. Important agents of social change are technology, population, the natural environment, revolution, and war.

Section 2: Theoretical Perspectives on Social Change

Main Idea: The functionalist perspective depicts societies as relatively stable. Following a major change, these integrated systems seek a new equilibrium. According to the conflict perspective, societies are unstable systems that are constantly undergoing change. Symbolic interactionism identifies decreasing shared values as a source of social instability.

Section 3: Collective Behavior

Main Idea: Collective behavior describes how people behave when they are united by a single short-term goal. Rumors, fads, fashions, mass hysteria, and panics are examples of collective behaviors. Contagion theory and emergent norm theory describe crowd behavior.

Section 4: Social Movements

Main Idea: Social movements are more permanent and more organized than other types of collectives. Theories to explain how social movements develop include value-added theory and resource mobilization theory.

SOCIOLOGY Online

Self-Check Quiz
Visit the *Sociology and You* Web site at soc.glencoe.com and click on **Chapter 17—Self-Check Quizzes** to prepare for the chapter test.

Reviewing Vocabulary

Complete each sentence using each term once.

a. social movement
b. contagion theory
c. rumor
d. revolution
e. fashions
f. fads
g. crowd
h. collective behavior
i. emergent norm theory
j. social change
k. technology

1. New societal behaviors with long-term and relatively important consequences are called _____.

2. _____ is the knowledge and hardware used to achieve practical goals.

3. _____ is a type of social movement that may involve the violent toppling of a political regime.

4. The spontaneous and unstructured social behavior of people who are responding to similar stimuli is known as _____.

5. _____ is a widely circulating story of questionable truth.

6. The unusual behavior patterns that spread rapidly, are embraced zealously, and then disappear in a short time are called _____.

7. _____ are behavior patterns that are widely approved but expected to change periodically.

8. A temporary collection of people who share a common interest is known as a _____.

9. _____ emphasizes the irrationality of crowds, created when members stimulate one another to higher and higher levels of emotional intensity.

10. _____ stresses the similarity between daily social behavior and crowd behavior.

11. The form of collective behavior that has the most structure is called _____.

CHAPTER 17 ASSESSMENT

Reviewing the Facts

1. Use a diagram similar to the one below to show the cause and effect relationship between the three major social processes and social change.

SOCIAL PROCESSES

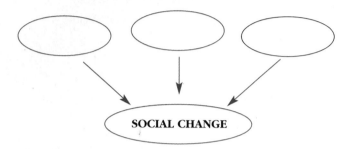

SOCIAL CHANGE

2. Identify and describe the three theories of crowd behavior.
3. What are the five important agents of social change?
4. In your own words explain the value-added theory of social movements.
5. List and describe the four primary types of social movements.
6. Explain the resource mobilization theory of social movements.

Thinking Critically

1. **Applying Concepts** Once upon a time, a family decided to grow orange trees. After several years of hard work and struggle, the first oranges appeared on the trees. Every year after that, when the oranges appeared, the father would say, "Everyone is entitled to choose one orange from the crop." The business thrived and expanded. The children were puzzled that even when the orange grove had grown to include over a thousand trees, they were allowed only one orange a year. Finally, when the children were grown and had children of their own, one of the grandchildren said, "Grandpa, every year we produce hundreds of thousands of oranges, and every year you tell us that we can have only one orange. Why is that?" Grandpa replied, "Because that's the way it's always been." In what way is this story a metaphor for society?

2. **Analyzing Information** Television shows often mirror changes taking place in some segments of society. Sometimes, these changes have not yet reached the mainstream culture. (One popular program centers many of its scenes in a unisex workplace bathroom.) What role do you think television has in changing society? Do you think its influence is more positive or negative?

3. **Evaluating Information** In this country, it is common to read about rumors circulated by the media, especially tabloid newspapers and television news magazine programs. How justified are newspapers and news reporters in publicizing unverified information? Should viewers be responsible for evaluating the information themselves? Should the news sources be penalized for not investigating or verifying rumors? What are the consequences for society if news sources are not reliable?

4. **Drawing Conclusions** Twenty years ago, body piercing (other than for earrings) was considered deviant behavior. Today, it is fast becoming a social norm in many classes and social categories. Do you think that body piercing is a fad or a fashion? What factors might cause a behavior that is not desirable in one generation to become accepted just one generation later?

Sociology Projects

1. **Technology** Over the next few days, look for new technologies that have initiated social changes within the last five years. For example, Web TV is a fairly new technological invention. Make a list of such items, including things that you have heard are coming but have not yet been released. For each item write down what earlier development made the new item possible. For example, high-definition TV was a result of knowledge gained from aerospace

satellite projects. Share your findings with classmates. You will probably be amazed at how extensive your list is. Post it in the classroom, and add to it as you hear about more changes.

2. **Fads** Look through old and new magazines for examples of fads that have appeared since you were born. (Examples might include retro platform shoes and Beanie Babies.) Create a collage illustrating those fads. Are some of the fads still around? Have they been replaced by similar fads? Ask your parents or grandparents what some fads were when they were teenagers. Find pictures, or ask them if they can provide you with examples. Make a poster or arrange the pictures in a booklet format that explains some of the unusual fads.

3. **Crowd Behavior** As an experiment in crowd behavior, try to start a new fad or fashion in your school. For example, get everyone in your group or class to agree to start wearing necklaces with metal washers on them or unmatched socks. If several of you do this, you might be able to convince others that a new fad has begun. If the fad does not catch on, list reasons why you think your peers were resistant to change in this case.

4. **Rumors** Search the library magazine catalog or Internet for rumors concerning a public figure. Identify the source and evaluate its credibility. Or, research a lawsuit filed by a public figure over the publication of a false story.

5. **Fads and Fashions** Working in groups, collect some old high school yearbooks from parents and relatives. Comb through them looking for examples of fads and fashions from different decades. Present your findings to the whole class.

6. **Rumors and the Media** As an extension to "Thinking Critically," question number 3, consider and list the options that a news reporter has when he or she receives unverified stories to report. Suggest possible consequences associated with each option.

Technology Activity

1. Jan Harold Brunvand coined the term *urban legend* to describe a type of rumor that is long lasting and widely believed. This term is commonly used now, and if you search the Internet, you will find many sites devoted to this subject.

   a. Select a few of the web sites (two good ones are at http://www.urbanlegends.com/ and http://www.snopes2.com/) and review them. Be prepared to share one or two of them with your class.

   b. What common elements do these urban legends have? Do your observations correspond with those of Urbanlegends.com?

   c. What role do you think the Internet plays in spreading these urban legends?

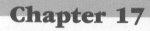

Chapter 17
Enrichment Reading
Falling Through the Net

Computer technology is changing the face of American society. Access to personal computers and the Internet is even affecting the nature of social stratification. Digital technology has become such an important tool for economic success that it threatens to create a new divide between haves and have-nots.

Information tools, such as the personal computer and the Internet, are increasingly critical to economic success and personal advancement. *"Falling Through the Net: Defining the Digital Divide"* finds that more Americans than ever have access to telephones, computers, and the Internet. At the same time, however, . . . there is still a significant "digital **divide**" separating American information "haves" and "have nots." Indeed, in many instances, the digital divide has *widened*. . . .

The good news is that Americans are more connected than ever before. Access to computers and the Internet has soared for people in all demographic groups and geographic locations. At the end of 1998, over 40 percent of American households owned computers, and one-quarter of all households had Internet access. Additionally, those who were less likely to have telephones (chiefly, young and minority households in rural areas) are now more likely to have phones at home.

Accompanying this good news, however, is the persistence of the digital divide between the information rich (such as Whites, Asians/Pacific Islanders, those with higher incomes, those more educated, and dual-parent households) and the information poor (such as those who are younger, those with lower incomes and education levels, certain minorities, and those in rural areas or central cities). The 1998 data reveal significant **disparities,** including the following:

❖ Urban households with incomes of $75,000 and higher are more than *twenty times* more likely to have access to the Internet than those at the lowest income levels, and more than *nine times* as likely to have a computer at home.

❖ Whites are more likely to have access to the Internet from home than Blacks or Hispanics have from *any* location.

❖ Black and Hispanic households are approximately *one-third* as likely to have home Internet access as households of Asian/Pacific Islander descent, and roughly *two-fifths* as likely as White households.

❖ Regardless of income level, Americans living in rural areas are lagging behind in Internet access. Indeed, at the lowest income levels, those in urban areas are more than twice as likely to have Internet access than those earning the same income in rural areas.

For many groups, the digital divide has *widened* as the information "haves" outpace the "have nots" in gaining access to electronic resources. The following gaps with regard to home Internet access are representative:

❖ The gaps between White and Hispanic households, and between White and Black households, are now more than five percentage points larger than they were in 1997.

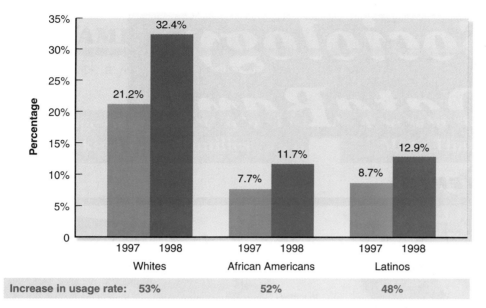

Increase in usage rate:	**53%**		**52%**		**48%**

Figure 17.5 Minorities and the Internet.   *This figure reveals the digital divide in the United States between whites, African Americans, and Latinos. What do you think are the most important consequences of this divide?*

Source: "Report Finds Net Users Increasingly White, Well Off," *Washington Post,* July 9, 1999, p. A20.

❖ The digital divides based on education and income level have also increased in the last year alone. Between 1997 and 1998, the divide between those at the highest and lowest education levels increased 25 percent, and the divide between those at the highest and lowest income levels grew 29 percent.

  Nevertheless, the news is not all bleak. For Americans with incomes of $75,000 and higher, the divide between Whites and Blacks has actually narrowed considerably in the last year. This finding suggests that the most affluent American families, **irrespective** of race, are connecting to the Net.

Source: "Falling Through the Net: Defining the Digital Divide," a Report on the Telecommunications and Information Technology Gap in America (Washington, DC: National Telecommunications and Information Administration, U.S. Department of Commerce, July 1999)

What Does it Mean ?

divide
as a noun, something that separates two areas; a point or line of division

disparities
marked differences in quality or character (usually where you would not expect them)

irrespective
regardless; without relation to

Read and React

1. What is the main idea of this report on Internet access?
2. What does the term *information rich* (in the third paragraph) mean?
3. Who is more likely to have Internet access, whites or Asian/Pacific Islanders? How can you tell?
4. Why do you think urban Americans are more than twice as likely to have Internet access as rural Americans with the same income level?
5. In what category has the gap between African Americans and whites significantly narrowed? What explanation would you offer for this?
6. Do you think the federal government is now (or should be now) attempting to bridge the digital divide in the U.S.? Why or why not?

Reported Voting by Age Group—Presidential Elections, 1976–1996

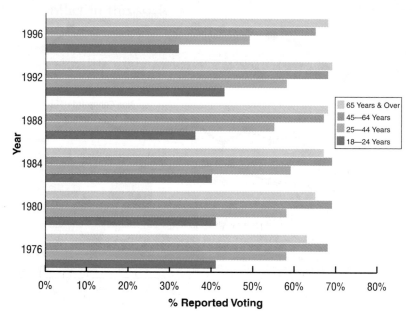

Source: Federal Election Commission

Voter Turnouts in National Elections in the 1990s

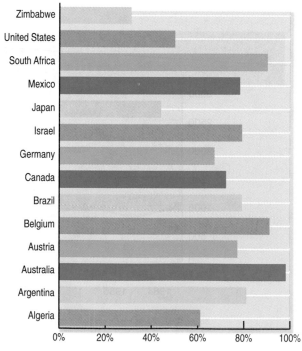

Source: Federal Election Commission

THE ECONOMY

The *economy* is the social institution that regulates the production and distribution of goods and services for a society.

What Jobs Do Women Have?

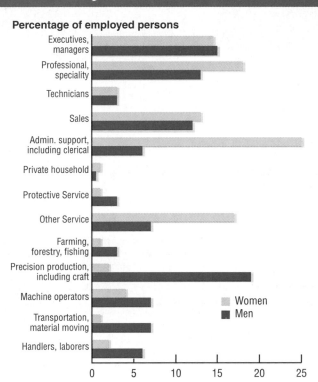

Percentage of employed persons

Source: *2000 United States Population Data Sheet.*
Washington, DC: Population Reference Bureau, 2000.

Sociology Databank

Who's Entering and Staying in the Labor Force?

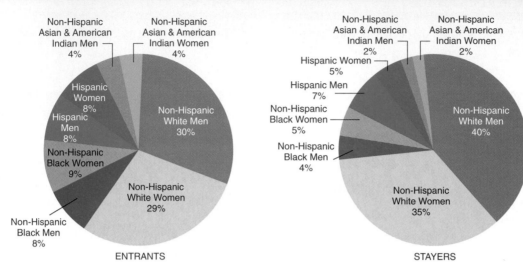

ENTRANTS

- Non-Hispanic Asian & American Indian Men 4%
- Non-Hispanic Asian & American Indian Women 4%
- Non-Hispanic White Men 30%
- Hispanic Women 8%
- Hispanic Men 8%
- Non-Hispanic Black Women 9%
- Non-Hispanic White Women 29%
- Non-Hispanic Black Men 8%

STAYERS

- Non-Hispanic Asian & American Indian Men 2%
- Non-Hispanic Asian & American Indian Women 2%
- Hispanic Women 5%
- Hispanic Men 7%
- Non-Hispanic Black Women 5%
- Non-Hispanic Black Men 4%
- Non-Hispanic White Men 40%
- Non-Hispanic White Women 35%

Source: *2000 United States Population Data Sheet.*
Washington, DC: Population Reference Bureau, 2000.

Median Net Worth of Households by Monthly Household Income Quintile Groups: 1993 and 1995

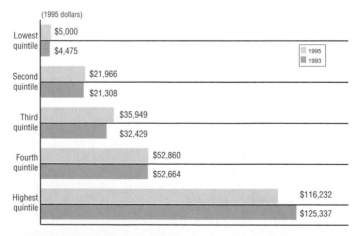

(1995 dollars)

Quintile	1995	1993
Lowest quintile	$5,000	$4,475
Second quintile	$21,966	$21,308
Third quintile	$35,949	$32,429
Fourth quintile	$52,860	$52,664
Highest quintile	$116,232	$125,337

Source: U.S. Bureau of the Census. *"Household Net Worth and Asset Ownership."* Washington, DC: U.S. Government Printing Office, 2000.

Gross National Income in Purchasing Power Parity Per Capita for Selected Countries, 1999

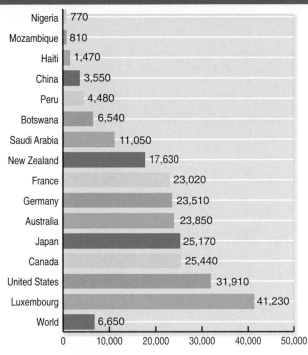

Country	Value
Nigeria	770
Mozambique	810
Haiti	1,470
China	3,550
Peru	4,480
Botswana	6,540
Saudi Arabia	11,050
New Zealand	17,630
France	23,020
Germany	23,510
Australia	23,850
Japan	25,170
Canada	25,440
United States	31,910
Luxembourg	41,230
World	6,650

Source: *2001 World Population Data Sheet.*
Washington DC: Population Reference Bureau, 2001.
Note: Figures given in U.S. dollars

Percentage of Workers Who Are Self-Employed (3-year average 1997–1999)

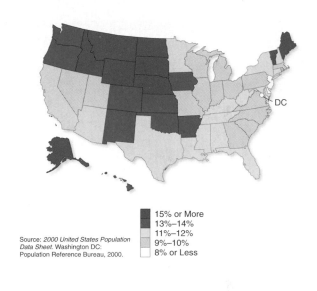

DC

- 15% or More
- 13%–14%
- 11%–12%
- 9%–10%
- 8% or Less

Source: *2000 United States Population Data Sheet.* Washington DC: Population Reference Bureau, 2000.

RELIGION

Religion is a unified system of beliefs and practices concerned with sacred things.

Percentage of Americans Who Think Religion Is Increasing or Losing Its Influence

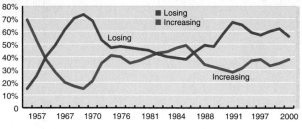

Source: The Gallup Organization

U.S. Per Capita Income/ Per Member Giving as a Percentage of Income

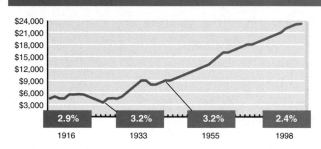

Percentage of Americans Who Believe that Religion Can Answer All of Today's Problems or Is Old-Fashioned

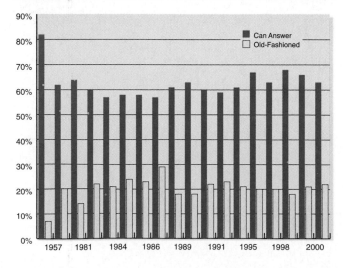

Source: The Gallup Organization.

Giving as a Percentage of Income and Membership as a Percentage of U.S. Population, 1968–1998

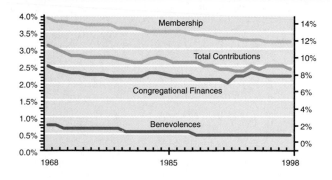

SPORT

Sport is a set of competitive activities in which winners and losers are determined by physical performance within a set of established rules.

Participation in High School and NCAA Sponsored Sports, 1982 to 2000

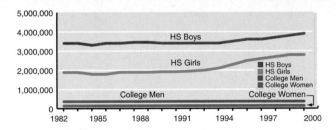

Sources: National Federation of State High School Associations and the National Collegiate Athletic Association.

Interest in Professional Sports Based on Attendance At Professional Sporting Events: United States by Demographics

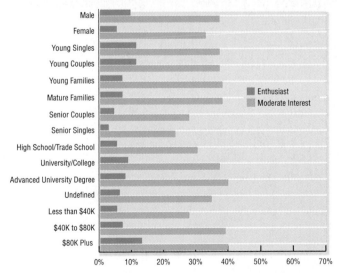

Source: Lang, David. *"Interest in Professional Sports (As a Spectator) Profile Report."* April 2001.

Racial Composition of Players in Men's Professional Leagues and the WNBA

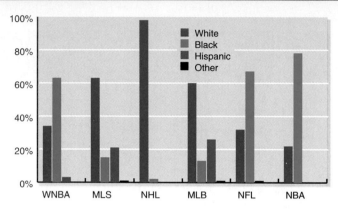

Source: Lapchick, Richard E., and Kevin J. Matthews (1998). *"1998 Racial and Gender Report Card."* Boston: Northeastern University's Center for the Study of Sport in Society.

Percentage Increase in Applications to Colleges and Universities in the Three Years Following a National Championship

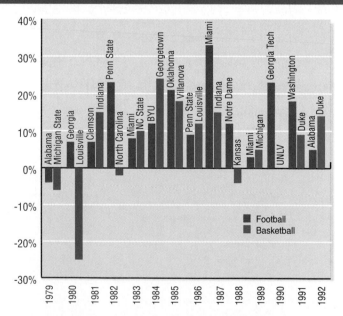

Source: Toma, J. Douglas, and Michael E. Cross (1998). *"Intercollegiate Athletics and Student College Choice: Exploring the Impact of Championship Seasons on Undergraduate Applications."* Research in Higher Education 39, 633—661.

AMERICAN SOCIOLOGICAL ASSOCIATION'S CODE OF ETHICS

The American Sociological Association's (ASA's) Code of Ethics sets forth the principles and ethical standards that underlie sociologists' professional responsibilities and conduct. These principles and standards should be used as guidelines when examining everyday professional activities. They constitute normative statements for sociologists and provide guidance on issues that sociologists may encounter in their professional work.

The Preamble and General Principles of the Code are aspirational goals to guide sociologists toward the highest ideals of sociology. Although the Preamble and General Principles are not enforceable rules, they should be considered by sociologists in arriving at an ethical course of action and may be considered by ethics bodies in interpreting the Ethical Standards.

The Ethical Standards set forth enforceable rules of conduct by sociologists. Most of the Ethical Standards are written broadly in order to apply to sociologists in varied roles, and the application of an Ethical Standard may vary depending on the context. The Ethical Standards are not exhaustive. Any conduct that is not specifically addressed by this Code of Ethics is not necessarily ethical or unethical.

Preamble

This Code of Ethics articulates a common set of values upon which sociologists build their professional and scientific work. The Code is intended to provide both the general principles and the rules to cover professional situations encountered by sociologists. It has as its primary goal the welfare and protection of the individuals and groups with whom sociologists work. It is the individual responsibility of each sociologist to aspire to the highest possible standards of conduct in research, teaching, practice, and service.

The development of a dynamic set of ethical standards for a sociologist's work-related conduct requires a personal commitment to a lifelong effort to act ethically; to encourage ethical behavior by students, supervisors, supervisees, employers, employees, and colleagues; and to consult with others as needed concerning ethical problems. Each sociologist supplements, but does not violate, the values and rules specified in the Code of Ethics based on guidance drawn from personal values, culture, and experience.

General Principles

The following General Principles are aspirational and serve as a guide for sociologists in determining ethical courses of action in various contexts. They exemplify the highest ideals of professional conduct.

Principle A: Professional Competence   Sociologists strive to maintain the highest levels of competence in their work; they recognize the limitations of their expertise; and they undertake only those tasks for which they are qualified by education, training, or experience. They recognize the need for ongoing education in order to remain professionally competent; and they utilize the appropriate scientific, professional, technical, and administrative resources needed to ensure competence in their professional activities. They consult with other professionals when necessary for the benefit of their students, research participants, and clients.

Principle B: Integrity   Sociologists are honest, fair, and respectful of others in their professional activities—in research, teaching, practice, and service. Sociologists do not knowingly act in ways that jeopardize either their own or others' professional welfare. Sociologists conduct their affairs in ways that inspire trust and confidence; they do not knowingly make statements that are false, misleading, or deceptive.

Principle C: Professional and Scientific Responsibility   Sociologists adhere to the highest scientific and professional standards and accept responsibility for their work. Sociologists understand that they form a community and show respect for other sociologists even when they disagree on theoretical, methodological, or personal approaches to professional activities. Sociologists value the public trust in sociology and are concerned about their ethical behavior and that of other sociologists that might compromise that trust. While endeavoring always to be collegial, sociologists must never let the desire to be collegial outweigh their shared responsibility for ethical behavior. When appropriate, they consult with colleagues in order to prevent or avoid unethical conduct.

Principle D: Respect for People's Rights, Dignity, and Diversity   Sociologists respect the rights, dignity, and worth of all people. They strive to eliminate bias in their professional activities, and they do not tolerate any forms of discrimination based on age; gender; race; ethnicity; national origin; religion; sexual orientation; disability; health conditions; or marital, domestic, or parental status. They are sensitive to cultural, individual, and role differences in serving, teaching, and studying groups of people with distinctive characteristics. In all of their work-related activities, sociologists acknowledge the rights of others to hold values, attitudes, and opinions that differ from their own.

Principle E: Social Responsibility   Sociologists are aware of their professional and scientific responsibility to the communities and societies in which they live and work. They apply and make public their knowledge in order to contribute to the public good. When undertaking research, they strive to advance the science of sociology and to serve the public good.

Ethical Standards

The complete text of the Ethical Standards can be found at the ASA web site. Excerpts from this code are reproduced here.

1. Professional and Scientific Standards: Sociologists adhere to the highest possible technical standards that are reasonable and responsible in their research, teaching, practice, and service activities.

2. Competence: Sociologists conduct research, teach, practice, and provide service only within the boundaries of their competence, based on their education, training, supervised experience, or appropriate professional experience.

3. Representation and Misuse of Expertise: Because sociologists' scientific and professional judgments and actions may affect the lives of others, they are alert to and guard against personal, financial, social, organizational, or political factors that might lead to misuse of their knowledge, expertise, or influence.

4. Delegation and Supervision: Sociologists provide proper training and supervision to their students, supervisees, or employees and take reasonable steps to see that such persons perform services responsibly, competently, and ethically.

5. Nondiscrimination: Sociologists do not engage in discrimination in their work based on age; gender; race; ethnicity; national origin; religion; sexual orientation; disability; health conditions; marital; domestic, or parental status; or any other applicable basis proscribed by law.

6. Non-exploitation: Whether for personal, economic, or professional advantage, sociologists do not exploit persons over whom they have direct or indirect supervisory, evaluative, or other authority such as students, supervisees, employees, or research participants.

7. Harassment: Sociologists do not engage in harassment of any person, including students, supervisees, employees, or research participants. Harassment consists of a single intense and severe act or of multiple persistent or pervasive acts which are demeaning, abusive, offensive, or create a hostile professional or workplace environment. Sexual harassment may include sexual solicitation, physical advance, or verbal or non-verbal conduct that is sexual in nature. Racial harassment may include unnecessary, exaggerated, or unwarranted attention or attack, whether verbal or non-verbal, because of a person's race or ethnicity.

8. Employment Decisions: Sociologists have an obligation to adhere to the highest ethical standards when participating in employment-related decisions, when seeking employment, or when planning to resign from a position.

9. Conflicts of Interest: Sociologists maintain the highest degree of integrity in their professional work and avoid conflicts of interest and the appearance of conflict. Conflicts of interest arise when sociologists' personal or financial interests prevent them from performing their professional work in an unbiased manner.

10. Public Communication: Sociologists adhere to the highest professional standards in public communications about their professional services, credentials and expertise, work products, or publications, whether these communications are from themselves or from others.

10.02 In working with the press, radio, television, or other communications media or in advertising in the media, sociologists are cognizant of potential conflicts of interest or appearances of such conflicts (e.g., they do not provide compensation to employees of the media), and they adhere to the highest standards of professional honesty (e.g., they acknowledge paid advertising).

11. Confidentiality: Sociologists have an obligation to ensure that confidential information is protected. They do so to ensure the integrity of research and the open communication with research participants and to protect sensitive information obtained in research, teaching, practice, and service. When gathering confidential information, sociologists should take into account the long-term uses of the information, including its potential placement in public archives or the examination of the information by other researchers or practitioners.

11.02 Sociologists may confront unanticipated circumstances where they become aware of information that is clearly health- or life-threatening to research participants, students, employees, clients, or others. In these cases, sociologists balance the importance of guarantees of confidentiality with other principles in this Code of Ethics, standards of conduct, and applicable law.

Confidentiality is not required with respect to observations in public places, activities conducted in public, or other settings where no rules of privacy are provided by law or custom. Similarly, confidentiality is not required in the case of information available from public records.

11.06 Sociologists do not disclose in their writings, lectures, or other public media confidential, personally identifiable information concerning their research participants, students, individual or organizational clients, or other recipients of their services which is obtained during the course of their work, unless consent from individuals or their legal representatives has been obtained.

When confidential information is used in scientific and professional presentations, sociologists disguise the identity of research participants, students, individual or organizational clients, or other recipients of their services.

12. Informed Consent: Informed consent is a basic ethical tenet of scientific research on human populations. Sociologists do not involve a human being as a subject in research without the informed consent of the subject or the subject's legally authorized representative, except as otherwise specified in this Code. Sociologists recognize the possibility of undue influence or subtle pressures on subjects that may derive from researchers' expertise or authority, and they take this into account in designing informed consent procedures.

12.04 In undertaking research with children, sociologists obtain the consent of children to participate, to the extent that they are capable of providing such consent, except under circumstances where consent may not be required.

12.05 Sociologists never deceive research participants about significant aspects of the research that would affect their willingness to participate, such as physical risks, discomfort, or unpleasant emotional experiences.

12.06 Sociologists obtain informed consent from research participants, students, employees, clients, or others prior to videotaping, filming, or recording them in any form, unless these activities involve simply naturalistic observations in public places and it is not anticipated that the recording will be used in a manner that could cause personal identification or harm.

13. Research Planning, Implementation, and Dissemination: Sociologists have an obligation to promote the integrity of research and to ensure that they comply with the ethical tenets of science in the planning, implementation, and dissemination of research. They do so in order to advance knowledge, to minimize the possibility that results will be misleading, and to protect the rights of research participants.

13.01 Planning and Implementation: In planning and implementing research, sociologists minimize the possibility that results will be misleading.

Sociologists take steps to implement protections for the rights and welfare of research participants and other persons affected by the research.

In their research, sociologists do not encourage activities or themselves behave in ways that are health- or life-threatening to research participants or others.

In planning and implementing research, sociologists consult those with expertise concerning any special population under investigation or likely to be affected.

13.04 Reporting on Research: Sociologists do not fabricate data or falsify results in their publications or presentations.

In presenting their work, sociologists report their findings fully and do not omit relevant data. They report results whether they support or contradict the expected outcomes.

Sociologists report sources of financial support in their written papers and note any special relations to any sponsor. In special circumstances, sociologists may withhold the names of specific sponsors if they provide an adequate and full description of the nature and interest of the sponsor.

14. Plagiarism: In publications, presentations, teaching, practice, and service, sociologists explicitly identify, credit, and reference the author when they take data or material verbatim from another person's written work, whether it is published, unpublished, or electronically available.

15. Authorship Credit: Sociologists take responsibility and credit, including authorship credit, only for work they have actually performed or to which they have contributed.

Sociologists ensure that principal authorship and other publication credits are based on the relative scientific or professional contributions of the individuals involved, regardless of their status. In claiming or determining the ordering of authorship, sociologists seek to reflect accurately the contributions of main participants in the research and writing process.

A student is usually listed as principal author on any multiple-authored publication that substantially derives from the student's dissertation or thesis.

20. Adherence to the Code of Ethics: Sociologists have an obligation to confront, address, and attempt to resolve ethical issues according to this Code of Ethics.

20.01 Familiarity with the Code of Ethics: Sociologists have an obligation to be familiar with this Code of Ethics, other applicable ethics codes, and their application to sociologists' work. Lack of awareness or misunderstanding of an ethical standard is not, in itself, a defense to a charge of unethical conduct.

20.02 Confronting Ethical Issues: When sociologists are uncertain whether a particular situation or course of action would violate the Code of Ethics, they consult with other sociologists knowledgeable about ethical issues, with ASA's Committee on Professional Ethics, or with other organization entities such as institutional review boards.

When sociologists take actions or are confronted with choices where there is a conflict between ethical standards enunciated in the Code of Ethics and laws or legal requirements, they make known their commitment to the Code and take steps to resolve the conflict in a responsible manner by consulting with colleagues, professional organizations, or the ASA's Committee on Professional Ethics.

20.03 Fair Treatment of Parties in Ethical Disputes: Sociologists do not discriminate against a person on the basis of his or her having made an ethical complaint.

Sociologists do not discriminate against a person based on his or her having been the subject of an ethical complaint. This does not preclude taking action based upon the outcome of an ethical complaint.

20.04 Reporting Ethical Violations of Others: When sociologists have substantial reason to believe that there may have been an ethical violation by another sociologist, they attempt to resolve the issue by bringing it to the attention of that individual if an informal resolution appears appropriate or possible, or they seek advice about whether or how to proceed based on this belief, assuming that such activity does not violate any confidentiality rights. Such action might include referral to ASA's Committee on Professional Ethics.

20.05 Cooperating with Ethics Committees: Sociologists cooperate in ethics investigations, proceedings, and resulting requirements of the American Sociological Association. In doing so, they make reasonable efforts to resolve any issues of confidentiality. Failure to cooperate may be an ethics violation.

20.06 Improper Complaints: Sociologists do not file or encourage the filing of ethics complaints that are frivolous and are intended to harm the alleged violator rather than to protect the integrity of the discipline and the public.

Honoring America

For Americans, the flag has always had a special meaning. It is a symbol of our nation's freedom and democracy.

Flag Etiquette

Over the years, Americans have developed rules and customs concerning the use and display of the flag. One of the most important things every American should remember is to treat the flag with respect.

- The flag should be raised and lowered by hand and displayed only from sunrise to sunset. On special occasions, the flag may be displayed at night, but it should be illuminated.

- The flag may be displayed on all days, weather permitting, particularly on national and state holidays and on historic and special occasions.

- No flag may be flown above the American flag or to the right of it at the same height.

- The flag should never touch the ground or floor beneath it.

- The flag may be flown at half-staff by order of the president, usually to mourn the death of a public official.

- The flag may be flown upside down only to signal distress.

- The flag should never be carried flat or horizontally, but always carried aloft and free.

- When the flag becomes old and tattered, it should be destroyed by burning. According to an approved custom, the Union (stars on blue field) is first cut from the flag; then the two pieces, which no longer form a flag, are burned.

★ ★ ★ ★ ★ ★ ★ ★

The American's Creed

I believe in the United States of America as a Government of the people, by the people, for the people, whose just powers are derived from the consent of the governed; a democracy in a republic; a sovereign Nation of many sovereign States; a perfect union, one and inseparable; established upon those principles of freedom, equality, justice, and humanity for which American patriots sacrificed their lives and fortunes.

I therefore believe it is my duty to my Country to love it; to support its Constitution; to obey its laws; to respect its flag, and to defend it against all enemies.

The Pledge of Allegiance

I pledge allegiance to the Flag of the United States of America and to the Republic for which it stands, one Nation under God, indivisible, with liberty and justice for all.

The Star-Spangled Banner

O! say, can you see, by the dawn's early light,
What so proudly we hail'd at the twilight's last gleaming?
Whose broad stripes and bright stars, thro' the perilous fight,
O'er the ramparts we watched were so gallantly streaming?
And the rockets' red glare, the bombs bursting in air,
Gave proof thro' the night, that our flag was still there.
O! say, does that Star-Spangled Banner yet wave
O'er the land of the free and the home of the brave?

On the shore, dimly seen thro' the mist of the deep,
Where the foe's haughty host in dread silence reposes,
What is that which the breeze, o'er the towering steep,
As it fitfully blows, half conceals, half discloses?
Now it catches the gleam of the morning's first beam,
In full glory reflected now shines on the stream.
'Tis the Star-Spangled Banner. O long may it wave
O'er the land of the free and the home of the brave.

And where is that band who so vauntingly swore,
That the havoc of war and the battle's confusion
A home and a country should leave us no more?
Their blood has wash'd out their foul footstep's pollution.
No refuge could save the hireling and slave
From the terror of flight or the gloom of the grave,
And the Star-Spangled Banner in triumph doth wave
O'er the land of the free and the home of the brave.

O thus be it e'er when free men shall stand
Between their lov'd home and war's desolation,
Blest with vict'ry and peace, may the Heav'n-rescued land
Praise the pow'r that hath made and preserv'd us a nation.
Then conquer we must, when our cause it is just,
And this be our motto, "In God is our Trust."
And the Star-Spangled Banner in triumph shall wave
O'er the land of the free and the home of the brave.

Glossary

A

absolute poverty the absence of enough money to secure life's necessities

achieved status a position that is earned or chosen

actuarial tables statistics of life expectancies; used as basis for life insurance costs

age stratification the unequal distribution of scarce resources based on age

ageism a set of beliefs, attitudes, norms, and values used to justify age-based prejudice and discrimination

agricultural society a society that uses plows and draft animals in growing food

alternative movement a social movement that focuses on bringing about limited changes in people

anomie a social condition in which norms are weak, conflicting, or absent

anticipatory socialization the voluntary process of preparing to accept new norms, values, attitudes, and behaviors

ascribed status a position that is neither earned nor chosen but assigned

assimilation the blending or fusing of minority groups into the dominant society

authoritarianism a political system controlled by nonelected rulers who usually permit some degree of individual freedom

authority the legitimate or socially approved use of power

averting turning aside; prevention

B

beliefs ideas about the nature of reality

bilateral family arrangement where descent and inheritance are passed equally through both parents

biological determinism principle that behavioral differences are the result of inherited physical characteristics

bourgeoisie class owning the means for producing wealth

bullish optimistic; hopeful

bureaucracy a formal organization based on rationality and efficiency

C

canon an accepted principle or rule

capitalism an economic system based on private ownership of property and the pursuit of profit

capitalist person who owns or controls the means for producing wealth

case study intensive study of a single group, incident, or community

caste system a stratification structure that does not allow for social mobility

causation the belief that events occur in predictable ways and that one event leads to another

census regularly occurring count of a particular population

central-city dilemma concentration of people in need of public services without tax base–generated money to provide for them

charismatic authority authority that arises from the personality of an individual

charter schools public schools that are operated like private schools by public school teachers and administrators

church a life-encompassing religious organization to which all members of a society belong

city dense and permanent concentration of people living in a specific area and working primarily in non-agricultural jobs

class conflict the ongoing struggle between the bourgeoisie (owners) and the proletariat (working) classes

class consciousness identification with the goals and interests of a social class

closed-ended questions questions a person must answer by choosing from a limited, predetermined set of responses

coercion interaction in which individuals or groups are forced to behave in a particular way

cognitive ability capacity for thinking abstractly

collective behavior the spontaneous behavior of a group of people responding to similar stimuli

collectivity collection of people who do not normally interact and who do not share clearly defined norms

compensatory education specific curricular programs designed to overcome a deficiency

competition system in which rewards are based on relative performance

concentric zone theory theory that describes urban growth in terms of circular areas that grow from the central city outward

conflict interaction aimed at defeating an opponent

conflict perspective approach emphasizing the role of conflict, competition, and constraint within a society

conformity behavior that matches group expectations

conglomerates networks of unrelated businesses operating under one corporate umbrella

contagion theory theory stating that members of a crowd stimulate each other to higher and higher levels of emotion and irrational behavior

contingent employment the hiring of part-time, short-term workers

control theory theory that compliance with social norms requires strong bonds between individuals and society

convergence theory theory that states that crowds are formed by people who deliberately congregate with like-minded others

cooperation interaction in which individuals or groups combine their efforts to reach a goal

cooperative learning instructional method that relies on cooperation among students

core tier an occupational structure composed of large firms dominating their industries

corporation an organization owned by shareholders, who have limited liability and limited control

correlation a measure of the relationship between two variables

counterculture a subculture deliberately and consciously opposed to certain central beliefs or attitudes of the dominant culture

crime acts committed in violation of the law

criminal justice system system comprising institutions and processes responsible for enforcing criminal statutes

crowd a temporary collection of people who share an immediate common interest

crude birthrate the annual number of live births per one thousand members of a population

crude death rate the annual number of deaths per one thousand members of a population

cult a religious organization whose characteristics are not drawn from existing religious traditions within a society

cultural bias the unfair measurement of the cognitive abilities of people in some social categories

cultural particulars the ways in which a culture expresses universal traits

cultural pluralism desire of a group to maintain some sense of identity separate from the dominant group

cultural universals general cultural traits that exist in all cultures

culture knowledge, values, customs, and physical objects that are shared by members of a society

D

de facto segregation denial of equal access based on everyday practice

de jure segregation denial of equal access based on the law

demographic transition theory theory that population growth is a function of the level of economic development in a country

demography the scientific study of population

denomination one of several religious organizations that most members of a society accept as legitimate

dependency ratio the ratio of dependent persons to economically active persons

dependent variable a characteristic that reflects a change

desocialization the process of giving up old norms, values, attitudes, and behaviors

deterrence discouraging criminal acts by threatening punishment

deviance behavior that departs from societal or group norms

deviant a person who breaks significant societal or group norms

differential association theory theory that individuals learn deviance in proportion to the number of deviant acts to which they are exposed

diffusion process by which one culture or society borrows from another culture or society

discovery process by which something is learned or reinterpreted

discrimination treating people differently based on ethnicity, race, religion, or culture

dispersed collectivity collectivity made up of people who are not physically connected but who follow common rules or respond to common stimuli

doubling time number of years needed to double the base population size

downsizing the process by which companies reduce their work forces

dramaturgy approach that depicts human interaction as theatrical performances

drive impulse to reduce discomfort

dysfunction negative consequence of an aspect of society

E

economic institution institution that determines how goods and services are produced and distributed

edge city a suburban unit specializing in a particular economic activity

educational equality condition in which schooling produces the same results for lower-class and minority children as it does for other children

elitism system in which a community or society is controlled from the top by a few individuals or organizations

emergent norm theory theory stating that norms develop to guide crowd behavior

endogamy marriage within one's own group as required by social norms

equalitarian family structure where authority is evenly shared between the husband and wife

equilibrium a society's tendency to react to changes by making adjustments to keep itself in a state of functioning and balance

ethnic minority group identified by cultural, religious, or national characteristics

ethnocentrism judging others in terms of one's own cultural standards

exogamy the practice of marrying outside one's group

exponential growth growth in which the amount of increase is added to the base figure each time period

extended family two or more adult generations of the same family whose members share economic resources and a common household

extrapolating predicting based on past experiences

F

fad an unusual behavior pattern that spreads rapidly and disappears quickly

false consciousness adoption of the ideas of the dominant class by the less powerful class

family a group of people related by marriage, blood, or adoption

family planning the voluntary use of population control methods

fashion a widely accepted behavior pattern that changes periodically

fecundity the maximum rate at which women can physically produce children

feminization of poverty a trend in U.S. society in which women and children make up an increasing proportion of the poor

fertility a measure of the number of children born to a woman or a population of women

fertility rate the annual number of live births per one thousand women aged fifteen to forty-four

field research research that takes place in a natural (nonlaboratory) setting

folkways norms that lack moral significance

for-profit schools schools run by private companies on government funds

formal organization a group deliberately created to achieve one or more long-term goals

formal sanctions sanctions imposed by persons given special authority

formal schooling education that is provided and regulated by society

fundamentalism the desire to resist secularization and to adhere closely to traditional religious beliefs, rituals, and doctrines

G

game stage Mead's third stage in the development of role taking; children anticipate the actions of others based on social rules

Gemeinschaft "community"; preindustrial society based on tradition, kinship, and close social ties

gender identity a sense of being male or female based on learned cultural values

gender socialization the social process of learning how to act as a boy or girl

generalized other integrated conception of the norms, values, and beliefs of one's community or society

genocide the systematic effort to destroy an entire population

gentrification the development of low-income areas by middle-class homebuyers, landlords, and professional developers

Gesellschaft "society"; industrial society characterized by weak family ties, competition, and impersonal social relationships

gross migration rate the number of persons per year per one thousand members of a population who enter or leave a geographic area

group at least two people who have one or more goals in common and share common ways of thinking and behaving

groupthink when thinking in a group is self-deceptive, based on conformity to group beliefs, and created by group pressure to conform

H

hate crime a criminal act motivated by prejudice

hidden curriculum the informal and unofficial aspects of culture that children are taught in school, such as conformity or cooperation

hidden unemployment unemployment that includes people not counted in the traditional unemployment categories

horizontal mobility a change in occupation within the same social class

horticultural society a society that survives primarily through the growing of plants

hunting and gathering society a society that survives by hunting animals and gathering edible foods

hypothesis of linguistic relativity theory stating that our idea of reality depends largely upon language

hypothesis testable statement of relationships among variables

I

"I" the part of the self that accounts for unlearned, spontaneous acts

ideal culture cultural guidelines that group members claim to accept

imitation stage Mead's first stage in the development of role taking; children begin to imitate behaviors without understanding why

in-group exclusive group demanding intense loyalty

incarceration a method of protecting society from criminals by keeping them in prisons

incest taboo a norm forbidding marriage between certain kinds of relatives

income amount of money received by an individual or group over a specific time period

independent variable a characteristic that causes something to occur

industrial society a society that depends on science and technology to produce its basic goods and services

infant mortality rate the annual number of deaths among infants under one year of age per one thousand live births

informal organization groups within a formal organization in which personal relationships are guided by norms, rituals, and sentiments that are not part of the formal organization

informal sanctions rewards or punishments that can be applied by most members of a group

instincts innate (unlearned) patterns of behavior

institutionalized discrimination unfair practices that grow out of common behaviors and attitudes and that are a part of the structure of a society

integrative curriculum an approach to education based on student-teacher collaboration

interest group a group organized to influence political decision making

intergenerational mobility a change in status or class from one generation to the next

interlocking directorates directorates that result when heads of corporations sit on one another's boards

intervening variable a variable that changes the relationship between an independent and a dependent variable

interview a survey method in which a trained researcher asks questions and records the answers

invention the creation of something new from previously existing items or processes

iron law of oligarchy theory that power increasingly becomes concentrated in the hands of a few members of any organization

L

labeling theory theory that society creates deviance by identifying particular members as deviant

latent function an action that produces an unintended and unrecognized result

law a norm that is formally defined and enforced by officials

legitimate justify or give official approval to

life expectancy the average number of years that persons in a given population born at a particular time can expect to live

life span the most advanced age to which humans can survive

looking-glass self an image of yourself based on what you believe others think of you

M

magnet schools public schools that focus on particular disciplines or areas, such as fine arts or science

manifest function an action that produces an intended and recognized result

marriage a legal union based on mutual rights and obligations

mass media means of communication designed to reach the general population

master status a position that strongly affects most other aspects of a person's life

material culture the concrete, tangible objects of a culture

matriarchy the pattern in which the oldest woman living in the household has authority over all other family members

matrilineal family arrangement where descent and inheritance is passed through the female line

matrilocal the pattern in which married couples live with or near the wives' parents

"me" the part of the self formed through socialization

mechanical solidarity social dependency based on a widespread consensus of values and beliefs, enforced conformity, and dependence on tradition and family

mechanization the process of replacing animal and human power with machine power

meritocracy a society in which social status is based on ability and achievement

migration the movement of people from one geographic area to another

minority a group of people with physical or cultural traits different from those of the dominant group in the society

mob emotional crowd ready to use violence for a specific purpose

monogamy a marriage consisting of one man and one woman at a time

monopolies companies that have control over the production or distribution of a product or service

mores norms that have moral dimensions and that should be followed by members of the society

mortality deaths within a population

multicultural education an educational curriculum that emphasizes differences among gender, ethnic, and racial categories

multinationals firms based in highly industrialized societies with operating facilities throughout the world

multiple causation the belief that an event occurs as a result of several factors working in combination

multiple nuclei theory theory that focuses on specific geographic or historical influences on urban growth

N

negative deviance involves behavior that underconforms to accepted norms

neolocal the pattern in which newly married couples set up their own households

net migration rate the annual increase or decrease per one thousand members of a population resulting from migration into and out of the population

nonmaterial culture ideas, knowledge, and beliefs that influence people's behavior

norms rules defining appropriate and inappropriate behavior

nuclear family family structure composed of one or both parents and children

nullifying causing to have no value or force; negating

O

obligations behaviors that individuals are expected to perform toward others

occupational sex segregation the concentration of women in lower-status positions

occupations categories of jobs that involve similar activities at different work locations

oligopolies combinations of companies that control the production or distribution of a product or service

open class system a system in which social class is based on merit and individual effort; movement is allowed between classes

open classroom a nonbureaucratic approach to education based on democracy, flexibility, and non-competitiveness

open-ended questions questions a person is to answer in his or her own words

organic solidarity social interdependency based on a high degree of specialization in roles

out-group group targeted by an in-group for opposition, antagonism, or competition

overurbanization when a city cannot supply adequate jobs and housing for its inhabitants

P

Pandora's box a source of trouble

participant observation a case study where the researcher becomes a member of the group being studied

pastoral societies societies where food is obtained primarily by raising and taking care of animals

patriarchy the pattern in which the oldest man living in the household has authority over the rest of the family members

patrilineal family arrangement where descent and inheritance is passed through the male line

patrilocal the pattern in which married couples live with or near the husbands' parents

peer group set of individuals of roughly the same age and interests

peripheral theory theory that emphasizes the growth of suburbs around the central city

peripheral tier an occupational structure composed of smaller, less profitable firms

perspective a particular point of view

play stage Mead's second stage in the development of role taking; children act in ways they imagine other people would

pluralism system in which political decisions are made as a result of bargaining and compromise among special interest groups

political institution institution that determines how power is obtained and exercised

political socialization informal and formal processes by which a person develops political opinions

polyandry the marriage of one woman to two or more men at the same time

polygamy the marriage of a male or female to more than one person at a time

population a group of people living in a particular place at a specified time or a group of people with certain specified characteristics

population control attempts by government to control birth rates

population momentum inability to stop population growth immediately because of previous high rate of growth

population pyramid a graphic representative of the age and gender composition of a population

positive deviance involves behavior that overconforms to social expectations

reference group—grupo de referencia grupo utilizado como autoevaluación y desarrollo de actitudes, valores, creencias, y normas

reflex—reflejo reacción automática a estímulos físicos

reformative movement—movimiento reformista movimiento social que intenta efectuar cambios limitados en la sociedad

rehabilitation—rehabilitación proceso para cambiar o reformar a un criminal por medio de la socialización

relative poverty—pobreza relativa sistema para medir la pobreza basado en la desigualdad económica existente entre aquéllos que se encuentran en el extremo inferior de la escala social y el resto de la sociedad

religion—religión sistema unificado de creencias y prácticas relativas a cosas sagradas

religiosity—religiosidad formas en que las personas expresan sus intereses y convicciones religiosas

replacement level—nivel de reemplazo tasa de nacimientos en la cual la pareja se reemplaza a sí misma sin aumentar la población

representative democracy—democracia representativa sistema de gobierno que usa a funcionarios elegidos para satisfacer los deseos de la mayoría

representative sample—muestra representativa muestra que refleja con exactitud las características de la población tomada en su totalidad

resocialization—resocialización el proceso de adoptar nuevas normas, valores, actitudes, y conductas

resource mobilization—movilización de recursos teoría de movimiento social que se centra en el uso de los recursos para lograr metas

retribution—punición castigo que tiene como objetivo que los criminales paguen compensación por sus actos

revolution—revolución derrocamiento repentino y total de un orden político o social

revolutionary movement—movimiento revolucionario movimiento social que intenta cambiar la estructura total de la sociedad

rights—derechos conductas que los individuos pueden esperar de otros

riot—disturbio episodio de violencia y destrucción aleatoria llevada a cabo por una multitud

role—rol la conducta esperada asociada a un estado social determinado

role conflict—conflicto de roles condición en la cual la ejecución del rol de un estado social interfiere con la ejecución del rol de otro estado social

role performance—desempeño de un rol la conducta real de un individuo en un rol

role strain—tensión de rol condición en la cual los roles de un solo estado social son inconsistentes o conflictivos

role taking—tomar un rol asumir el punto de vista de otra persona y usar ese punto de vista para moldear el concepto de sí mismo

rumor—rumor trozo de información de gran difusión que no ha sido verificada como verdadera o falsa

S

sacred—sagrado objetos e ideas que se ponen aparte y a las cuales se les da un significado especial que va más allá o trasciende la existencia inmediata

sample—muestra grupo de personas que representan una población mayor

sanctions—sanciones recompensas o castigos usados para estimular a las personas que sigan las normas

school desegregation—integración escolar el logro del equilibrio racial en una sala de clases

scientific method—método científico el reconocimiento y formulación de un problema, la recolección de datos a través de la información y la experiencia y la formulación y comprobación de hipótesis

secondary analysis—análisis secundario la utilización de información prerrecolectada para propósitos de recolección de datos e investigación

secondary deviance—desviación secundaria desviación en la cual la vida e identidad de un individuo están organizadas en torno al rompimiento de las normas sociales

secondary group—grupo secundario personas que comparten sólo parte de sus vidas mientras se centran en una meta o labor

secondary relationships—relaciones secundarias interacciones impersonales que involucran porciones limitadas de las personalidades

secondary sectors—sectores secundarios aquella parte de la economía que se ocupa de los bienes manufacturados

sect—secta organización religiosa que proviene de un deseo de reformar una organización religiosa ya existente

sector theory—teoría de sector teoría que enfatiza la importancia de las rutas de transporte en el proceso de crecimiento urbano

secularization—secularización el proceso a través del cual lo sagrado pierde influencia sobre la sociedad

self-concept—autoconcepto imagen de sí mismo como teniendo una identidad separada de la de otras personas

self-fulfilling prophecy—profecía autocumplida predicción que tiene como resultado una conducta que hace que lo esperado se convierta en realidad

sex—sexo clasificación de las personas en masculino o femenino basada en características biológicas

sexism—sexismo conjunto de creencias, actitudes, normas y valores usados para justificar la desigualdad de los sexos

significant others—personas importantes aquéllas personas cuyas reacciones son las más importantes para su autoconcepto

social aggregate—agregado social agrupaciones de personas al mismo tiempo en el mismo lugar

social categories—categorías sociales grupos de personas que comparten una característica social

social change—cambio social nuevas conductas sociales con consecuencias importantes en el largo plazo

social class—clase social segmento de la sociedad cuyos miembros poseen cantidades similares de recursos y comparten valores, normas y un estilo de vida identificable

social control—control social formas para estimular la conformidad a las normas sociales

social dynamics—dinámica social el estudio del cambio social

social exchange—intercambio social acción voluntaria llevada a cabo con la esperanza de obtener una recompensa a cambio

social interaction—interacción social el proceso de influenciar a otras personas mientras las personas se relacionan entre sí

social mobility—movilidad social el movimiento de individuos o personas entre clases sociales

social movement—movimiento social movimiento cuyo objetivo es promover o prevenir los cambios sociales; la forma mejor estructurada y racional de conducta colectiva

social network—red social red de relaciones sociales que unen una persona a otras personas y grupos

social processes—procesos sociales serie de pasos que llevan a un cambio en el nivel social

social sanctions—sanciones sociales premios o castigos que incentivan la conformidad con las normas sociales

social solidarity—solidaridad social el grado en que una sociedad está unida

social statics—estática social el estudio de la estabilidad y orden social

social stratification—estratificación social la clasificación de personas o grupos de acuerdo a su acceso desigual a los recursos escasos

social structure—estructura social las interacciones moldeadas de las personas en las relaciones sociales

socialism—socialismo sistema económico basado en la creencia que los medios de producción deben ser controlados por las personas como un todo

socialization—socialización el proceso de aprendizaje a participar en un grupo

society—sociedad territorio específico habitado por personas que comparten una cultura en común

sociobiology—sociobiología el estudio de la base biológica del comportamiento humano

sociological imagination—imaginación sociológica habilidad para ver el vínculo entre la sociedad y uno mismo

sociological perspective—perspectiva sociológica punto de vista que mira el comportamiento de grupos, no de individuos

sociology—sociología el estudio científico de la estructura social (conducta social humana)

spirit of capitalism—espíritu del capitalismo la obligación de reinvertir el dinero en negocios en vez de gastarlo

sport—deporte conjunto de actividades competitivas en las cuales los ganadores y los perdedores se determinan por el desempeño físico, bajo un conjunto de reglas establecidas

sport subculture—subcultura deportiva grupo que desempeña roles determinados, valores y creencias organizadas alrededor de una actividad deportiva

spurious correlation—correlación espuria relación entre dos variables que es realmente ocasionada por un tercer factor

stacking—relegación designación de jugadores a posiciones menos importantes sobre una base de raza o etnicidad

status—estado posición que ocupa una persona dentro de la estructura social

status set—conjunto de estados todas las posiciones que ocupa una persona en un tiempo específico

stereotype—estereotipo imagen distorsionada, exagerada o demasiado simplificada aplicada a una categoría de personas

stigma—estigma rasgo o calificación no deseada que se usa para caracterizar a un individuo

strain theory—teoría de tensión teoría que sostiene que las desviaciones ocurren cuando existe un espacio entre las metas culturales y la habilidad para lograr esas metas por medios legítimos

subculture—subcultura grupo que forma parte de la cultura dominante pero que difiere de ella en algunos aspectos importantes

subjugation—subyugación proceso por medio del cual se le niega a un grupo minoritario el acceso a los beneficios de una sociedad

suburbanization—suburbanización pérdida de población de una ciudad a las áreas circundantes

survey research—investigación por encuesta método en el cual las personas responden a preguntas

symbol—símbolo cualquier cosa que representa otra cosa y que tiene un significado acordado

symbolic interactionism—interacción simbólica enfoque que se centra en las interacciones entre las personas basadas en símbolos que ambas entienden

T

taboo—tabú regla de conducta cuya violación exige de un castigo severo

technology—tecnología conocimiento y herramientas utilizados par lograr metas prácticas

tertiary sector—sector terciario la parte de la economía que proporciona servicios

theoretical perspective—perspectiva teórica conjunto de suposiciones que se aceptan como verdaderas

total fertility rate—tasa de fertilidad total promedio de niños que tiene una mujer durante su vida

total institutions—instituciones absolutas lugares en que las personas son separadas del resto de la sociedad y controladas por los funcionarios a cargo

totalitarianism—totalitarismo sistema político en el cual un gobernante con poderes absolutos trata de controlar todos los aspectos de una sociedad

tracking—clasificación colocación de los alumnos en programas acordes a sus niveles de habilidad académica

traditional authority—autoridad tradicional formas de autoridad en las cuales la legitimidad de un líder tiene sus raíces en la costumbre

U

underclass—clase inferior personas típicamente desempleadas que provienen de familias que han sido pobres por generaciones

urban ecology—ecología urbans el estudio de las relaciones entre los seres humanos y el medio ambiente de las ciudades

urban legend—leyenda urbana una historia moralista que el narrador jura que le pasó a alguien que él o ella conocen

urbanism—urbanismo la idea que la urbanización involucra un estilo particular de vida

urbanization—urbanización proceso por medio del cual una porción más grande de la población mundial vive en las ciudades

V

value added theory—teoría de valor agregado teoría que sostiene que ciertas condiciones deben estar dadas para que los movimientos sociales ocurran

values—valores idea amplia sobre lo que es bueno o deseable compartida por muchos integrantes de una sociedad

variable—variable característica sujeta a cambios

verstehen—empatía la comprensión de la conducta humana poniéndose uno mismo en el lugar de otros

vertical mobility—movilidad vertical cambio hacia arriba o hacia abajo del estado ocupacional o clase social

victim discounting—clasificación de víctimas procedimiento mediante el cual se reduce la gravedad de los crímenes que dañan a personas de estratos bajos

voucher system—sistema de comprobantes sistema en el cual los fondos de las escuelas fiscales pueden utilizarse para subsidiar a escuelas públicas, privadas, o religiosas

W

war—guerra conflicto armado organizado que ocurre dentro de una sociedad o entre naciones

wealth—riqueza el total de los recursos económicos que posee una persona o grupo

white-collar crime—crimen de ejecutivos crímenes relacionados al trabajo cometido por personas de condición alta

working poor—trabajadores pobres personas empleadas en trabajos que requieren de un grado elemental de habilidad con los sueldos más bajos y que no ganan lo suficiente para salir de la pobreza

Z

zero population growth—crecimiento cero de la población situación en la cual las muertes están equilibradas con los nacimientos de modo que no crece la población

References

A

Acosta, R. Vivian, and Linda Jean Carpenter. "Women in Intercollegiate Sport: A Longitudinal Study—Nineteen Year Update, 1987–1996." Department of Physical Education, Brooklyn College, 1997.

Adelmann, P. K., T. C. Antonucci, S. E. Crohan, and L. M. Coleman (1989). "Empty Nest, Cohort, and Employment in the Well-Being of Midlife Women." *Sex Roles*, 173–189.

Adler, Emily Stier, and Roger Clark (1999). *How It's Done: An Invitation to Social Research*. Belmont, CA: Wadsworth Publishing Company.

Adler, Patricia A., and Peter Adler (1998). *Peer Power*. New Brunswick: Rutgers University Press.

Allport, Gordon (1958). *The Nature of Prejudice*. Garden City, NY: Doubleday.

American Sociological Association (1995). "Careers in Sociology." Washington, DC.

Andersen, Margaret L. (1997). *Thinking About Women*. 4th ed. Boston: Allyn and Bacon.

Asch, Solomon E. (November 1955). "Opinions and Social Pressure." *Scientific American 193*, 31–35.

Atchley, Robert C. (1999). *Social Forces and Aging*. 9th ed. Belmont, CA: Wadsworth.

Auguet, Roland (1972). *Cruelty and Civilization*. London: George Allen and Unwin, Ltd.

____. (1972). *Crueldad y Civilización: Los Juegos Romanos*. Barcelona: Aymá.

B

Baca Zinn, Maxine, and D. Stanley Eitzen (1998). "Economic Restructuring and Systems Inequality." In Margaret L. Andersen and Patricia Hill. (eds.), *Race, Class, and Gender: An Anthology*. 3rd ed. Belmont, CA: Wadsworth Publishing Co., pp. 233–237.

Bai, Matt, and Andrew Murr (January 25, 1999). "Go for the Greed." *Newsweek*.

Ballantine, Jeanne H. (1993). *The Sociology of Education*. 3rd ed. Englewood Cliffs, NJ: Prentice Hall.

Bardo, John W., and John J. Hartman (1982). *Urban Sociology*. Itasca, IL: Peacock.

Barlett, Donald L., and James B. Steele (1996). *America: Who Stole the Dream?* Kansas City, KA: Andrews and McMeel.

Barner, Robert (1996). "The New Millennium Workplace: Seven Changes that Will Challenge Managers—and Workers." *The Futurist 30*, 14–19.

Barnes, et al. (1998). *Growing Up in Stepfamilies*. New York: Oxford University Press.

Barr, C. (1995). "Pushing the Envelope: What Curriculum Integration Can Be." In E. Brazee and J. Capelluti. (eds.), *Dissolving Boundaries: Toward an Integrative Curriculum*. Columbus, OH: National Middle School Association.

Barron, James (September 16, 1988). "Fondly Recalling a Martian Invasion." *New York Times*, B1, B3.

Barry, Norman P. (1999). *Welfare*. 2nd ed. Minneapolis: University of Minnesota Press.

Beaton, Rod (February 25–27, 2000). "Braves Penalized for Illegal Signing." *USA Today* :1A.

Becker, Howard S. (1991). *Outsiders*. New York: Free Press.

Begley, Sharon (November 1, 1993). "Not Just a Pretty Face." *Newsweek*, 63–67.

____. (February 28, 2000). "Getting Inside a Teen Brain." *Newsweek*, 58–59.

Bell, Daniel (1999). *The Coming of Post-Industrial Society*. New York: Basic Books.

Bellah, Robert N., et al. (1991). *The Good Society*. New York: Knopf.

Belton, Beth (March 2, 1999). "Fear Forces Employees to Take Initiative." *USA Today*.

Benokraitis, Nijole V. (1999). *Subtle Sexism*. Thousand Oaks, CA: Sage.

____. (1998). *Marriages and Family*. Englewood Cliffs, NJ: Prentice Hall.

Berger, Peter L. (1990). *The Sacred Canopy: Elements of a Sociological Theory of Religion*. New York: Doubleday & Co.

Berk, Richard A. (1974). *Collective Behavior*. Dubuque, IA: William C. Brown.

Bianchi, Suzanne M. (June 1990). "America's Children: Mixed Prospects." *Population Bulletin 45*, 3–41.

Bierman, John (January 29, 1990). "Frustration and Fury." *Maclean's, 29*.

Blum, Debra E. (August 11, 1993). "Men Turn to Federal Anti-Bias Laws to Protect Teams from the Chopping Block." *Chronicle of Higher Education*, A33–A34.

Blumer, Herbert. "Collective Behavior." In Alfred M. Lee (ed.), *Principles of Sociology*. 3rd ed. New York: Barnes & Noble, 1969a, pp. 65–121.

____. (1969b). *Symbolic Interactionism.* Englewood Cliffs, NJ: Prentice Hall.

Booth, Alan, and Ann C. Crouter. (eds.). (1998). *Men in Families: When Do They Get Involved? What Difference Does It Make?* Mahwah, NJ: Lawrence Erlbaum Associates.

Bowen, William G., and Derek Bok (2000). *The Shape of the River: Long-Term Consequences of Considering Race in College and University Admissions.* Princeton, NJ: Princeton University Press.

Brajuha, Mario, and Lyle Hallowell (January 1986). "Legal Intrusion and the Politics of Fieldwork: The Impact of the Brajuha Case." *Urban Life 14,* 454–478.

Branscum, Deborah (March 1, 1999). "Go On, Break the Chain." *Newsweek, 58.*

Brinton, Crane (1990). *The Anatomy of Revolution.* New York: Knopf.

Brodie, Mollyann (1995). *The Four Americas: Government and Social Policy Through the Eyes of America's Multi-Racial and Multi-Ethnic Society.* A report of the Washington Post/Kaiser Family Foundation/Harvard Survey Project. Menlo Park, CA: Kaiser Family Foundation.

Brown, Susan L., and Alan Booth (August 1996). "Cohabitation versus Marriage: A Comparison of Relationship Quality." *Journal of Marriage and the Family 58,* 668–678.

Bruner, Jerome (January 1982). "Schooling Children in a Nasty Climate." *Psychology Today,* 57–63.

Brunvand, Jan Harold (1989). *Curses! Broiled Again!* New York: Norton.

Bulkeley, William M. (June 16, 1997). "Family Portrait: Web Pages Allow Families to Keep in Touch." *The Wall Street Journal,* R24.

Burgess, Ernest W. (1925). "The Growth of the City." In Robert E. Park, Ernest W. Burgess, and Robert D. McKenzie (eds.), *The City.* Chicago: University of Chicago Press, pp. 47–62.

Buss, David M., Neil M. Malamuth, and Barbara A. Winstead (1998). "Sex, Power, Conflict: Evolutionary and Feminist Perspectives." *Contemporary Psychology 43.*

C

Campbell, Frances A., and Craig T. Ramey (1994). "Effects of Early Intervention on Intellectual and Academic Achievement: A Follow-Up Study of Children from Low-Income Families." *Child Development 65,* 684–698.

Cantril, Hadley (1982). *The Invasion from Mars.* Princeton, NJ: Princeton University Press.

Caplow, Theodore (1991). *American Social Trends.* New York: Harcourt Brace Jovanovich.

____. (February 1998). "The Case of the Phantom Episcopalians." *American Sociological Review 63,* 137–145

Casbergue, Renee M., and Judith Kieff (Spring 1998). "Marbles Anyone? Traditional Games in the Classroom." *Childhood Education,* 143–147.

Casler, Lawrence (1965). "The Effects of Extra Tactile Stimulation on a Group of Institutionalized Infants." *Genetic Psychology Monographs 71,* 137–175.

Center for the American Woman and Politics. "Fact Sheet." April 1999.

Chagnon, Napoleon A. (1997). *Yanomamö.* 5th ed. Fort Worth: Harcourt Brace College Publishers.

Chamberlain, Gary (October 4, 1999). "Metal Wars." *Design News 115.*

Chambliss, William J. (November/December 1973). "The Saints and the Roughnecks." *Society, 11,* 24–31.

Chang, Iris (1998). *The Rape of Nanking: The Forgotten Holocaust of World War II.* New York: Viking Penguin.

Chandbasekaran, Rajiv (June 25, 1999). "Microsoft Trial Ends After 8 Months," *The Washington Post,* A1, A20.

Children's Defense Fund (1991). *The State of America's Children—1991.* Washington, DC: Children's Defense Fund.

Clark, Charles S. (May 7, 1993). "Cults in America." *C Q Researcher, 3,* 385–408.

"Closing the Gap." (September 2, 1995) *The Economist 74.*

Coakley, Jay J. (ed.). (1998). *Sport in Society.* 6th ed. Boston: Irwin/McGraw-Hill.

Cohen, David, and Marvin Lazerson (March/April 1972). "Education and the Corporate Order." *Socialist Revolution 2,* 47–72.

Coleman, James S., et al. (1966). *Equality of Educational Opportunity.* Washington, DC: U.S. Government Printing Office.

Coleman, James W. (September 1987). "Toward an Integrated Theory of White-Collar Crime." *American Journal of Sociology 93,* 406–439.

Cooley, Charles Horton (1902). *Human Nature and the Social Order.* New York: Scribner's.

Cox, Frank D. (1999). *Human Intimacy: Marriage, the Family, and Its Meaning.* Belmont, CA: Wadsworth Publishing Company.

Cox, Harvey (1977). *Turning East: The Promise and Peril of the New Orientalism.* New York: Simon and Schuster.

____. (1992). *Religion in the Secular City.* New York: Simon & Schuster.

____. (1996). *Fire from Heaven.* London: Cassell.

____. (1996). *Fire from Heaven: The Rise of Pentecostal Spirituality and the Reshaping of Religion in the Twenty-First Century.* Reading, MA: Addison Wesley Longman, Inc.

Cowgill, Donald O., and Lowell D. Holmes (eds.). (1972). *Aging and Modernization.* New York: Appleton-Century-Crofts.

Cowley, Geoffrey, and Anne Underwood (Winter, 1997–98). "Surgeon, Drop that Scalpel." *Newsweek* 77–78.

Crain, Robert L. (January 1970). "School Integration and Occupational Achievement of Negroes." *American Journal of Sociology 75,* 593–606.

Crain, Robert L., and Carol S. Weisman (1972). *Discrimination, Personality and Achievements.* New York: Seminar Press.

Cress, Daniel M., and David A. Snow (December 1996). "Mobilization at the Margins: Resources, Benefactors, and the Viability of Homeless Social Movement Organizations." *American Sociological Review 61,* 1089–1109.

Crewdson, John (March 13, 1994). "Fraud in Breast Cancer Study." *Chicago Tribune 1.*

Crosby, F. E. (1993). *Juggling.* New York: Free Press.

Crosby, John F. (1985). *Reply to Myth: Perspectives on Intimacy.* New York: Wiley.

Cuzzort, R. P., and E. W. King (1976). *Humanity and Modern Social Thought.* 2nd ed. Hinsdale, IL: Dryden Press.

D

Darder, Antonia, and Rodolfo D. Torres (1997). *The Latino Reader.* Malden, MA: Blackwell.

Davies, Bronwyn (1990). *Frogs and Snails and Feminist Tales.* New York: Pandora Press.

Deak, JoAnn (1998). *How Girls Thrive.* Washington, DC: National Association of Independent Schools.

Degler, Carl N. (1991). *In Search of Human Nature.* New York: Oxford University Press.

DeYoung, Alan J. (1989). *Economics and American Education.* White Plains, NY: Longman.

DiIulio, John J., Jr., and Anne Morrison Piehl (Fall 1991). "Does Prison Pay?: The Stormy National Debate Over the Cost-Effectiveness of Imprisonment." *The Brookings Review* 28–35.

Doreian, Patrick, and Frans N. Stokman (1997). *Evolution of Social Networks.* Amsterdam: Gordon & Breach Publishers.

Dornbush, Sanford M., et al. (1985). "Single Parents, Extended Households, and the Control of Adolescents." *Child Development* 56, 326–341.

Dudley, Kathryn Marie (1997). *The End of the Line: Lost Jobs, New Lives in Postindustrial America.* Chicago: The University of Chicago Press.

Dudley, William (ed.) (1999). *Media Violence.* San Diego, CA: Greenhaven Press.

Duke, Lynne, and Gabriel Escobar (May 10, 1992). "A Looting Binge Born of Necessity, Opportunity." *Washington Post* Al, A23.

Durkheim, Emile (1964a). *The Division of Labor in Society.* New York: Free Press.

____. *Suicide.* Translated by John A. Spaulding and George Simpson (1964b). Edited by George Simpson. New York: Free Press.

____. *The Elementary Forms of the Religious Life* (1995). New York: Free Press.

Dynes, Russell R., and Kathleen J. Tierney (eds.) (1994). *Disasters, Collective Behavior, and Social Organization.* Newark: University of Delaware Press.

E

Eccles, Jacquelynne, et al. (February, 1993). "Development During Adolescence: The Impact of Stage-Environment Fit on Young Adolescents' Experiences in Schools and in Families." *American Psychologist 48,* 90–101.

Eder, Donna (1995). *School Talk.* New Brunswick, NJ: Rutgers University Press.

Eitzen, D. Stanley (1993). *Sport in Contemporary Society: An Anthology.* 4th ed. New York: St. Martin's Press.

____. "The Dark Side of Competition." In D. Stanley Eitzen (ed.) (1996), *Sport in Contemporary Society.* 5th ed. New York: St. Martin's Press, pp. 185–192.

____. *Fair and Foul: Beyond the Myths and Paradoxes of Sport.* Lanham, MA: Rowman & Littlefield Publishers, 1999.

Eitzen, D. Stanley, and George H. Sage (1997). *Sociology of North American Sport.* 6th ed. Boston: WCB McGraw-Hill.

El Nasser, Haya (June 25, 1996). "Judges Say 'Scarlet Letter' Angle Works." *USA Today* 1A–2A.

Elikann, Peter T. (1996). *The Tough-On-Crime Myth: Real Solutions to Cut Crime.* New York: Plenum.

Elkin, Frederick, and Gerald Handel (1991). *The Child and Society.* 5th ed. New York: McGraw-Hill.

Ember, Carol R., and Melvin Ember (1999). *Anthropology.* 9th ed. Upper Saddle River, NJ: Prentice Hall.

Erikson, Erik H. (1964). *Childhood and Society.* 2nd ed. New York: Norton.

____. (1982). *The Life Cycle Completed*. New York: Norton.

Erikson, Kai. *Sociological Visions*. Blue Ridge Summit, PA: Rowman & Littlefield Publishers, 1997.

Erikson, Kai T. (1976). *Everything in Its Path*. New York: Simon & Schuster.

Espiritu, Yen Le (1996). *Asian American Men and Women*. Thousand Oaks, CA: Sage.

Etzioni, Amitai (October 1982). "Education for Mutuality and Civility." *Futurist 16*, 4–7.

Evans, Jean. *Three Men*. New York: Knopf, 1954.

F

Farley, Reynolds (1996). *The New American Reality: Who We Are, How We Got There, Where We Are Going*. New York: Russell Sage Foundation.

Fausto-Sterling, Anne (1987). *Myths of Gender*. New York: Basic Books.

Feagin, Joe R. (February 1991). "The Continuing Significance of Race: Antiblack Discrimination in Public Places." *American Sociological Review 56*, 101–115.

Fedarko, Kevin (December 6, 1993). "Bodies of Evidence." *Time 70*.

Federal Election Commission. (2001) "International Voter Turnout." http://www.fec.gov/.

Fine, Gary Alan (1987). *With the Boys: Little League Baseball and Preadolescent Culture*. Chicago: University of Chicago Press.

____. (1996). *The Culture of Restaurant Work*. Berkeley and Los Angeles: University of California Press.

Fischer, David Hackett (1977). *Growing Old in America*. New York: Oxford University Press.

Fishman, Mark, and Gray Cavender. (eds.) (1998). *Entertaining Crime*. Hawthorne, NY: Aldine de Gruyter.

Flanagan, William G. (1993). *Contemporary Urban Sociology*. New York: Cambridge University Press.

Fukuyama, Francis (May 1999a). "The Great Disruption: Human Nature and the Reconstitution of Social Order." *Atlantic Monthly 283*, 55–80.

G

Galloway, Joseph L. (March 3, 1999). "In the Heart of Darkness." *U.S. News & World Report*.

Gallup, George H., Jr. (2001). *The Gallup Poll*. http://www.gallup.com/poll/.

Gallup, George H., Jr. (1988). *The Gallup Poll*. Wilmington, DE: Scholarly Resources.

____. (1994a). *The Gallup Poll, Public Opinion 1993*. Wilmington, DE: Scholarly Resources.

____. (1996). *Religion in America 1996*. Princeton, NJ: The Princeton Religion Research Center.

Game, Ann, and Andrew W. Metcalfe (1996). *Passionate Sociology*. Thousand Oaks, CA: Sage.

Gamst, Glenn, and Charles M. Otten (Summer 1992). "Job Satisfaction in High Technology and Traditional Industry: Is There a Difference?" *The Psychological Record* 413–425.

Ganong, Lawrence, and Marilyn Coleman (1994). *Remarried Family Relationships*. Thousand Oaks, CA: Sage.

Gans, Herbert J. (1968). *People and Plans*. New York: Basic Books.

____. (July/August 1971). "The Uses of Poverty: The Poor Pay All." *Social Policy 2*, 20–24.

Gardner, David Pierpont (1983). *A Nation at Risk: The Imperative for Educational Reform*. Report of the National Commission on Excellence in Education. Washington, DC: U.S. Government Printing Office.

Garreau, J. (1991). *Edge City: Life on the New Frontier*. New York: Doubleday.

Gegax, T. Trent, and Matt Bai (May 10, 1999). "Searching for Answers." *Newsweek* 30–34.

Gelles, Richard J. (1997). *Intimate Violence in Families*. 3rd ed. Thousand Oaks, CA: Sage.

George, Yolanda S., Shirley M. Malcolm, and Laura Jeffers (May 1993). "Computer Equity for the Future." *Communications of the ACM 36*, 78–81.

Gerstel, Naomi, and Harriet Engel Gross (1995). "Gender and Families in the United States: The Reality of Economic Dependence." In Jo Freeman (ed.), *Women: A Feminist Perspective*. 5th ed. Mountain View, CA: Mayfield, pp. 92–127.

Gerth, H. H., and C. Wright Mills (eds.) (1958). *From Max Weber*. New York: Oxford University Press.

Gibbons, Tom (February 24, 1985). "Justice Not Equal for Poor Here." *Chicago Sun-Times* 1, 18.

Gibson, Margaret A., and John V. Ogbu (1991). *Minority Status and Schooling*. New York: Garland Publishing.

Giddens, Anthony (1987). *Social Theory and Modern Sociology*. Stanford, CA: Stanford University Press.

____. (1997). *Introduction to Sociology*. 2nd ed. New York: Norton.

Gilbert, Dennis (1998). *The American Class Structure*. 5th ed. Belmont, CA: Wadsworth Publishing Company.

Glazer, Nathan (1999). "The End of Meritocracy." *The New Republic*.

Glick, P., and S. L. Lin (February 1986). "More Young Adults Are Living with Their Parents: Who Are They?" *Journal of Marriage and the Family*, 107–112.

Goffman, Erving (1961a). *Encounters*. Indianapolis: Bobbs-Merrill.

____. (1963). *Stigma.* Englewood Cliffs, NJ: Prentice- Hall.

____. (1974). *The Presentation of Self in Everyday Life.* New York: Overlook Press.

____. (1979). *Gender Advertisements.* New York: Harper & Row.

____. (February 1983). "The Interaction Order." *American Sociological Review 48,* 1–17.

Golden, Frederic (December 31, 1999). "Albert Einstein: Person of the Century." *Time,* 62–65.

Goleman, D. (April 10, 1988). "An Emerging Theory on Blacks' IQ Scores." *New York Times Education Supplement,* 22–24.

Goode, Erich (1992). *Collective Behavior.* Fort Worth, TX: Sanders College Publishing.

Goode, William J. (1970). *World Revolution and Family Patterns.* New York: Free Press.

Gould, Stephen Jay (1981). *The Mismeasurement of Man.* New York: Norton.

Greenwald, Elissa A., Hilary R. Persky, Jay R. Campbell, and John Mazzeo (1999). *NAEP 1998 Writing: Report Card for the Nation and the States.* Washington, DC: National Center for Education Statistics.

Griffin, John Howard (1961). *Black Like Me.* Boston: Houghton Mifflin.

Gur, R. C., et al. (January 27, 1995). "Sex Differences in Regional Cerebral Glucose Metabolism During a Resting State." *Science 267,* 528–531.

H

Hagan, Frank E. (1994a). *Introduction to Criminology.* 3rd ed. Chicago: Nelson-Hall Publishers.

Hagan, John (1994b). *Crime and Disrepute.* Thousand, Oaks, CA: Pine Forge Press.

Hagedorn, John M. (1998). "Gang Violence in the Postindustrial Era." In Michael Tonry and Mark H. Moore (eds.), *Youth Violence.* Chicago: The University of Chicago Press, pp. 365–419.

Hammel, Sara, and Anna Mulrine (July 12, 1999). "They Get More than Just Game." *U.S. News and World Report.*

Handel, Gerald (ed.). (June 1990). "Revising Socialization Theory." *American Sociological Review 55,* 463–466.

Harlow, Harry F. (1967). "The Young Monkeys." *Psychology Today 5,* 40–47.

Harlow, Harry F., and Margaret Harlow (November 1962). "Social Deprivation in Monkeys." *Scientific American 207,* 137–146.

Harlow, Harry F., and Robert R. Zimmerman (August 1959). "Affectional Responses in the Infant Monkey." *Science 21,* 421–432.

Harris, Chauncy D. (1997). "'The Nature of Cities' and Urban Geography in the Last Half Century." *Urban Geography,* 15–35.

Harris, Judith Rich (1998). *The Nurture Assumption: Why Children Turn Out the Way They Do?* New York: Free Press.

Harris, Marvin (1974). *Cows, Pigs, Wars, and Witches.* New York: Random House.

Hawking, Stephen W. (1998). *A Brief History of Time.* New York: Bantam Books.

Hawley, W. D. (1985). "Achieving Quality Integrated Education—With or Without Federal Help." In F. Schultz (ed.). *Annual Editions: Education 85/86.* Guilford, CT: Dushkin Publishing, pp. 142–145.

Hawley, W. D., and M. A. Smylie (1988). "The Contribution of School Desegregation to Academic Achievement and Racial Integration." In P. A. Katz and D. A. Taylor (eds.), *Eliminating Racism.* New York: Plenum Press, pp. 281–297.

Heller, Mary Edna, Ruth S. Kempe, and Richard D. Krugman (1999). (eds.). *The Battered Child.* 5th ed. Chicago: University of Chicago Press.

Herbert, Wray (March 22, 1999). "Getting Close, But Not Too Close." *U.S. News Online.* http://www.usnews.com.

Herrnstein, Richard J., and Charles Murray (1996). *The Bell Curve: Intelligence and Class Structure in American Life.* New York: Free Press.

Hillier, Susan, and Georgia M. Barrow (1999). *Aging, the Individual, and Society.* 7th ed. Belmont, CA: Wadsworth Publishing Company.

Hilts, Philip (1997). "Smoke Screen." In Jerome H. Sknolnick and Elliott Currie (eds.), *Crisis in American Institutions.* New York: Longman, pp. 29–38.

Hirschi, Travis (1972). *Causes of Delinquency.* Berkeley: University of California Press.

Hochschild, Arlie R. (1997). *The Time Bind: When Work Becomes Home and Home Becomes Work.* New York: Henry Holt.

Hoebel, E. Adamson (1983). *The Law of Primitive Man.* New York: Atheneum.

Hoecker-Drysdale, Susan (1994). *Harriet Martineau.* Oxford: Berg Publishers.

Hoffman, Karen E. (November 9, 1998). "Internet as Gender-Equalizer?" *Internet World.*

Holt, John (1967). *How Children Fail.* New York: Dell.

Houseman, John (December 1948). "The Men from Mars." *Harper's Magazine 197,* 74–82.

Hoyt, Homer (1939). *The Structure and Growth of Residential Neighborhoods in American Cities.* Washington, DC: Federal Housing Authority.

Hunt, Stephen, Malcolm Hamilton, and Tony Walter. (eds.) (1998). *Charismatic Christianity: Sociological Perspectives.* New York: St. Martin's Press.

Hurley, Jennifer A. (ed.) (1998). *Racism.* San Diego, CA: Greenhaven Press.

Hurn, Christopher J. (1993). *The Limits and Possibilities of Schooling.* 3rd ed. Boston: Allyn and Bacon.

I

Ikeda, Keiko (1998). *A Room Full of Mirrors.* Stanford, CA: Stanford University Press.

J

Jacoby, Sanford M. (1997). *Modern Manors: Welfare Capitalism Since the New Deal.* Princeton, NJ: Princeton University Press.

Janssen-Jurreit, Marie Louise (1982). *Sexism.* New York: Farrar Strauss Giroux.

Jencks, Christopher, and Meredith Phillips (September-October 1998). "America's Next Achievement Test: Closing the Black-White Test Score Gap." *The American Prospect 40,* 44–53.

Jensen, Arthur (Winter 1969). "How Much Can We Boost IQ and Scholastic Achievement?" *Harvard Educational Review 39,* 1–123.

Johnson, David W., and Frank P. Johnson (1994). *Joining Together.* 5th ed. Boston: Allyn and Bacon.

Johnstone, Ronald L. (1996). *Religion in Society.* 5th ed. Upper Saddle River, NJ: Prentice Hall.

Jones, James M. (1993). *Bad Blood* (expanded ed.). New York: Free Press.

K

Karatnycky, Adrian (January/February 1995). "Democracies on the Rise, Democracies at Risk." *Freedom Review 26,* 5–10.

Katz, James E., and Philip Aspden (December 1997). "A Nation of Strangers?" *Communications of the ACM* 81–87.

Kelly, Delos H. (ed.) (1996). *Deviant Behavior.* 5th ed. New York: St. Martin's Press.

Kephart, William M., and William Zellner (1998). *Extraordinary Groups.* 6th ed. New York: St. Martin's Press.

Kids Count Data Sheet (2001). Baltimore, MD: The Annie E. Casey Foundation, 2001.

Kilson, Martin L. (1998). "The State of African-America Politics." In Lee A. Daniels (ed.), *The State of Black America 1998.* New York: National Urban League, pp. 247–270.

Kinsley, Michael (February 2, 1998). "In Defense of Matt Drudge." *Time* 41.

Kitano, Harry H. (1993). *Japanese Americans.* New York: Chelsea House.

Klee, Kenneth (December 13, 1999). "The Siege of Seattle." *Newsweek* 30–39.

Kleniewski, Nancy (1997). *Cities, Change, and Conflict.* Belmont, CA: Wadsworth.

Kohn, Alfie (1992). *No Contest: The Case Against Competition.* Revised edition. Boston: Houghton Mifflin Company.

Konner, Melvin (July-August, 1999). "Darwin's Truth, Jefferson's Vision." *The American Prospect* 30–38.

Kraybill, Donald B., and Marc A. Olshan (eds.) (1994). *The Amish Struggle with Modernity.* Hanover, NH: University Press of New England.

Kuhn, Thomas S. (1996). *The Structure of Scientific Revolutions.* 3rd ed. Chicago: University of Chicago Press.

L

Ladson-Billings, Gloria (1998). "From Soweto to the South Bronx: African Americans and Colonial Education in the United States." In Carlos Alberto Torres and Theodore R. Mitchell (eds.), *Sociology of Education.* Albany, NY: State University of New York Press, pp. 247–264.

Lamanna, Marianne, and Agnes Riedmann (1997). *Marriages and Families: Making Choices and Facing Change.* 6th ed. Belmont, CA: Wadsworth.

Lampert, Leslie (May 1993). "Fat Like Me." *Ladies Home Journal,* 154ff.

Landry, Bart (1988). *The New Black Middle Class.* Berkeley: University of California Press.

Lanier, Mark M., and Stuart Henry (1997). *Essential Criminology.* Boulder, CO: Westview Press.

Lapchick, Richard E., and Kevin J. Matthews (1999). *1998 Racial and Gender Report Card.* Center for the Study of Sport in Society: Northeastern University.

Lapchick, Richard E., and Kevin J. Matthews (2001). *2001 Racial & Gender Report Card.* Center for Study of Sport in Society: Northeastern University.

Laub, John H., and Janet L. Lauritsen (1998). "The Interdependence of School Violence with Neighborhood and Family Conditions." In Delbert S. Elliott, Beatrix A. Hamburg, and Kirk R. Williams (eds.), *Violence in American Schools.* New York: Cambridge University Press, pp. 127–155.

Lawrence, Frederick M. (1999). *Punishing Hate; Bias Crimes Under American Law.* Cambridge, MA: Harvard University Press.

Le Bon, Gustave (1960). *The Crowd.* New York: Viking.

Leacock, Eleanor Burke (1969). *Teaching and Learning in City Schools*. New York: Basic Books.

"Left Out." (March 21, 1983). *Newsweek* 26–35.

"Lego: Fighting the Video Monsters." (January 30, 1999). *The Economist 57*.

Lemann, Nicholas (1991). *The Promised Land*. New York: Knopf.

Lemert, Charles, and Ann Branaman. (eds.) (1997). *The Goffman Reader*. Malden, MA: Blackwell Publishers.

Lemert, Edwin M. (1972). *Human Deviance, Social Problems, and Social Control*. 2nd ed. Englewood Cliffs, NJ: Prentice Hall.

Leonard, Wilbert Marcellus, II. (1998). *A Sociological Perspective of Sport*. Boston: Allyn & Bacon.

Lester, David (1998). *The Death Penalty*. 2nd ed. Springfield, IL: Charles C Thomas.

Levin, Jack, and Jack McDevitt (1993). *Hate Crimes: The Rising Tide of Bigotry and Bloodshed*. New York: Plenum.

Levin, Susanna (1996). "The Spoils of Victory: Who Gets Big Money from Sponsors, and Why." In D. Stanley Eitzen (ed.), *Sport in Contemporary Society*. 5th ed. New York: St. Martin's Press, pp. 367–372.

Levine, Daniel U., and Rayna F. Levine (1996). *Society and Education*. 9th ed. Boston: Allyn and Bacon.

Levine, Rhonda (1998). *Social Class and Stratification*. Blue Ridge Summit, PA: Rowman & Littlefield.

Liebow, Elliot (1967). *Talley's Corner*. Boston: Little, Brown.

Light, Ivan (1983). *Cities in World Perspective*. New York: Macmillan.

Linden, Eugene (March 22, 1993a). "Can Animals Think?" *Time* 55–61.

Linder, Eileen W. (ed.) (2000). *Yearbook of American and Canadian Churches*. Nashville, TN: Abingdon Press.

Little, Suzanne (February 1975). "Sex Roles in Faraway Places." *Ms.,* 77ff.

Lofland, John (1993). *Polite Protesters*. Syracuse, NY: Syracuse University Press.

Longmire, Dennis R. (1996). "American Attitudes Among the Ultimate Weapon: Capital Punishment." In Timothy J. Flanagan and Dennis Longmire (eds.), *Americans View Crime and Justice*. Thousand Oaks, CA: Sage, pp. 93–108.

Lopreato, Joseph (1990). "From Social Evolutionism to Biocultural Evolutionism." *Sociological Forum 5,* 187–212.

Loprest, Pamela (1999). *Families Who Left Welfare: Who Are They and How Are They Doing?* Washington, DC: The Urban Institute.

Ludwig, Jack. "Gallup Social Audit On Black/White Relations In The U.S." (July 11, 2001). http://www.gallup.com.

M

Maccoby, Eleanor E. (1997). *The Two Sexes: Growing Up Apart, Coming Together*. Cambridge, MA: Belknap Press of Harvard University Press.

MacKenzie, Donald A., and Judy Wajcman (eds.) (1999). *The Social Shaping of Technology*. 2nd ed. Bristol, PA: Taylor & Francis, Inc.

Madon, S., L. Jussim, and J. Eccles (1997). "In Search of the Powerful Self-Fulfilling Prophecy." *Journal of Personality and Social Psychology 72,* 791–809.

Malthus, Thomas (1798). *An Essay on the Principle of Population*. London: Reeves and Turner.

Marriott, M. (August 11, 1991). "Afrocentrism: Balancing or Skewing History?" *New York Times* 1, 18.

Martin, Karin A. (August 1998). "Becoming a Gendered Body: Practices of Preschools." *American Sociological Review Association 63,* 494–511.

Martinez, Valerie J., R. Kenneth Godwin, Frank R. Kemerer, and Laura Perna (September 1995). "The Consequences of School Choice: Who Leaves and Who Stays in the Inner City." *Social Science Quarterly 76,* 485–501.

Mason, Philip (1970). *Patterns of Dominance*. New York: Oxford University Press.

Mathews, Tom (May 11, 1992). "The Siege of L.A." *Newsweek* 30–38.

Mauer, Marc. "The Crisis of the Young African American Male and the Criminal Justice System." http://www.sentencingproject.org/, 1999.

McCarthy, John D., and Mark Wolfson (December 1996). "Resource Mobilization by Local Social Movement Organizations: Agency, Strategy, and Organization in the Movement Against Drinking and Driving." *American Sociological Review 61,* 1070–1088.

McGinn, Daniel, and Joan Raymond (Winter 1997–98). "Workers of the World, Get Online." *Newsweek* 32–33.

McLaren, Peter (1997). "Multiculturalism and the Postmodern Critique: Toward a Pedagogy of Resistance and Transformation." In A. H. Halsey, et al. (eds.), *Education*. New York: Oxford University Press, pp. 520–540.

McNamee, Mike, and Joann Muller (December 21, 1998). "A Tale of Two Job Markets." *Business Week 3609,* 38.

McPhail, Clark (1991). *Myth of the Madding Crowd*. Hawthorne, NY: Aldine de Gruyter.

Mead, George Herbert (1934). *Mind, Self and Society*. Chicago: University of Chicago Press.

Mead, Margaret (1950). *Sex and Temperament in Three Primitive Societies*. New York: Mentor Books.

Menaghan, E. G., and T. L. Parcel (1991). "Parental Employment and Family Life: Research in the 1980's." In A. Booth (ed.), *Contemporary Families*. Minneapolis: National Council on Family Relations, pp. 361–380.

Merton, Robert K. (1968). *Social Theory and Social Structure* (enlarged ed.). New York: Free Press.

____. (1996). *On Social Structure and Science*. Chicago: University of Chicago Press.

Michels, Robert (1949). *Political Parties*. New York: Free Press.

Micklin, Michael and Dudley L. Poston, Jr. (ed.) (1998). *Continuities in Sociological Human Ecology*. New York: Plenum Press.

Milgram, Stanley (1963). "Behavioral Study of Obedience." *Journal of Abnormal and Social Psychology 67*, 371–378.

____. (1964). "Group Pressure and Action Against a Person." *Journal of Abnormal and Social Psychology 6*, 137–143.

____. (1965). "Some Conditions of Obedience and Disobedience to Authority." *Human Relations 18*, 57–76.

____. (1974). *Obedience to Authority*. New York: Harper & Row.

Miller, Greg, and Stuart Silverstein (February 5, 2000). "Even Corporate Perks Join the Dot.com Revolution. *The Los Angeles Times* A1.

Millicent, Lawton (February 12, 1992). "Schools' 'Glass Ceiling' Imperils Girls, Study Says." *Education Week* 17.

Mills, C. Wright (1959). *The Sociological Imagination*. New York: Oxford University Press.

Mills, Kay. *Something Better for My Children: The History and People of Head Start*. New York: NAL/Dutton, 1998.

Mitchell, B., and E. Gee (October 1996). "Boomerang Kids and Midlife Parental Marital Satisfaction." *Family Relations* 442–448.

Moen, Phyllis (1992). *Women's Two Roles*. New York: Auburn House.

Montagu, Ashley (1998). *The Natural Superiority of Women*. 5th ed. Thousand Oaks, CA: Altamira Press.

Moore, Joan, and Harry Pachon (1985). *Hispanics in the United States*. Englewood Cliffs, NJ: Prentice Hall.

Moorhead, Gregory, Richard Ference, and Chris P. Neck (1991). "Group Decision Fiascoes Continue: Space Shuttle Challenger and a Revised Groupthink Framework." *Human Relations 44*, 539–550.

Moorhead, Gregory, Christopher P. Neck, and Mindy S. West (February/March, 1998). "The Tendency toward Defective Decision Making within Self-Managing Teams: The Relevance of Groupthink for the 21st Century." *Organizational Behavior and Human Decision Processes* 327–351.

Morganthau, Tom (October 24, 1994). "IQ: Is It Destiny?" *Newsweek* 53–55.

Morris, Norval, and Michael Tonry (1990). *Between Prison and Probation*. New York: Oxford University Press.

Muldavin, Joshua (June 3, 1999). "Commentary: Market Reforms Breed Discontent." *Los Angeles Times* B9.

Murdock, George P. (1945). "The Common Denominator of Cultures." In Ralph Linton (ed.), *The Science of Man in the World Crisis*. New York: Columbia University Press, pp. 123–142.

Myers, David G. (1999). *Social Psychology*. 6th ed. Boston: McGraw-Hill College.

N

Nanda, Serena, and Richard L. Warms (1998). *Cultural Anthropology*. 6th ed. Belmont, CA: Wadsworth.

"National Television Violence Study: Executive Summary." Studio City, CA: Mediascope, Inc., 1998.

Newborne, Burt. (2001). "Reclaiming Democracy." *The American Prospect* (March 12–26):18–24.

Newman, Katherine S. (1993). *Declining Fortunes*. New York: Basic Books.

____. (1999). *Falling from Grace*. Updated edition. Berkeley, CA: University of California Press.

Nie, Norman H., and Lutz Erbring (February 17, 2000). "Internet and Society: A Preliminary Report." Stanford Institute for the Quantitative Study of Society.

Niebuhr, H. Richard (1968). *The Social Sources of Denominationalism*. New York: World.

Nisbet, Robert A. (1989). *The Present Age*. New York: Harper & Row.

Nixon, Howard L. II, and James H. Frey (1996). *A Sociology of Sport*. Belmont, CA: Wadsworth Publishing Co.

Nock, Steven L. (January 1995). "A Comparison of Marriages and Cohabiting Relationships." *Journal of Family Issues 16*, 53–76.

Nolan, Patrick, and Gerhard E. Lenski (1999). *Human Societies*. 8th ed. New York: McGraw Hill College.

Novak, Michael (1996). *The Unmeltable Ethnics*. 2nd ed. New Brunswick: Transaction.

Nydeggar, Corinne N. (1985). "Family Ties of the Aged in Cross-Cultural Perspective." In Beth B. Hess and Elizabeth W. Markson (eds.), *Growing Old in America*. New Brunswick, NJ: Transaction Press.

O

Oakes, Jeannie, and Martin Lipton. In Laura I. Rendon and Richard O. Hope (eds.) (1996). *Educating a New Majority: Transforming America's Educational System for Diversity*. San Francisco: Jossey-Bass Publishers, pp. 168–200.

O'Brien, Joanne, and Martin Palmer (1993). *The State of Religion Atlas*. New York: Touchstone.

O'Dwyer, Thomas (October 27, 1999). "The Taliban's Gender Apartheid." *The Jerusalem Post* 6.

Office of Management and Budget. "A Citizen's Guide to the Federal Budget." *Budget of the United States Government Fiscal Year 2000*, 1999. http://www.access.gpo.gov/usbudget/fy2000/guide02.html.

Ollman, Bertel (1998). *Market Socialism*. New York: Routledge.

Olzak, Susan, and Joane Nagel (eds.) (1986). *Competitive Ethnic Relations*. San Diego, CA: Academic Press.

Orfield, Gary A., et al. (1992). "Status of School Desegregation: The Next Generation." Report to the National School Board Association. Alexandria, VA: National School Board Association.

Ornstein, Robert, and Paul Ehrlich (1991). *New World New Mind*. London: Paladin.

O'Sullivan, Christine Y., Clyde M. Reese, and John Mazzeo (1997). *NAEP 1996 Science Report Card for the Nation and the States*. Washington, DC: National Center for Educational Statistics.

P

Palen, John J. (1997). *The Urban World*. 5th ed. New York: McGraw-Hill.

Passell, Peter (November 9, 1994). "'Bell Curve' Critics Say Early I.Q. Isn't Destiny." *New York Times* B10.

Patterson, James T. (1986). *America's Struggle Against Poverty: 1900–1985*. Cambridge, MA: Harvard University Press.

Patterson, Thomas E. (1999). *The American Democracy*. 4th ed. Boston: McGraw-Hill.

Pearson, Kent. "Subcultures and Sport." In John W. Loy, Jr., Gerald S. Kenyon, and Barry D. McPherson (eds.) (1981). *Sport, Culture, and Society*. 2nd ed. Philadelphia: Lee & Febiger, pp. 131–145.

Pearson, Patricia, and Michael Finley (1997). *When She Was Bad: Violent Women and the Myth of Innocence*. New York: Viking Penguin.

Peoples, James, and Garrick Bailey (2000). *Humanity: An Introduction to Cultural Anthropology*. 5th ed. Belmont, CA: Wadsworth.

Perry, Joellen, and Dan McGraw (September 6, 1999). "In Cleveland, It's a Back-to-School Daze." *U.S. News & World Review*.

Pfeffer, Jeffrey (1997). *New Directions for Organization Theory*. New York: Oxford University Press.

Phu, Vu Duy (December 14, 1998). "Vietnam—Anticipating IT." *Vietnam Economic News*.

Plog, Fred, and Daniel G. Bates. (1990). *Cultural Anthropology*. 3rd ed. New York: McGraw-Hill.

Pollard, Kelvin (1999). "U.S. Diversity is More than Black and White." Washington, DC: Population Reference Bureau.

Pontell, Henry N. (1984). *A Capacity to Punish*. Bloomington: Indiana University Press.

Popenoe, David (1999). *Life Without Father*. Cambridge, MA: Harvard University Press.

Popenoe, David, Jean Bethke Elshtain, and David Blankenhorn (1996). *Promises to Keep: Decline and Renewal of Marriage in America*. Lantham, MD: Rowman and Littlefield Publishers.

Pryor, Douglas W. (1999). *Unspeakable Acts: Why Men Sexually Abuse Children*. New York: New York University Press.

Q

Queen, Stuart A., Robert W. Habenstein, and Jill S. Quadagno (1985). *The Family in Various Cultures*. 5th ed. New York: Harper & Row.

Quintanilla, Michael (May 20, 1996). "Turning Off to Save the Family." *Los Angeles Times* E1–E2.

R

Redhead, Steve (1997). *Subcultures to Clubcultures*. Malden, MA: Blackwell.

Rendon, Laura J., and Richard O. Hope. (eds.) (1996). *Educating a New Majority*. San Francisco: Jossey-Bass Publishers.

Rennison, Callie Maroe (1999). "Criminal Victimization 1998, Changes 1997–98 with Trends 1993–98." U.S. Department of Justice, Bureau of Justice Statistics, Office of Justice Programs.

Reskin, Barbara (1993). "Sex Segregation in the Workplace." *Annual Review of Sociology 19*, 241–270.

Richmond, P. (January 19, 1986). "Weighing the Odds." *Colorado Springs Gazette Telegraph*, F1–F4.

Ridley, Matt (1996). *The Origins of Virtue*. New York: Viking.

Riederer, Richard K. (March 1999). "Battered by the World Financial Crisis." *33 Metal Producing 37*, 42–45.

Riley, Nancy E. (1997). *Gender, Power, and Population Change*. Washington, DC: Population Reference Bureau.

Ritzer, George (1996). *McDonaldization of Society*. Revised edition. Thousand Oaks, CA: Pine Forge Press.

____. (1998). *The McDonaldization Thesis: Explorations and Extensions*. Newbury Park, CA: Sage Publications.

Rochon, Thomas R. (1998). *Culture Moves: Ideas, Activism, and Changing Values*. Princeton, NJ: Princeton University Press.

Roethlisberger, F. J., and William J. Dickson (1964). *Management and the Worker*. New York: Wiley.

Rosenthal, Robert, and Lenore Jacobson (1989). *Pygmalion and the Classroom*. New York: Irvington Publishers.

Rosenzweig, Jane (July-August 1999). "Can TV Improve Us?" *The American Prospect 45*, 58–63.

Rosin, Hanna, and John F. Harris (August 3, 1999). "Welfare Reform is on a Roll." *The Washington Post* A1, A6.

Rubin, Lillian B. (1994). *Families on the Faultline*. New York: HarperCollins.

Rudolph, Frederick (1962). *The American College and University*. New York: Random House.

Rust, Michael, and Tiffany Danitz (March 9, 1998). "New Medium Fuels Ancient Passion." *Insight on the News* 22–23.

S

Sadker, Myra, and David Sadker (1995). *Failing at Fairness*. New York: Simon & Schuster.

Samuda, Ronald (1975). *The Psychological Testing of American Minorities*. New York: Dodd, Mead.

Samuelson, Paul A., and William D. Nordhaus (1995). *Microeconomics*. 15th ed. New York: McGraw-Hill.

Sandberg, Jared (July 19, 1999). "Spinning a Web of Hate." *Newsweek* 28–29.

Sapir, Edward (1929). "The Status of Linguistics as a Science." *Language 5*, 207–214.

Sapolsky, Robert (October 1997). "A Gene for Nothing." *Discover* 40–46.

Sarat, Austin. (ed.) (1998). *The Killing State: Capital Punishment in Law, Politics, and Culture*. New York: Oxford University Press.

Schaeffer, Richard T. (1993). *Racial and Ethnic Groups*. 6th ed. New York: Longman.

Schaeffer, Robert K. (1997). *Understanding Globalization*. Lanham, MD: Rowman & Littlefield Publishers.

Scheper-Hughes, Nancy (1983). "Deposed Kings: The Demise of the Rural Irish Gerontocracy." In Jay Sokolorsky (ed.), *Growing Old in Different Societies*. Belmont, CA: Wadsworth, pp. 130–146.

Schiff, Michel, and Richard Lewontin (1987). *Education and Class*. New York: Oxford University Press.

Schmidt, Steffen W., Mack C. Shelley, and Barbara A. Bardes (1999). *American Government and Politics Today*. Belmont, CA: Wadsworth.

Schnitzer, Martin C. (2000). *Comparative Economic Systems*. 7th ed. Cincinnati, OH: South-Western College Publishing.

Schrag, Peter (1977). "The Forgotten American." In John Walton and Donald E. Carns (eds.), *Cities in Change*. 2nd ed. Boston: Allyn and Bacon, pp. 129–137.

Schwartz, Barry (1987). *The Battle for Human Nature*. New York: Norton.

Scott, Martin B. (1981). "The Man on the Horse." In John W. Loy, Jr., Gerald S. Kenyon, and Barry D. McPherson (eds.), *Sport, Culture, and Society*. 2nd ed. Philadelphia: Lee & Febiger, pp. 146–156.

Seligmann, Jean (July 26, 1999). "Husbands No, Babies, Yes." *Newsweek* 53.

Sellin, Thorsten (1991). *The Penalty of Death*. Beverly Hills, CA: Sage.

Shapiro, Isaac, and Robert Greenstein (1999). *The Widening Income Gulf*. Washington, DC: Center on Budget and Policy Priorities.

Shapiro, Laura (May 28, 1990). "Guns and Dolls." *Newsweek* 54–65.

Shattuck, John (August 14, 1997). "Ending Africa's Tragedy." *The Christian Science Publishing Society,* 19.

Sidel, Ruth (1996). *Keeping Women and Children Last*. New York: Penguin Putnam, Inc.

Simmel, Georg (1964). *Conflict and the Web of Group Affiliation*. Translated by Kurt H. Wolff. New York: Free Press.

Simmons, J. L. (1969). *Deviants*. Berkeley, CA: Glendessary Press.

Simmons, Sally Lynn, and Amelia E. El-Hindi (November 1998). "Six Transformations for Thinking about Integrative Curriculum." *Middle School Journal 30*, 32–36.

Singh, Sarban (September 16, 1998). "Shift in Focus." *Malaysian Business* 54.

Sizer, Theodore (1996). *Horace's Hope: What Works for the American High School*. Boston: Houghton Mifflin.

Skolnick, Jerome H. (July-August 1998). "The Color of Law." *The American Prospect 39*, 90–95.

Sloan, Allan (February 26, 1996). "The Hit Men." *Newsweek* 44–48.

Smelser, Neil J. (1971). *Theory of Collective Behavior*. New York: Free Press.

____. (1976). *The Sociology of Economic Life*. 2nd ed. Englewood Cliffs, NJ: Prentice Hall.

Smith, Michael D. (December 1979). "Hockey Violence: A Test of the Violent Subculture Hypothesis." *Social Problems 27*, 235–247.

Snipp, C. Matthew (1992). "Sociological Perspectives on American Indians." *Annual Review of Sociology 18*, 351–371.

____. (November 1996). "A Demographic Comeback for American Indians?" *Population Today 24*, 4–5.

Snyder, Howard N., and Melissa Sickmund (1999). *Juvenile Offenders and Victims: A National Report*. Rockville, MD: Juvenile Justice Clearinghouse.

Spitze, G. (1991). "Women's Employment and Family Relations: A Review." In A. Booth (ed.), *Contemporary Families*. Minneapolis: National Council on Family Relations, pp. 381–404.

Spitzer, Steven (1980). "Toward a Marxian Theory of Deviance." In Delos H. Kelly (ed.), *Criminal Behavior*. New York: St. Martin's Press, pp. 175–191.

Spohn, Cassia C. (Winter 1995). "Courts, Sentences, and Prisons." *Daedalus 124*, 119–143.

Stacey, William, and Anson Shupe (December 1982). "Correlates of Support for the Electronic Church." *Journal for the Scientific Study of Religion 21*, 291–303.

Starr, Mark (February 7, 1994b). "She Can Skate, But She Can't Hide." *Newsweek 21*.

Starting Points April, 1994. The Report of the Carnegie Task Force on Meeting the Needs of Young Children. Carnegie Corporation of New York.

The State of America's Children: A Report From the Children's Defense Fund. Boston: Beacon Press, 1998.

Stavans, Ilan (1996). *The Hispanic Condition*. New York: Harper Collins.

Stefancic, Jean, and Richard Delgardo (eds.) (1998). *The Latinola Condition*. New York: New York University Press.

Stockard, Jean, and Miriam M. Johnson (1992). *Sex and Gender in Society*. 2nd ed. Englewood Cliffs, NJ: Prentice-Hall.

Stoll, Cliff (1995). *Silicon Snake Oil*. New York: Doubleday.

Strasburger, Victor C. (1995). *Adolescents and the Media: Medical and Psychological Impact*. Newbury Park, CA: Sage.

Straus, Murray A., David B. Sugarman, and Jean Giles-Sims (August 1997). "Spanking by Parents and Subsequent Antisocial Behavior of the Child." *Archives of Pediatrics and Adolescent Medicine*, 761–767.

Street-Level. http://streetlevel.iit.edu. 1999.

Sumner, William Graham (1906). *Folkways*. Boston: Ginn.

Sutherland, Edwin H. (1940). "White-Collar Criminality." *American Sociological Review 5*, 1–12.

____. (1983). *White-Collar Crime*. New Haven, CT: Yale University Press.

Swinton, David H. (1989). "Economic Status of Blacks." In *The State of Black America 1989*. New York: National Urban League, pp. 129–152.

Symonds, William C. (February 7, 2000). "For-Profit-Schools." *Business Week* 64ff.

T

Tax, Meredith (May 17, 1999). "World Culture War." *The Nation*.

Taylor, Shelley E., Letitia Ann Peplau, and David O. Sears (1997). *Social Psychology*. 9th ed. Englewood Cliffs: Prentice-Hall.

Tellegen, Auke, D. T. Lykken, T. J. Bouchard, Jr., and M. McGue (August 1993). "Heritability of Interests: A Twin Study." *Journal of Applied Psychology* 649–661.

Thomas, Evan (April 7, 1997). "The Next Level." *Newsweek* 28–36.

Thomas, Evan, and Lynette Clemetson (November 22, 1999). "A New War Over Vouchers." *Newsweek* 46.

Thornton, Russell (1984). "Cherokee Population Losses During the Trail of Tears: A New Perspective and a New Estimate." *Ethnohistory 31*, 289–300.

Tilly, Charles (1978). *From Mobilization to Revolution*. Reading, MA: Addison-Wesley.

____. *Social Processes* (1997). Lantham, MD: Rowan and Littlefield, 1997.

Tilove, Jonathan (May-June 1999). "The New Map of American Politics." *The American Prospect*.

To Establish Justice, To Insure Domester Tranquility: A Thirty Year Update of the National Commission on the Causes and Prevention of Violence. Washington, DC: The Milton S. Eisenhower Foundation.

Toch, Thomas, and Warren Cohen (November 23, 1998). "Public Education: A Monopoly No Longer." *U.S. News & World Report* 25.

Toland, John. *Adolph Hitler* (1976). Garden City, NY: Doubleday.

Tönnies, Ferdinand (1957). *Community and Society.* Translated and edited by Charles P. Loomis. East Lansing: Michigan State University Press.

Trigaboff, Dan (June 8, 1998). "Drudge Begrudged." *Broadcasting & Cable 55.*

Trimble, J. E. (1988). "Stereotypical Images, American Indians, and Prejudice." In P. A. Katz and D. A. Taylor (eds.), *Eliminating Racism.* New York: Plenum Press, pp. 181–202.

Troeltsch, Ernst (1931). *The Social Teachings of the Christian Churches.* New York: Macmillan.

Turner, Jonathan H., Leonard Beeghley, and Charles H. Powers (1989). *The Emergence of Sociological Theory.* 2nd ed. Chicago: Dorsey Press.

Turner, Ralph H. (1964). "Collective Behavior." In Robert E. L. Faris (ed.), *Handbook of Modern Sociology.* Chicago: Rand McNally, pp. 382–425.

Turner, Ralph H., and Lewis M. Killian (1987). *Collective Behavior.* 3rd ed. Englewood Cliffs, NJ: Prentice Hall.

U

Uchitelle, Louis, and N. R. Kleinfield (1996). "The Price of Jobs Lost." In *The New York Times* Special Report *The Downsizing of America.* New York: Random House.

U.S. Bureau of the Census. (2000c). "Educational Attainment, by Race, and Hispanic Origin." Current Population Reports. http://www.census.gov/population/www/socdemo/education.html.

U.S. Bureau of the Census. "Educational Attainment—Total Money Earnings in 1999 of Persons 18 Years Old and Over, by Age, Race, Hispanic Origin, Sex, and Work Experience in 1999." Washington, DC: U.S. Government Printing Office, 2000e.

U.S. Bureau of the Census (2000a). "Money Income in the United States: 1999." Current Population Reports, P60–209. Washington, DC: U.S. Government Printing Office.

U.S. Bureau of the Census. *Money Income of Households, Families, and Persons in the United States: 1992.* Current Population Reports. Series P-60. No. 184. Washington, DC: U.S. Government Printing Office, 1993a.

U.S. Bureau of the Census. (2000b). "Poverty in the United States, 1999." Current Population Reports, Series P60–210. Washington, DC: U.S. Government Printing Office.

_____. (1993e). *1990 Census of Population, Social and Economic Characteristics, American Indian and Alaska Native Areas.* Section 1 of 2. CP-2–1A. Washington, DC: U.S. Government Printing Office.

U.S. Bureau of the Census. (2000d). *Statistical Abstract of the United States:* 2000. Washington, DC: U.S. Government Printing Office.

_____. (1993i). *School Enrollment, Social and Economic Characteristics of Students: October 1992.* Current Population Reports. Series P-20. No. 474. Washington, DC: U.S. Government Printing Office.

_____. (1996a). *Statistical Abstract of the United States: 1996.* Washington, DC: U.S. Government Printing Office.

_____. (1996b). *Poverty in the United States: 1995.* Current Population Reports. Series P-60. No. 194. Washington, DC: U.S. Government Printing Office.

_____. (1998a). *Statistical Abstract of the United States: 1998.* Washington, DC: U.S. Government Printing Office.

_____. (1998c). Current Population Reports Series, P23–194, *Population Profile of the United States: 1997.* Washington, DC: U.S. Government Printing Office.

_____. (1999a). "Poverty 1997—Poverty Estimates by Selected Characteristics." *Current Population Survey, March, 1998.* http://www.census.gov/hhes/poverty/poverty97/pv97est1.html.

_____. (1999b). "Income 1997—Table B." *Current Population Survey, March, 1998.* http://www.census.gov/hhes/income/income97/in97dis.html.

_____. (1999e). "Asset Ownership of Households: 1993—Table F." http://www.census.gov/hhes/www/wealth/wlth93f.html.

_____. (1999f) "Resident Population Estimates of the United States by Sex, Race, and Hispanic Origin: April 1, 1990 to April 1, 1999." *Population Estimates Program.* http://www.census.gov/population/estimates/nation/intfile3-1.txt.

_____. (1993). U.S. Department of Labor, Bureau of Labor Statistics. *Employment in Perspective: Women in the Labor Force.* No. 865. Washington, DC: U.S. Government Printing Office.

_____. (1997a). *Employment in Perspective: Women in the Labor Force.* Report 860. Washington, DC: U.S. Government Printing Office.

_____. (1997b). *Employment and Earnings.* Washington, DC: U.S. Government Printing Office.

V

Valian, Virginia (1998). *Why So Slow? The Advancement of Women.* Cambridge, MA: MIT Press.

Vanhanen, Tatu (1997). *Prospects of Democracy.* London: Routledge.

Virnoche, Mary E. (1998). "The Seamless Web and Communications Equity: The Shaping of a Community Network." *Science, Technology, & Human Values, 23,* 199–220.

W

Walsh, Edward, and Roberto Suro (June 19, 1999). "NRA Achieves Its Goal: Nothing." *The Washington Post,* A1, A6.

Wallechinsky, David, and Irving Wallace (1981). *The People's Almanac #3.* New York: Bantam.

Wang, C. T., and D. Daro (1998). *Current Trends in Child Abuse Reporting and Fatalities: The Results of the 1997 Annual Fifty State Survey.* Chicago, IL: Prevent Child Abuse America.

Weeks, John R. (1999). *Population.* 6th ed. Belmont, CA: Wadsworth.

Weingart, Peter, et al. (eds.) (1997). *Human by Nature: Between Biology and the Social Sciences.* Mahwah, NJ: Lawrence Erlbaum Associates.

Westoff, Leslie Aldridge, and Charles F. Westoff (1971). *From Now to Zero.* Boston: Little, Brown.

White, Lynn, and David B. Brinkerhoff (September 1981). "The Sexual Division of Labor: Evidence from Childhood." *Social Forces 60,* 170–181.

Who Owns Whom 1998/1999 (1998). High Wycombe, UK: Dun and Bradstreet Ltd.

Whorf, Benjamin Lee (1956). *Language, Thought and Reality.* Edited by John B. Carroll. Cambridge, MA: MIT Press.

Whyte, William Foote (1993). *Street Corner Society.* 4th ed. Chicago: University of Chicago Press.

Wiesel, Elie (April 12, 1999). "The Question of Genocide." *Newsweek.*

Wildavsky, Ben (September 13, 1999). "Grading on a Curve: A New Controversy Erupts Over Race, Class, and SAT Scores." *U.S. News & World Report.*

Williams, Robin M., Jr. (1970). *American Society.* 3rd ed. New York: Knopf.

Wilson, Craig (February 25–27, 2000). "Why People Will Do Almost Anything to Get on TV." *USA Today* 1A, 2A.

Wilson, William Julius (1984). "The Urban Underclass." In Leslie W. Dunbar (ed.), *Minority Report.* New York: Pantheon, pp. 75–117.

_____. (1997). *When Work Disappears: The World of the New Urban Poor.* New York: Knopf.

Wingfield, Nick (June 15, 1998). "Family Planning: The Computer Server Promises to do to the Home What It Has Already Done for Business." *The Wall Street Journal* R18, R23.

Wirth, Louis (1945). "The Problem of Minority Groups." In Ralph Linton (ed.), *The Science of Man in the World Crisis.* New York: Columbia University Press, pp. 347–372.

Wolfe, Alan (1998). *One Nation, After All.* New York: Viking.

World Population Data Sheet. Washington, DC: Population Reference Bureau, 1999.

World Without Work. In Robert Staples (ed.) (1999), *The Black Family.* Belmont, CA: Wadsworth Publishing Company, pp. 291–311.

World Population Data Sheet. (2001). Washington, D.C.: Population Reference Bureau.

Wright, Kevin N. (1987). *The Great American Crime Myth.* New York: Praeger.

Wright, Robert (1996). *The Moral Animal.* New York: Pantheon Books.

Y

Yamagata, Hisashi, et al. (November 1997). "Sex Segregation and Glass Ceilings: A Comparative Statics Model of Women's Career Opportunities in the Federal Government Over a Quarter Century." *American Journal of Sociology 103,* 566–632.

Yap, M. T. (1995). "Singapore's 'Three or More' Policy: The First Five Years." *Asia-Pacific Population Journal 10,* 39–52.

Yorke, Liselle. (2000). "Joint Center Releases 1999 National Court of Black Elected Officials." Washington, DC: Joint Center for Political and Economic Studies.

Young, T. R. (January 1986). "The Sociology of Sport: Structural Marxist and Cultural Marxist Approaches." *Sociological Perspectives 29,* 3–28.

Z

Zamble, Edward, and Vernon L. Quinsey (1997). *The Criminal Recidivism Process.* New York: Cambridge University Press.

Zborowski, Mark (1952). "Cultural Components in Response to Pain." *Journal of Social Issues 8,* 16–30.

_____. (1969). *People in Pain.* San Francisco: Jossey-Bass.

Zellner, William W. (1999). *Countercultures: A Sociological Analysis.* 2nd ed. New York: St. Martin's Press.

Zigler, Edward, and Sally J. Styfco (eds.) (1993). *Head Start and Beyond*. New Haven, CT: Yale University Press.

Zimbardo, Philip G., S. M. Anderson, and L. G. Kabat (June 26, 1981). "Induced Hearing Deficit Generates Experimental Paranoia." *Science,* 1529–1531.

Zweigenhaft, Richard L., and G. William Domhoff (1998). *Diversity in the Power Elite*. New Haven: Yale University Press.

Index

Credits

Photo Credits

CHAPTER 1 **2** The Stock Market, Jon Feingersh **4** The Stock Market, Tom & Dee Ann McCarthy **6** Index Stock Photo, Andrea Booher **7**(1) Index Stock Photo, Omni Photo Communications, Inc. **7**(2) Index Stock Photo, Palmer Brilliant **7**(3) Index Stock photo, Frank Pedrick **7**(4) ©AFP/Corbis **8** Index Stock Photo, SW Production **10** ©Francis G. Mayer/Corbis **11** Index Stock Photo, SW Production **14** North Wind Picture Archives **15**(top) ©Corbis **15**(bottom) Brown Brothers **16** ©Archivo Iconografico, S.A./Corbis **17**(top) ©Bettmann/Corbis **17**(bottom) Brown Brothers **19**(left) ©Bettmann/Corbis **19**(right) ©Bettmann/Corbis **20** Index Stock Photo, Jeff Greenberg **21**(left) ©Bettmann/Corbis **21**(right) ©Bettmann/Corbis **25**(top) Index Stock Photo, Black Box **25**(bottom) Index Stock Photo **26** Tony Stone Images, Ben Edwards **31** Index Stock Photo, Jeffrey Blackman

CHAPTER 2 **36** ©PhotoDisc **38** ©Don Milici **40** Index Stock Photo, Grantpix **43** Associated Press, Christopher Pfuhl **44** Associated Press, Jean Whiteside **47** Associated Press, Elise Amendola **50** ©AFP/Corbis, Wayne Scarberry **54** ©Archivo Iconografico, S.A./Corbis **59** Tony Stone Images, Andy Sacks **60** Associated Press, Tom Uhlman **62** Tony Stone Images, Jed & Kaoru Share **66** Index Stock Photo, SW Production

CHAPTER 3 **68** Index Stock Photo, Omni Photo Communications, Inc. **70** (top left) Associated Press, Enric Marti **70**(top right) Associated Press, Lynne Sladky **70**(bottom left) Associated Press, David Longstreath **70**(middle right) Associated Press, Katsumi Kasahara **70**(bottom right) Associated Press **72** ©Kevin Fleming/Corbis **73** ©Michael Pole/Corbis **74** Index Stock Photo **75** ©Digital Art/Corbis **76** ©Joel W. Rogers/Corbis **76**(top) Index Stock Photo **77**(bottom) ©Werner Forman/Corbis **79** Index Stock Photo **81** Index Stock Photo **83**(left) ©Digital Stock **83**(right) ©Digital Stock **84**(top left) Associated Press, Eric Risberg **84**(bottom left) Associated Press, Gail Oskin **84**(right) Associated Press, Ruth Fremson **87** ©Digital Stock **89** Associated Press, Patrick D. Pagnano **90**(top) Index Stock Photo **90**(bottom) Index Stock Photo **92** Index Stock Photo **94** Index Stock Photo, Daniel Fort **95** Associated Press, Denis Farrell **96** Index Stock Photo **97** ©James Marshall/Corbis **98** Index Stock Photo **100** Associated Press, Frank Boxler **105** Index Stock Photov **106** ©Michael S. Yamashita/Corbis

CHAPTER 4 **108** The Stock Market **110** ©Hulton-Deutsch Collection/Corbis **111** Associated Press, B. K. Bangash **112** The Stock Market, Chuck Savage **113** Index Stock Photo, Ewing Galloway **115** Index Stock Photo, Omni Photo Communications, Inc. **118** Index Stock Photo **119** The Stock Market, Mug Shots **120** ©Hulton-Deutsch Collection/Corbis **121**(left) Index Stock Photo, SW

Production **121**(right) The Stock Market, George Shelley **123**(top) Tony Stone Images, Lori Adamski Peek **123**(bottom) ©Nik Wheeler/Corbis **124** Index Stock Photo, SW Production **126** The Stock Market, David Brooks **127** Index Stock Photo, SW Production **128** Associated Press, Brett Coomer **132** Index Stock Photo, Phil Cantor **136** Associated Press, Mark Van Manen

CHAPTER 5 **138** ©Adam Woolfitt/Corbis **140** Tony Stone Images, Karan Kapoor **141** Index Stock Photo, Powerstock-ZEFA **143** ©PhotoDisc **144** ©News Service, Stanford University **147** Index Stock Photo, SW Production **151** Index Stock Photo, SW Production **152** Tony Stone Images, Tony May **154** Tony Stone Images, Paul Chesley **156** Tony Stone Images, Nick Gunderson **157** ©Archivo Iconografico, S.A./Corbis **158** Associated Press, Dario Lopez-Mills **159** ©Bettmann/Corbis **160** ©Charles O-Rear/Corbis **162** Associated Press, Peter Morgan **164** Associated Press, Charles Bennett

CHAPTER 6 **170** Index Stock Photo, Bill Romerhaus **172**(left) Tony Stone Images, Don Smetzer **172**(right) Index Stock Photo, Patricia Barry Levy **173** Index Stock Photo, Stewart Cohen **175** Tony Stone Images, Jon Riley **176** Associated Press, Greg Baker **177**(left) Tony Stone Images, Robert E. Daemmrich **177**(right) ©PhotoDisc **178** ©Corbis Images **181** Associated Press, Jane Hwang **182** Darko Bandic/AP Wide World Photos **183** Index Stock Photo, Len Rubenstein **184**(top) Associated Press, Damian Dovarganes **184**(bottom) ©Bettmann/Corbis **187** Index Stock Photo, Chip Henderson **189** From the film "Obedience," copyrighted in 1965 by Stanley Milgram and distributed by The Pennsylvania State University, Media Sales **190**(top) Associated Press, Tsugufumi Matsumoto **190**(bottom) Tony Stone Images, Bruce Ayres **195** Index Stock Photo, SW Production **201** Associated Press, Vincent Yu

CHAPTER 7 **202** Associated Press, Tom Zubak **203**(top) Associated Press, Ed Wray **203**(bottom) Associated Press, Shane Harvey **207** Index Stock Photo, SW Production **208** ©Corbis **209** Associated Press **210** Associated Press, Kathy Willens **212** Index Stock Photo, SW Production **213** Associated Press, Lacy Atkins **215** Associated Press, William Plowman **216** ©Bettmann/Corbis **217** ©Bettmann/Corbis **218** Associated Press, Cheryl A. Miller **219**(left) Associated Press, Pat Sullivan **219**(right) Associated Press, Gregory Rice **221** Associated Press, Ron Edmonds **224** Associated Press, Frank Anderson **228** Index Stock Photo, Mauritius **229**(top) Associated Press, Paul Sakuma **229**(bottom) Associated Press, Dan Krauss **231** Index Stock Photo, John Boykin

CHAPTER 8 **238** Associated Press, H. Rumph, Jr. **240**(top) Index Stock Photo, Ted Wilcox **240**(bottom) Associated Press, Dale Fulkerson **242** Associated Press **246**(top) Associated Press, Brian Bohannon **246**(bottom left) Associated Press, Chris Pizzello   **246**(bottom right) Associated Press, Kevork Djansezian   **248** Index Stock Photo, Steven Begleiter   **249** ©Arte & Immagini SRL/Corbis   **250**(left) The Stock Market, John Maher   **250**(right) The Stock Market, Nancy Ney   **251**(top) Associated Press, Bob Mooney   **251**(bottom) Index Stock Photo, Craig Wikowski   **253** Index Stock Photo, SW Production   **255**(top) Associated Press, Richard Drew   **255**(bottom) Tony Stone Images, Frank Siteman   **257** Associated Press, Eric Draper   **258** Associated Press   **259**(left) Associated Press, David Longstreath   **259**(right) Associated Press, Mike Derer   **262** Associated Press, Lou Krasky   **264**(top) Index Stock Photo, Benelux Press   **264**(bottom) Associated Press, Don Ryan   **265** The Stock Market, Lester Lefkowitz   **266** Index Stock Photo, Steve Starr   **267** Associated Press, Stevan Morgain   **268** Index Stock Photo, Ami Katz

CHAPTER 9   **274** Associated Press, Charles Tasnadi **276** The Stock Market, Mug Shots   **277** The Stock Market, George Disario   **282** Woolaroc Museum, Bartlesville, OK **284**(top) ©Bill Aron, PhotoEdit   **284**(bottom) Associated Press, Leslie E. Kossoff   **285** Associated Press, Dan Loh **286** Index Stock Photo, Gary Conner   **289** Associated Press, William Thomas Cain   **290** Associated Press, Dave Martin **292** Associated Press, Bebeto Matthews   **293** Associated Press, Joe Marquette   **295** Associated Press, Eric Draper **296** Associated Press, Wilfredo Lee   **297** ©Corbis **299** Index Stock Photo, Phil Cantor   **301** Associated Press, Stephen Morton

CHAPTER 10   **308** The Stock Market, Dale O'Dell **310**(left) ©Jennie Woodcock, Reflections Photolibrary/Corbis **310**(right) ©Hannah Gal/Corbis   **312**(left) Associated Press, Amy Sancetta   **312**(right) ©Buena Vista Television/Shooting Star   **313** Associated Press/American Museum of Natural History   **314** Associated Press, Daniel Hulshizer **315** ©Corbis   **316** Index Stock Photo, Mitch Diamond **317** Index Stock Photo, Zephyr Pictures   **320** Associated Press, Wilfredo Lee   **322** Associated Press, Ben Margot **324** Associated Press, Shizuo Kambayashi   **328** Index Stock Photo, ZEFA-Motions Emotions   **329** Associated Press, Charles Rex Arbogast   **330** ©PhotoDisc   **332** Associated Press The Republic, Joe Harpring   **333** Index Stock Photo, Omni Photo Communications, Inc.   **335**(left) Associated Press, Ruth Fremson   **335**(right) Associated Press, Audrey Woods   **336** Index Stock Photo, Allen Russell

CHAPTER 11   **344** The Stock Market, Alan Schein **346** ©PhotoDisc   **348** The Stock Market, Jose Luis Pelaez, Inc.   **349** Associated Press, Tanya Breen   **351** Associated Press   **355** Werner Bokelberg/Getty   **356** Index Stock Photo, Phil Lauro   **357** Index Stock Photo, Kindra Clineff **359** Index Stock Photo, Myrleen Cate   **360** Associated Press, Anat Givon   **363** The Stock Market, Jose Luis Pelaez, Inc.   **367** ©Christel Gerstenberg/Corbis   **369** Associated Press, Mark Foley   **370** Index Stock Photo, Bonnie Kamin **371** ©Bettmann/Corbis   **372** AFP/Corbis   **374** Index Stock Photo, Benelux Press   **377** ©Corbis   **378** ©Digital Stock **380** Associated Press/Fox Broadcasting Company

CHAPTER 12   **386** The Stock Market, Jose L. Pelaez **388**(left) Associated Press   **388**(right) Tony Stone Images, Walter Hodges   **390** The Stock Market, Mug Shots **391** Associated Press, Tim Hynds   **392** ©Corbis **393** Associated Press, Lynsey Addario   **395** Tony Stone Images, Bob Daemmrich   **396** The Stock Market, Tom & DeeAnn McCarthy   **400** Associated Press, Joe Richard **401** Associated Press, Mary Ann Chastain   **403**(left) Index Stock Photo, Jim Scourietis   **403**(right) Associated Press, Pablo Martinez Monsivais   **405** Index Stock Photo, Frank Siteman   **406** Associated Press, Laurie DeWitt   **408** Associated Press/Herald-Leader, Dana Johnson **409** Associated Press/Clarksburg Exponent, Steven Wayne Rotsch   **410** ©Richard T. Nowitz/Corbis   **413** Associated Press, Nick Ut   **414** Tony Stone Images, Alan Levenson **421** Associated Press

CHAPTER 13   **422** Associated Press, Jon Kieckhefer **424** Associated Press, Daniel Portnoy   **425** Index Stock Photo, Table Mesa Prod.   **426**(top right) Associated Press **426**(left) Associated Press, Alan Greth   **426**(bottom right) Associated Press   **427** Associated Press, Sherwin Crasto **428** Associated Press, Michael Jung Pool   **430** Associated Press   **431** Associated Press, Jose Goitia   **432** Associated Press, Greg Baker   **433** Associated Press, Eric Draper **434**(left) Associated Press, Itsu Inouye   **434**(top right) Associated Press, Maribeth Brown   **434**(bottom right) Associated Press, Julia Malakie   **441**(top) Associated Press, Jeff Christensen   **441**(bottom) Associated Press, Chris Polk **443** Index Stock Photo, Tina Buckman   **444** Associated Press, Eugene Hoshiko   **445** Associated Press, Michael Caulfield   **446** Associated Press/The Cincinnati Enquirer **449** Associated Press   **450** Associated Press, Susan Ragan **451** Associated Press, Roger Werth   **453** Associated Press, Gary Tramontina   **454** Associated Press, John Hayes **456** Associated Press, Gail Oskin   **461** ©Mark Richards, PhotoEdit

CHAPTER 14   **462** Index Stock Photo: Omni Photo Communications, Inc.; Color Point Studio; Dennis Curran; Eunice Harris   **464** Index Stock Photo, Craig Brown **465**(top) Index Stock Photo, Image Port   **465**(bottom) Associated Press, Rose Palmisano   **466** ©AFP/Corbis **467**(top) Associated Press, Charles Becker   **467**(bottom left) Index Stock Photo, Kadir Kir   **467**(bottom right) Index Stock Photo, Daniel Bailey   **472** ©Archivo Iconografico, S.A./Corbis   **474** The Stock Market, Sanford/Agliolo **475** Index Stock Photo, Michael Long   **476** ©Bettmann/ Corbis   **477** ©Ted Streshinsky/Corbis   **478** Associated Press/Internet   **479**(left) Associated Press, Charles Dharapak **479**(right) Tony Stone Images, Bil Aron   **481**(top left) Associated Press, Joan Seidel   **481**(top right) Associated Press, Dave Martin   **481**(bottom left) Associated Press, Julie Vennitti   **481**(bottom right) Index Stock Photo, Dave Bartruff   **484** Associated Press/Union Rescue Mission Web **486** Associated Press, John Bazemore   **488** Associated Press **493** Associated Press, John Moore

CHAPTER 15   **494** Index Stock Photo, Bill Bachmann

496(top) ©Digital Stock   496(bottom) Index Stock Photo, ZEFA-Taste of Europe   497(top) Associated Press, Paul Vathis   497(bottom) Associated Press, Patricia McDonnell   498(top) Associated Press, Eric Risberg   498(middle) Associated Press, Eric Risberg   498(bottom) Associated Press, Chris Gardner   499 Associated Press   500 Associated Press/Vancouver Province, Gerry Kahrmann   501 ©Digital Stock   502 Associated Press, Stuart T. Wagner   503 Associated Press, Mark Duncan   507 Associated Press, Doug Pizac   508 ©Anne Griffith Betz/Corbis   511 The Stock Market, Mug Shots   513 Associated Press, Robin Nowacki   515 Associated Press, Orlin Wagner   517(top left) Associated Press, Denise L. Oles   517(top right) Associated Press, Mark Lennihan   517(bottom) Duomo/CORBIS   519 Associated Press, Paul Sakuma   525 Associated Press, Rhonda Simpson

CHAPTER 16   526 The Stock Market, George B. Diebold   528 The Stock Market, Jon Feingersh   530 Associated Press, Greg Baker   531 Associated Press, Susan Plageman   533 Associated Press, Dado Galdieri   539 ©Bettmann/Corbis   542 The Stock Market, Bob Krist   543(top) Associated Press, John McConnico   543(bottom) ©Owen Franken/Corbis   545 Associated Press, Elizabeth Ellis   547 The Stock Market, Chuck Savage   548(top) Index Stock Photo, Chris Minerva   548(bottom) Index Stock Photo, Phil Lauro   549 Index Stock Photo, Powerstock-ZEFA   552 Associated Press, Nick Ut   554 Associated Press, Eli Grothe   559 Index Stock Photo, John Connell   565 Index Stock Photo, Mark Gibson

CHAPTER 17   566 Associated Press, Dave Martin   571 Index Stock Photo, Dave Bartruff   572(top) Index Stock Photo, Stewart Cohen   572(bottom) Associated Press, Volodymyr Repik   573 ©Robert Holmes/Corbis   575 Associated Press, Lauren Rebours   577 Associated Press, Nell Redmond   578 Associated Press, Doglas C. Pizac   581 ©Bettmann/Corbis   582 ©Hulton-Deutsch Collection/Corbis   583(top right) ©Bettmann/Corbis   583(bottom right) ©Bettmann/Corbis   583(middle) Frank Capri/SAGA/Archive Photos   583(top left) Darlene Hammond/Archive Photos   583(bottom left) Associated Press, Mark Lennihan   584 Thomas E. Franklin/Bergen Record/Saba/Corbis   586(top) Index Stock Photo, Omni Photo Communications, Inc.   586(middle) Associated Press, Dave Duprey   586(bottom) Associated Press, Eric Draper   587 Associated Press, Bob Galbraith   588 Associated Press, Paris Saris   589 Associated Press, Mark Hertzberg   590 Associated Press, Eric Draper   593 ©Kevin R. Morris/Corbis   594 John Filo/Archive Photos   596 Associated Press, Jill Connelly

Handbook Credits

HB-1 Bob Daemmrich Stock Boston   **HB-2** Michael Newman/ PhotoEdit   **HB-3** David Young-Wolf/PhotoEdit   **HB-5** Reuters NewMedia Inc./Corbis   **HB-8** Jeffrey W. Myers/CORBIS   **HB-9** Steve Chenn/CORBIS   **HB-15** Pascal Quittemelle/Stock Boston   **HB-16** David Young Wolf/Stone

Cartoon Credits

18 © 1991, Mike Marland, (Reprinted with permission.)   30 *Tank McNamara*, © 1996, Universal Press Syndicate, Millar/Hinds. (Reprinted with permission.)   39 *Doonesbury*, © 1980, Universal Press Syndicate, G. B. Trudeau. (Reprinted with permission.)   53 © Sidney Harris, *The Chronicle of Higher Education*. (Reprinted with permission.)   88 *The Far Side*, © 1994 FarWorks, Inc. (Reprinted with permission.) All rights reserved.   91 *Calvin and Hobbes*, © 1990 Watterson. Reprinted with permission of Universal Press Syndicate. All rights reserved.   122 © 1993, Chronicle Features, Gail Machlis. (Reprinted with permission.)   131 *Cathy*, © Cathy Guisewhite, Universal Press Syndicate. (Reprinted with permission.)   142 © 1991, *The New Yorker Magazine, Inc.*, Francino. (Reprinted with permission.)   146 © 1998, *The New Yorker Magazine, Inc.*, C. Barsotti. (Reprinted with permission.)   153 *The Far Side*, © *The Far Side Gallery 5*, Gary Larson. (Reprinted with permission.)   185 © *The New Yorker Magazine*, Inc., Henry Martin. (Reprinted with permission.)   192 *Calvin and Hobbes*, © Bill Watterson, *Scientific Progress Goes Boink*, page 39. (Reprinted with permission.)   215 Tank McNamara, © Universal Press Syndicate, Millar/Hinds. (Reprinted with permission.)   244 © 1992, *The New Yorker Magazine, Inc.*, W. Miller. (Reprinted with permission.)   251 *Funky Winkerbean* by Tom Batiuk. © by and permission of News America Syndicate.   262 © Creator's Syndicate, Jeff Shesol. (Reprinted with permission.)   307 © 1996 *The New Yorker Collection*, Mick Stevens. (Reprinted with permission.)   311 © 1995, *The New Yorker Collection*, Donald Reilly. (Reprinted with permission.)   375 © Chronicle Features, Gail Machlis. (Reprinted with permission.)   379 ©1989, *The New Yorker Collection*, Henry Martin. (Reprinted with permission.)   395 *Calvin and Hobbes*, © Bill Watterson, *The Calvin and Hobbes Tenth Anniversary Book*. (Reprinted with permission.)   402 © 1998, *The New Yorker Collection*, Roz Chast. (Reprinted with permission.)   455 © Toles, *The Buffalo News*. (Reprinted with permission.)   479 *Calvin and Hobbes*, © Bill Watterson, *The Calvin and Hobbes Tenth Anniversary Book*. (Reprinted with permission.)   503 © 1999, *The Green Bay Press Gazette*, Joe Heller. (Reprinted with permission.)   510 Sidelines, © 1999, *The Green Bay Press Gazette*, Joe Heller. (Reprinted with permission.)   512 © 1991, Millar/Hinds, Universal Press Syndicate. (Reprinted with permission.)   536 © Toles, 1990, *The Buffalo News*. (Reprinted with permission.)   570 © King Features Syndicate, Jim Bergman. (Reprinted with permission.)   591 *The Far Side*, © Universal Press Syndicate, Gary Larson. (Reprinted with permission.)   **HB-7** *Calvin and Hobbes* © 1995, Watterson. Reprinted with permission of Universal Press Syndicate. All rights reserved.